THIRD EDITION

AMERICAN ECONOMIC DEVELOPMENT

The Progress of a Business Civilization

HERMAN E. KROOSS

Professor of Economics, New York University

Cop. b

PRENTICE-HALL, INC., Englewood Cliffs, New Jersey

Library of Congress Cataloging in Publication Data

Krooss, Herman Edward.
    American economic development.

    Includes bibliographies.
    1.-United States—Economic conditions. I.-Title.
HC103.K7 1974   330.9'73   73-20104
ISBN 0-13-024950-5

Printed in the United States of America

10 9 8 7 6 5 4 3 2 1

Prentice-Hall International, Inc., *London*
Prentice-Hall of Australia, Pty. Ltd., *Sydney*
Prentice-Hall of Canada, Ltd., *Toronto*
Prentice-Hall of India Private Limited, *New Delhi*
Prentice-Hall of Japan, Inc., *Tokyo*

CONTENTS

Century. What Americans Ate. What Americans Wore. The
Houses in Which Americans Lived. Education and Leisure in
the United States. How Long Americans Lived. Some of the
Reasons Why: *The physical environment; Regional
distribution of natural resources; The heritage from the
Old World; Social and political organization; The American
value system; The endogenous factors in the growth process.*

3

THE LAND AND THE POPULATION

The Importance of Land in Early American History. The
Growth of the American Population. Birth and Death Rates.
Immigration as a Factor in Population Growth. Why the
Immigrants Came. Government Restrictions on Immigration.
Where the Immigrants Settled. The Effects of Immigration.
*The Acquisition and Dispersion of the Public Land: How the
colonists acquired land; Federal land policy in the early
nineteenth century; The debate over Federal land policy;
Miscellaneous land disposals; The conservation movement;
The effects of government land policy; Land policy and
speculation; Other results of the land policy.* The
Westward Movement and the Safety Valve Doctrine. Population
in the Urban Areas: *The cities of 1800; The growth of the
city in the nineteenth century; The appearance of the
metropolitan area.*

4

THE FARMER IN AMERICAN ECONOMIC HISTORY

The Contribution of Agriculture to Early Economic
Development. Pioneer Farming in the North. The Problem
of Capital and Credit. Toward Commercial Farming. Southern
Agriculture Before the Civil War. Slavery and the Southern
Economy. Gradual Change in the Methods of Farming: *Better
cultivation and better crops; Bigger pigs and better cows.*
The Expansion of Farm Mechanization: *From the wooden to the
chilled-iron plow; Reapers, harvesters, binders, and
combines; The cotton gin.* The Early Nineteenth Century
Farmer as a Businessman—A Summary.

5

THE FARMER AS A BUSINESSMAN

Agriculture's Share of the National Income. Farm Production
and Prices. The Farmer in the Export Market. Why the Farm
Problem? Rising Productivity in Farming. The Forces that
Induced Higher Productivity: *The problem of mechanizing the
farm; The evolution of power; Changes in farm size; More*

PREFACE

Of all varieties of history, the economic is the most fundamental. Not the most important. . . . Economic advance is not the
same thing as human progress. . . . But economic activity with its
tools, fields, trades, inventions, and investment is the basement of
man's house.

Sir John Clapham
A Concise Economic History of Britain

This is the third edition of a book first published in 1955. What
made the first edition unusual was that it was the only text in
economic history organized topically. All the other texts then in
print treated the subject chronologically. It seemed to me then, as
it does now, that a topical organization makes more sense than
what was then the orthodox approach. Later events seem to
support this view, for the more recent books on the subject also
follow the topical method.

This new edition is not just an addendum; it is an entire
revision. In addition to bringing the material up to date, it
incorporates the findings of the remarkably fruitful research
produced in the 1960s. A new chapter has been added on money
and banking, and the chapters on the growth of the economy,
labor, domestic commerce, and land and population have been
greatly expanded, making this third edition considerably longer
than the second.

I have not intended to write an economic history from the

economist's point of view, nor from the *historian's* point of view. The intention has been to present economic history from the *economic historian's* view. In the words first quoted by W.J. Ashley, an economic historian should be "an economist without ceasing to be a historian." Or, as Sir John Clapham expressed it, "Economic history is a borderline study, lying along the frontiers of history and economics, with an ill-defined territory over which both the general historians and the economists require grazing rights."

With this in mind, this text is an attempt to explain how the American economy came to be what it is today, what problems were faced, what solutions were tried, and what institutions were created in the process.

I am deeply indebted and most grateful to the many users of the book and readers of the manuscript who offered their helpful criticisms to the publisher. Each suggestion was carefully considered and most of them have been embodied in the text. Without these criticisms, the extensive changes that have been made would not have been possible.

A special debt of gratitude is due to Miss Lee Silman, who has once again transformed my confused handscript into a readable manuscript.

Herman E. Krooss

Chapter One

THE PROGRESS
OF AMERICAN ECONOMIC LIFE:
THE NATIONAL INCOME

Before embarking on an account of what happened in economic history, it seems advisable to say a few words about what economic history is. In the simplest terms, economic history is the subject that deals with the ways in which man has made a living.

Since the day he first appeared, man has struggled to keep himself alive and to increase his worldly goods. In the process, he has been constantly forced to make economic decisions of one kind or another. Human beings have always had a vast variety of wants, but, unfortunately, nature has provided neither enough goods to satisfy these wants nor enough resources with which to produce them. In some parts of the world, there is not enough food or shelter to meet man's elementary needs. In other places, there are not enough beefsteaks, automobiles, and swimming pools to satisfy all who want them. And nowhere are there enough labor or capital resources available to grow or manufacture all that man would like to have.

Goods and resources being scarce and wants being apparently unlimited, human beings, in the course of making their living and spending their incomes, are constantly faced with the necessity of choosing among many alternatives. Because they cannot produce everything they desire, they must decide which wants they will satisfy first and allocate their resources accordingly. Every individual must decide what he will do with the income he receives from his productive efforts. Should he spend all of it, or should he save some of it and thereby increase his capital funds? How much should be spend on the necessities of life, and how much, if any, on luxuries? The mysterious subject known as "economics" seeks to answer these questions. *Economics deals with the ways in which man uses his limited resources to satisfy his wants.* Economics is, in a word, the art of economizing. In any economy in which very few goods are produced, a person's choice will be limited almost entirely to necessities; and in every economy there are some individuals who never earn enough to purchase anything else. In such cases, an individual's only choice may be between such alternatives as brown bread and white rice. But in an economy in which many goods are produced and in which some individual incomes are very high, a person may be confronted with an almost infinite number of choices. He still must set aside a certain amount of his income for the purchase of necessities, but other choices—whether to invest in a hundred shares of A. T. and T., or to buy a Picasso, a gold-plated attaché case, or a college education for his nephew—swim in upon him and require decision.

If man were motivated entirely by economic considerations, he would allocate his available resources in such a way as to insure himself maximum economic satisfaction. But because he is not so motivated, his economic choices are often choices in name only. In many instances, they are made almost automatically under the dictates of habit, heredity, and environment. John Jones may be a farmer because his forebears were farmers. He may continue to work long after he has acquired sufficient wealth to satisfy all his material wants because it is easier to go on than to stop. In an underdeveloped economy, he may spend far more on ceremonials than prudence would dictate simply because it is the thing to do. For much the same reason, but with less deleterious effects, people in a rich economy may also consume conspicuously. Regardless of his motivation, however, a man's economic status is measured by his level of living—by the number of wants he has satisfied or is able to satisfy.[1]

What applies to the individual applies equally to a nation. A nation, through the collective judgment of its individual citizens, decides how to allocate its scarce resources and how to combine the four factors of production—land, labor, capital, and enterprise—in the productive process. A nation must decide how much to produce; how to use its labor supply, its raw materials, and its capital equipment; how much to consume and how much to save. Just as surely as in the case of the individual citizen, a nation's economic choices will reflect its philosophy, customs, habit, tradition, and folklore. But, as with the individual

---

[1]The term "level of living" applies to the way people actually live; "standard of living" refers to the way they would like to live. In a society in which there is a large degree of social mobility, the gap between the standard and the level of living is far greater than in a society in which there is relatively little mobility.

citizen, a nation's economic success must be judged by how much income its individual citizens earn in the process of making their living.

If this is economics, then what is history? It is not, as Voltaire so cleverly said, a pack of tricks that we play on the dead, nor is it, as Goethe put it, the invention of historians. History includes all man's past activities— economic, social, political, aesthetic, and intellectual. *It is the study of how man has come to be what he is and how he has come to believe as he does.* "Economic history" is, therefore, a specialized subdivision of a broad area of learning. *It is the branch of history that deals with the ways in which man has used his limited resources to satisfy his wants and with the institutions[2] he has developed to organize his economic activities.*

Every discipline must have a framework, or it becomes a confusing melange. This book is primarily concerned with the economic development and growth of the United States. Most of our attention is, therefore, centered on the changes that occurred in the level of living as measured by the national income accounts.[3] We are chiefly interested in what each factor of production contributed to the national income and what it got out of it. But this is by no means the whole story. There are other themes in economic history besides the swelling of the national income. Economic history is also concerned with the economic aspects of the social institutions of the past, regardless of their direct effect on the national income. Thus, we are interested in such phenomena as the Westward movement, the evolution of the money and banking system, the ubiquitous farm problem, the trials and tribulations of early railroading, the historical whims of the antitrust policy, and many more pieces of economic history, even though their relationship to changes in the national income may be rather remote. Some fifty years ago, a great pioneer in American economic history described the intricacies of the subject very well when he wrote that the economic historian's "subject ought to be the wealth of nations in the literal sense of that phrase. He ought to make clear what factors have determined the ability of each nation to produce wealth at any particular time and what ones have influenced its distribu-

[2]Institutions are the social structure and the machinery through which human society organizes, directs, and executes its activities. See Harry Elmer Barnes, *Social Institutions* (Englewood Cliffs, N.J.: Prentice-Hall, Inc., 1942). As the term is used in this book, *institutions* include organizations, such as labor unions and trade associations, as well as more abstract concepts, such as the profit motive and freedom of contract.

[3]There are four principal national income accounts: gross national product, national income, personal income, and disposable income. *Gross national product* (GNP) purports to measure all the goods and services produced, including depreciation but not including goods used in the process of production. *National Income* is the total of what is paid out in the form of wages, salaries, interest, rent, and profit to the factors of production in exchange for productive services. *Personal income* subtracts corporate income and counts only that part of national income paid to persons. *Disposable income* is personal income after deducting personal taxes.

tion; he should also reveal the forces which have acted to change economic conditions from time to time, producing economic progress or economic decline; and he must know in detail how individuals and communities have made a living and what circumstances have affected their ability to do so. "[4]

All the variety of subject matter in economic history is intermeshed in an intricate pattern. Economic history is like a well-constructed jigsaw puzzle. It is impossible to pick up one piece without lifting the whole. It is difficult to answer the question of which came first, to separate cause from effect. Nothing occurred in a vacuum. Things fed on each other. Capital, for example, came from income, but increments of capital increased income, producing more capital, and so on. Or, to take another example, the growth of manufacturing affected or was affected by the declining importance of agriculture, the expansion of the labor supply, the accumulation of capital, the appearance of large-scale business enterprise, the development of transportation and marketing facilities, the expansion of governmental powers, and so on and so forth.

The ramifications extend even further than this. Economic history is intimately related to political history, social history, and economic theory. To what degree economic factors are interrelated with the political framework is still a matter for heated argument, but that each wields an influence on the other is indisputable. In the American experience, attitudes on such fundamental economic matters as land policy, the tariff, the farm problem, and monetary and fiscal policy were immensely potent influences in shaping the form and structure of political parties and institutions. In turn, political decisions, such as the efforts to keep the nation out of the Napoleonic Wars, or the attempts of the government to throw off the great depression of the 1930's, certainly shaped the form and figure of the American economy.

The relationship between economic and social history is much more one-sided than the connection between economics and politics, for social history is concerned with the end results of the process of economic development. Social history treats of such matters as the way Americans lived, the use of leisure time, and the rise of the city. These are not really subjects of economic history, but the results of the spinning of economic history. Thus, urbanization, with all its problems and all its implications, was a product of the growth of commerce and manufacturing; and the accumulation of leisure time, with all its mysteries, was the result of a constant rise in productivity.

The link between economic history and economic theory is so close that occasionally attempts have been made to make one the subdivision of the other. The German historical school and some American institutionalists tried to eliminate theory and concentrated on collecting data. Some theoreticians, going

[4]Guy S. Callendar, "The Position of the American Historian," *American Historical Review*, Vol. XIX (1913).

to the other extreme, have tried to eliminate the history from economic history. Thus far, none of these attempts has completely succeeded. Economic history still remains a vehicle for illuminating economic theory, and theory is still a valuable tool in the historian's kit. Theory, by posing questions and hypotheses, provides the framework on which economic historians mostly depend in arriving at their explanation of what happened in economic history. History, in turn, provides the only laboratory in which there is some possibility of testing the questions and hypotheses posed by theory.

To a great extent, economic history must be an exercise in description, but it can be more than that. Ideally, it should help to explain past economic events in terms of their causes and effects. It should seek to answer such fundamental questions as: What changes occurred in the individual's economic status? How did institutions develop? Why did these changes and developments happen? and What were their effects on the nation's individual citizens and on the political, social, and economic environment?

Practical men will immediately ask: What use is all this? If it is true, as Dean Inge once caustically remarked, that "the things we know about the past may be divided into those which probably never happened or those which do not much matter," then economic history, along with all other history, has little value. But the "Gloomy Dean" was wrong, for in the last analysis, almost everything depends on history. Admittedly, it is not true that history repeats itself in the sense of an absolute periodic duplication of events. But every true historian knows that there is no such thing as revolution, only evolution. He also knows that yesterday's problems will return again, and that there are always enough familiar elements in every new situation to enable people and nations to learn from what has gone before. Hence, by studying how economic systems have developed and functioned in the past, we shall better understand how our own works today.

It is a natural human trait to think that the time in which one lives—the century, the decade, and even the year—is in no way related to the past, that each day exists by itself unconnected with the past and auguring nothing for the future. Thus, each generation is tempted to believe that it is living in a "new era" and that "times are altogether different from what they used to be." A moment's reflection should demonstrate that this is a delusion. To quote the oft-paraphrased quotation of George Santayana: "Progress, far from consisting in change, depends on retentiveness. When change is absolute there remains no being to improve and no direction is set for possible improvement; and when experience is not retained, as among savages, infancy is perpetual. Those who cannot remember the past are condemned to repeat it."[5]

[5]George Santayana, *The Life of Reason* (New York: Charles Scribner's Sons, 1905), Vol. I, p. 284.

THE NATIONAL INCOME AS A MEASURE OF
ECONOMIC PROGRESS

As has been said, one way of measuring a nation's economic progress is to analyze the changes that took place over a period of time in real per capita income, that is, in the amount of goods and services available to each person. If the national income advanced faster than the combined increase in population and the price level, real per capita income went up and the level of living improved. Thus, if population doubled and the price level also doubled, money national income had to more than quadruple in order to accomplish an improvement in real per capita income.

Valuable as it is, the national income approach should not be called upon to do more than it can or was intended to do. Up to the present, national income estimates are the best yardsticks that have been invented for measuring economic progress. They provide the most objective tool for drawing generalizations and making comparisons relative to economic growth. But they are by no means perfect. They are estimates, and as such they can never be more than approximations. They are aggregates or averages and, therefore, somewhat unreal. Although they are objective, they nevertheless abound in value judgments.

Perhaps the most striking disadvantage of the national income accounts is that they do not include any intangibles or anything that cannot be measured. GNP, for example, does not include the income from nonmarket transactions. It includes imputed rents and income in kind, but not household manufacturing, the production of housewives, or other do-it-yourself activities. Another weakness of national income accounts is that they do not include costs; they measure output but not input. This is misleading, for if income remains the same but hours of work fall, life has improved even though real per capita income has not changed. Similarly, there are some costs incidental to earning a living that are ignored in the income accounts. For example, a given dollar of urban income costs more than a given dollar of rural income, because of the expenses of portal-to-portal time, training for more complicated jobs, and the expenses of city life in general. Nor do national income accounts measure changes in quality. Also, they assume something that everyone knows to be incorrect, that is, that everything in the national income is there because someone wants it for its economic value. Police departments, fire departments, and defense departments are wanted for protection, not because they satisfy material wants. Because of these weakenesses, national income does not measure *welfare* as the word is ordinarily defined by the layman. A rising gross national product usually means that we are better off economically, but it does not necessarily mean that we are any better off in the broader meaning of the term.

Some final words of caution. Even under the best conditions, data are never complete. They have to be manipulated on the basis of reasonable assumptions.

Comparisons over time and between different countries are especially vulnerable to scepticism. They require adjustments for price differentials, which are not easy to determine because radical differences in the goods and services produced at different times in history and at different places on the globe make it impossible to find a common denominator for accurate comparison. One need think merely of the differences between life in colonial times and today to get the point. How can one equate the prices of the products we use with those of the rural, horse-and-buggy, household manufacture of yesterday?

Yet, despite all these weaknesses, it is well to repeat that national income accounts are the best yardsticks that we have for measuring economic growth.

The growth of production and income

Economic historians know little about how much Americans produced or earned in the years before the Civil War. At various times, courageous scholars have made estimates,[6] but there are few raw data with which to work. Consequently, the findings, as one would expect, differ widely. Suspect as they are, however, they give us considerable insight into the trends of early American economic development. First impressions of the Colonial Period might lead one to believe that economic progress in those years was universally slow, for there were no startling innovations, either in business or in technology. Yet, some highly respected students have come to a different conclusion regarding colonial economic development. George Rogers Taylor has estimated American output in 1710 at about $10 million, or $30 per capita. In dollars of 1840 purchasing power, Taylor's estimates would be $15 million and $45 per capita.[7] Taylor further hypothesized that "until about 1710 growth was slow . . . from about 1710 to 1775, the rate was relatively rapid (perhaps 1 percent per capita or even a little higher) and from 1775 until 1840 . . . *average* per capita production showed little if any increase." If Taylor is correct, per capita income in 1800 would have been approximately $120, based on the *price level* in 1800. According to another conjecture, output in 1799 was $667 million or about $130 per capita in 1799 prices.

The most widely respected figures we have for 1839-1869 are the product of the energy and skill of Professor Robert E. Gallman. According to his data,

---

[6]The earlier estimates have been collected by Paul Trescott and appear in National Bureau of Research, "Trends in the American Economy in the Nineteenth Century," *Studies in Income and Wealth,* Vol. 24 (Princeton, N.J.: Princeton University Press, 1960), p. 360. See also Robert E. Gallman, "Estimates of American National Product Made Before the Civil War," in Ralph Andreano, ed., *New Views on American Economic Development* (Cambridge, Mass.: Schenkman Publishing Co., Inc., 1965).

[7]George Rogers Taylor, "American Economic Growth Before 1840," *Journal of Economic History,* Vol. 24 (1964), pp. 427-44, reprinted in Andreano, *op. cit.*

output totalled (in current prices) $1.5 billion in 1839 and $7 billion in 1869.[8]
If these estimates are within the boundaries of reasonable accuracy (which they
certainly are), the United States in 1839 enjoyed a national income equal to
two-thirds that of Britain. It was, therefore, hardly a poor country. Indeed,
judged by comparison with today's underdevleoped countries, it was rich.

Estimates of national product for the period after the Civil War are more
reliable than those for earlier years, and figures for the period since World War I
are still more reliable. They show that gross national product rose to about $80
billion in 1919 and to over $1 trillion today, or about 1,000 times in a little less
than 175 years. But these are *aggregate* figures expressed in *money* rather than in
real terms. Even if the estimates were precisely correct, they would not mean
that either the country as a whole or the average citizen is 1,000 times better off
today than in 1800. For one thing, population increased almost 40 times, so that
production per head in dollar terms is only 25 times as great as in 1800. Meanwhile, too, prices have risen, so that each dollar of income buys less than it used
to. Between 1800 and 1970, prices advanced at a rate that averaged out at 1.25
percent a year. Taking these price changes into account, *real per capita* GNP
(output of goods and services per head) is about 12 times as high today as it was
in the early nineteenth century. To put this in a different way, the average
citizen produces about 12 times as much in goods and services as his great-
great-grandfather did.

A nation's potential GNP can be reduced to a simple formula: its labor
force times the hours worked times productivity. Differences in *potential
aggregate* GNP between one year and another are, therefore, a function of
increases or decreases in labor force (including hours worked), productivity, and
the price level. Differences in *potential real* GNP are a function of changes in the
labor force and productivity. In turn, differences in *real* GNP *per capita* are the
result of changes in productivity (i.e., the output per unit of resources—labor
and capital).

Whether a country achieves its potential depends on how fully its labor,
capital, and managerial resources are utilized. In short, the difference between
potential and actual GNP depends on the extent of unemployment. But that is
another story that will be taken up later. Suffice it here to say that of the
increase in aggregate output in current dollars between the early nineteenth
century and today, population accounted for approximately two-fifths (40

[8]The lowest estimate of output in 1799 is $470 million; the highest $730 million. The
$677 million figure is Robert F. Martin's estimate of *realized income.* The 1839 and 1869
figures are based on Gallman's estimate of *commodity* output. Martin's estimates have been
severely criticized because they show that *real* income was higher in 1799 than in any other
decennial year before 1849. Robert F. Martin, *National Income in the United States, 1700-
1938* (New York: The National Industrial Conference Board, 1939), Robert E. Gallman,
"Output, Growth, and Price Trends," *Studies in Income and Wealth,* Vol. 24, *op. cit.*

percent), price inflation for one-quarter (25 percent), and productivity for one-third (35 percent). In the nineteenth century it was population growth that was the chief propelling force for total output; in the twentieth century it has been productivity. In the 1800s about 64 percent of the rise in commodity output came from population growth; in the 1900s, only 19 percent. The remainder in each case came from productivity. To put this another way, commodity output

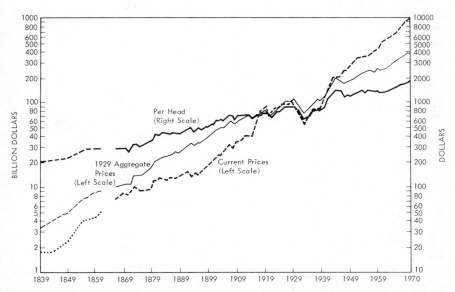

CHART 1. Aggregate gross national product, current and constant (1929) prices and real GNP per capita (1929 prices), 1839-1970.

per worker increased 26 percent in the twentieth century and 16 percent in the nineteenth.

Admirable as they may be for measuring a country's accomplishments, GNP and total output lack significance for the individual because they do not represent what individuals receive directly. GNP represents total production, including depreciation and corporate income. If we deduct depreciation and undistributed corporate profits, we find that the *personal income* of today's average American family is approximately $10,000 in today's prices, compared with $5,000 a generation ago, and $3,000 in grandfather's time. Of this personal income, taxes and a trivial amount of nontax payments took 1 percent from grandfather and 3 percent from father. By contrast, they take 15 percent from today's average American. And of the disposable income that each had, about 92 percent was spent for consumption and 8 percent represented personal saving.

Table 1

AGGREGATE AND PER CAPITA REAL INCOME, 1839-1970
(1929 dollars)

Year	Aggregate	Per Capita[1]
1839	$ 3.4 billion	$ 200
1849	5.2	220
1859	8.4	270
1869	10.3	260
1879	16.8	330
1890	24.6	390
1900	36.4	480
1910	60.8	650
1920	73.3	690
1929	104.4	860
1932	76.4	610
1940	121.0	920
1950	187.1	1,220
1960	246.8	1,370
1970	364.3	1,780

Average Annual Rates of Change in GNP

1840-80	4.0%	1.3%
1880-1920	3.5	1.6
1920-60	3.2	1.8
1840-1960	3.6	1.6
1960-70	4.0	2.7

[1]Rounded to the nearest $10.
SOURCE: 1839-1879, Gallman, *op. cit.;* 1890-1900, Simon Kuznets, *Capital in the American Economy;* U.S. Department of Commerce, *Long Term Growth, 1860-1965; Survey of Current Business;* Simon Kuznets, "Notes on the Pattern of Economic Growth" in Robert Fogel and Stanley Engerman, *The Reinterpretation of American Economic History.*

The expansion of wealth

As everyone should know, wealth, both national and individual, results from what is saved and retained out of income. If it is not easy to measure national income, it is an immensely difficult task to count the country's wealth. Yet, some estimates have been made. Raymond Goldsmith has estimated that total wealth increased from $10 billion in 1850 to $4.1 trillion in 1960. Calculations based on Security Exchange Commission data estimated total national assets at $6.5 trillion in 1968.

Table 2 shows what has happened to the composition of the asset side of the national balance sheet in the twentieth century. Note the increase in the relative share of claims and the decline in the share represented by tangible assets. Note also that structures and durable goods (both producers and consumers) represent about the same share today as in 1900. Land, on the other hand, accounts for a considerably smaller proportion of total assets than in 1900, although its share is about the same as in 1929. Corporate stock also has had its ups and downs. It represented ten cents of every asset dollar in 1900, 20 cents in 1929, and 15 cents in 1968.

International comparisons

How does American economic growth compare with that of the world's other developed economies? In terms of aggregate real output over a long period of time, Japan has led the world with an average annual increase of just over 4 percent. Our growth rate in the aggregate is close behind at over 3.5 percent a year. In per capita terms, many countries have done better than we have. In the last 80 years, Japan's per capita product has grown at a rate of almost 3 percent a year; Sweden's, at 2 percent a year for almost 100 years; and ours, at 1.75 per year for over 100 years. Yet there are only four countries (U.S., Canada, Switzerland, and New Zealand) in which per capita real income is over $1,000 at 1953-54 prices, and per capita real income here is 1.5 times as high as in any other place in the world.

How can this double paradox be explained? First of all, we experienced the highest rate of population growth of any of the developed countries—2 percent per year contrasted with 1.2 percent in Japan, 0.64 percent in Sweden, and 0.24 percent in France. This extraordinary rate of increase in the numbers of people explains why our aggregate output increased disproportionately to our per capita increase. The solution to the second paradox is that our output—both aggregate and per capita—must have been far higher at the beginning of our measured period than was the case in the other countries at the time they began to count their output. Starting at a much lower base, they would have had to grow at a considerably faster rate than we grew just in order to catch up to what we had already attained.

Long-run trends in the growth of income and wealth

To sum up what has been said about our economic progress as measured by national wealth and national income, aggregate wealth rose at an annual rate of about 6 percent. Aggregate income, as measured by the gross national product in current dollars, advanced from about 1840 on at an average rate of 5 percent a year; output in dollars of the same purchasing power rose about 3.5 percent a year; and output per person in constant dollars about 1.75 percent a year. But just how did this progress take place? Was it a relatively steady movement? Or did it take place in a series of long waves in which energetic spurts were followed

Table 2

NATIONAL ASSETS, 1900-1968
(billions of current dollars)

	1900		1929		1945		1958		1968	
	Amount	Percent	Amount	Percent	Amount	Percent	Amount	Percent	Amount	Percent
Total tangible assets	91	58	428	46	578	38	1,678	47	3,096	48
Land	31	20	115	12	121	8	311	9	715	11
Structures	35	22	190	20	285	19	833	23	1,537	23
Producers durables	7	5	38	4	49	3	200	6	377	6
Consumer durables	6	4	42	5	46	3	179	5	233	4
Other	12	8	43	5	77	5	155	4	234	4
Claims[1]	49	33	340	34	761	51	1,477	41	2,501	38
Against government	3	3	33	3	296	20	335	9	436	7
Against financial institutions	12	8	88	9	298	20	539	15	926	14
Against consumers	6	4	51	5	28	2	172	5	392	6
Other	28	18	168	17	139	9	428	12	747	11
Corporate stock	14	9	187	20	147	10	457	12	983	15
Total assets	154	100	955	100	1,486	100	3,609	100	6,580	100

Note: Totals do not add to 100 percent because of rounding.

Rate of Growth in National Wealth

	Current dollars		Constant dollars	
	Aggregate	Per capita	Aggregate	Per capita
1850-1880	6.2%	3.6%	4.7%	2.1%
1900-1929	6.5	4.9	4.0	2.4
1929-1945	2.9	2.0	1.3	0.4
1945-1958	6.9	5.2	3.3	1.6
1850-1900	5.7	3.3	5.1	2.7
1900-1958	5.6	4.2	3.1	1.7
1850-1958	5.6	3.7	4.1	2.2

[1] Assets in the form of claims really do not exist. In a *national* balance sheet, they are canceled out by offsetting liabilities. For example, bank deposits are an asset to depositors, but an equal liability to the banks.

SOURCE: Raymond W. Goldsmith, *The National Wealth of the United States in the Postwar Period* (Princeton, N.J.: Princeton University Press, 1962); Goldsmith, "Balance Sheets and Tests of Inflation," *Science*, June 1962; U.S. Department of Commerce, Bureau of the Census, *Statistical Abstract.*

by tired lags? Or did it occur in stages—that is, in a few giant steps widely separated in time?

Conclusions about the relative steadiness of economic progress depend upon the way one interprets the word "relative." It becomes a matter of judgment resting upon the length of the time periods examined and the importance placed on the business cycle. Over 40-year periods, as one can see from Table 1, the rate of increase in aggregate and per capita real income did not vary much, ranging from 3.7 percent to 4.0 percent in the aggregate and from 1.3 percent to 1.8 percent in the per capita. Shorter periods were something else again. For example, the rate of growth in 1859-1869 averaged only 1.99 percent per year for the aggregate and minus 0.39 percent for the per capita. Again, in the dismally depressed 1930s, both aggregate and per capita product declined. On the other hand, in the late 1890s, product advanced 5.03 percent and per capita soared upward 3.19 percent per year. The explanation for this wide disparity lies of course in the vagaries of the business cycle.

THE HISTORICAL PATTERN IN THE BUSINESS CYCLE [9]

Although economic fluctuations, that is, ups and downs in business activity, occurred as far back as colonial times, they were not associated with industrial activity and, consequently, are not customarily included in the history of business cycles. More or less arbitrarily, economists consider that the first real business cycle occurred in the years around the War of 1812. They have been happening ever since. The National Bureau of Economic Research which has devoted hundreds of thousands of man-hours to the study of the subject, has constructed a set of dates that mark the turning points in the 27 business cycles that it has discerned in the last 125 years. These demonstrate that, from low point to low point, cycles have varied in length anywhere from a little over a year to a little less than ten years, but the mode has been three to four years. From the data gathered by the Bureau and by the Cleveland Trust Company, it appears that since 1815, the American economy has experienced, on the average, about one and a half years of expansion to every one of contraction. Thus, the

[9]There is a sizable literature on business depressions, but not so much on the cycle. See Rendigs Fels, *American Business Cycles, 1865-1897* (Chapel Hill, N.C.: University of North Carolina Press, 1959); Norman A. Silberling, *The Dynamics of Business* (New York: McGraw-Hill Book Company, 1943); Walter B. Smith and Arthur H. Cole, *Fluctuations in American Businesses, 1790-1860* (Cambridge, Mass.: Harvard University Press, 1935); Murray Rothbard, *The Panic of 1819* (New York: Columbia University Press, 1962); Reginald C. McGrane, *The Panic of 1837* (Chicago: University of Chicago Press, 1924); George W. Van Vleck, *The Panic of 1857* (New York: Columbia University Press, 1943); Broadus Mitchell, *Depression Decade* (New York: Holt, Rinehart & Winston, Inc., 1947); K. D. Roose, *The Economics of Recession and Revival: An Interpretation of 1937-38* (New Haven, Conn.: Yale University Press, 1954). See also Samuel Rezneck, *Business Depressions and Financial Panics* (New York: Greenwood Publishing Company, 1968).

process of climbing the ladder of economic progress was one of falling back two rungs for every three that were scaled.

All business cycles were not of equal duration or magnitude. As can be seen from Table 3, some were much shorter than others, some were extremely mild, and other were relatively intense. Each recession was not more serious or less serious than the previous one, nor was each recovery more, or less, vigorous than the last. The longest depression occurred between 1873 and 1878; the most severe, between 1929 and 1932. The longest sustained recovery, prior to World War II, took place from 1932 to 1937, but the economy climbed upward for almost as long a period between 1848 and 1853. Some recovery periods were very strong, but others, such as those of 1911 and 1919, were tired almost from the day they began. Many recessions, those of 1869, 1927, and 1960, for example, hardly scratched the course of economic development. On the other hand, a few depressions, notably those of 1907, 1921, and 1937, were very deep, but also very short. Thus, there have been relatively few cycles distinguished for both length and depth. The years of boom prosperity and deep depression surrounding the seven panics of 1819, 1837, 1857, 1873, 1882, 1893, and 1929 exhaust the list.

Historians, thinking in the sweeping terms of long-run developments and emphasizing the social effects of business fluctuations, customarily focus their attention on the major depressions, de-emphasizing the prosperity phase of the cycle and ignoring recessions almost entirely. It is hard to understand why prosperity has attracted so little attention, but there is much logic in de-emphasizing minor recessions. These mild downturns were the result chiefly of changes in inventories and did not cause critical social disturbances. Only economists seem to have noticed them. In history, they were light thundershowers on an otherwise clear day. Consumer spending held up well, bankrupticies were not extraordinarily numerous, and personal income declined only slightly, if at all. To be sure, unemployment rose, but to disturbing, rather than alarming, levels. Recessions did not result in a widespread loss of faith in the long-run future of the economy, and, as soon as inventories were substantially liquidated, recovery set in.

Major depressions, on the other hand, were periods of severe deflation. They were associated primarily with a fall in the money supply and with steep and prolonged declines in capital nvestment. All business activity dropped precipitately.[10] Consumer spending weakened, unemployment rose to tragic heights, and prices and real per capita income skidded downward, bringing hardship and ruin to many in the community—businessmen as well as others. Depressions

[10]It is tempting to fall into the trap of describing business depressions as the result of overspeculaiton in the previous boom period. This widely repeated explanation is not logically defensible, as has been pointed out by J.R.T. Hughes and Nathan Rosenberg in "The United States Business Cycle Before 1860: Some Problems of Interpretation," *Economic History Review*, Second Series, Vol. XV (1963).

influenced the rate of population growth, the quantity of immigration, and the internal movement of population. The economic devastation that accompanied the great cataclysms required radical readjustments for the farmer, the worker, the businessman, and the investor. Severe depressions left in their wake wide-spread social and economic dissatisfaction and contributed to political reforms designed to alleviate future social disaster or to expunge the sources of economic misfortune. Depressions did irreparable damage to the "American Dream," caused a re-evaluation of economic progress, and shook people's faith in the future of the economy, with resulting basic changes in the money system, the structure of institutions, and the role of the government in the economy.

Although all business cycles shared the same basic characteristics, they differed from each other in detail. The cycles of the first half of the nineteenth century were associated with the extensive development of an overwhelmingly agrarian economy. Most of the working force were farmers. Indeed, agriculture, it has been estimated, accounted for well over 50 percent of all production. Some manufacturing did take place, but judged by modern standards, it was minuscule, accounting for less than 15 percent of production. Altogether, the so-called service industries produced 25 percent of total production.[11] There was little domestic commerce because of the primitive nature of transportation facilities and the relatively limited market area. Foreign commerce, however, was very active, making the balance of trade and the flow of foreign capital ex-tremely strategic factors in the alternation of recession and recovery. Since the public seemed to need little in the way of public services, government played a minor role, although it did add to the social capital on a federal as well as a local level.

The financial structure was also quite different from what it has since become. In a farm economy heavily involved in international trade, capital investment went into "making a farm," shipbuilding, and the construction of turnpikes, canals, and, toward the middle of the century, railroads. Most of the capital needed for these uses came from the farmer's own labor, and the sale of securities. In such an environment of direct financing, there was far less need for financial intermediaries—the middlemen who bring together savers and invest-ors—than there is today. With the exception of commercial banking, which was a thriving industry before the end of the eighteenth century, financial inter-mediaries were still in their infancy or early adolescence. To be sure, general insurance companies were already venerable institutions; but savings banks, life insurance companies and savings and loan associations were just beginning to show their influence. Pensions, credit unions, and investment companies hardly existed. Investment banking did exist in a precarious sort of way, but stock markets did little business; Americans exercised their speculative propensities by dabbling in land, real estate, and lotteries rather than by buying securities.

[11] The estimates are from Robert Gallman, *op. cit.,* and Thomas Weiss, "The Service Sector in the U.S., 1839-1899," summary of an unpublished Ph.D. dissertation, *Journal of Economic History,* Vol. 27 (1967).

Table 3
DURATION AND AMPLITUDE OF BUSINESS
CYCLES, 1855-1960

Expansion, trough to peak			Contraction, peak to trough		
Years	Duration in months	Amplitude in percent	Years	Duration in months	Amplitude in percent
1854-57	30	12.3	1857-58	18	21.0
1858-60	22	16.8	1860-61	8	14.1
1861-64	46	18.1	1864-67	32	11.4
1867-69	18	6.9	1869-70	18	7.9
1870-73	34	18.4	1873-78	65	26.9
1878-82	36	27.6	1882-85	38	27.9
1885-87	22	22.7	1887-88	13	11.2
1888-90	27	16.6	1890-91	10	17.0
1891-92	20	16.3	1892-94	17	30.7
1894-95	18	25.3	1895-96	18	24.3
1896-99	24	26.6	1899-1900	18	14.4
1900-03	21	14.2	1903-04	23	14.4
1904-07	33	20.2	1907-08	13	29.5
1908-10	19	25.6	1910-11	24	12.0
1911-13	12	13.6	1913-14	23	23.2
1914-18	44	29.8	1918-19	7	22.0
1919-20	10	17.9	1920-21	18	34.7
1921-23	22	38.0	1923-24	14	21.8
1924-26	27	17.8	1926-27	13	9.3
1927-29	21	16.7	1929-32	43	75.1
1932-37	50	63.7	1937-38	13	45.4
1938-44	80	72.7	1944-46	8	41.0
1946-48	37	14.7	1948-49	11	17.5
1949-53	45	23.9	1953-54	13	14.3
1954-57	35	13.9	1957-58	9	22.7
1958-60	25		1960-61	9	
1961-69	118		1969-70	12	

SOURCE: NBER, *Business Cycle Indicators;* Dept. of Commerce, Business Cycle Developments.

Most of the funds that were not supplied directly came via loans from the commercial banks—loans for long-term projects as well as for merchants and manufacturers. Through their paper money issues, the banks supplied all of the economy's money stock, except the hard money or high-powered money represented by specie (i.e., gold and silver).

Judged by today's standards, commercial banking in the early nineteenth century was conducted in a loose and freewheeling fashion. Yet, on the whole, the system, if it can be so called, seems to have provided a sufficient amount of money to keep the economy well lubricated. In the last analysis, the whole money supply depended upon the volume of high-powered money, which in turn depended upon the operation of an international specie standard. Although legal reserve requirements existed in only a few states, any prudent banker maintained a specie reserve against his note issue and his deposits.[12] Since these reserves were in the form of high-powered money, they were the plaything of international specie movements. Consequently, the money spply (note issue and deposits) fluctuated widely.

The interregnum period of the late nineteenth century could be regarded as the age of railroads, steam, and steel. Industrialism made extraordinary strides, while the relative importance of agriculture rapidly diminished. Toward the end of the century, agriculture accounted for an estimated 20 percent of total output, manufacturing for 30 percent, and services for 45 percent. The industrialization and urbanization of the country opened up new and vaster channels for capital investment in railroads, in mass urban transportation, in residential housing, and in capital-intensive manufacturing. At the same time, capital institutions underwent a fundamental transformation. A dual banking system that incorporated nationally-chartered as well as state-chartered banks replaced the state banking of the early period and added a factor of safety that had previously been absent. But for most of the half century, both the banking system and the money supply continued to be subject to the arbitrary vagaries of an international gold standard.

The cycles that occurred in the twentieth century reflected still different features. This was the era of intensive development—the age of the automobile and electricity. During these years, the importance of agriculture diminished absolutely as well as relatively. The gap was filled both by manufacturing and, much more so, by the expansion of the so-called "service industries."[13] The institutional structure underwent a subtle evolution. Government emerged as an immensely important participant in the economy, accounting for 6 percent of national income in 1929, 10 percent in 1950, and 16 percent in 1970. The banking structure achieved greater safety after the depression of the 1930s under the influence of an increasingly powerful Federal Reserve System helped by reassurance from the Federal Deposit Insurance Corporation. Capital investment continued to pour into residential housing, and also into producers' durable goods, public utilities, urban office construction, highways, and, eventually, space exploration.

[12]It is well to remember that bankers have always faced the dilemma posed by the conflicting objectives of maximizing profits and at the same time maintaining safety. The more that bankers extend loans, which are the source of their profits, the closer they come to jeopardizing the safety of their deposits.

[13]In 1970, agriculture accounted for only 3 percent of national income; manufacturing, for 28 percent. Within the service sector (62 percent of national income) transportation and communication produced 8 percent; trade, 15 percent; finance, 11 percent; and services, 13 percent.

LONG WAVES IN ECONOMIC PROGRESS

By de-emphasizing the influence of the business cycle, it can be argued that real output per capita increased steadily and did not deviate very much from the long-run average gain of 1.75 percent per year. Professor Raymond Goldsmith has demonstrated this very graphically. To reduce somewhat the effects of cyclical fluctuations, he translated annual changes in real production into a set of five-year moving averages, which he superimposed on the basic trend line. Observed values departed somewhat from the average, but on the whole they conformed closely. In only three instances—the years around the Civil War, the great depression of the 1930s, and World War II—did the actual values deviate by more than 10 percent above or below the long-run trend.

By applying different statistical techniques to the same basic data, some students[14] of economic history conclude that growth, as measured by national income, took place in a series of long waves, or long swings, or, as they are sometimes called, trend cycles. These long waves were altogether different from the business cycle, because they were much longer and involved much wider fluctuations in economic activity.

Scholars differ somewhat on the precise chronology of long waves,[15] but it is generally agreed that they centered around the dates of the great panics—the aforementioned 1819, 1837, 1857, 1873, 1882, 1893, and 1929.

The anatomy of the long wave

Each long wave consisted of three phases. In phase one, the economy expanded very rapidly under the driving forces of an atypically large volume of capital investment and a forward spurt in productivity. This expansion phase did not last long. Accelerated economic activity soon filled the gaping hole left by the previous great depression and quickly absorbed unemployed resources. Once this was accomplished, phase two set in. The pace of economic advance slowed down to one-half or one-third the rate that had prevailed at the height of prosperity.

---

[14]Notably, Moses Abramovitz. Instead of using a five-year moving average, Abramovitz averages not for a specific number of years, but over the actual number of years in each cycle. Business cycles have thus been ironed out completely.

[15]The late professor Schumpeter, one of the foremost proponents of the longwave approach, divided economic history into three Kondratieff cycles: (1) from the 1780s to 1842—the Industrial Revolution, (2) from 1842 to 1897—the age of steel and steam, (3) from 1898 on—the era of electricity, chemistry, and motors. Each Kondratieff was divided into six Juglar cycles eight to ten years in length. See Joseph A. Schumpeter, *Business Cycles* (NewYork: McGraw-Hill Book Company, 1939), Vol. I, p. 170. Abramovitz cites the following dates as peaks of the long waves: 1814, 1834, 1846, 1864, 1881, 1889, 1899, 1914, 1923, and 1938.

Retardation continued progressively and finally culminated in the unusually severe depressions that marked phase three. Once again, capital spending and productivity were important controlling factors. At the bottom of the long swing, both were far below their peak levels. But capital spending lagged behind the curve of economic activity, whereas productivity led it. That is, in the ordinary sequence of a downturn, retardation first hit man-hour output, then economic growth in general, and then capital investment.

There is some evidence, though inconclusive, that the long waves in economic growth are weaker than they used to be. Raymond Goldsmith's conclusions on the rate of growth of national assets show that there has been a slowing down in the twentieth century. He found that national wealth accumulated at a rate of 2.7 percent per person per year in the last half of the 1800s, but at only 1.7 percent in the first half of the 1900s. Some scholars believe that any slump in the rate of economic growth has been due to a falling off in labor and capital input per head. In other words, if growth is not what it used to be, it is because the rewards of economic progress have been increasingly taken in the form of increased leisure and increased consumption rather than in increased income and increased saving.

Two examples, one from early American history and one from the more recent past, may serve to illustrate the course of typical long swings. Some evidence has already been presented showing a healthy rate of growth in the Colonial Period. Thereafter the economy seems to have fallen on difficult years. It does not seem to have become reinvigorated until the 1830s or 1840s. It was in this latter period that the railroads first became really significant and technology had its first great spurt in agriculture. It was also the era that has been associated with the "rise of the common man," when enterprising, hustling entrepreneurs first appeared in some profusion and the country first gave evidence that its overwhelming objective was economic growth. For these reasons or perhaps for others, the economy entered a new phase of recovery and prosperity.

In our second example—the 1920s—the economy emerged from World War I and the sharp downturn of 1920-1921 to embark upon a boom. By 1923, the *rate* of economic advance had reached its peak. The economy continued to climb for the next six years, interrupted twice by the mild recessions of 1924 and 1927, the pace became progressively slower until it finally culiminated in the great depression of the 1930s. Part of this history has been repeated in the 1950s and 1960s. The economy again emerged from a major war and began a substantial expansion. By the middle 1950s, the rate of growth had visibly slowed. Between 1947 and 1955, real GNP advanced about 4.5 percent a year, but after 1955 it slowed to about 2.5 percent a year until the mid 1960s when real growth advanced to 4.5 to 5.0 percent a year. If the pattern of the past should repeat itself, it would mean a severe and prolonged depression in the near future. But, although this is by no means impossible, such a development would come as a great surprise to most economists.[16]

Some explanations of the long wave

It has already been implied that long waves are closely interrelated with the volume of capital investment. Therefore, whatever explains variations in the one also explains variations in the other. A text in economic history is not an appropriate medium for a long description of the many explanations that have been offered for these long waves, but even at the risk of gross over-simplification, the most important should at least be briefly mentioned.

All of the widely accepted explanations of long waves have much in common, but they differ in the relative emphasis they place on primary causes. First of all, there are those that stress the strategic importance of the entre-preneur. According to the simplest of these interpretations, the economy runs down because entrepreneurs become tired, careless, and slack. Success inevitably breeds inefficiency, and nothing much can be done about it. A variant of this—more associated with the cyle than with long waves—is that business downturns are the creatures of variations in profit margins. In the initial stages of recovery, costs—especially labor costs—are low and profit margins are high. But as recovery proceeds, costs gradually increase, profit margins fall, capital investment loses much of its economic fascination, and the economy cracks up.

Joseph A. Schumpeter, in his *Theory of Economic Development,* offered still another variant of the entrepreneurial explanation. Schumpeter argued that long-wave variations in economic activity were set in motion by *innovations,* which may be defined as "doing things differently in the realm of economic life"; or, to put it still another way, innovation is a process of combining factors of production in a new way. Upswings in long waves began when entrepreneurs carried out innovations. These new methods of combining factors lowered per-unit costs of production and raised profits. The prospect of profits in turn attracted adaptive businessmen, and, as they invaded the field, production rose

[16]Their opinion rests upon the belief that the great depressions of the past were associated with a decided slowing down in capital investment and were aggravated by misguided fiscal and monetary policies. Most economists believe that institutional changes have eliminated both. It is argued that the Federal Reserve System will not permit a drastic contraction of the money supply. An extreme curtailment of capital investment is also con-sidered unlikely because the presence of a battery of so-called "economic stabilizers," including the magnitude of government expenditures, the flexibility of the progressive tax structure, unemployment insurance, and Social Security payments will maintain demand at a high level and thus keep both consumption and investment spending from tobogganing downward.

and profit margins sank. The impulse to innovation had spent itself and the long wave entered its desultory phase.[17]

A second set of explanations emphasizes demand rather than supply as the causal factor in long waves. Here the argument is that faltering demand dissuades businessmen from increasing their capital investment, and, as investment slackens, the economy gradually deteriorates. Faltering demand has been explained in many different ways. Underconsumptionists believe that demand falls because consumer wants have been satiated, or because population growth begins to lag, or because of an inequitable distribution of income. Others put most of the onus on a disequilibrium between planned saving and planned investment. Still a third group insists that the difficulty lies in a failure of the money supply to grow in pace with general economic activity.

Another explanation for long waves puts the blame on exogenous factors, such as sun spots, atmospheric disturbances, and, most especially, war. Major wars, according to the story, not only raise the demand for military goods during the conflict itself, but also bequeath to the postwar world a backlog of demand for civilian goods. Thus, major wars stimulate spending, prices, and general economic activity and propel the economy into boom prosperity. However, like all good things, this too must come to an end. Eventually, the backlog of demand fills up, competition increases, and costs rise. As the effect of the war-produced stimulant runs down, so does economic activity, and the bloom of prosperity fades.

LONG WAVES IN PRICE MOVEMENTS

Efforts to establish the existence of long-wave movements in population, production, construction, and prices similar to those in economic growth have met with varied success. Wave-like movements of about twenty years duration occurred in many basic American time series at least as far back as the early nineteenth century. There have been observable cycles in building construction, railroad construction, and immigration that roughly synchronized with the broader waves of economic activity,[18] but whether long swings characterize such economic phenomena as the growth of population and production is debatable. There is no doubt, however, that very definite long swings occurred in the history of prices, and that these were intimately related to war and its aftermath.

[17]See Schumpeter, *Business Cycles,* Vol. I, pp. 84-174; "The Creative Response in Economic History," *Journal of Economic History,* Vol. 7 (1947); *The Theory of Economic Development* (Cambridge, Mass.: Harvard University Press, 1934).

[18]Walter Isard has suggested the following peaks in the construction cycle: 1836, 1853, 1871, 1890, 1909, and 1925. See "Transport Development and Building Cycles," *Quarterly Journal of Economics,* Vol. 57 (1942). Compare these with Abramovitz's peaks cited in a previous footnote.

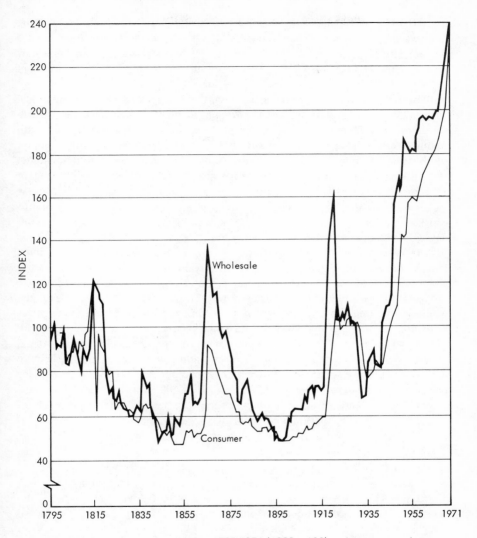

CHART 2. Wholesale price index, 1795-1971 (1929 = 100) and consumer price index, 1800-1971 (1929 = 100)

As we may see from Chart 2, fluctuations in wholesale prices and the cost of living were a prominent feature of American economic life even during short intervals of time. But by eliminating these cyclical oscillations, we can easily discern long-term trends in price movements. These lasted anywhere from 12 to 32 years—roughly, from the price peaks reached in wartime to the troughs plumbed at the bottom of major depressions. Wholesale prices declined secularly from 1814 to 1843, then moved upward until the end of the Civil War. A long, downward spiral occurred between 1864 and 1896, when prices fell to exactly the same floor as in 1843. Then a substantial recovery set in, reaching a new ceiling at the end of World War I. The price index again trended downward from 1920 to 1932, crept upward to 1940, and soared to another new high at the end of World War II. For a short time thereafter, it appeared that the historical pattern would reassert itself, but the Korean incident carried the index to still another high. Then, after a few years of small increases interspersed with stability, prices again took off as a result of a rapidly expanding money supply, the Vietnam involvement, and a high volume of business investment spending. Over the long run, the price index, as has already been stated, rose by roughly 1.25 percent a year. This statement, however, is somewhat deceiving, because it makes no allowance for changes in the quality of goods. If these were taken into consideration, the gap between today's prices and those of the day before yesterday would be much smaller than it actually is.

At first glance, it might seem that declining prices raised the real national income because they made it possible to buy more goods and services with a given money income. It might also seem that rising prices deterred economic progress because they cut purchasing power. However, this is by no means the whole story. Declining prices were not an unmixed blessing, and rising prices were not an unmitigated evil. Indeed, it has been argued that rising prices, by causing an increase in the dollar value of inventories and a decline in real wages, showered businessmen with windfall profits and thereby encouraged them to increase capital expenditures.[19] Whether this hypothesis is true or not, rising prices would be what one would expect to result from high-level economic activity. They were symptoms of expanding production, intense demand for resources, and rising national income. To be sure, each dollar had less purchasing power as prices rose, but also people had more dollars. Conversely, declining prices often accompanied declining national income, so that, even though each dollar of money income bought more, there were less dollars of income available. Thus, the dollar bought the most goods and services in 1843, 1896, and 1932, when prices were very low, but these were also extreme depression years when national income was very low. Oppositely, the dollar bought less when prices were high in 1864, 1920, and 1960, but in these years national income was very high. Moreover, business contractions tended to be longer when the trend in prices was downward and shorter when prices were rising. According to the National Bureau's chronology, when prices were in a rising trend, there were three years of upswings in business activity for each one year of retardation; but during waves of falling prices, there was less than one year of prosperity for each year of retardation. Of course, this does not mean that price inflation caused prosperity; prices were an effect, not a cause.

[19]See Earl J. Hamilton, "Prices as a Factor in Business Growth," *The Journal of Economic History,* Vol. 12 (1952).

However, on balance, rising prices were more symptomatic of economic growth than were falling prices. The outstanding exceptions occurred when prices fell during the economic upswing following the Civil War and when they remained stable during the boom of the 1920s.

The stages theory of economic growth

Stage theories have intermittently enchanted historians because their neat patterns offer a plausible explanation of what happened in the past. The German historians of the late nineteenth and early twentieth centuries were especially fond of explaining history as a procession of successive stages, each one replacing the preceding one in a quite orderly fashion. But most contemporary economic historians are cold to stage theories of any sort. They insist that there is little, if any, evidence to support them. They also point out that economic history is not discontinuous. It is a flow, rather than a set of upward thrusts. Stage theories, therefore, mask rather than reveal long-run trends in economic progress. There is, however, nothing wrong with a stage approach, provided it is not expected to do more than it can do. It is a convenient means of classification, an excellent pedagogical device. But if it is overdone, it may, as Professor Cairncross has said, "make good drama or supply the element of myths required for a popular manifesto; but it does not make . . . good history."[20]

Professor Walt W. Rostow has been the most articulate spokesman for the "stages" explanation of economic growth. He argues that a society goes through five stages in the course of economic development.[21] First is the Traditional Society, in which there is a low ceiling on the level of output because the potentialities of technology are either unavailable or not applied. Second comes the Precondition Period, the transitional stage in which the preconditions for "the Take-off" are developed. Then comes stage three: the all-important Take-off, when growth becomes the normal condition. Rostow dates this, in the United States, with the coming of the railroads in the 1830s.

According to Rostow the precipitating force in launching the Take-off is a sharp increase—perhaps a doubling—in the rate of capital formation. In short, effective investment rises to a significant fraction of the national income. But that is not all. There are two other characteristics of the Take-off: the development of one or more substantial manufactures, and "the existence or quick emergence of a political, social, and institutional framework which exploits the impulses to expansion."

[20] A. K. Cairncross, *Factors in Economic Development* (New York: Frederick A. Praeger, Inc., 1962), p. 132.

[21] Walt W. Rostow, *The Stages of Economic Growth* (London: Cambridge University Press, 1960); Walt W. Rostow, "Take-off into Self-Sustained Growth," *The Economic Journal,* Vol. LXVI, No. 261 (1956).

Some sixty years after the Take-off, an economy reaches stage four: a state of Economic Maturity in which the society can produce, not everything, but anything it chooses. The last stage, the Diffusion Stage, is an "age of high mass consumption," characterized by large-scale purchases of consumer durable goods and services.

Like all stage theories, Rostow's has been thoroughly criticized. Professor Simon Kuznets viewed the concept of the Take-off with something more than skepticism. He found no statistical evidence to confirm a sudden acceleration in the rate of investment and saving. Indeed, the most substantial increases in the rate of capital formation came after rather than before the presumed dates of the Take-offs. A second criticism was that there was no clear distinction between the pre-condition stage and the take-off. And finally, there is no such thing as self-sustained growth.[22]

Other critics have joined in roasting Rostow's thesis. Yet, despite the widespread criticism, the majority of those who have investigated early economic growth believe that the economy did take off in the 1830s or 1840s.[23] The logic is all on the side of a take-off for two reasons. We can be positive that real output per person could not have advanced steadily at a rate of 1.75 percent a year from the beginning of the nation's history. For, if it had, output in the early years would have been absurdly low—indeed, much too low to sustain life. Growing at an annual rate of 1.75 percent, output doubles every 40 years. If real per capita production was somewhere in the vicinity of $400 at about 1840, it would have been less than $20 at around 1650. This seems quite impossible. The Pilgrims were poor, but not that poor.

Looking at the problem from the other side of the glass also supports a take-off. The rates of increase in the 1840s were high. If these rates were extrapolated back, 1799 would be 60 percent of 1839. It is highly unlikely that output increased by 2/3 between 1799 and 1839. It follows, therefore, that either there must have been some point in the early years of our history when the curve of economic growth veered sharply upward, or there must have been alternate and almost equal bursts of progress and regression, which is hardly likely.

THE DISTRIBUTION OF THE NATIONAL INCOME

Thus far we have been concerned with the historical interrelationship between national income and economic progress, but only in terms of averages.

[22]Simon Kuznets, *Economic Growth and Structure* (New York: Norton, 1965).

[23]Gallman "is inclined" to believe that acceleration began with the forties or before. Goldsmith accepts the view that the railroad and a sharp spurt occurred simultaneously. Taylor also thinks that in the thirties the economy took off. But for a skeptical view, see Paul A. David, "The Growth of Real Product, in the U.S. Before 1840: New Evidence, Controlled Conjecture," *Journal of Economic History,* Vol. 27 (1967).

And averages can be most deceiving, as we know from the sad story of the man who drowned in a pool of water that averaged three feet deep. Unless we know something about how the income is distributed, averages are almost meaningless. An economy may boast a high average income, but, because of an extremely unequal distribution, many people may be living in poverty. It is not likely, however, that such a combination of high average income and extreme maldistribution could long continue. For, if a few people were receiving extraordinarily large shares and the rest very small shares, consumption would be so low that it would put a discouraging obstacle in the way of economic progress. On the other hand, if national output were cut into exactly equal pieces, no one would be able to save much, capital accumulation would be low, technological progress would be handicapped, and the prospects for high-level economic growth would not be very promising.

Historical data on the distribution of income are fragmentary, but it seems safe to assume that in early colonial times the small amount that was produced was fairly equally divided. There is no way of knowing what proportion went to the wealthiest one-third or to the poorest one-third of the population, but it is probably true that incomes were more evenly divided in New England than in the South, and there certainly was less difference between the income of the richest person and that of the poorest person in colonial New England than there is in the United States today.

What little data we have demonstrate that beginning in the late colonial period and continuing until 1929, income became more unevenly distributed by region and by occupation as well as among the different income groups. To be sure, those who were writing in the early nineteenth century had opposite views. They saw the United States as a vast experiment in equalitarianism. "The country," said a typical observer in 1855, "is not so rich as it seems at first sight though its wealth is more equally diffused than in England."[24] But present-day students of income and wealth concentration do not see such a diffusion, and judged by logic alone, they have the best of the argument. All the evidence that can be mustered demonstrates that economic growth is accompanied by a more unequal distribution of income and wealth. American economic growth was no exception. As the size of the national pie increased, everybody tended to get a larger piece, but the shares received by the fortunate few at the top of the income scale tended to grow faster than the shares received by the lower-income groups. In nineteenth-century America, in other words, the rich grew richer faster than the poor became less poor.

The growth in the number of large fortunes gives us a clue to income concentration in the nation's early years. Stories of the magnificent fortunes of some of the colonial fathers are highly exaggerated and romanticized. It is very unlikely that Thomas Hancock, Robert Morris, John Carroll, or George Washington succeeded in accumulating a fortune of over $1 million. Indeed, there were

[24]James Robertson, *A Few Months in America,* quoted by *Hunts Merchants Magazine,* Vol. 33 (1855), p. 54.

probably very few fortunes in excess of $500,000, for New Yorkers and Phila-delphians considered $100,000 comfortable and $300,000 great wealth.

By the early nineteenth century, however, some shrewd and aspiring in-dividuals had succeeded in becoming multimillionaires. Thomas Willing and William Bingham, Philadelphia merchants, were millionaires before 1800. Stephen Girard left over $6 million to found a home for orphans, and John Jacob Astor accumulated a staggering estate of $25 million. In 1843, a news-paper estimated that five men had fortunes of over $5 million, and 20 had fortunes of more than $1 million. This seems too low. It is more likely that there were at least 60 millionaires in the country in 1840. At about the same time, Philadelphia had 350 fortunes of $100,000 or more; New York had 300; Boston, 150; and Brooklyn, 26. Fifteen years later, in 1855, it was estimated that there were 91 millionaires in New York City alone. By the end of the century, millionaires had become so common (4,000 in 1892) that no one bothered to make a fuss over them. Instead, newspapers were giving their readers a vicarious thrill by writing intimately about fortunes of $100 million or more. Commodore Vanderbilt left an estate of over $100 million in 1877, and by 1889 there were six such fortunes. Forty years later, the wealthiest Americans rivaled the nabobs of India and made Croesus seem a pauper. Three men had accumulated close to $1 billion each, and wealth was being measured not in terms of $100 million, but in yearly incomes of $1 million or more. In 1929, there were 513 such individuals. The great depression reduced this number to 20 in 1932, and by 1941 only 57 were in the select circle. In the affluent 1960s, when more millionaires were reared than during any other period in American history, the Internal Revenue Service reported that 398 persons filed returns on incomes of over $1 million a year.

Fascinating as it is, the unqualified story of the growth of the great American fortunes gives a distorted picture of income concentration. We can get a better understanding of what happened to income distribution by dividing income recipients into groups according to size of income and then estimating what share of the total income each group received.

Unfortunately, there are no estimates of this kind for the years before 1900, but there are estimates of wealth holdings. They all show an increasing concen-tration. Studies based on Chester County, Pennsylvania, and Boston in the late seventeenth century conclude that the richest 10 percent owned 25 to 40 percent of total wealth. By 1780, their share had risen to over 50 percent and by 1860 to over 70 percent. But the wide discrepancy in the conclusions reached by different studies is well illustrated by the estimates for the 1890s which put the share of the upper 10 percent at 50 to 70 percent of total wealth, less than it was in 1860.[25]

[25] Edward Pessen, "The Egalitarian Myth and the American Social Reality," *American Historical Review,* Vol. 76 (1971), pp. 989-1034; Jackson T. Main, "Trends in Wealth Concentration Before 1860," *Journal of Economic History,* Vol. 31 (1971); Alice Hanson Jones, "Wealth Estimates for the New England Colonies about 1770," *Journal of Economic History,* Vol. 32 (1972); Robert E. Gallman, "Trends in the Size Distribution of Wealth,"

For the years since 1910, a number of consecutive series on income distribution are available. According to one study, covering the early years of the twentieth century, the shares received by the different income groups did not vary very much. The share of the top 30 percent of income recipients ranged between 56 and 62 percent. The share of the middle 40 percent did not go below 29 percent or above 32 percent, whereas the bottom 30 percent received between 8 and 14 percent. Another study found that the share of the top 1 percent ranged from 14 to 17 percent. Thus, income distribution did not shift very much in the first quarter of the century, but what shift did take place was in the direction of more inequality. Cyclical variations tended to blur this long-run trend. Invariably, the *relative* share of the higher-income brackets climbed in prosperity and fell somewhat in recession. Oppositely, the *percentage* share of those in the lower brackets was highest in depression and lowest in prosperity. The reasons for this are readily understandable. The lowest groups were so close to subsistence that they could give up little of their income without it disappearing altogether. The upper-income groups received most of the property income, and property income, especially profit, was high in boom years and low in depressions.

Every estimate of income distribution concludes that the tendency toward somewhat greater concentration of income, which had continued from the beginning of the American economy, came to an end with the depression of the 1930s.[26] Indeed, a decided shift in the other direction took place during World War II. The whole population moved up the economic ladder, but the poor moved up much faster than the rich. Between 1929 and 1946, the share of total income going to the lowest two-fifths rose from 12.5 to 16.1 percent, whereas the share of the highest two-fifths fell from 73.7 to 67.9 percent. The top 5 percent fared even worse. Their share fell from about 30 percent to 20 percent, and the share of the top 1 percent did still worse, falling from 17 to 10 percent. During the same years, wealth was becoming more equally distributed along with income. In 1929 the wealthiest 1 percent owned almost 40 percent of all personal assets. By 1949, their share had fallen to less than 25 percent.[27]

NBER, *Studies in Income and Wealth,* Vol. 33 (1969); James A. Henretta, "Economic Development and Social Structure in Colonial Boston" in Robert W. Fogel and Stanley L. Engerman, eds., *The Reinterpretation of American Economic History* (New York: Harper & Row, 1971).

[26]See Selma Goldsmith, "Size Distribution of Income since the Mid-Thirties," *Review of Economics and Statistics,* Vol. 36 (1954), Robert Solow in Ralph Freedman, ed., *Postwar Economic Trends in the United States* (New York: Harper & Row, Publishers, 1960); Herman P. Miller, *Income of the American People* (New York: John Wiley & Sons, Inc., 1955); Irving B. Kravis, *The Structure of Income* (Philadelphia: University of Pennsylvania Press, 1962).

[27]Robert J. Lampman, *The Share of Top Wealth-Holders in National Wealth, 1922-1956* (Princeton: Princeton University Press, 1962), p. 209. In 1896, it was estimated that the top 1 percent of income recipients took about one-quarter of the "national income" and owned a little over half the national wealth. Charles B. Spahr, *An Essay on the Present Distribution of Wealth in the United States* (New York: Crowell Publishing Company, 1896).

Meanwhile, too, income was being redistributed geographically, for per capita income was rising faster in the "poorest" sections than in the higher-income regions. Yet the difference between the poor and the rich was still very great indeed. Even in 1946, after a number of years of redistribution, the bottom 40 percent was still getting less than the top 5 percent, but they had succeeded in earning more than the top 1 percent. Theoretically, the new turn of events, by shifting income from those with a high propensity to save to those with a high propensity to consume, should have invigorated consumption and diminished saving. Actually, little change occurred. The marginal propensity to save seems to have been greatly exagerated. One study, concerned with the years 1929-1947, found that when the share of the upper 5 percent was cut almost in half, the share of disposable income spent on consumption rose insignificantly.

Some of the causes of the shift of income that occurred during the great depression and World War II were self-evident. The improved position of those in the lower-income bracket was a result of a sharp upward trend in nonproperty income. Income from interest, rent, and dividends began to decline after 1929. Wages and noncorporate income, on the other hand, zoomed upward during World War II, especially in the very low-income occupations: unskilled labor, service work, and farm labor. Median earnings in each of these three groups almost tripled between 1939 and 1946.

The unusual upsurge in the share of the total that went to nonproperty income occurred because of the depression, the demands of war, the influence of government, and a change in the behavior of business management. As noted above, nonproperty income held up better than property income during deep depressions. Then when war came, wartime controls reduced income from rents, and cheap money policies held down interest income. On the other hand, the intense wartime demand for food and fiber multiplied the farmer's earnings. The need for labor in defense work erased unemployment, created opportunities for overtime, and pushed up wage rates, while businessmen, under the necessity of turning out production at any price, diminished their resistance to wage increases. Government tax policy was not a primary factor in the reversal of the long-term trend in income distribution, for the shift took place in income before taxes. What tax policy did do was to narrow further the gap between the cap wearers and the top hat wearers.

At the end of the War, it was generally believed that the "revolution" in income distribution would be more or less permanent. This has not turned out to be the case. Since the end of World War II, there has been little change in the pattern of distribution. Between 1947 and 1970, the share of the bottom 40 percent rose from 16.8 to 17.9 percent, whereas that of the top 40 percent fell from 66.1 to 64.4 percent, and the income of the top 5 percent continued to fall from 17.2 to 14.7 percent of the total. These figures are before taxes; but, odd as it may seem, after-tax distribution would not be very much different. In

Table 4

**SIZE DISTRIBUTION OF AGGREGATE INCOME BY FAMILIES,
1929 to 1969**

Family income	1929	1947	1960	1969
lowest 1/5	4.0%	5.0%	4.9%	5.6%
middle 1/4	14.0	17.0	17.6	17.6
highest 1/5	54.0	43.0	42.0	41.0
top 5%	30.0	17.2	16.8	14.7

SOURCE: *Survey of Current Business,* April 1964; *Statistical Abstract,* 1971.

1960, for example, the richest 5 percent received 20 percent of pre-tax personal income and about 18 percent of what was left after taxes. The poorest 40 percent took 15.6 percent of pre-tax and 16.4 percent of after-tax income.

The problem of poverty

There are many ways of defining poverty, none of which is altogether satisfactory. Indeed, some definitions of the concept are absurd. One definition sets the poverty level to include an arbitrary proportion of the population (for example, one-third or one-fifth) at the bottom of the income stream. By this measure the proportion of society in poverty would always remain the same. It is, therefore, a definition of the poor rather than of the poverty-stricken. Another group defines poverty to include all those beneath a fixed amount of income, such as $3,000 or $4,000. In 1962, the Council of Economic Advisers determined that $3,000 was the income level that separated the poverty group from the rest of society. More recently, some people have decreed that $6,500 marks the upper boundary of bare subsistence for the average-size family. But the use of either of these fixed figures to describe poverty in the past leads to ludicrous conclusions. The $3,000 bare subsistence income in 1962 would equate with $1,700 in 1929 after correcting for changes in the price level. Seventeen hundred dollars in 1929 was not considered a low income. Almost half of all American families made less, and it would be unrealistic to conclude that almost half of American families in 1929 were at the poverty level. If we pushed the calculations back to colonial times, we would be forced to the untenable conclusion that 90 percent of colonials were below the minimum decency level.

The most objective definition labels the poverty-stricken as all those whose incomes are below the level of subsistence or what is sometimes called a minimum decency level. On the basis of budgets drawn up at different points in time, minimum decency at any time would be equal to approximately half of real per capita GNP.

The historian's chief difficulty with any definition of poverty is that poverty is not the same for all times and all places. To most of the Indians in Calcutta, the idea of poverty in America is laughable. But it is very real to an Indian in Monument Valley. The man with an income of $100,000 a year considers the $12,000 a year man poor; to him who makes $3,000, he is rich.

Nor should the measure of poverty be the same over periods of time. The yardstick is a flexible one that is constantly expanding. Poverty, in short, is a relative concept. As David Ricardo brilliantly observed many years ago, the standard of living is that to which one becomes accustomed. A "minimum decency" level includes more and more goods and services as time goes on; that, after all, is progress.

No matter what the definition, the incidence of poverty in the United States has fallen significantly. In terms of 1967 dollars, 27 percent of American families were below $3,000 in 1947 contrasted with 9 percent today. By this definition of poverty, we have gone 66 percent of the way to the elimination of poverty. Measured in dollars of the same purchasing power, the proportion of families making $6,000 or more a year has more than quadrupled since 1929 and more than doubled since 1947.

There is still another way of looking at this. In 1929, it was estimated that 20 percent of Americans earned a bare subsistence income[28] or less with another 25 percent in the bare subsistence plus group. In 1969, the Bureau of the census estimated the poverty-stricken at 12.2 percent of the total population. The corresponding figure for 1959 was 22.4 percent. Looking at the income stream from the top down, less than 3 percent of Americans earned $10,000 or more in 1947. By 1960 this group had climbed to 14 percent and by 1969 to 46 percent. Of course, it must be remembered that many units that have a bare subsistence income may also enjoy a more than comfortable level of

Table 5
DISTRIBUTION OF FAMILIES AND UNATTACHED INDIVIDUALS BY REAL INCOME LEVELS

Personal Income (1963 dollars)	1929	1947	1963	1969
Below $2,000	30%	16%	11%	7%
$2,000-$5,999	54	54	38	22
$6,000-$9,999	10	21	30	38
$10,000 and over	6	9	21	33

SOURCE: *Survey of Current Business,* April 1964; 1969 based on data in *Current Population Reports.*

[28]Bare subsistence is just enough to hold body and soul together. A comfortable income is one in which 25 percent or more of income can be spent on other than necessities. It must be remembered that one man's necessities are another man's luxuries and vice versa.

living. For example, some retired and temporarily unemployed families may be living comfortably on previously accumulated capital. But even allowing for this, we still have a long, long way to go to attain the affluent society that some people are sure we have already achieved.

SUGGESTED READINGS

(On specific topics, consult the readings cited in the footnotes in the chapter.)

Denison, E.F., *The Source of Economic Growth in the United States and the Alternatives Before Us* (New York: Committee for Economic Development, 1962).

Galman, Robert E. and Edward S. Howle, "Trends in the Structure of the American Economy Since 1840," in Robert W. Fogel and Stanley Engerman, eds., *The Reinterpretation of American Economic History* (New York: Harper & Row, Publishers, 1971).

Harte, N.B., ed., *The Study of Economic History* (London: Frank Cass, 1971).

Kuznets, Simon, "Notes on the Pattern of U.S. Economic Growth" in Fogel and Engerman.

Miller, Herman, *Income Distribution in the U.S.* (New York: Social Science Research Council, 1966).

Pessen, Edward, "The Egalitarian Myth and the American Social Reality," *American Historical Review,* Vol. 76 (1971), pp. 989-1034.

Taylor, George Rogers and Lucius F. Ellsworth, eds., *Approaches to American Economic History* (Wilmington, Del.: Eleutherian Mills-Hagley Foundation, 1971).

U.S. Congress, Joint Economic Committee, *Employment, Growth, and Price Levels,* Hearings, Part 2, "Historical and Comparative Rates of Production, Productivity, and Prices," 1959. Papers by Abramovitz and Goldsmith. These have been reprinted in Ralph Andreano, ed., *New Views on American Economic Development* (Cambridge, Mass.: Schenkman Publishing Company, Inc., 1965).

Bibliographies in Economic History

American Economic Association, *Index of Economic Journals,* Vols. I-VII, 1886-1966.

Daniels, Lorna, *Studies in Enterprise: A Selected Bibliography of American and Canadian Company Histories and Biographies of Businessman* (Boston: Harvard Business School, 1957). Extended in *Business History Review,* No. 2 of 1959-62 and No. 3 of 1963-64.

Larson, Henrietta M., *Guide to Business History* (Cambridge, Mass.: Harvard University Press, 1948).

Lovett, Robert W., *American Economic and Business History Information Sources* (Detroit, Mich.: Gale Research Company, 1971).

Taylor, George Rogers, *American Economic History Before 1860* (New York: Appleton-Century-Crofts, 1969).

The source for most statistics in economic history is U.S. Department of Commerce, Census Bureau, *Historical Statistics of the United States, Colonial Times to* 1957; *Continuation to 1962.*

Chapter Two

THE PROGRESS
OF AMERICAN ECONOMIC LIFE:
THE WAY AMERICANS LIVED

There are two ways of looking at the progress of the American economy. One is by the tables of national income. This we have been through in Chapter One. The other attempts to describe how Americans actually lived. But before embarking on this task, a digression is in order.

Economic history, no matter how much the members of the guild may protest, is an amalgam of history and economics. And like many marriages, it has not always been a happy one. Historians accuse economists of being concerned with nothing else but numbers and theory to the neglect of the human being. Economists indict historians for their failure to be precise and their tendency to tell the story of what happened in the past to the neglect of explaining the past. And so the disagreement goes on. But the truth of the matter is that we must have both the economics and the history. Man does not live by bread alone, and numbers give even less nourishment. To understand the past, one has to go much beyond mathematical analysis and theory. But as Lord Kelvin said long ago, "When you can't measure what you are speaking about and express it in numbers, your knowledge is of a meagre and unsatisfactory kind." Without theory and some elements of measurement, economic historians are lost in a sea of vagary.

Those who are wedded wholly and solely to economics think there is only one way—the national income way—to measure

35

economic progress. But for many others, this technique has little appeal. For them, GNP and all its subdivisions are mystical abstractions with little relation to reality. They contend that, even if the statistics are true, what they add or seem to add to exactness, they subtract from interest and appeal. Some of the critics of GNP seek a better understanding of change in the scale of living by comparing how people actually lived at different periods of history. They are not interested in total production, price indexes, or average income. They would much rather know how much John Smith made and how much he paid for beef, bread, and beer. The subjects they want to describe in broad, impressionistic brush strokes are how Americans made their living, how they spent what they made, what they ate, where they lived, how they wasted or invested their leisure, how long they lived, and what they died of.[1]

This "way of living" approach presents history in a series of vignettes rather than in a series of statistical tables. It is therefore closer to life; but, although it answers many questions that cannot be answered by national income accounts, it also presents some fresh problems of its own. It is general and subjective. There has never been an "average American," and, therefore, no average way in which Americans lived. Levels of living have differed among occupational groups, income strata, geographical regions, and differing ethnic backgrounds. But, despite the difficulties, it is possible to draw some conclusions about the changes that took place in the way our nation's citizens lived.

Early America was a predominantly rural society in which the vast majority of the labor force was engaged in primary production. Contemporary America is a commercial-industrial, urban-suburban-exurban society in which more workers are engaged in providing services and keeping records than in actually producing or processing goods. One of the most striking features of this transformation has been a remarkable increase in the quantity, the variety, and—romantic nostalgia to the contrary—the quality of the goods that make up the level of living. Thus, what were luxuries for one generation became necessities for the next and trash for the third. Yet, with all the plethora of goods, consumer wants were not satiated. Over the course of time, the level of living increased, but it increased arithmetically, while the standard of living increased geometrically. Americans understood this very well. "My father wanted fifteen things," remarked a Cape Cod sea captain. "He didn't get 'em all. He got ten and worried considerable because he didn't get the other five. Now I want forty things, and I get thirty, but I worry more about the ten that I cannot get than the old man used to about the five he couldn't get." To express the same idea in the less picturesque language of statistics, in 1910, a person with an income of $2,500 in terms of

---

[1]These by no means cover the entire gamut of living, but they are the questions in which the economic historian is primarily interested. Behavioral scientists are interested in much different but equally important aspects of life: social organization, religious beliefs and customs, courtship and marriage, and so forth. But these change minutely, if at all, over time, and they are not very helpful in assaying the level of living.

1950 purchasing power not only enjoyed a high level of living, but he was able to save about 10 percent of his income. Since then, however, the level of living has increased so markedly that the same $2,500 income today would be inadequate to maintain a "reasonable" consumption pattern, let alone permit any saving.

Somewhat paradoxically, as the array of goods and services improved in quantity, quality, and variety, there was also a tendency toward greater standardization among different geographical sections and income groups. This was especially marked in dress. In colonial times, for example, clothes were a badge of station, and in the early nineteenth century, an immeasurable gulf still existed between the pioneer in his homespun and the Charleston plantation owner or the Boston merchant in his finery. The first great spurt in economic growth dramatically blurred these distinctions, and as early as the middle of the nineteenth century there was little outward difference between the types of dress worn by the different strata of urban society. And with the further passage of time, the differences between the tycoon and the clerk, the big-city resident and the small-towner, were much more in quantity and quality of goods owned and in the amount of saving set aside than in the fundamentals of living.

Consumption always loomed very large in American life, but the increase in the level of living was by no means confined to material things alone. Although these were undoubtedly regarded as the most precious, there were comparable, if somewhat undervalued, intangible gains. Successive generations of Americans progressively ate a more varied diet. They could look forward to a longer life expectancy. They put in many less hours of work and expended less physical energy to earn a much larger income. Many more Americans attended school, and those who did stayed longer than their forebears had.

HOW AMERICANS MADE THEIR LIVING

The ways in which a nation's people earn their living is a good indicator of its economic status. In an underdeveloped economy, most resources must be devoted to producing the necessities of life. The vast majority of workers are farmers or fishermen. Early America was no exception. As in all underdeveloped areas, most Americans worked in agriculture. Indeed, at the end of the Colonial Period, 90 out of every 100 Americans worked on farms, or in the forest, or as fishermen; manufacturing and construction absorbed another five; and trade and services were practically nonexistent.

With economic progress, fewer workers were needed to produce the elemental necessities. Immense strides in agricultural productivity, together with the fact that Americans did not increase their food consumption, made it possible to rapidly shift resources out of farming. By the close of the nineteenth century, the gap between employment on the farm and in the factory had

Table 6

INDUSTRIAL DISTRIBUTION OF THE WORKING FORCE, 1800-1970

	Agriculture, forestry & fishing	Mining	Manufacturing & construction	Transport	Trade	Personal & professional services	Government	Not specified
1800	74.5%	–	–	2.1%	–	2.1%	–	21.3%
1840	64.1	–	13.9%	1.8	6.2%	4.2	–	9.8
1870	50.4	0.2%	23.3	4.7	6.4	10.8	0.2%	4.0
1890	43.0	0.2	26.0	6.3	7.6	11.8	0.3	4.8
1920	27.4	0.3	31.5	9.6	9.8	13.5	4.5	3.4
1950	11.8	1.7	31.9	8.0	16.0	18.1	8.8	3.7
1970	4.7	0.8	30.6	6.2	20.2	20.5	17.0	–

SOURCE: NBER, *Studies in Income and Wealth*, Vol. 11, 1949; Vol. 24, 1966; 1970, Census Bureau.

perceptibly narrowed. By then, agriculture employed less than 50 out of every 100 workers; another 25 were in manufacturing; and 31 were in the so-called service industries.

In the wake of further gigantic strides in productivity, the shift in manpower continued into the twentieth century. The exodus out of agriculture gained in speed and intensity, but the expansion of manufacturing employment slowed down perceptibly. Today, less than 5 out of 100 Americans work in agriculture. But, unlike what happened in the late 1800s, very few of the 25 who left the farm in the past 50 years went into the factory, for the proportion of the labor force in manufacturing—about 30 percent—is almost the same as it was in 1920. On the other hand, services, distribution, and government have grown spectacularly, employing 20, 25 and 17 percent of the labor force. In sum, the American economy was heavily agrarian in the early nineteenth century; became highly industrialized in the late nineteenth century; and shifted toward a so-called service economy in the twentieth century.

THE OCCUPATIONS IN WHICH AMERICANS WORKED

A radical shift in the things workers did accompanied their redistribution from agriculture to manufacturing, trade, and finance. One hundred years ago, it was an odds-on chance that a stranger in the land would have been more likely to meet a farmer than anyone else. Today, he would probably meet a white-collar worker.

We have no systematic data telling us what occupations Americans pursued in the early years. But we know that around 1800, over 70 percent of the working population were farmers. Most of the others were independent artisans, laborers, storekeepers, and the classic professionals. There could not have been very many clerks, certainly no typists, and extremely few secretaries, accountants, and technicians. The situation was not so amazingly different at the beginning of the twentieth century when the great change in the occupational structure really began. Since then, the trend has been steadily and continuously toward the more sedentary occupations. Between 1910, the first year for which we have adequate statistics, and today, the number of farmers declined not only relatively but absolutely, the number of blue-collar workers doubled but white-collar workers increased almost five-fold. Not all white-collar occupations expanded at the same speed. The number of clerks and professionsls increased almost seven times, managers tripled, and sales workers more than doubled.

It was mostly office workers who were responsible for the spreading white collar; it was certainly not the classic professions. Between 1910 and 1970, population just about doubled. The number of accountants multiplied ten times; engineers and technicians, seven times; and stenographers and secretaries, over four times. Dentists and teachers kept step with the population rise; undertakers did somewhat better; but the number of lawyers, clergymen, and physicians did not increase as fast as population. Indeed, there were just about as many physicians per one thousand of population in 1970 as there had been 100 years before.

The great transformation that occurred in the ways Americans earned their living could be described in a different way. In 1870, 75 percent of all Americans were absorbed in producing goods. Another 10 percent distributed the goods, and the remainder provided the few professional and business services that were needed. Today, only 40 percent of the working population are involved in primary production; 25 percent are in the business of distribution; 20 percent provide professional and other services; and 15 percent coordinate business operations in a clerical occupation of one kind or other. There has been a shift from working with things to working with people, or, as the more cynical would express it, from manipulating things to manipulating people. Whether for good or ill, we have become a nation of office workers and memo writers. How much paper work has come to mean is spectacularly illustrated by the information that the Pentagon, a giant among office colossi, sells ten tons of waste paper every day to junk dealers.

The revolution in the occupational structure has also had the effect of diminishing the American's direct stake in private property. At the beginning of the nineteenth century, about 85 percent of all working Americans were self-employed; by 1860, the self-employed were down to 60 percent; and 100 years later, they were below 15 percent. The small yeoman farmer and the independent artisan no longer represented the majority. Much more typical was the property-less manufacturing worker, the dispenser of services in private and public enterprise, the worker in trade and transportation, and the man or woman who kept the files, books, accounts, and records of America's many economic activities.

HOW AMERICANS SPENT THEIR INCOMES

The American economist who, in the early twentieth century, said, "Tell me how you spend your income and I will tell you what you are," possessed a deep understanding of the American way of life. In the United States, where tradition, family background, and class stratification have been relatively insignificant and money values have been relatively important, the spending of money has been a most important determinant of an individual's social standing. Thrift has never been one of our chief attributes. Perhaps because nature was not as niggardly and opportunities seemed greater here than in some other parts of the world, Americans usually preferred the joys of present spending to the security of providing for a rainy day. Individuals saved a relatively small percentage of annual income and spent the rest. Income might rise or fall sharply over short periods of time, but consumption increased steadily though gradually, so that,

Table 7
OCCUPATIONAL MAKE-UP OF LABOR FORCE
(1910 and 1970)

	Percent of labor force, 1970	Change in number, 1910-1970
Clerks	17.4	690
Professional	13.8	635
Accountants	.80e	1500 e
Engineers	1.40	1430
Nurses	.90	850
Draftsmen	.40	690
Teachers	3.32	437
Clergymen	.45	300
Lawyers	.35	245
Doctors	.40	200
Musicians	.25	150
Service	10.5	470
Sales	6.1	275
Semiskilled	18.2	265
Managers	10.2	330
Skilled	12.8	240
Labor force	100.00	210
Private household	2.0	88
Unskilled	5.0	82
Farmers	2.1	28
Farm labor	1.8	29

e estimated

SOURCE: *Historical Statistics of the United States*. U. S. Department of Labor, *Handbook of Labor Statistics*, 1971; *Occupational Outlook Quarterly*, Spring, 1972.

over long periods of time, the average annual percentage of personal income saved remined about the same.

The entirely different pattern of living was a continuous source of wonder to European visitors. In the 1850s, a British traveler was astonished at the American pattern of living:

> The people of the United States are not only "profuse" in their "expenditures," but extravagant to a degree amounting to prodigality. We sincerely believe that Americans, particularly in the city of New York, are the most extravagant people on the face of the earth. There are men, merchants in that city, who live in houses costing $100,000, and expend at the rate of $25,000 or $30,000 per annum, and some of the wives of these men and merchants wear thousand-dollar shawls, and other things to match. The sound, wholesome, prudential, and

Table 8
PERCENTAGE ALLOCATION OF THE CONSUMER'S DOLLAR
(1909-1971)

	1909	1929	1933	1945	1971
Food	25.6	24.4	23.6	28.0	20.5
Clothing	13.9	13.4	11.3	16.2	10.1
Housing & Utilities	24.0	18.0	22.6	13.9	14.9
Total	63.5	55.8	57.5	58.1	45.5
House operation	11.8	16.4	15.7	13.3	14.1
Transportation	5.2	9.9	8.9	5.8	13.6
Medical	2.8	3.7	4.4	4.1	7.8
Recreation	3.0	4.8	4.0	5.0	6.4
Education (private)	1.4	1.5	1.8	0.8	1.7
Religion and welfare	2.8	1.8	2.2	1.5	1.4
Other (alcohol, tobacco, personal care, & miscellaneous)	9.6	6.2	5.6	11.4	9.5

SOURCE: J. Frederick Dewhurst, *America's Needs and Resources* (New York: Twentieth Century Fund, 1955); U.S. Dept. of Commerce, *National Income Supplement*, 1954; *U.S. Income and Output,* 1958; *Survey of Current Business,* July, 1972.

Table 9
WORKING-CLASS BUDGETS, 1874-1970

	1874	1901	1929	1935	1950	1970
Food	57.4	43.1	39.0	37.2	34.5	28.0
Clothing	14.2	13.0	12.0	9.0	11.6	13.0
Housing[1]	22.6	23.8	24.5	35.1	25.8	28.6
Transportation	—	—	—	7.3	13.8	10.4
Medical care	—	—	—	4.6	5.1	6.5
Other	6.1	20.1	24.5	6.8	9.2	13.5

[1] includes house operation and fuel.

SOURCE: 1901, *Eighteenth Annual Report,* Commissioner of Labor; 1929, Standard Statistics Co.; 1874, 1935, 1950, *Historical Statistics of the United States*; 1970, *Statistical Abstract*, 1971, p. 341.

economical proverbs of honest Ben Franklin are repudiated, and we have heard them designated as "scoundrel maxims."

Again in the 1920s, the reaction of the French journalist, André Siegfried, was typical:[2]

European luxuries are often necessities in America, and where Europe, and especially Asia, will stint, America consumes without reckoning.... American ideas of extravagance, comfort and frugality are entirely different from European as we soon discover if we ask what the Americans mean by economy. In America, the daily life of the majority is conceived on a scale that is reserved for the privileged classes anywhere else.

American wants seemed utterly unlimited, and we strove continually to improve our scale of living whether we could "really afford" it or not. This characteristic of the American way of life had already appeared in the Colonial Period, for it was then reported that many middle-class wives in colonial Boston "spurred their spouses into getting ahead by demanding a higher scale of living than they either desired or could provide."[3]

How did Americans apportion their incomes for spending purposes? According to one of the best-known principles in economics, Engel's Law, as the income of any person or group increases, a smaller *percentage* of total income will be allocated to the purchase of food, clothing, and shelter—the necessities of life—and a larger share will be spent on luxuries. This follows because the satisfaction derived from the consumption of necessities diminishes sharply with each increase in the number of units consumed. The demand for necessities is, therefore, relatively inelastic, that is, it will not vary very much regardless of what happens to prices or income. It follows, therefore, that as income and the scale of living rise, food, clothing, and shelter absorb an ever-decreasing percentage of income, and other goods and services a larger share.

In American history, percentage expenditures for the so-called necessities did decline, but not as much as one would expect. However, beyond the needs of subsistence, food, clothing, and shelter ceased to be mere necessities and became luxuries. Then as income rose, Americans did not allocate the entire increment to genuine luxuries, but bought more varied, better quality, and fancier "necessities."

---

[2]The Robertson item is from *Hunts Merchants Magazine,* Vol. 33 (1855), pp. 53ff; André Siegfried, *America Comes of Age* (New York: Harcourt, Brace & World, Inc., 1927), p. 160.

[3]Carl Bridenbaugh, *Cities in Revolt* (New York: Alfred A. Knopf, Inc., 1955), p. 149.

THE CONSUMPTION PATTERN IN COLONIAL AND
NINETEENTH-CENTURY AMERICA

We have no way of telling how much of his income the ordinary person in late colonial America spent for the necessities of life. The cost of subsistence, however, was extraordinarily low by present standards. The expenses of a Princeton student around 1750 were only $63 a year, and bids as low as $12.50 were made to provide a year's food and lodging for the destitute. Bonded servants and slaves, who made up the great majority of the working class, lived at a subsistence level and had nothing to spend for luxuries. But from the meager data that are available, it seems clear that for the small farmer, tradesman, shopkeeper, and artisan, life was comfortable, and income, although not substantial, was high enough to provide something over and above the necessities of life.

We have ample evidence that the standard of consumption was very high, if not extravagant, among the very rich and even among the well-to-do. Luxuries were imported in relatively great profusion from England. A steady stream of excellent furniture—desks, highboys, chests, chairs in oak, walnut, mahogany, and olive wood—flowed from Europe into the homes of the rich. Silver plate, china, laces, silks and satins, and a variety of gadgets and curios joined the parade. The physical survivals of life among the colonial rich, and available records of inventories of upper-class colonial homes further attest to a pattern of luxury equal to that of England.

By the early nineteenth century, "to make a living" meant something decidedly more than merely existing. By modern standards, prices of necessities were very low. Around the turn of the century, one could stay at the best hostelry in the South for $1.60 a day, if "he ate a cold supper and was content with one quart of toddy." By the 1830s prices were lower. William E. Dodge rented a two-story house in New York City for $300 a year. Henry Wadsworth Longfellow paid tuition of $8 a semester at Bowdoin College; his board cost $27 for 13 weeks and his room $3.30. Late in the decade, Nathan Trotter, a prosperous Philadelphia merchant, bought a barrel of flour for $7.75, a barrel of sugar for $23.62, half a barrel of beer for $3, and a gallon of Madeira for the same price. From 1839 to 1852, his annual family expenditures only twice exceeded $3,500, and the family lived very comfortably. Philip Hone, wealthy merchant and one-time mayor of New York, thought nothing of paying $4.50 for a bottle of wine, but he complained bitterly in his diary for 1837 that he had spent the extravagant sum of $17.31 for a 14-pound bass, two small turkeys, three pairs of chickens, one pair of partridge, 21 pounds of veal, 12 pounds of mutton, and 6 sweetbreads.

Prices of the ordinary things in life did not increase much before the galloping inflation of the Civil War. Around 1850, eggs were 20 cents a dozen and "steak," 18 cents a pound. Ready-made suits cost $8 to $30. The tariff at the Fifth Avenue Hotel was $2.50 a day, American plan. At other New York hotels, prices ranged from $1 to $4 for room and board but at a hotel in San Francisco, in the heady atmosphere of the Gold Rush, one egg cost $1. A college student's ordinary expenses were about $260 a year. Sidney Fisher, a member of Philadelphia's upper set, had a comfortable house, servants, a good table, country residence, and a full wardrobe on $3,000 a year.

Because incomes were increasing and the prices of necessities were low, consumers had more leeway in deciding how to spend their money. Yet most of them did not reduce appreciably their relative expenditures for necessities. Instead, they bought more and better food and household furnishings, increasing only slightly their expenditures for luxuries, social and cultural activities, medical care, and recreation. Most people had little time for anything but working, eating, and sleeping. The working day was long, holidays were few, and vacations were almost unknown. Few luxuries were available, and, of those that did exist, many were too expensive for the ordinary consumer. There were, for example, few household appliances on the market, and these were expensive. Books and newspapers were cheap, but a college education was not. The ordinary citizen could not afford to send his sons to college when the cost at such institutions as Williams, Brown, Yale, Harvard, and Pennsylvania was $120 to $200 a year.

Table 10
PRICES OF SELECTED ITEMS

	House[1]	Man's Suit	Restaurant dinner[2]	Beef[3]
1840-1850	750	19	.50	.18
1890-1900	1,200	12	.60	.35
1910-1913	1,600	25	1.25	.20
1930-1932	3,700	25	2.00	.29
1950	12,309	100	12.00	1.00
1970	23,400	150	30.00	1.20

[1] 1840-1930, average cost; 1950-70, median sales price
[2] The "best" in New York City.
[3] "Steak" per lb.

The middle class, of which this country has fortunately always had a large number, lived comfortably, but the working class, which was much more numerous than in colonial days, had a difficult time trying to make ends meet and had little money for anything but the bare necessities. Only the rich and the well-to-do spent large amounts on luxuries. They owned horses and carriages, indulged in elaborate house furnishings, and traveled widely. They sent their sons and occasionally their daughters to college, and they supported the social and cultural activities that thrived in all the cities.

SPENDING IN THE LATE NINETEENTH AND TWENTIETH CENTURIES

Prices fell rather steadily during the latter part of the nineteenth century. In the 1870s, city-dwellers paid 50 cents a pound for butter, 50 cents a dozen for eggs, 35 cents a pound for beef, $1 for a case of beer, and $30 for a good suit. By 1900, these prices had been cut in half, and one could live sumptuously on what had been and would again be regarded as a modest income. A well-known Eastern university offered an eminent professor a salary of $3,500 a year and explained that $162 a month would cover his expenses for rent, food, utilities, and two servants, leaving about $130 a month for discretionary spending. Students at another well-known university paid 14 cents for a "combination lunch" of soup, Irish stew, cranberry sauce, desert, and beverage. Inns in the vicinity of Baltimore charged 25 cents for dinner. An average hotel in San Francisco offered a menu on which most of the items cost 10 cents. The Waldorf-Astoria, the most luxurious hotel in New York, charged 60 cents for a roast beef dinner. A shirt cost less than $1; eggs, 32 cents a dozen; rib roast, 20 cents a pound; and a haircut, 30 cents.

But disparities in the scale of livng were still very wide. In the 1870s, some people insisted that they had to economize on an income of $6,000. In the 1890s there were still some who thought they could not afford to marry on $4,000 a year. A handful of Americans lived on a scale that would have made an ancient Sybarite blush. The marginal utility of money meant very little to the Philadelphia lady who discovered that "gold bathroom fixtures were very economical because they didn't have to be polished." But these examples of flamboyantly conspicuous consumption were few. For most consumers, spending for "necessities" had not declined impressively, for other alternatives were still not sufficiently attractive. In 1909, as in previous decades, consumers in general were still devoting about two-thirds of their total spending to food, housing, and clothing. Apparently, they were buying better food, better housing, and better clothing, rather than a much larger amount of "non-necessities."

A decided change in spending patterns occurred in the 1920s. Consumers began to spend less of their incomes on primary needs and more for goods and services that were more in the "want" than in the "need" class. It was estimated that, before World War I, from 70 to 80 percent of consumers' purchases were for goods and services not subject to violent fluctuations. After the war, the percentage fell to 60 to 65 percent. By 1929, the average consumer divided his spending somewhat in this fashion: 47.7 percent for nondurables, 40.6 percent for services, and 11.7 percent for durables. Food still took about one-quarter of the consumer's dollar, but housing was down to less than 20 percent. Meanwhile, the cost of maintaining a home had increased until it was almost equal to the amount spent for rent. More and more labor-saving devices were being brought into the house. Along with the right to vote, urban and suburban housewives were acquiring washing machines, vacuum cleaners, gas ranges, and electric refrigerators. But the influence of the automobile was all-pervasive. Automobile registrations almost quadrupled in the 1920s. As they did, the share of the dollar going to transportation rose from a nickel in 1909 to a dime in 1929.

The allocation of expenditures changed little in the great depression and World War II. During the gloomy years of the 1930s, prices of everyday goods dropped to less than two-thirds the 1929 level. Eggs, butter, and steak could be purchased for about 30 cents a dozen or a pound, and an excellent suit for $25. But income plummeted just about as much, so that the typical consumer was not able to improve his command over goods. During World War II, shortages of consumer goods, restrictions on gasoline consumption, more equal income distribution, and government controls, especially on rents, pushed up percentage expenditures for food and clothing but depressed the shares spent for housing, household maintenance, and transportation. As a result, spending for so-called necessities took about the same share—58 percent—in 1945 as in 1933.

The depression and war years were abnormal interruptions of a long-run trend. As soon as peace returned, spending for necessities resumed its gradual slide as consumers rushed to buy the durable goods that they had so long done without. At the end of the war, approximately half of American homes owned automobiles, washing machines, and vacuum cleaners; almost 70 percent used electric refrigerators; but practically none had television and air conditioning. By 1970, more than 90 percent had refrigerators, washers, and television sets. About 80 percent had automobiles, and 40 percent had air-conditioning equipment. Spending for durables had risen more than 30 percent above 1929, whereas expenditures for nondurables had dropped and those for services were somewhat higher.[4] The boom environment of the postwar years cut deeply into average expenditures for food and clothing. At the same time, spending for health, recreation, education, and household operation ballooned upward. By 1970, less than half of total expenditures were allocated to necessities and the share for recreation was almost double what it had been 50 years before.

As had always been the case, there was a wide disparity between the consumption habits of the high- and low-income brackets. High-income groups conformed closely to the letter of Engel's Law. Proportionately, they spent much less on necessities than did those at the lower end of the income scale. In 1935, it was estimated that expenditures for food took over 40 percent of low-income budgets but less than 30 percent at the top end. By 1950, despite some redistribution of income, 33 percent of low budgets and 26 percent of high budgets went for food. Housing expenditures followed pretty much the same pattern. But the share spent by the comfortable and the well-off for clothing was roughly double that of the poor in both 1935 and 1950.

---

[4]The percentages were 15.6 for durables, 41.9 for nondurables, and 42.6 for services. But this is somewhat deceiving, for the quality of durables was vastly better than it had been a generation before.

Over the long run, changes in the consumption pattern reflected an increase in the level of living. The majority of 1970 Americans lived on a scale that only the rich enjoyed 100 years ago. Percentage expenditures for food, clothing, and rent dropped, whereas those for health, transportation, recreation, and household operation rose. However, aside from housing, the magnitude of change was not very impressive. Except for short periods, proportional spending for necessities declined gradually and not spectacularly. In the absence of sufficiently attractive alternatives, Americans seem to have preferred to spend their larger incomes on necessities of higher quality rather than on luxuries. This can be demonstrated by comparing the actual decline in the percent spent for food with the decline that would have occurred if consumers had always bought the same selected list of foods. Lower-income groups probably spent 50 percent of their income for food in 1830 and about 30 percent in 1960. However, if they had consumed the same amount of the same foods in 1960 as in 1830, food would have taken 15 percent in 1960, instead of 30 percent.

WHAT AMERICANS ATE[5]

In a primitive or poor economy, food is an end in itself. Appetites are not jaded, bread is the staff of life, and quantity rather than quality is the important thing. As an economy develops and the level of living rises, food consumption becomes less a biological matter and more a social function. Bread ceases to be the staff of life and more emphasis is placed on quality. Changes in eating habits are, therefore, symptomatic of changes in the level of living; and the historical trends in American eating habits illustrate quite forcefully a persistent rise in the level of living. Even though we still have a long way to go before achieving a universally adequate and balanced diet, food consumption has improved generation by generation.

The most striking long-run trends in American food consumption have been the extremely small increases in per capita consumption, the continuous progress toward a more varied and healthful diet, and the greater degree of standardization among different geographical sections and different individuals. Eating habits, along with many other things, were influenced by the change from a rural to an industrial economy. As the economy shifted from the farm to the office, Americans ate less meat, potatoes, and wheat flour and more sugar, dairy products, vegetables, and fruits. At the same time, less food was produced at home, and the custom of "eating out" became more general. As food production moved to the factory, improvements in processing and distribution made it possible to break down the most glaring geographical differences in diet. Thus, at

[5]See Richard O. Cummings, *The American and His Food* (Chicago: The University of Chicago Press, 1941).

one and the same time, diet became more varied but also more standardized. More importance was placed on new types of food, but people tended more and more to follow much the same food-consumption patterns no matter in which section of the country they lived. We can see these trends developed by comparing American diets at three different periods: the late colonial era, the late nineteenth century, and the mid-twentieth century.

Certain foods were abundant in colonial America, but generally the diet was plain and lacked variety. Game, fish, and berries were plentiful. As on every American frontier then and later, honey, maple sugar, and molasses were widely used for sweetening; and turnip greens, cabbage, sweet potatoes, and corn in every variety were consumed on a large scale. But although the diet was plentiful, there were decided differences between the eating habits of the rich and the poor. The rich ate meat at least once a day, but the poor in the cities and even in the rural areas were almost vegetarians. Fresh meat was rare because there was no really effective means of refrigeration. Pork was the chief meat in the diet, along with some beef and veal, but almost no lamb or mutton was consumed.

By the early nineteenth century, the pace of life had become much faster, and America had become a nation of hustlers. The "quick lunch" was introduced early in the 1830s, and most people regarded the whole process of eating as an annoying interference with work, the really important part of life. Most cooking was atrocious by any standard. Food was customarily prepared by drowning it in grease; when served, it frequently was a sodden, half-cooked, indigestible mess. Indigestion and dyspepsia were chronic aliments and would have been even more common if people had not lived active, outdoor lives with plenty of sunshine and exercise. Even so, Americans drank large quantities of alcoholic beverages to "settle the stomach." There was little public drunkenness, but many people were habitually "high," and children of 12 years or even less "tipped their drams."

These eating and drinking habits continued well into the nineteenth century. There was some improvement in cooking in the large cities as the more sophisticated adopted French culinary techniques, but Americans by and large still deserved, in the words of the Frenchman Volney, the *grand prix* for a scheme of living designed to injure the stomach, teeth, and health in general.

In Europe, where land was scarce in proportion to population, people rarely wasted food. Their chief staple was grain, which yields more calories per acre than any other food. In the United States, on the other hand, wasting food was common. Having so much land, Americans could afford to feed grain to animals and eat meat, even though meat yields far less calories per acre than grain. In the first half of the nineteenth century, as the land area expanded, as livestock became more plentiful and of better quality, and as improved methods were developed for bringing animals to the market, meat consumption increased markedly. By 1850, it is estimated that the average person consumed over 180 pounds of meat a year. For most Americans, eating was a constant round of meat and potatoes. Judged by modern standards, the diet was bountiful and cheap. A "modest" Northern hotel, in the middle of the nineteenth century, charged $2 a day American plan and served for dinner: soup; fish; six boiled, three cold, and six roasted meats; a variety of vegetables; pastry; pudding; and ice cream.

Although the American diet continued to be bountiful, it was still monotonous for most people. Before the development of fast and convenient methods of transportation, Americans in each section ate those foods that were produced in the local market area plus a small amount of nonperishables brought from other areas. Diet was also limited by the vagaries of climate. During the early nineteenth century, it was almost impossible to preserve food. Cold cellars and spring houses were only partly successful and, consequently, early Americans preserved their food by drying, salting, or smoking it. These processes, of course, were unsatisfactory because only certain foods could be preserved in this way and because salting or smoking destroyed a great deal of food value.

But new developments were in the wind and were soon to alter the situation. Rapid industrialization, accompanied by technological innovations in processing, refrigeration, and transportation, brought fundamental changes in the American diet. An improved method of refining sugar, introduced by Havemeyer and Moller in 1858, cut the time from 2 weeks to 24 hours and the price from 10 cents a pound to 1 cent. Sugar consumption jumped from 30 to 70 pounds per capita and meat fell from 180 to 150 pounds as the number of office workers, who needed less meat, fats, and starches than farm and rural workers, increased.

Better methods of preserving food were worked out early in the nineteenth century, but, as with most technological developments, they were not widely adopted until much later. Thomas Moore, a Maryland farmer, built a refrigerator in 1803, but it did not come into wide use until 1827, when Nathaniel Wyeth invented an ice cutter. Foods were first canned in the United States in 1820, but sterilization and the manufacture of tin cans were still extremely crude processes, and canned food was, therefore, very expensive. A small can of tomatoes cost 50 cents, and at such prices few could afford the luxury of eating commercially preserved foods. The canned foods industry did not really begin to blossom until 1855, when the first machine-made cans appeared. Even then it did not immediately become a large-scale business. It was the Civil War that gave commercial canning its greatest impetus. The Union Army used large quantities of canned foods, and many soliders carried their acquaintance with canned products over into the postwar era, thus boosting demand. The Van Camp Company began to can food in 1861 and Gail Borden began to can milk in the same year. By 1870, 30 million cans of food were being processed yearly—six times as many as in 1860.

Meanwhile, the spreading railroads contributed most significantly to the rising level of living. They brought fresh milk to the cities from the surrounding rural areas, Southern fresh fruits and vegetables to the North, Eastern fresh seafood to the Middle West, and fresh meat from the Middle West to the East. At first, the railroad's bounty was confined to the high-income groups, but it gradually spread to the rest of the urban population as the economy became more industrialized and as railroad techniques improved.

Still, it was a long while before these changes affected the rural or outlying areas. Big cities like New York and urban areas in general provided a mass market, and therefore attracted such quantities of produce that food differed little regardless of the season of the year. On the other hand, a rural area did not constitute a large enough market to attract food from distant points, and until the twentieth century rural people had to content themselves with two distinct but still very plain diets: one for the winter and one for the summer. The winter eating of a Middle Western family with a moderate income in the 1890s consisted of roasts, macaroni, potatoes, turnips, fried applies, stewed tomatoes, Indian pudding, rice, cake, and pie. They never thought of having fresh fruits and vegetables and could not have gotten them if they had.

By the middle of the twentieth century, the trends in food consumption begun in the late nineteenth century had reached their fruition. Meat consumption slipped steadily to an all-time low of about 130 pounds in 1930, but then climbed to about 160 pounds in 1960. Butter consumption was very stable from 1900 to the great depression. Thereafter, it fell steadily from about 20 to 8 pounds per capita. On the other hand, Americans in 1960 ate, on the average, about one-third more sugar and twice as much vegetables as at the beginning of the century.

Constant improvements in transportation, refrigeration, and processing tended to standardize the types of food consumed in different sections of the country. By the middle of the century, intersectional differences still existed in the subleties of eating. The "unwashed salad bowl and the perfectly adequate little red wine" were typical of New York's Greenwich Village and San Francisco's North Beach, dried corn was peculiar to the Pennsylvania Dutch country, and black-eyed peas were common in the South, but these differences were hardly fundamental. The continued shift from home to factory processing was one of the most important causes of increasing standardization. As time passed, there was less of "the bread that mother used to bake." Even in rural areas, families relied increasingly on commercial baking, canned goods, pre-prepared mixes, and frozen foods.

The whole system of food distribution had also changed radically. At the beginning of the century, food retailing was carried on in small neighborhood stores. The comfortable and the well-off bought their supplies in bulk—a sack of potatoes, a crate of apples, a case of canned goods at a time. But for the most part, the store owner doled out five cents' worth of this and ten cents' worth of that. From behind the counter in his dingy establishment, he ground coffee, candled eggs, ladled milk out of a container, and scooped loose butter out of a tub. The arrangement was picturesque, but neither sanitary, efficient, nor satisfactory. By the beginning of the second half of the century, it had been largely replaced by the supermarket. By then, except for very low-income groups, Americans were eating far differently from their grandparents. In 1918, it was estimated that a quarter of American children were "undernourished." During the depression, it was said that one-third of the nation was "ill-fed." By 1960, this could be said of only one-tenth. In the same year, moreover, it was estimated that Americans consumed $100 million of dietary foods. Perhaps nothing else so well illustrated the advance in the level of living.

WHAT AMERICANS WORE

In colonial America, the way one dressed marked one's scale of living. The wealthy male was plumed in a velvet, tailor-made suit. He wore silk stockings and lace collars, a three-cornered hat, and silver buckles on his shoes. He carried a gold-headed cane and a silk handkerchief. In every way, he was a fit match for Beau Brummell; but he paid a high cost for his finery, for the expenditure on a single outfit might run as high as $500 in today's money. People of the lower-income groups, however, dressed inexpensively and very plainly. They wore leather and linsey-woolsey, wool stockings, and coarse shoes.

Dress rapidly ceased to be a very good indicator of differences in scales of living. The spread of democracy in the Jeffersonian and Jacksonian eras put an end to the wearing of knee breeches and lace by 1830. The growth of the American cotton textile industry made clothing relatively inexpensive, virtually eliminating the wearing of linen and curtailing the wearing of wool. Ready-made clothing first appeared in the 1830s and left and right shoes in 1850. By the middle of the century, there was virtually no home production of cloth, though finished clothing was still made in the homes of farmers and low-income city-dwellers.

Compared with the Colonial Period, clothing for the well-to-do was very cheap by the middle of the nineteenth century. A good suit could be bought for $30 and an excellent overcoat for $24. The price of women's clothing had also declined substantially, but this was offset by the quantity of the clothing worn. Women in the upper-income brackets wore about 100 yards of clothing in 1860, compared with 15 yards at the most in the middle of the twentieth century.

By the early twentieth century, there was little difference between the clothing worn by different income groups, and only the expert could distinguish milady's clothes from those of the shop girl. Even more was this true of men. Ready-made men's clothing was almost impossible to distinguish from tailor-mades. All types of Americans could, if they wished, dress like ladies and gentlemen, and clothing ceased to be a mark of class.

In the nineteenth century, no decided changes occurred in clothing fabrics; but in the twentieth, new synthetic fibers became increasingly important. On the whole, clothing was also more expensive. In 1916, a good ready-made suit could be bought for $25; by 1929, it cost $50. At the bottom of the depression, it was back to $25. In 1970, the same brand suit cost $150. Average expenditures for men's and boys' clothing were about the same in constant dollars in 1970 as in 1917, but women spent, on the average, half again as much in 1970 as in 1917.

THE HOUSES IN WHICH AMERICANS LIVED[6]

In 1800, indeed throughout American history, within individual cities and within individual rural areas there was less similarity in the houses in which men lived than there was in the food they ate or the clothes they wore. Housing in any specific area ranged from the magnificent to the squalid, from the luxurious mansion on the hill to the weather-beaten shack on the wrong side of town. Differences in income were more easily distinguished by the houses people lived in than by anything else, for a man's house was his badge of conspicuous consumption.

Frontiersmen in 1800 usually lived in one-room log cabins. Farmers in the more settled rural regions generally lived in one-and-a-half-story or two-story frame houses of from four to seven rooms. Wealthy city-dwellers lived in Georgian frame, or, more rarely, brick homes containing six or more rooms. There were no glass windows in the frontier home, and nonurban dwellings were usually unpainted. Only the homes of the rich contained fine furniture, rugs, wallpaper, chandeliers, clocks, silver, china, glass, and brass and copper cooking utensils. Other homes were stocked with crude home-made furniture, wooden or pewter dishes, and tin or iron cooking utensils. Pine knots, candles, or whale oil furnished light, flints were used for ignition, and heat was provided by a fire-place. The wealthy, of course, might have several fireplaces, foot warmers, or a Franklin stove.

At the middle of the nineteenth century, the usual residence in the rural regions was much the same as in colonial times. Frontier people still lived in log cabins, although on the Great Plains, where wood was scarce, pioneers erected sod houses. On farms in the more settled areas, the average house was still a two-story, four-to-seven-room affair.

In the large cities, to which more and more Americans were moving, the wealthy were building more brick homes, but the lower-income groups still lived in frame houses. An outstanding innovation—the balloon-frame house—appeared in 1833 and made it possible to build houses more easily and quickly. Previously, heavy posts and beams were used without nails in construction. In the balloon type, two-by-fours and nails were used in the basic structure. The

---

[6]See James Ford, *Slums and Housing* (Cambridge, Mass.: Harvard University Press, 1936).

average cost of a frame house in 1860 was $800—only $50 more than it had been in 1840. At the same time, a two-story house with an unfinished attic cost $1,500, and an 11-room house with "all conveniences," $7,500. A Boston flat rented for $5.86 a month, and middle-class hotels in downtown New York charged $2 to $4 a week.

The growth of population caused much overcrowding in the large cities. The average house in 1860 contained five or six inhabitants; but in Boston this same home provided living space for 9 and in New York for 14 or 15. In rural areas, newly married couples lived with their parents and relatives; but in the cities, the groom who could not afford to buy a home carried his wife across the threshold of Mrs. Smith's boardinghouse. Almost every family among urban lower-income groups took in lodgers, for the apartment house, although very old in France, first appeared in the United States in New Orleans in 1849. It did not catch on quickly and was very expensive. In 1875, when New York contained 198 apartment houses occupied by 3,000 families, eight-room apartments in excellent neighborhoods rented for $75 to $150 a month.

Central heating and inside plumbing were still rare. Even in the best homes, they were considered curiosities. In hotels and in the homes of the rich, hot air, steam, or hot water was used for central heating. Gas was first used for lighting in 1816 on the streets of Baltimore. Thereafter, it was gradually adopted, and by the 1840s, homes were commonly illuminated by gas. Bathtubs probably did not exist before 1820, for the first that we know about were installed in 1832 by intrepid citizens of Philadelphia, who paid an annual cost of $36 per tub. By 1836, there were 1,530 tubs in Philadelphia; but the stationary bathtub with plumbing first appeared in Cincinnati in 1842 and as late as 1848 bathtubs were still considered so much of a novelty that they were prohibited in Boston except on medical advice. Even at the outbreak of the Civil War, few houses had inside plumbing. Albany, with a population of 62,000, had only 19 private baths and 150 lavatories, or about 1 for every 80 dwelling units.

Many other household conveniences had appeared by the middle of the nineteenth century. Paint, glass windows, plaster walls, and pine planks were common in all parts of the country. Coal for heating was first used in 1815, and about the same time iron ranges and stoves, tinware, glass, and china came into more common use. The first matches appeared in 1827, but they were not widely used until 1850. The invention of the mechanical saw in 1814, the power circular saw in 1820, and the turning lathe and rip saw in 1838 made cheap furniture possible, but the factory product only slowly superseded the hand-made. The cylinder press greatly lowered the cost of wallpaper and made it widely available by 1860. Rugs were now more common, for carpets sold as low as 59 cents a yard. There were even some mechanical labor-saving devices, such as the carpet sweeper and the washing machine, though the washboard was still the most common piece of capital equipment in the housewife's inventory.

The 58 million dwelling inits in which Americans lived in the middle of the twentieth century represented a collection of heterogeneous structures accumulated in a century of home development. They included a few of the brownstones left over from the middle of the previous century; the large, gingerbread homes of the Benjamin Harrison era; the English tudor; French chateau; semi-detached, and small box-like homes that were constructed at the outskirts of the cities in the first quarter of the century; and the enormous apartments of the large cities and the split-level and ranch-type homes built in suburbia and exurbia after World War II. About one-tenth of all dwelling units were in slum or blighted areas. Two-thirds of the homes contained less than six rooms—considerably smaller than a century before, but somewhat larger than just after World War II; but the number of people per unit had also declined from about five in 1890 to three in 1970.

Once urban concentration became part of reality, neighborhoods deteriorated rapidly. As early as the late 1850s, a study by the New York State Legislature found:

> As the city grows, the store and workshop encroach upon the dwelling house and dispossess its occupants. The weathier citizens move. Their houses become boarding houses or pass into the hands of real estate agents. In the beginning, the tenant house was a real blessing to the industrious poor. Rents were modest and a mechanic with family could hire two or more comfortable apartments in a house once occupied by wealthy people for less than half what he was required to pay for narrow and unhealthy quarters. This state, however, did not last long, for the rapid march of improvement speedily enhanced the value of property, rents rose, and accommodations decreased. . . . Rooms were partitioned and they became inhabited by the dregs of society.[7]

Housing costs varied greatly between the height of prosperity and the depth of depression. It cost three times as much to build a house in 1920 as in 1913, but only one and a half times as much in 1933. After the depression, there was a steady increase; by 1970, a dwelling unit cost nine times as much to construct as before World War I. Rents also had their ups and downs. In the 1920s, it was said that one tenant paid $75,000 a year to rent a 54-room triplex apartment, but $25 to $35 a month was probably closer to reality for the average American. Much better information on rents is available after 1940. According to Census figures, the median rent in 1940 was about $25 a month. By 1970, it was up to $90. But although rents just about doubled, the construction cost of the average house tripled, and the median value soared seven-fold from about $2,400 to $17,000. Yet, the urge to buy a house continued with ever-greater enthusiasm, for by 1970 two-thirds of the population lived in their own homes.

[7]*Ibid.*, pp. 131-32.

EDUCATION AND LEISURE IN THE UNITED STATES

The progress of education in the United States is another impressive illustration of the very real advance that has been made in the level of living. For, as has been increasingly emphasized by experts on economic growth, income varies directly with the scope of education. Education, or investment in human capital, to use a more precious phrase, is a most important contributor to productivity.

In the early 1800s, 80 percent of Americans did not go beyond primary school and only 3/4 of 1 percent attended college. In the next 60 years, some progress was achieved, steadily and rather slowly. By 1890 about half of the population between 5 and 20 years old was attending school. About 4 percent of those between 18 and 21 were in the nation's 1,000 colleges, which, in that year, granted somewhat less than 30,000 degrees. But total expenditures for education were about half a billion dollars, 10 percent of the population was illiterate, and only 6 percent had graduated from high school.

In contrast to the first 100 years, the educational advance of the last 70 years has been fantastic. The total educational budget doubled every decade, by 1970 reaching $70 billion—a little less than the cost of national defense. Almost 90 percent of those of school age were attending school, 50 percent of the 18- to 21-year group were in college, and the nation's 3,000 colleges conferred almost one million degrees. Education was becoming more intensive as well as more extensive. In 1970, over 26,000 doctor's degrees were granted—26,000 times as many as in 1870 and 75 times as many as in 1900.

Despite the remarkable strides made in education, many social commentators became increasingly uneasy about what they referred to as "the problem of spending one's leisure." If not possessed by an almost fanatical compulsion to work, Americans at least regarded inactivity with distrust. As a consequence, they enjoyed the highest level of living ever achieved. But in the opinion of their severest critics, they never mastered the problem of dealing with the rewards that their superb economic achievements made possible.

In the eighteenth and early nineteenth centuries, the rich seemed to have enjoyed the same leisure activities that prevailed in Western Europe. They traveled widely, raced horses, and played cards. But for most people in rural America, work and play were interrelated. Play was a by-product of the business of earning a living. Fishing, hunting, corn-husking, barn-raising, and quilting parties were economic activities but at the same time offered a recreational outlet. In the few hours of leisure that interrupted work, frontier Americans engaged in bull-baiting, cock-fighting, gouging, and other esoteric amusements. Politics was avidly discussed. and argued, and some newspapers were read, but there was little other reading or writing. Letter writing, at which the rich were industrious, averaged about one a year per adult, but then it cost from 8 to 12

1/2 cents to mail a letter. Gentlemen had private libraries, but in all the public libraries in the whole country in 1800 there were hardly 50,000 volumes, and about one-third of these were in the field of theology. Noah Webster looked upon his countrymen and found them woefully ignorant. But many dissented from this judgment. Timothy Dwight thought that the common man in the United States knew less about his job than his European counterpart but much more about other things. Many European travelers shared this view. Henry Bradshaw Fearon thought that American farm laborers surpassed the English in intelligence and information. John Bristed wrote in 1818 that the mass of Americans excelled every other people in shrewdness, general intelligence, and willingness to experiment.

As industrialism gradually replaced agrarianism, commercialized recreation became more common, for there was little chance to combine work and play in the urban office or factory. Reading, especially of newspapers, the theater, and Sunday outings began to feature leisure-time activity. The penny newspaper appeared in 1840, and by the time of the Civil War, newspapers had a circulation of 1.5 million while books were a $16 million-a-year industry. Although the summer vacation spread rapidly among nonmanual workers from the 1870s on, home continued to be the usual place for entertainment until well into the 1900s. Almost every parlor boasted its amateur musician. In the early 1900s, a piano could be bought for less than $100, and one social historian has claimed that America had more pianos than bathtubs.

In the 1920s, a variety of new recreational activities appeared and a new pattern of leisure-time occupation emerged. Commercialized sports, automobile driving, and the movies lured Americans from their homes. The number of pages offering musical instruments in the Sears, Roebuck catalog slumped from 60 in 1905 to 12 in 1925. When the radio appeared, General Harboard, president of Radio Corporation said, "Of all that may be said of radio, the best is that it will tend to keep the young people on the farm and put the American woman back in the house."

The twentieth-century American worked hard at filling his leisure time. Activity was the rule and reflection, the exception. He was the most widely traveled human being in the world, and he saw all the sights worth seeing. He read enormously; in fact, at mid-century, Americans were buying twice as many books as they had been buying before the war. He was the world's greatest joiner of clubs, lodges, and fraternities. He took an active part in civic life and followed the news through the press, radio, and television. Yet, despite the relative broadness of their information and their feverish activity in acquiring more, Americans for some unexplainable reason had what amounted to a national inferiority complex regarding themselves as less cultured and less informed than the peoples of some older nations.

HOW LONG AMERICANS LIVED

It is not uncommonly believed that the American's feverish pursuit of activity in work as well as in leisure had made him a prey to tension, frustration, ulcers, heart attacks, and death in his late forties. But it is also said that the United States is the "most over-medicated, most over-operated, most over-innoculated country in the world." The truth lies somewhere between. Actually, Americans can expect to live about as long as any people in economically advanced areas and much longer than people in the underdeveloped areas. It seems safe, therefore, to conclude that poverty does not lengthen life.

The American born in the underdeveloped economy of 1800 had a life expectancy of about 35 years. Fifty years later, if we may take Massachusetts experience as typical, life expectancy was still only 38 years; but by 1900 it had reached a little over 47 years. The principal reason for this limited span of life was an inordinately high infant mortality rate. In 1900, 141 of every 1,000 live births in Massachusetts died within a year. The most common diseases of the day—tuberculosis, peneumonia, typhoid, and a catch-all known simply as "fever"—attacked the young much more than the old and played havoc with the expectancy of life. In the larger cities, pestilence was seasonal. Typhoid came every spring, malaria every summer, and smallpox every winter.

The twentieth century brought real progress in extending the length of life. In general, this was so because of the progress of the scale of living. More specifically, it could be traced to the adoption of sanitary regulations, a more balanced diet, more healthful housing, better clothing, and improvements in medical science and medical service. Whereas it had taken the whole of the nineteenth century to add 12 years to the life cycle, it took less than one-quarter of the twentieth century to add another 12 years. By 1970, expectancy of life at birth had passed the Biblical quota of 70 years; but women could expect to live seven and a half years more than men, because the nation was becoming constantly more urbanized, and the city was more deadly to the male than to the female.

The extension of the life span did not mean, however, that either women or men could expect to reach "a grand old age." Indeed, there were probably just about as many *very* old in 1800 as in the 1950s. The expectancy of life for those who were 40 years old was only about five more years in 1970 than it had been in 1850. The greatest success in prolonging life came through substantial reductions in the mortality of the very young. It was not so much that more Americans were living to an advanced age, but that more newborn Americans were living to middle age and early old age.

Medical science has achieved remarkable success in checking the epidemic diseases that have been especially fatal to the young. This can be seen in Chart 3. But science has had much less success in combating the illnesses that hit the middle-aged and the old. The communicable diseases have been either almost

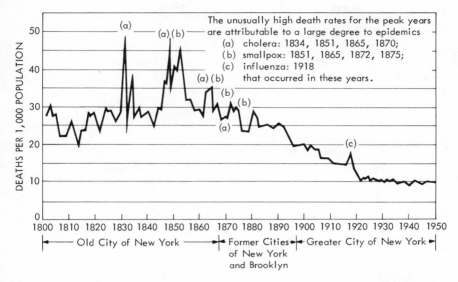

CHART 3. Number of deaths per 1,000 of population, New York City, 1800-1950

eliminated or substantially reduced. On the other hand, the degenerative diseases have become more common and frequently more fatal. In 1900, pneumonia and tuberculossis were the greatest killers, annually accounting for 202 and 194 deaths per 100,000 of population. Cancer and heart disease were not nearly so fatal, causing only 64 and 137 deaths. By mid-century, the situation was reversed. Heart disease and cancer caused 363 and 147 deaths; pneumonia and tuberculosis, 30 and 26 per 100,000. Surprisingly, deaths from accidents also fell impressively. In 1900, accidents killed more people than cancer. In 1960, even with the automobile, deaths from accidents were one-third less than in 1900.

SOME OF THE REASONS WHY

By whatever criteria one may judge, whether by national income or by progress in the amenities of life, twentieth-century Americans enjoy a much higher scale of living than their forebears did. They have more income, more education, better food, better housing, more luxuries, and better-quality goods. They live longer, and during their lifetime they enjoy more leisure and put up with less drudgery.

Perhaps in an absolute sense, the growth of the American economy has not been so remarkable. Certainly, the performance has not been perfect; one-eighth to one-sixth of our population is still immersed in or on the border of poverty.

Relatively, however, American economic growth has not been matched, and for those of us who believe that nature is niggardly and economic progress a long, hard, frustrating struggle, the performance has been remarkable.

Many explanations have been offered and many reasons given for the success of the American economy. But, as with all exceedingly complicated questions, there is no universally accepted theory of economic development. Nor is there any simple explanation of American economic development in particular. A multiplicity of causes lay at the root of American economic growth. We are not sure that we know them all or that we can say which of them are the most important; but we do know that all of them are closely interrelated.

It is well to repeat that at any given time, the potential height of a country's scale of living is equal to the percent of the population in the labor force times hours worked times output per man-hour. Economic growth, therefore, is a function of the increase in any one or more of three variables: the size of the labor force, the length of the work year, and productivity. In the past, the percent of population in the labor force has been very stable. Hours of work declined erratically, but often a reduction in hours resulted in a proportional increase in man-hour output, so that the labor force, working less hours, produced about the same amount of goods and services. From all this, it is clear that output per hour was the true variable and held the key to economic growth. What raised productivity raised the scale of living.

But this very valuable piece of information does not answer the riddle of economic progress; it raises a new and even more complicated question: What caused productivity to rise? The reasons that are most often given fit into half a dozen different categories: the physical environment, the European heritage, the social and political organization, the institutional framework, the culture or value system, and, finally, a set of factors operating within the economy itself.

The physical environment

Some scholars think that climate is the basic factor influencing the rise of civilizations. They insist that economic progress requires moderate changes in temperature from one day to the next. Ellsworth Huntington, the most extreme champion of this view, believed that the average temperature most conducive to optimum physical effort was 60 or 65 degrees, and that mental activity was at its best when the temperature averaged about 40 degrees. A large part of the United States fitted these requirements. The average annual temperature ranged between 40 and 70 degrees, and there was a relatively wide gap between maximum and minimum temperatures.

The climate of the United States made possible a crop-growing season of five or more months over 55 percent of the nation's area. But favorable agricultural conditions required good soil and adequate rainfall as well as favorable temperature. Good soil was plentiful, and the average annual rainfall of over 26 inches was well in excess of the 20 inches required by agriculture. Piled on top of all this was a land mass far in excess of the next centuries' potential population growth. The combination of favorable temperature, good soil, adequate rainfall, and a most fortuitous man-land ratio enabled the United States to cultivate extensively, to emphasize man-hour output, and to produce foodstuffs far in excess of the amount needed to feed her population.

In addition to advantageous agricultural conditions, nature had sprinkled the American continent liberally from her cornucopia of resources. The fantastic tales of untold wealth that had lured early Spanish adventurers into the interior of the continent on fruitless quests proved to be not so fantastic after all. True, gold and silver were not lying free on the face of the earth; the storied Seven Cities of gold were never found. But this was more a blessing than a loss, because the country was stocked with resources far more valuable than gold and silver. All she demanded was that her bounty be felled, dammed, quarried, and mined.

The area of the United States originally included almost 850 million acres of timberland, and, even though forests were rapidly felled and denuded and timber reserves were fast depleted, there was still more than enough to satisfy the nation's requirements for many generations to come. Energy-producing resources—petroleum, natural gas, and coal—were also spread throughout the country in enormous supplies. The land also contained large mineral deposits. Iron, the chief ingredient of four-fifths of the metal consumed in the United States, existed in such ample quantities that, despite consumption of over 100 million tons a year, there are still enough reserves to last hundreds of years. Nonferrous metals did not exist in the original colonies, but the opening of the West uncovered large deposits of tin, copper, and lead. The United States also had adequate supplies of some of the additive metals whose use was practically unknown before 1900. There were large reserves of molybdenum, tungsten, and vanadium, but very sparse supplies of the more commonly used ferro-alloy metals (for example, bauxite for aluminum) and rubber.

Regional distribution of natural resources

Although nature endowed the whole of the United States with more than its share of natural resources, these resources were not distributed evenly. Climate and topography were neatly apportioned, so that each region was able to contribute importantly to the country's aggregate economic development.

The United States may be divided into eight rather distinct regions: New England, the Middle Atlantic, the South, the Middle West, the Great Plains, the Mountain, the Southwest, and the Pacific Coast. In only three of these regions— the Great Plains, the Mountain region, and the Southwest—were economic resources too meager to support more than a sparse population. The Great Plains—that vast stretch of land between the 97th meridian and the Rocky Mountains—was suitable for raising livestock, but not much else. The climate was not conducive to best physical and mental effort. The crop-growing season was less than 150 days—in some parts less than 90 days. Annual rainfall was much less than 20 inches. The region, therefore, could not support much agriculture. It had no timber for constructing dwellings and little iron and coal for heavy manufacturing.

The Mountain region was equally unsuited for agriculture and industry. Its land, with few exceptions, was poor and did not possess sufficient diversity of minerals to support heavy industry. It had, however, large amounts of copper, silver, gold, and lead, and it furnished much of the raw material used in the country's manufacturing centers. The Southwest was very similar to the Mountain states, but water, provided through irrigation, made possible a growing season that lasted for as much as nine months and produced as many as five crops.

The Pacific Coast is remarkably versatile. In some parts, rainfall is over 60 inches a year, and the arid areas, which resemble the Southwest more than the rest of the Coast, produce with the help of irrigation vast quantities of fruit, vegetables, rice, cotton, and wheat. In addition, the Far West, particularly Oregon and Washington, is by far the largest lumber-producing area in the nation. California is still the nation's leading gold producer, and its oil fields are second only to those in mid-continental America—the Texas-Oklahoma area. The Pacific Coast has few deposits of coal or iron ore, but its tremendous water-power resources enable it to take a leading role in aluminum production, shipbuilding, and aircraft construction.

Since shortly after its original settlement. the Middle West has been the agricultural center of the United States, producing more wheat, corn, hogs, and rye than the rest of the nation put together. Its temperature was ideal for efficient mental and physical activity. Rainfall varied between 28 and 40 inches a year. The crop-growing season lasted over 150 days, the land was flat, and the soil excellent, thus combining the best possible conditions for mechanized farming of staple crops. Though rightfully known as the "Bread Basket of the World," the Middle West could stake an equal claim to fame as an industrial center. It was rich in coal, iron, and oil, and its excellent natural waterways provided cheap and efficient means of transportation. The Middle West now produces more automobiles, fabricates more rubber, packs more meat, and manufactures more farm equipment than any other place in the world.

The Middle Atlantic section also had the natural resources needed for a diversified economy. Its excellent harbors, its relative nearness to European markets, the advantage of an early start, and its natural and man-made transportation faciliites thrusting into the interior quickly made it the center of the nation's commerce and finance. Its basic mineral resources were good enough to give the region a pioneer position in iron and steel production, and a mass market close at hand early stimulated the manufacture of consumer goods. Emphasizing trade and manufacturing, the Middle Atlantic region developed an urban civilization, but it also had the natural advantages—good soil, adequate rainfall, and a propitious growing season—to create an agriculture suitable for an urban region's demand for perishable and specialized crops.

New England's geographic environment was not nearly so favorable, but the impetus of an early start still enables her to support a relatively dense population and to make an important contribution to the nation's economy. New England's poor soil and a short crop-growing season were not conducive to a thriving agriculture. She also lacked the resources necessary for heavy industry. However, her long coastline lying near the famous fishing banks of the Atlantic stimulated the growth of a large-scale fishing industry. Good harbors encouraged trade and commerce, and excellent water-power sites gave New England an early advantage in light manufacturing, especially of textiles.

The South had many of the resources necessary for an integrated economy. The South Atlantic was rich in water power and timber; the lower Mississippi Valley had excellent soil and plentiful supplies of coal, iron, and petroleum. But climate and the slavery system led the South to specialize in cotton, tobacco, and sugar. The South made a heavy contribution to early American growth through her cotton crop that loomed large in foreign trade, but the section did not, ironically enough, share proportionately in the national income. Many critics, notably De Bow, the editor of the South's most influential publication, attributed this economic lethargy to the "absence of a spirit of enterprise." More recently, the South has turned to livestock, iron, steel, and textile manufacturing. Since the latter part of the nineteenth century, she has made as much progress in industrialization as any other section of the country.

The heritage from the Old World

The physical environment was immensely important in American economic growth, but by itself it is not enough to explain the rapidity and the lavishness of our development. For growth was well under way before most of our resources were discovered. Colonial New England, it is well to remember, had a most promising economy in the midst of unpromising resources, whereas the South lagged behind the rest of the nation even though her resources were at least equal to those of the North. Then, too, other nations have possessed a plethora of natural resources without enjoying a plethora of wealth.

But then, in addition to her natural gifts, America had the by no means insignificant advantage of being a late starter rather than a pioneer in economic development. America built upon Old World contributions and developed a cultural background and an institutional framework that brought forth a less conservative, less restrictive, less limited, and more spectacular economic growth than that experienced by the nations from which we had taken our roots.

By the time the United States signed the Declaration of Independence, the Old World, especially Europe, and most especially England, had already experienced a long and rich economic development. England had already gone through a "commercial revolution," and "agricultural revolution," and was in the midst of an "industrial revolution." It was on this foundation that America built. She borrowed freely of Europe's people and of Europe's capital; she copied Europe's technological know-how, and she transplanted Europe's institutions. Above all, European culture supplied the germ from which eventually emerged, although not without significant mutations, the values, beliefs, behavior, and attitudes that may be summed up in the often badly used phrase, the "American character."

Social and political organization

But once again, this is not the whole story. Europe contributed much, but other lands and other people were also in a position to learn from Europe's lessons, without always doing so. It has been said that this was because other nations did not have our political and social organization or our economic institutions. Ours, it is argued, was from the beginning a democratic, free-enterprise society which emphasized competition and frowned upon monopoly. Government did not discourage economic growth, but encouraged it by allowing market forces free play, except to strengthen them by guaranteeing freedom of contract, protecting the rights of private property, and acting as a policeman in preserving a competitive environment.

This point of view has never lacked articulate champions, and in the euphoria of their enthusiasm, they have made some most preposterous claims in behalf of their argument. They seem to have forgotten that other nations with quite different attitudes toward competition, democracy, and free enterprise have also made impressive strides in raising the level of living. Economic and political institutions are not a root cause of economic growth. They are symptoms of more fundamental forces; they reflect a philosophy, a system of values.

The American value system

Anthropologists and sociologists have long believed that a nation's culture, that is, its value system, offers the most revealing explanation of economic development, for the value system includes, reflects, and transcends all the other factors, such as natural environment, contributions from other nations, and the political institutions that are often used to explain economic progress.

Very few social scientists believe that there is such a thing as a "national character" in the sense of a set of inherent traits peculiar to one nation or to one people, and very few social scientists believe that one culture is superior to another. Nor do most social scientists believe that a value system persists without change from generation to generation, or that it manifests itself to the same degree in every individual in the nation.

It is often said that a burger of Lyons is closer in type to a burger of Bremen or Buffalo than to a factory worker in his own country, but in the ordinary things of life—meals, games, marriage, and so forth—this is not so. To be sure, there is no such thing as the "average American" or "average Frenchman." The personality differences that separate the proper Bostonian from the Midwestern farmer, and the Breton fisherman from the Parisian *bon vivant,* are marked and deep. Yet, despite differences among its citizens, every nation has its own culture, its own system of values, its own spirit that transcends individual differences and gives the society a collective psychology and philosophy that manifests itself in a credo or set of beliefs. "The statistical prediction can be made that a hundred Americans, for example, will display certain defined characteristics more frequently than will a hundred Englishmen comparably distributed as to age, sex, social class, and vocation."[8]

In the United States, the great desideratum was material prosperity. Nothing in the fabric of American values stood higher than the achievement of economic success, and dollars were the counters by which success was measured. In the "American Dream," economic success meant much more than family background and much more than intellectual, military, or professional pursuits or attainments. The dream, of course, did not always burn with the same intensity. It was brightest in prosperity and dimmest in the great depressions. And for many millions, the dream never became a reality. Nevertheless, throughout most of our history and for most of our people, the substance of the American dream was economic success symbolized by the house on the hill, the Cadillac in the driveway, and the swimming pool in the backyard.

The obsession with success made the attainment of a competitive goal far more important than the attainment of personal satisfaction. Enterprise and competitiveness were more prominent in America than in most other cultures. It was very hard for many Americans to understand or pay sympathy to any other way of life. In early America, a trapper who had journeyed to the Spanish settlements of the West was amazed to find that "the people live apparently unconscious of the paradise around them. They sleep and smoke and hum Castilian tunes while nature is inviting them to the noblest and richest rewards of honorable toil."

To say, however, that the American spirit was materialistic would be to oversimplify. Money had a lower marginal utility in the United States than in many other parts of the world. Money was a prize to be won in the competitive game, but it was not a thing to be hoarded. Europeans were very early impressed with America's high propensity to consume. Because nature had been so

[8]Clyde Kluckhohn and Henry A. Murray, eds., *Personality in Nature, Science, and Culture* (New York: Alfred A. Knopf, Inc., 1953), pp. xiv, 36, and 39.

generous with them, Americans were not so inclined to save for future emer-
gencies. Where material success was the measure of status, possessions were the
badge of success. Spending, therefore, was a national pastime, and the heavy rate
of consumption, engendered by spending, acted as a stimulus to increased
production just as increased production stimulated a high rate of consumption.

The American spirit was profit- and risk-minded, not security- and thrift-
minded. Material rewards were very important, but activity and work were
regarded as the substance of life. Leisure was sinful and contentment regarded,
at best, with suspicion. De Tocqueville, like many other Europeans, pointed out
that Americans regarded work as the necessary, natural, and honest condition of
existence. In the United States, he said, a rich man would think himself in bad
repute if he employed his life solely in living.

The emphasis on work, the all-pervading importance of "the game," sank
deep into the structure of society and permeated much of American life.
Intellectuals decried and ridiculed it, moralists questioned its ethical implications, and psychologists pointed to it as an example of national neurosis. The
competitive game offered no real stability, nor real security; and, because only a
few could achieve great success, most lived at best only modestly successful. But
although this did not make for individual serenity, it did prove an ideal philosophical foundation for economic development and expansion, for no success
was ever completely attained; it was onward, ever onward toward new goals of
achievement.[9]

Infused with such a spirit and fed by an environment rich in natural resources, the American people spun an economic philosophy that went a step
further than it had in Europe. The original settlers for the most part had left
Europe because of dissatisfaction with much of what existed there. They
brought to the New World those aspects of European life that they found
pleasing and rejected the institutions they disliked.

Here and there, in the Colonial Period, some attempts were made to
establish feudal institutions, but without permanent success. They died either at
birth or in infancy. Attempts to establish a guild system failed. Quitrents, entail,
and primogeniture were declining before the end of the Colonial Period and were
completely obliterated after the War of Independence. Other European attitudes
and obsessions found the new American climate equally hostile. Americans were
more interested in the practical than the abstract; they were thing-minded, not
spirit-minded. Europeans were more concerned with religious, military, and
governmental matters than with business. Even in Great Britain, the home of the
Industrial Revolution, more homage was paid to the landowner, the cleric, the
military man, and the civil servant than to the businessman. But America paid
tolerant respect to the cleric, honored the military man in time of war, regarded

---

[9]One of the most recent and provocative nondeterministic explanations for economic
growth is David C. McClelland, *The Achieving Society* (Princeton: D. Van Nostrand Co.,
Inc., 1961). See also the review of the book by Fritz Redlich in *Explorations in Entrepreneurial History,* Series II, Vol. I (1964).

the civil servant as a rather inept creature who had learned to accept his own limitations, and lavished its admiration, sometimes concealed by envy, on the man who had achieved success in business.

A new country, constantly growing and possessing abundant supplies of land, stimulated enterprise by holding before everyone the possibility of profit. As a result, Americans tended to be venturesome and optimistic. This was reinforced by the selective force of emigration which peopled America with persons more energetic, more independent, and more aggressive than those who hesitated to leave their ancestral homes. In such an environment and with such a people, the characteristics of Western Europe were pushed to extremes. In the United States, the family and the state were less important than in Europe. The individual, not the family or the clan, was the center of the universe. The western respect for self-reliance and individualism was, therefore, carried even further. Americans believed that the individual was master of his fate; he could take credit for his successes, but he also had to assume the blame for his failures. His destiny was in his own hands, and Henley's *Invictus* was the national poem.

But the complete rugged individualism of the "every man for himself" variety, with its abhorrence of collective action, was a rarity. Quilting bees and barn raisings were among the leading social events on the frontier, and societies and associations filled the same function in the cities. All over the country, government activity, although frowned upon in theory, was welcomed if it gave promise of helping the cause of economic growth and progress.

There were always, it is true, some segments of society who derided what they considered the American obsession with economic gain. Southern planters, along with patricians and intellectuals in all parts of the country, shared the European aristocrat's hostility toward industrialism;[10] but in general, Americans were always stalwart champions of the entrepreneurial frame of mind, with its admonitions to work productively, to make a profit, and to plow it back. It has been said that, because of the depression and World War II, the American value system has changed in recent years, that the traditional beliefs have lost much of their glamor, and that the Protestant ethic, with its emphasis on work and achievement, has declined. But if this is so, there is very little real evidence to prove it. By and large, Americans allow no conflicting aesthetic, political, or ecclesiastical values to distract them from the main goal of achieving economic progress.

The endogenous factors in the growth process

Economists have shied away from explanations of economic growth couched in terms of value systems. Some economists believe that abstract explanations of

---

[10]For example, Emerson, Jefferson, Calhoun, and Theodore Roosevelt, but even in some of these cases, the abhorrence of industrialism was not uncompromising.

growth have no merit whatsoever. They believe that all people are pretty much alike, and they think in terms of market forces rather than in terms of different cultures. They are technicians rather than philosophers, and their explanations of economic growth are relatively deterministic.

There are other economists, however, who take cultures and value systems for granted. They assume an aspiration for economic growth and proceed to analyze the process in terms of the construction and operation of the economy. In this type of analysis, American economic growth has been the result of, among other things, a favorable land-man ratio, technological progress in agriculture, the broadening of the market area, an expanding money system, imaginative and adaptive businessmen, an ambitious and mobile labor force, a benevolent government, and relative freedom from war. The chapters that follow are designed to give more detail on how these factors contributed to a growing scale of living.

SUGGESTED READINGS

(On specific topics, see the sources cited in the footnotes in the chapter.)

Adams, T.M., "Prices Paid by Vermont Farmers for Goods and Services and Received by Them for Farm Products, 1790-1940," *Bulletin 507*, Vermont Agriculture Experiment Station, Burlington, 1944.

Davis, Lance, "And It Will Never Be Literature," in Ralph Andreano, ed., *The New Economic History* (New York: John Wiley & Sons, Inc., 1970).

Hofstadter, Richard and Seymour M. Lipset, eds., *Turner and the Sociology of the Frontier* (New York: Basic Books, 1968).

Martin, Edgar W., *The Standard of Living in 1860* (Chicago: University of Chicago Press, 1942).

Potter, David M., *People of Plenty: Economic Abundance and the American Character* (Chicago: University of Chicago Press, 1954).

Redlich, Fritz, "Potentialities and Pitfalls in Economic History," in Andreano, cited above.

Sawyer, John E., "The Social Basis of the American System of Manufacturing," *The Journal of Economic History,* Vol. XIV (1954).

U. S. Department of Labor, *How American Buying Habits Change* (Washington, D.C.: U. S. Government Printing Office, 1959).

QUESTIONS

1. Currently, there is much argument about the pace of economic growth. Some argue that a 6 percent growth rate is likely. Others say that 6 percent is much too optimistic. On the basis of the historical record, which view do you support?

2. What are the advantages and disadvantages of using national income data to measure economic progress? What other methods of measuring economic progress are there?
3. Draw a rough graph showing the course of prices in American history. Draw a similar graph to show the movement of the business cycle. Is there any correlation between the two?
4. Which seems to have been most associated with economic growth: rising prices, stable prices, or falling prices? On what evidence do you base your answer?
5. How has American economic growth compared with that of other industrialized countries?
6. Why are the 1837 and 1893 panics and depressions given more attention than the recessions of 1869 and 1927?
7. "The economic growth of the United States has been unusually spectacular." Do you agree or disagree? Why?
8. What, in your opinion, have been the most striking changes that have occurred in the occupational make-up of the American population? Why have these changes occurred?
9. Contrary to some oft-expressed opinions, the share of the consumer dollar expended on food has not declined steadily. Why?
10. Contrast the "average" American of today with the "average" American of 1860 in respect to (a) his probable occupation, (b) how he spent his income, (c) what he ate, (d) where he lived, (e) how long he lived and what he died of.
11. Contrast 1800 with today in respect to the percentage of all workers engaged in farming. Approximately when were 50 percent of all workers engaged in farming?
12. Which point of view do you agree with and why: American economic growth took place in (a) stages, (b) slowly and steadily, (c) in a series of long waves?
13. One of the great "revolutions" of recent years has been the transformation in the "occupational mix." What has been the nature of this transformation, and why did it occur?
14. In recent years, much has been made about the redistribution of income. Has income been redistributed? If so, how and to what extent?

Chapter Three

THE LAND
AND THE POPULATION

A nation's output and the level of living of its people can never rise above the limit set by the available supply of the scarcest factor of production, for what an economy lacks most restricts its ability to utilize its more plentiful resources. If one factor is scarce in proportion to the others, the scarce one will be "dear" and the others will be "cheap." In order to obtain optimum production from its resources, an economy should try to maximize the output of the scarce factor, not the plentiful factors; in other words, it should minimize the use of what it has little of and waste what it has in abundance. In one sense, therefore, economic growth is a process of increasing the supply of the relatively scarce factors of production.

If land and natural resources are scarce in proportion to population, a nation will not be able to produce enough food for its people. If capital (machinery, tools, and equipment) as well as land is scarce, there is little possibility of creating an industrial or commercial economy to support a large mass of people. Forced to cultivate its land intensively and with little incentive to substitute "dear" capital for "cheap" labor, the economy's output, measured in terms of man-hours, will be extremely low. Because it is difficult, if not impossible, to reduce population drastically, and because the physical supply of land cannot be increased, such a nation is in a most wretched position insofar as its prospects for future economic growth are concerned. Its people are doomed to a subsistence existence and move under the threatening shadows of pestilence and famine. The only possible way to raise the level of living is to increase the supply of scarce capital so as to increase man-hour production. But as long as production provides a people with no more than the bare necessities, there is little opportunity to create a surplus that can be used for capital accumulation and technological progress.

On the other hand, if land and natural resources are plentiful compared to labor and capital, land should be used extensively. Emphasis should be placed on man-hour output rather than per-acre output. To make the most of its resources, it would be best for such an economy to economize in the use of labor and capital and to "waste" the land.

Prospects for long-run economic growth are better for an economy where population density is low than for one with a high man-land ratio; for, whereas the physical supply of land is fixed, the labor supply can be increased through population growth, capital can be accumulated through the production of a surplus, and capital can be substituted for scarce labor, enabling the whole system to produce more.

THE IMPORTANCE OF LAND IN EARLY AMERICAN HISTORY

Up to 1860 and probably until the end of the nineteenth century, land was the most influential factor in American development. Because it was very plentiful, it was "cheap" while labor and capital, being scarce, were "dear." The long-run economic problem was to increase the supply and output of labor and capital in proportion to land, for it was in this way only that total output and the level of living could be raised. Thus, the abundance of land acted as an incentive in increasing the supply of other factors. It is not difficult to understand how this applied to labor. The existence of a large, undeveloped land mass fairly bursting with natural resources offered great opportunity for economic progress. To be sure, the settlement of the land required work and capital, but to an optimistic population, this was unimportant, for it seemed almost impossible not to achieve economic success when land was practically unlimited and available almost for the asking. The golden opportunity offered by almost unlimited land attracted immigrants from across the ocean. It also encouraged early marriages and large families, for developing a farm on readily available land required little apprenticeship, and every increase in the family meant an additional worker to till the fields and handle the animals. But, even with an astonishingly high rate of population growth, a vast gap still remained between plentiful land and scarce labor. To fill this gap, Americans at every opportunity resorted to the use of capital equipment to increase labor output. Thus, the plentitude of land also encouraged the rapid technological development that has characterized economic growth.

The land also spurred investment spending. Americans were anxious to work their acres; and, as they fell to it, a demand was created for capital investment in the form of tools, building construction, and, somewhat later, machinery. Moreover, the enormous expanse of land, the sheer distances separating the Atlantic Coast from the Far West, soon revealed a need for transportation facilities. The construction of these facilities—turnpikes, canals, and railroads— required an extraordinary amount of investment spending met by a substantial volume of American and foreign saving.

To some extent, land itself offered the means by which the investment needs of the expanding economy were financed. Federal and state governments gave generous land grants to private entrepreneurs, some of whom succeeded in selling part or all of the land, using the proceeds to meet some of the costs of constructing transportation facilities. In some instances, governments also used the proceeds of land sales to pay for internal improvements constructed under their own auspices. Actually, this was an early example of deficit financing. Instead of spending money in excess of receipts, governments were spending their physical assets. In so doing, they were subsidizing private enterprise in a great colonization venture much as England had done in the era of mercantilism and much as other governments were to do in a later era of neo-mercantilism.

Land was also used in other ways to finance early American capital investment. It produced a surplus of agricultural products that could be exported in exchange for the manufactured goods of the older and more industrialized economies of Europe. And, in a few instances, sales of land were made directly to Europeans. Robert Morris, William Duer, and other entrepreneurs of early American land companies sold tracts to the British, the Dutch, and the French, and through such land sales Americans obtained foreign capital funds that were used to expand the general economy. Land also was an important factor in early Federal and state government borrowing, for governments frequently earmarked the proceeds of public land sales to meet the payments of interest and principal on public debt. Finally, both the government and the banks used land as the basis for the money supply. In colonial times, almost every colony at one time or other established a land bank that issued paper money against mortgages on land. Even as late as the 1830s, the State of Mississippi formed a bank that operated like the colonial land banks, printing money that it loaned against mortgages on land. And from the time they first appeared, private banks created deposits or printed notes against loans made against the security of land.

We should also pause for a moment here to consider the importance of the vast expanse of land in determining the sectional and economic interests which exerted such a profound influence on American political history. As we shall see, the problem of disposing of land became involved with the tariff issue, the slavery question, the debate over whether the Federal government should finance internal improvements, and the scope of government spending and tax raising. The land issue was as important as any issue in causing the sharp differences between the political attitudes of the West, the South, and the North. And it was also of great importance in the political cleavage between the industrialist, the laborer, and the farmer.

But the abundance of land was not an unmixed blessing. It led, inevitably, to methods of agricultural production that were "wasteful." As long as the land appeared inexhaustible, it was not practical to conserve it, especially at the expense of labor and capital, which were in short supply. Moreover, the abundance of land helped to make the American a land speculator. Yet it was this speculative opportunity, which land provided, that made the settlement of the West so dramatic. It was the land that formed the basis for projecting the American frontier, the most dynamic factor in early American agricultural history.

THE GROWTH OF THE AMERICAN POPULATION

Even though population density in 1970 was less than 60 per square mile,[1] a fairly small figure, the United States had, in the previous 150 years of its existence, experienced the most extraordinary population increase in world history. During the Colonial Period, the population doubled about every 23 years. There were about 50,000 people in the colonies in 1650, and about 1.2 million in 1750—approximately half the number now living in Philadelphia. During the long period from the signing of the Constitution to the outbreak of the Civil War, the population continued to double approximately every 23 years, increasing about one-third every decade. In 1790, when the British Isles contained about 15 million and France 25 million, there were 4 million in continental United States. By 1812, the population had doubled. It doubled again by 1835, and again by 1858.

Intelligent observers took the rate of population growth to be a law that would never be repealed. President Lincoln pointed out that from the beginning population had grown at an average rate of 34.60 percent per decade and had never varied more than 2 percent above or below this. He therefore forecast a population of 103.2 million in 1900 and 251.7 in 1930.[2] But forecasts that combine a specific number and a specific date are booby traps for the credulous. The Civil War with its extraordinary mortality depressed sharply the population growth rate. Yet, the increase still averaged 25 percent every decade between 1860 and 1890, 20 percent between 1890 and 1910, and 15 percent between 1910 and 1930. During the great depression of the 1930s, the population grew

---

[1] This compares with 819 per square mile in the Netherlands, 720 in Japan, 593 in the United Kingdom, and 239 in France; but 47 in Sweden, 29 in Russia, 26 in New Zealand, and only 5 in Canada.

[2] Population in 1900 turned out to be 76 million and in 1930, 123 million.

by only 7 percent. But this decline was reversed during the war and the following prosperous decades. Population increased 14.5 percent per decade in the forties and 18.5 percent in the fifties—about the same rate as at the beginning of the century. Then the trend resumed its historical downward slope, for in the sixties, growth was only about 13 percent.

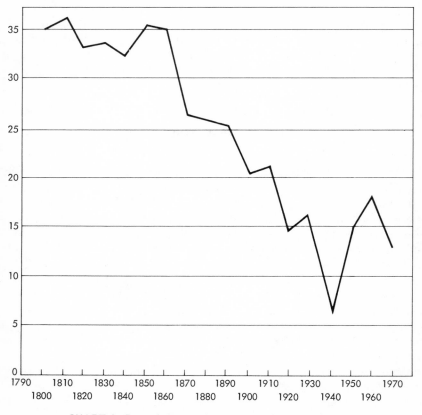

CHART 4. Rate of change of total population, 1790-1970

    The extraordinary nature of the long-run American population explosion may be judged by considering that at present Latin America is presumed to have the highest rate of population growth in the world, over 2 percent per year. In the most thriving years of her economic development, Great Britain's population increase probably never exceeded 20 percent per decade.

    In absolute terms, the population of the United States grew from about 30 million in 1860 to approximately 50 million in 1880, by which date we had become the largest western power. During the twentieth century, even though the rate of increase fell off, the population reached 100 million in 1915, 150 million in 1950, and over 200 million in 1970. With 3.5 billion people in the whole world, the United States had a little less than 6 percent of total population.

As the rate of population growth declined and the length of life increased, Americans naturally grew older, but the aging process took place slowly. In 1800 the median age was 16 years; it did not exceed 20 until 1870. By 1900 it was hardly 23 years, and in 1970 it was somewhat less than 30. In 1900, less than 5 percent of the population was 65 or older, whereas 35 percent was younger than 15. But the number of older people increased and the number of very young declined as the curve of population growth fell. By 1970 almost 10 percent of the population was over 65, but only 30 percent was below 15. In terms of economic growth, the gradual increase in the median age of the population was favorable, for it meant a continual increase in the percentage of the population of working age.

Despite the growth of population, density per square mile did not increase substantially in the first half of the nineteenth century, because the nation constantly acquired new territory and restless Americans moved to occupy it. In 1790 there were less than five people per square mile—about the same as the present density in the state of Montana—and by 1860, only a little more than ten. After the middle of the century, however, the density began to climb. By 1890, when the Census Bureau announced the end of the frontier line, there were more than 20 per square mile, and by 1970 there were more than 60 per square mile in continental United States.

BIRTH AND DEATH RATES

In general, population grew so rapidly and extensively in the United States because of the opportunities offered by the almost unlimited mass of land and resources, the absence of rigid caste lines, and the high percentage of people living in the rural regions. But more specifically, population expanded because of a high birth rate, a low death rate, and immigration.

The birth rate in the early United States was much higher than in Europe. Benjamin Franklin claimed that the average number of children in a colonial family was twice that of England. In 1820, the birth rate was estimated at the extraordinary figure of 55 per 1,000 population—about twice as high as in recent years. Even though this is higher than the rate in any contemporary country, the estimate seems quite plausible. The high rate of population growth lends credence to it. Then, too, the economy was overwhelmingly agricultural, encouraging early marriages, which in turn were conducive to a high birth rate. In the Southern states, for example, where agriculture reigned, it was not unusual for girls to marry at 13 or 14; many were grandmothers at 40 and some at 27. In all sections of the country, most girls were married before they were 20 and most men by the time they were 22.

For the next century and through the depression of the 1930s, the birth rate declined secularly, dropping to less than 40 by 1880, to 30 in 1910, and below 19 in 1933. At times the rate fell below that of western Europe. Throughout the period, the curve of population growth was declining; the economy was becoming steadily more industrialized; and people were not marrying quite so young. In the 1920s, new elements began to influence the picture. As early as the immediate post-Civil War era, the dissemination of birth-control information had caused some people to live in fear of imminent race suicide, but information on birth control did not really become widespread until the twentieth century.

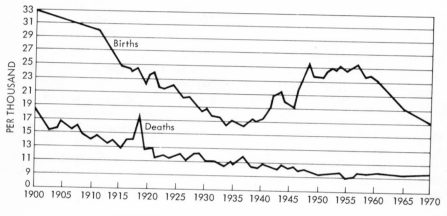

CHART 5. Birth and death rates, 1900-1970

The emancipation of women and the declining importance of the family added to the pressures. In the 1930s, the slump in the birth rate was further accentuated by the deep and prolonged depression. During World War II and the prosperous postwar years, the downward trend was reversed, at least temporarily. In the 1950s, the birth rate was 23 to 25 per 1,000 of population—approximately the same as before World War I, but then in the 1960s, it fell drastically, and by 1972 it was less than 17 per 1,000. To express this a different way, in the 1940s, the population below age five soared by over 50 percent, a record high; in the 1960s, it fell by over 15 percent, also a record high.

The historical trend in the American birth rate offers no conclusive evidence in support of any of the leading population theories. The Malthusian dictum that population tends to increase to the limits set by available subsistence is not borne out by American experience, for population growth in the United States showed signs of diminishing long before the limits of subsistence were reached. Nor does the American story substantiate the theory, propounded by Herbert Spencer and more fully developed by Corrado Gini, that fertility declines as civilization advances and that the birth rate will decline as the standard of living rises and education and culture are advanced. The growth rate curve, for example took on fresh vigor in the decade of the 1940s, when industrialism and urbanization were at an all-time high. The American experience does demonstrate that prosperity and depression affect the rate of population growth. Thus, the percentage rise was slightly smaller than normal during the depression years of the 1830s and 1870s and perceptibly lower during the great depression of the 1930s. But there has certainly not been any one-to-one relationship between economic well-being and an increase in the number of people. Population growth declined during the very prosperous 1920s and it declined secularly, good times or bad times, from the Civil War to World War II. Prosperity no doubt had much to do with the surge in numbers of people in the 1950s but better reasons are the migration to suburbia and a renewed and different interest in the family. The move from the country to the city depressed population growth; the move from the city to the suburbs temporarily gave it new life.

Like the birth rate, the death rate in early America was conducive to rapid population growth. It was very high in comparison with today, but low in comparison with other nations at that time. Primarily, this was so because of the abundance of land, which eased the problem of making a living, and the geographical dispersion of the population, which lowered the incidence of disease. The historical statistics on the death rate are not very good. They were not collected by the Federal government until 1900, and up to 1920 the data were gathered from a limited but growing number of states and cities and were, therefore, questionable. Nevertheless, there were some early estimates. One placed the death rate between 25 and 30 per 1,000 population in 1800. In Massachusetts, morbidity fluctuated narrowly around 20 per 1,000 all through the last half of the nineteenth century; then came solid improvement. Federal statistics show the same substantial progress; the death rate dropped from 17.2 in 1900 to 13.2 in 1915 and 9.5 in 1960. But up to 1933, the birth rate was going down even faster, and it was this accelerated falling off that was primarily responsible for the declining rate of population growth.

IMMIGRATION AS A FACTOR IN POPULATION GROWTH

Immigration did not contribute as much to the over-all growth of American population as did the increase in the domestic population. If we take crude and unrefined figures, immigration in the years from 1850 to 1930 accounted for anywhere from 1.7 percent (1920-1930) to 22.9 percent (1850-1860) of the increased population. However, this assumes that every immigrant added one person to the population, an assumption that many would deny. Indeed, some authorities, notably Francis Walker, insisted that immigration had no effect at all on the size of the American population. Walker pointed out that the population grew just as rapidly before as after the great influx of immigrants. It is well known that the greater the degree of urban concentration, the lower the birth rate. Walker argued that, because immigrants tended to settle in the crowded cities, they lowered the birth rate, and instead of being additions to the population, they were merely replacements. Thus, according to Walker, the population would have expanded at the same rate, immigration or no immigration. The only question was whether the names of the additions would be Smith or Schmidt.

It is hard to accept this theory in its entirety. Altogether about 65 million immigrants came to the United States between 1820 and 1970 and perhaps 30 million went back, leaving a net of 35 million remaining. It is difficult to believe that an influx of 35 million people had no effect whatsoever on population growth. Certainly, there is no evidence of a one-to-one correlation between immigration and the fall in the birth rate. The years of greatest immigration were not the years of substantial drops in birth rates. Nevertheless, there seems to be some germ of truth in the idea that not all immigrants represented a net increase in population. Students of the subject think that the birth rate first began to decline impressively at about the middle of the century when urban concentration became clearly noticeable and immigration first became sizable. Immigrants did contribute to increased urban concentration, and, because city birth rates were lower than rural birth rates, increased urban concentration tended to accelerate a decline in the domestic birth rate. It seems, therefore, that Walker was at least partly correct.

Prior to 1870, the vast majority of immigrants came from northern Europe, especially from the United Kingdom and Germany. Of the 19.6 million people living in the United States in 1850, 2.2 million, or approximately 11 percent, were foreign-born, and of these over 40 percent were Irish, about 25 percent were German, and 15 percent were from England, Scotland, and Wales. After 1870, because of political troubles, cheaper transportation, and chronic economic hardships, immigration from southern and eastern Europe, the so-called "New Immigration," increased and eventually surpassed that from northern Europe, accounting for two-thirds to three-quarters of annual immigration from 1890 to World War I. After World War I, immigration fell off sharply; but, of the smaller number of immigrants who did come over, about 70 percent came from northern Europe, for Federal laws restricting the number of immigrants favored northern Europe as against southern and eastern Europe.

Most of the new arrivals, especially in the nineteenth century, were from rural backgrounds. Immigration was, in other words, another manifestation of a world-wide phenomenon, the drift from the farm to the city. The overwhelming mass had no particular occupation, or else were agricultural workers, laborers, or domestic servants. The Census of 1860 reported that, of 5½ million passengers who had arrived since 1820, roughly half listed no occupation, a little more than 15 percent were laborers, and a little less than 15 percent were farmers. Of the immigrants who came in the last years of the century, 47 percent had no known occupation, 25 percent were laborers, and 7 percent were farmers. After they arrived here, few immigrants immediately became farmers. Instead, most of them entered occupations with which they were at best only vaguely familiar. They filled the ranks of the unskilled, the domestic servants, and the jobs with which the native American was not in the least bit infatuated. In 1855, in New York City, well over half of the foreign-born were unskilled laborers or in the service occupations; about 10 percent were storekeepers, 4 percent were clerks, and only 2 percent were professionals. In the whole country in 1870, only 10 percent of the farmers were foreign-born, but 40 percent of the unskilled had come from abroad.[3]

Census data indicate that during the whole period of heavy immigration, well over 60 percent of the newcomers were males, with the proportion being highest when the volume of immigration was highest. For example, in the peak year of 1907, over 72 percent were males. It was, moreover, the middle-aged male, not the young boy or the old man, who populated the immigrant ranks. Over long periods of time, between two-thirds and four-fifths of the immigrants were in the 15-to-44 year age groups. Thus, immigration was an important factor in making the population of the United States more male than female and in raising its median age.

Aside from some radical political refugees, whose influence has been greatly exaggerated, immigrants were conservative, law-abiding people. They were also energetic, productive, and ambitious, for coming to the New World was no holiday outing. It could take as long as two months to get here from Europe, and even in 1850 the average journey covered 12 days. It was not until the late 1890s that the time was reduced to less than a week, and a journey on the high seas of more than a week in the nineteenth century indicated that the average immigrant wanted to get here "in the worst way."

Immigration was greatest during periods of high world prosperity. (See Chart 6.) We can pick out four great immigration waves. From 1847 to 1854, about 300,000 came to the United States annually. During the second great wave—from 1866 to 1873—about 350,000 arrived annually, with a peak of 460,000 in 1873. During the early 1880s, there were over 600,000 a year—789,000 in 1882 alone. From 1903 to 1914, there was an average of over 1 million a year, with an all-time high of 1.3 million in 1907. Immigration spurted again in the years immediately following World War I, but government legislation and the panic of the 1930s depressed the figure once again.

WHY THE IMMIGRANTS CAME

Prosperity encouraged immigration; depressions discouraged it. The depression of the 1870s, for example, cut immigration to one-third its former size; the panic of 1884 and the depression of the 1890s reduced it to half its former level. The vast Irish immigration, induced by the great famine of the

---

[3]Robert Ernst, *Immigrant Life in New York City, 1825-1863* (New York: Columbia University Press, 1949); Stanley Lebergott, *Manpower in Economic Growth* (New York: McGraw-Hill Book Company, 1964).

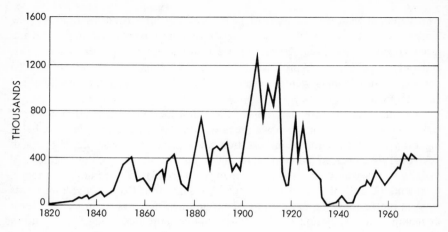

CHART 6. Immigration into the United States, 1820-1970

1840s, can be considered an exception, but even short recessions in the midst of secular uptrends in business activity caused a quick and decided drop in the number of immigrants. Thus, immigration declined from 316,000 in 1867 to 139,000 in 1868, and from 1.3 million in 1907 to 752,000 in 1909.

There were many reasons why people were more prone to migrate during boom times than in bad times. Although the cost of passage was low in dollar terms—$30 to $40 in the early 1800s, $18 to $25 in 1850 and $10 to $15 in the late 1800s—it was high in proportion to the income of the average European, especially during periods of depression. Migration, moreover, entailed an intense psychological conflict. Almost all roots with the past had to be broken. Optimism was a prerequisite, and periods of economic depression were hardly conducive to such a state of mind. Then, too, many immigrants were persuaded to leave home by the encouraging reports they received from friends or relatives who had already emigrated. The human tendency to romanticize when the going was smooth and to pall when the curve of economic activity turned downward reflected itself in the letters that were sent home and did much to encourage or discourage others from migrating. Finally, during depression, American businessmen and organizations soft-pedaled their efforts to encourage migration.

Immigrants left their homelands to escape from abuses and disadvantages of one sort or another. During the nineteenth century, the European farmer toiled under constant pressure, which induced heavy emigration. Population was rising, and with it rents were skyrocketing and more and more marginal land was being exhausted. The farmer's costs were multiplying and the increasing competition from an ever-rising volume of cheap American agricultural exports was compounding his plight. It was move or be ruined. He could either go to the city to join the growing army of industrial workers, or he could go to America. And there were many who were eager to help him on his way. Landlords and individual philanthropists sent off the poor in "wagon loads." One in Ireland is said to have paid the passage of some 15,000. Charitable institutions, societies, and religious organizations, such as the Society of Friends, and the Tuke Society in the 1880s, aided many others to emigrate. Trade unions, parishes, towns, and villages also assisted the poor, the unemployed, paupers, and criminals to depart.

But, in addition to being pushed out of his native land, the immigrant was also pulled by the opportunities that America promised. And the United States was as eager to have him as Europe was to see him go, for American population was relatively low and the labor supply relatively sparse. Shipping companies romanticized the economic and scenic wonders of the New World. Free land was offered by land companies and railroad promoters, who sent agents to Europe and distributed advertising in order to persuade Europeans to pack up and leave Bremen and Budapest for the haven of Ellis Island.[4] State governments also used free land in an effort to encourage immigration. Wisconsin had an immigration officer and a press agent in New York in the 1850s who flooded Europe with attractive inducements and dazzled the immigrant with honeyed descriptions of the state. After the Civil War, Minnesota and Iowa joined the competition by establishing boards of immigration.

Social and political conditions in central Europe also helped to swell the immigrant tide. Whereas the Irish, Scotch, and British were attracted more by the economic opportunities that America offered, many continental Europeans saw in the New World a chance to escape from the oppression of autocratic rule, both on a national and a local level. Compulsory military service, unsuccessful revolutions, and pogroms against minority groups led many Germans, Austrians, Poles, and Russians to flee to the United States.

Technological progress was also a factor in swelling immigration. Constant improvements in transatlantic shipping reduced the cost and increased the safety of the arduous voyage to the New World. At the same time, the multiplication of steamship lines made transportation accessible to more and more foreigners who were eager to leave home.

GOVERNMENT RESTRICTIONS ON IMMIGRATION

From the beginning of the great waves of immigration, there had always been resentment against the immigrant in some quarters of American society. There was always an articulate minority of nationalists who were decidedly hostile toward "the foreigner," Phillip Hone told his diary in 1832: "The

[4]Railroad entrepreneurs were especially active in trying to encourage emigration. See Paul W. Gates, *The Illinois Central Railroad and Its Colonization Work* (Cambridge, Mass.: Harvard University Press, 1934); R. C. Overton, *Burlington West* (Cambridge, Mass.: Harvard University Press, 1941).

boast that our country is the asylum for the oppressed in other parts of the world is very philanthropic and sentimental, but I fear that we shall before long derive little comfort from being made the almshouse and place of refuge for the poor of other countries."[5] To this upper class, articulate minority, labor added its voice, especially in periods of depression.

Resentment against the Irish immigrants who settled in New England in the 1840s culminated in the formation of an extremely nationalistic political party, the Native American Party, more familiarly referred to as the "Know Nothing" party. The Know Nothings achieved little practical success, but their emergence was unmistakable evidence of a rising tide of anti-immigration sentiment among the middle class and the lower-income groups.

As the nineteenth century wore on, anti-immigration sentiment increased. By the 1880s, labor organizations were enthusiastically urging the government to restrict immigration because it reduced the American level of living. They argued that immigrants swelled the labor supply and competed with native labor, that immigrants were willing to work for very little money and were depressing the whole level of wages. In essence, the anti-immigration forces were arguing that there was only so much work to be done. Immigration would, therefore, mean less work for each laborer and would force wages downward. The effectiveness of this essentially wages-fund theory of wages increased as the supply of free land began to be exhausted, for many people believed at the time that free land acted as a safety valve, drawing off the excessive population from the crowded urban centers and thus neutralizing the effects of a large inflow of foreign labor. Meanwhile, however, entrepreneurs, interested in maintaining a large supply of labor for their factories, supported free immigration. They argued against labor's demands for restriction on the ground that freedom of population movement was an essential ingredient of free enterprise, a sacred American doctrine by this time. But to this, labor spokesmen replied that business had already abandoned free enterprise. They argued that business had protected itself against international competition by persuading the Congress to erect tariff barriers that effectively prevented the free movement of goods and that, therefore, labor had the right to demand protection against competition by campaigning for the imposition of regulations against immigration.

The agitation against immigration began to achieve some small successes in the 1880s. In 1882, the Federal government excluded Chinese immigrants, imposed a head tax of 50 cents on each immigrant, regardless of his country of origin, and prohibited the entry of certain types of undesirables: convicts, lunatics, idiots, and persons likely to become public charges. Subsequent acts in the 1890s and early 1900s extended exclusion to many more types of undesirables, including the alcoholic and the diseased. Meanwhile, the shift of emigration from northern to southern and eastern Europe intensified native

[5] Allan Nevins, ed., *The Diary of Philip Hone* (New York: Dodd, Mead & Co., 1927), Vol. I, p. 79.

hostility, resulting in more vigorous agitation for more restrictive legislation. In 1885, contract labor was prohibited. In 1907, by agreement with Japan, Japanese laborers were excluded from immigration. Meanwhile, attempts to impose a literacy test were vetoed on four different occasions, but such regulations were finally passed in 1917.

After World War I, the sentiment that opposed free immigration became stronger. The power of organized labor was greater than ever, nationalism was probably more intense than at any time since the end of the War of 1812, and businessmen's fears of alleged immigrant radicalism began to outweigh their desire for a large labor supply. Regardless of the merit of these sentiments, the Federal government began, in the early 1920s, to adopt legislation that effectively limited the number of immigrants who might enter the country. Congress in 1921 limited annual immigration for each country to 3 percent of the number of such nationality living in the United States in 1910. The act of 1924 reduced the percent to 2 and pushed the quota back to 1890. Then, by the National Origins Act of 1929, the total number of immigrants to be admitted each year was restricted to 153,929. Each nation was allowed a quota on the basis of the same ratio to 150,000 that the number of persons of that national origin bore to the total population as of 1920. There were, however, many exemptions: certain close relatives of American citizens, professors, ministers, citizens of the Western Hemisphere, and a few minor groups. The depression of the 1930s made the quota acts academic, for by 1932 more people were leaving than were coming in. The end of World War II, however, seemed to foretell another resurgence in immigration, but this was nipped in 1952 by the passage of the Walter-McCarran Act, which substantially reaffirmed the quota act which had been put into effect in 1929.

WHERE THE IMMIGRANTS SETTLED

Because most of the immigrants were of rural background, it would be logical to assume that they would settle in the rural sections of America. And because free land was such an important inducement to emigration, it would also be logical to assume that many immigrants went West to set themselves up as farmers. But such was not the case. Although there were some outstanding exceptions, most of the older immigrants remained in the East, and, no matter where they went, they tended to be city-dwellers. Only a handful went South, and of the greater number who went West, not all became farmers and very few were pioneers. Many worked on the railroads and settled in the growing cities. Those who became farmers ordinarily did so only after long years of saving, and then by buying land that had already been partly cultivated by the trapper and the pioneer farmer—usually native Americans. The Boones and the McCleods were the pioneers; the Hansons, Johnsons, Petersons, and Schmidts, who were by no means typical of all the immigrants, came later. They were the fillers in the process of settlement. In the 1830s, immigrant farmers began to settle in western New York, Pennsylvania, and Ohio. They moved into Missouri, Illinois, and Wisconsin in the 1840s, into eastern Iowa and Minnesota in the 1850s and 1860s, and into the Great Plains in the 1870s.

Census data support the argument that most of the early immigrants congregated in the East, that a large number of the minority pushed on to the Middle West, and that hardly any settled in the South. The Census of 1850 estimated that New York, Pennsylvania, Massachusetts, and Ohio, with 40 percent of the total population of the United States, contained 60 percent of the 2.2 million foreign-born. Illinois, Missouri, and Wisconsin,[6] with 9 percent of the total population, contained 13 percent of the foreign-born. Thus, seven states with about half the total population contained almost three-quarters of the foreign-born.

Not all national groups followed the same pattern of settlement. Almost two-thirds of the 960,000 Irish in the country in 1850 lived in New York, Pennsylvania, and Massachusetts. A similar fraction of the 380,000 English lived in New York, Pennsylvania, and Ohio. The 580,000 Germans were more widely dispersed. Slightly more than half lived in New York, Ohio, and Pennsylvania, but there were many on the farms and in the cities of Wisconsin, Missouri, and Illinois. In 1850, only the first slow trickle of Scandinavian immigration had begun. There were only 18,000 in the whole country, and of these over half lived in Wisconsin. And, to buttress the statement that European immigrants were slow to enter pioneer territory, there were only 12 Scandinavians in the whole Minnesota Territory in 1850.

Census data also show that the early immigrant tended to settle in the city and not on the farm. In 1850, about one-third of the foreign-born population, as compared with less than one-tenth of the total population, lived in the 12 largest cities. Foreign-born constituted about one-third the population of Boston and Philadelphia, a little less than half the population of New York and New Orleans, and about half the population of Brooklyn, St. Louis, and Cincinnati.

If the city was a magnet for the older immigrants, it was even more so for the members of the so-called "new immigration," the immigrants from eastern and southern Europe in the late nineteenth and early twentieth century. Of the northern European groups, the Germans and the Irish tended increasingly toward the cities, but the Scandinavians continued to keep their eyes fixed on the farms of the Middle West.

By 1900, the foreign-born made up about 14 percent of the American population. Almost 40 percent of them lived in cities of over 100,000 popula-

[6]Wisconsin had been extremely successful in its deliberate campaign to encourage immigration, and by 1850, it was a Mecca for immigrants. Of its population of roughly 300,000 over one-third were foreign-born. This was the highest percentage of all the states in the Union; but, in absolute terms, its 100,000 foreign-born was much less than New York's 650,000.

tion; roughly two-thirds, as compared with one-third of the native-born, lived in cities with a population of 2,500 or more. Irish immigrants constituted 23 percent of New York State's urban population and only 12 percent of the population of the rest of the state. They represented 16 percent of Pennsylvania's urban population, but only 4 percent of its rural population. If there had ever been any doubt about the immigrant's destination, it had been dispelled by the latter nineteenth century. For every one who went to the farm, two stayed to work in the city's trade and industry.

There were good reasons why the great majority of immigrants remained in the city. Most of them had barely enough money to see them safely to the American coast, let alone carry them hundreds of miles into the hinterland. Nor did American agriculture offer attractive prospects for the immigrant. Cotton raising was alien, and the agricultural methods current in the great West differed so radically from those in vogue in Europe that the immigrant's knowledge of farming was more a hindrance than a help. The great open spaces of the American West were quite different from the tightly packed farm plots he had known in Europe, and farming in the United States was much more extensive and much more mechanized than in Europe.[7] The immigrant, moreover, was a gregarious person, and, like most human beings, he sought the company and companionship of those who had interests and backgrounds similar to his own. The relatives and friends who preceded him had settled in the cities and he therefore tended to do the same.

THE EFFECTS OF IMMIGRATION

From a sociological viewpoint, immigration had many disadvantages. It was difficult for American society to assimilate the immigrant; the "melting pot" did not melt that thoroughly. Never completely accepted by native Americans, the immigrant tended to live to himself in a small circle of friends and relatives, and concentrated on minding his own business. He could not immediately take part in civic affairs and was usually apathetic to the problems of local and national government. His entrance into industrial life created class lines in the ranks of labor, for the native worker regarded him with distrust or outright antagonism.

It is more difficult to generalize about what the immigrant did to the American economy. It has been argued that he created an excess supply of unskilled labor and thereby depressed wages, lowered working and living standards, discouraged the use of capital, and retarded the growth of unionism. But a more convincing case can be made for exactly the opposite conclusion. Immigration was, in a way, an automatic stabilizer. In the long run, it adjusted itself to

[7]For a most poignant treatment of the immigrant farmer's social, economic, and psychological problems, no scholarly work can surpass Ole Rolvaag's novel, *Giants in the Earth.*

the demand for labor, being high in prosperity when costs were high and low in depression when costs were low. If immigration flooded the supply of unskilled labor, one would expect that unemployment would have been higher in areas where immigrants were most numerous. To the contrary, unemployment was no higher among immigrants than among native workers and no higher where immigrants were most numerous. No doubt, the docile immigrant laborer was often exploited by entrepreneurs, but so was the native American worker. The clothing industry, for example, was a sweatshop industry before immigrants entered it on a large scale, and native American labor in the South undermined the Northern immigrant's economic position in the textile, mining, and metal industries.

On balance, the immigrant did little, if any more, to depress the status of labor than did the native American. On the other hand, he made some immensely important positive contributions to the productive capacity of the American economy. At a time when labor was scarce, every added worker helped to redress the balance among the factors of production, thereby enabling the economy to make better use of its more plentiful resources and adding to the national income. The immigrants, furthermore, were potential workers from the day they arrived. Society did not have to pay the cost of rearing them, as would have been the case with the native workers. Immigrants were a windfall to the American economy, not only because they arrived ready to work, but because they brought with them a willingness to work, an admiration and ambition for material success, and, in many cases, skills that were in short supply.

Immigrants were ordinarily very poor, so that they brought little capital, except for their own productive capabilities. Douglass North suggests that the pre-Civil War immigrants brought in about $350 million, $25 to $100 for each immigrant. Friedrich Kapp, in 1870, estimated the capital value of the average immigrant at $1,125. Andrew Carnegie, who had a talent for such things, thought that each year immigrants added to the wealth of the United States an amount in excess of twice as much as all that the gold and silver mines produced. He estimated the cash value of immigration in 1882 at $1.25 billion; each immigrant brought $125 in cash and was worth $1,500 (the price of a slave).[8]

THE ACQUISITION AND DISPERSION OF THE PUBLIC LAND

How the colonists acquired land

Land has always been relatively plentiful in the United States in proportion to the population. For the most part, therefore, Americans usually could acquire land cheaply and easily. This was certainly true from colonial times to the end of

[8]For the pros and cons of the economic effects of immigration, see Oscar Handlin, ed., *Immigration as a Factor in American History* (Englewood Cliffs, N.J.: Prentice-Hall, Inc. 1959), Chap. 3; Henry P. Fairchild, *Immigration* (New York: The Macmillan Company,

the nineteenth century. Colonial proprietors, anxious to populate their grants, encouraged settlement by making the land easily accessible to those who would come in and work it. After the War of Independence, the various states were equally liberal in giving land away; and when the states' bounty was exhausted, the Federal government began to give land away with a lavish hand.

Before the Revolution, climatic and topographical characteristics, as well as social and cultural beliefs, determined the ways in which land was disposed of. New England, with its stern climate and its rocky soil, was unsuited for large-scale agriculture. Consequently, landholdings were small. Land was given to groups of individuals who divided it among themselves in small lots, and people lived in villages with a township type of local government.

Farming on a larger scale was possible in the middle colonies, but, although there were some very large holdings in the Hudson River Valley, where attempts were made to set up a feudal system of land tenure, land was usually granted to single individuals in only slightly larger plots than in New England. The somewhat wider distribution of land in the middle colonies resulted in a mixed form of local government; the county type prevailed, although the township was not unknown.

A plantation economy developed early in the South, for southern climate and terrain were much more suited to large-scale agriculture than were those of either New England or the middle colonies. Most colonies, especially outside of New England, used the system of head rights to encourage settlement. Proprietors granted 50 acres of land to every settler who came over at his own expense and 50 more to every person who brought over another settler. Virginia supplied every family with 12 acres, a four-room house, and tools and provisions. The colonies had so much land that most of them also sold it in 50- to 100-acre parcels for a small fee.

Throughout the colonies, colonial administrators made determined attempts to institute feudal forms of land tenure. A few proprietors attempted to impose feudal obligations, and all proprietors and the Crown insisted upon levying quitrents which, theoretically, amounted to $100,000 a year in 1775. These attempts, however, were largely unsuccessful. They were the cause of constant disputes between proprietor and tenant, and the expense of collecting them hardly justified their imposition. Down through the Colonial Period, primogeniture (the right of the oldest son to inherit) and entail (the system of disposing of landed property in one piece) were the only legal methods of disposing of intrafamily land. After the Revolution, however, rising democratic sentiments put an end to these laws.

As a result of the Revolution, the original 13 colonies acquired the vast landholdings of the British Crown and expropriated or bought the estates of the loyalists who had refused to join the rebellion. Pennsylvania paid William Penn's

---

1925); J. W. Jenks and W. J. Lauck, *The Immigration Problem* (New York: Funk & Wagnalls Co., 1922).

heirs £130,000 and Maryland paid Lord Baltimore's heirs £10,000. These lands, some of which ran to the Mississippi, gave the states immense acreages that they sold at ridiculously low prices or gave away to land companies and individuals. In New York, for example, William Cooper, the father of James Fenimore Cooper, acquired 750,000 acres, and James Wadsworth acquired extensive holdings which he rented out on lifetime leases.

Federal land policy in the early nineteenth century

When the Treaty of Paris was signed with Great Britain in 1783, the whole area of the United States embraced a little more than half a billion acres. After that, another one and one-half billion acres were added, bringing the total acreage to almost two billion acres, or approximately three million square miles, about the same size as Australia and Brazil, three times as large as western Europe, half the size of Russia, and three-quarters the size of Canada.

Of the two billion acres that comprise continental United States today, the Federal government at one time or another owned 1.4 billion, or 70 percent. The accumulation of the public domain began as a by-product of the Articles of Confederation. The six states that had no claims to Western land refused to ratify the Articles unless the seven states that had such claims ceded their outlying territories to the Federal government. In 1780, New York did so, and the others followed between 1784 and 1802. This original acreage was later augmented by purchase and appropriation. The Louisiana Purchase, in 1803, doubled the original area at a cost of $15 million or less than 3 cents an acre. In 1819, 46 million more acres were added when Florida was bought from Spain for $5 million. In 1846, diplomacy settled a boundary dispute with Great Britain and attached to the rapidly growing nation 183 million acres of Oregon territory. At the close of the Mexican War in 1848, $15 million was paid to Mexico for 339 million acres in New Mexico and California; and in 1853, the Gadsden Purchase brought our government 19 million acres more for $10 million.[9]

At the same time that the government was acquiring land, it was also disposing of it. Indeed, in a period of less than 150 years it sold or gave away about one billion acres. The manner in which this was done was of inestimable importance in determining how rapidly the land would be settled and of equal importance in affecting the American scale of living.

In formulating its land policy, the Federal government had a number of choices. It could keep the land as a national heritage; it could make it available in large or small parcels to individual settlers, groups of settlers, or speculators, or offer it as a subsidy to business enterprise; it could sell it on credit or for cash at a high or low price; or it could give it away. Over the course of history,

[9]The annexation of Texas in 1845 increased the area of the United States, but not the public domain, by 249 million acres.

Federal land policy evolved gradually, covering the whole gamut of alternative choices, except sales at a high price. As a generalization, however, it can be said that the objective changed from revenue raising, to rapid settlement, and, finally, to conservation.

The early emphasis on revenue raising is easily understandable. Emerging from the Revolution with a vast debt and without adequate sources of income, the government naturally relied on its one great resource, the public domain, as a means of obtaining money. The first important land ordinance, adopted in 1785, set up mechanics for the sale of land that remained in effect as long as the public domain was available for settlement. The government was to survey an area six miles by six miles. This area comprised a township of 36 sections of 640 acres of one square mile each. The township received one section, section 16 (and, after 1848, section 36 as well), as an endowment for education. Congress retained sections 8, 11, 26, and 29, and mineral lands were reserved to be leased by the government. The remaining land was to be sold at auction in parcels of 640 acres at a minimum price of $1 an acre. Soon after the original ordinance, Congress also provided for the sale of land in wholesale quantities at prices well below $1 an acre. This, of course, gave great encouragement to land speculation. In fact, as early as 1796, a European observed that the best way of describing the United States in one sentence was "a land of speculations."

After the ratification of the Constitution, the government continued to regard the public domain as a source of revenue. Both Alexander Hamilton and Albert Gallatin favored selling land in small parcels at low prices. It has been argued that they would have been better advised to recommend selling land in small parcels at a high price, for this would have encouraged serious argiculture instead of speculation. Congress, however, insisted upon continuing the unrealistic and dubious policy of sales in large blocks. Under the land act of 1796, prospective purchasers still had to buy at least 640 acres, but the minimum purchase price was raised to $2 an acre. Payment could be made in cash or in evidence of public debt, but purchasers were allowed a year to complete payments. This act, and all later acts that permitted buying land on the installment plan, stipulated that in the event of default, the purchaser forfeited all money already paid, but this provision was largely theoretical, for Congress was always passing legislation giving relief to those in arrears.

The act of 1800 reduced the minimum purchase to 320 acres, and, although the minimum price remained at $2 an acre, the terms of purchase were liberalized by lowering the down payment to 50 cents an acre and allowing four years for the payment of the balance. In 1804, land was made purchasable in 160-acre parcels at $1.64 an acre with the same credit terms as before. Sales increased thereafter, but the returns lagged far behind expectations. By the War of 1812, only about 3.5 million acres had been sold for about $7 million, of which about $1.7 million remain unpaid. The land policy had failed to swell the Federal exchequer appreciably. One fault lay in the laws themselves—they were not liberal enough. The older states were offering more attractive land at prices much below $1 an acre. Massachusetts, between 1783 and 1821, sold about five million acres at about 17 cents an acre. Kentucky sold 400-acre plots at 25 cents an acre, and Georgia offered land at 6 to 8 cents an acre.

A second obstacle in the way of success for the land policy was that it required superhuman courage or extreme foolhardiness to settle in the Northwest Territory. The roads through the mountains were little more than Indian trails, dangerous in dry weather and utterly impassable when wet. If he were fortunate enough to reach the West, the settler faced even greater dangers. Although Indians did not lurk behind every bush, the chances were about even that they would eventually remove the scalp of the intrepid settler. If both terrain and the Indians were overcome, there was still a third reason why the sale of land was sluggish. The minimum parcel was too big. Without adequate help and with virtually no capital, the settler could just about manage 80 acres, but he faced the prospect of having to farm a sprawling 160 acres, the smallest plot the government offered for sale.

The public domain became more attractive at about the end of the War of 1812. The constant increase in population and the exhaustion of state lands caused would-be settlers and land speculators to look for new outlets. The removal of the Indians made the West less dangerous. The extremely high prices of farm products, especially cotton, which sold at 30 cents a pound, made the West a land of opportunity. The construction of the Cumberland Road by the Federal government made the West more accessible. The government sold over one million acres in 1814 and three and one-half million in 1818—about as much as the aggregate sales in the entire period before 1812. Indiana's population increase from 24,000 in 1810 to 147,000 in 1820 was ample proof that the westward movement had begun.

The debate over Federal land policy

As the demand for Western land accelerated, Federal land policy became the subject of heated debate in which the arguments were mostly determined by sectional economic interests. The West favored a liberal land policy, the North was split on the question, the South was opposed, and the border states favored compromise.

Westerners supported a liberal land policy because it would encourage rapid settlement, and rapid settlement would raise land values. Moreover, the influx of new settlers would increase the political power of the West, for, as population rose, new states would be created, adding to the section's power in the Senate. At the same time, the area's representation in the House, based as it was on population, would rise. Perhaps the most important reason why Western farmers favored a liberal land policy was that such a policy would enable them to become commercial farmers. Adequate transportation facilities were essential in their scheme of things. Without these, they could not market their goods, but it was not economically feasible to build railroads and turnpikes through sparsely populated territory, and private capital could not or would not build them without government assistance. A liberal land policy would encourage the rapid settlement that was needed in order to make transportation facilities feasible and give the West the political power to obtain government subsidies. The chief spokesman for the Western point of view in Congress was Thomas Benton, of Missouri, who favored selling land at graduated prices, with the poorest land being given away free.

Western arguments fell on many sympathetic ears in the East. City wage earners believed that free land would offer them an easy escape from the hardships of industrial life. Northern industrialists, however, opposed a liberal land policy, fearing that it would drain away the Eastern labor supply. There was also a very small group, mostly in New England, who believed that the public domain should be kept as a national heritage. John Quincy Adams, the spokesman for this group, proposed to use the public lands as an endowment for national education and for cultural projects. His viewpoint, rational and farsighted though it may have been, was not popular and had no possibility of being adopted.

As the South became convinced that its future lay in cotton culture and slavery, it increasingly opposed a more liberal land policy. Free land would multiply Western population and inflate Western political power and thereby weaken the South. Free land also implied high tariffs, for the government's only important sources of revenue were the public lands and the tariff. If land were sold at low prices or given away, the government would have to raise tariffs to compensate for the money lost because of reduced land revenue. High tariffs reacted to the disadvantage of the South because the area's economic existence depended on the export of cotton and indirectly on the import of British manufactured goods which paid for the cotton exports.

The border states, Kentucky and Tennessee, which were neither completely Southern nor completely Western, were caught in a dilemma. Cheap lands in the New West would drain population out of the older states and thus reduce the value of their land. On the other hand, Kentucky and Tennessee could not altogether oppose the Western demand for free land, because they needed internal improvements almost as much as did the states to the west. The border states, therefore, compromised on the issue. Their great political figure, Henry Clay, became the "Great Compromiser," favoring a policy of distributing Federal land among the states for them to do what they would with it.

As time passed, the arguments against a liberal land policy began to lose their force. Surpluses, not deficits, characterized Federal finance in the nineteenth century, and surplus revenue was a nuisance, not an asset. Consequently, those who supported public land sales as a revenue-raising device were having the ground cut out from beneath them and their arguments.[10]

[10]Half of aggregate federal revenue in 1836 came from the sale of public lands, and the surplus in that year was equal to more than half the total expenditures. Instead of seeking

At the same time, the groups who favored a more liberal land policy increased their political strength, while that of the opposition weakened. Western political influence increased while that of the South declined. Northern industrialists shifted from hostility to neutrality as it became clear to them that the westward movement was not significantly affecting the Eastern labor supply. Moreover, the rising democratic spirit engendered in the early nineteenth century by wide extensions of the suffrage caused many people to support a more liberal land policy on the ground that it would benefit the lower-income groups.

Government land legislation under a liberal land policy

By 1820, it was evident that the Western viewpoint was winning out. This should not have come as a surprise to anyone who understood the American culture. Given the habits and philosophy of the people, the abundance of land, and the popular desire for land, a liberal land policy was inevitable. Theoretically, a more conservative policy might have been followed. Land might have been sparingly distributed in order to preserve tighter and more compact settlement. It might have been sold at higher prices. It might have been retained by the government and leased to private enterprisers, or a policy of conservation might have been adopted much earlier. Other countries adopted these alternatives with good results. But the policy that was actually followed in the United States was the only policy possible for Americans. "Wasteful" as it might have been, it did offer the American an opportunity to satisfy his yearning for a piece of land of his own, and it fitted America's desire for rapid economic growth.

In 1820, the minimum purchase was reduced to 80 acres and the minimum price to $1.25 an acre. So much land was offered by the government that bids always remained around the minimum. Because of reduced terms, the 1820 law prohibited purchases on credit. Although the insistence on cash payment appeared to make the policy more stringent, in actual practice, would-be purchasers still had little difficulty in purchasing land on credit, for instead of owing the government for the land, they borrowed from state banks, using the purchased land as security.

By mid-century, it was apparent that the goals and motives of the land policy had definitely changed. Increasingly liberal, it was no longer designed to produce revenue but to encourage rapid settlement. In 1832, some land began to be sold in 40-acre parcels, and in 1841 Congress passed the very important Pre-emption Act, which gave permanence to a practice first begun in 1830 of

means of increasing revenue, the Treasury was confronted with a problem of getting rid of the surplus. See Paul Studenski and Herman E. Krooss, *Financial History of the United States* (New York: McGraw-Hill Book Company, 1963), pp. 99-102, for the nature of the surplus revenue problem and the role of land sales in creating the problem.

allowing squatters to pre-empt 160 acres at the minimum price of $1.25 an acre. Squatters were a constant source of consternation for land policy makers. They formed "claims clubs" and "squatters associations" to protect their interests, sometimes violently. Although the pre-emption law confined the allowance to only 160 acres, squatters, through their claims clubs, often preempted 320-480 acres.

The beginnings of a robust movement for free land appeared in 1844, and ten years later Congress adopted the Graduation Act, for which Senator Benton had been fighting for years. Under this act, the government disposed of its previously unsold land (at least 80 million acres) at prices ranging from $1 an acre for land that had been for sale for ten years, to 12 1/2 cents for land that had been on the market for 30 years. The average price in this great bargain sale was 32 cents an acre. By 1862, when the act was repealed, it had dispersed 40 million acres. The liberal land policy culminated in the Homestead Act, passed in 1862 after the South had left the Union. Ostensibly designed to benefit the lower-income groups by providing free land, it permitted any citizen or prospective citizen who was head of a family or over 21 years of age to file a claim for 160 acres (80 acres within the lateral lines of a railroad). After paying a registration fee of approximately $25 and living on and working the land for five years, the settler would own it. Or, if five years seemed too long a time, he could pre-empt the land in six months for $1.25 an acre.

After the Civil War, a whole series of new land laws were passed to plug up the loopholes in existing legislation and to provide a land policy more adaptable to the peculiar conditions of the arid, treeless Great Plains. The Timber Culture Act of 1873 granted 160 acres of land to settlers if they would plant trees on a small portion of their plot. Under the terms of the Desert Land Act of 1877, a settler could acquire 640 acres of unwatered land for $1.25 an acre if he irrigated it within three years, the acreage being amended to 160 acres in 1890 and 80 in 1891. The Timber and Stone Act of 1878 provided for the sale of 160 acres of nonmineral land at a minimum price of $2.50 an acre. Up to 1890, one individual, taking advantage of all his opportunities under the various land acts, could acquire 1,280 acres at a cost of $1,400 plus some filing fees.

Miscellaneous land disposals

Not all Federal land disposals were made in the manner just described. Land also was used to reward veterans and to encourage the development of education and the construction of internal improvements. In using the land in this way, the Federal government had ample precedent from colonial times. The colonies and the English government gave land to soldiers to encourage enlistments in the colonial wars. The colonies also gave land to encourage higher learning: Harvard, William and Mary, Yale, and Dartmouth each received a grant of land.

Similarly, the colonies made grants to individuals who contracted to erect forts, manufacture gunpowder, and build iron and copper works.

During the Revolution and after the War of 1812, the Federal government continued to use land to reward soldiers. These acts were crude and did not work well, but in 1850, after the Mexican War, the government passed a more comprehensive act giving all military veterans warrants for 160 acres of land.

At first, these warrants were not assignable, but in 1852 this provision was removed, much to the profit of speculators, who bought the warrants at 50 cents to $1 an acre. Altogether the Federal government gave approximately 60 million acres to veterans, but only a small percentage of the recipients ever actually settled on the land.

The Federal government also made extensive land grants to the states throughout the nineteenth century for the purpose of financing education and public improvements, such as roads and canals. When Ohio was admitted to the Union in 1803, the Federal government agreed to earmark 3 percent of all receipts from Ohio land sales to the state for building roads on condition that no taxes be levied on such homesteads for five years. This early grant-in-aid was extended to each public-land state that was later admitted. In 1841, certain Western states were given 500,000 acres each. Some states also received specific grants for use in financing social welfare projects. In addition, about 65 million acres of swamp lands were given to the states within whose boundaries they lay.

Governments also gave land to the railroads. Between 1850, when it made a grant of 2.5 million acres to the Illinois Central Railroad, and 1872, the Federal government gave 131.4 million acres to the railroads, and 48.9 million more were given through the states. In addition, over 40 million acres that had been granted were forfeited because of failure to meet the terms of the grant. The value of these net grants of 180 million acres has been variously estimated at anywhere from $130 million to $2.5 billion. By 1940, the railroads had received $434.8 million from sales and still retained 16 million acres valued at $60 million. The grants, however, were not without a *quid pro quo*. In some cases, for example that of the Illinois Central, the road agreed to pay a stipulated percent of annual revenue to the state. Also, the roads—both the land-grant roads and their competitors—gave the government in exchange for the land a rate reduction on its shipments. With few exceptions, this amounted to 20 percent on mail and 50 percent on all else. By 1947, when this privilege ended, the Federal government had received an estimated $1 billion in reductions, mostly during World War II.

The rationale for these land grants was that they would aid in meeting the costs of railroad construction, help develop the West, fulfill military needs, and serve the Orient trade. Whether these grants were "fair and equitable" or whether they gave promoters a windfall profit at the expense of the rest of the nation is still being debated.[11] It is, however, true that the land subsidy acceler-

[11] Robert S. Henry, "The Railroad Land Grant Legend in American History Texts," *Mississippi Valley Historical Review,* Vol. XXXII (1945); comments on Col. Henry's article

ated rapid settlement, enhanced land values, and encouraged overextension of railroad construction. Whether the price for these advantages and disadvantages was too high is a matter of subjective values.

The Federal government also used its public lands to subsidize education. By the Morrill Act of 1862, every state received 30,000 acres of land for each senator and representative it had in Congress in order to provide an endowment for colleges in agricultural and mechanical arts. About 11 million acres were disposed of under the original Morrill Act; eventually, the Federal government gave a total of 99 million acres to encourage education. This government subsidy, mainly to the farmer's education, was of unmeasurable importance in developing a farm population that was willing to experiment with new crops, new machinery, and new agricultural practices.

The conservation movement

In 1890, when the Census Bureau announced that the frontier line no longer existed and when population increase began to taper off, a new trend began to appear in the public land policy. The nation at long last was beginning to think seriously about the plundering of natural resources that had inevitably resulted from the liberal land policy. More and more, serious people began to think of ways in which their precious heritage of land could be preserved.

In 1891, Congress empowered the President to declare timberland a reservation. President Cleveland in 1897 used this power to create 13 reservations, but vociferous opposition from the West and from rugged individualists caused Congress to modify the President's ruling, and conservation made little progress until early in the twentieth century. The comment of Uncle Joe Cannon was typical. Said the Speaker of the House, "Why should I do anything for posterity; what has posterity done for me?" Under Theodore Roosevelt's administration, however, over 230 million acres of timber, mineral, and water lands, which had hitherto been available virtually free, were withdrawn from the public domain. At the same time, a Forest Service was established to supervise the conservation of what remained of America's timber resources. By the Newlands Act of 1902, the proceeds from land sales in the semiarid states were set aside to finance the construction of irrigation projects. During and after World War I, the government established a leasing system for some of its land. Conservationists believed they had achieved final victory in 1935, when all remaining public lands were withdrawn from settlement.

But in the midst of the conservation trend, vestiges of the liberal land policy still remained. Between 1868 and 1897, the Homestead Act disposed of 70 million acres, and between 1898 and 1917, when conservation was in the

---

in the same journal, Vol. XXXIII (1946); Lloyd J. Mercer, "Land Grants to American Railroads: Social Cost or Social Benefit," *Business History Review,* Vol. XLIII (1969). See also below pp. 358-59.

ascendancy, total land disposals amounted to 100 million acres, or more than had been given away during the entire liberal land-policy period. In 1909, with the passage of the Enlarged Homestead Act, 320 acres instead of 160 were made available to settlers, and in 1912 the residence requirement was reduced to three years. In 1946, an executive order reversed the edict of 1935, and homesteading was restored.

The effects of government land policy

The government was extraordinarily successful in disposing of the public domain. In a very short time it sold 255 million acres for cash and gave 255 million acres to individuals, 250 million acres to the states, 130 million acres to the railroads, and 60 million acres to veterans.

The land policy certainly accomplished the rapid settlement of the country. No other colonization venture in history took place with such speed as the settlement of the American West. In the short run, this accomplishment accelerated the early discovery and utilization of America's natural resources and raised the level of living, but it is questionable whether the long-run effects were as beneficial as alternative policies might have been. The liberal land policy encouraged immigration, internal migration, and the dispersion of population. It played an important role in the development of transportation facilities, and it was an equally important influence in shaping government fiscal policy and in molding the economic and social institutional framework within which a large part of American society moved. Despite what it accomplished, however, it failed in its primary objectives. It did not produce as much revenue as was anticipated; it did not help the poor; and it did not develop the land. It fell so far short of meeting this last objective that a thoughtful and ordinarily tolerant authority has said: "The early record of Federal land grants is so dismal that one can explain its continuance and expansion only on some irrational basis not yet identified." [12]

The brief for this broad indictment of the land policy is that it encouraged speculation, beggared bona fide settlers, led to soil butchery, aggravated farm overproduction, and reduced the national income from what it otherwise would have been.

Some of the charges that have been leveled at the land policy are inconsistent. The policy, for example, has been criticized for encouraging over-production by attracting too many settlers, and at the same time it has been crit-

[12]Thomas LeDuc, "Public Policy, Private Investment, and Land Use in American Agriculture, 1825-1875," *Agricultural History,* Vol. 37 (1963); LeDuc, "History and Appraisal of U.S. Land Policy to 1862," Howard Ottoson, ed., *Land Use Policy and Problems* (Lincoln, Nebraska: University of Nebraska Press, 1963), pp. 3-27.

icized for not being liberal enough to settlers. It is evident that these charges are mutually contradictory. It should also be remembered that the land policy was not the only dog in the manger. What agricultural distress existed was world-wide and had more basic reasons than land policy alone. The fundamental reasons for the farmer's plight were economic. He lived in a peculiar world of pure competition and inelastic demand and supply schedules, and nothing could be done about it. Be that as it may, the majority of the critics argue that the liberal land policy, especially in the last thirty years of the nineteenth century, brought too many resources—land, labor, and capital—into farm cultivation. The land policy, therefore, caused overproduction and thereby produced chronic depression in agriculture. The indictment goes on to say that the agricultural labor force was not only too large, but consisted to a large extent of misfits. The land policy attracted people who because of physical disabilities, inexperience, or lack of knowledge could not farm efficiently.

The indictment has considerable appeal, and at first blush it is more than plausible. Economic theory, moreover, would give some support to the critics' main contentions. According to theory, the resources flowing into agriculture would be much greater than those flowing into manufacturing. This would follow because agriculture was closer to pure competition than manufacturing and would therefore operate closer to full capacity than manufacturing which, even in the nineteenth century, exhibited monopolistic characteristics.

Unfortunately, the evidence that history offers does not give much support to the theoretical analysis. Nor does it substantiate the devastating criticisms that have been leveled at the land policy. If agriculture was overloaded with resources in proportion to manufacturing and trade, then it would follow that agriculture must have suffered from continuous depression; farm prices must have declined faster than other prices; interest rates and equity returns on the farm must have been lower than in the cities; and wages must have been lower.

On the basis of existing evidence, which is admittedly far from conclusive, none of the dire effects listed above seems to have occurred. The last 30 years of the 1800s were not a time of constant depression in farming, and farm prices did not fall steadily. Nor did they fall faster than other prices.

It is especially difficult to draw judgments on the relative returns to the different factors of production. Real wages on the farm did not rise as fast as those in manufacturing, but in the West, where the land policy was in effect, they held their own with manufacturing. It seems hard to believe that returns on farm equity compared favorably with returns on other forms of investment, but some scholars have insisted that they did.

Whatever the evidence, it is clear that the land policy was hardly as myopic as it has been painted. Perhaps the real reason for the hostility to the policy lies in the critics' belief that the land policy's most important effect was that it encouraged widespread speculation, a type of economic behavior which most people regard as sinister and anti-social.

Land policy and speculation

The government's liberal land policy was idealistically designed to favor the bona
fide settler and the lower-income groups on the farms and in the city. But,
although the policy did encourage rapid settlement, critics have insisted that it
benefited speculators much more than the settlers, the city laborers, and low-
income groups whom land-reform leaders had in mind. To begin with, the
low-income groups did not have the money to move and to set up a farm, and
the land policy provided only the land—not the funds to get there. Then, too, of
those who bought land, only a minority intended to cultivate it permanently.
The majority hoped to sell and reap a quick profit. Settle and sell, rather than
settle and cultivate, became the rule of Western agriculture. An English commentator thought that not more than half of 1 percent of those who moved west
did so with the intention of settling permanently. De Tocqueville observed: "It
seldom happens that an American farmer settles for good upon the land which
he occupies." If it appears that the Englishman and the Frenchman were looking
at the American farmer with a biased eye, consider the remark of an American
who suggested that not one settler in ten made a permanent impression on the
landscape of the great West. If land speculation is defined as the act of buying
land with no intention of cultivating it or of holding it permanently, the settler
was more a speculator than a farmer, and, unlike the European, he was more
disposed to gamble on land prices than to make money on crops.

Although most of the farmers who took part in the westward movement
tended to end up as speculators, their operations were on a small scale. There
were, however, some large-scale speculators—shrewd, enterprising men—who
took advantage of the public land laws in spite of all the government's attempts
to close the loopholes which they manipulated. Many speculators acquired
enormous tracts from the various state governments. Robert Morris and his
North American Land Company bought six million acres from state governments. Others lapped up Federal lands, whole empires, for next to nothing. John
Cleve Symes bought one million acres in the Miami River Valley of Ohio for $1
an acre. The Ohio Company bought one and one-half million acres at about 10
cents an acre by paying for the land with depreciated government securities. The
Scioto Company bought five million acres, and William Duer one and one-half
million, for about the same price under the same arrangement. Later speculators
bought land warrants from veterans at depreciated prices. Paul Gates reports that
brokers acquired some 60 million acres on the prairies at 50 to 80 cents an acre.
A careful study of Iowa land history estimates that speculators owned half of
the state in 1860. Speculators also evaded the spirit of the land laws by filing
claims in the names of dummies. Under the Homestead Act, for example, more
land was pre-empted than was given away, and most of the pre-emptions were
made by speculators. William S. Chapman owned over one million acres in
California and Nevada. The Miller and Lux ranch covered 450,000 acres. William

Scully owned 250,000 acres. Easley and Willingham put together 146,000 acres in the Middle West. From these examples, it would seem that land speculation must have been an easy road to formidable riches, but such was not the case. The occasional spectacular bonanza was the exception, not the rule. In most cases, speculators overreached themselves; if they did strike it rich, they stayed too long.[13] The Bogues conclude that returns to speculators in Indiana and Illinois varied from a loss to 125.3 percent. But in the years of largest sales, the return was high—above 15 percent. Returns on Nebraska land were somewhat less, but still robust. Since interest on mortgages varied from 8 to 12 percent, the Bogues conclude that speculative land paid. But Robert Swierenga's research on Iowa land returns does not come to so unequivocal a judgment. Approaching the problem in a different way, he concludes that speculative land was sold for $3 an acre, whereas non-speculative land sold for $5.27, or $4.21 an acre if the costs of improvements are deducted.

Other results of the land policy

In the early years, when the Treasury considered itself desperate for funds, land policy did not raise nearly as much revenue as had been hoped. Even though land was formally sold at auction, the minimum price tended to be the only price. Aside from occasional years, such as the middle 1830s, aggregate revenue was not very large. Land sales also tended to follow the business cycle; land was, in other words, income-elastic. In periods of prosperity, when revenue was apparently least needed, the government did a "land-office business." In periods of recession and depression, when it was thought that revenue was desperately needed, land sales fell away to insignificance. (Note, for example, the extreme peaks and troughs on Chart 7.) Land sales also accomplished an enormous fiction in fiscal affairs. When the government sold land, it commingled these receipts with its other revenue from taxes, tariffs, and miscellaneous sources, none of which involved a surrender of assets or an increase in liabilities. The treasury tried to operate on a balanced budget in terms of money and ordinarily succeeded, but this was deceiving because the receipts from sales of public lands were not really revenues, being offset by a surrender of assets. The federal government was, in other words, very often operating under a kind of deficit financing.

[13]The saga of easy riches remains perennially fascinating. See A.M. Sakolski, *The Great American Land Bubble* (New York: Harper & Row, Publishers, 1932); Allan and Margaret Bogue, "Profits and the Frontier Land Speculator," *Journal of Economic History,* Vol. XVII (1957); Paul Wallace Gates, "Land Policy and Tenancy in the Prairie States," *Journal of Economic History,* Vol. I (1941); Paul Wallace Gates, "The Role of the Land Speculator in Western Development," *Pennsylvania Magazine of History and Biography,* Vol. LXVI (1942); Robert P. Swierenga, *Pioneers and Profits* (Ames, Iowa: The State University of Iowa Press, 1968).

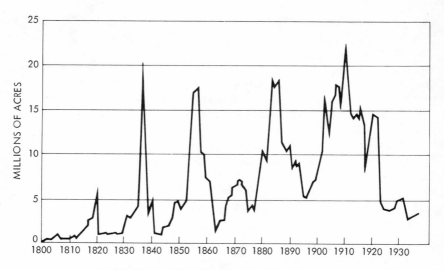

CHART 7. Original land entries, 1800-1934

There was one more link between land sales and fiscal affairs. By giving the land away or by selling it at very low prices, the government sacrificed what might have been an important source of revenue. Because the idea of a balanced budget in money terms was deeply ingrained, revenue to meet expenditures had to come from somewhere. Given the bias in favor of free or cheap land, federal revenue had to depend almost exclusively on the tariff. The land policy, therefore, buttressed a regressive system of taxation, for tariff duties and excise taxes were passed on to the consumer and fell more heavily on those in the low-income brackets, who spent all their income, than on those in the high-income brackets.

Land policy also affected the size of the American farm. Together with the speculative activities of American citizens, land policy caused wide discrepancies in the size of the American farm. In the early years, the land parcel was far larger than the optimum; with little machinery and little labor, the farmer could not handle the 640-acre tract of the first land law, or even the 160-acre tract of ten years later. After what has been called "the revolution in farm technology," that is, the appearance of machinery on a large scale, the land policy distributed a parcel that was much smaller than the optimum. On the Great Plains, for example, the 160-acre grant was totally unrealistic. As far back as 1878, John Wesley Powell urged that not less than 2,500 acres be offered on the treeless, flat, and arid Great Plains. In New Mexico and Arizona, where rainfall varies from 3 to 15 inches a year, it takes 40 acres to sustain one cow. Unless he is willing to live in a rural slum, a rancher needs 350 to 400 cattle, which means that anything less than 14,000 acres is uneconomic.

To the extent that land policy did benefit the small settler, it encouraged the continued existence of the family-sized farm, the 160-acre tract of the Homestead Act. On the other hand, because it was easy to evade the spirit of the law, the land policy also encouraged speculators to amass huge areas. Thus, to speak of an average-size farm is very unreal; typical American farms were either much smaller or much larger than the average. In either case, the effect on the economy was not good. The small farm was uneconomic because it could not take advantage of the economies of mechanized mass production; the bonanza farm often remained uncultivated, either because it was too large or because the owner was merely holding it until he could get a good price for it. If it was cultivated, it soon passed the point of diminishing returns and encouraged tenancy or inefficient farming.

THE WESTWARD MOVEMENT AND THE SAFETY VALVE DOCTRINE

The government's land policy was a prime factor in accelerating the westward movement, but it was by no means the only factor. By itself, land would not have caused the westward movement. There had to be a demand for it, and it had to be made easily available. Prosperity and population growth, especially in the rural areas, created the demand for land; government policy made the land easily accessible.

As population pressed upon the boundaries of civilization, the frontier bulged westward, but it moved sporadically, not steadily. Nor did it always move west. The line of settlement went north from Connecticut, east from New Hampshire, south from Tennessee, and east from California. The first real surge toward the West occurred after the War of 1812 and ground to a halt with the depression of 1819. At this time, the frontier line was fixed at the outer fringe of the Northwest Territory and the western extremities of the New South of Alabama and Mississippi. The next great wave of western settlement occurred during the great prosperity of the 1830s; when it ended with the depression of 1837, the frontier had reached the Mississippi River. In the prosperous 1850s, the frontier line took another great jump and, by the outbreak of the Civil War, it had arrived at the 95th meridian. During the prosperity of the 1870s and 1880s, the Great Plains were settled, and in 1890 the Census Bureau made its famous announcement that there was no longer any American frontier line.

It has been a favorite thesis of American historians that it was the West, and, more especially, the frontier, that determined the course of development of the American people. The theory was expressed many times, but it was best enunciated by the great historian, Frederick Jackson Turner. In 1893, Turner said that American social development had been continually beginning over again at the frontier, and that it was the great West, not the Atlantic Coast, that held the clue to the history of the nation and the development of our political, social, and economic institutions. Because the frontier imported its notions along with its people, this thesis can easily be exaggerated. Yet there is no doubt that the westward movement did accentuate the American admiration for economic success. On the frontier, family background, education, and culture meant little; economic accomplishment meant a great deal. Moreover, the movement of population into new frontiers constantly reaccentuated the casual nature of American life. We have been a nation of movers, finding it difficult to settle down and plant roots. From 1850 on, when data on the subject were first collected, every census reported that over one-fifth of native Americans had migrated from the state of their birth. This fluidity of population, which, however, was mostly agricultural, would certainly not have occurred without the liberal land policy.

The Turner thesis implied a subsidiary theory of even greater significance for economic history. Turner expressed this theory—the "Safety Valve Doctrine," as it came to be called—as follows:

> Whenever social conditions tended to crystallize in the East, whenever capital tended to press upon labor or political restraints to impede the freedom of the mass, there was this gate to the free conditions of the frontier. . . Men would not accept inferior wages, and a permanent position of social subordination, when this promised land of freedom and equality was theirs for the asking. [14]

This idea that the West offered a haven for the oppressed laborers of the East, exerted an upward pressure on wage rates, and acted as a healing unguent for the sores of depression, was a very old and perennially popular thesis. Turner uncovered a 1634 version of it. Washington and Jefferson, Horace Greeley, Henry George, and Karl Marx believed it. In the late nineteenth century, it was quoted with considerable effect by those who favored immigration restrictions. Today it is one of the most important premises of those who believe that the American economy is a mature economy. Yet, venerable as the theory was and persistent as it remains, modern research indicates that it overromanticized the real influence of the frontier and the West on American history.[15]

It was true that economic life had a "perennial rebirth" at the frontier. Each newly settled area went through a gradual transformation from self-sufficient farming to commercial farming, from household manufacturing to factory manufacturing, from economic infancy to economic adolescence, and from a capital-less, subsistence level of living to a more comfortable level. And it seems just as true that the westward movement and the frontier did diffuse population. The great West grew much faster than the rest of the nation. From 1790 to 1860, the West doubled its population every decade, whereas the whole of the

[14]Frederick Jackson Turner, *The Frontier in American History* (New York: Holt, Rinehart, & Winston Inc., 1920), p. 259.

[15]See Fred A. Shannon, "The Homestead Act and the Labor Surplus," *American Historical Review,* Vol. XLI (1936). For a more sympathetic view, see H. C. Allen, *British Essays in American History* (New York: St. Martin's Press, Inc., 1957).

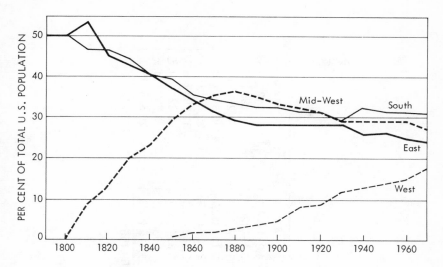

CHART 8. United States population by sections--census years 1790-1970

United States was averaging only a 34 percent gain. Of every 100 Americans in 1800, 24 lived in New England, 28 in the Middle Atlantic States, and 45 in the South Atlantic States. This pattern of population changed constantly, with New England and the South Atlantic States falling continually. The westward dispersion of population did slow down at about 1880; but in 1970, the West was still growing more rapidly than the East. In 1970, only 65 percent of the population lived in the East, compared with 90 percent in 1850.

This great emigration did not spring from the Eastern urban centers. Indeed, city population in the first half of the nineteenth century increased five times as fast as the national population. Although the density of population for all the United States increased from six per square mile in 1800 to 51 per square mile in 1960, population was packed much more closely in the small, highly industrialized states of the East. The population of Rhode Island increased from 69 per square mile in 1800 to 903 in 1970 and compared with the most densely populated areas of Western Europe. By 1950, all the industrialized sections in the East had population densities in excess of 100 per square mile; but in the great expanses of the agricultural West, density was much less than 100 per square mile.

The frontier offered no haven for presumed excess population in periods of depression. The mere desire to go west was not enough. Besides desire, the would-be settler needed money and a certain courage and faith. Neither money nor faith was very conspicuous during depressions. Sales of public lands were highest and the movement of the frontier line most rapid in boom periods, showing quite clearly that the West's drawing power was much more irresistible in prosperity than in depression. Indeed, the westward movement slowed from a

Table 11

DISTRIBUTION OF POPULATION BY SECTIONS, 1800-1970

(in thousands)

	1800	1850	1880	1970
New England	1,233 (24.2%)	2,728 (11.3%)	4,011 (8.0%)	11,842 (5.8%)
Middle Atlantic	1,403 (27.6)	5,899 (25.4)	10,497 (20.9)	37,199 (18.3)
East North Central	51 (1.0)	4,523 (19.5)	11,207 (22.3)	40,252 (19.8)
West North Central	—	880 (3.8)	6,157 (12.2)	16,319 (8.0)
South Atlantic	2,286 (45.3)	4,679 (20.1)	7,597 (15.1)	30,671 (15.1)
East South Central	109 (2.1)	3,363 (14.5)	5,585 (11.1)	12,803 (6.3)
West South Central	—	940 (4.5)	3,334 (6.7)	19,321 (9.5)
Mountain	—	73 (0.3)	653 (1.3)	8,282 (4.1)
Pacific	—	106 (0.6)	1,115 (2.3)	26,523 (13.0)
	5,082	23,191	50,156	203,212

SOURCE: U.S. Census Bureau.

104

stampede in prosperity to a lockstep in depression. At any time, it was difficult for an indigent laborer to pick up and move out to where nature was presumed to be more generous. As the cynical Gouverneur Morris put it realistically: "It is absurd to suppose that a person with scarce a second shirt to his back can go 2 or 300 miles to survey a farm and return to clear the title." It took at least $1,000 to establish a farm in the West in the 1850s. This was a sum far beyond the means of most people during hard times—in fact, at any time. The most fortunate Eastern worker earned less than $1,000 annually, hardly sufficient to allow him to accumulate enough capital to make the long jump to the frontier. Even if he were financially able, he lacked the necessary know-how to be a farmer. Moreover, he was bound to the city by habit, custom, and pure inertia.[16]

Who, then, did settle the West? For the most part, it was the migrant farmer. Each area was settled by farmers who migrated from a contiguous area. For example, Kansas was occupied mainly by people from Missouri, Illinois, and Iowa. Although Americans moved frequently, they usually moved in short jumps; the long safari from the East to the frontier was exceptional.[17] Great-great-grandfather moved from Connecticut to Ohio in the early 1800s; great-grandfather moved from Ohio to Illinois in the 1830s; grandfather migrated to Iowa in 1860; father pushed on to Nebraska in the 1880s; and junior made the long jump to California in the 1920s. The migrant to new lands was occasionally, but not commonly, a tenant farmer, an ordinary day laborer, or an Eastern storekeeper. Much more often, he was an independent farmer who had sold his previous holdings, or the son of an established farmer who had worked for other farmers, saved part of his income, and, with the aid of father or father-in-law and a mortgage, had bought a farm.

POPULATION IN THE URBAN AREAS

No one generalization can explain the American experience in a completely satisfactory manner. Certainly, the frontier hypothesis is not a sufficiently adequate explanation of the American value system, and the safety valve doctrine does not fill the bill in economic history. It was not the farm that was a

[16]Miriam Beard, *A History of the Businessman* (New York: The MacMillan Company, 1938), p. 613; Murray Kane, "Some Considerations of the Safety Valve Doctrine," *Mississippi Valley Historical Review,* Vol. XXIII (1936); Clarence H. Danhof, "Farm Making Costs and the 'Safety Valve,' 1850-1860," *Journal of Political Economy,* Vol. XLIX (1941).

[17]Census data for the years 1870-1940 offer evidence for this contention. In 1890, a little over 10 percent of those born east of the Mississippi were living west of the Mississippi. This was the highest percentage recorded. In 1870, only 8 percent of those born east of the Mississippi were living west of the Mississippi, and in 1940 only 5.5 percent. Even in the period after World War II, when migration was relatively high, only 2 percent of the population migrated between noncontiguous states during a given year.

safety valve for disgruntled and dejected city people so much as it was the city that was the safety valve for escaping farmers. The pioneer who left the wide-open spaces was a much more typical American than the pioneer who went to the great open spaces. In describing what happened to America, the swift rise of the city, the stampede to the boulevards and the back alleys, was just as important as the trek to the frontier. Perhaps it was more important, even though not as much has been made of it. The farms produced the raw materials; the city's factories and human beings consumed them. The frontier fostered individualism; the city fostered collectivism. Problems that were unknown on the farms and in the sparsely populated areas were not only annoying but critical to the teeming urban masses. Whether they were right or wrong, city people became convinced that police protection, fire prevention, sanitation, and education could only be provided collectively. Thomas Jefferson, the champion of agrarianism, fully realized this. In his desire to maintain a "happy" and individualistic society, he warned: "When they (Americans) get piled upon one another in large cities, as in Europe, they will become as corrupt as in Europe." By the end of the nineteenth century, Jefferson's vision of "a chosen country with room enough for our descendants to the thousandth and thousandth generation" seemed curious indeed.

The cities of 1800

In the overwhelmingly agrarian society of 1800, only a small number of Americans—about 6 percent—lived in cities. The Census of 1800 counted a total of 33 urban places, but most of these were not even overgrown villages. [18] There were four cities with a population of 25,000 or more; but, of the total population of 5,000,000, only 200,000 lived in the five largest cities: Philadelphia, New York, Baltimore, Boston, and Charleston. But, although only 4 percent of Americans lived in what were considered big cities, urban life was in a sense more distinctive then than it is today. The line of demarcation between town and country life was very sharply marked, whereas today, when almost everyone lives within an hour's drive of a city of 100,000 or more, rural life is no longer isolated.

The large cities of 1800 had also been the metropolises of the Colonial Period. They had grown because of their strategic importance in marketing. Naturally, all of them were on the Atlantic Coast, for their distinction was that they were frontier outposts of European commercial expansion. They were the trading posts, the distributing centers for bringing manufactured goods to the hinterland and for exporting raw materials to Europe and the Caribbean. [19]

[18] The Census has at different times used different definitions of an urban place, but it would not be too incorrect to say that, in general, urban population has been defined to include all the people living in incorporated places of 2,500 or more.

[19] There is a mine of interesting information about early cities in Henry Adams, *The*

Philadelphia was the pride of the United States. It was the second largest
city in the English-speaking world. Objective observers deemed it "one of the
most beautiful cities in the world." In urban amenities, it was far ahead of its
rivals, for it was well-paved, partly drained, and had an excellent water system.
New York was like most foreign seaports, badly paved, undrained, and "as foul
as a town surrounded by tides could be." Every few years, an outbreak of yellow
fever drove the gentry way uptown to Greenwich Village. Yet, the city already
showed signs that it would lead in establishing the supremacy of economic
values. Unlike its rivals, it had a bustling exciting air, and its citizens complained,
as they would 150 years later, about the gravity of city problems—snarled
traffic, crime, noise, and urban sprawl.

Boston resembled an English market town. It had cobblestoned streets and
sidewalks, some lighting, and, like all other cities, a wholly inadequate police and
a mostly inadequate fire service. Wealthy and conservative, it had a reputation
for being old-fashioned. It was already following a pattern that would be cut
over and over again. As the market changed, the strategic importance of some
cities would deteriorate. They would cease to grow and would be rapidly overtaken and passed by cities in a more favorable position with more adventurous
entrepreneurs. Boston had been the largest city in 1750, but by 1800 it was
much smaller than Philadelphia and New York and had just ceded third place to
Baltimore. The fishing industry, shipbuilding, and shipping did not hold the
opportunities that were offered by agriculture and the processing of farm
products.

Northern cities, even in 1800, were either interested in or enthusiastic about
economic progress. Farther South, conditions were quite different. It was not
that Southern cities did not have geographic advantages. Lloyd's of London is
said to have thought that New Orleans would become the greatest port in the
world. Charleston could serve a market area such as no other city except New
York could boast. But perhaps life was too easy. Business was conducted on a
personal basis in coffee houses or wine shops. There was no business organization and no desire for it. Gracious living was the real business of life in an
atmosphere of gaiety, ease, and leisure. The citizens expected no public
services—schools, sewers, a water supply, and so forth—and resisted every effort
to create any. They wished only to be let alone, secure in the illusion that the
strategic location of their cities made them immune from competitors. As the
death rate mounted, men of property danced at the St. Cecilia Ball, and the
American economy passed them by.

Formative Years (Boston: Houghton Mifflin Company, 1947); Carl Bridenbaugh, *Cities in
the Wilderness* (New York: Alfred A. Knopf, Inc., 1938); Constance M. Green, *American
Cities in the Growth of the Nation* (London: The Athlone Press, 1957); Carl Bridenbaugh,
Cities in Revolt, 1743-1776 (New York:Alfred A. Knopf, Inc., 1956); Charles N. Glaab, *The
American City: A Documentary History* (Homewood, Illinois: Dorsey Press, Inc., 1963).

The growth of the city in the nineteenth century

The decade of 1810 to 1820 was the only one in American history in which the urban population did not increase faster than the rural.[20] As if to make up for that lapse, urban population rose an average of 75 percent a decade for the next 40 years, the highest rates in the American experience. Yet rural life was so dominant that, despite this extraordinary advance, city population was less than 20 percent of the total in 1860. The big-city dweller was still a rarity: only about 5 percent of the population lived in cities of over 100,000 in 1850.

In the last half of the century, cities continued to grow rapidly, although, to be sure, the pace was somewhat slower than the previous frenetic rate. By 1890, one out of three Americans was a city-dweller, and cities of over 100,000 housed one out of every six Americans. Like everything else, urbanization took part in the westward movement. In 1890, the ten largest cities included three that had hardly existed in 1850. Cities were becoming ubiquitous, enabling everyone suddenly to recognize a transition that had been taking place for 70 years: the rapid shift from a nation of farmers to a nation of urbanites.

Birth rates among city people were not high enough to enable the cities to reproduce themselves, but immigrants and fleeing ruralites poured into the centers, creating a density of population that contrasted ironically with the otherwise realistic picture of the United States as a vast land sparsely inhabited. The most congested areas of the East Side of New York, for example, held 523.6 people per acre, the highest density in the western world. "The growth of the large cities," wrote one observer around 1890, "constitutes perhaps the greatest of all problems of modern civilization."[21]

Crime and vice, poverty and filth, were hallmarks of the big city. Squeezed to suffocation by the influx of great numbers, city population had to spill over into the suburbs. Suburbs had always existed, for they were nothing more or less than the outer fringes of the expanding city. What was new about the suburbs in the 1890s was that they were far away from the run of economic activity. They were not within walking distance of "downtown". Commuting became a national pastime. To be sure, there had been some commuting as early as 1850, but its real importance began in the 1890s, for it was then that such famous suburbs as Greenwich, Connecticut; Chestnut Hill, Pennsylvania; and Lake Forest, Illinois, began to attract city-dwellers in large numbers. An assist in this change was given by a major technological improvement in the street railway; the interurban electric trolley car appeared in the middle 1880s. In constant dollars, the value of its plant and equipment attained an all-time high in 1916. By the 1890s, the street railway was the largest user of capital in the economy.

[20] During the great depression of the 1930s, urban population growth barely exceeded rural growth.

[21] Adna Ferrin Weber, *The Growth of Cities in the 19th Century* (New York: Columbia University, 1899), p. 2.

Table 12

THE TEN LARGEST CITIES IN THE UNITED STATES, 1810-1970

1810	1850	1890	1960	1970 (Metropolitan Areas)
New York	New York	New York	New York	New York
Philadelphia	Philadelphia	Chicago	Chicago	Los Angeles
Baltimore	Baltimore	Philadelphia	Los Angeles	Chicago
Boston	Boston	St. Louis	Philadelphia	Philadelphia
Charleston	New Orleans	Boston	Detroit	Detroit
New Orleans	Cincinnati	Baltimore	Baltimore	San Francisco
Salem	Brooklyn	Pittsburgh	Houston	Washington, D.C.
Providence	St. Louis	San Francisco	Cleveland	Boston
Richmond	Albany	Cincinnati	Washington, D.C.	Pittsburgh
Albany (9,400)	Pittsburgh (46,601)	Cleveland (261,000)	St. Louis (750,000)	St. Louis

SOURCE: U.S. Census Bureau.

Table 13
NUMBER OF CITIES IN THE UNITED STATES, 1800-1970

	1800	*1850*	*1890*	*1930*	*1970*
Total	33	236	1,348	3,165	7,061
25,000 to 50,000	2	16	66	185	519
50,000 to 100,000	2	4	30	98	240
100,000 to 250,000		5	17	56	100
250,000 to 500,000		—	7	24	30
500,000 to 1,000,000		1	1	8	20
over 1,000,000		—	3	5	6

SOURCE: U.S. Census Bureau.

The appearance of the metropolitan area

The movement toward the suburbs gathered momentum in the twentieth century, aided by the subway, the elevated railroad, and the telephone. It gathered speed after World War I and again after World War II under the driving force of the automobile and ever-better roads. It is estimated that suburbia held 7 million people in 1910, 16 million in 1930, 21 million at the end of World War II, and 50 million in 1970. The limits of the city, seldom more than ten miles in the nineteenth century, increased to 35 miles and, in some cases, to 60 miles as the twentieth century rolled on. The concept of the city ceased to have much meaning. A new term, the *metropolitan area*,[22] had much more practical value under the new living arrangements of the twentieth century.

In the United States of 1900, there were 44 standard metropolitan areas, in which about one-third of the country lived. By the 1970s, there were over 200 such areas containing almost two-thirds of the population. Within these areas, another considerable change had taken place. In 1900, the number of people living in the central city outnumbered the outsiders by more than three to one. By 1970, the population of the satellites was larger than the number living in the core.

In 1970, there were 33 metropolitan areas in the United States with a population of 1,000,000 or more each. New York was well ahead with over 11.5 million; Los Angeles followed with seven million; and Chicago was close behind with just under seven million. In all but 14 of these areas, the population of the central city fell between 1960 and 1970. The most extreme example was New York, where the population at the center was less in 1970 than it had been in 1900. The movement to suburbia was also well illustrated in the Detroit Metropolitan Area, where the central city's population fell almost 10 percent, whereas

[22]A standard metropolitan area consists of at least one city of 50,000 or more, together with contiguous counties that are more industrial than agricultural and that are socially and economically integrated with the central city.

the population outside the core more than doubled. But the best example of the modern metropolitan area is Los Angeles. The city itself had a population of less than 50,000 in 1890. By the early 1960s, less than 75 years later, its population had passed two and one-half million. It was the core of a vast area in which the inhabitants of the fringe areas outnumbered those in the core by four to three.

In the nineteenth century, some cities grew faster than others even though their advantages were inferior quantitatively and qualitatively. Chicago, for example, grew much faster than St. Louis, and New Orleans and Baltimore failed to fulfill the great expectations of their boosters. A similar phenomenon was apparent in the metropolitan areas of the twentieth century. Location theory could hardly explain why Houston surpassed Galveston. The answer lies more in the nature of the value system and the drive of the city's entrepreneurs.

The movement to suburbia and exurbia, and the appearance of the metropolitan areas, had broad ramifications in the American economy and in the level of living. Individual for individual, suburbia was the most lucrative market area in the country. Its residents were younger than those in the rest of the country. Most of them owned their own homes and were interested in raising families. Suburbanites had much to do with the "population explosion" of the post-World War II era. Because it was the home of a high propensity to consume, suburbia helped to raise the rate of consumption and to reduce the rate of saving. It led to the decentralization of economic activity and it created a multitude of new occupations. The spread of the city and its surrounding areas made America and American life altogether different from what it had been. But the process took place so rapidly and so differently in different sections of the country that it is doubtful whether the population as a whole comprehended what had happened. In the middle of the twentieth century, the problems of urban living—and there were a plethora of them—were being met to a large extent by answers that were rural in origin and philosophy.

SUGGESTED READINGS

(On specific topics, see the readings cited in the footnotes in the chapter.)

Danhof, Clarence H., "Farm Making Costs and the 'Safety Valve,' 1850-1860," *Journal of Political Economy*, Vol. XLIX (1941).

Gates, Paul Wallace, "The Homestead Law in an Incongruous Land System," *American Historical Review*, Vol. XLI (1936).

Glaab, Charles H. and Theodore A. Brown, *A History of Urban America* (New York: The Macmillan Company, 1967).

Hansen, Marcus L., *The Immigrant in American History* (Cambridge, Mass.: Harvard University Press, 1940).

Hansen, Marcus L., *The Atlantic Migration* (Cambridge, Mass.: Harvard Company, 1949).

Hibbard, B.H., *A History of the Public Land Policies* (New York: The Macmillan Company, 1924).

Robbins, Roy, *Our Landed Heritage* (Princeton: Princeton University Press, 1942).

Taylor, George R., ed., *The Turner Thesis* (Lexington, Mass: D.C. Heath & Company, 1949).

QUESTIONS

1. The United States experienced the most phenomenal growth of population in world history. Why? What were the effects of this population growth? The outstanding characteristic of population growth after 1850 was a slowing down in the rate of increase. Explain why this occurred.

2. The importance of immigration as a factor in increasing population has been well emphasized. How important a factor was it?

3. What is meant by the statement: "Immigration was in a way an automatic stabilizer"?

4. What were the similarities and differences between immigration into the United States and migration to the West?

5. Trace the history of immigration from about 1850 to the present. Mention changes in the aggregate number of immigrants, country of origin, and legislation. How do you explain the changing attitude of people toward immigration during this period? On the basis of the American experience, would you recommend a policy of free immigration for underdeveloped countries?

6. What were the principal effects of the man-land ratio on American economic development?

7. "Federal land policy became the subject of heated debate in which arguments were mostly determined by sectional economic interests." What was the substance of the debate?

8. The Federal government sold land and gave it away to individuals, but it also used it to encourage the construction of "social capital." Describe what it did in this direction.

9. A noted authority has said: "The Homestead Act was one phase of an incongruous land system." Explain what he meant.

10. What was the "Safety Valve Doctrine"? How valid do you think it was?

11. What principal changes took place in Federal land policy? About when did they take place? Why did they take place? What were the principal effects of the land policy on economic development?

12. The land policy of the Federal government was liberalized during the nineteenth century, but even the liberalized land policy was not very effective in making entry into farming very easy. Why not? What does

"to do a land-office business" mean? Did land offices always do a land-office business? Explain.

13. Comment on the following statement: "It was not the farm that was a safety valve for disgruntled and dejected city people so much as it was the city that was the safety valve for escaping farmers."

Chapter Four

THE FARMER
IN AMERICAN ECONOMIC HISTORY

In the early stage of its development, an economy must necessarily rely upon agriculture for most of its economic goods, for a primitive or a developing economy does not possess enough resources to create an industrialized society. It lacks capital, a mass market, transportation facilities, and a large supply of skilled labor. But land usually is abundant, and farming and the other extractive industries offer the quickest way of producing the things—food, clothing, and shelter—that people must have in order to live. The productive process cannot be anything but simple, uncomplicated, and rudimentary, for resources must be allocated to the production of those goods that directly satisfy human wants.

Some economies never emerge from this primitive phase of development; but others, using agriculture as a base, accumulate the capital, build up the mass market, and develop the transportation facilities that make possible the emergence of an industrial society. Soon, industry rather than agriculture comes to anchor the economy. Agriculture may still constitute an important segment of the overall economy and may continue to expand, but its growth will be absolute, not relative. The real economic pacemaker will be manufacturing, growing not only absolutely, but also at the expense of other sectors of the economy. Eventually, industrialism may become so dominant that agriculture will begin to decline not only relatively, but absolutely as well.

THE CONTRIBUTION OF AGRICULTURE TO EARLY
ECONOMIC DEVELOPMENT

During most of our history—at least four-fifths of it—we were a nation of farmers rather than artisans; the small farmer, not the city-dweller, was the typical American. In 1800, more than 95 percent of the population was rural. In 1820, rural residents in nonagricultural occupations exceeded the entire city population, and in 1850 country dwellers still constituted almost 85 percent of the population. For the better part of the first century of our national existence, agriculture was indisputably predominant in the American economy. It produced the major share of national commodity output—71 percent in 1839 and 60 percent in 1850. The growth of farm gross product in the early nineteenth century, 3.11 percent annually, was by no means trivial, although it was somewhat lower than the overall growth. The heavy volume of farm production made possible much of the nation's manufacturing progress, for it was large enough to produce surpluses that could be exchanged in world markets for the capital goods that were needed in the development of American manufacturing.

Agriculture also accumulated much of the capital in the early nineteenth century, for its invesment per dollar of income was larger than that of any other sector in the economy. In the economist's language, agriculture's externalities were greater than those in other industries, which, simply put, means that the farmer used more producer's goods, such as iron and tools, than anyone else in the economy. Agriculture also employed the overwhelming majority of workers and largely determined the mode of American life.

Agriculture also profoundly influenced the American political and social scene. During the first half of the nineteenth century, the farm, rather than the factory, determined in which direction the nation moved. Agrarian spokesmen in Congress stumped for a liberal land policy, extensive internal improvements, an aggressive foreign policy, and tariffs for raising revenue. As long as agriculture was of overwhelming importance, the American economic and political sphere featured a land policy devoted to rapid settlement and a forceful foreign policy that contributed to territorial expansion. Gradually, however, the agrarians' grip began to slip. By the latter part of the nineteenth century, American foreign policy was based on protectionism and the domestic policy on sound currency and a national banking system. Not until he managed to close ranks in the early twentieth century and, more effectively, in the 1930s was the farmer again able to wield great political power. Then, through his "farm bloc" representatives in Congress, he succeeded in having legislation passed that gave him government assistance in the form of outright cash subsidies.

In the first half of the nineteenth century, American agriculture was more extensive than intensive and more self-sufficient than commercialized. It was more a way of life than a business, not because the farmer wanted it that way, but because farming for the most part was concerned with pioneering, with the settlement of the land, and with speculation in land. Labor and capital were scarce; but an almost unlimited land mass beckoned and provided a proving ground for changing agricultural methods. The job of settling the land required people to work the land, raise dwellings, and establish communities. Settlements also called for people who were mobile. It was the farmer who best met this challenge. He was the most prolific of Americans. It was his sons and daughters who peopled the land. He, more than anyone else, gave American life its casual character. Of all Americans, he was most willing to pull up stakes and start out anew. Unlike his European counterpart, the American farmer was "here today and gone tomorrow," hardly pausing long enough to cultivate one strip, always eager to push on to where grass lay greener and water might flow deeper.

Because land was plentiful and labor and capital were scarce, the early nineteenth-century farmer could not cultivate his land scientifically. He necessarily "wasted" land and economized in the use of labor and capital. This behavior was well recognized and understood. According to George Washington: "The aim of the farmers (if they can be called farmers) is not to make the most they can from the land which is cheap, but the most of labor which is dear." In order to get the most from his resources, he had to emphasize man-hour output, not output per acre. He cultivated extensively because he could not afford to spend his scarce factors and conserve his plentiful factor. He was, therefore, more often interested in land speculation than in land cultivation; he was more a colonizer than a patron of husbandry. Although he was always eager to be a commercial farmer, that is, to sell most of his products in the market, he could not do so to the extent he wished. Isolated from large markets by the lack of transportation, most of what the farmer grew went on the family table or on the family backs. To be sure, many Southern planters and Middle Atlantic farmers were doing a thriving business in raising tobacco, cotton, indigo, sugar, and naval stores, distilling whiskey, and breeding cattle for the commercial market, but they were the exceptions rather than the rule.

The focus of this chapter and the next is on the farmer as a businessman facing business problems. The basic farm problem has always been the failure of the farmer to receive what he considers a "fair share of the national income." There have always been subsidiary business problems that contributed to this major headache. In the early nineteenth century, however, these subsidiary problems were relatively few: raising capital, finding lenders, the high cost of labor, and the problem of getting goods to market. The economics of farming also pressed an omnipresent thorn in the side of the farmer who wanted to break out of the confines of a way of life into the world of business, and this thorn could not be blunted. The demand for farm products was extremely inelastic. That is to say, the consumption of farm products remained pretty much the same regardless of what happened to their prices or to the income of consumers. Similarly, the supply of farm products was inelastic in the short run. In the long run, the demand for farm products grew steadily, for it conformed to the growth of population. Supply, on the other hand, increased in steps, because it was to a large extent dependent on the opening of new lands. This was notice-ably true of cotton in the period around the 1830s. The price of cotton soared under the pressure of rapidly increasing demand. But when new lands were brought into cultivation, the price collapsed.

PIONEER FARMING IN THE NORTH

Pioneer farming was never easy at any place or any time. The forest prime-val, the thickly grown virgin forest, so beloved by the poet, was nothing but an economic headache to the Eastern pioneer farmer. To a slight extent, the Indian had shown the pioneer the way, had girdled trees and planted about one million acres in corn before the appearance of the white man. But where the Indian had not cultivated, the settler could clear about five acres a year. It therefore took three or four years before the investment of time and labor began to pay off, and about 40 years to convert 200 acres. Clearly, this was an important form of capital formation, but the results were very hard to measure. One authority has estimated that clearing the land occupied more labor than fencing, ditching, and farm building combined.[1] Because his task was to clear the forest, the pioneer in the area east of the Great Plains had to be more a woodsman than a farmer; his most precious tools were the axe and the rifle, not the plow and the shovel.

Because he had little aptitude for farming, the pioneer rarely settled permanently. He remained just long enough to clear a small piece of land and build a crude cabin before moving further west. Usually his place would be taken by another pseudo-farmer who cleared a larger area and planted a few vegetables. But he also moved at the first opportunity, making way for the permanent settler who was fast on his heels. When the land had been finally cleared, the labor that had been allocated to this job was no longer necessary; it had become excessive and could be used to feed the infant factories in the towns.

On the Great Plains frontier, the obstacles confronting the first settler were quite different but equally disheartening. Instead of too many trees, there were none at all. Consequently, there was no wood for fuel, nor timber for houses, nor rails for fencing. The pioneer used buffalo chips for fuel and built a sod-house, but he could not fence in his acres until barbed wire had made its appear-ance. Nor was there enough rainfall, and the weather, as a whole, was extremely variable. Few settlers were encouraged to remain and take up farming perman-ently.[2]

Even if "making a farm" had not been so difficult, "settle and sell" would still have been one of the first principles of early Northern farming. As long as there was plenty of land, and as long as the government followed a liberal land

[1] Martin L. Primack, "Land Clearing in the Nineteenth Century," *Journal of Economic History*, Vol. XXII (1962).

[2] The trials and tribulations of the Great Plains farmer are well described in Everett Dick, *The Sod-House Frontier, 1854-1890* (New York: Appleton-Century-Crofts, 1937).

policy, the easiest course of action was to sell quickly, earn a capital gain, pack up, and move westward. The pioneer farmer was well aware that, in the end, his profits would come largely from rising land values. Moreover, his prestige in the community would be based largely on how much land he owned. Usually, therefore, the pioneer farmer tried to buy more land than he could utilize.[3]

THE PROBLEM OF CAPITAL AND CREDIT

Whether one bought it from the government or from a prior purchaser, land was cheap, but it still required capital to make a farm. A going farm could be purchased for $30-$40 per acre. The best location would command $100 per acre, and government land was, of course, much cheaper.

The tendency to buy too much land left the farmer short of working capital. In any case, his optimistic nature often lulled him into grossly underestimating what he would need to put his land into cultivation. Many farmers agreed with a French traveler of the late eighteenth century who estimated the average pioneer's capital requirements at about $125. He made a down payment on 150 to 200 acres and arrived with a cow, a few pigs, a couple of indifferent horses, and a stock of flour and cider. He felled a few small trees and girdled the large ones, cleared one to three acres a year, and planted corn. It is evident that the traveler's estimate was on the very sanguine side. Much of what the pioneer needed, such as a place to live and something to live on until the acreage began producing, was omitted in the calculation. *American Husbandry* was much more realistic when it said: "only those who have a good sum of money— $2,000-$5,000—should go into farming." This estimate included the value of the land. But conservative and knowledgable advisers to would-be farmers thought that $2,000 was the minimum necessary to operate a 100-acre farm in the east in 1850, and the figure was not very much different at any other time during the early 1800s. In the early 1830s, for example, it was said that a farmer, just for labor and subsistence, needed working capital equal to 60 percent of his annual product. The $2,000 estimate just cited allowed $1,000 for livestock, $475 for implements, and $525 for seed, labor, and food while waiting for the crop. But this was for a going farm. New land would also require $25 an acre for fencing and clearing. Since 15 acres was about as much as could be brought into production in a year, fencing and clearing would add another $375 a year.

For most people in the early 1800s, $2,000-$3,000 was a gigantic sum, even though at today's prices it may appear to be a trifle. The embryonic farmer had already strapped himself in order to buy his land. In the 1830s, for example, half the farms in the East and a great many in the West were mortgaged. Now he was

---

[3]Paul W. Gates, *The Farmer's Age: Agriculture, 1815-1860* (New York: Holt, Rinehart, & Winston, Inc., 1960), p. 399.

faced with the problem of borrowing to put his newly-acquired farm into operation. He had two sources from which to produce short-term funds: trade credit and bank credit. It was common practice to borrow from the country store and to settle the bill once a year at harvest time. Agricultural implements were bought "on time" from manufacturers or selling agents. Banks provided funds directly and indirectly through loans to merchants.

Borrowing was expensive. The stated interest rate was 6-7 percent, but there were many ways of getting around this, so that actual interest rates were more on the order of 10-12 percent than 6-7 percent. Since the cost of credit and the amount of capital required were so high, tenancy and share cropping were common by the 1840s, if not earlier.

TOWARD COMMERCIAL FARMING

On the frontier, where there were no readily accessible markets or transportation facilities, farmers were forced to be self-sufficient producers. They raised their own provisions, obtained their clothing from sheep, cattle, deer, or raccoon, and built their houses, without benefit of glass or iron, from the timber and sod that Providence had provided. Buttons were made of horn, and brooms of reed, thorns were used for pins and skewers, and gourds for dippers. Farmers who lived near a city or near navigable waters raised crops commercially, and here the degree of self-sufficiency was considerably less. Shops, which were combined taverns and stores, kept almost everything that was needed—sugar, coffee, tea, spices, clothing, books, ironware, and spirits—and bartered them for the farmer's produce.[4]

In 1820, according to a "reasonable approximation," only 20 percent of farm output was sold in urban markets. The general absence of commercial farming in the North was attested by the British economist McCulloch, who wrote in 1841: "It is needless to take up the reader's time by entering into detail with respect to the grain trade of the United States. It is abundantly clear that we need not look to that quarter for any considerable supplies." As late as 1853, when commercial farming was widespread, it was still not universal even in the East, as is evidenced by a commentator who, in surveying the agricultural picture, estimated that a farmer in the Connecticut River Valley spent $100 a year in cash, compared with $10 in 1820. He was still producing on his own farm most of the things he used.

Without capital and with little labor, there was a limit to the amount that a farmer could plow, sow, and reap. One man could harvest only 20 or 30 acres of wheat with the awkward tools in use before the development of the reaper or mower. Consequently, the early nineteenth-century Northern farmer needed

[4]Rodney Loehr, "Self-Sufficiency on the Farm," *Agricultural History*, Vol. 26 (1952).

only a small farm. The average-sized farm was only 100 to 200 acres in New England and about 150 acres in Pennsylvania. There were only ten million acres, or two acres per capita, in crops in 1800, and four-fifths of these were in corn and wheat with the former accounting for about three times as much as the latter.

In time, as the surpluses and scarcities in the economy were smoothed out and a better balance was achieved in the proportion of the available factors of production, the economic organization of agriculture changed. Farmers, helped by better access to markets, became more specialized and more commercial, producing more for the market than for their own consumption.

In the early nineteenth century, a farmer could market his crop as far away as 15 miles, but this required an overnight trip and was quite impossible for highly perishable products, whose market area extended five to eight miles. Evidently, the further progress of commercialization required marketing facilities. It called for specialized middlemen, storage facilities, and the construction of roads, canals, and railroads. The urban areas of the East had such facilities very early, and, as fast as they were opened, the farmer took advantage of them. By 1820 in the Middle Atlantic states, and by 1830 in New England, farming had become much more commercial than self-sufficient. The steamboat, the opening of the Erie Canal, and the mania for canal building that followed in the 1830s made it possible for many Middlewestern farmers to commercialize their activities. But before 1850, most Western farmers still had only two main routes for reaching the market: the Mississippi River and the Great Lakes. Although these were remarkable arteries of commerce, neither was completely satisfactory. But the rapid expansion of the railroad network after 1850 remedied the situation. As the *American Agriculturist* expressed it: "If the farmers had taxed themselves to build all the railroads in the country and given them away to companies who would stock and run them, the increased value of their lands would have well repaid all the outlay."[5]

As marketing facilities developed, each section was able to restrict its production to those commodities for which it was best adapted. The East turned more and more to manufacturing and commerce; the South to cotton; the Northwest to wheat; the Middle West raised hogs; and the Great Plains, cattle. Cash crops moved westward under the pressure of rising land values and declining yields. Industrialism and urban concentration skyrocketed land values in the East. At the same time, agricultural yields in the East declined, for wheat, the cash crop, rapidly depleted the soil, and cattle and other livestock needed grazing space. During the Colonial Period, New England grew corn; the Middle Atlantic states, wheat and corn; and the whole Eastern seaboard raised livestock. Gradually, the East switched to perishable crops, and wheat, corn, and livestock moved westward to areas where the farmer had a comparative advantage over his Eastern competitor in growing the staple crops. New England was the first

[5]Quoted in Clarence H. Danhof, *Change in Agriculture: The Northern United States, 1820-1870* (Cambridge, Mass.: Harvard University Press, 1969), p. 5.

section to shift to perishables: Pennsylvania and New York continued to raise large flocks of sheep until 1840, and Pennsylvania was still the largest wheat producer in 1850. But by the Civil War, the whole picture of Northern farming had changed. Sheep raising in New England declined 50 percent between 1840 and 1850 and 35 percent in the next decade. The number of pigs in Massachusetts, Connecticut, and Rhode Island fell from 300,000 to 165,000 between 1840 and 1860. By 1860, Pennsylvania was only fifth among states producing wheat, and the five states of the old Northwest produced nearly the entire national crop. Also, by 1860, corn production had become concentrated in Illinois, Ohio, and Missouri. In 1850, the center of both wheat and corn production was around Columbus, Ohio; by 1890, corn had moved to Illinois and the center of the wheat belt was west of Des Moines, Iowa. Equally evident of the transition from staples to perishables in the East was the fact that New England and the Middle Atlantic states, with 34 percent of the population, were producing 70 percent of American cheese and 50 percent of American butter in 1860.

By increasing specialization, agriculture made more use of the principle of comparative advantage and operated on a more efficient basis, contributing heavily to the nation's over-all economic development. Specialization on the farm also meant the abandonment of household manufacturing, which, in turn, meant that those people who had previously been involved with manufacturing on the farm could move to the city and take jobs in manufacturing. This movement from the farm to the factory raised the level of living, for each shift from farm to industry meant an increase in the national income.

Specialization also enabled each section of the nation to produce a surplus that it could exchange for other commodities, either intersectionally or internationally. From 1820 to 1850, agriculture accounted for 60 percent of total exports. Cotton was by far the leading export but, in addition, the United States also exported tobacco, wheat, corn, flour, and provisions. Without the westward movement, the extension of marketing facilities, commercial farming, and division of labor, these exports would not have been possible, and without these exports the United States would not have been able to import as much European manufactured and semimanufactured goods as it did. However, commercial farming also created a pool of surplus farm labor; it tended to increase urban concentration; and it made the farmer more dependent on others than he had been in the days of relative self-sufficiency.

SOUTHERN AGRICULTURE BEFORE THE CIVIL WAR

There was some resemblance between Southern and Northern agriculture before the Civil War, but there were more differences than there were similarities. Like Northern agriculture, Southern agriculture was diversified, self-sufficient, and extremely extensive. As in the North, crops moved westward as new frontiers opened. But in the South, the average-size farm was much larger, commercialized crops were much more important, international trade played a far greater role, slavery was prominent, and class lines were rigidly drawn.

Although small farms dotted the mountain regions of the upper South and were a common sight in the border states, the plantation was the principal farming unit in the South. Consequently, the average Southern farm was much larger than the average Northern farm. Indeed, by 1860, four-fifths of the farms of 500 acres or more were in the South.

The plantation system made it possible for Southern agriculture to be both self-sufficient and commercialized. In the upper South, the small farmer never progressed beyond the self-sufficient stage, but the plantation owner raised commercial crops, such as cotton, rice, sugar, tobacco, and indigo, and also grew enough of the incidental crops to make his enterprise self-sustaining.

In the antebellum South, cotton was indisputably king. Indigo, an important commercial crop in the Colonial Period, disappeared during the Revolution. Tobacco was always an important cash crop in the upper South, but it could not be grown in the West and it wore out the soil very quickly. Rice and sugar, requiring specialized climatic conditions and a very large outlay, were important in the deep South; but in seven of the eleven Southern states that finally seceded from the Union, cotton was the economic darling. It was the commercial crop that the South exchanged for manufactured goods from other areas, especially Great Britain. Indeed, it was the base on which foreign trade was built.

The return from cotton was extremely low. If it sold at 10 cents a pound, it returned an average of $15 to $20 an acre, for the best soil produced but 300 pounds an acre and the poorest only 100 pounds. But, despite this relatively low return, the South raised more cotton at every opportunity. But intensive planting soon wore the soil thin, and the center of the Cotton Belt began to move westward as new lands were opened for settlement. After 1830, Alabama and Mississippi were the leading producers, and by 1850 Texas grew more cotton than South Carolina. The westward movement of the cotton crop, however, had far different effects on the South than the westward movement of grain crops had on the North. As the center of cotton production moved westward, the value of the older lands in the Southeast declined, for, unlike the North, the Southeast did not switch to raising other crops or to industry, despite the fact that it could not hope to compete successfully with the fat cotton crops that the richer lands of the Southwest were producing.

Because it brought an extremely low return in proportion to the man hours invested, cotton growing could never have established itself in the South unless low-cost labor had been available. Consequently, cotton growing meshed very well with slavery, for slave labor, at least in the short run, was cheap labor.[6] In

[6]If it is assumed that factors are worth what they produce, there is, of course, no such thing as cheap labor and no such thing as cheap land.

this harmony between cotton cultivation and the slavery system, it mattered little whether slavery encouraged cotton growing, or if cotton growing encouraged slavery. Regardless of which came first, cotton culture, which could not be carried on without cheap labor, encouraged slavery; and slavery, which was thought to be cheap labor, encouraged cotton culture. This mutual encouragement determined the economic organization of all Southern agriculture and cannot be ignored in explaining the nation's economic development.

Although cotton required some tending for nine months out of the year, it required special care for only short periods. Slaves could not be laid off; and when they were not busy in the cotton fields, they planted corn and other crops for local consumption. As a result of this diversification, the South contributed a substantial part of the nation's total agricultural production and was, if anything, more self-sufficient than the North. In 1860, the South supplied 43 percent of the nation's corn and 26 percent of the wheat; it raised 54 percent of the hogs and 36 percent of the dairy cattle. However, cotton, and to a lesser extent, sugar, rice, and tobacco were the chief crops, for they were marketable. Raising grains and animals was incidental to the main business of raising cash crops for the commercial market, and little pains were taken to raise them efficiently. General farming was, therefore, less efficient than in the North. In 1860, for example, the South owned proportionately as many cows as the North, but its butter production was less than half as much and it produced no cheese at all.

SLAVERY AND THE SOUTHERN ECONOMY

Was slavery really cheap? Or, to put the question as it is usually posed: was slavery profitable? The riddle has been debated for more years than anyone cares to count, primarily because it requires so many answers to so many equally difficult questions: Profitable for whom? For the large slaveholder? For all Southerners? For the economic growth of the South and, therefore, the nation as a whole? [7]

Slavery was a peculiar institution in more ways than one. One of its special peculiarities was that it was by no means universal. Over half of Southern families owned no slaves at all. Only 2 percent owned more than 50, and perhaps only 4 percent owned enought to replace them without purchase in the open market. What was profitable for the large slaveholder might not be for the small slaveowner, and what was profitable for the slaveowner was not necessarily profitable for the South.

[7]Harold D. Woodman, "The Profitability of Slavery," *The Journal of Southern History,* Vol. XXIX (1963); Robert Evans, Jr., "The Economics of American Negro Slavery, 1830-1860," Universities-National Bureau, *Aspects of Labor Economics* (Princeton: Princeton University Press, 1962).

Taking the questions one at a time, it seems evident that slavery was as profitable for the largest slaveowners as any other investment. If the average price of a slave was $500, and the interest rate on his investment 8 percent, the annual cost of a slave, including upkeep and supervision, was $84. If cotton sold at 10 cents a pound, the value of a slave's annual product was $130, leaving a profit of $46. Departing from this accounting approach, Conrad and Meyer used a capital-value formula in analyzing the profitability of slavery. They pointed out that slavery had two production objectives: the output of slaves and the output of cotton. They concluded that the rate of return varied from 2.2 to 13 percent, with 50 percent of the cases paying better than 6 percent. Where land was good, profits came from cotton; and where land was poor, profits came from selling slaves.[8]

For those Southern families who had to buy slaves in the market, the slave system posed a critical problem. Because the importation of slaves was prohibited by law, the supply did not increase as fast as the demand and, consequently, the price of slaves rose secularly. A good field hand cost $400 in 1800; by 1860, the figure had tripled. To those who raised slaves and to those who sold them, this increase meant a profit, but for the majority it was in the nature of a calamity for, while the price of slaves had been spiraling upward, the price of cotton had stabilized. It could, of course, be argued that planters would not have bought slaves unless it had paid to do so, but the small farmer faced very much the same dilemma that the Northern small farmer faced with respect to machinery: he was lost if he bought and lost if he didn't. The small Southern farmer sought to escape from his trap by supporting the reopening of the African slave trade, and in time this became one of the chief causes of the Civil War with all its impact on the economy of the whole nation.

It has been argued that regardless of slavery's profitability to the individual Southern planter, the slave system prevented the South from achieving the same rate of economic growth experienced by the North because it destroyed incentives, discouraged productivity, prevented the growth of a supply of skilled labor, absorbed whatever surplus the South produced, and prevented the accumulation of other types of capital. Moreover, slavery, by discouraging widespread education, also reduced capital below what it would otherwise have been.

Admittedly, the South's commercial institutions were very feeble. It was estimated that in 1860, 40 cents out of every cotton dollar went to the North, chiefly to New York, for interest, insurance, and shipping charges. Immigration to the South was almost nonexistent and the density of population was very low. In 1830, population was 6.4 per square mile in the South, in comparison

---

[8]Alfred H. Conrad and John R. Meyer, "The Economics of Slavery in the Ante-Bellum South," *Journal of Political Economy,* Vol. LXVI (1958); see also Alfred H. Conrad, et al., "Slavery as an Obstacle to Economic Growth in the United States: A Panel Discussion," *Journal of Economic History,* Vol. XXVI (1966).

with 31.5 per square mile in New England. With a much smaller population density, the South did not improve its land as rapidly as the North, nor did land values rise as rapidly. In 1860, only 29 percent of Southern land was improved, compared with 60 percent in the North. Land and improvements averaged about $10 an acre in the South, $20 in the Central States, and $24 in New England.

Anyone who believes that cultural values have anything to do with economic growth cannot be convinced that slavery did not hurt the South's economic progress, for it seems on the face of it that slavery could not help but erode the entrepreneurial spirit upon which growth thrived. The spirit of the South was a feudal spirit. Unlike the North, where economic motivation was of primary importance, the Southern social system laid little stress on economic values. Southern planters were landed proprietors who had little enthusiasm for trade, widespread education, the machine, or higgling in the market place. They emphasized chivalry and hospitality rather than acquisitiveness, pride in family rather than pride in business, the good life rather than economic growth. Whereas his Northern counterpart busied himself with account books and ledgers, the Southern planter leafed through the pages of Scott's novels and read there of a way of life that at times seemed very close to his own. It was a state of mind under which slavery flourished, or perhaps slavery was a system under which such a state of mind flourished. In either case, slavery was, directly or indirectly, importantly responsible for DeBow's plaintive lament: "We. . . most sadly want enterprise, which God, we implore, will give to our children, should it so happen that we are irreclaimable and past all hope."

Most people's impressions of the antebellum South reflect the picture that has just been drawn, a picture that resembles Hinton Rowan Helper's South much more than the South of *Gone With the Wind*. Helper's South was a stagnant society lagging far behind the North's economic progress. This is the popular impression and has been for years. But, flying in the face of everyone's impressions, recent research has concluded that the antebellum South was growing just as fast as the North.

Admittedly, the conclusion is tentative, but it is safe to say that most economic historians accept it as accurate. Certainly, the revisionists, that is to say those who contend that slavery was profitable, found nothing surprising in the discovery that the South was not as economically backward as it has always been described. The revisionists had ready answers to the indictment of slavery. If it was debilitating, so too was Northern labor; if slaves did not rush to work, neither did free labor. The revisionists also deny that slavery prevented productive saving, or that it took capital away from other uses. If some in the South consumed conspicuously, so did many in the North and in England where slavery did not exist. Nor did the investment in slaves destroy capital funds; it only transferred them from the slave buyer to the seller. The purchase only added another link in the chain of saving and investment.

Among the small group who still insisted that the South's economy lagged badly behind the North's, there were many who did not find slavery at fault for any of this. Instead, they blamed the Southern way of life. If the South was backward, it was not because of slavery, but because of its climate, its natural resources, its location, its means of transportation, the character of its white population, and its overwhelmingly agricultural orientation.

As distasteful as it may be, the economic historian on the present evidence has no choice but to conclude that slavery paid.

GRADUAL CHANGE IN THE METHODS OF FARMING

It is no exaggeration to say that American agricultural methods in use around 1800 were about the same as those that characterized English farming at about 1600. Most farming was extensive and mined the soil quickly. The average farmer[9] paid little or no attention to animal husbandry, was either ignorant or contemptuous of scientific farming, and used almost the same implements as his Saxon predecessor of the eighth century. The typical plow was crude and awkward, the sickle was of ancient invention, the flail had not been changed since Biblical days, and even the clumsy cradle was a rarity. The whole system of agriculture was typified by the "old oaken bucket that hung in the well." It might instill the poet with a feeling of nostalgia, but to the economist it represented the inefficiency and sparse productivity of a system based primarily on human energy and the slow-moving traction power of oxen.

Gradually, farming methods changed, basically influencing not only the farmer's level of living but also the level of the whole economy. Chemistry and crop rotation changed the methods of land cultivation; eugenics changed the shape and the size of hog, cow, and sheep; and machinery sowed and reaped the crop. Productivity on the farm in the first half of the nineteenth century increased at a higher rate than in the second half. By the middle of the nineteenth century, the farmer had certainly abandoned the old-oaken-bucket way of life. Of course, the process of progress was continuous. Productivity was to rise much faster in the twentieth century. By the middle of the twentieth century, the farmer would be using tools and machines to do more than 60 percent of his work. The value of his mechanized equipment had risen to $25 billion, and he had become interested in new processes of fertilization, crop rotation, soil conservation, and scientific animal husbandry.

---

[9] Like all averages, "the average farmer" is an abstraction that may not exist in reality. Farmers differed widely in different sections and according to the crops they grew. There was, for example, little similarity between the Western grain grower and the Eastern truck farmer. But the term, "average farmer" is, nevertheless, the most expedient one to use in generalizing about the condition of agriculture.

Better cultivation and better crops

With few exceptions, crop rotation and the use of fertilizers were almost unknown in early America. Hardly anyone knew anything about soil chemistry, and farmers planted the same crop over and over again until the yield diminished significantly. They took what they could from the land and then moved on to greener pastures. Fields would then lie fallow, weeds would grow, and some productive power would be restored. Even the use of stable manure was not universal, for it was common practice to compute the expense of moving the barn or removing the manure pile, and frequently the barn was moved as the less expensive job of the two.

In colonial America new land produced 20 to 40 bushels of wheat per acre, and a yield of 80 to 120 bushels of corn was not unusual. By the middle of the nineteenth century, Western lands produced 20 to 25 bushels of wheat and 40 to 50 bushels of corn per acre. In Massachusetts, however, wheat yielded only 15 bushels per acre; in New York, only 7½ bushels. Even in Lancaster County, Pennsylvania, considered the best farm country in the East, the yield was only 20 to 30 bushels.

As early as the 1850s, mining of the soil was a commonly accepted fact. Horace Greeley's *Tribune* editorialized in 1851: "There are whole counties, almost whole states which once yielded 20 bushels of wheat or 40 bushels of corn, yet now average 5 and 20." Some farmers recognized the peril, but the majority remained indifferent. Said one: "To talk of manuring all our farms is simply ridiculous. With the present scarcity and high price of labor, how is the farmer to find time and money or labor to manure his farm of from one hundred and sixty to fifteen thousand acres?" [10]

The farmer could have farmed more efficiently, for there were many books, almanacs, newspapers, journals, and societies to give him advice. The American Philosophical Society, founded in 1743, was interested in agriculture. In 1785, Philadelphia founded a society "for Promoting Agriculture." New Jersey followed in 1790, New York in 1791, Massachusetts in 1792, and Virginia in 1811. By 1820, it was estimated that there were more than 100 such societies, and by 1858 at least 1,000 could be counted. These societies were instrumental in founding journals and newspapers to bring the word to the farmer. Between 1819 and 1860, some 250 agricultural magazines were founded. As early as 1810, private fairs were held in Massachusetts to spread information on better farming methods. By 1850, these fairs were drawing enormous crowds; over

[10] Quoted in Fred A. Shannon, *The Farmer's Last Frontier* (New York: Holt, Rinehart & Winston, Inc., 1945), p. 170.

500,000 people, for example, attended the Connecticut State Fair in 1855. Governments also attempted to encourage better methods of farming. States offered bounties to encourage farmers to grow special crops. They also contributed toward agricultural education. Quite early they began to subsidize the fairs, and in 1857 Michigan founded the first agricultural college. The first Federal assistance came in 1839, when $1,000 was appropriated to the Patent Office for the importation of foreign plants and seeds, the distribution of seeds, and the collection of agricultural statistics. Until the Civil War, however, the interests of agriculture occupied a small pigeonhole in the many activities of Washington.

Here and there some farmers took the exhortations seriously. The Pennsylvania Germans were rotating crops before the Revolution. When Justus von Liebig made his valuable contributions to the science of soil chemistry around 1840, he had some effect. Soil exhaustion, declining land yields, and the increasing scarcity of good land drove home the lessons to be learned from scientific farming. By 1800, crop rotation was common in New England, spreading to the rest of the East by 1840 and to the West by the 1860s. Gypsum, marl, and lime were being used in the East early in the nineteenth century. Commercial sales of South American guano began in 1843, and commercial fertilizers were first sold in Baltimore in 1849. By the 1850s, fertilizers were being used to replenish the soil of the Old South; and by the time the first shells fell on Fort Sumter, phosphorous, potash, and nitrogen were revitalizing worn-out land in many parts of the country. Yet American farmers used only 53,000 tons of commercial fertilizers in 1850.

Bigger pigs and better cows

The American Indian had no domestic animals except the dog. With no indigenous supply, colonial Americans had to import their animals, usually at considerable difficulty. Those animals that were imported probably wished they had stayed in the old country, for the care and feeding of animals in early America was a far cry from what we refer to today as "animal husbandry." Hogs ran wild in most parts of the frontier region and resembled the razorbacks of Arkansas or the wild boars of Europe. At 18 months, an eighteenth-century Eastern hog weighed about 200 pounds; an early nineteenth-century Western hog weighed even less. Mostly legs and bones and incredibly fast, the porkers made butchering a hazardous occupation.

American Husbandry had very few compliments for the early American farmer. After having described rural management in most parts as miserable, it said: "Most of the farmers in this country are, in whatever concerns cattle, the most negligent, ignorant set of men in the world . . . They depend on plenty of land as a substitute for all industry and good management." Cows roamed almost at will and were housed in barns only during the winter. Left to fend almost entirely for themselves, they were a pretty poor species. In the eighteenth century, most seven-year-old cows and oxen weighed about 400 to 500 pounds dressed, although in Massachusetts weights were considerably higher; and George Washington reported that a well-cared-for cow could be made to yield two pounds of butter per day and 1,000 pounds of meat. Colonial sheep fared somewhat better than hogs and cows. They were about 30 inches high, produced two or three pounds of wool per shearing, and weighed 10 or 15 pounds per quarter; but the wool was not of fine quality and the mutton not the most tender.

As long as animals were allowed to pick their own companions, as was the good-natured custom in most of early, labor-scarce America, scientific breeding was impossible. But this difficulty was gradually rectified. Gentlemen farmers, aware of European improvements in breeding, imported prize animals with an enthusiasm that at times became fanatical. Suffolk, Essex, Berkshire, and Poland China hogs were imported. Beginning in 1817, English shorthorn cattle—Devons and Herefords for beef and Ayrshires, Guernseys, and Jerseys for dairy products—began to appear. At about the beginning of the nineteenth century, a craze for Spanish merino sheep developed, and fantastic prices were paid for prize specimens. The panic of 1819, with the resultant drop in the price of wool, brought this to a halt, but later the Saxon merino sheep began to be imported.

THE EXPANSION OF FARM MECHANIZATION

Because of the chronic shortage of labor, there was always a need for more machinery on the American farm. Improvements in technology, therefore, began to appear at a very early date, but they had no significant effect on productivity until 1850. Increased production hardly paid if the product could not be shipped to the market. Thus, the underlying cause for the adoption of agricultural machinery was a scarcity of labor, but the precipitating cause for its gradual adoption was the development of transportation and marketing facilities. Farms did not begin to use machinery until they had some method of getting goods to market. As a rule, every important agricultural implement existed in Europe before it appeared in the United States; but as soon as domestic economic conditions warranted it, the implement was adopted, changed to fit American conditions, and manufactured on a mass-production basis.

The colonial farmer had very few tools; Plymouth had no plows during its first ten years, and Massachusetts Bay had only 30 in 1636. The farmer of 1800 used about $15 to $20 worth of tools, probably including a plow of sorts, a sickle, a flail, a hoe, a pitchfork, and a shovel. Then, as commercial farming appeared in the East, more tools and equipment were used, but on a relatively small scale because of the nature of the terrain and the comparatively small

Table 14
CHANGES IN AGRICULTURE, 1800-1850

	1800	1850
Farm population	4.3 million	15.8 million
Number of farms	335,000	1,449,000
Gross production per worker (1910-14 dollars)	$292	$294
Farm wage rates (index, 1910-14 = 100)	33	49
Total gross output (1910-14 dollars)	$343 million	$1,521 million
Gross investment in land and buildings (" ")	$33 million	$124 million
Investment in machinery (" ")	$2 million	$11 million
Total gross investment	$51 million	$190 million

SOURCE: Towne and Rasmussen in National Bureau of Economic Research, *Studies in Income and Wealth,* Vol. 24, 1960.

landholdings. On the other hand, the West was ideally suited to machine farming because of its flat, rockless terrain, its relatively large landholdings, and its comparative advantage as a grain grower. Consequently, the West quickly adopted machinery once enough transportation facilities appeared to make large-scale commercial farming profitable. By 1857, even the family-sized, 80-acre farm had about $400 worth of tools. In self-defense and because its labor costs were constantly rising as industry expanded, the East was forced to increase its use of machines; but the South, with its emphasis on cotton culture, was not so much affected by Western competition and did not find it so necessary to invest in machinery. In other words, the progress of technology was delayed and halting as well as being uneven between regions.

From the wooden to the chilled-iron plow

Changes in agricultural technology began, logically enough, with improvements in the plow, and the evolution of this tool illustrates how marketing facilities and the change from self-sufficiency to commercialization resulted in the wider adoption of agricultural machinery.

In the Colonial Period, even wooden plows were scarce, and hoes were often used to break up the soil. It then took two men and two or three horses one day to plow one or two acres. Despite the fact that a cast-iron plow was made in Scotland as early as 1763, it was not until 1797 that Charles Newbold patented the first one in the United States. Even then it was not enthusiastically received. It was made in one piece and was very expensive. Moreover, farmers believed that it made weeds grow, an allegation that was more than accurate, because the improved plow made everything grow better.

Many suggestions were made for improving the Newbold plow, but it was not until 1819 that Jethro Wood patented a plow that incorporated them. Instead of consisting of one piece of cast iron, Wood's plow had three separate parts bolted to a frame: a moldboard, a share, and a landside.[11] Each was standardized and could either be replaced quickly or removed for quick repair by a blacksmith. As commercial farming spread throughout the East, Wood's plow was widely adopted, and it was in common use by 1830. But because heavy soil sticks to cast iron, the Wood plow did not scour well in the sticky loam of the Middle West after the first or second year of cultivation.

It was quickly recognized that what was needed for the Middle West was a less brittle, more durable plow with improved scouring qualities and a more scientific moldboard. The problem of making a plow that would break the prairie was solved as early as 1833 when John Lane plated a wooden moldboard with saw steel. But it was not until 1846 that John Deere began to manufacture steel plows in Moline, Illinois, and it was not until 1850 that these plows were in wide use. Deere sold only 1,000 in his first year but ten times as many in 1857. Once again, a relatively expensive innovation had to wait until commercial farming developed. The final phase in the basic improvement of the plow came in the 1870s, when James Oliver's chilled-iron plow received wide acceptance.

Because of the chronic shortage of labor, rising man-hour output was the great ambition of the commercial farmer, and the evolution of the plow was the first step in accomplishing this. With the crude wooden plow, two men and four oxen could plow one acre a day; with the cast-iron plow, one man and two oxen could plow an acre and one half in a day. Metal plows, moreover, meant better yields as well as more rapid plowing, for a wooden plow cut only a shallow furrow of about four to five inches, compared with an ideal depth of six to seven inches cut by the metal plow.

Reapers, harvesters, binders, and combines

The evolution of the plow was, of course, basic, but it may be argued that the development of harvesting machinery made an even greater contribution to economic development. With a sickle, harvesting required two man-days per acre. An energetic farmer could cut about one acre a day, and it took him another day to bind and shock an acre yielding 20 bushels of wheat. The best scythe wielder could cut three acres a day. With a cradle, an expert could cut four acres a day, or four times as much as a sickle wielder. But cradling was extremely heavy work, and it was not practical in a heavy stand or with ripe grain.

[11]The moldboard is the part of the plow that lifts, turns, and pulverizes the soil. The share is attached to the moldboard and cuts the furrow. The landside guides the plow and receives the side pressure when the furrow is turned.

It was easier, for example, to cradle three acres each yielding 20 bushels of wheat than two acres yielding 30 bushels. Consequently, the early farmer could choose between the slower harvesting time of the sickle or the lesser yield of cradling. But, sickling or cradling, harvesting was the major bottleneck in wheat production, for it was limited by natural conditions to between 10 and 20 days. Consequently, about 400 bushels was the maximum that one man could reap, rake, and bind per harvest. The improved plow that increased the acreage that could be sown intensified the problem.

From ancient times, man had been attempting to break the harvesting bottleneck, and between 1786 and 1831 more than 50 different reapers had been patented. Reapers were not widely used in Europe, and none was successful in the United States. They would not work in the peculiar terrain of the East, for they left the stubble uneven; the blades often broke in the rocky soil; and they were costly. Obed Hussey patented a reaper in 1833, and Cyrus McCormick patented one in 1834. McCormick later admitted that his machine was of little practical value before 1845, and up to 1847 he sold only 1,278. Hussey was equally unsuccessful. [12]

It was not until McCormick settled in Illinois in 1848 that the reaper was extensively adopted. The flat plains and the rockless soil of the Middle West offered ideal conditions for machine farming, and McCormick really struck it rich in the boom of the 1850s. He sold 1,000 machines in 1851 and 15,000 in 1855. By 1860, the reaper was cutting 70 percent of the wheat in the Middle West.

The early reaper, crude though it was, greatly increased man-hour output. As early as 1851, nine men with a reaper could do the work that formerly had required 14 cradlers. A few years later, McCormick thought that eight cradlers and eight binders could harvest 16 acres by hand at a cost of $20. With the reaper, the same 16 acres could be harvested by two men, five binders, and four horses at a cost of $10. Continuous improvements added materially to the increase in productivity, and by the Civil War the reaper could cut 12 acres a day, or as much as four to six cradlers or 12 sickle wielders. The reaper, furthermore, made binding easier and in this way eliminated the need for additional manpower.

Once the problem of cutting the grain by machine had been substantially solved, experimenters turned their attention to mechanizing the other processes of harvesting—raking, binding, and shocking. A self-raker was patented in 1854, but it did not become popular until the Civil War. At about the same time, headers which cut off the heads of grain and raised them to a wagon were widely used in the dry regions. In 1861, the Marsh brothers made a harvesting machine which facilitated binding by attaching to a reaper a traveling apron that elevated

[12]The best source of information on the reaper is William T. Hutchinson, *Cyrus Hall McCormick* (New York: Appleton-Century-Crofts, 2 vols., 1930, 1935).

the grain into a receiving box so that men standing on a platform next to the apron could bind the grain without stooping. Yet, like the early reaper and the early plow, the Marsh harvester was a long time coming into its own. William Deering took over the Marsh patent in 1870, but he made only 1,000 machines. Meanwhile, Deering had also developed a wire binder, but it was not very successful. But by 1876, the harvester had begun to catch on, although even as late as 1879 farm equipment manufacturers produced only 26,000 harvesters, headers, and binders, compared with 35,000 reapers and 55,000 combination reapers and mowers.

In the 1880s, the last fundamental development in harvesting machinery—the Appleby twine binder, which had been invented in 1878—came into common use and displaced the self-raking reaper and the harvester. Using a self-binder, one man could cut and bind eight acres of wheat a day, a job that previously had called for eight men using a cradle or for three men operating a harvester. This was an achievement that rivaled the very substantial advances in productivity being made by manufacturing industry.

Plows and harvesting machines were the most important innovations in grain growing, but the process of mechanizing agriculture included a wide variety of other devices. Some of these were fundamental, but others were merely elaborations of existing machines. In each case, considerable time elapsed between the initial development and its wide adoption. Combines, for example, were used in California before the Civil War. Pulled by 20 to 40 horses, they harvested 25 to 45 acres a day, but they were not practical for use on smaller farms.

As reapers were improved, the bottleneck in grain cultivation shifted from harvesting to threshing. The Pitts thresher, which appeared in 1837, solved this problem, for it could thresh 30 bushels a day, but it was not widely used until the late 1840s. Improvements in the plow created a demand for better methods of seeding and cultivating. The grain drill and the corn planter appeared in the 1850s and gradually replaced broadcast sowing, for the drill used only about half as much seed as did hand sowing. Harrows and cultivators were being turned out early in the nineteenth century, but the spring-toothed harrow did not come into its own until the late 1870s and the disk harrow, not until the early 1890s. The corn binder was in wide use by the 1890s.

The cotton gin

In 1793, Mrs. Nathaniel Greene, the widow of the Revolutionary War general, had a problem. On her plantation near Savannah, Georgia, an expert field hand could pick better than 200 pounds of cotton a day, but the most nimble hand could clean only about ten pounds a day. This bottleneck, requiring 20 cleaners for every picker, became an obsession to Mrs. Greene, her overseer, and her neighbors, and they explained it at considerable length to every guest who came to partake of the Greene hospitality. One of these was Eli Whitney, Yale '93, a would-be school teacher. Almost as soon as the problem had been explained to him, Whitney hit upon the solution. Within ten days, he had built a small-scale model for a cotton gin, which came as close to revolutionizing an economy as any single invention could.[13]

The Whitney gin consisted of two cylinders, revolving in opposite directions against one another over a hopper covered by wire ribs. One cylinder had teeth that pulled the cotton through the wire ribs, separating it from the seeds. The other cylinder held a brush that removed the lint from the cotton as the cylinder revolved. The device was extraordinarily simple—so simple, in fact, that it was adopted without compunction and without monetary acknowledgment throughout the South.

The gin more than broke the bottleneck in cotton production, for, built on a much larger scale than the original model, it made it possible to clean cotton faster than it was picked. A gin house, therefore, became a community affair in the cotton lands of the South, and the crops of various planters were cleaned at a central point. With the bottleneck broken, cotton culture expanded as rapidly as new lands became available. In 1790, the South produced 3,000 bales. By the end of the century, it was producing 40,000 bales. In spite of the increased supply, however, the price of cotton rose, for the industrial demand for the crop rose even more rapidly than the supply. The textile mills of Great Britain, created by what has been called "the Industrial Revolution," consumed almost half the Southern output and cried for more. Consequently, the price of cotton in New York rose from a satisfactory 14.5 cents a pound in 1790 to a lucrative 36.3 cents in 1800.

With the opening of new lands in the West, cotton production increased even faster. By the late 1820s, the South was producing over 600,000 bales a year, of which over 500,000 were exported. Demand, however, was no longer rising as fast as supply, and the price of cotton dropped to around 11 cents a pound. After 1830, cotton production continued to increase, but, aside from cyclical fluctuations, the price remained relatively stable. By 1860, cotton production was almost four million bales annually, and the price was slightly over 10 cents a pound.

THE EARLY NINETEENTH CENTURY FARMER AS A BUSINESSMAN: A SUMMARY

For reasons already explained, the early nineteenth-century Northern farmer, especially on the frontier, could not produce in large quantities. The

---

[13]A gin had previously been developed for cleaning Sea Island cotton, but it cleaned only 25 pounds a day. Whitney immediately gave up his ideas of being a teacher. Education's loss, however, was society's gain, for Whitney later made valuable contributions to the machine tool industry.

abundance of land, the scarcity of labor, the lack of capital, and the absence of marketing facilities prevented him from producing the maximum per acre. Free land emphasized the attractiveness of a settle-and-sell policy; the scarcity of labor forced him to cultivate extensively; the lack of capital limited his total output; and without marketing facilities, he was forced to be almost wholly self-sufficient. Consequently, he could not institute a system of specialization and division of labor on his own farm or on an area-wide basis. His objective had to be "to cultivate with a minimum amount of labor the largest possible acreage planted in the most immediately valuable crops."[14] Jack-of-all-trades and master of few, he was fortunate if at the end of the year he made $100 over and above upkeep for himself and his family. Yet, low as this is by modern standards, it was quite respectable compared to the average income of that time. It represented economic success, or, in other words, a farmer's success as a businessman.

Most farmers, however, were not good businessmen, or good managers. They tended to buy too much land. They ignored the costs of maintaining unused land. They did not have enough working capital or enough labor. Then too, there was more than a world of difference separating the commercial farmer from the subsistence farmer. The subsistence farmer, who incidentally was one of society's objects of affection, refused to accept the notion that farming was a business, and he was in the vast majority even in 1850. His methods of farming ignored the value of time. He used "cheap" methods in order to save investment outlays. But he did so by sacrificing speed. The commercial farmer's outlook on labor, time, and capital investment was entirely different. In the interest of saving time, he emphasized "dear" methods. He specialized, and he was eager, not reluctant to make capital outlays.

A glaring example of the difference between the successful commercial farmer and the plodding subsistence farmer occurred quite early. The commercial farmer was quick to substitute the "expensive" but much faster horse for the subsistence farmer's "cheap" but slow ox.

Whether a farmer succeeded or failed was not to be explained in terms of diversity or quality of land or quantity of capital, but in terms of differences in the skills of management, which included entrepreneurial ability and mechanical talents.

SUGGESTED READINGS

(For suggested readings and questions, see the next chapter.)

---

[14]Danhof, *op. cit.,* p. 252.

Chapter Five

THE FARMER
AS A BUSINESSMAN

After the middle of the nineteenth century, it was apparent that American agriculture as a whole had matured. It was less speculative, less extensive, more scientific, and more commercial. The change did not take place overnight, nor did it occur simultaneously in every section of the country. It was a gradual process, and it took place in one section at a time as population increased, markets developed, and transportation facilities appeared. In some areas, such as New England and the Middle Atlantic states, the change from speculative, extensive, and self-sufficient agriculture occurred long before the Civil War; in other areas, like the Great Plains, the evolution had not even begun by the end of the War. For the country as a whole, however, agriculture by the late nineteenth century was more a business than a way of life.

The growth of population had narrowed the gap between the supply of land and labor; extended transportation facilities had given the farmer access to markets; specialization and division of labor had become characteristic of most agricultural areas. By the middle of the nineteenth century, the fundamental developments in agricultural machinery had appeared and some progress had been made toward scientific farming. The West was rapidly filling up; the frontier line was about to disappear; and the extensive development of the agricultural economy had been largely accomplished. From relative self-sufficiency, agriculture had developed into a complicated business. But now that he had achieved what he had always wanted, the farmer, like most human beings, found that it was not quite so sweet as he had anticipated. He found himself beset by business problems that had not bothered him too much in the pioneer stage. How well each individual farmer solved them determined his economic success or failure.

AGRICULTURE'S SHARE OF THE NATIONAL INCOME

It has already been said that at the heart of the so-called "farm problem" is the farmer's belief that he is not getting a "fair share of the national income." In proportion to the number of people employed, agriculture's share in the national income has always been lower than the share accruing to the other participants in the economy. Per capita farm income has always been below the average for the United States, whereas per capita manufacturing income has about equaled the average, and per capita income in the services has exceeded it. There is nothing new or unique about this; it has been typical for agriculture in all nations and for all periods of time. It was evident in early nineteenth-century America, in nineteenth-century Britain, and wherever else students have looked.[1]

Table 15
FARM WAGE AND FACTORY WAGE, 1910-1970

Years	Average Farm Wage	Index (1910-14 = 100)	Manufacturing Production Workers	Per capita personal income			
				Index	Farm	Nonfarm	Farm as % of Nonfarm
1910-14	$ 338	100	$ 547	100	—	—	—
1920	660	195	1,353	247	$ 343	$ 729	47.2
1934	360	107	946	173	166	512	32.4
1948	1,842	545	2,762	505	963	1,529	63.0
1960	2,058	609	4,665	853	1,255	2,309	54.4
1970	3,682	1089	6,954	1271	1,841	3,798	48.5

SOURCE: Department of Agriculture, *The Farm Income Situation,* 1955; *Statistical Abstract.*

Agriculture's share of the national income has ordinarily been equal to 40 to 60 percent of its share of the labor force, and its per capita share of personal income has varied between one-third and two-thirds of nonfarm personal

[1] J.R. Bellerby, *Agriculture and Industry, Relative Income* (London: Macmillan & Co., Ltd., 1956).

income. Farmers comprised about 60 percent of the 1860 labor force, but they received only slightly better than 30 percent of the national income. Constituting about one-third of the gainfully employed from 1899 to 1908, they averaged about 17 percent of the national income. In the prosperous year of 1929, agriculture's share in the national income equaled 38 percent of its share of the labor force. During the depression years, it fared much worse, dropping to about 30 percent. During the war years, the farmer's relative position was at its best. In 1946, he made up about 13 percent of all workers and received 9 percent of the national income. Subsequently, the statistics reverted back to trend, and in 1970 agriculture's piece of the national pie was equal to about 58 percent of its participation in the working population.

Like the farm operator, the farm worker did not do as well as his counterpart in industry. Money wages on the farm increased steadily and slowly after 1850, but not as rapidly as those in non-farm occupations. Between 1850 and 1900, farm wages, it is estimated, jumped about 30 percent, but nonfarm wages soared 70 percent. During the 1920s and the 1930s, farm workers shared the depressed economic conditions that characterized agriculture in general. In fact, during the great depression, one-fourth of all farmers were on relief. From the late 1930s, however, farm wage rates resumed their upward climb, and during World War II they rose more than at any other time. By 1970, they were almost ten times as high as they had been in 1910. For most of the period, however, manufacturing wages rose even more sharply. In 1960, in absolute dollar terms, the man who ran a factory machine earned more than twice as much as the man who milked the cows. (See Table 15). But in the next decade the farmer's superior performance in raising man-hour output succeeded in raising farm wages by 80 percent while factory wages rose by 50 percent.

The farmer's apparently desperate economic plight must be sharply qualified. First of all, there were psychic factors that helped to compensate for the discrepancy in money income. Second, farm income has always been unequally distributed, so that not all farmers were members of the group that President Roosevelt once described as the "ill-clothed, ill-housed, and ill-fed." In 1929, half the commercial farmers had an income of less than $1,000 a year, but they produced only 11 percent of farm output. In the 1960s, at the peak of prosperity, one-tenth of the commercial farmers received half the farm income; more than 20 percent had an income of less than $2,000 per year. Less than 20 percent of all farms sold more than $20,000 worth of produce; but they accounted for two-thirds of all farm sales; 16 percent sold less than $2,500. Entrepreneurial income on the most profitable farms was over 60 times as much as on the least profitable.[2]

[2]A "farm" is defined as a place of ten acres or more selling at least $50 of produce a year, or a place of less than ten acres selling at least $250. Before 1960, the definition of a farm included any place of three or more acres selling or producing $150. A commercial farm includes those that sell $2,500 or more or $50 or more provided the operator is under 65 and does not work off the farm 100 or more days a year. Only a little more than half of the 2.2 million farms are classified as commercial.

A third mitigating factor is that farming has become for many so-called farmers more and more a part-time job. For many years, one-third to one half of farm families have been receiving more income from nonfarm than from farm occupations; 30 percent work off the farm for 100 or more days a year. Finally, despite low incomes, per capita net worth has averaged about the same for farm as for nonfarm families.

The explanation for the seeming paradox between low income and relatively high net worth lies in what happened to the price of farm land. It is usually assumed that land values are determined by capitalizing actual or anticipated rents. Thus, when prices go up and rents rise, land values also rise, and when prices and rents fall, land values should also fall. But this tidy assumption ignores the double-barreled effect that rising farm population and able entrepreneurs will have in increasing the demand for land. If population increases, land values may rise despite declining farm prices. At the same time, able entrepreneurs, who can get more out of a given piece of land than the average farmer can, may bid up land prices, even though average returns are declining. Up to the end of World War I, the price of farm land rose regardless of whether farm commodity prices went up or down, because farm population, although declining relative to urban population, continued to increase absolutely, while the quantity of land remained stationary. The value of land and buildings climbed from an average of $16.30 an acre in 1860 to $21.30 in 1890, despite falling commodity prices. When production stabilized and farm commodities began to command a better price, values rose even more. By 1910, even though farm population was beginning to level off, the average value per acre was $39.60, about double the price it had commanded in 1900. Very good land did even better. The price of an acre of improved Iowa land rose from $6 to $96 between 1850 and 1910.

Encouraged by inflated prices during World War I, farmers tried to expand their landholdings, and, as the demand increased, the value of land and buildings rose to $69.39 an acre in 1920. After the war, land prices began to decline secularly for the first time in history. Declining farm population, falling prices, and stable per-acre yields pushed the price of an average acre down to below $50 in 1930 and to less than $20 at the bottom of the depression. The demand for farm products in World War II brought substantial recovery. This continued as the more successful farmers bid up the price of higher-yielding farm acreage, and real estate subdivisions cut the supply of farm land in the postwar era. By 1970, the value of land and buildings was six times the average for 1912-1914, with the price of land alone over $180 an acre—more than twice as high at the end of World War II.

The rising price of land encouraged the farmer to continue the "settle and sell" policy that had so strongly characterized the earlier years. Thus "no matter the age of the community, between 50 and 80 percent of any new group of farmers were gone ten years later."[3] Although this was written about northern

[3]Allan G. Bogue, "Farming in the Prairie Peninsula, 1830-1890", *Journal of Economic History*, Vol. XXIII (1963).

Illinois and Iowa, it applied anywhere else in the Middle West. Rising land prices also made it unprofitable to grow low-price staples. Wheat and cotton, for example, did not pay on high-priced land, for their yield per acre was not high enough to cover all costs, including implicit interest on a large investment in land. Most important of all, the rising price of land was the one bright spot in the generally bleak farm picture, because it still left the farmer with the alternative of selling out and realizing a capital gain if he could not make farming itself pay. Thus, farming was one of the few occupations, if not the only one, in which a participant could go along year after year hardly holding his head above water and yet emerge to live comfortably on his savings.

Clearly, some farmers did well, but most did very poorly. Reduced to its lowest common denominator, therefore, the farm problem has been concerned not with agriculture as a whole but with the great bulk of farmers at the bottom of the agricultural ladder. Some of the discrepancy in income between those at the top and those at the bottom depended on the nature of the crop and much, of course, depended on the nature of the individual.[4] In the long run, apparently only those who were able businessmen and who raised livestock really made money.[5] Those in staples—tobacco, cotton, and grains—had much less chance of achieving a comfortable status.

FARM PRODUCTION AND PRICES

Between 1850 and 1970, the gross product of farming[6] multiplied about seven times, but population increased almost nine times. This hardly substantiates the widely held view that the farmer was "guilty" of overproduction. (See Chart 9).The disparity between farm product and population was even greater in the twentieth century. Between 1900 and 1970 farm output did not quite double but population more than doubled, again giving evidence that the farmer did not overproduce. But any conclusions based on data covering 120 years are much too neat. The composition of farm production is significantly different today from what it was in 1900, let alone 1850. Consumption of most grains,

---

[4]All of which could also be said of manufacturing, trade, or any other business, and may be what makes a business a business.

[5]Livestock operators could not count on making large profits year after year. Overproduction was a constant threat and brought with it heavy losses. Yet "no ordinary business could compare in profitableness with the open-range cattle business in its halcyon days, say from 1866 to 1885," Joseph Schafer, *The Social History of American Agriculture* (New York: The Macmillan Company, 1936), p. 101.

[6]Gross farm product includes cash receipts from marketing, plus or minus change in inventories, plus board and housing less value of intermediate products consumed. All of which leaves a large margin for error.

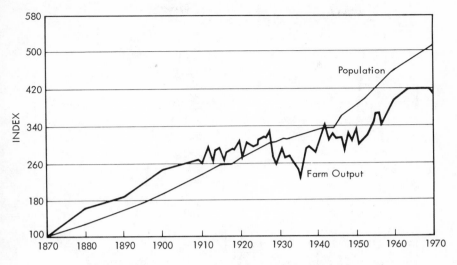

CHART 9.   Population and farm output, 1870-1970 (1870=100)

cotton, and potatoes has declined while beef, dairy products, and vegetables are much more important. America is living much leaner and much higher on the hog. Moreover, the displacement of farm animals by the tractor has had a significant impact on grain farming. The industrial use of farm products has also changed, and exports have been ignored in comparisons of farm product and population. Statistics on farm output, therefore, do not tell the cautious generalizer very much. We can learn much more by examining the movement of prices.

In the last 120 years, agricultural prices experienced two periods of depression, two wartime periods of unprecedented prosperity, and two that, for want of a better word, may be called normal. These five periods were closely connected with the "overproduction" or "underproduction" of farm commodities. In general, the farmer's economic status shifted from good to bad as production expanded. The exceptions were during major wars, when expanded production was more than offset by increased demand.

Most agricultural prices declined from the end of the Civil War to the late 1890s. Increased mechanization, perhaps helped by the government's land policy, boosted production. This was sometimes alleviated by increased exports, but it was also occasionally accentuated by declines in urban disposable income. Thus, during the late nineteenth century, agricultural conditions were especially bad during the depression years but reasonably tolerable in other years. The production of the three basic cash crops—wheat, corn, and cotton—rose faster than did the population throughout most of the period and their prices declined commensurately. In the 30 years from 1870 to 1900, there were only eight years when wheat sold at more than $1.00 per bushel and only seven years when corn

CHART 10.   Parity ratio, 1910-1970

sold at over 45 cents a bushel and cotton at more than 10 cents a pound.[7] But agriculture's position was not completely bleak. Cattle prices held up well. They fluctuated around $4.50, except for 1889 when they dropped to $3.90 and 1882 when they hit $6.25. Moreover, farm prices did not fare any worse than prices in manufacturing. Wholesale farm prices were the same in 1900 as in 1850, but the prices of all commodities were slightly lower at the end of the century than in 1850. During the long price decline from 1864 to 1896, farm

---

[7]Per capita wheat production increased from 6.4 bushels in 1870 to 7.9 bushels in 1894. Its price declined from $1.04 to 49 cents. Corn production per capita increased from 28 bushels in 1870 to 38 bushels in 1896, while its average price fell from 52 to 21 cents. Cotton production almost doubled, while the price per pound declined from 12 to 6 cents.

prices dropped 65 percent, but so did the all-commodity index and home furnishing prices. Metals dropped to 25 percent of their 1864 level which was a decidedly greater decline than the drop in farm prices.

Falling prices for farm products benefited urban wage earners by increasing their real wages. They also swelled the volume of foodstuffs exported to Europe, thus allowing these overseas nations to withdraw some of their resources from agriculture and channel them into industry. But, although the city dweller and Europe benefited from falling prices, the farmer did not. He was a chronic debtor and, with each decline in the price of his commodity, he had to sell a greater quantity to meet the interest charges on his fixed obligations. Whenever prices fell, therefore, the farmer turned to any scheme that promised to reverse this trend; but whether he put his faith in monetary panaceas, as he did in the late nineteenth century, or in government price supports, as he did later, the problem seemed unsolvable.

Because production stabilized, agriculture recovered and enjoyed relatively mild prosperity from 1900 to 1913. Per capita production of wheat remained at virtually the same level that it had reached at the end of the nineteenth century; corn production per capita fell below the 1870 level; cotton production continued to increase faster than population; aggregate farm production remained about the same. Meanwhile, something was happening on the demand side. Consumer spending rose 73 percent in the first decade of the twentieth century, as compared with an increase of only 16 percent in the last decade of the nineteenth century. Most prices climbed back to their post Civil War levels. Wheat sold at 99 cents a bushel in 1914, and corn at 64 cents a bushel, but the price of cotton sank to 7 cents a pound.

World War I brought the farmer unprecedented prosperity, despite the fact that he greatly expanded his production. Wheat production exceeded one billion bushels in 1915, corn passed the three-billion-bushel mark in 1920, but cotton production, while increasing, fell far short of the record crop of 1914. As production expanded, total demand, buoyed up by foreign buying, increased even more. Consequently, prices shot upward. By 1919, cotton sold at 36 cents a pound, corn at $1.50 a bushel, and wheat at $2.15 a bushel. At the same time, the parity ratio, that is, the ratio of prices received by the farmer to prices paid, rose to 120.

Immediately following the war, agriculture went into a slump. The European demand, which had been maintained during the war by government loans to the Allied powers, fell off when the loans ceased and when Europeans resumed their own production. Domestically, consumers spent a smaller percentage of their incomes on food and shifted their diet so radically that the farmer could not keep up with the change. In the face of declining demand, farmers were unwilling or unable to curtail production sufficiently to keep prices from falling drastically. In 1931 and 1932, at the bottom of the depression, corn and wheat production were almost as high as during the war and cotton production was at its second highest in all history. Prices of farm products sank to the levels of the 1890s: 30-cent corn, 40-cent wheat, and nickel cotton. The parity ratio fell to 80 in 1920, came back to 95 in 1925, and then plummeted to 58 in 1932. (See Chart 10.)

In the middle 1930s, agriculture slowly recovered. Much of the New Deal legislation was intended to curtail crop production, and nature gave the policy-makers in Washington a helping hand. From 1934 to 1936, extensive droughts hit agricultural production, especially in the Great Plains region. Corn production fell to less than one and a half billion bushels, and wheat to about half a billion bushels. The prices of both rose sharply, passing 80 cents in 1934. By 1935, farm prices in general averaged 66 percent above 1932 and 8 percent above the prewar level. But government policy and the widespread drought notwithstanding, they still had not recovered as much as had been hoped.

No matter what World War II did to the general economy it produced a distinct turn for the better for the American farmer. Agricultural trends with a long and sustained history were reversed, and the farmer began to enjoy the greatest prosperity he had ever experienced. Like all wars, World War II multiplied the demand for farm products. Export demand increased, gross national product more than doubled, and consumer spending for food increased as fast as the gross national product. To meet the rising demand, the farmer relied more on intensive than extensive methods. He increased production but in a new way. He multiplied the yield from his available acres and brought less new acres under cultivation than he had done during the Civil War and World War I. He grew 50 percent more food than in World War I and 35 percent more than the 1923-1932 average. Corn production increased 17 percent over the prewar ten-year average and wheat increased 50 percent. Even so, production did not rise as fast as demand, and farm prices rose sharply. By February 1948, they were almost double the 1926 level, and the parity ratio was at 115, illustrating once again that farm prices were more flexible than other prices.

With the end of hostilities, agriculture experienced a slight recession, and farm prices once again fell more sharply than other prices, but a repetition of the extreme collapse of the 1920s did not seem likely in the foreseeable future. Overproduction seemed less a menace than previously. The rate of population growth, which had declined decade by decade after the Civil War, increased during the 1940s, providing new consumers for farm products. Because farm exports were not relatively high, as in 1920, there was less likelihood that they would drop significantly. Even if a surplus were produced, the Federal government was committed to protect the farmer through subsidies or some other form of financial aid. Much of this optimistic outlook was doomed to disappointment. Farm production again began to rise. It was 6 percent higher in 1960 than during the War. Wheat and cotton farmers were producing half again as much; corn farmers, one-third as much. To be sure, prices did not collapse. It was 30-cent cotton, $1 corn, and $2 wheat; but the parity ratio was down to 80, about the same as in 1920. The problem of agricultural overproduction had not been solved; its costs had been socialized. The farmer no longer carried the whole burden of overproduction; it was shared to a great extent by taxpayers and urban consumers.

THE FARMER IN THE EXPORT MARKET

If the farmer overproduced, as most people assumed he did, the surplus had to be absorbed by an increase in per capita domestic consumption or else exported to foreign markets. Because per capita consumption did not increase much, surpluses were exported. The American farmer had an absolute advantage in growing farm products because of cheap land and, more so, because of high man-hour output. In 1850, wheat could be grown in the Middle West and shipped to England as flour for $4.40 a barrel. At the same time, English flour sold for $6.90. In the 1880s, wages on an American wheat farm were four times as much as in Prussia; yet the cost of production in Prussia was 80 cents a bushel compared to 40 cents in the United States.[8] The rise in production in the late nineteenth century pushed up exports. Crude material exports amounted to 10 percent of value added in 1850 and 13 to 20 percent after 1879. In the nine years from 1874 to 1883, the United States exported more grain than it had in the previous 50 years. Wheat exports alone rose from 91 million bushels in 1873 to 186 million in 1880. But this extraordinary increase in exports occurred only because prices were falling, and in a sense, therefore, it represented a benefit to foreign consumers at the expense of foreign and domestic farmers.

During the 1880s and early 1890s, exports declined somewhat and contributed to the problem of agricultural overproduction. For a short time thereafter, exports recovered strongly and strengthened the position of the farmer. In the early 1900s, however, Russia, Argentina, Australia, and Canada gradually increased their exports, cutting into the market formerly held by the United States. Shortly after 1900, exports of all the basic crops except cotton declined. Wheat exports reached a peak of 155 million bushels in 1902; beef exports were at their highest in 1906 at 732 million pounds, pork exports hit a high of 1.5 billion pounds in 1901. The average export of wheat in the ten years before World War I was only 15 percent of the crop, compared with 41 percent in 1900. By 1910 the United States was even importing beef.

During World War I, exports again increased. In 1915, 260 million bushels of wheat were exported—more than double the amount before the war. Other crop exports increased similarly. With the end of war and the resumption of European production, American farm surpluses once again could be exported

[8]Hutchinson, *op. cit.*, Vol. I, p. 378; the contrast between Prussia and U.S. quoted by Robert Gallman in *Studies in Income and Wealth*, Vol. 24, 1960, p. 20.

only if drastic reductions in prices were offered. Thus, the physical volume of exports remained almost the same, but their dollar value fell from almost $4 billion to $2.5 billion.

The events of the decade of the 1930s reduced farm exports even more. Natural disaster reduced the American surpluses, and government legislation raised prices, handicapping the farmer in the foreign market. Farm exports totaled $1.6 billion annually in 1927-1931, but only $713 million in 1932-1936. World War II, like World War I, restored the export market, and in 1947 farmers sold $3.6 billion internationally. Unlike World War I, peace brought a very small decline in farm exports, and they were still valued at $5.1 billion annually in 1957-1970.

WHY THE FARM PROBLEM?

The primary reason why farmers did not obtain what they considered a fair share of the national income was inherent in the economics of agriculture. There were two principal reasons why the economics of farming could not be shaped to conform to the pattern of industrial economics: farmers operated in a market that was generally characterized by pure competition, and the demand for agricultural products in the aggregate was highly inelastic.

Industrialists operated in a market of imperfect competition. That is, there were relatively few sellers, and any one of them could influence the market. As demand declined, industrialists met the problem by cutting production as well as by lowering prices. Farmers, on the other hand, were more subject to the dictates of a nonpersonalized market. Because there were many sellers of farm commodities, the individual farmer's product could not influence total production significantly. The individual farmer, therefore, had no control over market prices, and it was obviously impossible for the mass of farmers to cooperate to exert effective control over either production or prices. Thus, the individual farmer tended to operate at full capacity; he did not cut production when aggregate demand declined, nor did he increase his production proportionately as aggregate demand rose. Consequently, prices declined markedly when demand fell and rose sharply as demand increased. The fact that the demand for agricultural commodities in the aggregate was relatively inelastic, whereas the demand for many industrial products was much more elastic, accentuated this rise and fall of prices. Farm prices were generally more sensitive than industrial prices; with the passage of time, they seemed to be becoming more so, for the disparity between farm and industrial prices became sharper with each succeeding period of economic change.

All the farmer's problems could not be traced to the peculiar market structure in which he operated. Many of them were the result of a multitude of noneconomic factors and were not amenable to the solutions offered by classical economic theory. Classical theorists assumed that inefficient farms would be eliminated by the operation of the market. If overproduction occurred, prices would be driven so low that many farmers would not be able to meet costs and would be forced out of business. In reality, farmers did leave the farm, and they left not in bunches or in groups, but in swarms and in hordes. Farm population declined relatively from the beginning of settlement, and it has been declining absolutely throughout the twentieth century. Indeed, the number of farmers is about the same today as it was in 1830. In spite of this drop, however, the farm problem still remains.

The decline in the farm population was not in any sense caused by a decline in the rural birth rate or by an increase in the urban birth rate. As in every Western nation except Ireland, the rural birth rate consistently exceeded the urban birth rate. From 1905 to World War II, the net reproduction rate (the number of potential mothers born to each woman) in urban areas was not high enough to maintain a stationary population. The rural-nonfarm rate was much higher, and the rural-farm rate was highest of all.

The agricultural states consistently registered the highest birth rates, while the lowest occurred in the highly industrialized states. New Mexico, Arizona, Mississippi, Utah, and Louisiana had birth rates of over 27 per 1,000 in 1960. Connecticut, New Jersey, New York, and Rhode Island each had a birth rate of less than 22 per 1,000.

Rural population failed to increase as fast as urban because farmers were much more mobile. Because the demand for manufactured goods was elastic, the demand for labor to produce them was much less limited than the demand for agricultural workers. Town and industry could, therefore, absorb far more labor than agriculture and thus could attract the rural population far more effectively than the country could attract the city-dweller. As a result, the flow of population was from the farm to the city, not from the city to the farm. It was estimated that, in the days when the frontier was still being settled, 20 farmers came to the city for every city laborer who moved to the farm.[9] In the mid-twentieth century, farmers were still the most restless Americans. The occupancy of the average farm was less than 12 years, and the net migration averaged almost one million a year.

Although they left the farm in great numbers, farmers still did not leave rapidly enough to satisfy the economics of the case, for there were important noneconomic factors that kept the farmer in business despite falling prices. Even though farmers might not be as well off in money terms as urban dwellers, high birth rates, inertia, habit, custom, lack of alternatives, and a desire for independence kept too many of them on the farm. Even so, however, it was questionable whether the problem of overproduction could have been solved by an even more massive exodus from farm to city. If 30 percent of the marginal

[9]Fred A. Shannon, *The Farmer's Last Frontier* (New York: Holt, Rinehart & Winston, Inc., 1945), p. 357.

farmers (not including those who are farmers for tax purposes only) were eliminated, total farm production would fall by only 3 percent.

It was not so much that there were too many farmers and too many acres, but that there were too many *poor* farmers. Astute students of agricultural history have not tired of pointing out that either by "push" or by "pull," many of those who went to new lands should have stayed home. "Real estate agents, railroads, state immigration commissions, and general busybodies," writes Theodore Saloutas, "drew pictures of a heavenly existence very much opposed to the truth. Sufferers from pulmonary, bronchial, and malarial diseases . . . young ladies suffering from neurasthenia and ennui would get healthy by a short residence in Dakota." In one eastern Montana settlement, it was found that 51 percent of the settlers had no capital, and many were incapable of farming: "two circus musicians, a paper hanger, a sailor, two wrestlers, two barbers, an undertaker, a deep sea diver, six old maids, a milliner, and a professional gambler." Paul Gates has put the matter even more bluntly: "It was greed, to put it baldly, that drove many Americans, but by no means all, to go West to acquire quantities of low-priced land. Farm-making and farming were not their principal interests; rather they wanted to get their share of Uncle Sam's domain which they might sell at a handsome price when values rose. Because that increase in value did not come sufficiently rapidly to permit them to live on their gains, many of these petty speculators—for that is what they were—had perforce to turn to farming somewhat reluctantly. Their reluctance combined with their greed did not make them good farmers."[10]

The weaker farmers did not plan for the long run. They were crushed in depression, and were in the van of those who sought government aid. The more efficient farmers, driving on to be successful businessmen, made it more and more difficult for those who would not or who could not play the game, that is, the inefficient farmer or the nonconformist farmer, to remain in existence.

Just as it was an oversimplification to say that the farm problem was "too many farmers," it was an oversimplification to say that the farm problem was "too many farms." Most indices of farms and land cultivation showed a sharply rising trend until the bottom of the depression. Then the pattern went into reverse. In 1850, there were about 1.5 million farms in the United States; in 1935, there were 6.8 million; and today there are about 3 million—about the same number as 100 years ago. It took 80 years to quadruple the number of farms; it took 10 years to cut the number in half. In Lincoln's day, there was one farm for every 15 people; today, there is one for every 60 people.

The retirement of acres has been quite as remarkable as the elimination of farmers and farms. The number of harvested acres is less than it was in 1900, and land in crops is rapidly backtracking toward the figure of 1900.

---

[10] Theodore Saloutas, "The Spring Wheat Farmer in a Maturing Economy, 1870-1920," *Journal of Economic History,* Vol. VI (1946); Paul W. Gates, *Journal of Economic History,* Vol. XXII (1962).

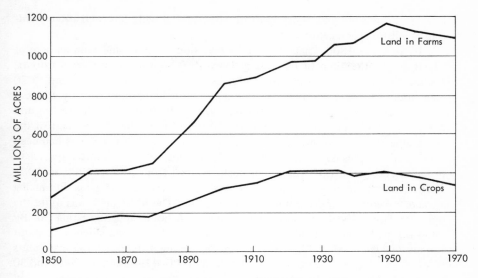

CHART 11. Land in farms and in crops, 1850-1970, in millions of acres

RISING PRODUCTIVITY IN FARMING

It must be clear by this time that the need for increased output was manifested not in too many farmers or too many acres. It was in the multiplying productivity of those farmers and of those acres.

Throughout the nineteenth and early twentieth century, per-acre yield remained about the same. Corn yielded about 25 bushels per acre in 1850 and about 25 bushels per acre in 1930. Wheat yielded 15 bushels per acre in 1840 and the same about 90 years later. In most of the years between 1910 and 1937, crop production per acre varied from 75 to 85 percent of the 1947-1949 average. The exceptions were the very depressed years of the early 1930s, when productivity fell to less than 60 percent of the postwar average. By contrast, beginning in 1937, and at a rising tempo thereafter, production per acre made impressive progress. By 1970, it was 40 percent above the 1947-1949 average, or three times as high as at the bottom of the depression. The basic crops did even better, corn yielding almost 80 and wheat 25 bushels an acre. At the same time, yields from cows and poultry increased commensurately. A dairy cow, for example, produced 4,500 pounds of milk in 1928. Today a cow produces 8,000 pounds.[11]

Man-hour output, in contrast to per-acre yields, just about doubled between 1850 and 1900. It doubled again between 1900 and 1947, and doubled a third

[11] The best farms produce three to four times as much as the average.

time between 1947 and 1960. In short, labor productivity has risen about eight-fold in a little over a century.

It took the 1800 wheat farmer 16 man hours to sow and tend an acre of wheat up to the time of harvesting. Harvesting consumed another 40 hours, making 56 man hours in all. By 1880, the total time had been reduced to 20 man hours (8 hours before harvesting and 12 for harvesting). But by 1970, it required less than 3 man hours, divided almost evenly between preharvesting and harvesting. Thus, in a period of about 150 years, more than 90 percent of the labor time required to produce an acre of wheat in the United States had been eliminated. Expressed in another way, the number of man hours required to produce 100 bushels of wheat had been reduced from 370 in 1800 to 10 in 1970. Production of corn and cotton also showed remarkable gains. Producing an acre of corn in 1800 required 86 man hours. The bottleneck was quite the opposite from wheat; preharvesting required 56 hours and harvesting 30. By 1880 this had been cut to almost 46 hours, and by 1970 it had fallen to 6, about equally divided between harvesting and preharvesting. It required 185 man hours to produce an acre of cotton in the South in 1800, 119 hours in 1880, and 30 hours in 1970.

Table 16

MAN HOURS PER UNIT OF FARM PRODUCT

	1800	1880	1900	1940	1965-69
Wheat, per 100 bushels	373	152	108	47	11
Corn, per 100 bushels	344	180	147	83	7
Cotton, per bale	601	318	280	191	30

SOURCE: Historical Statistics K83-97; Department of Agriculture, *Agricultural Statistics.*

Other crops demonstrated similar gains in productivity, so that whereas one farm worker provided food for 4.5 people in 1820 and for 10 people in 1920, he supports almost 50 people today. This increase in productivity occurred sporadically, not steadily. Gross farm production per worker moved up slowly from 1850 to 1920. Indeed, at times it showed no progress at all. There were, for example, only small gains in the 1880s and during World War I. From 1920 on, however, the curve was sharply upward, with the most remarkable rise occurring in World War II and thereafter. For the first time in the recollection of man, output per worker improved faster in agriculture than in manufacturing. With only 5 percent more land available and 10 percent less workers contributing, farmers produced 50 percent more in World War II than they had in World War I. If all farmers had used the same methods in 1944 as had been used in World War I, it would have taken nine billion more man hours to produce the 1944 crop. In the 1950s, the achievement was equally brilliant. The farmer increased his output by about 10 percent with 40 percent less land and labor.

Because per capita consumption of farm products remained fairly stable throughout American history, agriculture required less workers as productivity increased. Furthermore, as the farmer became self-sufficient, he became more dependent on the market and bought, rather than made, the manufactured goods he needed, thereby eliminating the need for home-manufacturing workers. Thus, three things—relatively constant per capita food consumption, increases in agricultural productivity, and a decline in the number of people engaged in home manufacturing—combined to release millions of farm workers for ever-expanding, nonagricultural economic activities.

Higher productivity was, of course, a good thing for society in general; it is the goal which economists urge society to seek, because it is the ladder to a higher scale of living. No doubt, too, improvement in productivity benefited some farmers. It is probably true, however, that it hurt more farmers than it helped. In order to achieve agriculture's rising potential, the individual farmer was forced to make a series of hazardous business decisions. He had to decide how much land to buy and what to plant on high-priced land. He also had to decide whether to use machinery, how much of it to use, when to substitute it for human and animal energy, and whether to buy it, rent it, or use it cooperatively. He had to be more concerned with production functions, that is, putting the factors of production together. In short, he had to be a businessman, and this was not easy.

THE FORCES THAT INDUCED HIGHER PRODUCTIVITY

The problem of mechanizing the farm

The forces that were responsible for burgeoning farm productivity were mechanization; scientific farming, including education, better methods of cultivating soil and handling animals, the use of fertilizers, and disease and pest control; and the government, which disseminated the information.

The so-called "Agricultural Revolution" began at least as early as the 1830s. By the 1850s, most of the elementary farm machinery had appeared: plows, harvesters, the combine, threshers, harrows, and so forth. Yet, in 1850 the typical farm still was not using very much machinery. Then, because of the opening of the vast West, the shortage of labor, the falling price of farm machinery, and, most important of all, the construction of efficient arteries of transportation, it behooved the farmer to use machinery in much greater quantities. In constant dollars, the farmer used 40 times as much machinery in 1960 as in 1850,[12] and the machinery was far better in quality. Between 1850

[12]In 1926 dollars, he owned $200 million in 1850, $4.1 billion in 1930, $3.2 billion in 1940, and $8.7 billion in 1960.

and 1930, the amount of machinery multiplied 20 times. The depression temporarily stalled this march, but after World War II it again doubled. It was estimated in 1900 that a well-managed Northern farm needed $785 worth of tools. By 1970 the average farm owned over $10,000 of farm equipment.

The evolution of power

In the technological evolution, power was almost as important as farm machinery. Indeed, without the power evolution, it would have been quite impossible to develop some of the more elaborate farm equipment.

Oxen and, more frequently, human beings supplied the power used on the colonial and early nineteenth-century farm. Gradually, horses and mules and, to a small extent, steam replaced the slow-moving ox and the tired human being. Then, in the twentieth century, gasoline and electricity rapidly replaced animal energy.

Horses and mules could perform farm work with more speed than oxen, even though they were not so strong. Compared with human beings, however, they were superior in both speed and strength. But the gasoline-driven tractor, which first appeared in 1905, was many times superior in speed and pulling power to both man and animal, besides possessing abilities unknown to either ox, horse, or human being.

One gasoline tractor could replace 20 horses on a wheat farm. Because it did not have to rest, it could be used at any time, thus making possible more thorough and more timely operation. Because it did not consume any products of the farm, it released land that had previously been used to raise food for work animals, thereby enabling the farmer to increase his production for the market. The tractor was also more efficient than the horse in performing such common farm chores as threshing, wood-cutting, ditch-digging, and removing stumps and rocks. It enabled the farmer to plow deeper and work the seed bed more thoroughly. The gasoline-powered truck and the automobile reduced the time of marketing, widened the market area in which the farmer could sell, increased the efficiency of distribution, and made it possible to prolong the hours of work by using labor shifts. Also, gasoline and electricity could be used for jobs that the horse could never accomplish—pumping, grinding, and milking, for example.

With such obvious advantages, it is small wonder that farmers adopted gasoline and electricity as quickly as possible. The only obstacle was lack of capital, and in periods of prosperity this disadvantage became relatively unimportant. In 1910, farmers owned 51,000 tractors, motor trucks, and automobiles. Shortly thereafter, the original tractor that was clumsy and enormously heavy gave place to a smaller, less expensive, and more practical machine. By 1930, farmers owned almost 6 million such machines; and by 1970, over 10 million. Meanwhile, the number of horses and mules decreased correspondingly. In 1910, there were 24 million horses and mules, or almost one for every member of the farm population. By 1930 there were 19 million and in 1960, only 3 million, or one for every five people living on a farm.

Changes in farm size

Each improvement in power and mechanization required for its most efficient use a larger-size farm. Systems of slavery, serfdom, and small, peasant proprietorship relied on human energy; the family-size farm utilized horsepower economically; but only large-scale acreage could justify and permit mechanized mass production of agricultural crops. The American system of land tenure was not completely geared to such large-scale farming. Because of the early shortage of labor and machinery, and because of government land policy, the average-size farm in 1850 was less than 200 acres. After the Civil War, the breakup of the large plantations in the South pushed the size of the average farm down even further. In ten Southern states, the number of farms of less than 100 acres increased by over 50 percent. The average size shrank from 402 to 230 acres in the South and to 130 acres in the country as a whole by 1880. It remained at around 150 acres from 1900 to the Great Depression, when it began to move up sharply. Yet even in 1970, the average of 400 acres was still short of the optimum size for power-driven machinery.[13] Agricultural economists think that there are decided economies of scale up to 260 acres for any kind of farming, and far beyond that for the staple crops. It should be pointed out, however, that diseconomies of scale rise very rapidly once optimum size is passed.

The whole problem of technology confronted the small-scale farmer with a dilemma. Unless he mechanized, he could not produce efficiently or competitively. If he did invest in machinery, he could not use it effectively on his small holdings. In time, various solutions were tried with varying degrees of success. During the three decades following the Civil War, "bonanza farms," huge accumulations of acreage, were organized in the West. At one time there were 29 farms comprising 21 million acres in the area. One owner, operating over 100 square miles, could grow with 400 men what it took 5,000 men to produce in France. Yet the giant farms were not as common as is sometimes supposed. In 1890, there were 428 farms in Iowa and 383 in Illinois of 1,000 acres or more. They were abortive, and most of them turned out to be unsuccessful. By the 1930s, there were only 130 farms in Iowa and 190 in Illinois with 1,000 acres or more. Another solution, tried on a much wider scale, was the renting and cooperative use of machinery. But the cooperative idea was alien to

[13] Tiresome as it may be, it must be emphasized once again that averages are misleading. At mid-century, when the national average was 300 acres, the average in North Carolina was 83; in Kansas, 481; and in Arizona, 5,558.

the American ideal of independence and self-sufficiency and to the average American's admiration for small business. In the long run, therefore, farmers as a whole did not succeed in solving their capital goods dilemma. They did not spend enough on mechanization to achieve optimum productive efficiency, but, on the other hand, more farmers probably failed through over- than underinvestment in machinery.

The rising price of land and the greater use of farm machinery required an ever-larger fixed investment per dollar of output. Indeed, farming ultimately required a larger relative outlay of capital than the investment required in manufacturing. To establish a 200-acre farm in the Old Northwest in 1835 required about $1,500; the investment required for a 1,600-acre cotton plantation in the antebellum South was less than $100,000; but to set up a farm in 1900 on less than $10,000 or in 1960 on less than $50,000 was extremely risky.

More scientific farming

Machines raised the output per man-hour while better use of soil and animals raised the output per acre. Until the twentieth century, however, not much progress was made in raising bigger and fatter animals, and no progress at all was made in making the land yield more. Indeed, it was estimated that the grossly unscientific methods of the American farmer had irreparably damaged one-fifth of the land and badly damaged another one-third. It has been reiterated again and again that this occurred because the farmer was doing what was best for him. Emphasis on per-man production gave him a higher income in the short run than if he had devoted part of his resources to replenishing the soil.

The course of events changed in the early twentieth century; first rather slowly with the recognition that the era of free land was over, then radically, under the impact of government policy which gave the farmer immense incentive to increase the product of his acres. In 1890, farmers used 1.4 million tons of commercial fertilizer. The quantity had doubled by 1900, again by 1910, once more by 1943, and tripled by 1970, when farmers used over 38 million tons. Crops were improved by using better seeds, new plant strains, and disease and insect controls. Insecticides and disease repellents culminated in the development of DDT and sulfa drugs; hybrid seed corn, first introduced in 1929, was planted on 25 percent of corn acreage by 1945 and increased the yield by 15 to 20 percent. In addition, scientists contributed chemicals to remove leaves from cotton plants before picking and to kill potato plants before harvesting; crop dusting by airplane, which cut the cost to less than 10 percent of hand labor; hormones to kill weeds and increase animal fertility; artificial insemination, which made it possible for a bull to father 2,000 calves a year instead of 40; and vitamins to increase the weight of poultry and hogs up to 30 percent.

Government's relation to production and productivity

Before 1850, state governments had given some spiritual and financial support to private attempts to encourage more scientific farming. At the same time, the Federal government, through its land policy, had significantly helped to inflate farm production.

In the late nineteenth century, the state governments continued to encourage better farming. Almost every state, beginning with Connecticut in 1875, added an experiment station to carry on research in plant and animal disease, to develop new seeds and plant forms, and to experiment with new methods of farming.

Gradually the Federal government shifted its position, and in the twentieth century the pattern that was to become characteristic of government intervention was followed in agriculture. As the economy became more complicated, the Federal government seemed to be in a better position than the states to take care of the more complex needs of agriculture, and it gradually supplanted state governments in providing for the farmer's needs. In 1862, Congress created the Department of Agriculture as a service agency. Its functions expanded continuously, and Congress gave it full cabinet status in 1889. Eventually the department became an enormous center of research and a statistical agency for agriculture. The Federal government's new assistance was designed to make the farmer a better producer. Under the Morrill Act, the government gave each state 30,000 acres of land for each of its representatives and senators in Congress, the sales proceeds to be used to establish colleges of agricultural and mechanical arts. A small annual cash subsidy, which was increased by later amendments, accompanied the land grant. Using the state agricultural colleges as a base, the government took steps to encourage scientific agricultural research. Beginning with the Hatch Act of 1887, it gave financial aid to each state to establish an agricultural experiment station. As a direct outgrowth of the experiment stations, it began, in 1902, an active campaign against plant and animal diseases and pests, especially against the boll weevil.

In time, Federal aid to agricultural education was carried to the farmer himself. By the Smith-Lever Act of 1914, extension courses were established for farmers outside the land-grant colleges. The act also created county agents to give advice and help to practicing farmers. The Federal government gave additional positive help to the farmer by providing agricultural credit. To alleviate the farmer's inability to obtain capital funds, it established Federal Farm Loan Banks in 1916 to make mortgage loans to farmers. Later it created Intermediate Credit Banks to discount paper for farm cooperatives, Regional Agricultural Credit Corporations to refund short-term indebtedness, and a system of banking for cooperatives.

THE FARMER'S CAPITAL PROBLEMS

In current dollars, farmers had an investment of about $4 billion in 1850 and about $250 billion in 1970. Total capital investment took place very rapidly up to about 1920 and slowly thereafter. Because the number of farms multiplied faster than the volume of investment, investment per farm fell between 1870 and 1900. It then rose slowly until 1940, and has soared since then.

The amount of investment and the return on investment varied greatly among different crops. The typical investment on a Wisconsin dairy farm is about $36,000, and the return is a little over 10 percent. On a huge wheat farm, the average investment is somewhere around $78,000, but the net income is only $3,000. In cotton production, a typical investment of $12,500 may pay $1,200.

In most cases, the financial resources of the farmer or would-be farmer were far less than the ideal capital outlay required to set up a farm. He therefore had to borrow most of his capital funds, chiefly by mortgaging his land. Farm debt in 1890 was about $1,200 per farm, or about one-third the value of land and buildings. Half the farms in the country were mortgaged, and in the Wheat Belt of the Great Plains there were as many mortgages as there were families. Farm mortgage debt continued to increase until the 1920s, when it passed $10 billion. The farmer's other debts added another $5 billion. Three-quarters of the farms were mortgaged, for the farmer continued to expand by incurring fresh indebtedness.

As long as prices were high, farmers could meet their fixed charges; but when prices declined, the burden of debt increased correspondingly and many farmers were wiped out by foreclosure. In the decade after 1925, almost one-third of all farms changed hands through forced sales, but a large amount of indebtedness was liquidated. Prosperity during World War II reduced farm debt even more, and by 1946 mortgage debt was down to $4.8 billion. Debt increased very rapidly thereafter. Mortgage debt was over $28 billion by 1970, and nonmortgage debt was up to $30 billion. Yet, 60 percent of all farms were mortgage-free and total mortgage debt was equal to only 10 percent of the value of the land.

Although his debt increased almost constantly, the farmer did not find it easy to borrow money, because the money market, by and large, was not geared to making farm loans. Under the early land laws, farmers could buy land from the government on credit. After 1820, when the government insisted on cash payment, land buyers usually borrowed from a state bank. But the state banks declined in number after the Civil War, and the national banks that replaced them were not permitted to make real estate loans. Thus, the supply of funds for agriculture in the post-Civil War era could not keep pace with the farmers' increasing demand.

Nevertheless, the farmer managed to borrow, often at rates exceeding 12 percent. In the South, the economic effects of the lack of capital facilities were most devastating. The Civil War had destroyed the existing banking structure, and nothing was created to take its place. Southern farmers, both the ex-plantation owners and the far more numerous yeoman farmers, found themselves with neither money nor the facilities to raise it. The proprietor of the local country store stepped in to fill the breach. The farmer borrowed from him, pledging his crop as security, while the storekeeper usually borrowed from a Northern factor or commission house. Enormous rates of interest were charged, although they were sometimes disguised by charging the farmer stepped-up prices for the goods he purchased.

In order to protect himself against this highly inefficient system, the store-keeper insisted that the farmer grow the staple Southern crops—cotton, tobacco, and sugar. Thus, the tendency toward a one-crop system that had been discernible in the South before the Civil War was accentuated during Reconstruction, to the detriment of both the farmer and the general economy. The system or lack of system ruined economic incentives. The Southern farmer became a perpetual debtor and, as the years went by, saw no prospect of extricating himself. Each harvest was used to pay off the previous year's debt, and the new crop was planted with the help of new loans. It was said that in the vicious cycle that resulted, the farmer skinned the land, and the landlord skinned the farmer.

In time, as the nation's supply of funds increased and as policymakers came to realize that new solutions for the farmer's problem had to be found, the farmer found it easier to obtain credit. Although the growth of life insurance companies added one new source of borrowing, the Federal government became the chief agent in easing agricultural credit. By the Federal Reserve Act, national banks were permitted to make farm loans, although on a very restricted basis. The Federal Farm Loan Act of 1916 created a source for long-term farm loans, and in 1923 the Federal Intermediate Credit Act provided farm funds for terms of six months to three years. The creation of a system of farm credits enabled the farmer to borrow money as easily as the industrialist, and at the same rates.

The rising price of land and the capital outlay required to operate a mechanized farm prevented many potential farmers from becoming entre-preneurs. They tended instead to become tenant farmers. Even before 1850, leasing farms was not uncommon but thereafter it became a popular activity. Tenants operated one-quarter of the farms in 1880 and over 40 percent in 1930. Thereafter, because of the depression, government policy, and the war, the tide was reversed, and tenancy began to fade. Today, only 20 percent of the farms are so operated. Like all small business, agriculture has been plagued by too many chiefs and not enough Indians, but here again the picture has shown rapid improvement. Not long ago there were four owners for every hired man. The number of hired men has remained about the same, but the number of owners has dropped sharply, so that there are now less than two owners for each hired worker.

Tenancy varied from section to section. It was most prominent in the South and least prominent in New England. Wherever it appeared, however, it impeded economic progress, for the tenant had no incentive to make long-run improvements on a farm that he intended eventually to leave. Sociologically, he did not own property, the American badge of status, and he therefore lacked a sense of security and had no interest in maintaining the stability of society.

THE FARMER'S MARKETING PROBLEMS

The farmer's relatively inferior economic status was as much a result of distribution as of production and consumption. Everything about farming presented a paradox. The average farmer could not use machines efficiently, but without machines he could not compete with his neighbors. Without marketing facilities, farming was an avocation rather than a vocation; but when these facilities appeared, they created new economic problems. The farmer became dependent on "monopolistic middlemen" who took what the farmer thought was more than a fair share of the ultimate price charged the consumer.

As early as colonial times, the tobacco farmer complained because he received only 35 percent of the ultimate sales price. Other commercial farmers fared as badly. But the self-sufficient farmer was probably worse off. Although independent of middlemen, he was doomed to a subsistence existence.

Farmers had high hopes that the railroad would increase their ability to market goods, and, although it accomplished this, it also presented new disadvantages. Where one railroad competed with another, price cutting was fashionable; but where a railroad had a monopoly, it charged all that the traffic would bear. In order to prevent the financial disaster that would be the inevitable outcome of unbridled competition, railroads entered into gentlemen's agreements and pools to fix rates. But these arrangements were loose and intermittently broke down in violent rate wars. Many railroads charged small shippers standard rates while offering substantial rebates to large shippers. Where competition was most intense, rates were cut to the bone, the railroad hoping to balance its losses by charging heavily where it had a monopoly. Consequently, rates for long hauls were very often lower than rates for short hauls. The freight rate from Fargo to Duluth, for example, was double the rate from Minneapolis to Chicago, although the latter distance was twice as far.

The farmer had little sympathy for the railroads and regarded their attempts to solve their difficulties as monopolistic abuses. Initially eager for railroads, he came to resent them bitterly as long- and short-haul discrimination, rebating, and pools became more common in the latter part of the nineteenth century. He also resented the other middlemen in the economy and blamed them for the fact that he was not getting any larger share of the consumer dollar than he had received in colonial days. Ordinarily, he got about 40 cents out of every dollar spent for food, but he got as high as 55 cents during war prosperity and as low as 30 cents in the depression.[14]

THE FARMER'S SOLUTION TO HIS PROBLEMS

As long as prosperity ruled, the farmer maintained his relative position in the economy; and, even though that position was relatively inferior, the farmer, for the most part, accepted his lot without excessive complaint. But when depression came and farm income declined more than other income, the farmer eagerly sought ways and means of solving his suddenly pressing business problems. The effects of prosperity and depression on the farmer's attitude were succinctly expressed in the 1920s: "When corn is $1 a bushel, the farmer is a radical; when it's $1.50 a bushel, he's a progressive; and when it's $2 a bushel, he's a conservative."[15] Basically, he followed three methods: the formation of farm cooperatives, the creation of farm organizations, and reliance on government assistance.

In order to solve the problem of distribution, farmers formed marketing associations or cooperatives. This movement achieved its greatest development after each war. In 1915, there were 5,400 farm business associations with a membership of 650,000 and a business of $636 million. In contrast, by 1925, there were almost 11,000 with a membership of 2.7 million and a business of $2.4 billion. After the 1920s, the number of associations declined, although the membership and dollar volume increased. In 1969, there were 7,700 cooperatives with 6.3 million members, transacting a $7 billion business. Cooperatives were especially successful in highly specialized crops, such as dairy products; on the other hand, although they did a substantial business in grain and livestock, they were unsuccessful in the great staple crops where the difficulties of organizing many widely spread producers were too great to surmount.

It took a long time for the American farmer to consolidate his forces, but in the latter part of the nineteenth century he began to form organizations to protect his interests and to solve his economic problems. During their early history, farmers' organizations did well in periods of extremely depressed business activity but declined as soon as prices began to recover. After the great depression, however, farmers never again lost their enthusiasm for organization,

[14]The percent of the consumer's dollar obtained by the farmer is, of course, not necessarily an indication of the farmer's welfare. In some cases, he does better with products from which he gets a smaller share of the final price.

[15]Quoted by Eric Goldman, *Rendezvous With Destiny* (New York: Alfred A. Knopf, Inc., 1953), p. 298.

and farm groups prospered in periods of great prosperity as well as in periods of agricultural recession.

The first really prominent farm organization, the Patrons of Husbandry, better known as the Grange, was formed shortly after the Civil War. It carried on social and educational activities, formed cooperatives, and lobbied for legislation that would benefit the farmer. Although it had some success in effecting the passage of state legislation regulating the railroads, its political and economic influence had declined by the end of the nineteenth century. The Farmers' Alliance of the 1880s, the second farm organization, was chiefly political and eventually was swallowed up by the Populist Party. The Farmers' Union was founded in 1902 and the American Farm Bureau Federation in 1922. Both had strong political overtones and illustrated the farmer's increasing departure from individualism.

The departure from individualism toward collective action, illustrated by the formation of farmer organizations, was also evidenced by the farmer's changing attitude toward politics and government assistance.[16] During periods of depressed prices in the nineteenth century, farmers were absorbed by political conflict, but they supported indirect, not direct, controls. Being debtors, they were inflationists with an abiding faith in the quantity theory of money. They believed that the government could raise prices through monetary policy and thus solve the agricultural overproduction problem. They therefore lobbied for government action to increase the money supply, either by printing more paper money or by coining free silver. Farmers were the most powerful group in the unsuccessful struggle to increase the amount of greenbacks in circulation at the end of the Civil War. Their supporters constituted the majority in the fight for free silver in the latter nineteenth century and were instrumental in passing the Bland-Allison and Sherman Silver Acts.[17] At various times, they also supported tariffs, such as the McKinley Act of 1890, in the vain belief that protectionism would help them against foreign producers. On the other hand, they gave only halfhearted support to legislation for agricultural education, experiment stations, and disease and pest control.

Monetary measures and tariff bills, however, did not help the farmer, and in time his enthusiasm for them cooled, although he never abandoned them altogether. After World War I, he continued to support easy money and he also supported the Fordney-McCumber tariff, but he switched his main allegiance to direct controls. By then, too, farm organizations were achieving a new prominence as spokesmen for the farmers. The Farmers' Union had a relatively small membership at the end of World War I, but the American Farm Bureau Federation, usually called the Farm Bureau, had a membership of almost 500,000. The

[16]For an exhaustive study of government activities in agriculture, see Murray R. Benedict, *Farm Policies of the United States, 1790-1950* (New York: The Twentieth Century Fund, 1953).

[17]See Chapter 9.

bureau represented the commercial farmer. Initially, it was mainly interested in education and government legislation, but later it became disenchanted with government aid and moved toward a much more conservative position. In the 1920s, the bureau was instrumental in forming the "Farm Bloc," which became a powerful legislative mechanism in the interests of the farmer.

Spokesmen for the farmer believed that the businessman set his prices and fixed his production in a monopolistic market. They proposed to follow his example by modifying the almost purely competitive system under which farmers operated. Because there was little prospect of combining all farmers in a cooperative effort to cut production or to fix prices, spokesmen for the farmer determined to persuade the government to pass legislation fixing farm prices. The Farm Bloc supported the McNary-Haugen bills of the 1920s, which proposed to fix agricultural prices domestically and to dump surpluses on foreign markets at whatever prices they might bring. These bills were passed by Congress but vetoed by the President. In 1929, under the more sympathetic Hoover administration, the government adopted legislation under which loans were made to farm cooperatives against farm crops. No attempt was made, however, to curtail the supply of farm products and the system failed, for the Federal Farm Loan Board, which made the loans, simply became a dumping place for surplus farm commodities.

The failure of the McNary-Haugen bills and the farm loan program merely increased the farmer's demands for direct controls. At the bottom of the depression of the 1930s, he was attempting, through his spokesmen and through the Farm Bloc, to obtain legislation providing both direct controls over farm production and indirect controls, through monetary policy, to raise the general price level. When the administration refused to give him what he wanted, he expressed his dissatisfaction by using force to prevent further mortgage fore-closures and by switching his political allegiance from the Republican Party to the New Deal of Franklin D. Roosevelt.

The New Deal farm program

Early in its history, the New Deal attempted to help the farmer by passing legislation intended to restore "parity prices," that is, prices for farm commodities that would give the farmer the same purchasing power that he had had in the years 1909-1914. The legislation also had other aims, such as encouraging soil conservation and protecting the farmer against natural disaster, but these were incidental to the main goal.

The objective of the Agricultural Adjustment Act of 1933 was to cure the farm problem by cutting the supply of farm commodities by one-third. Under the act, farmers were paid subsidies for reducing their acreage planting of the basic crops. The subsidies were financed through taxes on the processing of farm commodities. On the face of it, the legislation was one of the most inconsistent measures passed during the New Deal. It proposed to assist the farmer by paying him to cut his acreage production, but it financed the subsidies by a processing tax that fell most heavily on low-income groups. The act, therefore, discouraged the increase in demand that other New Deal legislation was trying to encourage.

The first AAA was admittedly stopgap legislation that the administration intended to replace with a more long-range program whenever it was feasible. The precipitating action came when the Supreme Court declared the AAA unconstitutional in 1936 on the ground that a tax to help farmers was not a tax for the general welfare. The administration immediately proposed the Soil Conservation Act, under which the farmer was paid to shift production from soil-depleting to soil-conserving crops. The Soil Conservation Act was expanded in 1938 by the second Agricultural Adjustment Act, or the ever-normal granary plan. Retaining the soil-conservation features of the 1936 legislation, the second AAA proposed to restore parity prices by reducing crops rather than acreage. If the prospective supply of a farm commodity exceeded normal, the Secretary of Agriculture was authorized to proclaim a quota. This quota was translated into acres on the basis of estimated yields per acre. The new measure, therefore, still continued to approach the farm problem through acreage rather than crops, and it could therefore be nullified if yields per acre rose.

The quotas provided for in the 1938 law could not be imposed unless they were accepted by two-thirds of the growers affected. Sales in excess of quotas were taxed heavily; but, if the farmer kept his surplus off the market, he could obtain loans equal to not less than 52 or more than 75 percent of parity. These loans were nonrecourse, noninterest-bearing; that is, they did not have to be repaid and they carried no interest. To protect the farmer against natural disaster, the AAA of 1938 also established a Federal Crop Insurance Corporation under which the farmer was insured for an amount up to a specific percentage of his normal yield. As a further concession to the farmer, various exceptions were written into the law. For wheat, for example, the minimum acreage quota was fixed at 55 million, and farmers growing less than 15 acres of wheat were not included.

The farm program since World War II

During World War II, in order to encourage farmers to increase their production, existing farm legislation was amended by giving farmers the right to obtain loans equal to 90 percent of parity against basic, storable commodities. Thus, if the price of basic farm commodities fell below parity, the Commodity Credit Corporation would step in with a loan that was in essence the same as an outright subsidy. The provision was of no importance during the War, because prices remained high. The provision was to continue for two years after the end of belligerency. This came in 1948, and for the next few years farm legislation was extended with minor changes, the most important of which was the replacement of the 90 percent support price with flexible supports.

By 1956, it was plain even to its most enthusiastic champions that the farm program was something less than perfect. The cost was running at a rate of over $2 billion a year, and before the decade was over it would cost over $22 billion. The Commodity Credit Corporation owned in excess of $7 billion of farm products. The program had not solved the "farm problem," and it could not do so without some effective way of controlling supply. The Eisenhower Administration approached the problem in two ways. In 1956, it proposed, and Congress adopted, a Soil Bank. Farmers were paid for "renting part of their land to the government" and for putting land in a "soil bank" for conservation purposes. Payments were from $10 to $13 an acre, and 28 million acres were taken out of production in 1960.

Meanwhile, Secretary of Agriculture Benson had become more and more convinced that if price supports were lowered, supplies would be cut drastically. He believed, in other words, that the agricultural supply was elastic. Following his theory, the support price for corn in 1960 was set at 90 percent of the average price in 1956-1958, the lowest since World War II. The farmer responded by growing 4.4 billion bushels, the biggest crop on record.

The Kennedy Administration, torn between a desire to help the farmer and a desire to keep the cost of such help at a minimum, made a determined effort to cut the supply. It moved against the most flagrant culprit, wheat. In 1962, Congress drastically amended the wheat program. It removed the 55-million-acre floor. It included the small farmer in the program. It fixed the support price of wheat at $1.30 instead of $2, but provided certificates which gave the farmer a $2 support on part of his acreage. The program was subject to a referendum, and when the votes were counted in 1963, wheat farmers, far from giving it a two-thirds majority, voted against the program. One year later, Congress passed a new law providing for $1 billion in subsidies to wheat and cotton raisers. In 1970, the farm program was again weakened. Although total subsidies ($3.8 billion) would remain the same as they had been in 1969, payments to any one farm were limited to $55,000 a year, more acres were to be "set aside" from production, and minimum price supports were reduced to $1.25 for wheat, $1 for corn, and 35 cents or 65 percent of parity for cotton. The bill passed the Senate, 48 to 35.[18]

At best, the solution of the "farm problem" through government action was far from satisfactory. It did not cut production, for farmers offset acreage controls with increased productivity. It was not of much help to the 10 percent at the bottom of agriculture who make up almost one-quarter of America's nonaffluent. They grew too little to be helped very much by price supports. On

---

[18]By an act of August 1973, direct price subsidies were ended to be replaced by government payments to farmers if prices fell below "target" prices set in the law.

the other hand, large operators, like the Mississippi State Penitentiary, received what many people considered huge loans—in cotton, as high as $900,000, and in wheat, in excess of $300,000. Government price supports for agriculture meant supporting a declining industry, for every shift from agriculture to manufacturing to service raised the national income and increased the level of living. Economically, therefore, it was not an ideal method of using resources. When emphasis shifted to stabilization, the result was to create an obstacle in the way of economic growth, for economic growth means more production, whereas the agricultural program not only meant less production, but also a shift of income from producers to nonproducers. In the international market, this was especially bad, for it damaged our competitive position. Socially, it also left much to be desired. There was the general dissatisfaction because of the illusion that the program was making the rich richer. There was also the dissatisfaction of the great mass of the urban population who insisted that they were paying the bill through increased taxation.

Despite all its faults, the program was not a one-way street of disadvantages. The program certainly encouraged the farmer to raise per-acre yields. It also helped to push reluctant farmers from less economic to more economic pursuits. Cotton was a case in point. Partly because of the control program, the price of cotton raced upward. The foreign market fell in half, and farmers shifted production to livestock and other crops. The assassination of King Cotton may, however, have been a good thing, for raising livestock brought a better return than raising cotton.

Some economists defended the program on the ground that, in the absence of subsidies, farm purchasing power would decline and reduce the demand for industrial products. Still others argued that, in the absence of subsidies, farmers would be forced out of agriculture and would not be able to find employment elsewhere. A third argument, completely outside of economics, was that it was necessary to have ample amounts of farm products to maintain a great degree of self-sufficiency for purposes of military security. If the farm program reflected a conflict between economic values and survival values, only one solution was possible: the needs of survival had to take precedence even if it meant a relatively lower level of living.

SUGGESTED READINGS

(On specific topics, see the readings cited in the footnotes in the chapter.)

Bentley, Arthur F., *The Condition of the Western Farmer* (Baltimore: The Johns Hopkins University, 1893). Reprinted in Sigmund Diamond, ed., *The Nation Transformed* (New York: George Braziller, Inc., 1963).

Bidwell, Percy W., and John J. Falconer, *History of Agriculture in the Northern United States, 1620-1860* (Washington, D. C.: The Carnegie Institution, 1925).

Danhof, Clarence H., *Change in Agriculture: The Northern United States, 1820-1870* (Cambridge, Mass.: Harvard University Press, 1969).

Edwards, E. E., "American Agriculture—The First 300 Years," *Yearbook of Agriculture* (Washington, D. C.: Government Printing Office, 1940).

Gates, Paul W., *The Farmer's Age: Agriculture, 1815-1860* (New York: Holt, Rinehart, & Winston, Inc., 1960).

Gray, Lewis Cecil, *History of Agriculture in the Southern United States to 1860.* (Washington, D. C.: The Carnegie Institution, 1918).

Hutchinson, William T., *Cyrus Hall McCormick* (New York: Appleton-Century-Crofts, 1930-1935).

Meij, J. L., ed., *Mechanization in Agriculture* (Chicago: Quadrangle Books, 1960), Chapters 1, 3, 4.

Rogin, Leo, *The Introduction of Farm Machinery* (Berkeley: University of California Press, 1931).

Shannon, Fred A., *The Farmer's Last Frontier* (New York: Holt, Rinehart & Winston, Inc., 1945).

QUESTIONS

1. What is meant by the statement that in the early nineteenth century American agriculture was dynamic, self-sufficient, extensive, and a way of life; thereafter, it became more static, more commercialized, less extensive, and more of a business?

2. (a) What do you understand by the "commercialization" of agriculture?
   (b) Why did it take place?
   (c) How did it affect the susceptibility of the farmer to changes?

3. The farmer has complained that he has always received less than his fair share of the fruits of economic progress. Do you agree? Why?

4. "More and more, each section restricted its production to those products for which it was best adapted." What does this mean, and why did it happen?

5. Do you think that slavery paid? Why, or why not? In view of the defects of the slave system, how do you explain the success of the plantation system?

6. What agricultural conditions stimulated the invention and adoption of farm machinery?

7. Explain carefully what problems of agricultural economics each of the following solves: (a) the cotton gin, (b) the plow, (c) the reaper.

8. Today the farmer has as many business problems as the urban industrialist. What forces created these problems?

9. How did government land policy and war influence the farmer's economic position?

10. What are the similarities and differences between the economic problems of the late nineteenth-century farmer and those of today's farmer? To what factors do you attribute the agricultural distress between 1866 and 1897? What other explanation did the farmer give? What practical acts did they promote to carry out their ideas?

11. Why have farmers been unhappy during declines in the price level? What have they tried to do about it? Discuss with references to the periods after the Civil War and World War I.

12. How did the New Deal attack the farm problem?

13. Discuss the historical factors that have given rise to the present government policy of giving financial assistance to the farmer.

14. A European economist once said that exports of American farm products after the Civil War had far greater effects on the European economy than the silver exports of the sixteenth century. Why did he think that farm exports at the end of the Civil War were so extraordinarily important?

Chapter Six

THE CONTRIBUTIONS
OF BUSINESS ENTERPRISE
TO THE AMERICAN ECONOMY

In American economic history, the protagonist was the business entrepreneur, not the statesman, the military leader, or the intellectual. From its beginnings, the United States was devoted to the business ideal. Business influenced the American's habits, customs, manners, folklore, and way of thinking much more than politics, philosophy, or religion. The American spirit was a business spirit; the American system was a business system. The business game was always a pervasive feature of American culture, because it was so intimately related to our way of life. Even the farmer, as we have seen, and the labor union, as we shall see, were imbued with the business spirit.

Henry Seidel Canby, the critic, recalled that in his boyhood days in Delaware, the businessman was the most admired member of the community. If occupations had been graded, the radical thinker would rate an E; the contented idler, D; the deeply religious person, scientist, or journalist, C; a good parent, an honest man, or a good retail salesman, B; a wholesale salesman, A; and a first-rate businessman, A plus. "Business," said Canby, "was much more than an occupation—it was a philosophy, a morality, and an atmosphere."[1]

Polticians and statesmen, from the pragmatic city boss to the intellectual liberal, recognized this very well. Richard Croker, the leader of Tammany Hall in the 1890s, told Lincoln Steffens, "Everything is business." Calvin Coolidge expressed the idea

[1]Quoted in Eric Goldman, *Rendezvous with Destiny* (New York: Alfred A. Knopf, Inc., 1953).

better in his oft-quoted: "America's business is business." And according to Woodrow Wilson, "Business underlies everything in our national life."

President Wilson has never been included in the list of staunch champions of the business system. But no person influential in political life, at least since 1830, has been anti-business. A great many, indeed the majority, have been anti-big-business, but this has been more than offset by a vociferous championship of small business. Even William Jennings Bryan, orator for the agrarian left, was not anti-business. In his famous Cross of Gold speech, he made it clear that he was only trying to draw the business circle a little larger than was customary.

In a society in which economic values loomed very large, these expressions were not odd. For throughout most of American history, the businessman in commerce, industry, and finance more than anyone else made the decisions that determined the trend and the speed of economic development and growth. In the terminology of the economist, it was the businessman who determined the production function; it was he who combined the other factors of production and decided how resources were to be allocated. To the student of management, it was the function of the businessman to manipulate the seven Ms of management: Men, Methods, Money, Machines, Materials, Management, and Marketing. In a word, it was the businessman who determined the volume of production, the quantity of investment, and, in the last analysis, the extent of technological development.

But it has been argued that these decisions were made for him by forces beyond his control. Like any other factor of production, the businessman was an impotent creature of market forces. It was not really he who determined the mix of resources. He hired as much labor, borrowed as much capital, and used as much raw material as was required to produce what the market demanded. If this were true, it would also be true—and some people insist it is true—that any chimpanzee could run a business.[2] But this would not explain why some businessmen were vastly successful and others failed, why some consistently made money and others did not.

To be sure, economic change was fundamental in changing business behavior. Every successful businessman had to adjust himself and his business to changes in the economic structure. The most successful readily adapted their business tactics and institutions to the requirements of such exogenous factors as population growth, technological progress, and the expansion of the market area. Businessmen built large-scale enterprises, evolved new forms of business organization, and transformed the managerial structure. All this was done within the context of an economy run by market forces. But this is not the same as

---

[2]Twenty years ago, Joseph Schumpeter prophesied that eventually the entrepreneurial function would be taken for granted. *Capitalism, Socialism, and Democracy* (New York: Harper & Row, Publishers, 1946). Ironically, it is the emphasis on the market forces which he so much admired that is contributing to this downgrading of the entrepreneur.

saying that businessmen were mere puppets operated by the strings of market forces. Some were mere puppets, but others shaped and reshaped business enterprise by making major decisions and influencing the external environment.

As every student should know, generalizations are booby traps for the unwary and snares for the naive. The notion of a business class in the sense of a solid phalanx of businessmen sharing a unanimous ideology, behaving in much the same way, and exerting much the same influence is a myth. Businessmen have differed from each other in the influence they have exerted just as much as they have differed in appearance. Only a small fraction of the total number of businessmen have been in a position of being able to change the economy. A quick look at the United States Census will illustrate this. In 1960, there were about 4,500,000 business firms in the country. Less than 3 percent employed 50 or more employees, and about 1 percent employed 100 or more. If the yardsticks were adjusted for the changing size of the economy, it is probably true that this same small percentage would be seen to have prevailed in the past. It is on the businessmen who led these comparatively few firms that economic historians concentrate as they describe what happened in business history.

Businessmen have also differed in their philosophy and behavior. The big businessman in manufacturing did not share the opinions of the great merchant, and neither shared the opinions of the banker. The owners of "small business," the anonymous managers of large- and medium-sized businesses, and the even more anonymous little businessmen, ranging from the delicatessen store owner in the large city to the trading-post proprietor in the Southwest, did not behave in the same way or believe in the same things. Admittedly, all businessmen extolled the middle-class virtues of self-reliance, hard work, and frugality. All of them urged conformity to traditional social mores. But beyond these few glittering, vague, but important generalities, unanimity ended. The outstanding entrepreneurs, that is, the businessmen with whom we are concerned, differed from the run-of-the-mill businessmen in that they did new things or did old things in a new way. In their business practices, they showed little reverence for traditional ways of doing things.[3] In their deviant behavior, they reacted upon the external environment just as the external environment reacted upon them. Thus, change in the business environment was precipitated by both internal and external forces. It is the purpose of this chapter to summarize the course of this change.

[3]See Arthur H. Cole, "An Approach to the Study of Entrepreneurship," Supplement to the *Journal of Economic History,* Vol. VI (1946); Joseph A. Schumpeter, "The Creative Response in Economic History," *Journal of Economic History,* Vol. VII (1947); Werner Sombart, "Capitalism," *The Encyclopedia of Social Sciences* (New York: The Macmillan Company, 1930). On the deviant behavior of the business leader, see Thomas C. Cochran, "Role and Sanction in American Entrepreneurial History," in *Change and the Entrepreneur* (Cambridge, Mass.: Harvard University Press, 1949).

THREE THEORIES OF BUSINESS HISTORY

The late Professor N. S. B. Gras some 30 years ago formulated what is probably the most widely known theory of business history. The Gras theory is a stages theory, in which each stage was dominated by a distinctive type of businessman.[4] The metamorphosis from one stage to the next came less as a result of human action than of market forces and changes in the external environment, such as wars, competition, and long-wave movements in prices and business activity. The entrepreneur was an important, but somewhat passive figure who took advantage of the economic forces that controlled human life. Although Gras would have been shocked by the judgment, his theory was heavily deterministic and resembled the models spun by Karl Marx and, more especially, by Werner Sombart.

According to Gras, early business was dominated by the "petty capitalist," by whom Gras meant the small businessman, i.e., the peddler, the traveling merchant, the country store proprietor, and the town and village artisan. In time economic change bypassed the petty capitalist, and his dominant position was usurped by the sedentary merchant, who specialized in exporting, importing, and wholesale and retail trade, but who also had a small or large interest in every kind of business in the late eighteenth and early nineteenth century. He was a diversified entrepreneur and, as such, he could not cope with the business problems that arose as American manufacturing came of age. What was required was a specialized entrepreneur, not a jack-of-all-trades. This specialist appeared in the person of the industrial capitalist, who concentrated on production and dominated business life in the middle years of the 1800s. He, in turn, lost his eminent position as a consequence of the constant seesaw between specialization and diversification. In the 1890s, or thereabouts, the finance capitalist, the banker with multitudinous interests, took over the dominant position in a world that required law and order instead of the competitive chaos spawned by the industrialist.

Like all stages theories, the Gras thesis is much too neat. As with all sweeping generalizations, there were many significant exceptions to the general rule. But Gras was not describing all businessmen or even a modal businessman. He was attempting to isolate the dominant businessman at different periods of time and the dates he used were deliberately vague. It could be said that what he was describing were the arithmetic means of a series of standard deviations. As such, his model is a handy tool of description.

[4]N.S.B. Gras and Henrietta M. Larson, *Casebook in American Business History* (New York: Appleton-Century-Crofts, 1939), pp. 3-15; N.S.B. Gras, "Capitalism," reprinted in Frederic C. Lane and Jelle C. Riemersma, eds., *Enterprise and Secular Change* (Homewood, Ill.: Richard D. Irwin, In.c, 1953); Alfred D. Chandler, Jr., *Strategy and Structure: Chapters in the History of the Industrial Enterprise* (Cambridge, Mass.: Massachusetts Institute of Technology Press, 1962).

Arthur H. Cole has suggested an entirely different theory of business history, in which the entrepreneur dominated the process of change and the external environment was relatively unimportant. Cole suggested that entrepreneurship had traveled through a series of categories: empirical, or rule-of-thumb, entrepreneurship; rational, or informed, entrepreneurship; and cognitive, or sophisticated, entrepreneurship. The differences among the three were largely a matter of the breadth of knowledge a businessman could gain and the span of operations he had to oversee. "The business leader of modern decades," wrote Cole, "not only must know more facts about more subjects . . . synthesize more appraisals of experts and advisors, and be cognizant of more services from more service institutions, but he must relate his decisions to a longer time space of past and future."

Gras viewed business history as the history of the subjects taught in schools of business. Cole thought in terms of the businessman's expanding range of knowledge and information. Alfred D. Chandler, Jr., who in recent years has written extensively on business history, concentrates on business management, or, more accurately, on the decision-making process in the successful company.

Chandler's thesis is that in the successful firm, structure must follow strategy. Strategy is defined as "the determination of long-term goals and objectives, and the adoption of courses of action, and the allocation of resources for carrying out these goals." Structure is "the degree of organization through which the enterprise is administered."

In the early years, the business firm handled a single product and a single function. It marketed its products through a wholesaler or commission merchant, and it did not control the sources of its raw materials. To be sure, the phrase "single function" should not be taken too literally. It really meant that the firm concentrated on one function and as far as possible left the others to independent enterprises.

Population growth, urbanization, economic crises, and technological development, especially the railroad and new types of power, put great pressure on industrial firms and their executives. If they were to continue to be successful they would have to keep their resources fully employed. They therefore had no choice but to adopt a strategy of expansion in order to assure more satisfying marketing facilities or to have more certain supplies in order to employ more fully existing plant and personnel.

In the last part of the nineteenth century, aggressive entrepreneurs, dissatisfied with the ways in which outsiders were marketing their goods and encouraged to expand because of external influences, began to integrate vertically. They changed from single-product, single-function companies to single-product, multifunction companies. In the process they freed themselves from dependence on wholesalers and raw material producers. At the same time they began to spread out geographically by creating field offices to take care of the widening market area. Administration now had to be carried on at two levels instead of one—at general headquarters and in the field offices. The structure or organization had to be changed to fit the new strategy if the firm was to continue to be successful.

In reshuffling the organization, manufacturing industry had an excellent model to follow in the railroads, which as the first really big business, had long since altered their structure to fit the strategy of expansion.

Like the railroad leaders, far-sighted industrialists soon learned that a departmentalized structure best fitted the multifunction company that strategy had produced. In the last of the nineteenth century, most large industrial firms were operating under such a structure. The tendency was also toward a more centralized organization, either in individual top executives or in centrally located committees. Chandler points out that these changes were not adopted universally, and when they were adopted, it was gradually and under considerable pressure. It was faltering demand, for example, that forced firms into adopting centralized inventory control, coordination of production to demand, and budget and capital appropriation procedures. All of this in turn tended to confine the top executives to overall planning and to separate them from day-to-day operations.

Yet there were glaring weaknesses in the departmentalized, centralized structure. The empire builders who had created the firm were unable to mind their own business. Instead of concentrating on entrepreneurial activities, they constantly interfered in day-to-day operations. Decision making was very often a matter of negotiation between departments, each supporting its own interest instead of the interest of the firm itself.

These weaknesses were not crippling so long as business did not expand in new ways and forms. But business growth is a continuous process. Firms continued to be forced to expand under the pressure of external economic forces and the drive of the aggressive entrepreneur. Strategy had to change so that resources might continue to be used to the fullest extent. In the twentieth century, as firms reached the limit of the existing market, some of their executives began to reach out to new and entirely different markets or to new and entirely different products. Thus the basic change in strategy was toward diversification of product and toward the extension of the market area internationally.

The change in strategy made obsolete the departmentalized structure which had been successful in the multifunction, single-product company. Diversification required a new structure. The multifunction, multiproduct company required a divisionalized, decentralized administration, rather than a departmentalized, centralized administration. To be sure it took an economic crisis to persuade even the innovators to adopt the change, but it was done. What emerged was a four-tier structure. A general office decided upon long-range goals and policies. A central office handled divisions. The department headquarters supervised the departments within the divisions. The field units—sales, plant, and so on—took care of nothing but day-to-day operations.

Chandler's thesis may be summed up by reemphasizing the importance of the market. Those companies that sold semifinished products to a relatively few large customers required a simple structure. Those that sold a larger variety of one major line consistently centralized their activities. Those that made and sold different lines for increasingly differentiated groups of customers turned to multidivisional structures.

But these rules applied to the successful firms, and not all firms were successful. Some were not willing to adopt their structures to their strategy of expansion. The primary reason for this was the inertia of their chief executive or executives. In general, the firms whose control remained within the family were slow to adopt organizational change; individualistic, empire-building entrepreneurs resisted change; and the first professional managers, who were specialists rather than generalists, were not interested in change.

In the Chandler model, technology, the market, and the personality of the entrepreneur were of ultimate importance. Other factors faded into the background. This is especially true of government behavior: "The market, the nature of their resources, and their entrepreneurial talents have, with relatively few exceptions, had far more effect on the history of large industrial firms than have antitrust laws, taxation, labor and welfare legislation, and comparable evidences of public policy."

In the pages that follow, it would be well to keep these three theories in mind, for each provided a framework for what happened in business history.

BUSINESS ENTREPRENEURSHIP IN THE PRE-RAILROAD ERA[5]

During most of the colonial period, petty capitalism—that is, extremely small business—dominated the American business scene. Most American businessmen were peddlers, blacksmiths, and small shopkeepers. They operated as sole proprietors, for they had no need for partners or stockholders in hawking their wares or in serving a closely confined town community. Here and there, however, some businesses were beginning to expand. Goods had to be imported from abroad and distributed to a market area that was constantly growing. Ordinarily, the petty capitalist did not have the capital or the acumen necessary to cope with the needs of the widening market. Although he never disappeared,

---

[5]A footnote cannot encompass the immense literature on the histories of firms and industries and the biographies of businessmen. There are three valuable bibliographies: Henrietta M. Larson, *Guide to Business History* (Cambridge, Mass.: Harvard University Press, 1948); Lorna Daniells, *Studies in Enterprise* (Cambridge, Mass.: Harvard University Press, 1957). An annual addition to the latter appeared in the *Business History Reviews,* 1959-64; Robert W. Lovett, *American Economic and Business History Information Sources* (Detroit, Mich.: Gale Research Company, 1971). An article by Ralph W. Hidy (*Business History Review,* Vol. XLIV (1970) brings the literature up to date.

his place of dominance was quickly taken over by a group of versatile merchants who were better able to take care of the international, metropolitan economy that the colonies had become as an important part of the British Empire.

There came into existence in the cities large retail "general stores," as well as shipping, brokerage, and wholesale houses owned and operated by merchants who directed from their countinghouses far-flung shipping and trading enterprises. The era of this merchant entrepreneur spanned the century from about 1750 to about 1850. Thomas Hancock, Stephen Girard, and John Jacob Astor were merchant capitalists, and so were the Darbys, Cabots, Higginsons, Livingstons, Beekmans, Roosevelts, Crowninshields, and many others. Shortly before the Revolution, there were at least 100 leading merchants in each of the three big cities, Philadelphia, Boston, and New York, and 50 in Newport and Charleston.

These merchants were not business specialists. Most of them sought to create the kind of life that they thought existed in England; they desired to become landed aristocrats. For the most part, they were engaged in foreign trade, but they could not confine themselves to only one slice of business, because they served a small, widely scattered population; transportation was poor; there was a chronic shortage of specie; and it was difficult to find a cargo for England. If they wished to be fully employed, they were forced to diversify their activities by carrying on wholesale and retail trade, warehousing, insurance, brokerage, banking, and occasionally, investing in manufacturing. The career of Thomas Hancock, probably the leading colonial merchant, was typical. He began as a bookseller, but he constantly broadened his activities, and at the height of his prosperity, he was involved in every type of business activity. He was a merchant and a shipper. He provided an informal mail service and did some banking. He was constantly concerned with bills of exchange and the other complications of foreign trade. He dabbled in manufacturing and played an important role in the whale-oil industry. As a supplier for the British army, he made windfall profits in the eternal wars with the French.[6]

Although the merchant's business interests were varied and prosperous, they were still on a small scale and required nothing more than a simple organization. Sixty-one of the members of the New York Chamber of Commerce in 1775 were partnerships and 43 were sole proprietorships. Operations were carried on within a closely knit, extended-kinship family structure,[7] for, in the Age of Reason,

[6]See Virginia D. Harrington, *The New York Merchant on the Eve of the Revolution* (New York: Columbia University Press, 1935); W. T. Baxter, *The House of Hancock* (Cambridge, Mass.: Harvard University Press, 1945).

[7]See the essay by Robert K. Lamb, 'The Entrepreneur and the Communty," in William Miller, ed., *Men in Business* (Cambridge, Mass.: Harvard University Press, 1952). For the importance of family relations with English merchants, see Bernard Bailyn, *The New England Merchants in the Seventeenth Century* (Cambridge, Mass.: Harvard University Press, 1955), p. 35.

nepotism had many more advantages than disadvantages. The corporate form of organization, which could bring outsiders into the business, held no fascination for the merchants. They were more interested in preserving public faith and retaining their decision-making powers than in maintaining continuity, ensuring limited liability, and obtaining large capital resources.

In the merchant's counting house, there was no need for business administration as we know it today. A simple line organization was more than adequate to treat the relatively uncomplicated problems that might arise. At most, five or six people occupied the office: a clerk or two to keep the books, to wait on customers, and to write an occasional letter; an apprentice or two to do the chores and learn the business; and the owner himself, who made decisions, sought new business, collected bills, and communicated with customers and competitors at the coffee house or the exchange. The profuse ancillary institutions that serve business today were hardly known in the early years of the American economy. Of course, lawyers were prominent, but many of them were directly involved in a mercantile business. There were insurance companies to underwrite the more obvious disasters, but there were no business advisory services, no management consultants, public relations men, and the like. Even banks did not exist until the 1780s and 1790s, and accounting was extremely primitive. Crude single entry was the rule, trial balances were impossible, gross mathematical errors were common, balanced statements were drawn up only on special occasions, and, of course, there were no public accountants. But the merchant really did not need any advanced accounting. At most, he handled 40 transactions a day. On such small-scale operations, accounting could not fulfill its primary purpose of enabling him to make or save more money. The merchant knew where he had been and he needed no accountant to tell him where he was going. The second important function of accounting—to act as a means of control over what one cannot personally see—was equally wasted on the merchant. He needed no substitute for on-the-spot observation, for he was always on the spot and he was required to answer to no one but himself.

Despite the fact that he was a jack-of-all-trades, the early merchant did not work very hard. Typically, he wrote four to six letters a week. Hancock, whose sales averaged 15 a week, wrote only a few more than 60 letters a year, hardly a killing rate of correspondence.[8] Even at a later date, when the tempo had accelerated and there was more business to be done and more money to be made, successful merchants were not slaves to their offices. John Jacob Astor, for example, could rarely be found in the business community after two o'clock.

Because he could not specialize, the merchant's capital requirements were two to four times as much as those of his English counterpart. Yet it did not require much more than $5,000 to become a merchant of some standing; and

---

[8]See the interesting article by Arthur H. Cole, "The Tempo of Mercantile Life in Colonial America," *Business History Review,* Vol. XXXIII (1959).

even on a small capital, there were promising possibilities of amassing a fortune. In the late Colonial Period, Thomas Hancock, Oliver DeLancy, and Colonel Bayard were worth $200,000 to $300,000 each. A quasi-census of wealth taken at Newport in 1761 estimated merchant holdings to be worth on the order of $12 million, three-quarters of which was inventory.[9] It is certain that the merchants in larger cities had amassed an even greater estate. From this rapid accumulation of fortunes, we may infer that the rate of economic growth in the Colonial Period must have been considerably higher than average.

Because the merchants could use only a limited amount of capital in their main business, they could not plow back much of their profits. Yet, wedded as they were to the Puritan ethic, they could neither retire nor waste their substance in riotous living. They therefore launched their sizable capital funds into varied outside investment.[10] Then, as later, the businessman's need for a place for his multiplying resources was one of the main reasons for the constant metamorphosis of business enterprise.

Much of the merchant's wealth went into real estate. There were a few exceptions in New York, but it was only in New England that the deviations were very significant. Even before the Revolution, New England capital had already begun to pour out of trade and into manufacturing and finance. The four Brown Brothers, Providence merchants, were deep in manufacturing spermaceti candles by the early 1760s, and less than 30 years later the family launched Samuel Slater on the road to fortune in cotton-textile manufacture. But there was no really large-scale manufacture and no factory, in the true sense of the word, until the interruption of international trade that came with the War of 1812. Then a group of 15 families, the Boston Associates, organized the Boston Manufacturing Company in 1814. During the next century, the merchant fortunes mobilized in Boston would feed New England manufacturing, Michigan mining, western railroads, southern utilities, and much else that needed the nourishment that money gives.

The concentration of capital that was taking place in the early nineteenth century brought into being some large-scale enterprise in manufacturing and transportation. But it is well to emphasize that this change occurred very slowly before 1820, somewhat less slowly between 1820 and 1840, and more rapidly thereafter. At the middle of the century, big business was still a rare phenomenon. Almost all industrial firms were agriculturally oriented and dealt in a small, localized market. They produced a single product and handled a single function—manufacturing. They procured their raw materials from an inde-

[9]Carl Bridenbaugh, *Cities in the Wilderness* (New York: Alfred A. Knopf, Inc., 1938) and *Cities in Revolt, 1743-1776* (New York: Alfred A. Knopf, Inc., 1956) contain much interesting material on the colonial merchant.

[10]Colonial merchants were not overwhelmed by a flood of capital, but what they had was apparently enough to meet their needs. See Robert A. East, *Business Enterprise in the American Revolutionary Era* (New York: Columbia University Press, 1938).

pendent organization and marketed their product through sales agents, commission merchants, distributors, and other outsiders.

BUSINESS ENTERPRISE IN THE LATE NINETEENTH CENTURY

The railroad, urbanization, and industrialism

As the economy continued to grow, new conditions created a need for new forms of business leadership. The building of a railroad network immeasurably widened the market area. Technological progress diminished the relative economic importance of agriculture and, along with the continued increase in population, accelerated the growth of cities. In 1850, there were less than 10,000 miles of railroad, and only 15 percent of the population lived in cities. By 1870, there were over 50,000 miles of railroad and 25 percent of the population lived in cities. Mass production, mass marketing, and mass consumption were now possible; but, to make the most of its opportunities, industrialism required a system of business enterprise that would go beyond the techniques of trade and small-scale production to include techniques for expanding business plant, for mass marketing, for financing large-scale business, and for supervising a large labor force. As Alfred Chandler has put it, technological achievement, population shifts, and the need to utilize resources led to fundamental changes in the strategy and structure of business.

To fill this need, the industrial capitalist appeared[11] and took over the dominant position formerly occupied by the merchant. It is possible to draw a composite portrait of this industrial capitalist. To be sure, few, if any, businessmen possessed all of his attributes in an unqualified fashion, but the great empire builders—Carnegie, General Henry DuPont, Duke, Ford, McCormick, Rockefeller, Swift, Westinghouse, and the like—did not differ greatly from the prototype. Those who conformed most closely had magnificent strengths, but they also possessed some magnificent weaknesses. Their financial policies brought many of them very close to disaster. They underestimated the value of carefully formulated managerial practices—a weakness which ultimately made it impossible for them to adjust to new economic circumstances and to new business needs, just as many merchants found it impossible to adapt themselves to rapid economic growth. But, on the other hand, their abilities in production enabled them to fill an untapped market in an incredibly short span of years. This

---

[11] "Industrial capitalist" is N. S. B. Gras' term. He has also been called "empire builder," "heroic entrepreneur," and "robber baron" by those who have viewed him in a friendly, neutral, or hostile fashion. By whatever name he is called, he had certain characteristics and represented a composite of the influential entrepreneurs of the era, but never the entire business universe.

multiplication of production at consistently declining prices contributed in no uncertain fashion to economic growth and a rising scale of living. Andrew Carnegie's performance in the steel business affords an excellent illustration of what the industrial capitalist accomplished. In 1872, just before Carnegie and his partners opened the Edgar Thomson works, the United States produced less than 100,000 tons of steel; 25 years later, the Carnegie enterprises had so thoroughly taken advantage of the conditions produced by market forces that they turned out 4 million tons of steel, almost half of total American production, and prices had dropped from $65 to $20 a ton.

The industrialist had the peculiar abilities that were required to exploit an expanding, largely virgin market. He was primarily a specialist who, in the words of Carnegie, put all his eggs in one basket and then watched the basket. His talents and interests were chiefly in production, to a lesser extent in marketing, still less in management, and practically nonexistent in corporation finance.

Like most human beings, businessmen in general were not enthusiastic about change. They were reluctant to replace obsolete equipment if the product was satisfactory. The temptation to save the heavy cost of drastic change was very great indeed. Even the business leaders were no radical exceptions to this generalization. They were not always the first to accomplish technological innovation. McCormick, for example, was very late in manufacturing a good mower, and Carnegie apparently expressed what most industrialists believed when he said that pioneering doesn't pay. But once they decided on a policy, they pushed it with all the vigor of their disciplined determination and ample resources. "In no other country," it was said, "has skill in the organization and administration of productive enterprises been so highly developed as in the United States. Our 'captains of industry' are quick but sure in their judgments, self-reliant, and of boundless energy. They are less conservative than their competitors abroad, more ready to seize upon improved methods, and to incur risks where there is a fair chance of conspicuous success."[1 2]

The industrialist was more concerned with increasing supply than with increasing demand. Indeed, operating in a virgin market, he often took demand for granted. Typical was Henry Ford's well-known comment that a customer could have any color car as long as it was black. If he started on a small scale without benefit of family as some of the most successful did, the late-nineteenth-century entrepreneur's chief problem was raising capital. He borrowed from whatever source he could, from relatives, friends, small town bankers, big city bankers, international investment bankers, and life insurance companies. Yet he had a chronic distrust of the financial world and financial mechanisms, such as the stock exchange, a proliferation of different kinds of securities, and earnings per share. He thought a stockholder, again to quote Henry Ford, was a

[1 2]W. Paul Strassmann, *Risk and Technological Innovation* (Ithaca, N.Y.: Cornell University Press, 1959); *Report of the Industrial Commission*, 1902, Vol. 19, p. 519.

man who bet his money on other people's brains. He plowed earnings back into the business, and if he was successful in business, he himself became a source of capital. John D. Rockefeller, for example, became a fount of capital funds equal to a large city bank.

The individualistic, successful owner-entrepreneur believed in centralized authority and did his best within the limits of human capability to run a so-called "one-man business." He was an optimistic, nonintellectual hunch player, who scoffed at managerial theory. He regarded all office work except accounting with contempt. He maintained a paternalistic attitude toward his employees and gave almost no thought to public relations. Although he probably had never heard of it, the philosophy of Social Darwinism was at the root of his social code; he believed that economic life was governed by the principle of survival of the fittest and the operation of inexorable economic laws. He thoroughly distrusted government officeholders. He doubted the wisdom, honesty, and efficiency of politicians, and thought that "there was never anything more absurd and ridiculous than that prosperity can be brought to a country by legislation." In the hierarchy of his values, the interests of his business came first, and "he had no duty or right to sacrifice that for anything or anybody." Although the profit motive loomed large in his thinking and behavior, he also had an immense drive for accomplishment and an exaggerated power complex. He was, therefore, respected and heartily disliked by those who did not have his ambition or, perhaps, his ability. Willis L. King of Jones and Laughlin thought that Carnegie had done more than any other man to improve the practice of steel making, but "his unreasonable competition was childish and against public policy."[13]

The Alger legend

Until recently, the typical businessman of the nineteenth century has been portrayed as a poor boy who rose to success in Horatio Alger fashion through intense work and painful experience in the school of hard knocks. A moment's reflection must lead one to conclude that it would be a strange state of affairs if this were true. It would be an irrational world indeed if those who had every advantage of wealth, education, and prestige would be less successful than those who started from less fortunate circumstances. In any event, students who have closely examined this once widely held view have demonstrated that it is largely a legend. "Poor immigrant and poor farm boys who became business leaders,"

---

[13]The most systematic attempt to analyze the beliefs and opinions of the nineteenth-century entrepreneur is Thomas C. Cochran, *Railroad Leaders, 1845-1890: The Business Mind in Action* (Cambridge, Mass.: Harvard University Press, 1953). The King quotation is from Strassmann, *op. cit.*, p. 46.

wrote William Miller, "have always been more conspicuous in American history books than in the American business elite."[14] According to Gregory and Neu, the successful businessman of the 1870s was usually "American by birth, of a New England father, English in national origin, urban in early environment, born and bred in an atmosphere in which business and a relatively high social standing were intimately associated with his family life." Over half of the business leaders had fathers who were businessmen; only one-quarter came from farms; and only one-tenth were sons of workers.[15]

The Gregory and Neu sample consisted of about 200 industrial and railroad leaders rather heavily weighted by the textile business, but different samples showed about the same results. Cochran found that 51 of 61 railroad leaders were born east of the Alleghenies and north of the Mason-Dixon Line; two-thirds were middle class; one-third had been to college, mostly to Harvard and Yale.[16] Miller's study of 190 businessmen of the early twentieth century found that three out of every four were fourth-generation Americans; half were from the upper class; and more than half came from a business family in a city or a town. Miller also demolished the implausible myth that those who started to work at an early age rose to the top before the late starters. Actually, almost half of the late starters and about one-quarter of the early birds found room at the top by age 45. The rags-to-riches story was not even typical among the spectacular "robber barons," despite Carnegie and Vanderbilt.

Analyses of the origins of more recent business leaders show, surprisingly enough, that the Alger legend is less unrealistic than it was a few generations ago. It is not easy—indeed, it is most difficult—for the boy from the other side of the tracks to achieve business success; but, contrary to popular belief, it is less difficult for him than it was for his father or grandfather. About 20 percent of today's business leaders came from working-class families and another 10 percent from the farm. The prerequisite for business success today, as in the past, is education. More than one-third of Gregory and Neu's business leaders went to college when hardly anyone else did. Today four out of five business executives have been to college.[17]

[14]William Miller, "American Historians and the Business Elite," *Journal of Economic History,* Vol. IX (1949); Irwin G. Wylie, *The Self-Made Man in America* (New Brunswick, N.J.: Rutgers University Press, 1954).

[15]Francis W. Gregory and Irene D. Neu, "The American Business Elite in the 1870s," in William Miller, ed., *Men in Business* (Cambridge, Mass.: Harvard University Press, 1952). See also Seymour Martin Lipset and Reinhard Bendix, *Social Mobility in Industrial Society* (Berkeley: University of California Press, 1959), Chap. 4.

[16]Cochran, *Railroad Leaders.*

[17]Frank W. Taussig and Carl S. Joslyn, *American Business Leaders* (New York: The Macmillan Company, 1932); Mabel Newcomer, *The Big Business Executive* (New York: Columbia University Press, 1953); W. Lloyd Warner and James C. Abegglen, *Occupational Mobility in American Business and Industry, 1928-1952* (Minneapolis: University of Minnesota Press, 1955).

The problem of competition in the late 1800s

Many of the outstanding entrepreneurs of the late 1800s catapulted toward business success in the 1870s and early 1880s. Charles Pillsbury organized C. A. Pillsbury and Company in 1872. In the same year, General DuPont formed the Gunpowder Association. Carnegie and his associates erected the Edgar Thomson works in 1873. Philip Armour moved to Chicago as head of the firm in 1875. Wanamaker opened the Grand Depot in 1876, and Gustavus and Edwin Swift created their partnership in 1878. The original members of the "Standard Oil Crowd"[18] had all taken their places by 1879. Duke began to manufacture cigarettes by machine in 1881.

Burgeoning entrepreneurship was not a mere coincidence or freak of nature. By 1870, railroad construction and urbanization had proceeded far enough to create a mass market for both consumer and producer goods. Industrial firms met the challenge by stepping up production at a tempo that exceeded the impressive gains in demand. Total manufacturing production was twice as high in the early 1880s as it had been in the early 1870s.

With productive capacity multiplying faster than demand, businessmen were quickly confronted by the problem of excess capacity and the specter of ruthless price competition. The businessman recognized that price wars might benefit the consumer, but he also knew that they would cause a large number of business failures. Naturally therefore, he tried to prevent price wars from occurring.

Traditional methods of controlling price competition centered around the trade association. Because written contracts aiming to fix prices or to curtail output were forbidden by common law, competitors resorted to so-called "gentlemen's agreements" and pools. These devices were almost as old as economic history. In the United States, they were used by the early transportation companies in a desperate but frustrated effort to regulate rates. However, it was not until the 1850s, when the textile and metal industries had grown to some size, that agreements through associations appeared regularly in manufacturing. For the next 20 years, they were tried with more persistence than success. Ohio salt manufacturers formed a joint-stock company in 1851 to regulate the quantity of salt manufactured and to regulate prices. In 1853, the American Brass Association was formed to "meet ruinous competition." In 1854, the Hampton County Cotton Spinners Association was organized, and in 1855 the American Iron Association appeared.

Gentlemen's agreements and pools were informal or formal cartel agreements which divided the market by fixing quotas or by setting up single selling agencies. They rarely lasted for very long because they offered no positive solution to the problem of competition in a climate of excess capacity. They

[18] John D. and William Rockefeller, Flagler, Payne, Bostwick, Pratt, Warden, Brewster, Archbold, Rogers, Lockhart, and Vandergrift.

neither cut costs nor increased demand. They could work only if each member refrained from producing as much as he could. Time soon showed that not all the gentlemen in a gentlemen's agreement were gentlemen and that not all the participants in a pool could be trusted to behave themselves. Market forces may not have worked as perfectly in the real world as in the theorist's model, but they worked well enough to break almost all voluntary combinations. Supply eventually exerted itself in a rough way. Members found it easy to evade the self-imposed restrictions. Sooner or later, one party sold below the agreed-upon price, and the whole delicately contrived scheme collapsed.

Pioneering in horizontal and vertical integration

One way of avoiding the frustrations inherent in the pool was to eliminate dependence on voluntary agreement by buying a substantial or a controlling interest in rival companies. Such horizontal integration was very popular in older industries producing goods that were characterized by inelastic demand. Price competition in such products was especially disastrous because, even if prices were cut to the proverbial bone, the quantity sold increased very little.

The Michigan Salt Association, formed in the late years of the calamitous depression of 1873, was called a "pool," but it was really an example of successful horizontal integration. Each member owned one share of Association stock for each barrel of daily capacity. All the salt that was produced was turned over to the Association for marketing, and the proceeds were distributed to the stockholders. The Gunpowder Association was another outstanding example of horizontal integration. It was a self-confessed "agreement to minimize competition." It gave the industry "long and profitable protection against price cutting and the unsettling effects of free competition,"[19] but it did so because General Henry DuPont owned a block of stock in each of the member companies, and the General knew exactly what his objectives were and how to achieve them.

Horizontal integration could not be a final answer to the businessman's most pressing problems. If he succeeded in buying out his competitors, he emerged as a large-scale replica of his predecessors with most of their weaknesses. He was still directing a single-product, single-function firm and was still terribly hampered in using his resources effectively. The pressures were toward cautious rather than aggressive operation. In order to gain more elbow room, the entrepreneur had to break out of his traditional area and gain control of the market. The leading entrepreneurs of the 1870s and 1880s did this by integrating vertically, that is, by expanding forward to the consumer or backward to the producer of the raw material. They began to add other functions to that of

[19]Ernest Dale, "DuPont: Pioneer in Systematic Management," *Administrative Science Quarterly,* Vol. 2 (1957). Reprinted in Ernest Dale, *Great Organizers* (New York: McGraw-Hill Book Company, 1960).

manufacturing, and emerged as multifunction, single-product enterprises. The initial expansion was usually in the direction of the consumer. The pioneers gradually took over the marketing of their products, a function that had previously been performed by middlemen. For a big producer this made sense, for it was cheaper to distribute directly than through a middleman. It was easier to coordinate supply and demand if a firm handled its own distribution. Then, too, a middleman who handled the products of a number of firms could not be expected to push the products of any one at the expense of the others.

Vertical integration was a relatively long-drawn-out process—an evolution that took a firm about 20 years to accomplish. Different entrepreneurs pursued different tactics in achieving their objectives, but almost all of them headed in the direction of the consumer by building marketing organizations. Before 1850, direct selling by manufacturers was very rare. Almy and Brown, the Providence textile manufacturers, tried the idea as early as 1803, but the experience was abortive.

The real pioneers in building a marketing organization were the McCormick Reaper Company and the Singer Sewing Machine Company. Before 1850, McCormick began to sell his products through commission agents. Gradually, this built up to a franchise agent system, which later became common in the automobile business. In the sewing machine business, Edward Clark, the marketing brain in the Singer Company, like McCormick in agricultural equipment, intuitively recognized that his company would have to demonstrate the machine and give instructions and service to the customer. In order to do this, he established branch stores, the first in Boston in 1852; by 1859, there were 14 of them. Singer also sold through commission agents who bought the machines at discounts ranging from 20 to 40 percent. Commission agents were also supposed to provide demonstration and repair service, but they did not perform these services well. Moreover, the franchise method became increasingly expensive. To give better service and to cut costs, the company gradually took over the agencies. This move toward vertical integration—for that was what it was— received encouragement from the peculiarities of Civil War taxation. The Federal government levied a tax on each sale. A final product that passed through the hands of a series of different producers carried as many taxes as there were producers. On the other hand, products made by an integrated producer were taxed only once. Integration, therefore, offered obvious tax advantages, and Clark took advantage of this. By 1867, when it began to make its own cabinets, Singer was integrated from raw material to final customer.[20]

Producers of both new and old consumers' goods also invaded the national market in the late nineteenth century. Swift, who had the novel idea of shipping

---

[20]Andrew B. Jack, "The Channels of Distribution for an Innovation: The Sewing Machine Industry in America, 1860-1865," *Explorations in Entrepreneurial History,* Vol. IX (1957).

refrigerated meat, and Duke, who introduced a new product called cigarettes, built national marketing organizations from the ground up. Swift opened a chain of branch offices that sold to and sometimes controlled retail outlets. Duke set up headquarters in New York City in 1884 and, with salesmen and advertising, soon had a coordinated distribution organization. Milwaukee brewers, finding their local market too narrow, broke its boundaries in the late 1870s. Pabst, for example, began to sell nationally through salesmen and commission agents. From the early 1880s on, it added to its advertising and, like other brewers, bought retail outlets all over the country and rented them to saloonkeepers. By the 1890s, therefore, Pabst was selling directly to the consumer.[21]

The Standard Oil alliance, whose experiences have been described in great detail by the Hidys, traveled an entirely different route to gain control of the market.[22] In 1870, the Rockefeller brothers and Henry M. Flagler reorganized their oil-refining business as Standard Oil (Ohio). By then, the industry was suffering from overexpansion. Prices were falling sharply and profit margins were slipping even more alarmingly. Rockefeller and his associates used every stratagem to reverse the tide. They joined traffic pools, such as the notorious South Improvement Company, followed an aggressive and ruthless policy of horizontal integration by absorbing rival refineries, and initiated a long-range plan for vertical integration. At first, they expanded toward the consumer and back to the raw material, but in 1878 they temporarily quit producing crude oil. They continued, however, to make gestures toward adding marketing to manufacturing. In 1871, they bought two New York selling agents, and in 1873 they purchased an interest in the leading Southern jobber. At the same time, they began to build pipelines and to forge a chain of 130 bulk selling stations to sell directly to retailers from the Midwest to New England. Despite these significant moves, Standard was in the early 1880s still much more dominant in refining than in selling. The company had moved at an incredibly heady pace toward mass manufacturing, but much more slowly toward mass marketing. It was committed to an aggressive policy in pipelines, but its marketing affiliates, Chess-Carley and Waters-Pierce, were semiindependent, and Standard salesmen dealt with many outside wholesalers. Foreign marketing was even less systematized, even though about half of all production was exported. The company sold almost exclusively through outsiders. Its only foreign marketing outlet was an agency established by an affiliate in Germany in 1880.

Slowly the picture changed. During the 1880s and early 1890s, Standard continued to buy small marketing businesses, often operating them under their old names. It also acquired the remaining minority interest in its marketing affili-

[21]Thomas C. Cochran, *The Pabst Brewing Company* (New York: New York University Press, 1948).

[22]Ralph W. and Muriel E. Hidy, *Pioneering in Big Business, 1882-1911* (New York: Harper & Row, Publishers, 1955).

ates, organized new units, and accumulated miles of pipelines and fleets of tankers, tank cars, and tank wagons. Meanwhile, the company, in order to assure itself of supplies, also drifted back into crude-oil production in the early 1880s and more seriously and systematically in the 1890s. By the outbreak of the panic of 1893, Standard was fully integrated from the well to the pumping station.

Some of Standard's directors were most unhappy about integrating back to the raw material. They considered crude oil production very speculative and preferred to stay out. In the steel business, Carnegie felt the same way, but he too was persuaded to acquire guaranteed sources of raw materials. The Frick coke properties were added in 1882, but the Oliver iron deposits were not acquired until the 1890s, some time after the consolidation of a marketing organization.

By the 1890s, most of the large companies had orderly arrangements for obtaining supplies; at the other end they were selling directly to the retailers. The textile industry was an outstanding exception. In the 1890s, only one mill sold directly to retailers. It was not until the late 1920s that the others fell into line.

BUSINESS ORGANIZATION IN THE LATE NINETEENTH CENTURY

Vertical integration required much more sophisticated business methods than had sufficed for the merchant and the small businessman of the early nineteenth century. The pioneers in industrial expansion needed far more capital and much more complicated forms of business organizations. In addition, they had to develop an administrative structure, something that had not been necessary in the previous generation.

The corporate form of organization was used in a small number of cases as far back as the Colonial Period and increasingly thereafter.[23] In the early years, corporate charters were granted by special act of legislation. Gradually, however, this requirement of a special legislative act was eliminated, and so-called "free incorporation" replaced it. Connecticut in 1816 was the first state to have a general incorporation statute for *non-bank corporations.* Bank incorporation continued to require a special legislative act until the late 1830s when Michigan and New York passed free banking laws. Connecticut's example was eventually followed by other states and by 1850, free incorporation prevailed throughout the country.

[23]See J.S. Davis, *Essays in the Earlier History of American Corporation* (Cambridge, Mass.: Harvard University Press, 1917). See also James Willard Hurst, *The Legitimacy of the Business Corporation in the Law of the United States 1780-1790* (Charlottesville, Virginia: The University Press of Virginia, 1970).

In other ways too, corporate law became increasingly liberal. Limited liability for stockholders against third-party claimants offered a case in point. Early corporate charters did not limit the liability of stockholders, but court decisions during the first half of the nineteenth century held over and over again that a corporation charter conferred limited liability by implication unless there was clear provision to the contrary. Gradually, the states by specific enactment wrote into the law what the courts had already granted. But this is not to say that liability was altogether limited. Most states imposed many specific qualifications to limited liability as a *quid pro quo* for their overall generosity. Bank stockholders were specifically excluded from limited liability. Leading industrial states also required shareholders to be liable for any unpaid stock subscription. Some states made stockholders liable for double the original investment, and most states excluded unpaid wages from the protection against liability.

Massachusetts offers as good an example as any of increasingly liberal corporate law. It was an industrial state, and its experience seems to have been typical. From 1809 to 1830, Massachusetts granted, by special act of legislation, liberal corporation charters but without limited liability. From 1830 to 1850, corporation charters, although still given by special act of legislation, usually included limited liability. After 1850, no special act was required, and most corporate nonbank charters limited the liability of shareholders to what they had paid for their stock.

Limited liability, although important, was not the cardinal consideration in incorporating, for about the same number of corporations were formed in the less lenient states as in the most lenient. What made the corporation more and more appealing was that it fitted the needs of a growing economy better than did the proprietorship and the partnership. Through the sale of stocks and bonds, entrepreneurs could raise a much larger capital. This was of primary importance to land companies, turnpikes, banks, canals, and, especially, railroads that required much more capital than a group of partners could raise in a local area. These ventures were also speculative, and potential investors naturally desired some assurance that their possible losses would be limited. At the same time, stockholders were excused from assuming any of the burdens of management and they could sell their interest at any time without interrupting the continuity of operation. From the entrepreneur's point of view, the corporation had one disadvantage: dissident stockholders could annoy and even interfere with management.

Because of its apparent advantages, industrialists resorted more and more to the corporation charter in the late nineteenth century. The experience of two industrial states—New Jersey and Ohio—illustrated the trend. In 1870, they issued about 450 charters, one-third of them to manufacturing companies. In 1883, they issued about 900, about half to manufacturers. Most of these were so-called "closed corporations"; that is, they were really incorporated partnerships whose stock was not bought and sold in the open market. In the late

1880s, the Pullman Company was the only large manufacturing company listed on the New York Stock Exchange. The stock of some textile companies—Amoskeag, Wamsutta, and so forth—had a public market, but these companies were not very large.[24] Most of the large firms, including Armour, McCormick, Singer, and Swift, were closely held corporations. The Carnegie enterprises were typical. There were 25 stockholders, whose ownership interest ranged from less than 1 percent to 58½ percent. Under the terms of an "ironclad agreement," stockholders could sell their shares only to the company. Moreover, any holder's stock could be bought at book value if 75 percent of the stock so voted. This type of arrangement, of course, assured control to the insiders, but it also prevented the corporation from taking full advantage of its capital-raising powers. In almost all companies, management had to rely on a small group of stockholders, retained earnings, and bank borrowing to raise the sizable capital it needed. Retained earnings, for example, swelled the size of the Carnegie enterprises from $700,000 in 1873 to over $400 million in 1900. Standard Oil paid out only a little over half of its prodigious earnings in the decade of the 1880s.

The trust device

Corporation lawyers and business entrepreneurs soon created a new form of organization that gave more flexibility to the corporate form by expanding its capital-raising powers and at the same time confining control to a small group of insiders. This new refinement, called the *trust,* first appeared in the Standard Oil Trust of 1879 and the second and more famous Standard Trust of 1882. The innovation was essentially the brain child of Standard's brilliant legal adviser, Samuel C. T. Dodd, but many others contributed their ideas. Under the 1882 agreement, 41 stockholders in 40 different companies turned their stock over to nine trustees in exchange for $70 million in "trust certificates," representing all the stock in 14 companies and most or a large block in 26 others. Stockholders continued to receive dividends. In the extraordinary world of legal magic, they owned the companies but they had no vote in the trust. In the trust, in other words, ownership was effectively separated from control.

The trust idea caught on very quickly, and trusts were soon formed in cottonseed oil, whiskey distilling, sugar refining, cordage manufacture, and other businesses. It was easy to see why the device was so popular. It enabled a group of entrepreneurs to control many different companies in many different states—a practice that was not permitted under existing corporation law. It also enabled them to raise capital and convert some of their holdings into cash without relinquishing any of their control, for trust certificates could be bought and sold

[24]Thomas R. Navin and Marian V. Sears, "The Rise of a Market for Industrial Securities, 1887-1902," *The Business History Review,* Vol. XXIX (1955).

in the open market. Indeed, a few of them quickly became important playthings for stock exchange investors and speculators.

"Trusts" soon became synonymous with "monopoly," and states began action to dissolve them by antitrust proceedings. Louisiana attacked the cotton-seed oil trust in 1887. In 1888, New York attempted to break up the sugar trust. Nebraska in 1890 ordered a Nebraska distiller to withdraw from the whiskey trust. But it was Ohio, in 1892, that accomplished a ten-strike when it broke up the Standard Oil Trust by ordering Standard Oil of Ohio to withdraw. In that very famous case, the Court, anticipating a later debate, said:[25]

> Much has been said in favor of the objects of the Standard Oil Trust and what it has accomplished. It may be true that it has improved the quality and cheapened the costs of petroleum and its products to the consumer. But such is not one of the usual or general results of a monopoly; and it is the policy of the law to regard, not what may, but what usually happens. Experience shows that it is not wise to trust human cupidity where it has the opportunity to aggrandize itself at the expense of others.

By then, however, ingenious lawyers and promoters had developed another form of organization, the holding company, which promised an equally expedient method of exercising control. Actually, a type of holding company had appeared in the railroads as early as 1833 and in public utilities in 1868, but these relatively rare episodes were under special acts of legislation. The holding company first became really important when New Jersey in 1889 passed a law permitting its corporations to hold stock in other corporations. This act, copied as it was by other states, permitted a group of entrepreneurs acting through a parent company to exercise control over a large number of subsidiaries scattered over a large area at the price of a relatively small investment.

Administration in the late-nineteenth-century vertically integrated enterprises

The growing size and increasing complexity of the integrated firm, the variety of functions that had to be carried on, and the need for expert advice and information required an administrative structure that transcended the "one-man organization." Indeed, the notion that a single individual "ran the whole show" in the large firms of the late nineteenth century is as much a legend as is the rags-to-riches success story popularized in the Alger stories. The great empire-building entrepreneurs were undoubtedly the central driving figures in their

---

[25]Hans B. Thorelli, *The Federal Antitrust Policy* (Baltimore: The Johns Hopkins Press, 1955), p. 82.

companies, but they received invaluable assistance from their associates. In Standard Oil, few men made decisions or recommendations solely on their own. It was a community of interest led by John D. Rockefeller. The DuPont company owed as much to H. M. Barksdale, J. A. Haskell, and others as it did to General Henry DuPont. Carnegie had the help of his brother Thomas and his friend Henry Phipps, the production genius of Captain Billy Jones, and the executive ability of Henry Clay Frick.

A group of men managed each large firm. In the process, they built up a highly centralized organization. They set up a number of departments, each of which took care of one or more of the various functions performed by a large, integrated business. All activity was supervised by the central office. In some cases, the executives created committees, and, although many of them hated to do so, they conscripted an office force to provide data and information for the officers, the committees, and their aides. Strange things were happening in business life—things that must have created some uneasiness among the individualistic industrialists. The administrative end of the business was growing, and it was apparent that nothing could be done to stop it. For example, Cyrus McCormick, certainly no champion of office work, watched his office staff grow from two or three clerks who had barely enough to do in 1854 to 16 men who were hard pressed to answer the correspondence in 1879.

Like every other business action and intellectual process, what was occurring in administration was not brand new. It had its antecedents in the army, the church, and the large railroad. Some business administrators certainly knew this. For example, H. M. Barksdale, who contributed so much to the DuPont organization, [26] was well aware of the railroad experience, for he had been trained in the Baltimore and Ohio. According to James Stillman, of the National City Bank, the Standard Oil Company "borrowed" its idea of "strong centralized government (with certain other doctrines) from the Roman Catholic Church."[27] But in most cases, those who put together an administrative structure were unaware of the existing precedents. Their organizations were slapped together or just grew as expedience and necessity dictated. It is true that the organizations worked, but in a chaotic fashion. There were no clear lines of authority or responsibility and no separation of long-term planning and day-to-day operations. Some holding companies were also operating companies, and the functions of one committee or department overlapped those of others.

The historians of the Standard Oil Company have given us a detailed account of the evolution of the company's business administration, its success, and its trials and tribulations.[28] From the beginning, the company took a long-

[26]Ernest Dale and Charles Meloy, "Hamilton MacFarland Barksdale and the DuPont Contribution to Scientific Management," *Business History Review,* Vol. XXXVI (1962).

[27]Anna Robeson Burr, *Portrait of a Banker* (New York: Duffield & Co., 1927), p. 70.

[28]Ralph W. and Muriel E. Hidy, *Pioneering in Big Business,* pp. 32-40, 55-76, 323-39.

range point of view which required gathering information, consulting, planning, and centralized policy formation. The trustees were, of course, responsible for management, but Rockefeller soon began to delegate details and to disperse responsibility by building up a committee system. By 1886, the committee system had been completed. By then, too, a series of departments had been created, including auditing, legal, crude stock, and a number in manufacturing and marketing. At the top of the whole pyramid stood the executive committee, which consisted of those top managers who happened to be at the home office on any given day. Theoretically, the executive committee's function was to determine general policy, leaving the operating managers to carry it out. In actual practice, however, it handled not only general policy, but also routine management. For example, it had to approve any appropriation of more than $5,000 and it considered all raises on salaries of over $600. It was entrepreneur, administrator, and manager rolled into one.

The executives of Standard Oil spent their time at the office running from one meeting to another and still did not have enough time to decide all the matters that required a decision. A similar confusion existed among all the committees and departments. Because functions were vaguely defined, there was often friction between executives and managers, and equally often subsidiaries refused to follow the decisions and recommendations of the holding company headquarters.

Contrasted with the ideal, the Standard Oil organization left much to be desired. Even such tolerant critics as the Hidys point out that the organization had developed over time and emerged as "an uncommonly heterogeneous mixture" which such an orderly mind as that of S. C. T. Dodd could not unravel. But they also point out that the arrangement worked. As John D. Rockefeller put it, in 1886, "We are not free from the annoyance and trouble incident to this smooth running business, but it seems to me we have every reason to be grateful when we compare it with any other."

Ancillary institutions

In developing an administrative structure, businessmen relied more on ancillary institutions than had been their habit in the early 1800s. They saw no pressing need for public relations advisers, management consultants, or the more sophisticated assistants of the present day, and, as long as they could, they tried to avoid investment bankers. But the handful of business enterprises that were growing to gigantic size in the 1880s found it advisable to employ specialized corporation lawyers to solve the legal riddles associated with growth. They also depended heavily on the very large commercial banks to meet part of their immense needs for capital funds. There were, however, very few of these gigantic banks. Even at the outbreak of World War I, there were only about a dozen that were large enough to lend $1 million to one customer.

The increasing complexity of the manufacturing process affected accounting more than any other ancillary. The pressures of competition, the need to depreciate a huge capital investment, and the more intricate processes of round-about production necessitated more careful record-keeping and made somewhat more advanced accounting an indispensable adjunct to efficient business. Public accounting, academic training in accounting, and the first book on cost accounting appeared in the 1880s. But again the advance was confined pretty much to big business. Carnegie and Rockefeller were well aware of the value of better record-keeping, but the first controller of an industrial enterprise was not appointed until 1892; even as late as 1918, at least one relatively large and long-established manufacturing firm was still using single-entry bookkeeping.

CONSOLIDATION OF BUSINESS ENTERPRISE IN THE EARLY 1900s

The years around the turn of the century marked a period of consolidation that contrasted sharply with the previous era of frenzied activity. Business in general continued to grow, but not at the same rate of speed. On the other hand, individual business firms grew at a much faster rate, but by way of merger rather than internal expansion. Bankers and professional managers, who were more interested in serenity and in law and order, began to play a more important role in the conduct of business. Many more corporations became publicly owned, and new methods were developed for dealing with the ever-present problem of competition. By the outbreak of World War I, which temporarily interrupted the continued adjustment of business to new conditions, the large, bureaucratic, oligopolistic corporation had become the dominant institution in the market place.

The investment banker in business change

By whatever label we may know him, the industrialist, industrial capitalist, owner-entrepreneur, or empire builder of the late nineteenth century carried business enterprise to the brink of bigness and, in some few cases, even beyond. But by the end of the century, his place of dominance had begun to diminish. He was at his best in dealing with the vast untapped market created by the city and opened up by the railroad. His mills, packinghouses, factories, and refineries turned out a flood of goods. But once the initial demand had been filled, the empire builder's aptitudes lost much of their value and glamor. By the last quarter of the century, it was clear that his kind of business system could not continue without much modification. Very often, his financial policies were too weak to withstand the rigors of business depression, or his managerial organization was not geared for smooth operation of mass-production enterprise. He did not disappear altogether, and he returned in full force each time a new product

requiring capital-intensive production appeared or a new market called for
invasion. So, at a later date, Henry Ford, who perhaps most closely resembled
the composite industrial capitalist, took full advantage of the infant automobile
industry. By 1900, however, most of the spectacular, often flamboyant, owner-
entrepreneurs who had starred in the great growth that began in the 1870s had
retired from active business life. Clark retired from the Singer presidency in
1882. McCormick died in 1884. Pillsbury sold his flour mill in 1889. Rockefeller
and Armour began to withdraw from management in the early 1890s. Carnegie
and his associates sold their holdings to United States Steel in 1901. Swift died
in 1903.

The old order was giving place to new both in personalities and in behavior.
Either by force of circumstances or by voluntary decision, steps were taken to
change or improve the existing structure and to overcome some of the weaknesses
of the enterprise system. Frequently this change came from outside industry.
Thus, when a great industrialist's vast enterprises began to totter for want of
cash, or when price competition threatened to "demoralize" an industry, it was
not uncommon for the investment bankers of Boston's State Street or New
York's Wall Street to step in to protect their own interests or those of other
creditors or stockholders.

Bankers had been active participants in the railroad and textile businesses
for years, but it was only in the last quarter of the nineteenth century that their
intervention in general business became more and more frequent. Some writers,
such as Werner Sombart and N. S. B. Gras, have used the term *finance capitalism*
to characterize this new amalgam of industry and investment banking.

In their business policies, the investment bankers differed quite sharply
from the industrialists. Unlike most industrialists, who specialized in a single
branch of production, the bankers spread their influence over many different
industries. Consequently, their interests were too diversified to permit them to
assume an active and continuous entrepreneurial role. Within the firm, they
delegated to managers most of the actual power to make decisions.

As one might expect, investment bankers were more interested in financial
policy than in any other aspect of business activity. They preferred the discipline of corporate finance to that of industrial management. Income statements and balance sheets, earnings per share, security prices, capitalization, and
security flotations interested them much more than the index of industrial
production, the output of pig iron, or the volume of car loadings. Because
bankers and industrialists were so different, it is not surprising that bankers
disliked industrialists and that production men loathed bankers. Morgan thought
that Carnegie was a dangerous man who had "demoralized" the steel industry.
For his part, Carnegie abhorred promoters and boasted, not without reason,
that he could operate a steel business much better than a lot of "stock-jobbers"
who paid more attention to security manipulation than to steel-making.

Because they were so much concerned with financial matters, the investment bankers were more at home in reorganizing and consolidating existing

business than in creating and building new ones. They were not particularly venturesome or bold in expanding production. They were more interested in dividends, stability, and the protection of stockholders' interests than in plowing back earnings and expanding plant. They were opposed to ruthless price competition and favored, instead, a spirit of "live and let live," with stable rather than volatile prices. With such a set of beliefs, it was not surprising that the bankers exerted an important influence in bringing to the fore a concept of "fair prices" vaguely similar to the "just price" of medieval times. Judge Gary, of the United States Steel Corporation, a managerial representative of the bankers, expressed the idea very well when he said: "I think any of us would rather have the prices of our tailor or our grocer substantially uniform, assuming that they are fair and reasonable, than to have the prices very low in time of panic and depression, and then in other times very high and unreasonable."

Ultimately, this drift away from market-determined prices toward "fair and reasonable prices" invited government regulation and even government control; for, if prices were no longer determined by the market, they might just as well be administered by government as by businessmen and bankers. A representative of the new management, Theodore N. Vail, who was very much opposed to government ownership but very much in favor of government regulation, said in 1912, "There are few big captains of industry who can run a great corporation, but there is any quantity of men who could review their acts and who . . . could say whether or not the men who were doing things were doing them right."

Big business becomes a reality

Investment bankers, like Kuhn, Loeb and August Belmont and J. P. Morgan, had the advantage of being able to marshal huge aggregations of capital funds to finance their ventures. The resources at the beck and call of the House of Morgan were especially awesome. Beside their own assets, the Morgan partners could call on their close allies: in Boston, on Kidder, Peabody; in Philadelphia, on Drexel and Co.; in New York, on George Baker of the First National and James Stillman of the National City. One member or another in this entente had a controlling voice in a number of commercial banks, trust companies, and insurance companies, including the Bank of Commerce, the Bankers Trust, the Guaranty Trust, the Mutual Life, the New York Life, and the Equitable Life. The Pujo Committee, which conducted an investigation of the money market in 1912, asserted that the Morgan "money trust" controlled $13 billion worth of financial assets. The conclusion was misleading, for it included many firms in which the Morgan interest was represented but not dominant. The "money trust" was a pragmatic alliance that could exist only as long as all members of the inner circle were satisfied that their individual interests could best be served by cooperation and agreement. George F. Baker, for example, cooperated with Morgan, not because of subservience, but because the relationship offered mutual advantages. Executives of industrial corporations cooperated as long as they were relatively free to make business decisions and as long as their positions as executives depended on the acquiescence of the bankers. But the prevalent early-twentieth-century fear that the bankers had the American economy in thralldom was highly exaggerated. What did exist was an entente cordiale among bankers and industrial executives, an entente, however, that was so tenuous that it would be broken at the first slight change in the balance of power.

But there is no reason to quibble; investment bankers did control sizable funds. And with these huge pools of capital, by reorganizing and consolidating existing firms, they acted as the catalytic agents in producing the phenomenon known as "big business."

Actually, *big business* in the absolute sense of the word is a very modern creation. According to Myron W. Watkins, a careful student of business concentration, no single plant of the early 1800s controlled as much as 10 percent of the output of any manufactured product. In the late 1880s, when a company with a net worth of $10 million was relatively as large as the billion-dollar corporation of today, there were only about a half-dozen industrial giants. Each of the ten largest railroads was worth over $100 million; but the Carnegie Company, very conservatively valued to be sure, was presumably worth only $5 million and the McCormick reaper business only $2.5 million. The first billion-dollar company—United States Steel—was not born until 1901, and then it was by far the nation's largest business. At that time, 100 companies were valued at over $10 million, but only 40 were worth over $50 million. Thus, in one generation, giants had become commonplace in the business world.

The first merger wave, 1898-1906

In American history, mergers occurred in three great waves: the first between 1898 and 1906, the second in the 1920s, and the third following World War II. Although it is often assumed that mergers commonly took place in periods of business stagnation, this was not the case. To the contrary, each merger epidemic occurred in a boom economy; and apparently a prerequisite was an active, spiraling stock market.

The first merger movement was the most important one of the three. All the giant corporations that sprang to the top of American business in the early 1900s were the product in whole or in large part of mergers. During the years 1898–1906, more than 3,200 mergers took place in manufacturing and mining. Over 350, or more than 10 percent, involved major firms;[29] and 22 firms,

[29]R. L. Nelson, *Merger Movements in American Industry, 1895-1956* (Princeton, N.J.: Princeton University Press, 1959); Shaw Livermore, "The Success of Industrial Mergers," *Quarterly Journal of Economics,* Vol. XXXVII (1935).

including United States Steel, American Tobacco, American Smelting and Refining, and American Can, grew to massive size as a result of merger.

In general, mergers were the result of the same basic causes that had produced vertical integration in the previous generation. One purpose was to gain market control and eliminate competition. To some extent, mergers succeeded in attaining this objective, for big business brought the problem of competition under much more satisfactory control. At least 71 mergers succeeded in attaining some monopoly power.[30] By 1900, concentration had proceeded far enough to alter the structure of the market. Sporadic price cutting still occurred but, in general, prices conformed much more closely to what large-scale enterprise apparently regarded as ideal. They were not high enough to encourage competitors to expand and not low enough to set off disastrous price wars.

But to maintain any semblance of control over the market, entrepreneurs had to strain toward consolidation, for as soon as the merger movement began to lag, control by the very large firms began to weaken. According to one estimate, the 100 largest firms in manufacturing, mining, and distribution held 17.7 per cent of all industrial corporate assets in 1909 and 16.6 percent in 1919.[31]

Businessmen also resorted to mergers in order to relieve the stresses and strains of declining profit margins. It was generally assumed that large-scale enterprises created by integration and consolidation could gain substantial economies that were not available to small- and medium-size business. Indeed, it was thought that the economies of mass production were infinite—a theory that would not be seriously challenged for another generation. These economies of scale, as economists call them, could be achieved both in production and in administration. The large firm had decided advantages in buying raw materials and in distributing goods. It could use specialized machinery. It could get along with less inventory and could attract more skillful management than smaller business could. All this added up to lower costs in producing and selling a unit of output. Big business could also use ancillaries, such as lawyers, banks, and accountants, that were not available on the same scale to small firms.

Yet, although it would not be recognized for another 50 years, the economies of scale that could be attained by merger were often greatly exaggerated. Undoubtedly, the initial growth of business firms lowered the unit costs of production. Intraplant economies, such as mechanization, mass production, and

---

[30] Jesse M. Markham, "Survey of the Evidence and Findings on Mergers," in Universities-National Bureau of Economic Research, *Business Concentration and Price Policy* (Princeton, N.J.: Princeton University Press, 1955).

[31] Norman R. Collins and Lee E. Preston, "The Size Structure of the Largest Industrial Firms, 1909-1958," *American Economic Review,* Vol. LI (1961). See, for a quite different estimate for 1909, A. D. H. Kaplan, *Big Enterprise in a Competitive System* (Washington, D.C.: The Brookings Institution, 1964).

the use of scientific management techniques, could be accomplished more easily in a large plant than in a small one. But once the individual plant had passed its optimum size, further economies of scale ceased to exist. A multiplant structure could enable a firm to achieve further economies, provided the firm could erect a managerial structure equal to the task of overseeing the whole. But this, too, would come to an end when the firm, as well as the plant, passed far beyond the point of diminishing returns. An analysis made in 1937 of the cost structures of the firms in 59 industries revealed that the largest firm had the lowest unit cost in only one industry. Medium-sized firms had the lowest cost in 21 industries, and small firms in the remaining 37. These conclusions have been severely attacked; but, no matter how they are revised, they, and other subsequent findings, show that the economies of scale were not infinitely unlimited. They were often phantom economies and served as a rationale to cover a multitude of other complex motives that drove business firms in the direction of mergers. In many instances, mergers were little more than early manifestations of Parkinson's Law. Some businessmen who took part in extravagant consolidations were empire builders who were interested in growth for growth's sake. Others were more interested in acquiring financial control and in making profits on security transactions than in improving the process of production. When economic logic was subordinated to financial objectives or to a drive for power regardless of cost, mergers turned out disastrously. In fact, about half of the major mergers of the 1890s ended in failure.

The collective ownership of big business

Big business and finance capitalism had to be accompanied by something new in capital institutions: the appearance of a broad and open securities market.[32] In the transition to big business, ownership passed from a handful of partners to a much larger number of widely scattered stockholders. This occurred in railroads in the 1850s, but it was not until the 1890s that it took place in industrial firms. Between 1898 and 1902, the New York Stock Exchange welcomed a whole array of corporate giants, including United States Steel, International Harvester, American Can, American Car and Foundry, and United Fruit. On a sample day in 1903, trading took place in 136 industrial securities, one-third of which are still listed.

There were many reasons for this important institutional change. Big business on a broad scale could exist only under conditions of diverse ownership, and this could be accomplished only by inviting "the public" in. Investment bankers, who were now playing a major role in business, naturally used the milieu with which they were familiar: the stock exchanges and the securities

[32] See the article by Navin and Sears previously cited.

markets. Savers, who had previously invested their surplus in real estate, railroads, and government securities, welcomed an opportunity to diversify their investments through stock ownership. Finally, the industrialists, despite the suspicious hostility which some of them evinced toward bankers and security markets, had much to gain by "going public." It was much more difficult to sell a closely held business than to sell one's shares in a public corporation. Even if a sale could be successfully consummated, the sales price would be much lower than for a widely owned company. It was a common rule of thumb that a closed company was worth about three times what it earned, whereas shares in widely traded companies were typically valued at ten times earnings. To be sure, men who had taken part in building a business were not driven by money alone. They thought the game was worth the candle, but they were certainly not averse to cashing some of their gains before the wick burned away completely.

The story of how the Carnegie Company struggled over the issue of going public illustrates some of the complications of the problem. Like all the large companies of the day, except Pullman and the railroads, the Carnegie enterprise was until 1900 nothing more than an incorporated partnership; there was no public trading in its securities. The company was capitalized at its book value, which in 1892 was set rather arbitrarily at $25 million. In the event of death, dismissal, or resignation, a stockholder was paid the book value of his shares. Most of the executives felt, with good reason, that the company was worth much more than a meager three times annual earnings. Henry Clay Frick, theoretically the company's chief executive, felt this especially strongly, for he owned 6 percent of the company. If he left, he would receive $1.5 million, but he insisted that his share was worth at least 20 times as much. He therefore began a campaign to persuade the owners of Carnegie Steel into making it a public corporation. In short order, he converted all the partners except Carnegie himself. Finally, in 1900, Carnegie grudgingly surrendered to the views of his associates. The company was reorganized as the Carnegie Company, Incorporated, and its shares became eligible for public purchase.

Clearly the monetary benefits of going public were greater for Carnegie than for any of the other owners. His share was worth only $14.6 million under the old book value, $100 million under the new capitalization, and $280 million when the company was sold to United States Steel in 1901. Yet, despite the obvious advantages that Carnegie could gain, he remained hostile to turning the business over to "a lot of stock jobbers." His view still remains the popular one. The idea still persists that Carnegie's evaluation of the company was the fair and correct one. So, too, persists the corollary belief that, when the House of Morgan formed United States Steel, it scandalously overcapitalized the company by recklessly watering the stock, that is, by issuing stock far in excess of the company's value. The shoe was really on the other foot; the old Carnegie Company was grossly undercapitalized. The value attached by Morgan was much more realistic for, after a few very shaky years, United States Steel settled down and became part of the bedrock of the Stock Exchange. If the company had been so flagrantly overcapitalized, the so-called "water" in the stock would not have dried up nearly so fast.

SUGGESTED READINGS

(For suggested readings and questions, see the next chapter.)

Chapter Seven

THE CONTRIBUTION
OF BUSINESS:
BUSINESS ENTERPRISE SINCE 1920

The previous chapter sought to emphasize that in order to thrive, and in some cases even to survive, businessmen had to adjust their tactics and organization to changes in economic and political institutions, to shifts in market forces, and to technological evolution. In the nineteenth century, both the internal structure of business and the external environment it faced were relatively simple and posed few problems. Most businesses were small and, except in the giant railroad, the owner-manager was the typical entrepreneur. Labor unions were weak and the political system was as friendly as businessmen could realistically expect. The most dynamic features of the economy were the extraordinary growth of a highly mobile population and the construction of a railroad network, with all that that implied.

At all times, the entrepreneur's chief problem has been to use his resources most rationally in a world of rapidly shifting market forces. Intermittently, usually after a war, businessmen faced the pleasant prospect of operating in a sellers' market, that is, a market in which demand was greater than supply at existing prices. This entrepreneurial utopia was in each case short-lived. Prices spurted upward, productive capacity expanded very quickly, demand dwindled, and excess capacity took the place of a huge, unsatisfied backlog of demand. Nineteenth-century entrepreneurs met the problem by feverishly pursuing horizontal and vertical integration, often with the objective of achieving a monopoly position. In its effect on economic progress, this was laudatory, for nothing encourages economic growth as much as the deliberate pursuit of monopoly, provided the goal is never reached.

The problem of adjusting to major changes assumed different overtones in the twentieth century and, like everything else, it became much more complicated. In the institutional environment, there were three very important developments that taxed the resiliency of the entrepreneur. The ownership of the large corporation became constantly more fractionalized and more widely dispersed. In the labor field, business unionism finally emerged victorious over welfare unionism. In the political field, the Federal government played a more and more active role in economic life in general.

The ramifications of these developments sank deep into the foundations of business life. First of all, the professional manager replaced the industrialist and the financier as the prototype of the influential entrepreneur. This, in turn, brought forth a whole series of enigmatic and previously unheard-of problems which could be subsumed under the general heading "The Corporation Problem," and which included such matters as the separation of ownership from control, the stultifying effects of corporate bureaucracy, and the legitimacy of the corporate hierarchy.

Changes in economic and political institutions also led the businessman to put much more emphasis on functions that had previously been largely neglected. Public relations, labor relations, and government relations assumed an importance they had never enjoyed in the past. Business literature devoted more and more space to the businessman's social responsibility. Alarmed by this seeming departure from profit-mindedness, some critics charged that the businessman had become a manipulator of people rather than a manipulator of things, as his predecessor had been.

The behavior of market forces in the twentieth century was also different enough to create new problems of adjustment for the businessman.[1] Population growth slowed down, and, although new and important means of transportation were devised, they did not open new areas as the railroads had. Because the market did not expand as rapidly as in the past, businessmen had to be much more ingenious in dealing with the problem of so-called "excess capacity." They had to exercise much more active initiative in developing markets. In response to the challenge, they opened up a whole bag of tricks. They tried to stimulate the domestic market by multiplying the quantity and intensity of their advertising and their use of consumer credit. In addition, entrepreneurs diversified their activities on a broad front. They began intensively to exploit international markets. They created new products through research and development, and

---

[1] Some students of the English economy think that a prime reason for England's lagging growth in this century has been the entrepreneur's weakness in adjusting to new conditions. Derek K. Aldcroft and Harry W. Richardson, *The British Economy, 1870-1939* (New York: The Humanities Press, 1970).

they diversified by branching out into entirely new businesses. The net of all this was a change in the nature of competition and an equally important change in the internal organization of business. Competition became more a struggle between marketing departments and less a battle of prices. Internally, the centralized organization of the empire builder gave way to the decentralized organization of the career manager.

DIVERSIFICATION AND DECENTRALIZATION[2]

The most important developments in the last 40 or 50 years of business enterprise, or the most original within the limits that anything in history can be original, have been the diversification of business activities and the decentralization of business organization.

By the 1920s, most large firms were organized in centralized structures. They operated under departments, such as production, sales, law, and so forth. Although they had many functions, with few exceptions they still dealt in a single product. But to utilize their expanding resources and at the same time to assure a further measure of security against the vicissitudes of the business cycle, entrepreneurs inauguarated campaigns of ambitious diversification. They moved exactly opposite to Andrew Carnegie's famous dictum which admonished industrialists to put all their eggs in one basket. Electric-machinery manufacturers entered the appliance market, meat packers manufactured soup, automobile producers turned out refrigerators, oil companies expanded their international activities, and so on, through a long list of businesses, until only the metal companies and the processors of a few agricultural products were not diversified.

Some pioneering entrepreneurs were quick to recognize that diversification required an entirely different kind of managerial approach. The structure that had worked so well for a single-product firm did not suffice for a multiproduct firm. The top executives were too often busy with administrative rather than entrepreneurial decisions. The heads of departments ran into difficulties in handling a number of diverse products. Sales departments, for example, did not find it easy to sell both automobiles and refrigerators. Procurement of raw material and routing the production of different goods caused continuous headaches.

According to Chandler, DuPont, General Motors, Sears Roebuck, and Standard Oil were the business pioneers in solving the problem of adapting the managerial structure to the strategy of diversification. In the 1920s, they were the first to decentralize their organizations, to operate through divisions rather

[2]The research and writing of Alfred D. Chandler, Jr., have done much to illuminate this subject. See especially *Strategy and Structure.*

than departments, and to divorce their chief executives from day-to-day administration, leaving them free for long-range planning. During the 1930s, the shift
from a centralized to a decentralized structure quickened, and it attained a rapid
tempo after World War II.

Decentralization was selective. It came most quickly in companies that had
grown mostly by merger, in firms with diversified product lines and heavy investment in research and development, in businesses that were very complex, and in
companies headed by career executives. It came most slowly or not at all in
companies headed by the "empire-building" executive and in lines with no
diversification and little research and development. Indeed, Chandler, on the
basis of a large sample of companies, concludes that the three *Ds* traveled
together: diversification and development could not succeed without decentralization. Decentralization appeared unnecessary without the other two.

The experiences of the DuPont Company illustrate how strategy and structure changed in an immensely successful firm. Before World War I, DuPont,
principally because of the efforts of H. M. Barksdale, J. Amory Haskell, and A.
J. Moxham, developed a successful, departmentalized, centralized managerial
structure. The loss of an antitrust suit in 1912 and the stimulus of World War I
caused the company to diversify into other lines. Barksdale foresaw, "When the
war is over, our difficulty is going to consist of making a creditable showing in
earnings because of the huge increase in manufacturing facilities." Peace would
pose for DuPont a problem of resource utilization. Further expansion in explosives was not attractive because the demand would decline, and in any event
it was not possible because of the antitrust judgment. The company, therefore,
poured its resources into a varied series of investments. In addition to investing
substantially in General Motors, it began to manufacture and market, through its
existing departments, chemicals, paints, celluloid, dyestuffs, and synthetic fibers.

To its surprise, DuPont suffered heavy losses on its diversified lines. By
1921, these losses were about $30 million, and management was taking a very
hard look at major changes in its organization. The young men were sure they
understood the problem. Diversification had greatly increased the demands on
the administrative office, and the departmental structure was not attuned to
many different products. Selling paints, it was clear, was not the same as selling
explosives; a specialist in buying pigments was not an expert in procuring raw
materials for explosives. In 1920, the young group proposed as a solution a
reorganization on the basis of product, not function; but after much thought,
the idea was vetoed. However, when the company lost another $1.3 million in
early 1921, the veteran executives capitulated. The company adopted a new
structure of five autonomous divisions (cellulose, paint, purolin, dyestuffs, and
explosives) supervised by a general office with staff specialists and general
executives. Each division head was responsible for administrative decisions, and
the central office was relieved of all day-to-day operations.

THE FURTHER COURSE OF CONCENTRATION AND CONTROL

At first blush, it would appear that diversification must have accentuated the trend toward business concentration and control that had been one of the highlights of the late nineteenth century. The problem is not that simple. Whether big business has become bigger and whether big business controls more or less of the total business universe than it did 50 years ago are two halves of a highly controversial question. The answer to the first half is undoubtedly "yes," but the answer to the second half is still a subject of argument. Big business has certainly been getting bigger in an absolute sense ever since the beginning of American history, but whether competition has declined seriously in the twentieth century is not at all a settled matter.[3]

There can be no argument that big business is one of the facts of the modern economic world. Corporations originate over 80 percent of all business income. Among these corporations only 0.2 percent control over 60 percent of all corporate assets. One giant corporation employs over half a million people and gives employment to another 400,000 in dealerships. Another corporate colossus employs 800,000 and is owned by approximately 2,000,000 stockholders.

Although it is evident that big business has continued to grow, no such clear-cut answer can be given to the question of whether business has become more concentrated, that is, whether small business has been rapidly disappearing and whether the economic area not occupied by agriculture and the government has been completely usurped by big business. For the economy as a whole, there has been some tendency toward greater concentration, toward the relative importance of the very large corporations. The 100 largest manufacturing firms produced 17 percent of total value added in 1919, 28 percent in 1935, and 33 percent in 1970.[4] Between 1929 and 1960, the 100 largest manufacturers increased their share of total assets in manufacturing from 36 percent to 46 percent. In the next decade, however, their share only increased to 48 percent. Let us look at the problem in another way. There are approximately 100 manufacturing firms with assets of $1 billion or more; they control almost half of all corporate manufacturing assets and receive over half of all corporate manufacturing profits. The almost 2,000 corporations with $10 million or more in assets receive 88 percent of total corporate manufacturing profits.

---

[3]See, for example, G. Warren Nutter, *The Extent of Enterprise Monopoly in the United States, 1899-1939* (Chicago: University of Chicago Press, 1951); M. A. Adelman, "The Measurement of Industrial Concentration," *Review of Economics and Statistics,* Vol. XXXIII (1951); Solomon Fabricant, "Is Monopoly Increasing?" *Journal of Economic History,* Vol. XIII (1953).

[4]Norman R. Collins and Lee E. Preston, *American Economic Review,* Vol. LI (1961). Nutter, *op. cit.*; Federal Trade Commission, *Economic Report on Corporate Mergers,* 1970.

The evidence seems to support the contention that concentration in the whole of manufacturing has been continually increasing. But within individual industries, available evidence supports the view that concentration has not been increasing significantly, if at all. The reason for the disparity between concentration in the total economy and concentration in individual industries is clearly the proliferation of conglomerates in the last few decades. Actually, there are more businesses in proportion to population than there were in 1900. Moreover, the proportion of small businesses to the total business population is a little higher today than it was then. There is still a third piece of evidence leading to the conclusion that individual industries have not become more concentrated; it is estimated that monopolistic firms constituted 32 percent of the manufacturing population in 1899, 28 percent in 1937, 24 percent in 1947, and about 33 percent today. In the last 25 years, the share of total output produced by the four largest companies increased in about half of all industries and fell in the others.

As industries matured, most of them showed a tendency toward greater concentration. The number of firms shrank and, in some instances, one giant emerged as the clearly dominant firm. In the motor industry, for example, most firms disappeared and, of the few that remained, Ford at first and General Motors later clearly dominated. In the steel industry, on the other hand, the number of firms fell continuously, but no giant emerged. Indeed, the trend was the other way as smaller companies whittled away the dominant position of U.S. Steel. This may have been because some firms had easier access to capital funds, or it may have been because some entrepreneurs analyzed demand factors more accurately. Then again, it may have been because government antitrust policy acted as an obstacle to further expansion. But whatever the reason, it could be said that in general those firms that survived and grew did so because of astute management and good fortune and of these astute management was clearly the more important.

In the normal backing and filling that took place within the total business population, the largest corporations were not assured of maintaining their position in the upper stratosphere.[5] The composition of the largest 100 corporations changed sporadically, but not continuously, and the change was basically the result of technological development which took place in long swings. This proposition may be stated in another way: the degree of mobility among the largest firms was relatively small over a long period of time, but it was significant in shorter periods when technological change shook the economy. Of the 100 largest firms (by assets) in 1909, 39 had dropped out for one reason or another by 1919. Mobility slowed measurably between 1919 and 1958, for there was no new industry to raise havoc with existing large firms as the automotive industry

[5]Kaplan, op. cit.; Collins and Preston, op. cit.; Fortune, 1959-1971; Thomas R. Navin, "The 500 Largest American Industrials in 1917," Business History Review, Vol. XLIV (1970).

had done in the previous period. In the 40 years after 1919, at least 174 companies appeared at one time or another in the list of the 100 largest industrial firms. Of 1919's original 100, only 46 had dropped out by 1958; 13 disappeared as a result of mergers, 4 failed, and 29 dropped below the 100 class. Only 16 of the 100 largest in 1958 had not appeared in the list before 1948.

Between 1958 and 1970, 138 companies appeared among the 100 largest. Of the 100 largest in 1958, 30 were not on the list in 1970; 11 had disappeared because of mergers; the other 19 because of changing tastes and technological development. A 30 percent mobility rate certainly argues for high instability. But if a smaller sample were taken, it would bolster the argument that once a firm attained a large size, it was very difficult to dislodge it. Of the 30 firms that dropped from the 100 largest by 1970, only three were in the largest 50 in 1958, and all three lost their identity because of a merger, not because they failed or because they were surpassed by other firms. Of the 25 largest firms in 1909, 11 were still among the 100 largest in 1970. But this argues more for the stability of the American economy and the astuteness of management than it does for anything else.

Table 17
25 LARGEST INDUSTRIALS (BY ASSETS) 1909-1970

	1909	*1919*	*1958*	*1970*
U.S. Steel	1	1	3	11
Standard Oil (N.J.)	2	2	1	1
American Tobacco	3	22	38	43
International Merc. Marine	4	12	(2)	—
International Harv.	5	13	24	36
Anaconda Copper	6	16	23	54
U.S. Leather	7	36	(2)	—
Armour	8	3	85	(3)
American Sugar Ref.	9	35	(4)	—
Pullman	10	26	(4)	—
U.S. Rubber	11	8	55	83
Am. Smelting & Ref.	12	20	82	(4)
Singer Manufacturing	13	28	78	61
Swift	14	4	58	(4)
Consolidation Coal	15	27	94	—
General Electric	16	11	11	12
A.C.F. Industries	17	37	(4)	—
Col. Fuel & Iron	18	80	(4)	—
Corn Products Ref.	19	38	88	(4)
New England Navig.	20	(2)	—	—
American Can	21	41	32	73
Lackawanna Steel	22	64	(3)	—
American Woolen	23	42	(3)	—

Table 17 (continued)

	1909	*1919*	*1958*	*1970*
Westinghouse Elec.	24	29	17	21
B.F. Goodrich	25	24	65	84
General Motors	(4)	5	2	2
Beth. Steel	34	6	12	22
Ford	(4)	7	7	4
Socony Mobil	(4)	9	5	7
Midvale Steel	(4)	10	(3)	—
Sinclair Oil	(4)	14	16	(3)
Texaco	91	15	6	3
Phelps Dodge	49	17	83	(4)
DuPont	29	18	8	19
Gulf Oil	(4)	19	4	5
Union Carbide	(4)	21	14	20
Magnolia Petroleum	(4)	23	(3)	—
Standard Oil (Cal.)	(4)	25	10	10
Standard Oil (Ind.)	(4)	32	9	13
Shell Oil	(4)	(4)	13	15
Phillips Petroleum	(4)	(4)	15	23
IBM	(4)	(4)	18	6
Chrysler	(4)	89	19	14
Western Electric	55	46	20	18
Aluminum	(4)	49	21	30
Cities Service	(4)	(4)	24	37
Republic Steel	31	48	25	51
General Telephone	(4)	(4)	(4)	8
I. T. & T.	(4)	(4)	30	9
Atlantic Richfield	(4)	65	41	16
Tenneco	(4)	(4)	(4)	17
Eastman Kodak	60	71	34	24
Continental Oil	(4)	(4)	56	25

(2) Failed

(3) Merged

(4) Not in first 100

MERGER WAVES IN THE TWENTIETH CENTURY

As any historian would expect, much of what took place in business enter-prise in the twentieth century was a repetition, with different emphasis, of nineteenth-century phenomena. Thus, the merger movement of the late 1890s was repeated during the speculative 1920s and again when the stock market took off in the years after World War II. But there were some significant differences between 1890, 1920, and 1950. Fewer giant corporations participated in each successive merger wave. In the 1890s, the very large corporations consummated many of the alliances; in the 1920s, it was the middle-size group; and in the post-World War II era, most of the participants were small. As George Stigler described it, "In the early period, the leading firms seldom merged less than 50 percent of the industry's output; in the later period the percentage has hardly ever risen this high. The new goal of mergers is oligopoly."[6] A second difference was that in the twentieth century, bank mergers were as fashionable as mergers in manufacturing, mining, and transportation. Finally, the later merger movements were more concerned with conglomerate consolidations. In the 1890s, mergers continued the horizontal and vertical integration of the previous 20 years; in the 1920s, mergers of firms in different industries were interspersed with vertical integration; in the post-World War II period, diversification was the prevailing theme.

In relative numbers, the rate of merger in the 1920s has not been equaled at any time before or since. In absolute terms mergers in the 1920s surpassed all other periods except the 1960s. Mergers averaged 680 a year in the 1920s in comparison with about 360 a year in 1898-1900, 460 a year in 1948-1960, and 1,250 a year in the 1960s. In the years of the great bull market, 1925-1929, mergers averaged over 900 a year, reaching a high of 1,245 in 1929. Qualitatively, the merger movement of the 1920s rivaled its predecessor and far surpassed its successor. As has been said, giants merged in the 1890s, very large companies merged in the 1920s, and small companies joined forces in the 1950s and 1960s. Indeed, if merger movements were defined to encompass only major consolidations, the post-World War II era would not qualify as a merger movement. On the other hand, the 1890s would be memorable for having produced big business and the 1920s for having narrowed the gap between the big and the very big.

GOVERNMENT REACTION TO BUSINESS CONSOLIDATION

As soon as the first faint signs of giantism appeared in business, governments began to do something about it. All governments have always abhorred uncontrolled or unregulated monopoly. Yet most businessmen who had a possibility of achieving a monopolistic position strenuously exerted themselves to do so. Some governments, such as England, met the problem by putting some monopolies in the hands of a chosen few and attacking all others through the common law. Other nations, such as Germany, deliberately encouraged industrial firms to collaborate with each other in cartels under stringent government regulation. In the United States, by contrast, monopoly was considered an

[6]George J. Stigler, "Monopoly and Oligopoly by Merger," *American Economic Review,* Proceedings, Vol. VL (1950), reprinted in Richard B. Heflebower and George W. Stocking, eds., *Readings in Industrial Organization and Public Policy* (Homewood, Ill.: Richard D. Irwin, Inc., 1958).

inherent evil that restricted production and inflated prices, thereby exploiting the consumer and giving undeserved windfall profits to an antisocial few. Monopoly, or a market structure close to monopoly, was to be tolerated only when no alternative was possible. In the debates on what course of action should be followed in regulating business, it was taken for granted that free competition was the norm, the advantages of which were "too self-evident to be debated, too obvious to be asserted." Consequently, the economic rationale that underlay what came to be known as antitrust policy freely assumed that the elimination of monopoly would produce competition. Behavior and policy, therefore, were devoted to opposing monopoly rather than to shoring up competition.[7]

Although ostensibly concerned solely with economic issues, antitrust policy was just as much the offspring of social and ethical values. Indeed, at times economic considerations played an out-ot-tune second fiddle to social and ethical considerations in the enforcement of the antitrust laws and the regulation of business. Sociologists and anthropologists have pointed out that Americans have always admired control over things, but have resented control over people. Laymen have always been impressed with the American's sympathy for the underdog. Thus, in government regulation of business, the objective of protecting the weak in the economic market place has been as important as the elimination of monopoly and certainly more important than the shoring up of competition. In antitrust activity, this has meant attacking big business and protecting small business even at the possible expense of economic growth. As Judge Learned Hand put it:

> Throughout the history of these (antitrust) statutes it has been constantly assumed that one of their purposes was to perpetuate and preserve, for its own sake and in spite of possible cost, an organization of industry in small units.

Business leaders found this hard to understand. Their bewilderment was well expressed by James J. Hill when he heard that the Supreme Court had ruled against the Northern Securities Company, a merger of three important railroads. "It really seems hard," said Hill, "when we know that we have led all Western companies in opening the country and carrying at the lowest rates, that we should be compelled to fight for our lives against the political adventurers who have never done anything but pose and draw a salary."

The Sherman Act

Government regulation of business in America began in the Colonial Period. At that time, when goods were scarce relative to the economic ambitions of the

---

[7]Some interesting insights on antitrust policy from Coke to Theodore Roosevelt can be culled from the great detail in Hans B. Thorelli, *The Federal Antitrust Policy* (Baltimore: The Johns Hopkins Press, 1955).

citizens, and when medieval and mercantilist thought prevailed, governments used medieval precepts in trying to protect consumers. The concept of a "just price" was deeply ingrained in the legislation of the times, and the colonies enacted laws designed to prevent anyone from gaining a monopoly or cornering the market.

As production increased and laissez faire economics, with its emphasis on market forces, attained respectability, direct government regulation of business diminished. Under the assumption that the normal forces of competition would constrain the businessman's propensity to monopolize, the Federal government did not try to regulate competition or the internal operation of business, and on the state and local level, regulation was on a small scale. But a deep distrust of big business in the guise of the corporation always prevailed. In the Pennsylvania Constitutional Convention of 1837, it was proposed that no charter should be granted for the accomplishment of a project which individual activity could accomplish. In 1851, Ohio discussed the possibility of substituting partnerships for corporations. Maine changed its mind five times between 1821 and 1856 about whether to permit corporations to enjoy limited liability.

State government regulation became more active in the late nineteenth century. Acting under the common law, various states moved against the trusts, which had become a popular form of business organization. Their actions seemed to have been signally successful, for the trust device was abruptly abandoned. But perhaps this was more because business entrepreneurs had discovered in the holding company a more effective method of consolidation than because of state activity. In any event, the use of the holding company immunized large-scale enterprises from effective local regulation. As in other instances, the elimination of the state as a policeman, instead of shaking confidence in government regulation, led to a popular demand for Federal participation.

The national government first entered the business of formal regulation with the Interstate Commerce Commission in 1887, and then on a broader basis with the Sherman Act of 1890. The Sherman Act ("An act to protect trade and commerce against unlawful restraints and monopolies") made illegal "every contract, combination in the form of trust or otherwise, or conspiracy, in restraint of trade or commerce among the several States, or with foreign nations." Every person who monopolized, attempted to monopolize, or conspired to monopolize any part of interstate trade or commerce was guilty of a misdemeanor subject to a fine of up to $5,000 and imprisonment for up to one year.

Short and very much to the point, the Sherman Act seemed quite straightforward, but this quickly proved to be an illusion. The law soon broke down in a morass of halfhearted enforcement, widely different legal interpretations, and endless semantics. Corporation lawyers immediately busied themselves asking each other a set of enigmatic questions, the answers to which are still far from clear. What was trade? Was it any different from commerce? Did Congress mean every restraint of trade, or only "unlawful" restraints? What was an unlawful restraint of trade? Did this mean monopoly, and if so, what was a monopoly? Did huge size by itself constitute restraint of trade? Or was some predatory action required?

Over the years, the courts and Congress have produced a wide variety of answers to these questions, veering from one view to a quite different one, and then back again. Antitrust policy and its administration and interpretation have never fitted a long-range, preconceived pattern. Instead, government regulation has been a patchwork evolving pragmatically and reflecting the business cycle, the public image of the businessman, the prevailing social and economic philosophy, and the composition of the courts.

The Sherman Act got off to a very slow start. For one thing, the officials who were supposed to enforce the legislation had neither the funds nor the inclination to do so. In fact, one of the early attorney generals once characterized antitrust policy as "a little narrow pinchbeck policy." Given this disinclination, it was not surprising that the Sherman Act was invoked only 18 times in its first ten years, and four of these cases involved labor unions.

The first case to reach the Supreme Court was *U. S.* v. *E. C. Knight Co.* (1895). The American Sugar Refining Co., which refined 65 percent of American sugar, purchased E. C. Knight and three other producers to bring its capacity up to 98 percent. The government tried to enjoin the purchase, arguing that it would produce a monopolistic combination in restraint of trade. The Court decided against the government on the ground that "manufacture and commerce are two distinct and very different things. The latter does not include the former."

The sugar case is usually considered a milestone in antitrust history, but its importance has been greatly exaggerated. It is charged that the Court's ruling dealt a critical, almost fatal, blow to antitrust policy, because, if manufacturing was not interstate commerce, most of the so-called trusts could not be touched. But this charge makes little sense in light of the fact that only half a dozen cases had been raised under the Sherman Act. Moreover, the Court's extremely parochial definition of commerce, which could not continue very long, destined the *Knight* case to antiquarian importance. The narrow definition of *commerce* began to break down when the Court in *Addyston Pipe and Steel Company v. U. S.* (1899) held that manufacturers had violated the Sherman Act by setting up a system of collusive bidding. It was completely shattered by the *Northern Securities* case (1904) and *U. S. v. Swift and Co. et al.* (1905), which held that "whatever combination has the direct and necessary effect of restricting competition is in restraint of trade." In subsequent decisions, the courts have continuously broadened the definition of interstate commerce until today it may include almost any economic behavior, including the operation of a small country store in a small country town.

The rule of reason and the Clayton Act

Meanwhile, the courts were turning their attention to the fascinating question of whether Congress really meant *every* restraint of trade or whether it meant *unreasonable* restraints. At first, the courts took the congressional language literally. In *U. S.* v. *Trans-Missouri Freight Association et al.* (1897), the majority held that the language meant just what it said, but Justice White, in the dissenting opinion shared by three others, enunciated what later became known as "the rule of reason." "The words restraint of trade," he said, "embrace only contracts which unreasonably restrain trade, and, therefore, reasonable contracts, although they, in some measure, restrain trade, are not within the meaning of the words."

During the Progressive Era, a significant body of opinion in politics and economics openly questioned the traditional view that competition was the norm of economic life even in a free society. Writers such as Herbert Croly and Charles Van Hise argued that policy makers should resign themselves to the proposition that large-scale enterprise was inevitable, and they should cut their cloth accordingly. President Roosevelt was much impressed by this view. "Combinations in industry," he said, "are the result of an imperative economic law which cannot be repealed by political legislation. . . . The way out lies, not in attempting to prevent such combinations, but in completely controlling them in the interest of public welfare." The Supreme Court was also much impressed by the so-called "new competition." The rule of reason which had been in the minority now emerged as the prevailing view. The majority first enunciated the doctrine that there were good and bad combinations and that the good combinations were not to be dissolved or frowned upon as an *obiter dictum* in the *Northern Securities* case (1904), but it was fully explored in the *Standard Oil* and *American Tobacco* cases of 1911. In the *Standard Oil* case, Chief Justice White, now speaking for a clear majority, held that the Sherman law was intended to prohibit unreasonable restraints of trade where there was an intent to monopolize and where unfair competition ruled in the place of free competition.

The promulgation of the rule of reason was the last of a series of incidents that convinced many original proponents that the Sherman Act had not accomplished its mission. It had not clarified the perennial confusion over the nature of competition nor had it eliminated and outlawed all monopolistic practices. Indeed, some overzealous critics labeled the act "the mother of trusts," for, although it apparently prohibited agreements among independent firms (so-called "loose-knit" combinations), it did not forbid close-knit combinations, that is, mergers or consolidations.[8] Moreover, the law had fallen much

---

[8]The trusts were a rare species of polygenetic anthropomorphism, for they had many

more heavily on labor unions than its original supporters had intended. In order to clear the antitrust air, Congress, in 1914, passed the Clayton Act and the Federal Trade Commission Act.

The Clayton Act was designed to prevent monopolies before they happend. It prohibited interlocking directorates, price discrimination, and the acquisition of competitors where the result would be a substantial lessening of competition. The Federal Trade Commission was supposed to prevent unfair competiton.

During the 1920s, antitrust policy reverted to the doldrums that had been so characteristic in the early 1890s. Prosperity and the political climate were primarily responsible for this, but businessmen also lent a helping hand. Judge Gary's tactics, for example, were always colored by a concern for the Sherman Act. The annual reports, the news conferences, and the definite pursuit of good public relations were not unmindful of the fact that United States Steel was frequently in the antitrust courts.

Although it was a time of good feeling between government and business, at least two cases in this era were of more than passing significance as benchmarks in antitrust history. In 1920, the Supreme Court extended the rule of reason in deciding against the government in the *U.S. Steel* case. The majority opinion interpreted the government's brief as contending "that strength in any producer or seller is a menace to the public interest and illegal, because there is potency in it for mischief." After dismissing this as a "manifest fallacy" the Court continued, "The corporation is undoubtedly of impressive size. . . . But we must adhere to the law, and the law does not make mere size an offense, or the existence of unexerted power an offense." Much of this thinking was to be abandoned in less than a generation. A similar fate was to meet the Court's logic in *Thatcher Manufacturing Co. v. Federal Trade Commission* (1926). Here the Court held that the Clayton Act strictures against the purchase of a competitor applied only to stock purchase. This meant that there was no violation of the Clayton Act where one competitor bought the assets of another. In 1950, this peculiar interpretation was specifically negated by the Celler Amendment to the Clayton Act.

Government's flight from competition during the great depression

At various times during the Progressive Era and after, the government had been chipping away at the faith in competition that underlay the antitrust policy. In 1918, Congress passed the Webb-Pomerene Act, which permitted cartels in international trade by exempting them from the antitrust acts. In 1920, the Transportation Act encouraged combination in railroading. During the 1920s,

---

mothers. Free-traders referred to the tariff as the "mother of trusts," critics of the Sherman Act called it "the mother of trusts," and some students of economics thought that economic growth was the "mother of trusts."

too, the so-called new competition further infiltrated business thinking. A new breed of businessmen, the professional managers, disapprovingly looked back upon the old breed's competitive tactics. The new theory of competition, with all its inconsistency, was perhaps best stated by Judge Elbert H. Gary. After paying lip service to "the natural law of supply and demand," Gary continued by saying: "We never reach out intentionally to get a competitor's business. If the price of a commodity has been sufficiently established to secure publication in the journals, we never cut under that price . . . for two reasons: first, it would not be the fair thing to do; and secondly, it would only be a question of time before . . . we would feel the effects of it, because someone else might cut our prices . . . even worse than we had cut their prices. . . ."9

In line with the tenets of the new competition, there occurred a proliferation of trade associations which intentionally or unintentionally were designed to circumvent the Sherman Act by restricting competition. Their activities included "fair trade practices" and "open price" arrangements which published each member's prices and production for all to see. These cooperative activities had the blessing of the political administration. Secretary of Commerce Hoover said of them, "We are . . . in the middle of a great revolution . . . We are passing from a period of extremely individualistic action into a period of associational activities." Hoover's aide, Julius Klein, emphasized as "conspicuous among the newer forces of control, the vastly increased cooperative and collaborative element in modern business."10

Perfect cooperation, however, was, like perfect competition, more a state of mind than a reality. At least, business seemed to find it necessary to create artificial means to control man's "propensity to compete." This became quite evident during the great depression of the 1930s when, under economic stress, cooperation quickly reverted to "cutthroat competition." A number of businessmen, business spokesmen, and sociological economists urged that something be done about this unfair competition. They believed that overproduction had caused the depression. Almost as soon as the gloomy era began, they called for changes in the antitrust laws to permit business "to enter into contracts for the purpose of equalizing production and consumption." The United States Chamber of Commerce and other influential organizations argued that economic recovery could be greatly advanced through business cooperation under the aegis of Federal and state legislation. They urged the administration to adopt the Swope plan,11 or something similar. The Hoover administration rejected the whole idea with a sweeping condemnation, "There is no stabilization of price

9*Addresses and Statements of Elbert H. Gary* (privately printed, no date).

10Charles A. Beard, *Whither Mankind?* (New York: Longmans, Green & Co., Inc., 1928), p. 104; *Journal of Commerce,* October 29, 1921.

11A plan for the "self-regulation" of business proposed by Gerard Swope, head of General Electric. Many businessmen objected to all such plans.

without price fixing. . . . It is the most gigantic proposal of monopoly ever made in history."

But other administrations were much more amenable. In 1931, California passed a "fair trade" law, permitting producers to establish by contract with dealers minimum retail prices for their goods. Within a short time, 43 other states had adopted similar legislation. But the most extreme departure from the traditional American policy of resisting monopoly and economic collusion came with the National Industrial Recovery Act of 1933. Through the NIRA, the government tried to persuade the firms in each major industry to create, through a trade association, a code of fair practices, setting minimum prices, minimum wages, and production quotas. It was hoped that this elaborate blueprint for industry planning would protect the economically weak and enable the economy to pick itself up by the bootstraps, so that depression would give way to recovery.

In retrospect, the NIRA appears to have been a completely irrational piece of business; it seems never to have happened, for as soon as it was declared unconstitutional in 1935, the New Deal reversed its policy and inaugurated the most vigorous antitrust campaign in history. At roughly the same time, the Supreme Court began to press a much harder line, but Congress, ostensibly to protect small business, continued to restrict competition. In 1936, it passed the Robinson-Patman Act. In a sense, this law encouraged competition by prohibiting price discrimination on sales that were otherwise identical. But the act was really designed to protect small business, for it prohibited firms from sellling more cheaply in one part of the country than another and selling at "unreasonably low prices for the purpose of destroying competition." A second example of Congress' restrictions on competition came in 1937 with the Miller-Tydings Amendment, which exempted fair-trade contracts from the Sherman Act. Later, when resourceful businessmen invented ways and means of avoiding fair-trade restrictions, Congress passed the McGuire Act (1952), which not only continued the exemption of price maintenance, but gave firms the right to enforce fair-trade agreements against nonsigners and to fix prices not only at a minimum, but at any point. Again, however, resourceful businessmen cut the underpinning from this legislation, this time by attacking fair-trade laws in the state courts. Today, there are only 23 states in which nonsigners of price agreements are bound by fair-trade laws.

In the effort to protect the weak and at the same time to preserve competition, the policies of the different branches of government became a mixture of inconsistencies. On the one hand, the executive department attempted to encourage pure competition by attacking business concentration and resisting mergers on the theory that the consumer's bargaining position was weak and that free enterprise could not retain its dynamic character in an atmosphere of concentrated business power. On the other hand, Congress, on the theory that the weaker, small businessman needed protection, discouraged price competition and made prices less sensitive to changes in the market forces of supply and demand.

Antitrust and the courts since 1945

In the 40 years between the enactment of the Sherman Act and the outbreak of the depression, certain interpretations of the antitrust laws achieved a status of respectability. Among these were the principle that the Sherman Act applied only to unreasonable restraints of trade and the doctrine that size alone was no proof of monopoly. This line of reasoning evolved during a period when economists defined competition as a condition in which two or more sellers each tried to maximize income without regard to the action of the other. But then in the depression, under the influence of imperfect competition theory, competition took on a quite different meaning. "Pure competition" was defined as a situation in which many sellers, no one of whom could influence the price, dealt in products that were exactly the same. "Monopoly" continued to be defined as a one-seller market. Both pure competition and monopoly were very rare. The most common market structure—indeed, the only market structure in manufacturing and distribution—was a combination of competition and monopoly recognized as monopolistic competition, imperfect competition, or oligopoly.

Some economists looked upon imperfect competition as a fact of life about which nothing could be done. In formulating policy, they examined the behavior of a given market structure. To express this in the current language of the economist, they were more interested in performance than in structure. Their yardsticks for deducing the existence of insidious monopoly were not the number of sellers or the ratio of concentration, but ease of entry, effect on economic growth, price behavior, unused capacity, and technological innovation. Where a given industry scored well on the above tests, the market structure was described as one of "workable competition," the effects of which were analogous to pure competition.

It is, of course, impossible to say how much influence the new concepts had on the courts, but the latter did refer increasingly to imperfect competition theory. Impressed by the alleged evils of oligopoly, the courts jettisoned the rule of reason and the strictures against regarding huge size as evidence of monopoly. Judgment of antitrust violation reverted to questions of structure rather than of predatory performance. In five of the most important antitrust cases decided between 1945 and 1962, four rested on the criterion of size and only one referred to the doctrine of workable competition.

In the *Cellophane* case, the United States brought a judgment against the DuPont Company, charging an illegal monopoly in cellophane. The district court held in favor of the company on two grounds: first, that DuPont acted like a competitor and not like a monopolist; second, that, although DuPont had substantial control over cellophane, it had only a small share of flexible packaging. The Supreme Court in 1955 affirmed the judgment, emphasizing that the flexible packaging market, not the cellophane market, was the relevant one for determining market control. The *Cellophane* decision was the only important victory for a large industrial firm. It was also an uneasy victory, becaue it was a four-to-three decision. In four other decisions, size and market control ruled as the decisive factors in government victories.

In 1945, in the celebrated *Alcoa* case, Judge Hand effectively obliterated both the rule of reason and the concept that size alone was not evidence of monopoly. In holding the Aluminum Company in violation of the Sherman Act, Judge Hand said, "Congress did not condone 'good trusts' and condemn 'bad' ones; it forbade all." He put the question of monopoly strictly on a yardstick basis: a 90 percent share of the market "is enough to constitute a monopoly; it is doubtful whether 60 or 64 percent would be enough, and certainly 33 percent is not."

In the *Bethlehem-Youngstown* case (1958), the companies took the then novel position that the number of competitors in a market was much less important than the strength of the individual competitors. They argued that a market of four competitiors, one very large and three small, was less competitive than a market in which there were two competitors of like size. The government argued that the proposed merger would substantially lessen competition because it would make Bethlehem too large a steel company even though its capacity would be about 20 to 25 percent of total steel production. The district court held that the proposed merger violated the Celler Amendment to the Clayton Act because there was a reasonable probability that it would substantially lessen competition.

The decision in *Brown Shoe Company* v. *U. S.* (1962) carried antitrust to much greater lengths. The government sought to nullify Brown Shoe's purchase of the Kinney Shoe Chain. Brown argued that, even though it was the third largest shoe producer, it accounted for only 1.2 percent of all sales. Moreover, the companies were in different lines of commerce, the one in medium- and the other in low-priced shoes. The Court held that the Celler-Kefauver Amendment of 1950 intended "to arrest mergers at a time when the trend to lessening competition in a line of commerce was still in its infancy." It therefore decided in favor of the government.

One other case touched on so many points that it deserves to be quoted in somewhat more detail. In 1949, the government brought a Clayton Act suit against the DuPont Company, seeking to force it to divest itself of its 23 percent share in General Motors. The government contended that DuPont's stock interest gave it an unfair advantage in selling finishes and fabrics to General Motors. The government pointed to the fact that DuPont supplied two-thirds of

General Motors' finishes. The defendant pointed to the equally incontestable fact that this was only 3.5 percent of DuPont's production. Which, then, was the relevant market, General Motors or the universe of finish users? The Court in 1957 held in favor of the government. In doing so, it said:

> . . . The inference is overwhelming that du Pont's commanding position was promised by its stock interest and was not gained solely on competitive merit.
>
> We agree with the trial court that considerations of price, quality and service were not overlooked by either du Pont or General Motors. Pride in its products and its high financial stake in General Motors' success would naturally lead du Pont to try to supply the best. But the wisdom of this business judgment cannot obscure the fact . . . that du Pont purposely employed its stock to pry open the General Motors' market to entrench itself as the primary supplier of General Motors' requirements for automotive finishes and fabrics.
>
> Similarly, the fact that all concerned in high executive posts in both companies acted honorably and fairly, each in the honest conviction that his actions were in the best interests of his own company and without any design to overreach anyone, including du Pont's competitors, does not defeat the Government's right to relief. It is not requisite to the proof of a violation of Section 7 to show that restraint or monopoly was intended.
>
> The statutory policy of fostering free competition is obviously furthered when no supplier has an advantage over his competitors from an acquisition of his customer's stock likely to have the effects condemned by the statute.

Judge Brennan ended in a burst of pyrotechnics: "The fire that was kindled in 1917 continues to smolder. It burned briskly to forge the ties that bind the General Motors' market to DuPont, and if it has quieted down, it remains hot, and, from past performance, is likely at any time to blaze and make the fusion complete."

The effect of antitrust policy on economic growth

Antitrust policy has never been guided by a set of specifically defined objectives. Its goals, as near as they can be discerned, have been to resist monopoly, to prevent business concentration, and to protect (for moral, ethical, and sentimental reasons) the social structure of what is vaguely known as *small business*. Although at times economic growth was considered to be an indirect goal ancillary to the prevention of monopoly, antitrust policy was never designed to promote or encourage economic growth directly. The Attorney General's National Committee on the Antitrust Laws made this clear in 1955. In its opinion, a company that practiced "undue restraints of competition" could not be excused by proof that its actions represented progressive managerial policy or that it had performed acceptable social service or benefited the public. In other words, competition was desired not so much for its economic efficiency as for its constraint with respect to economic power.

In similar fashion, antitrust policy has been evaluated much more on moral and ethical grounds than on its addition to or subtraction from economic growth.[12] Business critics have concentrated on the fairness of the policy. Probably the most extreme expression of this view was delivered by Henry Lee Higginson, the Boston banker. "The Sherman Law," said he, "is probably the most vicious and unreasonable law that was ever passed by a legislative body." Other critics have been concerned with its success in breaking up so-called monopoly as though that was a desirable end in itself. It is not nearly so easy to measure the effects of antitrust on economic growth. Viewed by its severest critics, the effect has been most deleterious: to some, because it did not prevent further concentration of business; to others, because it did. According to its staunchest defenders, antitrust policy has signally aided economic growth. Which view one accepts depends on the weight put on the benefits of competition, the measurement of the efficiency with which market forces operate, the estimate of the gains to be gathered from economies of scale, the evaluation of the efficiency of large-scale business enterprise, notions of the causes of economic growth, and judgments on the executive and judicial enforcement of the antitrust statutes.

Antitrust policy has discouraged the natural tendency to resort to the more invidious forms of market control: price fixing, collusive bidding, and the division of the market. It has also been a necessary spur to counteract an inevitable disposition to let well enough alone. It has, in other words, kept big business "on its toes." But beyond this, its effects become very fuzzy. Supporters of rigid antitrust policy rest their case on three heroic premises. They equate pure competition with economic growth. They imply that big business is inefficient. They assume that political-legal action can produce pure competition. It is at least somewhat questionable whether pure competition always did a better job than imperfect competition in fostering economic growth. It is also questionable whether big business was inefficient in an absolute sense or in comparison with small business. What is most questionable is whether political-legal action could break down business concentration and produce a purely competitive market structure. Here, defenders of antitrust policy tend to exaggerate both its potentials and its accomplishments. It has been argued that stringent interpretation of the laws has had a significantly restraining effect on consolidation whereas loose interpretations have excessively encouraged combination and monopoly. Thus, it is said that the *Sugar* case was a great victory for

<hr/>

[12]For a broad discussion of the effects of antitrust, see Clair Wilcox, *Public Policies toward Business* (Homewood, Ill.: Richard D. Irwin, Inc., 1971), Chap. 11.

monopoly. Yet the American Sugar Refining Company, which won the great victory, controlled 98 percent of the business in 1895 but less than 50 percent when Henry O. Havemyer, its entrepreneur, died in 1907. From the time of its victory, it was beset by new competitiors, notably Spreckels and Arbuckle, who entered the field and stayed to be successful. In 1910, when the company manufactured 42 percent of the sugar, it owned 7 of the 21 cane sugar refineries and had an interest in 33 of the 68 beet sugar factories.

It is also claimed that the *Sugar* case inaugurated the merger movement of the 1890s and the *Northern Securities* case ended it. But the merger movement really did not begin until 1898, three years after the *E. C. Knight* case, and it did not end until 1906, two years after the *Northern Securities* decision. To be sure, the great merger movement of the 1920s took place in an environment of relaxed antitrust enforcement, but the same could not be said of the period since 1950. The growth of big business, whether fed internally or externally, seemed to proceed along a trend line regardless of the lax or rigid attitudes of antitrust enforcers.

THE SEPARATION OF OWNERSHIP AND CONTROL
IN THE LARGE CORPORATION

In the 1957 *DuPont* case, the Supreme Court ordered DuPont to divest itself of its stock interest in General Motors. This decision was much more than a trivial incident in the DuPont-General Motors chronicle or in the perennial contest between the government and big business. For 40 years, some member of the DuPont managerial hierarchy had taken an active part in General Motors, ostensibly to protect DuPont's substantial investment. The 1957 decision was, therefore, a kind of benchmark in the continuous trend toward the separation of the ownership and control of business enterprise. A few economists, especially the late Joseph Schumpeter, thought that this trend was one of a parcel that posed a much greater threat to economic growth and the continued existence of the free enterprise system than did the evils of imperfect competition.

The separation of ownership from control was an inescapable result of the growth of big business and the influence of finance capitalism. For, almost by definition, ownership was split off from control as soon as it became distributed through shares that could be bought and sold on stock exchanges. Even if shareholders had the desire and the knowledge to make the many intricate decisions involved in running a mass-production business, they could not do so, for it was physically impossible for all of them to meet together and to formulate policy in a kind of entrepreneurial town meeting.

Instead of being in the hands of those who owned the business, control in the sense of the power to make important decisions vested more and more in a group of professional executives whose ownership stake in the companies they managed was either small or nonexistent. This was another link in the ever-lengthening chain of division of labor. The "industrial revolution" and the factory system separated the worker from the instruments of production. Large-scale enterprise, in turn, did the same thing to the owners. But here again, a word of caution is necessary. The ascendancy of the career executive did not take place overnight. There was no managerial revolution. The evolution began in the railroads around the middle of the nineteenth century,[13] and it began there because they were gigantic businesses. It appeared in manufacturing and trade almost simultaneously with the appearance of large-scale enterprise. In 1912, Andrew Carnegie, in what must have been for him a moment of painful frustration and deep depression, told a congressional committee: "Private partnerships are out of fashion. There is not a big concern in America that I know today that is managed except by officers under salaries."

Carnegie was very farsighted, and his judgment was a little premature. It is estimated that in 1910, approximately 80 percent of all nonfarm managers were still self-employed, and one-quarter of the capital stock of a large sample of sizable companies was owned by executives. But the movement was well under way, and it proceeded at an accelerated rate. One study has shown that 76 percent of the business executives born in 1771-1800 were owner-operators; 5 percent were career managers. Of those born in 1831-1860, 56 percent owned businesses they had built; 21 percent were "bureaucrats." Of the 1891-1920 group, 18 percent were owner-operators; 48 percent were career men. In 1950, 60 percent of managers were still self-employed; but by 1970, only 25 percent owned their own businesses, whereas 75 percent worked for someone else.[14]

The professional manager was a person of very diverse talents. According to Crawford H. Greenewalt, past president of DuPont, "Specific skill in any given field becomes less and less important as the executive advances through successive levels of responsibility. Today, for example, there are thousands of people in the DuPont Company whose expertness in their special field I can only regard with awe and adminiration."[15]

The career executive's role was to act as trustee for a collective enterprise in which management, owners, creditors, workers, competitiors, consumers, and government had much more than passing interest. It was his function to keep all of these sometimes antagonistic groups as happy as their divergent interests would

[13] See pp. 318-20.

[14] Committee on Investigation of United States Steel Corporation, 1912; F. W. Taussig and W. S. Barker, "American Corporations and Their Executives," *Quarterly Journal of Economics*, Vol. XL (1925); *Historical Statistics of the United States*, p. 75; Bureau of Labor Statistics, *Employment and Earnings;* Reinhard Bendix, *Work and Authority in Industry* (New York: John Wiley & Sons, Inc., 1956), p. 229.

[15] Herrymon Maurer, *Great Enterprise* (New York: The Macmillan Company, 1955), p. 146.

permit. This meant broadening the motives and objectives of business enterprise. The profit motive worked very well when business only had its owners and customers to satisfy. In the new environment, business enterprise had to emphasize new motives and new objectives in order to placate the government, the public, and the conflicting strata of management. The profit motive still dominated, but it was much more qualified and less uncompromising. According to Thomas C. Cochran, "Good organization men were probably less aggressive risk takers, less relentless in the quest for profits than the owner managers of smaller enterprises."[16] The professional manager thought more in terms of long- than short-run profits, and his profit goals were always tempered by prestige objectives. Growth for growth's sake in terms of the firm's share of the market and the slope of its sales curve were very high on his slate, as were the desire for personal security, personal prestige, and the perpetuation of the business.

Ideally, the career executive was the cognitive or sophisticated entrepreneur described by Arthur Cole. He was supposed to be concerned, not with day-to-day activities, but with long-range plans and objectives. He required a broad knowledge of the total business situation as well as a knowledge of his own company. No single entrepreneur possessed this breadth of knowledge or the time and energy necessary to make the thousands of decisions that daily faced the large-scale enterprise. Management, therefore, broke its activities into specialized pieces, just as it had previously split the job on the production line.

Although nothing completely replaced what is referred to vaguely as "business judgment," management used applied mathematics, advanced accounting, statistics, economics, sociology, psychology, and the magic of the computer to help solve its riddles. Executives came to depend on large internal administrative staffs and ancillary institutions for information and data. Thus, a vast office force came into being. Again, this phenomenon had appeared at a much earlier date in the railroad business. In 1860, for example, the Delaware and Hudson Canal Company needed an entire building to house the administrative staff that directed its 4,200 employees. But the great armies of office workers in manufacturing and trade are the product of the last 15 or 20 years of managerial rationalization. Office workers have multiplied from 8.5 percent of the working population in 1910 to 12.5 percent in 1930, 17 percent in 1950, and 30 percent in 1970.

By necessity, the modern corporation became a bureaucratic structure. For splitting down complicated decisions, creating intricate organization charts, cataloging office workers as staff or line, and sorting the staff into departments meant routine and systematic administration, and systematized administration is the essence of bureaucracy.

[16]Thomas C. Cochran, *The American Business System* (Cambridge, Mass.: Harvard University Press, 1957), p. 180.

The corporation problem and economic growth

In the vast literature on the place of the businessman and the business corporation, comparatively little space has been given to an evaluation of the role of
business enterprise in economic growth. It is not easy to generalize about
whether the separation of ownership and control and the ascendancy of the
professional manager advanced or retarded economic growth. It would seem
logical to conclude that the division of managerial responsibility and the greater
degree of specialization of recent decades made business enterprise more rational
and more efficient, leading to a more effective use of economic resources.
Experts helped to make the decisions in each field. Research became more
scientific, more a matter of routine than of vision.

But the new system also had many disadvantages. Large-scale enterprise
bred bureaucracy, and bureaucracy deadened intiative and deemphasized risk. It
emphasized stability and security, thereby weakening the effectiveness of the old
buisness incentives. The career executive in the large corporation, the indictment
ran, was less flexible than the "socially irresponsible captain of industry" of a
century ago. Alfred P. Sloan, who was a large stockholder as well as president of
General Motors, recognized the nature of the problem when he said:

> In practically all of our activities, we seem to suffer from the inertia
> resulting from our great size. . . . I cannot help but feel that General
> Motors missed a lot. . . . Sometimes I must be forced to the conclusion
> that General Motors is so large, its inertia so great, that it is impossible
> for us to be real leaders.[17]

In many respects, the problems of managing big business were the same as
the problems of managing big government, big labor, big education, or big anything. Many members of the managerial group adopted the same psychology and
the same working plan held by the typical civil service employee. Admittedly,
the effects of the opiate of bureaucracy were most prominent in the lower
echelons; but even among top executives, there was a tendency to avoid risk and
to seek stability. In the early 1900s, the enervating effects of bureaucracy and
the seemingly pleasant rewards of large-scale enterprise for the top echelons were
being pointed out in the large insurance companies.[18] To some, the preservation
of the job became the paramount goal. The ideal was to become an anonymous
cog in an enormous machine. Initiative was repressed, because "going out on a
limb" might imperil the security of the jobholder. In the middle 1920s, an

---

[17]Quoted in House Committee on the Judiciary, *Study of Monopoly Power*, Part 2-B,
1949, p. 1214.

[18]Morton Keller, *The Life Insurance Enterprise,1885-1910* (Cambridge, Mass.: Harvard
University Press, 1963).

executive of a utility trade association viewed the entrepreneurial world from the depth of discouragement:

> We are raising a lot of thoroughly drilled "yes ma'ams" in the big corporations, who have no minds of their own; no opinions. As soon as the old individualists die, and there are not so many of them left, I think the corporations will have a lot of trouble in getting good executives. After a man has served 20 or 30 years in one of these monstrous corporations, he is not liable to have much of a mind of his own.[19]

As with any blanket indictment, there were important exceptions to the bureaucratic bill of particulars. Business bureaucracy differed in one extremely important respect from other bureaucracies: the criteria of success or failure were much clearer; they appeared in the profit or loss that showed upon the income statement. And this elemental difference vitiated much of the criticism deduced from the assumption of unqualified bureaucracy. The career executive may have been much less flexible than the old-time entrepreneur, but there is little evidence to support the notion. Actually, it was the new-style businessman who carried through diversification and decentralization, the major change in business enterprise in the twentieth century. The empire-building owner-entrepreneur was either unwilling or unable to cope with the problem of adjusting to the changes it necessitated.

Somewhat inconsistently, critics argued that losses were less effective in discouraging mistakes in the twentieth century than in the nineteenth century. The members of the new managerial class had relatively little stake in the business they operated. They therefore did not have to pay for their own mistakes with their own money. For the same reasons, it was argued that profits had lost most of their effectiveness in stirring entrepreneurs to ever-greater heights. But neither the older nor the newer entrepreneur worked for money alone. When Alfred P. Sloan said in 1938, "Making money ceased to interest me years ago. It's the job that counts,"[20] he was reiterating what John D. Rockefeller and Andrew Carnegie had said somewhat differently a generation before. Generalizations on what made the businessmen run are more dangerous than most generalizations; but, when all is said and done, the contribution of business to the economy rested more on the managerial ability of individual businessmen than on the size, the legal structure, or the bureaucratic nature of the business organization. Some businessmen had the ability to make intelligent adjustments; others did not.

The critics were on safer ground in insisting that the separation of ownership and control tended to weaken the businessmen's position in American

---

[19]Carl D. Thompson, *Confessions of the Power Trust* (New York: E. P. Dutton & Co., Inc., 1932), p. 14.

[20]*Fortune*, March 1938.

society. As the process of running a business became more routine, it seemed to the general public that making business decisions required no unusual effort or ability. It appeared so easy that it came to be accepted as part of ordinary day-to-day existence. As Oswald Knauth, a thoughtful and sympathetic managerial executive, expressed it, "The degree of success that management must produce to remain in office is surprisingly small."[21] The businessman began to lose his glamor; society was no longer impressed by him but began to take him for granted. Professor Schumpeter recognized this as threatening the whole structure of capitalist society when he wrote, "Success no longer carried that connotation of individual achievement which would raise not only the man but also his group into a durable position of social leadership. . . . Since capitalist enterprise, by its very achievements, tends to automatize progress, we conclude that it tends to make itself superfluous—to break to pieces under the pressure of its own success."[22]

BUSINESS PERFORMANCE

The mortality rate among business firms

Of all the species known to the economist, the business enterprise has one of the shortest life expectancies. The median age of all concerns in the United States is seven years. The chances of a firm reaching the age of ten years under the same ownership is about one in five. To put this the other way around, more than four out of five businesses disappear before they reach their teens. It may, however, be of some scant comfort for the would-be entrepreneur to know that the mortaility rate has dropped quite significantly in recent years.

In the early nineteenth century, according to Nat Griswold, a very successful businessman, 7 out of 100 merchants succeeded in business. The other "93 in the 100 of untold thousands, were bankrupts." In 1840, General Henry Dearborn, one-time Collector of the Boston Port, estimated that a mere 5 of every 100 commercial traders in 1800 were still in business. At about the same time, a Boston banker said that only 6 out of a thousand accounts of 1798 were still in existence. In 1950, the *Bankers' Magazine* declared it "a notable fact, in the history of mercantile life in the United States, that of the number who engage in it full seven-tenths fail from one to three times."

Dun and Bradstreet has kept figures on business failures[23] since 1857. The

[21]Oswald Knauth, *Managerial Enterprise* (New York: W. W. Norton & Company, Inc., 1948), p. 45.

[22]Joseph A. Schumpeter, *Capitalism, Socialism and Democracy* (New York: Harper & Row, Publishers, 1947), pp. 133-34.

[23]Not including finance, insurance, real estate, amusements, and railroads.

failure rate did not vary very much in the 60 years from the 1870s to the end of the Great Depression. The record number of annual failures, 242 per ten thousand goes back to 1857. In each of the three major depressions (1873-1878, 1893-1897, and 1930-33), failures averaged 125 to 129 per ten thousand firms. With the exception of the 1920s, the rate was just about as sticky during the prosperous years that preceded panics. Failures averaged 76 per ten thousand annually in the early 1870s, 78 in the 1880s, and 85 in the early 1900s. Between 1923 and 1929, failures averaged 102 per ten thousand firms. In contrast to this, failures have averaged the extraordinarily low rate of 44 per ten thousand since 1950.

Bankruptcies have not occurred with the same frequency in all businesses. Their incidence is high in retail trade and relatively low in wholesaling and finance. Three-fourths of all wholesale firms, but only three-fifths in retailing, survive their first year. Surprising as it may seem, efforts to protect the small independent operator by attacking his large competitor seem to have had just the opposite effect. Small retailers seem to have thrived best in competition with chain stores. [24]

Business profits in the nineteenth century

Data on profits are the least adequate statistics available to the economic historian. But it is safe to say that at any time in American history, a person who staked his all in a business venture had a very remote possibility of striking it rich, a somewhat better opportunity of making a fair living, and a strong probability of losing everything. Risks were great, losses were heavy, and failures were frequent, but profits were sometimes very large, and there was no discernible tendency for them to equalize among industries or among the firms in any individual industry.

There are no figures on aggregate or average business profits before the twentieth century. The scattered data that we have show rather high and very volatile rates of return. The Boston Manufacturing Company paid dividends of 15 to 22.5 percent in both the very good and the very bad years from 1817 to 1824, but profits sank in the depressed 1840s. The Glasgow Company, a gingham mill, earned 50 percent in good times and 20 percent when times were "dull." Paper companies in Holyoke, Massachusetts, also earned 50 percent and sometimes more. The Pepperell Company earned over 20 percent on sales in the prosperous years of the last half of the nineteenth century but as low as 4 percent in the depressed years. The Ames Manufacturing Company, a producer of durable goods, paid dividends of over 20 percent in the 1840s, 10 percent in

---

[24]Mabel A. Newcomer, "A Study in Business Mortality: Length of Life of Business Enterprises in Poughkeepsie, N. Y., 1843-1936," *American Economic Review,* Vol. XXVIII (1938).

the early 1850s, nothing during the 1857 depression, 10 to 25 percent during the Civil War, and 8 percent or less after the Civil War. Dividends in the iron industry were commonly 10 to 25 percent and sometimes climbed to 40 to 60 percent.

There is another and less happy side to the story. The ebb and flow in business conditions reflected itself in wide fluctuations in the price of securities and in the number of business failures. Companies that began at the peak of a long wave had very rough sledding; and even companies that began at the trough had some extremely painful experiences.[25] It was said in 1832 that the original owners of woolen mills had lost all the money they had invested. In the 1840s, almost one-third of all the iron mills in eastern Pennsylvania passed through bankruptcy.

These scattered bits of information which could, of course, be multiplied, are very interesting, but they are also suspect. What we have is a biased sample. In addition, most early businessmen kept such poor accounts that it was impossible for them to tell whether they were making or losing money. Then, too, the figures that purport to represent profits ordinarily include payments to other factors beside the entrepreneur. Most businessmen not only managed the companies they owned but also invested their capital funds in the business and sometimes worked the machines. Consequently, profit data, which were derived by deducting total expenditures from total revenue, did not represent the return to business enterprise alone, but included payments made to capital and sometimes to labor. If these payments of interest and wages were deducted, the return to enterprise as such would be much less than was pictured. As Samuel Slater recognized: "It is in this triple capacity of money lender, employer, and laborer, that our most successful manufacturers have succeeded. . . . Yet would their gross profits fall very short of a fair remuneration to each, if those profits should be divided among three distinct classes of persons, such as our theorists have supposed."[26]

No matter how poor the data, some authorities have considered it safe to draw some generalizations about business profits in the nineteenth century. Caroline Ware concluded that, after allowing something to the entrepreneur for wages on his labor and interest on his investment, cotton-textile earnings in the early nineteenth century averaged about 3 percent a year. In the 1830s a contemporary observer reported to the Secretary of the Treasury:[27]

[25]There is a discussion of the effect of long waves on business in Gras and Larson, *Casebook in American Business History* (New York: Appleton-Century-Crofts, 1939), pp. 661-744.

[26]Caroline F. Ware, *The Early New England Cotton Manufacture* (Boston: Houghton Mifflin Company, 1931), p. 131.

[27]*Report of the Secretary of the Treasury,* "Documents Relative to the Manufactures in the United States," House Executive Documents, 22nd Congress, 1st session, No. 308, Washington, D.C., 1833.

It will be perceived that there is a great difference of opinion . . . with regard to the average profit of capital. . . . I am inclined to think it does not differ materially from the market value of money. . . . As a general rule, a man with prudent management, who invests a few thousand dollars in trade and devotes his time to business will make 12 or 15 percent, but . . . when the value of his labor is deducted, he will not be a greater gainer than he would be if he had loaned his money at interest and hired out his services. It is, in general, very much the same in regard to the profits of capital invested in land.

Toward the end of the nineteenth century, according to Clark, Massachusetts manufacturers averaged under 5 percent after allowance for depreciation. In Clark's judgment, profits were higher in small companies than in large ones.[28]

Profits in the twentieth century

Much information is available on profits in the twentieth century, especially for the period since 1929. We have statistics on unincorporated business income as well as on corporate profits. But again, they leave much to be desired. The unincorporated income figures are not much more than calculated guesses; there is still no agreement on the definition of profits; and the intricacies of depreciation are a tribute to the genius of the accountant and the tax attorney.[29] Yet they are better than what is available for the nineteenth century.

On the dubious premise that any numbers are better than no numbers at all, Table 18 reproduces the course of profits since 1929. At least one conclusion can be safely drawn: profits have been extremely volatile. However, if the effect of the business cycle is eliminated by averaging profits for decades, the range is much less erratic, especially if profits are calculated as a percentage of national income. From 1870 to 1960, corporate profits plus unincorporated income varied from an annual average of a little less than 35 percent of national income in the decade 1910 to 1919 to a little less than 20 percent in the depressed 1930s. The average for the whole period was 26.4 percent, with five decades above the average and four below it.[30]

---

[28] Ware, *op. cit.*, p. 156; Victor S. Clark, *History of Manufactures in the United States* (New York: McGraw-Hill Book Company, 1929), Vol. 1, p. 373.

[29] Consider, for example, the experience of corporate business in the 20 years after 1940. Total receipts increased about five and a half times; before-tax profit, five times; after-tax profit three and a half times; and cash flow, five times. Which one best illustrates corporate performance? See Robert E. Graham and Jacqueline Bowman, "Corporate Profits and National Output," *Survey of Current Business,* Nov. 1962.

[30] D. Gale Johnson, "The Functional Distribution of Income in the United States, 1850-1952," *Review of Economics and Statistics,* Vol. XXVI (1954); *Historical Statistics; Statistical Abstract.*

Table 18

CORPORATE PROFITS AND UNINCORPORATED INCOME
1929-1970

(billions of dollars)

	Corporate pre-tax	Corporate after tax	Unin-corporated	Business capital consumption
1929	$ 9.9	$ 8.6	$ 8.8	$ 7.9
1932	−2.3	−2 7	3.0	7.4
1946	24.6	15.5	21.6	9.9
1950	42.6	24.9	24.0	18.3
1955	48.6	27.0	30.3	31.5
1960	49.7	26.7	34.2	43.4
1969	84.2	44.5	50.3	81.1
1970	75.4	41.2	51.0	87.6

SOURCE: Department of Commerce, *National Income,* 1954; *U.S. Income and Output,* 1958; *The National Income and Product Accounts,* 1929-1965; *Survey of Current Business.*

Profits continued to differ widely among different firms. If an investor had put $10,000 in to each of the 101 industrial stocks listed on the stock exchange in 1913, he could have watched his million-dollar investment grow to over $20 million 50 years later. His capital gain would have averaged 6.75 percent a year and, in addition, he would have collected a substantial sum in dividends. Some of the individual stocks performed in real life as they did in optimistic dreams. The $10,000 invested in one stock had grown to well over $1 million. But there were also the equities that never got off the ground. Nine companies ended in total loss, and 22 others were selling for less in 1960 than in 1913.

A more recent study concludes that investments in all the stocks listed on the exchange in 1926 would have returned between 6.84 and 9.03 percent, depending on the investor's tax bracket.[31]

Was the difference in performance a function of the size of the company? Did the economies of scale make big business more profitable, or did the bureaucratic malaise of the large company give the biggest profits to small business? The question is still being debated, with most authorities apparently believing that gigantic size is more a hindrance than a help.

Some studies correlating profits with the size of business go back as far as 1910. An investigation of profits as a percentage of permanent investment in the period 1910-1929 concluded that small companies (under $2 million) had by far the best rate of return—11.6 percent. Very large companies ($50-100 million) came in second best with 9.8 percent, and giant companies were close behind at

[31] Lawrence Fisher and James H. Lorie, "Rates of Return on Investments in Common Stocks," Center for Research in Security Prices, University of Chicago, 1963.

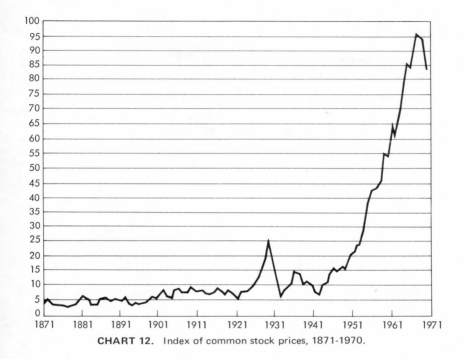

CHART 12. Index of common stock prices, 1871-1970.

9.5 percent. Medium-sized companies made the poorest showing (8.8 percent). But the TNEC (Temporary National Economic Committee) in 1940 announced that in most industries, the medium-sized company had the highest profit. A study by the Twentieth Century Fund in 1937 found that the larger the firm, the more rigid and stable its earnings. Small business, that is, companies with less than $50,000 capital, made much larger profits in prosperity but suffered greater losses in depression.

More recent statistical compilations, based on much broader divisions of the business universe, show big business consistently earning a higher rate of return than small business. In the prosperous first quarter of 1957 for example, companies with over $100 million in assets earned 24.5 percent on stockholders' equity, whereas companies whose assets were less than $1 million earned 15.6 percent. In the recession in the first quarter of 1961, the largest companies made 14.1 percent and the smallest, 6.3 percent.[32]

[32]H. B. Summers, "A Comparison of the Rates of Earning of Large-Scale and Small-Scale Industries," *Quarterly Journal of Economics,* Vol. XLVII (1932); TNEC, Monograph No. 13, *The Relative Efficiency of Large, Medium-Sized, and Small Business* (1940); *How Profitable is Big Business?* (New York: The Twentieth Century Fund, 1937); William L. Crumm, *Corporate Size and Earning Power* (Cambridge, Mass.: Harvard University Press, 1939); House Committee of the Judiciary, Study of Monopoly Power, Part 2B, 1949; FTC-SEC, *Quarterly Finance Reports for Manufacturing Corporations.*

What Caroline Ware said of the early cotton industry has always been true of business in general:

> The financial history of the early cotton industry, the way in which it attracted capital and the return which it brought, foreshadowed the later history of many an American industry. Someone believed in the possibilities of the business while the public held aloof; the idea took hold and there was a rush to join in the enterprise; a few people made large profits for a short time . . . ; others, though earning little, were led on by the few successes; they never prospered. . . . Such was the course of the early cotton industry and such has been the course of many industries from that day to this.[33]

SUGGESTED READINGS

On specific topics, see the readings cited in the footnotes in the chapter.

Chandler, Alfred D., *Strategy and Structure* (Cambridge, Mass.: The MIT Press, 1962).

Cochran, Thomas C., *The American Business System* (Cambridge, Mass.: Harvard University, Press, 1957).

——, *Railroad Leaders, 1845-1890: The Business Mind in Action* (Cambridge, Mass.: Harvard University Press, 1953).

Cole, Arthur H., "An Approach to the Study of Entrepreneurship," *Journal of Economic History,* Vol. VI, Supplement (1946). Reprinted in Frederic C. Lane and Jelle C. Riemersma, eds., *Enterprise and Secular Change* (Homewood, Ill.: Richard D. Irwin, Inc., 1953).

Gras, N. S. B., "Capitalism." Reprinted in Lane and Riemersma, eds., *Enterprise and Secular Change* (Homewood, Ill.: Richard D. Irwin, Inc., 1953).

Krooss, Herman E. and Charles Gilbert, *American Business History* (Englewood Cliffs, N.J.: Prentice-Hall, Inc., 1972).

Latham, Earl, ed., *John D. Rockefeller—Robber Baron or Industrial Statesman?* Amherst Readings in American History (Boston: D. C. Heath & Company, 1949).

Schumpeter, Joseph A., "The Creative Response in Economic History," *Journal of Economic History,* Vol. VII (1947). Reprinted in Joseph T. Lambie and Richard V. Clemence, eds., *Economic Change in America* (Harrisburg, Pa.: The Stackpole Company, 1954).

QUESTIONS

1. Which description of changes in the business system—Gras, Cole, Chandler, or any other—seems to you most valid? Why? Cite some specific examples to support your opinion.

---

[33]Ware, *op. cit.,* p. 160.

2. Show the way in which the business forms and methods of the nineteenth century rested on the technology of that period.

3. How did Astor and Carnegie differ as businessmen? How did Morgan differ from Carnegie?

4. Comment on the following: "Business enterprise has been more successful than labor or agriculture in adapting itself to economic change."

5. Business underwent vast changes in the last half of the nineteenth century. What were these changes? Why did they take place? Was "big business" inevitable? Why or why not?

6. Describe the changes that have occurred in the administration of business enterprise (the managerial structure). Why did they occur?

7. What were the causes of the movement for industrial combination in the last quarter of the nineteenth century? What devices were used to avoid competition?

8. (a) In what sense is it true that there has been a "decline in competition" in this country since about 1875? In what sense is it untrue?

   (b) Was the National Industrial Recovery Act, with its codes of fair competition, a reversal of our usual national policy toward monopoly? In what way?

9. Discuss the rise of "finance capitalism" as a dominant force in the American economy. What were its main contributions? What were its weaknesses?

10. In regulating business, has the government always been guided by the goal of maintaining competition? Describe the changes in the way the courts have viewed the Sherman Act.

Chapter Eight

CAPITAL ACCUMULATION
AND THE DEVELOPMENT
OF FINANCIAL INSTITUTIONS

Previous chapters have often alluded to the problem of raising capital. The task of this chapter is to describe in some detail the extent of capital formation and the mechanics by which capital was accumulated. But before embarking on a history of capital accumulation in the United States, it would be well to define the complicated subject we are talking about.

Economists define *capital* in many different ways. Classical economists defined it as "produced instruments of production," that is, goods that were used to make more goods. This would confine "capital" to plant and equipment—factories, machines, and the like. Recently, the tendency has been to broaden the concept and to define *capital* as an addition to wealth. Under this definition, capital accumulation, or investment, as it is usually called, could include additions to the stock of consumer goods: a bag of flour on the pantry shelf or a set of blocks in a child's toy chest. For purposes of manageability, however, the only consumer goods that are ever included are durable goods, such as houses, automobiles, washing machines, and the like. Some economists argue that the costs of education should be included, on the ground that accumulated stocks of knowledge contribute more toward increasing productivity than any other single factor. Despite the attractive logic of this argument, economic historians usually use a definition close to that of the classical school. They ordinarily define capital formation as the addition to the stock of goods in the hands of business and government plus residential housing and net claims against foreign countries. Capital formation or capital accumulation, therefore, includes construction, but not repair; new producers' durable goods, but not small tools; the net change in business and government inventories; and the net change in foreign claims.[1]

When economists use the term *capital,* they are referring to goods, not money. When financiers or students of finance refer to capital, they are really talking about capital funds, that is, the money value of capital as represented by bonds, promissory notes, mortgages, and the like. These capital funds are claims against real capital and in themselves they are nothing more than pieces of paper that represent both debts and credits. From the point of view of society as a whole, these pieces of paper have no net value and therefore have no real substance. When expressed in dollars of the same purchasing power, capital funds represent real capital (that is, goods), just as dollar income, when reduced to constant prices, represents real income. It is also necessary to point out that there is a difference between *gross* capital formation and *net* capital formation. Gross capital formation is the total capital investment in any given year, but part of each year's capital must be used to replace previously accumulated capital that has been worn out or become obsolete. Deducting this capital consumption, or depreciation, from gross capital formation gives us net capital formation or the amount that has been added to total capital.

Without capital formation, there can be little economic growth. To be sure, gains in productivity can be eked out without capital. Workers can learn to use their hands more efficiently, and businessmen can improve their methods of directing the labor force. But an economy must have some tools and machinery, some plant and equipment, before it can hope to create a comfortable scale of living. This is the same as saying that an economy cannot grow very much without saving, for all capital must come from saving; one is the obverse of the other. Businessmen who build plants and stock them with tools, farmers who fence their acres, and governments that build schools and highways may obtain the capital for their investments from their own saving or they may beg, borrow, tax, or steal other people's saving. But regardless of how they do it, the important point is that there can be no capital accumulation without saving, and an economy cannot grow very much without capital formation. It may be that capital accounted for 50 percent or more of the total economic growth that took place in the early nineteenth century. Dennison has estimated that 35 percent of the growth from 1909 to 1929 came from capital and that 15 percent has risen from capital since then.

Although the processes of capital accumulation and economic growth are

[1] The addition of residential housing to the classical definition of capital is, of course, illogical. Housing is certainly a large part of the country's wealth, and for most home owners it represents a huge "investment," but a house that is a home is hardly an instrument of production.

closely interconnected, the connection is not as absolute as it is often portrayed. Important as it is, the contribution of capital can be highly exaggerated. There is no one-to-one relationship between capital accumulation and economic growth. Some nations with relatively low rates of capital accumulation have experienced high rates of economic growth, and the opposite has also been the case. The range of capital formation between developed and underdeveloped countries is not immense; perhaps 10 percentage points separate them.

In nations that have enjoyed better-than-average economic progress, growth in total production has always exceeded increases in the quantity of labor and capital poured into the economy. In the United States, for example, the rise in total output averaged for many years about 3.5 percent a year, or about twice as much as the 1.7 percent increase in the inputs of labor and capital. Some specialists in the economics of economic development have advanced the theory that the "take-off" into accelerated economic growth requires a spectacular rise in the rate of capital accumulation. There is no empirical evidence to support this plausible hypothesis. Indeed, in some nations, vigorous economic growth preceded a rise in the rate of capital formation by many years. This would suggest that capital accumulation is more passive than active; it is more a result than a cause of high-level economic activity. Moreover, it is not so much the volume of capital that contributes to economic growth as it is the way it is used. More efficient use of capital is much more effective than an increase in its quantity. Finally, units of capital formation were not homogeneous in respect to their contribution to aggregate production. The amount of capital divided by output (the capital/output ratio, as the economist calls the relation between capital formation and gross national product) differed sharply for different industries. For example, so-called capital-intensive industries such as agriculture and the railroads showed a low output per unit of capital. The capital/output ratio also varied for different periods of time. In the early years of American industry when capital was in short supply and the economy seems to have been growing satisfactorily, the ratio was of course low; it rose from the 1880s to World War I and has declined since the 1920s.[2] This would, of course, be what one would expect, for technology improves over time, and with its improvement each unit of capital can be expected to produce more than its predecessor did. What might and what did neutralize this expected development was a shift in the industrial structure of the economy.

TRENDS IN CAPITAL FORMATION AND WEALTH

The abundance of land and the shortage and consequent high wages of labor in the United States acted as an incentive for capital accumulation, for only by

[2]Simon S. Kuznets in *Economic Development and Cultural Change*, July 1960; July, 1961; A.K. Cairncross, *Factors in Economic Development* (New York: Frederick A. Praeger, Inc., 1963), Chap. 7.

using tools and machines could the small labor force convert the nation's vast natural resources into finished products. This fact of economic life was well recognized early in American history. Tench Coxe, for example, took pains to stress "the peculiar value of labor-saving machinery to a nation of moderate numbers, dwelling in a country of redundant soil." [3]

As a general proposition, the American economy was characterized by a chronic shortage of capital and capital funds. At times, to be sure, the demand for capital faltered, and savers had to seek outlets for what they had accumulated. The prosperous early-nineteenth-century merchants, for example, seemed to have had a surplus of capital funds. But, by contrast, the early railroad promoters and the pioneer entrepreneurs in large-scale manufacturing enterprise had to go to considerable pains to raise the capital they needed.

Undoubtedly, much of the demand for capital was induced by what economists call the "accelerator principle." That is, it was demand-induced in the sense that businessmen invested in plant and equipment in response to an increase in demand for the products they produced. But much of the demand was also autonomous. It did not result as a reaction to increases in consumer demand, but because of exogenous factors, such as a desire to lower the costs of production or to make a better-quality product. David McCord Wright in an inspired moment explained autonomous demand as follows: "The better beer, the cheaper beer, and the bull-headed brewer would build a new brewery even though the volume of beer sales might be falling." In the United States, much of the investment in railroads was autonomous in the sense that it preceded rather than followed demand. The same could, of course, be said of much public construction and of some manufacturing investment, such as Carnegie's steel mills that were built and refurbished in periods of business depression.

Systematic data on capital formation are not available for the years before 1869, but there are estimates that shed some light. Robert Gallman has estimated that gross capital formation from the 1830s to the 1850s averaged 12 to 15 percent of gross national product depending on the definition used. This, as we shall see, was considerably lower than the estimated rate of capital accumulation after the Civil War. [4]

Another way of measuring the extent of capital formation is by comparing the stock of wealth at different points in time. Samuel Blodgett, Jr., in 1806 estimated that national wealth had increased from about $1.2 billion in 1790 to $2.4 billion in 1800, or by over 10 percent a year. Horatio Burchard in 1880 estimated national wealth at about $3.3 billion in 1825 and at $6.1 billion in 1845. According to Burchard's estimates, the increase in wealth in the 1850s was more rapid, for by 1860 the country's wealth approximated $16 billion. Both Blodgett and Burchard, of course, included land and consumer goods, so that

---

[3] *American State Papers, Finance,* Vol. II, p. 676.

[4] National Bureau of Economic Research, *Studies in Income and Wealth,* Vol. 30 (Princeton, N.J.: Princeton University Press, 1966).

they exaggerated the volume of capital and savings. No definition of capital formation includes the former, but definitions that emphasize the growth of wealth rather than the growth of productive assets naturally include consumer durables.

Working with the estimates supplied by Blodgett and Burchard and with data supplied from other sources. Raymond Goldsmith developed some figures on real, durable, reproducible, tangible wealth per capita. According to these estimates, real per capita wealth grew at an annual rate of approximately 2 percent from 1805 to 1960. The gains, however, fluctuated quite sharply. In the first half of the nineteenth century, the increase ran at about 2.25 percent a year; in the last half, it rose to 2.5 percent. From 1900 to 1930, it was barely 2 percent. During the depression and the war years, real wealth per person actually declined, but it reached its highest rate of growth (over 4 percent) in the years after World War II.[5] For the whole period, 1930 to 1960, per capita wealth increased by about 1 percent a year. In dollars of constant purchasing power, wealth increased from $700 per capita and $2,100 per worker in 1869 to $2,500 and $6,500, respectively, in 1960.

More comprehensive statistics on capital formation have been developed by Simon Kuznets for the years 1896-1955.[6] His figures show that, over that period, *gross* capital formation did not vary much. In constant prices, it amounted to about 23 percent of gross national product in 1869-1888 and 20 percent of GNP in the 1946-1955 period. The range was narrower if measured in current prices, because capital goods' prices rose more than the general price level. Indeed, in current dollars, gross capital formation takes a greater share of today's production (24 percent) than it did in the last part of the last century (20 percent).

Although gross capital formation remained about the same, capital consumption (obsolescence and depreciation) climbed continuously. Of every $1.70 that was saved in the nineteenth century, 70 cents was used to replace old or worn out plant and equipment, leaving $1 of net capital formation. Under today's conditions, $1.70 of gross capital formation leaves a net of about 55 cents. In other words, it now takes $3 of gross to produce $1 of net, whereas it used to take only $1.70. Because gross capital formation remained about the same and capital consumption rose, *net* capital formation as a percentage of net national product fell. In constant prices, net capital formation equaled about 15 percent of net product in 1869-1888, but only 6 percent of net product in

[5]International Association for Research in Income and Wealth, *Income and Wealth of the United States,* ed. by Simon S. Kuznets (Cambridge, England: Bowes and Boees, 1952); Raymond W. Goldsmith, *The National Wealth of the United States in the Postwar Period* (Princeton, N. J.: Princeton University Press, 1962).

[6]Simon S. Kuznets, *Capital in the American Economy* (Princeton, N.J.: Princeton University Press, 1961), Chap. 9. Kuznets' definition includes government but not consumer durables; Goldsmith includes the latter but not the former.

1946-1955. In current prices, it amounted to 13 percent in the early period and 7 percent more recently.

Data for more recent years show that the rate of capital formation and saving by the orthodox definition continued to recede, but at a slower pace than formerly. According to the Federal Reserve's *Flow of Funds,* gross saving (calculated differently than the 1869-1955 estimates) averaged 15.9 percent of GNP in the 1946-55 years and 14.8 percent of GNP in the 1960s. Net capital formation averaged 10.2 percent of net national product in the 1946-1955 era, and 6.9 percent in 1960-1970.

Because net capital formation is the most important single measure of capital accumulation and saving, it may be concluded that there has been a downward trend in the rate of saving. But this took place slowly at first and much more rapidly in recent years. Up to the depression of the 1930s, the average annual percentage of income that went into saving and capital formation was relatively stable. Net capital formation, in constant prices, ranged from 16 percent of net product in 1889-1898 to 11 percent in 1919-1928.

Different definitions would lead to different conclusions in regard to the trend in capital formation. If we included consumer durables as well as government in the definition, we would find that the rate of saving did not decline. It either increased or remained stable. If we went further and looked upon educational expenditures as an investment, the rate of saving would show an upward trend. Thus, it has been estimated that annual investment in education has risen from about half a billion dollars in 1900 to more than $40 billion today, or from 10 percent to 40 percent of gross capital formation. And if we confine saving to personal saving alone, we find another stable relationship. It was 5 percent of disposable income in 1929; in 1947 to 1970, it ranged from 4.9 in 1960 (a recession year) to 7.9 percent in 1970.[7]

Who exerted the demand for capital, and where did the accumulated capital go? Households and farmers use less capital than they once did, and governments use far more. According to Kuznets, households invested about one-third of net capital in the last part of the nineteenth century but only about one-fifth in the second quarter of the twentieth century. Governments, on the other hand, used only one-twenty-fifth in 1869-1898 but over one-third in 1929-1955. Business was responsible for the remainder—three-fifths in the early period and two-fifths more recently. But these estimates disregard consumer durable goods. If we include consumer durables, the picture is altogether different, for they have loomed continuously larger in the country's spending and saving pattern. From Table 19, it can be seen that major household equipment has come to exceed both producer durables and residential housing as a demander of capital.

As in all economies, construction declined as a consumer of net saving. It

[7]Board of Governors of the Federal Reserve System, *Flow of Funds;* Theordore W. Schultz, "Capital Formation by Education," *Journal of Political Economy,* Vol. LXVIII (1960).

Table 19

RANGE OF COMPONENTS OF GROSS FIXED CAPITAL FORMATION, 1897-1962
(billions of dollars)

Years	Single family residential	Other private construction	Major household equipment	Other household durables	producers durables
1897-1919	$ 0.3 (1897)	$ 1.0 (1898)	$ 0.3 (1897)	$ 0.6 (1897)	$ 0.6 (1897)
	1.3 (1919)	3.1 (1919)	3.4 (1919)	2.4 (1919)	5.0 (1918)
1920-1929	$ 1.4 (1920)	$ 3.0 (1921)	$ 3.5 (1921)	$ 2.3 (1921)	$ 3.1 (1921)
	3.2 (1925)	6.8 (1926)	6.2 (1929)	3.3 (1929)	5.8 (1929)
1930-1939	$ 0.6 (1932)	$ 0.8 (1933)	$ 1.9 (1932)	$ 1.7 (1932)	$ 1.6 (1933)
	2.2 (1939)	2.4 (1937)	4.6 (1937)	4.6 (1937)	5.1 (1937)
1940-1962	$ 0.7 (1944)	$ 1.3 (1943)	$ 1.9 (1944)	$ 4.6 (1944)	$ 4.0 (1943)
	22.5 (1962)	22.6 (1962)	32.4 (1962)	17.0 (1962)	29.0 (1962)

SOURCE: F. Thomas Juster, *Household Capital Formation and Financing* (New York: Columbia University Press, 1966); F. Thomas Juster and Robert E. Lipsey, "Consumer Asset Formation in the United States," *Economic Journal*, December 1967.

238

once absorbed almost three-quarters of net capital, and of this, residential construction accounted for half; more recently, construction takes about one-third, divided about equally between housing and other construction. The slack left by construction's decline has been picked up by producers' durable equipment. But again, different definitions and different times alter the findings. On a gross basis, net expenditures on residential housing, that is, the cost of land and buildings minus the depreciation on existing homes, took about one-fifth of *household* saving from 1897 to 1908, about one-quarter in the 1920s, and again about one-fifth in the post-World War II years. But on a net basis, that is after deducting the increase in home mortgage debt, residential housing fell from about one-fifth in the early 1900s to one-seventh in the 1920s, and to almost nothing in the 1950s.

SOURCES OF SAVING

For as long as we have figures, individuals have accounted for about 60 percent of saving in ordinary times. The story of the increase in American capital is, therefore, essentially a story of individual saving. But it is a one-sided kind of story. The majority of Americans have never been able to save much and, hence, have made only a meager contribution to capital accumulation. True, over 90 percent of Americans at one time or another had some possessions and, therefore, must have saved something. Some workers managed to deposit part of their incomes in savings banks or purchase homes or set up businesses, but samples taken among the working population at different periods show that saving was more the exception than the rule. Most working-class families in the early textile mills, for example, could not make ends meet. Early in the twentieth century, some working-class families blessed with two or three breadwinners and with room enough to take in lodgers managed to save something, but the majority hovered perilously on the brink of subsistence. Many farmers managed to put part of their surplus production into capital investment by improving their fields, building barns and houses, and acquiring tools and equipment. But all the available evidence points to the conclusion that the vast bulk of savings was done by the upper-income groups.

More complete data for the years since 1929 substantiate this conclusion. The spending of the lowest one-third of the income stream always exceeded its income, and in some years the same was true of the middle one-third. The upper one-third of income receivers was, therefore, responsible for all net personal saving. In 1935, for example, the upper one-third saved 124 percent of aggregate personal saving, the extra 24 percent being what was necessary to offset the dissaving of the other two groups. In 1950, a prosperous year, the upper one-third accounted for 108 percent of aggregate saving. It would be approximately true to say that spending units with assets equivalent to $100,000 in today's

Table 20

THE DEMAND FOR NET CAPITAL

(percentage shares based on constant prices)

Years	Households	Business	Government	Construction	Producers' durables	Inventories	Foreign claims
1869-1898	36.4	59.2	4.4	73.4	11.1	17.8	-2.2
1899-1928	26.6	60.8	12.6	54.0	16.8	13.8	15.1
1929-1955	22.0	43.4	34.6	34.2	38.1	21.0	6.7

SOURCE: Kuznets, *Capital in the American Economy*, pp. 149, 178.

prices accounted for half of total personal saving at any given time and that the upper 5 percent on the income ladder saved three-fourths to four-fifths of all that individuals accumulated. Because the wealthy accounted for most of what was saved, policies that succeeded in accomplishing a more equal distribution of income also resulted in a lower rate of saving and a higher rate of consumption.

Businessmen, the group which undoubtedly did most of the dollar volume of investment over the course of history, obtained funds for gross capital formation in five different ways: short-term borrowing from banks, individuals, and institutions; long-term borrowing by mortgaging property or selling bonds; the sale of stock; undistributed profits; and allowances for depreciation and obsolescence. The first three of these are usually labeled "external financing" and the last two "internal financing."

In setting up a business, businessmen obviously could not rely on retained earnings and depreciation. They had to resort to external financing. In addition to whatever funds of their own they were willing to risk, they often borrowed the initial stake from banks and from relatives and friends in the upper-income groups. Research by Lance Davis suggests that over one-half of the capital funds invested in the early New England textile companies was borrowed from commercial banks. McCormick, Carnegie, Rockefeller, and even Henry Ford, who considered bankers somewhat less than human, all relied heavily on bank borrowing.

Once the business began to produce, internal sources provided funds for expansion. As long as ownership represented control of business enterprise, as under the partnership or closed corporation, plowing back profits was standard procedure. Indeed, it was one of the basic rules of the so-called "industrial capitalist." Samuel Slater, for example, accumulated some $690,000 over a period of 40 years by retaining earnings. Later in the nineteenth century, the Carnegie enterprises expanded chiefly by internal financing; and in the twentieth century, Henry Ford built his business assets from less than $50,000 to over $750 million without having to raise any additional long-term capital.

When corporations "went public" and passed into the control of stockholders who had little or no interest in the management of the enterprise, a conflict arose over financial policy. Stockholders emphasized dividend payments and were somewhat less than enthusiastic about the practice of retaining earnings. On the other hand, managers, who had a relatively small stock interest but who were intimately concerned with the long-run survival of the business, did not want to be dependent upon the usual sources of capital funds. It would seem reasonable, therefore, to suppose that they would try to retain a substantial part of earnings instead of paying them out in dividends, and that, as management increased its control over the corporate form of organization, reinvested business earnings would again become an important source of saving. But although there is some evidence that this has been the case, it is not possible to work out any clear-cut, indisputable trend,[8] for economic and managerial considerations were not the only governing factors. Legal considerations, such as tax legislation, could be equally persuasive.

Data for all nonfinancial corporations show that internal financing supplied 55 percent of gross capital needs in 1901-1912, 60 percent in 1913-1922, and 66 percent in 1957-70. The ratio was much higher for manufacturing and mining, where depreciation and undistributed profits supplied 81 percent of gross capital in 1960. In a painstaking analysis, Gertrude Schroeder showed that, in the major steel companies, the importance of external financing declined steadily at the expense of capital funds saved internally. In the first 20 years of the century, the steel companies financed over 55 percent of their gross property additions by the sale of common stock, bonds, and preferred stock. Between 1930 and 1950, securities paid for less than 25 percent of property additions.

Within the area of internal financing, the tendency seemed to be for retained earnings to decline as a source of capital while depreciation allowances seemed to be on the rise. For all corporations, retained earnings supplied about 30 percent of all capital funds in the early years of the century, but only about 15 percent in more recent years, whereas depreciation provided about 25 percent in the early period and 50 percent later.

As corporations and governments accumulated a larger share of capital, the individual had less choice over the relative amounts he might spend or save. Corporations and governments made the decision for him by retaining earnings instead of paying them out in dividends and by taxing away part of his income and using it for capital formation.

The extensive practice of using retained business earnings to finance investment spending had decided advantages and evident disadvantages. By eliminating the question of where capital funds were coming from, it removed many of the obstacles in the way of economic expansion. It also made business less dependent on the managers of the money market—the commercial and investment bankers, whose attitudes often were opposed to those of business management. On the other hand, the practice of retaining earnings reduced the mobility of capital, because it reduced the pool of corporate saving that otherwise might have been available to new enterprises or to would-be entrepreneurs with ideas but no ready cash.

Corporate saving also contributed to sporadic inflation and deflation, for it was one of the forces that upset the delicate balance between spending, saving, and investment. Corporation decisions to save were not guided by the mechan-

[8]Kuznets, *Capital in the American Economy;* Raymond Goldsmith, *Financial Intermediaries in the American Economy Since 1900* (Princeton, N.J.: Princeton University Press, 1958); John Lintner, "The Financing of Corporations," in Edward S. Mason, ed., *The Corporation in Modern Society* (Cambridge, Mass.: Harvard University Press, 1961); Sergei P. Dobrovolsky, *Corporate Income Retention, 1915-1943* (New York: National Bureau of Economic Research, 1951); Gertrude G. Schroeder, *The Growth of Major Steel Companies, 1900-1950* (Baltimore: The Johns Hopkins Press, 1953), pp. 145-48.

isms that were supposed to equilibrate saving and investment. According to one school of thought, fluctuations in the interest rate would keep saving and investment in balance. Thus, if investors needed more capital funds, they would offer higher rates of interest, which would encourage more saving. On the other hand, if savers were saving too much for current investment needs, interest rates would fall, saving would decline, and investment would increase. But even if this analysis were true for individuals, it did not apply to corporations, for the rate of corporate saving was not very much influenced by the rate of interest. That is, rising interest rates did not encourage corporations to save more, and falling rates did not cause them to save less. Indeed, corporations were not motivated to save because of impersonal economic reasons, but by rules of thumb, the fortunes of prosperity, and a desire to achieve stability. Depreciation was largely a legal and accounting device, and the division of net profits between retained earnings and dividends came to be much more a matter of custom and tradition than a decision made by market forces.

Capital imports as a source of capital accumulation

In dollar volume, capital imports were insignificant when compared with domestic saving. At its peak in the early twentieth century, net foreign investment in the United States was about $4 billion, or about 3 percent of all intangible assets. Small as they were, however, capital imports were extremely important in influencing the pace of American economic development, for they varied widely. High in some years and low in others, they were the marginal capital funds that reflected the difference between prosperity and depression. Capital importations were especially high during the prosperous years of the early 1830s, the middle 1850s, the early 1870s, and the 1880s. They fell off during the depression years following 1837, 1857, and 1873.[9]

Up to the late 1830s, foreign investment crept up slowly and erratically from $60 million to $100 million. These capital imports were undoubtedly of great benefit to the growth of the underdeveloped American economy, because they were used to buy desperately needed goods which Americans could not yet produce. Nevertheless, they were bitterly resented by die-hard nationalists who thought that foreigners would come to own and control the American economy and enjoy an unearned income from it.

Despite the resistance that it met, foreign investment in America increased rather than diminished. During the prosperous 1830s, foreign investors more than doubled their holdings, buying mostly government bonds and the stock of

[9]See Cleona Lewis, *America's Stake in International Investments* (Washington, D.C.: The Brookings Institution, 1938); Leland H. Jenks, *The Migration of British Capital to 1875* (New York: Alfred A. Knopf, Inc., 1927), Chaps. 3 and 4; National Bureau of Economic Research, *Trends in the American Economy in the Nineteenth Century* (Princeton, N.J.: Princeton University Press, 1962).

the United States Bank. The rapid increase in state indebtedness of these years was almost wholly financed by foreign investment, mostly British. An analysis of the public debt of Pennsylvania, for example, showed that, out of a total of $16 million, $9 million was owned abroad. From the beginning, foreign investors were reluctant to buy industrial, railroad, and utility securities, because they considered these far riskier than the securities issued by government and a few banks. Indeed, it was not until 1836 that a private American corporation, the Baltimore and Ohio Railroad, was successful in raising money abroad. But foreign investors did contribute indirectly in financing enterprises requiring venture capital. When foreign capitalists bought government bonds and bank stocks, the American investors who sold them could use the proceeds of the sale to buy industrial securities. Thus, foreign-capital inflow released American savings to finance industrial development.

During the depression of the late 1830s and early 1840s, many foreign investors suffered through default and repudiation, and, although they probably fared as well from their American investments as they did from their domestic ones, antagonism toward the United States became very intense, the flow of capital from abroad came to a virtual halt, and total foreign holdings dropped from $300 million to less than $200 million. As recovery set in, foreign investment once again soared. In the 1850s, the Secretary of the Treasury estimated that foreign investors owned about 20 percent of total American securities. They owned 46 percent of the Federal debt, 58 percent of the state debt, 26 percent of railroad bonds, and 23 percent of the local debt, but they owned only 10 percent of American stock issues.

Foreign investment continued to soar through the late 1860s and the boom of the next decade, reaching almost $2 billion in 1875, almost ten times as much as in 1850. But new developments were in the wind. The almost unparalleled economic expansion of the country during the latter nineteenth century increased domestic savings to such an extent that American investors now began to invade the international money market. In the late 1870s, J. P. Morgan participated in a Canadian loan. And by the end of the century, American bankers were helping to finance the construction of the Hankow-Canton Railroad, and were floating a $10 million loan for Sweden, a $20 million loan for Germany, and a $25 million loan for the construction of Russian railroads. By 1898, Americans had almost $700 million invested abroad, but their international liabilities were over $3.5 billion.

In the first decade of the twentieth century, Americans continued to import capital, but at the same time more and more foreigners were turning to us for loans. Consequently, although the net addition to America's international liabilities increased, it did so much more slowly than in the previous century. By 1914, net liabilities on the international account were $3.7 billion. However, all this and something extra was wiped out as a result of World War I. American investment bankers and the United States government tapped the capital market and lent such large sums to the Allied powers that the United States emerged from the war as an international creditor.

By the 1920s, the status of the United States in the international money market had undergone a complete change. Originally, the problem had been to acquire foreign capital funds and capital goods to supplement domestic saving, which in most years was inadequate to meet the investment demands of the economy. Gradually domestic saving increased and the problem became one of finding investment outlets for the surplus. By 1930, the United States had net foreign investments of about $9 billion. The depression reduced capital exports sharply, but World War II brought the Federal government back into the picture as a major lender. By 1962, postwar aid amounted to almost $100 billion, of which about $24 billion was in loans. Of the $100 billion, $30 billion was for military aid; $65 billion was for economic and technical assistance, and $5 billion was invested in international financial institutions. Meanwhile, American business also was acquiring a stake in international investment. In the 25 years after the War, net foreign investment by American business multiplied to almost $70 billion.

The increase in net foreign investment from 1945 to 1960 amounted to over 10 percent of the increase in the gross national product. This may at first glance seem like a great deal, but in comparison with other times and other countries, it was not. It was not as large relative to the size of the economy as the amounts exported in the late 1920s, and it was not nearly as large as the 40 percent of saving that Britain exported at the height of her power and prestige.

THE REWARDS FOR SAVING

With occasional exceptions due to the peculiar demands of war and boom prosperity, interest rates in the nineteenth century tended to drift slowly downward. At times the rate on call loans floated to buy securities on the stock exchange reached dizzy heights—18 percent in 1873, 16 percent in 1870, and 13 percent in 1880—but this was as unusual as it was spectacular. As can be seen by Chart 13, the yield on high-grade investment bonds varied from 3.5 percent to a little over 5 percent, interest rates on New York commercial paper dropped from about 8 percent in the Civil War period to 5.5 percent at the end of the century, and savings banks paid over 5 percent when they were very young and 4 percent when they were middle-aged in 1899.

During the first 45 years of the twentieth century, that is, through the quiet days of the first decade, the war and boom years, the depressed 1930s, and World War II, interest rates continued to sink. But since 1945 the picture has changed. Interest rates have climbed, and at times the increase has been the sharpest in our history. Chart 14 lends some plausibility to the theory that there

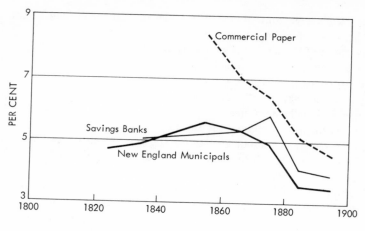

CHART 13.   Selected interest rates, 1820-1899

are long swings in interest rates as there are in many other features of economic history.

Cyclical fluctuations tended to obscure the long-swing movements. From 1900 to the outbreak of World War I most interest rates jumped significantly. Then they retreated in the first year of the war only to come back strongly in 1915-1920. In the ensuing short but precipitate depression, rates on high-grade bonds fell from 6.34 percent to 4.93 percent. Rates recovered in the early twenties, then slipped until 1927, and surged forward until 1929, so that high-grade bond yields ran from 6 percent in 1924 to 4.5 percent in 1927, and 4.8 percent in 1929.

With some exceptions (caused primarily by psychological factors and international tensions) interest rates fell during the depression of the 1930s. By 1937, triple A bonds were bringing only 3.1 percent and prime commercial paper was down to 0.75 percent.

During World War II, the Federal Reserve System held interest rates stable, but in the late 1940s and early 1950s, yields began to inch upward and in the 1960s, they soared. High grade corporates yielded 2.6 percent at the end of World War II; they passed 3 percent in 1955, 4 percent in 1959, 5 percent in 1966, 6 percent in 1968, and 8 percent in 1970.

No single cause was responsible for the abrupt changes that occurred in the movement of interest rates. Interest rates are the price of capital funds and are determined by the demand for and the supply of funds in the money and capital markets. On the demand side, consumers need funds to take care of everyday cash requirements, and investors want funds because they see possibilities of using them to make a profit. Expectations and forecasts regarding the future, therefore, play a large role in the demand for funds. The other half of the price mechanism—the supply of funds—is a function of the money stock plus total

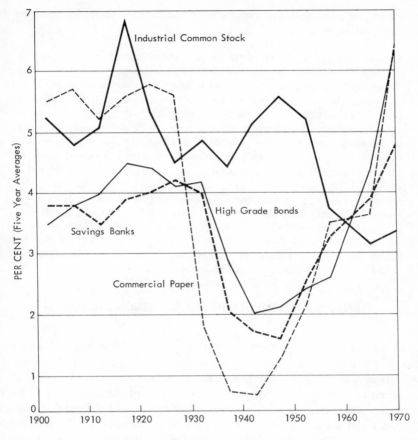

CHART 14. Yields and interest rates, 1901-1970

saving. Textbook models of what determines interest rates stress the role of money. Interest rates are supposed to vary inversely with changes in the money stock. For example, an accelerated increase in money is supposed to reduce interest rates on the logical ground that increases in supply result in lower prices. Conversely, a slower rate of money expansion is supposed to raise interest rates. Historical experience demonstrates that there is something wrong with this reasoning. Admittedly, the model works in the short run, but in the long run, increases in the money supply raised rather than lowered interest rates. The explanation for this is simple: the demand for funds increased faster than the supply of funds largely because of expectations of what would happen in the future. Ironically enough, this was well known by some of those who took part in the debates about money that dotted American history. But their arguments attracted little or no attention. In March, 1877, for example, Senator John Jones of Nevada, in arguing for an expansion of the money supply by restoring the coinage of silver, said:

> Equally fanciful and erroneous is the proposition that the rates of interest for money can be lowered by increasing its quantity. It is prices, and not interest, which depend upon the volume of money. The rates for the use of loanable capital depend upon entirely different factors; such as the current rates of business profits, productiveness of the soil, the security of property, the stability of government, pressure of taxation, and the fiscal policies of governments, such as the maintenance of public debts, which necessarily increase the rate of interest. In truth, increasing the amount of money tends indirectly to increase the rate of interest by stimulating business activity, while decreasing the amount of money reduces the rate of interest by checking enterprises and thereby curtailing the demand for loans. This is signally illustrated by the present condition of things in every part of the commercial world. The rate of interest should be, and under a correct money system would be, merely an expression of the rate of profit which could be made through the use of borrowed capital.[10]

FINANCIAL INTERMEDIARIES AND ECONOMIC GROWTH

In the modern, complicated world, those who do the saving are rarely the same people who do the investing (that is, the capital formation). Corporations save a large part of what they invest; governments save little of their capital formation; and most consumers have to go outside of their own coffers when they buy a house or a piece of consumer durable goods.[11] To put this another way, the investor's demand for capital funds must be matched with the saver's supply of funds. The matchmakers, the middlemen who bring the two together, are the financial intermediaries: commercial banks (including the Federal Reserve Banks), savings banks, savings and loan associations, postal savings system, credit unions, life insurance companies, mutual funds, and pension funds.

Banks and savings institutions create credit and provide capital funds, but they cannot create real capital, for there is no easy way to augment the stock of wealth. But, although they do not create capital goods, they nevertheless contribute most importantly to economic growth. They transfer funds from

[10]Herman E. Krooss, ed., *Documentary History of Banking and Currency* (New York: Mc-Graw Hill Book Company, 1960), Vol 3, pp. 1866-67.

[11]It can be argued, and often is, that all saving comes from people (households). This follows from the proposition that it is only people that count; corporations are people in the sight of the law, but not in a real sense; and governments can only exist as representatives of people. Whatever saving they do comes from the citizenry in the form of taxes or charges.

savers to investors, from those who have surpluses to those who wish to spend more than they have. By so doing, they make exchange and specialization possible, they reduce interest rates, and they facilitate the use of capital goods, enabling the economy to operate more efficiently. Indeed, without the financial institutions and the money and credit system for which they are largely responsible, an economy could not evolve from an underdeveloped state to a highly complex organization.

In a primitive economy, goods and services are traded in much the same way that small boys swap tops or gum wrappers. There is no monetary system in such a barter arrangement, and, in the absence of a medium of exchange, there is no common denominator in which prices of all commodities can be expressed. Consequently, there is no price system. Nor is there any banking system, because surpluses do not exist except on a very small scale; without considerable surplus, there can be no appreciable volume of lending or borrowing. Debtor-creditor relationships in a primitive economy are, therefore, virtually nonexistent.

As an economy develops and progresses, production increases, income rises, and surpluses appear. Here and there, a farmer raises a peck of corn, a bushel of wheat, or a calf in excess of his consumption needs. As consumption needs are more easily satisfied, the community can devote part of its efforts to the production of capital goods. Thus, capital goods appear and gradually accumulate. As specialization proceeds apace and as production becomes diversified, barter becomes too awkward and inefficient. The community, therefore, develops a medium of exchange, a money supply, to facilitate trade among producers of different types of goods and services. As money appears, capital goods are expressed in terms of the monetary unit. Thus, it is much simpler to say that Farmer A 's capital is $50 than to say that Farmer A has one shovel, one hoe, one sickle, and a cart.

Just as the creation of a money system improves and facilitates the process of exchange, so the creation of a banking system makes it possible to utilize surpluses or savings more efficiently. Savings from surplus production are scattered among different producers, many of whom have no intention of using their surpluses to increase production. Even if they were so inclined, their individual savings would be too small to be used effectively. On the other hand, many would-be entrepreneurs in the community are anxious to put the community's savings to effective use in some type of productive enterprise. At first, local merchants or storekeepers, by selling goods on long-term credit, by making loans, or by buying a piece of an enterprise, provide capital funds for ambitious but needy entrepreneurs.[12] But gradually the local merchant's role is usurped by banks, insurance companies, and investment bankers. Financial institutions create or transfer money, that is, the capital funds, that can be used

[12]Professor Postan estimated that the entire early textile industry in England could have been financed easily by the fortunes of a few merchants. The same could be said of early American industry.

to acquire capital goods. They encourage saving by providing a safe place of deposit. They gather up small amounts from scattered savers and transfer them to entrepreneurs for investment in plant and equipment. They increase the mobility of capital by transferring funds from one area to another.

In the beginning, an exchange economy is crude and makeshift but, as the system develops, the whole procedure by which capital funds are raised becomes more complex and more effective. As in any process of economic development, the first manifestations are extensive; the later manifestations, intensive. The framework is created rapidly, then the emphasis shifts to elaborating the rudimentary organization. Money, for example, is first represented by commodities, but as goods are exchanged more extensively, commodities give way to coin and paper money, which can be handled and transferred more easily, and to checks and drafts which represent bookkeeping entries in ledgers and journals. The banking system evolves from the elementary stage in which a merchant advances credit to a producer until in more developed form it consists of an array of specialized institutions, each advancing credit in a number of subtle ways.

None of the financial institutions that are common today existed in the Colonial Period, and some of them are only as old as the last generation. Once they appeared, however, they grew at a much faster rate than the total economy. Their per capita assets in constant dollars climbed at a rate of 2.5 to 3 percent a year, half again as much as the rise in real per capita production.

Table 21

ESTIMATES OF NET DEBT
(billions of dollars)

	1853	*1892*	*1913*	*1929*	*1929*
Government	$0.3	$ 1.7	$ 4.8	$ 33.4	$ 29.7
Corporate	0.9	5.7	18.8	43.8	47.3
Farm mortgage		1.1	4.9	9.5	9.6
Urban mortgage		4.9	8.8	33.1	31.2
Quasi-public	—	—	—	1.8	—
Total long term		13.3	37.3	121.6	117.8
Short term corporate	6.5	—	—	—	41.6
Farm nonmortgage ⎰	9.3	—	—	—	2.6
Nonfarm nonmortgage ⎱					28.9

SOURCE: 1853, *Report of the Secretary of Treasury,* 33 Congress, 1st Session, Exec. Doc. No. 42, March 2, 1854; 1892, *Hearings on H.R. 5181,* 55 Congress, 2nd Session, 1897-1898, p. 214; 1913, 1929, U.S. Senate, *Investigation of Economic Problems,* 1933, part 3, p. 376; 1929, *Historical Statistics.*

The impressive growth of financial institutions is also illustrated by the rise in the nation's aggregate debt, for most of the assets of the institutions are credits, and credits are, of course, the obverse of debt. We do not know how much debt there was the beginning of the nineteenth century. But in the last 50 years, total net debt has risen from about $80 billion to approximately $2 trillion. In dollars of current purchasing power, net debt rose from about $2,400 to $10,000, an annual rate of increase equal to that of the gross national product. Indeed, the correlation between debt and GNP is extraordinarily close as can be seen from Chart 15.

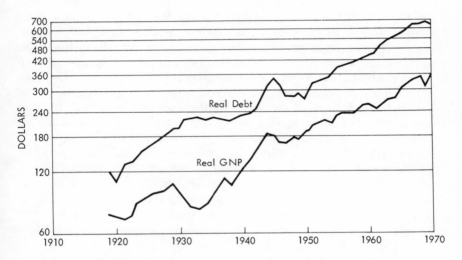

CHART 15.   Real GNP and debt in 1929 prices, 1919-1970

NONBANK FINANCIAL INTERMEDIARIES IN THE EARLY NINETEENTH CENTURY

The financial institutions that have just been cited differed from each other in respect to the public that they served and the services that they offered. Three of the eight intermediaries (commercial banks, savings banks, and savings and loan associations) are classified as thrift institutions. Life insurance and pension funds are designed to cover the hazards of death, disability, and old age. Mutual funds offer an investment vehicle; credit unions are in the small loan business; and postal savings no longer exist. But the most important difference among financial intermediaries exists between commercial banks and the other intermediaries, the so-called "nonbank intermediaries." Commercial banks provide capital funds by creating money. Other financial institutions create credit by physically transferring funds from savers to investors. In early American history, if a wholesaler, retailer, manufacturer, or any other businessman was unable or unwilling to borrow from a commercial bank, he might obtain credit from a merchant or a nonbank lender by giving his promissory note, by drawing a bill of exchange, or merely on the strength of his financial reputation. In any event, however, if he did not borrow from a commercial bank, he received (in exchange for his promise to repay) cash that had previously been saved by someone else.

In the Colonial Period and until about the middle of the nineteenth century, the credit system rested in large part on the foundation of foreign trade. Importers obtained credit from European commission merchants. By the 1830s, many importers were obtaining favorable discounts by paying cash. By advancing their own credit to their customers, they were taking over the functions of the English capitalist. Losses on credit transactions were not excessive if the few examples we have are of any worth. At first, a relatively long time—from six to nine months—was given for repayment, and the market was localized because merchants were forced to rely on their own limited knowledge or on the recommendation of other merchants. But by mid-century, the credit system had greatly improved. The invention of credit agencies, such as Lewis Tappan's Mercantile Agency, founded in 1841, and Bradstreet's Commercial Agency, provided merchants with a means of checking on borrowers, thus making it possible for them to extend credit over wider areas. At the same time, improvements in transportation and communication speeded the marketing of goods and led to a rapid reduction in terms to 30 to 60 days by the 1850s.

Aside from those that dealt in commercial credit, the financial institutions that acted as intermediaries between savers and investors were still in the development stage in the early nineteenth century. The Second Bank of the United States, the North American Trust Company, the Morris Canal and Banking Company, and I. L. and S. Josephs (agents for the Rothschilds) were pioneers in floating securities. All of these investment bankers failed, and, aside from Biddle and his bank, they were very small indeed. After the crash of 1837, a new group emerged, but even those who were most successful—Prime, Ward, and King and August Belmont of New York, Brown Brothers of Baltimore, Philadelphia, and New York, Corcoran and Riggs of Washington, and E. W. Clark and Co. of Philadelphia—had to depend heavily on the London money market for funds. In fact, London financed almost all the American export trade and, in addition, bought many of the securities issued in the United States.

The American market was so important in Britain that a group of houses, known as the Anglo-American merchant bankers, began to deal exclusively in facilitating export of capital to America. Some Anglo-American houses, such as Baring Brothers and, later, Morgan, Peabody and Company, specialized in underwriting American securities. Baring Brothers, especially, played a leading role in handling the securities of the Federal government and the Second Bank of the United States. Other British merchant houses, such as Peach and Pierce and Lascelles and Maxwell, played the part of American bankers by allowing American importers to draw drafts against them. These credits formed the basis for a further extension of credit in the United States. Thus, the dry-goods merchant who imported from Britain on the basis of British credit sold on credit to a jobber who in turn sold on credit to the retailer. A similar link existed between the Southern plantation owner and British bankers. The plantation owner borrowed from a factor in New Orleans or Charleston who was financed by a New York banker who, in turn, was financed by a member of the London money market.

In time, some American importers with strong British connections began to act as intermediaries for other American merchants, and gradually their foreign exchange business became so important that they dropped their importing business altogether and emerged as full-fledged bankers. Alexander Brown and Son, the founders of the present firm of Brown Brothers, Harriman and Company, was one concern that passed through this transition from importer to banker.

But investment banking was not very important in the United States until well after the Civil War. Stock transactions had been carried on in New York since 1792, but the New York Stock and Exchange Board was not founded until 1817, when seven firms and 13 individuals each contributed $25 to establish a formal organization. In 1800, Philadelphia, and in the 1830s, Boston had both opened exchanges. But in the nineteenth century, stock transactions in these and other exchanges were few and were limited to a small list. Government and bank stocks monopolized the early trading on the New York Stock Exchange. Railroad securities were not traded until 1830, although by 1850 there was more dealing in rail shares than in any other type of security. The first industrial shares (New York Gas Light and Schuylkill Coal) appeared in 1831 and 1832, but as late as 1867 there were only 15 industrial stocks listed on the New York Exchange, although in Boston the stocks of industrial and textile firms and of copper mining companies were somewhat more prominent. On all exchanges the volume of stock trading was relatively small. Before the speculative boom of the 1830s, brokers considered a one hundred share day as fair, but in the prosperous years, 1830 to 1834, one thousand share days were not unusual.

By the middle of the nineteenth century, the money market, like much else in the economy, was giving evidence of the gigantic status it would eventually attain. More new securities were being floated, the total outstanding being estimated at $1.5 billion by the Treasury Department in 1856. Stock market activity was also heavier. In one day during the boom of the 1850s, as many as 71,000 shares were traded on the New York Exchange, and aggregate trading over a four-week period reached almost one million shares. The term "call loan," referring to money loaned to purchase securities, was coming into common use. New York City, the securities center of the nation and the heart of the country's foreign trade operations, was achieving a pre-eminent position in the domestic money market. Bank reserves from all over the country flowed into New York to be loaned to those people or organizations who wanted to buy stock on margin. By the late 1850s, out-of-town banks had piled up balances of some $25 million. This pyramiding of bank reserves in New York aggravated panics, for, when the public's demand for money increased, out-of-town banks drew down their New York deposits, thus reducing the reserves of the New York banks and forcing them to call in their loans. Money became tight, and those who were conducting business on the basis of bank loans might be forced into bankruptcy.

Other capital institutions developed just as slowly as investment banking during the early nineteenth century. The trust company, as it is known today, was virtually unknown. Savings banks, which lent their deposits chiefly on real estate mortgages, appeared in the boom years following the War of 1812.

Like all financial institutions except the commercial paper house, American savings banks were copied from the savings banks of Europe and the British Isles. Founded by capitalists who were also active in commercial banking, insurance, and industry, the early savings banks were designed to provide a place where the poor could save.

The first savings bank, the Philadelphia Savings Fund Society, was founded in 1816. However, as long as savings banks were operated as a side line to more important financial activities and as long as they were more or less confined to serving the poor, their prospects for growth were extremely limited. In time, professional managers replaced the early founders; then banks broadened their investments, extended their hours of doing business, and sought the savings of those who were in the middle- and upper-income groups. By the late 1820s savings banks were growing impressively. By 1835 there were 52 banks with 60,000 depositors holding $10 million in deposits. By the middle of the century, savings banks were the fastest growing intermediary, and by 1860 they had at least $150 million in deposits.

Life insurance, the last of the giant financial intermediaries, also grew slowly. The Presbyterian Ministers' Fund of Philadelphia, the first association for the insuring of lives, began in 1759, a generation before the Constitution and long before commercial banks, the stock exchange, or savings banks. But despite life insurance's early beginnings, there were only 29 life insurance companies in 1840. To be sure, 37 new ones were started in the next decade; but in 1850, there was less than $100 million of life insurance in force, and the amount of saving in the form of insurance reserves was less than $10 million.

Thus, by the middle of the nineteenth century, savings banks were thriving, life insurance companies were in their infancy, trust companies had hardly made a beginning, and investment banking was still predominantly dependent on London. Commercial banking was, as we shall see, already well developed.

FINANCIAL INTERMEDIARIES IN THE LATE NINETEENTH CENTURY

Like its first years, the nineteenth century's last decades were characterized by outstanding changes in the cycle of innovation and integration that has featured economic history. The thirty years before 1860 was a time of solidification; the thirty years after 1860 was a time of new developments in finance. One of the major forces in this new burst of innovation was the Civil War. Whether the war advanced industrial progress and the national income is a moot question, but it undoubtedly had a profound effect on the evolution of financial institutions.

In proportion to the size and the national wealth, the Civil War was the bloodiest and most costly in the country's history. Thus it was bound to have an important effect on the financial structure. It was responsible for the National Banking System, and it gave an immense impetus to the insurance and investment banking businesses.

The war may also have had an indirect effect on the intermediaries. It may, as many students have argued, have given a mighty push to heavy industry and to the national income. But whether the war was or was not the cause, the late nineteenth century was the time when industry and the economy did come of age. It was the time of heavy industry. It was the age of steel and toward its end it was beginning to be the age of electricity and the internal combustion engine.

The last half of the century was also a time of rapid progress in the level of living. The amount of goods and services available to the average man, woman, and child almost doubled between 1860 and 1900. Industrial production multiplied more than six times. All of this was grist for the financial intermediation mill. With saving averaging about 20 percent of national income, expanding income provided an ever greater supply of capital funds. Heavy industry required immense amounts of these capital funds, but it could hardly raise what capital was needed by tapping individual savers directly; and it became less and less practical for savers to loan their funds directly to business, as had been the case when the population was small and face-to-face relations prevailed. However, it was practical for both the suppliers and the demanders of capital funds to deal with each other through the middlemen of finance. The more complicated the economy became, the greater the reliance on these middlemen.

The growth of financial intermediaries can best be measured by relating it to the growth of the national income and of national wealth. It has been said that during the period under discussion, the assets of the financial intermediaries increased at twice the rate achieved by the national income. Finance was, therefore, growing at a much faster rate than national wealth. As can be seen from the estimates in Table 22, the total assets of banks, life insurance companies, and building and loan associations (savings and loan associations) advanced from approximately $1 billion in 1860 to $14.7 billion in 1900. In the same years

Table 22

ASSETS OF SELECTED FINANCIAL INTERMEDIARIES, 1860-1970

(millions of dollars, except as noted)

	Total assets[1]	Commercial banks	Savings banks	Savings and loan associations	Life insurance	Credit unions	Noninsured pensions	Investment companies
1860	$ 1.0	$ 85.1	$ 149*	–	$ 24	–	–	–
1870	2.6	1,781	550*	–	270	–	–	–
1890	7.4	4,601	1,743	300	771	–	–	–
1900	14.7	10,011	2,430	490	1,742	–	–	–
1922	65.7	47,467	6,597	2,802	8,652	$ 11	$ 90	$ 110
1929	104.5	66,235	9,873	7,411	17,482	42	500	2,988
1933	87.0	47,127	10,758	6,231	20,896	37	700	1,283
1940[1]	118.5	67.8	11.9	5.7	30.8	0.3	1.0	1.0
1950[1]	284.1	169.9	22.4	16.9	64.0	1.0	6.5	3.4
1960[1]	547.7	258.4	40.6	71.5	119.6	5.7	33.1	18.8
1970[1]	1,206.8	581.5	79.2	176.2	207.3	18.0	97.0	47.6

[1] billions of dollars

* Deposits

SOURCE: *Historical Statistics of the United States; All Bank Statistics;* Raymond Goldsmith, *Financial Intermediaries in the American Economy Since 1900;* Annual Report of the Superintendent of Insurance, State of New York, 1961; Institute of Life Insurance, Division of Statistics and Research; National Association of Investment Companies; Insurance Information Institute; Federal Home Loan Bank; Bureau of Federal Credit Unions; Securities and Exchange Commission.

national wealth climbed from $12 billion to $60 billion. According to these conservative estimates, the intermediaries were growing at about 6.75 percent a year while national wealth was expanding at about 4 percent a year, so that the assets of the intermediaries represented about 10 percent of wealth in 1860 and 25 percent in 1900.

In real per capita terms, financial institutions were growing at about 3.5 percent a year, probably 25 percent higher than in the first half of the century. Yet, in 1900, some of our present financial intermediaries were almost unknown. Trust companies were not very old. They were, however, experiencing a phenomenal rise that had begun shortly before 1890. Pensions were rare and their dollar volume unimportant. To be sure, the Massachusetts Hospital Life Insurance Company was really an investment trust, but despite its great size—the largest financial institution in the country—it was hardly a household word. This meant that the entire increase in the activity of the financial institutions was accomplished by the commercial banks, the savings banks, and the life insurance companies. The number of commercial banks increased at least 11-fold; their assets at least 12 times. But savings bank deposits and life insurance reserves did even better. The former increased some 17 times, mostly between 1870 and 1890, and the latter expanded somewhat over 70 times.

Up to the panic of 1873, savings banks continued to enjoy a high rate of growth. A number of them had deposits of over $10 million each. The idea of savings banking was spreading, for there were such institutions in 18 states and the District of Columbia. Had the rate of growth experienced up to 1873 continued, savings bank deposits would have been over $5 billion by 1900. Actually, they were only about $2.5 billion. Apparently they had run into a stone wall. The first difficulty was the panic of 1873. Savings bank failures in the aftermath of this economic disaster were higher than at any other time in history. There were 123 suspensions between 1875 and 1879, 13 in the next five years, and 11 between 1885 and 1889. The chilling effects of this catastrophe, even though total dollar losses were minute, caused bank managers to swing to conservatism. At the same time state governments passed rigid laws to make savings banks impregnable. In 1875, New York passed a law restricting deposits to $5,000 and investments to United States and New York State and municipal bonds and those state bonds that had not been in default for ten years.

In other states, savings banks were stymied not so much by state regulation as by the activities of competing institutions. Savings banks continued to thrive in New York and New England, but they quickly deteriorated in other areas. In the West commercial banks caught most of the savings accounts in their interest-bearing, time-deposit net. In Pennsylvania the savings banks ran into the competition of building and loan associations.

Of all the financial intermediaries, life insurance experienced the most phenomenal growth. Between 1860 and 1890, life insurance companies watched their assets multiply to an amount more than twice as large as the assets in the hands of general insurance companies, although still considerably less than the assets of the savings banks. The amount of life insurance written in 1868 was greater than the national debt. The industry had become, in the words of the New York insurance commissioner, "one of the great business interests." By the end of the century, Americans owned more life insurance than the rest of the world combined.

There were five reasons for the extraordinary rise of life insurance. The first and most important was the stress that the life companies constantly put on marketing and aggressive salesmanship. A second reason was the revival of the hardy perennial of the insurance business—the tontine. The tontine originated with Lorenzo Tonti, an Italian physician and banker of seventeenth-century France. The original tontine stipulated that all sums deposited plus interest on such deposits would be paid to the last survivor of the group. This extreme form was never popular in the United States. But in its modified American version, the tontine was the seed for the birth of the Insurance Company of North America in the eighteenth century. Tontines fell out of favor in the early 1800s but the idea itself never died. In 1847 an article in *Hunt's* treated the advantages of endowments, annuities, and tontines. Then in 1867 Henry Hyde of Equitable, an extraordinary person in every way, resurrected the idea. It was then quickly adopted by his competitors in Mutual of New York and New York Life.

The tontine feature, coupled with aggressive salesmanship, enabled a few companies to take over the business and build up large reserves that enabled them to become important forces in the capital markets. Companies like Connecticut Mutual that refused to offer the tontine policy sank rapidly. Second largest in 1878, it had dropped to fourteenth by the end of the century.

A third innovation accounting for the growth of life insurance companies was the introduction of industrial life insurance. The regular life companies sold their policies primarily to the high- and middle-income classes. Generally, policies were not available with a face value of less than $500, which for the 1870s was no small amount. Moreover, the annual or semi-annual premium was a sum much in excess of what the average wage earner could afford. Not only were persons of limited means unable to acquire protection, but the life companies were failing to provide a means of gathering the small savings of these millions of individuals. It was to remedy these defects that the Prudential insurance Company of America, under the leadership of its founder, John F. Dryden, in 1877 brought industrial insurance into the United States from England, where it had originated in 1854.

Still a fourth reason for the industry's emergence was the liberalization of government restriction in the seventies and eighties. In 1869 New York, like many other states, had passed a law limiting investments to government securities and New York mortgages. In the seventies, investment power was broadened geographically, and in the eighties, New York companies were permitted to lend on mortgages anywhere in the United States. New England had long since made the same concessions to a national market.

The insurance companies were in a position to do something about capital mobility. They had the funds, and rates of return were higher in the West than in the East. All of them kept some of their deposits in banks far from the home office. According to a plan decided on at the time of its formation, Connecticut Mutual was the first to make substantial investments in Western securities. Other companies also advanced money on agricultural loans. The Aetna, in alliance with the Illinois Central Railroad, made many loans to small farmers in Illinois at 10 percent interest. The Northwestern had $30 million in Illinois mortgages, the Union Central was active in Indiana, and the Mutual Benefit spread all through the Middle West. The net effect of this giant step toward a national capital market was, of course, to narrow the spread in interest rates between different parts of the country.

The fifth reason for life insurance growth in the late nineteenth century rested with the ambitious, aggressive entrepreneurs who emerged as the heads of the fastest growing companies: Hyde of Equitable, Frederick S. Winston and Richard McCurdy of Mutual, William H. Beers and John McCall of New York Life, Dryden of Prudential, and Joseph F. Knapp of Metropolitan. These men shared an enthusiasm for growth at almost any cost. Profits and rates of return faded into the background, and the motive became not profit maximization but, as one competitor put it, "more, perhaps, for the pride in doing it than otherwise."

As the life insurance business grew to become a great fount of capital, the structure became honeycombed with bureaucracy; the leading firms became intermeshed with other financial intermediaries in the banking world; the aggressive entrepreneurs tired; and the business became a tool rather than an entity of its own. Home office staffs grew to awesome size. Prudential's staff rose from 89 in 1883 to 250 in 1890; Metropolitan's grew to 1,081 in 1897. The president of the latter company was referred to as "a business machine," and its home office proudly proclaimed that it had more typewriters than any other office building in the world. Boards of directors deteriorated to mere rubber stamps. Elaborate home office buildings were erected to house the trappings of bureaucracy. Inevitably, the leaders of yesterday could echo the words of John Hegeman: "The business some time ago outgrew me."

Investment banking comes of age

The growth of the financial intermediaries in the late nineteenth century was accompanied by similarly impressive development in other financial institutions: surging activity in the securities markets, the beginnings of the great days of investment banking and so-called security capitalism, the establishment of the commercial paper house, and a gradual decline in the relative importance of European bankers in the American money and capital markets.

On all sides, commentators of the day were impressed by the widespread activity in security speculation. Admittedly, there was then as there is now a tendency to exaggerate how much speculation actually existed, but the volume of shares traded on the New York Stock Exchange averaged slightly more than 50 million a year in the last of the 1870s, over 100 million a year in the early 1880s, and over 140 million in 1900. The booming economy was the main cause of what became known in some circles as "finance capitalism." The expansion of the national income, the much greater supply of dollar saving, and the larger number of wealthy individuals provided the fuel to stoke the furnace. Investment bankers appeared in much larger numbers to tend the furnace, and an eager public prepared to consume what the furnace produced. As the volume of transactions grew, improvements in the market's technical and business organization removed some of the more obvious bottlenecks and rigidities that might have interfered with expansion. In 1866 the Atlantic Cable began to operate. The stock ticker appeared the following year, and in 1878 telephones were installed on the floor of the Stock Exchange.

The investment bankers, who were so much involved in security capitalism, could be divided into four separate groups. First of all, there was a group headed by Jay Cooke. Cooke was unquestionably an innovator of more than ordinary importance, for as agent for the Federal Treasury during the Civil War, he was the one who introduced modern methods of distributing securities. Unlike his contemporaries, who dealt with only the very rich, Cooke placed loans with small banks and local capitalists. This practice stood him in good stead in selling Civil War securities. With a staff of 2,500 salesmen and with liberal use of throwaways and advertising that appealed to patriotism, he was phenomenally successful in selling the bonds and notes that raised most of the money the Union needed to finance the war.

The members of the second group—the German-Jewish group—sprang from quite different backgrounds. The founders of many of the firms were originally peddlers. Thus the Seligmans of J. & W. Seligman & Co., Abraham Kuhn and Solomon Loeb, Philip Heidelbach of Heidelbach, Ickelheimer, and Marcus Goldman of Goldman, Sachs progressed from peddling to banking via cotton brokerage, clothing stores, and dealing in commercial paper. Most of these houses climbed the ladder without any direct help; but some German Jewish houses grew and prospered with the help of talent and capital imported from the long-established banking houses of Frankfurt and Hamburg. The leading example was Kuhn, Loeb & Co., which benefited immensely through the infusion of Schiffs and Warburgs. Jacob H. Schiff, who came to the United States in 1865 and shortly became senior partner in the firm, married Theresa Loeb, and Paul Warburg married Nina Loeb.

A third group of bankers of considerable importance consisted of the non-Boston New Englanders: Levi Morton of Morton, Rose & Co. and Morton, Bliss & Co., Harvey Fisk, and, above all, J. Pierpont Morgan. Morgan's father was a partner in Peabody & Co. in London and later senior partner in J.S. Morgan & Co. J. P., therefore, had valuable connections with the leading British houses—the Rothschilds, and Barings, and naturally J. S. Morgan.

J. P. Morgan's personality was a cardinal factor in the House of Morgan's success, but it was by no means the only one. The firm was the best organized of any in the investment banking business. Moreover, Morgan had the supreme gift of the outstandingly successful entrepreneur—the ability to select men of great talent, weld them into the organization, and get the best out of their talents. The House of Morgan also had the ability of enlisting other financial institutions as allies in its ventures. At one time or another, most of the major financial houses participated in Morgan underwriting, but some relations were much more intimate than others. The alliance with George F. Baker of New York's First National Bank was the essence of an entente cordiale. In addition there were close associations with Morton, Bliss; the National Bank of Commerce; Lee, Higginson & Co.; Kidder, Peabody & Co.; James Stillman's National City Bank; and later an added number of insurance companies and trust companies.

The fourth group of bankers of unusual power in the world of finance were the Boston firms, chiefly Lee, Higginson & Co. and Kidder, Peabody & Co. Just as mysterious as most investment bankers, these houses, whose ancestry antedated all the others, played a quiet hand in almost every major financing that took place in the nineteenth century. But inbreeding, financial conservatism, and an imperfect managerial structure eventually had their effect; by the end of the nineteenth century, the Boston firms had become satellites of the more efficiently managed House of Morgan.

In addition to the better-known alliances and ententes, there were many smaller firms of private bankers, firms that have been virtually ignored in the preoccupation with commerical banking. As mentioned earlier, private bankers were much more important than can be gathered from the literature on banking and finance. The main reason for this oversight is that there are practically no data on how they conducted their business activities.

From the available information, we know there were at least 617 private banks in the United States in 1855, 830 in 1865 2,578 in 1880, and 4,365 in 1890. In the latter year, there were more private banks than state or national commercial banks, although their assets were much less. After 1890 and until World War I, the number of private banks remained about the same; then it dropped drastically.

The growth of private banking from the 1840s on was attributable more to geography than to finance. Private bankers needed little capital and they could supply personalized banking services to communities that were too small to permit incorporated banks. As the rural areas spread across the United States, private banking thrived, but its advantages disappeared with the end of the frontier.

Private banking could afford to be mysterious, and its practitioners did not feel any compulsion to report their activities to the Comptroller of the Currency. In 1890, for example, only 30 percent of the private bankers submitted reports. Their assets were equal to slightly more than 10 percent of state bank assets and 5 percent of those of national banks.

The establishment of the commercial-paper house

As has been noted, dealing in commercial paper was one of the private banker's most important activities. Commercial paper was also one of the most important media in the money market, and it deserves much more attention than it has thus far received.[13]

The modern commercial-paper house, unlike other economic institutions, is an American product. Indeed, it is the only financial mechanism that is indigenous to the United States. But like all other institutions, it is the product of a long process of pioneering and innovating. The first houses that bought and sold paper, instead of simply acting as brokers between borrower and lender, appeared early in the nineteenth century. The innovators, the specialists whose example would be generally copied, came on the scene just before the Civil War. One of the first specialists in commercial paper was Henry Clews & Co., founded in 1857. But his firm was small indeed compared with the giants that appeared at the end of the century. Then the business became truly cosmopolitan as houses were established in Chicago, Kansas City, and other Western centers, and as the home offices of the large Eastern commercial-paper houses hired traveling representatives to tour the country. It is easy to deduce what effect this activity had on capital mobility.

The total volume of commercial paper for the country as a whole is hard to estimate for the early years, but it certainly became a thriving business as soon as it started. One estimate of outstanding paper in 1862 puts the total at about $700 million. Volume presumably expanded after the panic of 1873. In 1882 a bank president said that New York banks were buying $1 million a day. In the same year, a prominent note broker handled $42 million in commercial paper.

One of the reasons for the popularity of commercial paper was that it was a cheaper way of borrowing for Southern and Western businessmen, because bank rates in their vicinity were much higher than rates in the East. Yet in boom times rates soared fantastically. Shortly after the peak of business—in November 1873, for example, paper was bought at a discount of 18 to 24 percent.

The relative decline of foreign banking

As the economy expanded in nineteenth-century America, the relative importance of foreign houses in domestic finance gradually declined. It was estimated that foreigners owned something under $1 billion of government debts and equities in 1866. By 1869, it was said that foreign holdings had multiplied to $1.5 billion, and in 1897 to $3.4 billion. Meanwhile of course, total debt had increased considerably more, and domestic intermediaries had grown over five times. Meanwhile, too, American investment bankers were becoming involved as

[13]The authority on the subject is Albert O. Greef, *The Commercial Paper House in the United States* (Cambridge, Mass.: Harvard University Press, 1938).

lenders in the international market. The first important international loan came in 1879 with a $3 million advance to Quebec.

There is a simple explanation for the relative decline of foreign investment. The unusual growth of the national income produced a supply of saving sufficiently large to enable the domestic market gradually to free itself of dependence on the older world. Yet the position of the foreign investors had been built up over such a long period and had become so solidly entrenched that it could tolerate years of erosion. As late as the early 1900s, long after the process of erosion had begun, Henry Clews, the garrulous banker, could still bemoan the eminence of Europeans in the financing of the export import trade. "In the present stage of our national development," he said "it is becoming a grave reflection upon our men of capital that we should remain almost entirely dependent on foreign bankers for transacting our immense foreign commerce."

THE GROWTH OF FINANCIAL INTERMEDIARIES IN THE TWENTIETH CENTURY

Financial institutions in the twentieth century continued to leap ahead at a breathtaking rate. Their aggregate assets grew by over 6.5 percent a year. They doubled every ten years, except for the 1930s when they declined depressingly and the 1960s when they rose two-and-a-half times.

Assets per head grew about 5 percent a year, outstripping national product by a wide margin. By the late 1960s, financial intermediaries were supplying 85 percent of the vast pool of funds in the credit markets compared to 75 percent of a much smaller pool in the 1950s.

But all the intermediaries did not grow at the same pace. As Chart 16 shows, commercial banks retreated somewhat from their awesomely dominant position. Savings banks steadily declined except for the depression years when they more than held their own. Savings and loan associations, on the contrary, suffered terribly from the depression, but then surged ahead. Life insurance companies progressed impressively until after World War II when their percentage of total assets dropped. Noninsured pensions, investment companies, and credit unions grew most impressively of all, but even in 1970, credit unions accounted for only 1 percent of the assets of private intermediaries. Understandably, as pension funds and investment companies loomed larger in the securities markets, investment banking declined.

A radical shift took place among the thrift institutions in the twentieth century. Time deposits in commercial banks and shares in savings and loan associations advanced rapidly when prosperity ruled. At the same time, savings in the more conservative savings banks and life insurance companies faltered. The changing fortunes of the thrift institutions can easily be seen in Table 23.

Savings banks that had four-tenths of thrift deposits in 1900 held only one-tenth in 1971. Time deposits in commercial banks doubled from two-tenths

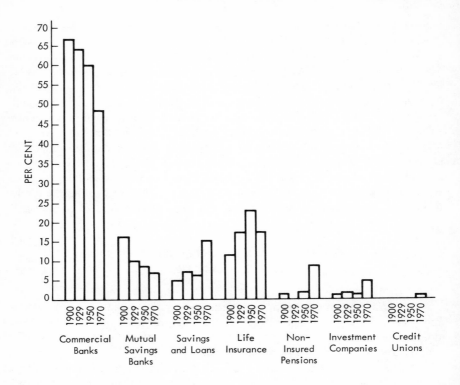

CHART 16. Distribution of assets, selected financial intermediaries, 1900-1970

to four-tenths. Life insurance reserves remain about the same, although in 1950, they were by far the largest depository of individual savings. Savings and loan associations experienced the most phenomenal growth, their share rising from less than 10 percent in 1900 and slightly more than 10 percent in 1950 to almost 25 percent in 1970.

The same factors that had troubled savings banks in the late nineteenth

Table 23

SAVINGS DEPOSITS AND SHARE ACCOUNTS BY TYPE OF INTERMEDIARY, 1900, 1950, 1970

	1900	1950	1970
Savings banks	41.2%	15.9	11.6
Savings and loan associations	9.8	11.1	23.5
Time deposits-commercial banks	21.6	29.6	38.0
Life insurance reserves	27.4	43.5	26.9

Totals may not add to 100% because of rounding.

century continued to erode their growth in the twentieth century. They were confined almost exclusively to the New England and Middle Atlantic States whose growth rate was lower than the rest of the country. In addition, throughout most of the period, the savings banks did not choose to compete aggressively with the savings and loan associations or one-stop-commercial banking. Thus it was that even in the East, they did not keep up with their rivals.

Savings and loan associations caught up to and then passed the savings banks. But in pursuing an aggressive strategy, they paid the price of experiencing a period of famine amid two periods of feast. They flourished in the building boom of the 1920s. Then they sagged during the depression. By 1935 they had lost one-third of the assets they had held in 1930. By 1940, there were almost 5,000 fewer associations than there had been in 1929. But with a new building boom following World War II, savings and loan assets came to exceed the combined assets of the 15 largest industrial corporations.

In the years preceding World War II, life insurance companies became the leading conduit for the personal saving of the American people. Their pre-eminence reflected the increased importance of contractual saving in American society. From one-twelfth of all saving early in the century, the share of contractual saving rose to one-eighth in the 1920s, and to three-tenths in the 1950s. But life insurance could not sustain its position despite the steadily increasing importance of contractual saving. In the 1950s and 1960s, continuous prosperity and continuous inflation changed the composition of the life insurance mix. The amount of insurance in force continued to soar, but the high-savings types of insurance (endowments and retirement incomes) gave place to policies with small reserves (term and group). Life insurance reserves in the 1950s and 1960s barely doubled while the ownership of financial assets more than tripled. The average size policy remained consistently at around 60 percent of average family disposable income. The amount of insurance in force multiplied six times in the twenty years after 1950, but premium income was up only three-and-a-half times. Group insurance grew 11 times, ordinary life only five times, and industrial insurance remained about the same.

The position of life insurance in contractual savings was rapidly taken over in the 1950s and 1960s by noninsured pension plans. By 1970, the assets of these intermediaries surpassed those of savings banks, were equal to more than half of savings and loan assets, and to about 45 percent of life insurance company assets. In twenty years, noninsured pensions had grown 16 times.

Investment companies followed much the same pattern as the savings and loan associations. They enjoyed a feast in the stock market boom of the 1920s, experienced a series of disasters in the 1930s, and came back strongly in the 1950s and 1960s.

The growth of pension plans and mutual funds came partly at the expense of orthodox investment banking. Investment banking retained its position of importance in the American economy until 1929. Just as Civil War financing had made the nation more conscious of security transactions, so the floating of

Liberty Bonds during World War I made many Americans more familiar with stock and bond dealings during the 1920s. Businessmen quickly turned to security issues to meet their needs for capital funds. New security issues totaling less than $3 billion in 1919 were about $10 billion in 1929.

The number of firms engaged in security selling increased almost as fast as the number of securities sold, creating a new type of competition in the money market and a fundamental change in investment banking leadership. Commercial banks expanded their investment banking business by forming security affiliates. The number of businesses engaged in selling securities increased from 485 in 1920 to 665 in 1929, while the number of branch offices expanded from 203 to 1,237. With one office for every 64,000 people, every whistle stop in the nation had its brokerage office complete with stock ticker and stock board. Activity on the New York Stock Exchange grew at the same hectic pace. In 1900, the Exchange handled over 100 million shares of stock, equal to a turnover of 172 percent of all listed shares. During the 1920s, volume averaged about 475 million shares. In 1929, business soared to a phenomenal 1 billion shares, a turnover rate of 119 percent of all listed stock.

The collapse of the stock market between 1929 and 1932 damaged the prestige of the investment banker and diminished his importance in mobilizing capital funds. In the next two decades, the security business failed to recover its previous position. Indeed, corporate security issues did not surpass the 1929 figure until 1955, when the gross national product was more than three times as high. Moreover, a higher portion of the security issues in the 1950s were bonds. In the 1920s, bonds accounted for 62 percent of security issues and common stocks for 24 percent. In the 1950s, the respective percentages were 77 and 17. The number of stockholders (at best an educated guess) did not keep pace with population growth, shrinking from ten million in 1929 to five million in 1950 and recovering to 12.5 million in 1960. Volume also fell far short of the pace of the 1920s. It averaged around 550 million shares a year. The stock exchange, for the first time since 1929, handled over 1 billion shares, but the turnover rate was only 15 percent of all listed shares. Despite relatively lower activity, however, prices reacted much as they had in the 1920s. Standard and Poor's stock index, based on 1941-1943 equaling 100, reached 260 in September 1929, a figure that was not surpassed until 25 years later. After 1954, the average again ran away, passing 900 in the 1960s.

There were a number of reasons why investment banking declined as a supplier of capital funds for business. When the market collapsed, emphasis on security temporarily replaced the "sky is the limit" psychology of the 1920s. Business itself contributed to the declining importance of investment securities, for "the new managers," with their new independence, found it less necessary to rely on investment bankers for capital funds. They therefore resorted more to internal financing than to the sale of securities. Government philosophy, legislation, and fiscal policy also contributed to the decline of the investment banker and the stock market. In the new era, government, largely because of popular sentiment, laid greater emphasis on security. It passed legislation separating commercial from investment banking, prohibiting pools and wash sales (fictitious sales such as between husband and wife), restricting margin trading, requiring publicity for new security issues over $300,000, regulating stock exchange operations, and requiring competitive bidding for certain types of new security issues. Government fiscal policy, by placing constantly greater emphasis on progressive taxation, reduced the number of persons who could afford to buy large blocks of securities. At the same time, it seemed to some observers to be foolish to buy risk securities in the face of high tax rates.

But investment banking, like other aspects of economic history, demonstrated long-wave tendencies. The return of boom prosperity mellowed the memories of the depression and brought security buying back into fashion. Corporate new issues totalled $6.4 billion in 1950, $10.2 billion in 1960, and $38.9 billion in 1970, representing a 60 percent increase in the 1950s and a 280 percent increase in the 1960s. The proportion of stock in these issues remained stable at about 20 to 25 percent.

To summarize, during the twentieth century, the mechanics of saving and investment showed a trend toward ever-greater emphasis on safety and de-emphasis on risk. Corporations relied less on commercial and investment bankers and more on retained earnings. Private savers turned toward life insurance, savings associations, pension funds.

Many economists were uneasy because of these developments. Deductive reasoning led them to believe that the trend toward security was inconsistent with continued economic growth, for it interfered with the mobility of capital funds. Experience, however, demonstrated otherwise, for the nation experienced great economic progress when the pursuit of security was especially noticeable. The new methods of mobilizing capital were apparently making it possible for the American people to enjoy security and economic growth at the same time. Whether this was a permanent development remained debatable. If investment outlets became filled, the rigidities that encouraged saving and, at the same time, reduced its mobility might tend to obstruct economic growth.

SUGGESTED READINGS

Goldsmith, Raymond, *Financial Intermediaries in the American Economy since 1900* (Princeton, N.J.: Princeton University Press, 1958).

Krooss, Herman E. and Martin R. Blyn, *A History of Financial Intermediaries* (New York: Random House, 1971).

Kuznets, Simon S., *Capital in the American Economy* (Princeton, N.J.: Princeton University Press, 1957).

Redlich, Fritz, *The Molding of American Banking* (New York: Hafner Publishing Company, Inc., 1946-1951). Reprinted by Johnson Reprint Corporation, 1968.

QUESTIONS

1. Comment on the statement, "The United States does not save as much as it used to."
2. Who did most of the saving in the American economy? Discuss the relative importance of domestic and foreign sources of capital funds before 1850 and after 1914.
3. Have interest rates moved in long waves? If not, how would you describe what happened to them?
4. Do you agree that interest rates vary inversely with the supply of money?
5. How do you explain why financial intermediaries have grown much faster than the overall economy?
6. Each financial intermediary experienced a sudden spurt in growth, and some intermediaries have been declining relatively. Explain why this has occurred.
7. What have the financial intermediaries contributed to economic growth?
8. What is meant by the comment: "Investment banking came into its own in the late nineteenth century"?

Chapter Nine

MONEY AND BANKING
IN AMERICAN HISTORY

History is, by one definition, the story of conflict. The history of American money and banking fits this definition very well, for from its first chapter it has been the story of a conflict between different philosophies and disparate beliefs over what money should do and how it should be controlled. In the oversimplified terms in which these battles are fought, the contest was one of "easy money" versus "sound money." Those who believed that easy money offered an excellent road to prosperity and maximum economic growth argued for a rapidly expanding money supply free from strict control by a central authority. Benjamin Franklin, for example, thought, "There is a certain proportionate Quantity of Money requisite to carry on the Trade of a Country and currently: More than which would be of no Advantage in Trade and Less, if much less, exceedingly detrimental to it."[1]

Franklin's views were opposed by those who believed in "sustainable" economic growth," that is, slow, steady progress under a central authority whose primary objectives were safety, solvency, and stability. The debate began before the Revolution and has continued ever since. The conflict is still far from

[1] "A Modest Enquiry into the Nature and Necessity of a Paper Currency," reprinted in Herman E. Krooss, ed., *Documentary History of Banking and Currency* (New York: McGraw-Hill Book Company, 1969), Vol. 1, p. 24.

resolved, but the trend has been slowly in the direction of growth and central-ized control.

The money and banking history of United States falls conveniently into five reasonably distinct periods: (1) the Colonial Period, (2) the years from the formation of the first commercial bank in 1781 to the end of the Second Bank of the United States in 1836, (3) the succeeding heyday of state banking, (4) the era of dual banking between the passage of the National Bank Act in 1863 and the formation of the Federal Reserve System, and (5) the period of modern central banking since 1914. The remainder of this chapter is intended to put some detail into this outline.

Colonial experiments with money

In early America, capital did not accumulate fast enough to raise the level of living very much. And because a high level of living was the focal point of American ambition, the enterprising citizenry sought to accumulate capital faster than they saved. Many people, acting on the assumption that money was the same as capital, thought that each addition to the money supply would automatically increase the stock of capital by the same amount. It was com-monly believed that a money system should have two functions: it should provide a medium of exchange, and it should augment the supply of capital. Although these two functions were largely contradictory, the colonists, in a desperate attempt to achieve them, ran through a whole series of ingenious monetary experiments in a relatively short span of time. These experiments ranged from primitive commodity money to the highly sophisticated modern system in which money represents nothing more than a set of numbers in over-sized ledger books. All of these experiments were resisted and sometimes thwarted by the British, who upheld the conservative view in the monetary debates of that period.

As in any underdeveloped economy, the colonies first used barter. Then, as barter became too awkward, commodity money—wampum, furs, tobacco, corn, livestock, and the like—was drafted into service. Meanwhile, even though accounts were kept in terms of British money, foreign coins, especially Spanish dollars, were used in those few transactions that required specie (gold or silver) payments.

By the middle of the seventeenth century, a mint had been established in Massachusetts, but it had scarcely begun to operate when it was closed by the British government. At about the same time, in order to increase their stock of metallic money, the colonies resorted to devaluation, that is, they cut the amount of metal in their silver coins. But this attempt to inflate the money supply was also prohibited by British edict. Refusing to accept the mother country's distaste for monetary inflation which stemmed from her position as a creditor, the colonies, which were deeply in debt, began to print paper money.

In 1690, Massachusetts issued £7,000 of one-year notes to pay returning soldiers. Theoretically, these were issued in anticipation of taxes, but in reality not enough tax revenue was ever raised to retire them. Yet, the experiment worked out so well that more paper money was quickly printed. Meanwhile, the other colonies, impressed by Massachusetts' ingenuity, also began to issue paper money. Some of these notes were issued by so-called banks, but there were no banks as we know them today. Colonial banks issued money against mortgages, but they did not accept deposits.

At first, paper money did not depreciate in value, and in some colonies, Pennsylvania being the best example, it never depreciated significantly. But in many colonies it was used unproductively and, after vast quantities had been issued, price inflation set in on a very broad scale. In Rhode Island, for example, the value of money fell 75 percent. Extreme inflation such as this disrupted the economy and caused widespread suffering among certain groups. However, paper-money depreciation did act to the advantage of colonial debtors and to the disadvantage of British creditors, who eventually prevailed upon the Crown to prohibit the printing of paper money.[2] According to Franklin, who viewed paper money sympathetically, the British antiinflation policy was one of the five causes of the Revolution.

AMERICAN COINAGE IN THE EARLY NINETEENTH CENTURY

The same circumstances that frustrated the colonies' efforts to work out a satisfactory coinage system forced the Federal government to set up an almost equally makeshift arrangement. In 1791, at the urging of Secretary of the Treasury, Alexander Hamilton, the United States established a bimetallic system. Gold and silver were freely minted into two types of coin, a $10 gold piece containing 247.50 grains and a silver dollar containing 371.25 grains. The price of gold at the mint was therefore $19.39 an ounce and the price of silver $1.2929 an ounce, a ratio of fifteen units of silver to one of gold.

Unfortunately, both the gold and the silver coins ceased to circulate a few years after the act of 1791. The price of gold in the international bullion market was over $20 an ounce, 61 cents more than the American mint price. Holders of gold, therefore, either sold it in the bullion market or hoarded it after it was coined. One of the incontrovertible laws of economics—Gresham's law, which says that in a bimetallic system the metal that is undervalued at the mint will cease to circulate—was operating to change a bimetallic standard into a *de facto* monometallic standard. But American silver coins also failed to circulate domestically. They were coined lighter than the Spanish dollars on which they were patterned. Consequently, they were exported to the Caribbean area, where

[2]See Richard A. Lester, *Monetary Experiments* (Princeton, N.J.: Princeton University Press, 1939).

they circulated at face value. Finally, in 1806, President Jefferson stopped the coinage of silver dollars entirely. Thus, the United States had a coinage system in theory only. In actual practice, no American coin higher than one cent circulated, and many transactions were still settled on a barter basis. As late as 1832, 18 out of 324 manufacturers stated that they disposed of their entire output, and 148 responded that they disposed of part of their product, by barter. Where the need for metallic money existed, foreign coins were used—Spanish dollars, Dutch guilders, and so forth—and were given legal tender status under American law.

By 1834 some gold deposits had been found in the Appalachian range of North Carolina. Although they produced far less than the later and more famous California, Alaska, and African fields, these mines did contribute enough new metal to make possible the establishment of a more effective specie standard. Taking advantage of the newly discovered gold deposits, the agrarian administration of Andrew Jackson, which was sympathetic to hard money, devalued the gold dollar. Its weight was reduced to 23.2 grains in 1834 and 23.22 in 1837, at which it remained until 1933. The silver dollar was kept at its old weight of 371.25 grains. The new bimetallic ratio was almost 16 to 1, and the price of gold at the United States mint was now $20.67 an ounce instead of $19.39. Gresham's law now began to drive silver out of circulation. As a result of the devaluation, therefore, the nation went on a *de facto* gold standard. Because silver was worth about $1.31 an ounce in the bullion market and $1.29 an ounce at the mint, it was sold as bullion or hoarded after being coined. On the other hand, the price of gold at the United States mint was higher than in the world market. Gold flowed into the United States to take advantage of the relatively high price, and the coinage of gold increased sharply. Later, the discovery of gold in California not only increased the specie available for export but also increased the amount of gold that could be turned into coins at the mint.

Although the economy now possessed gold pieces that circulated, it still had no subsidiary coinage, for the higher value offered for silver in the bullion market discouraged the coinage of half-dollars, quarters, and dimes, as well as dollars. In 1853 this situation was alleviated by reducing the weight of the silver in the subsidiary coinage. The half-dollar was cut from 185.625 grains to 172.8 grains, and the quarter and the dime were cut proportionately. For the first time, the United States had a coinage system under which coins from one cent to a $20 gold piece circulated. There was no longer any need for foreign coins, and Congress removed their legal-tender status completely in 1857. By the 1850s, the old practice of quoting price in terms of the Spanish dollar (7½ cents, for example) had disappeared.

The coinage system set up by the United States, even with its later modifications, could not provide enough money to take care of the country's economic needs. Paper money supplied the additional amount needed. Indeed, sometimes it supplied more than what was needed.

Prior to the Civil War, the Federal government did not issue any paper money, although some of its short-term securities issued during the War of 1812 and during the depression of 1837 circulated among private citizens as money. In addition, the government and some private institutions sometimes accepted government securities in payment of public dues or in payment of stock subscriptions. So it happened that government debt was converted into money or "monetized" even in early American history, but this monetization of the debt occurred so rarely and on so small a scale that it did not add substantially to the money supply. The vacuum in the money supply left by the inadequacy of government coinage and currency was filled by the commercial banks and, to a lesser extent, by an assortment of state-chartered corporations that had the power to issue paper money.

EARLY AMERICAN COMMERCIAL BANKING

Before the Civil War, commercial banks were already the most important type of financial institution in the country. They held deposits, made loans and discounts, and, most important of all, they created money in the form of bank notes which they issued to borrowers. Although these functions were the same as those carried on by modern commercial banks, nineteenth-century banks operated quite differently from modern banks.

In today's economy, commercial banks create money by making loans and investments. The borrowers are credited with demand deposits against which they can write checks. These deposits, it is apparent, serve the same functions as money and are, therefore, part of the money supply. To some extent, the amount of deposits that a bank may create is a matter of the banker's discretion. But a much more potent and much more important limitation, and in the final analysis the only limitation worth talking about, is the extent of the bank's reserves. Since these reserves are controlled by the central bank (i.e., the Federal Reserve System), it can be said that the Federal Reserve controls deposits, and, therefore, the money supply.

In the early nineteenth century, some banks also created money by entering deposits. But most banks created money by issuing bank notes to borrowers. Like the present banks, the early banks were also limited in their ability to create money by the extent of their reserves that, in those days, were determined by the amount of specie (gold or silver) in the bank's valults. Within the limits set by their specie stock, bankers could use their discretion in making loans and creating deposits. In addition, during forty years of the nineteenth century, the ability of the banks to create money was to some extent influenced by the policies and behavior of a quasi-central bank—the First Bank of the United States, 1791-1811, and the Second Bank of the United States, 1816-1836.

Banking practice in the big cities differed widely from methods followed in rural areas. Banks in all sections made "accommodation loans," that is, long-term loans to finance expenditures for fixed capital; but city banks also handled a large volume of short-term commercial loans. When a New York City merchant received a loan from a commercial bank, he submitted his note. In exchange, he received a bank deposit against which he could draw checks, or, less commonly, he received state-bank notes of varying denominations, ordinarily from $5 up. The borrower's note was payable in specie or bank notes at the end of 30 days, but it was usually renewable. In rural sections, the majority of loans were made to farmers and were for much longer periods than urban bank loans. Because American banking was predominantly of the rural variety, the early commercial banking system had little liquidity or shiftability. In the big cities, theoretically, loans could be liquidated, that is, turned into cash quickly by simply calling for payment, but this could not be done in the outlying areas. Nor could the security against which most loans were made be sold, that is, shifted to another agency, for no such agency existed.

Ostensibly, the notes issued by the commercial banks were secured by specie (gold or silver) and were redeemable on demand in specie. In actual practice, however, sporadic breakdowns occurred in the system of redemption. In fact, specie payments had to be abandoned either wholly or partly in the midst of every major recession and during every major war. During prosperity, banks increased their note issues up to the limits allowed by law or by the existing state of their reserves. When prosperity was suddenly succeeded by panic, some of the outstanding money supply became redundant. Holders brought their notes to the issuing banks and demanded coin as promised on the face of the notes. But because their assets were neither liquid nor shiftable, banks could not meet these demands for redemption as quickly as they were presented. In an effort to do so, they called loans, and the money supply diminished. But specie ran out faster than loans could be called and, consequently, specie payments had to be abandoned.

In the early years of the century, most bankers mistakenly regarded deposits as unprofitable and did not accept them with enthusiasm. The Massachusetts Bank in the first six years of its career (1784-1790) charged a fee for holding deposits. The Bank of Baltimore, as late as 1819, had only $17,000 on deposit. In the 1820s, the nine Massachusetts banks outside of Boston had $61,000 in deposits and $578,000 in outstanding notes. The District of Columbia banks in 1830 did one-third more business by notes than by deposits. But there were many exceptions to this prevailing picture, and it would be an error to think that deposits and checkbook money were unimportant in the early years. For the country as a whole, to be sure, checkbook money did not exceed pocketbook money until the 1840s, and in the rural areas this did not happen until late in the century. But banks in the financial centers of the big cities handled a substantial deposit traffic from the day they opened their doors. Around 1800, deposits in the Bank of New York were four times as large as note circulation; in the Bank of North America, deposits were certainly equal to note circulation;

and in the Massachusetts Bank, which made no effort to seek them, deposits were twice as large as note circulation.[3]

Some bankers actively sought both time and demand deposits. The Farmers' Bank of Maryland was the first to pay interest; in 1804, it offered 4 percent on time and 3 percent on demand deposits. Some Boston banks began to pay interest on deposits in the boom period following the War of 1812 and renewed the practice in each subsequent boom. The feverish competition for funds pushed interest rates up very rapidly. Legislators and others who believed themselves responsible for the public welfare became alarmed for fear that the high interest rates that banks agreed to pay would force them into high-risk investments which would end up with calamitous losses. These fears were not unfounded and occasionally came true. In order to prevent disaster, some states—for example, Massachusetts in 1834 and Connecticut in 1854—passed laws prohibiting or limiting interest on deposits. But these laws did not work, and the practice continued amidst the oft-expressed warnings of those who "viewed with alarm."

The growth of state commercial banks

In most of the early years of the republic, the commercial banking system was a dual one, consisting of a federally chartered central bank and a variety of state-chartered banks.

In the belief that banks could increase capital, the Federal government, under the influence of Hamiltonian federalism and against the opposition of agrarian spokesmen, who, in the words of Thomas Jefferson, "sincerely believed that banking establishments are more dangerous than standing armies," established the First Bank of the United States in 1791. Its charter was limited to 20 years and was not renewed on expiration.

Although the statistics are fragmentary, it seems safe to say that not many state banks were chartered while the First Bank of the United States existed. In 1800, there were only 29 state commercial banks, all located in the East. The first commercial bank west of the mountains was the Kentucky Bank, founded in 1802. There were less than one hundred state banks at the time the First Bank's charter expired in 1811. But during the War of 1812, state banks expanded rapidly. The main reason for this was the wartime financial policy of the Federal government. The government was reluctant to levy taxes to pay for the war, and it did not find it easy to borrow large sums from individuals. As a result, the Treasury became a magnificent customer for the state banks. It

---

[3]The 1814 balance sheet of the Bank of New York, one of the leading banks of the day, will give the reader an impression of the size and scope of commercial banking 150 years ago. The Bank's capital was $965,000; its circulation, $534,000; deposits, $984,000; and specie, $301,000.

borrowed heavily from them, selling securities in exchange for bank notes. Under this kind of encouragement, state banks experienced their first great period of growth. By 1815, there were over 200, and the bank notes they circulated had doubled (from $23 million to $46 million). As the volume of bank notes increased, reserves declined. The banks found it impossible to redeem their notes in coin and thus were forced to abandon specie payments. Thereafter, state-bank notes circulated at varying discounts and usually only in the region in which they were issued. Each city was surrounded by a set of rings, representing so many zones of different discounts. At Philadelphia, for example, Delaware notes circulated at 2 percent discount, those of Baltimore and Richmond at 3 percent, and those of western Pennsylvania and Ohio at 7 percent. The excellent notes of Boston and New York carried a 5 to 10 percent premium.

THE SECOND BANK OF THE UNITED STATES

With the end of the War of 1812, the conditions that had spawned the extraordinary monetary and price inflation disappeared. The Federal government no longer needed money, and instead of encouraging the expansion of the money supply as it had done during the war, it now tried rather half-heartedly to persuade the state banks to resume specie payments. When this effort failed, the Madison administration, which had followed the Jeffersonian tradition of considering central banking unconstitutional, reluctantly abandoned its ideological opposition and established the Second Bank of the United States. Again the charter was limited to 20 years, but in 1832, after Congress had passed a bill renewing the charter, President Jackson vetoed it and central banking did not return for 77 years.

The Second United States Bank was created to force the state commercial banks to restore specie redemption. Eventually, it not only succeeded in doing this, but also exerted considerable control over the whole commercial banking system. It acted as fiscal agent for the government, loaned money to state banks, handled intersectional exchange, dealt in foreign exchange, did a large discount business, and issued paper money. Control over its own paper money circulation gave the bank one means of regulating the money market. But, in addition, its activities in foreign exchange, its position as government fiscal agent, its central role in handling the complicated business of intersectional exchange, and its loans to state banks gave it the means of controlling state banks. Through its activities in collecting taxes, in receiving money in payment of loans, and in settling foreign and intersectional balances, the Bank was constantly receiving a stream of state-bank notes. It was, therefore, a creditor of the state banks and could exercise its creditor function to encourage expansion or contraction in the money market. By sending state-bank notes back for redemption in coin, the

bank could contract the money supply. By following a lenient policy in demanding redemption, the bank could encourage state banks to expand their
circulation.[4] But the bank was not all-powerful. It could not exert its powers
without regard to what the state banks might do in retaliation. Because the bank
also issued notes, it was vulnerable to attacks by the state banks which could
collect Bank of the United States notes and present them for redemption.

During the years immediately following the War of 1812, the bank made no
serious attempt to exert its powers to reduce the money supply. After specie
payments were restored, money inflation continued until 1819. By that time,
the bank itself was close to insolvency because it lacked enough specie to handle
the redemption of its notes. In order to survive, it instituted a policy of severe
deflation, which caused many bank failures and a drastic reduction in the money
supply, and initiated a severe panic and depression.

Because of its powers over the money market and its tendency to keep the
money supply under control, central banking in the form of the Second Bank of
the United States was not altogether popular in an economy that was beginning
to feel its oats. This unpopularity was clearly illustrated when the bank's charter
came up for renewal during the administration of Andrew Jackson. In the great
debate that culminated in Jackson's veto of the bank-charter bill, the bank had
the support of conservative, long-established businessmen and of state banks that
were strong enough to profit from a regulated money market. On the other
hand, the bank was opposed by those who, because of a belief in hard money,
distrusted all paper money and opposed all banks. This group, which included
President Jackson, Senator Benton, many agrarians, a number of monetary
theorists, and urban workers, drew no distinction between the central bank and
the state commercial banks. It mattered little to them that the central bank
tended to keep paper money issues within bounds. In their eyes, a bank was a
bank, whether it was conservative or wildcat; and, because the United States
Bank issued notes in excess of specie holdings, it was condemned along with all
other banks.

The bank also aroused the hostility of those who wanted more paper money
put into circulation. This easy-money group, consisting of small businessmen on
the make, many state bankers, and some debtor farmers, opposed the central
bank because its branches competed with the state banks, and because it tended
to limit the amount of available credit. Still a third group who opposed the bank
were those who feared the extensive economic power the institution possessed.
Many in this group thought the bank was unconstitutional, even though the
Supreme Court had upheld its constitutionality in the famous case of *McCulloch
v. Maryland.* They also considered the bank a monopoly, and, although this was
an exaggeration, the bank did control about one-third of the nation's banking

---

[4]For the most lucid explanation of the operations of the bank, see Walter Buckingham
Smith, *Economic Aspects of the Second United States Bank* (Cambridge, Mass.: Harvard
University Press, 1953).

capital and about one-fourth of its note circulation. Moreover, the bank's president, Nicholas Biddle, who made all the vital decisions concerning the bank's methods and operations, was rash enough to declare that he had the power of life and death over the state commercial banks.[5]

In one respect, the failure to renew the United States Bank's charter was an example of successful trust busting, a triumph of small business over big business. But, in another sense, the failure to recharter the bank represented a victory for loose banking over the restraints imposed by central banking; for, once the United States Bank was removed as a potent regulator of commercial banking, state bankers were free from one of the restraints on their power to expand their operations.

According to the traditional treatment of the events of the middle 1830s, the bank was the *only* force that kept other banks in line. Once its powers were clipped by Jackson's veto of the charter renewal, the state banks took advantage of their opportunities by starting on a second round of extraordinary growth. By 1837, there were almost 800 state banks—well over twice as many as had existed in 1830. Their circulation and deposits had more than tripled. They were flooding the economy with money, thus providing the fuel to feed speculation and inflation. The economy, so the argument runs, "overtraded"; it became embarked on what is now called "unsustainable growth." Once again specie reserves became badly strained, the economy collapsed in 1837, and specie redemption was once again abondoned. This orthodox explanation of what happened in the years 1834-1837 exaggerates the power of the bank, underestimates the importance of international factors, and omits some vital facts in the case.[6]

The early thirties were admittedly a period of inflation, but banks did not expand simply because the Bank of the United States no longer existed as a watchdog. Actually, banks had sufficient reserves to support the swelling money supply; as bank liabilities mounted, their specie reserves also mounted. So it cannot be said that banks "overtraded." Nor did the economy fall of its own weight. A logical succession of events brought the boom and the inflation to an end, and this succession of events began and ended in the English money market and centered around the American balance of payments.

---

[5]For different points of view on the controversy over rechartering the bank, see Ralph C. H. Catterall, *The Second Bank of the United States* (Chicago: University of Chicago Press, 1903); Arthur M. Schlesinger, Jr., *The Age of Jackson* (Boston: Little Brown & Co., 1945); Bray Hammond, *Banks and Politics in America* (Princeton, N.J.: Princeton University Press, 1957), Preface and Chaps. 7 and 11.

[6]Along with many others, this author also accepted the orthodox explanation without careful analysis. Recent research, expecially Peter Temin, *The Jacksonian Economy* (New York: W.W. Norton & Company, Inc., 1969), has damaged the orthodox view. See also George Macesich "Sources of Monetary Disturbances in the United States, 1834-1845", *Journal of Economic History,* Vol. XX (1960). What was wrong about the orthodox view was that it concentrated on the human actors in the drama and ignored market forces.

English bankers occupied a primary position in American finance at least until 1850. The most important of all were seven merchant banking firms known as the Anglo-American houses. Of these, Baring Brothers was especially important. Indeed, it is not too much to say that in this era the Bank of England and the Barings had a more potent influence on the American economy than did any American house, including the Bank of the United States. In fact, the behavior of the Bank of the United States itself depended largely on the actions of the English bankers.

The Barings, as early as 1832, became convinced that business "was not likely to be profitable for the coming few years and the utmost caution was in order." Therefore, they began to restrict their commitments and contracted stringently in the last quarter of 1835. What they refused to take, however, the other Anglo-American houses snapped up. In July and August 1836, the Bank of England, uneasy about the decline of its reserves, raised the discount rate to 5 percent. At the same time, it stopped discounting American paper and making loans against American securities. The money market tightened, and interest rates soared. The discount rate for first-class paper in New York and Boston was 5 percent in January 1835, 10 percent in December, and 36 percent in October 1836.

The British contraction, whether necessary or not, had a deplorable effect on the American economy and was a major factor in pushing the American economy into panic and depression. Cut off from European credit, the American economy sank. The money supply fell drastically, perhaps by as much as 25 percent from its high in 1836. Wholesale prices were cut almost in half. Most of the American states defaulted on their debts, the bulk of which were held abroad. State bank operations fell off sharply. By 1843, there were less than 700 state banks, their loans and investments had been cut in half, and their circulation and deposits had fallen to much less than half. With recovery, however, state banking embarked upon its third period of rapid growth, and by 1860 there were more than 1,500 banks, with loans of almost $700 million, $200 million of bank-note circulation, and $300 million of deposits—four times as much as 20 years before. These banks issued 7,000 different types of paper money, of which at least half were worthless or of dubious quality.

STATE BANKS AND ECONOMIC DEVELOPMENT[7]

State commercial banks influenced economic development and contributed to a rise in the level of living in two major ways. First, by making loans to

[7]Some of the histories of banking in the individual states are very helpful. These include: David M. Cole, *The Development of Banking in the District of Columbia* (New York: The William-Frederick Press, 1959); George T. Starnes, *Sixty Years of Branch*

would-be entrepreneurs or farmers, they encouraged production. Second, by issuing money, they facilitated the process of exchange and encouraged economic progress. However, the state banks had grave weaknesses. Scarcity of productive commercial loans, inadequate capital funds, and overly optimistic, sometimes dishonest, management created a poor foundation upon which to erect a commercial banking system. As a consequence, state banking fulfilled its functions at the expense of waves of bank failures and substantial losses to note-holders and depositors. Albert Gallatin counted at least 165 bank failures in 1811-1831. The capital of 129 of them was $24 million paid in. Since he was able to count only 329 banks with $110 million of capital in 1830, Gallatin's estimates show a high level of failures, more than half of all those that he could identify. Elliott estimated that, in the very depressed year 1841, there were 55 bank failures with $24 million in circulation. Knox, who thought that bank failures were greatly exaggerated, estimated the loss to noteholders at 5 percent per annum. But Jay Cooke, who was also close to the scene, went much further. Allowing for inefficiency and impropriety as well as insolvency, he said, "Fifty millions of dollars per annum, it is safe to say, would not cover the loss . . . growing out of broken banks, counterfeits, altered notes, and cost of exchange between different points."

The basic weakness of most state commercial banks lay in the fact that they were attempting to do a commercial banking business on the basis of savings bank assets that could not easily be turned into cash. Only in large cities were banks able to carry on genuine commercial banking, for only where industry was located could banks make enough short-term commercial loans to maintain liquidity. In small towns and country districts, banks made long-term loans against farm mortgages and issued short-term liabilities in the form of bank notes to borrowers. Borrowers, in turn, used the bank notes to purchase commodities—mostly capital goods—from industrial and commercial centers. When the notes were presented for redemption, banks were not always able to turn their assets into cash fast enough to meet these demands and found it difficult to maintain specie payments. Bank notes circulated at a discount and often became completely worthless. Thus, the outlying areas obtained capital goods at the expense of sellers in the more developed areas.

Most state banks also were plagued by a lack of adequate capital funds. Metropolitan areas, such as New York, Boston, and Philadelphia, quickly accumulated enough capital funds to provide sufficient bank reserves. But in other areas, especially on the frontier, capital funds were extremely scarce.

Banking in Virginia (New York: The Macmillan Company, 1931); N. S. B. Gras, *The Massachusetts First National Bank of Boston* (Cambridge, Mass.: Harvard University Press, 1937; Alfred C. Bryan, *History of State Banking in Maryland* (Baltimore: The Johns Hopkins Press, 1899); Walter W. Chadbourne, *A History of Banking in Maine; 1799-1930* (Orono: University of Maine, 1936); George D. Green, *Finance and Economic Development in the Old South: Louisiana Banking, 1804-1861* (Stanford, California: Stanford University Press, 1972).

Consequently, stock subscriptions were rarely paid in full in cash. The usual practice was to make a partial cash payment and then to submit a note for the balance. Banks operated on less than a shoestring, and their reserves were not adequate to meet redemption demands.

Probably the best way of evaluating the performance of the state banks is to examine what happened to the money supply. As has been said, most banks paid careful attention to their reserves and since these were basically dependent on the international specie standard, the banks were far from having complete control over how much money existed. Nevertheless, if we knew what happened to the money supply, we would have a basis for judging how well the system was working.

Accurate data on the nineteenth-century money supply do not exist. If information ever did exist on the early state banks, it has long since disappeared. What we have are pieces of information for scattered states and some estimates by contemporaries that have been carefully refined by present-day scholars.[8] In summary, the money supply seems to have risen from about $85 million in 1820 to $275 million in 1836. It then fell off sharply to about $210 million in 1840 from where it increased to about $325 million in 1850. If these figures are reasonably correct, the money supply increased at an average annual rate of 4.1 to 4.5 percent, somewhat faster than the assumed growth of real gross national product.

Estimates of the money supply are too rough to support narrow generalizations, but they do warrant a few broad conclusions. There is no doubt that money in circulation showed an upward secular trend. The money supply also tended to be elastic, that is, it varied more or less directly with the expansion and contraction in business activity. Thus, there was a sharp drop in the money supply following the panic of 1819 and during the depression of the late 1830s. There was also a close correlation between money in circulation and the price level. Prices and money were high in the boom of the 1830s and low in the depressed 1840s.

Early attempts to regulate banking

Whether the advantages of state banks offset their disadvantages is a debatable point. Suffice it to say that early commercial banking advanced the nation's overall economic development by supplying industry and agriculture, especially

[8]Samuel Blodgett in his *Economica* (1806) offered estimates on bank circulation and specie for the years 1774-1804. These were reprinted in John J. Knox, *A History of Banking in the United States* (New York: B. Rhodes and Co., 1900); also, in *Annual Report of the Comptroller of the Currency, 1915,* and in A. Barton Hepburn, *History of Coinage and Currency in the United States* (New York: The Macmillan Company, 1924). Albert Gallatin, in 1831, drew up some figures on the number of banks, their capital and specie, for 1811-1816 and also their deposits in 1820 and 1830. Jonathan Elliot, *The Funding System*

at the frontier regions, with capital funds, enabling them to obtain capital goods. But actually the advance was at the expense of the nation's older and more settled regions.

In time, commercial banking was sure to become safer and "sounder." With economic expansion, commerce and industry would appear, and commercial banks would be able to make short-term loans that could be liquidated in a crisis. True, there would be some bank failures, because in the course of liquidating their so-called "self-liquidating loans," some banks would suffer heavy losses. But at least banking would be safer than in the halcyon days of state banking.

One method of improving banking was by private enterprise putting its own house in order. Attempts of this kind, however, were rare. The outstanding example was the Suffolk System, a successful endeavor by the strong Boston banks to force the weaker and less conservative country banks into a mold of safety and solvency.

In the nineteenth century, city bankers wasted little love on their country cousins. The so-called foreign banks issued notes in a rather indiscriminate fashion, circulated them where they could, including the cities, redeemed them only after long delays or not at all, pushed city-bank notes out of circulation, and prevented city banks from getting their share of potential business. As soon as the first country bank appeared in New England, the problem of country bank notes presented itself. City people who received country notes could cash them in one of two ways, neither of which was particularly attractive. They could take them back to the place of redemption and exchange them for goods or specie, but this practice was expensive and inconvenient. More frequently, city holders of out-of-town bank notes sold them at a discount to a note broker, a step that was also expensive.

The Boston banks reacted to what they considered "funny money" by refusing to accept country-bank notes for deposit. The result, of course, was a severe blow to Boston merchants who had customers outside of Boston. A number of attempts were made to redeem systematically country-bank notes, but none of them succeeded until the Suffolk Bank of Boston undertook redemption and persisted in the task. Eventually it persuaded other Boston banks to join it and thus the Suffolk System came into existence in 1824. Essentially it was a collection clearing house for the New England banks. It attempted to do in New England what the Bank of the United States could in theory do for the whole country. Each country bank agreed, after much arm twisting by the city banks, to keep a deposit with the system in return for which the system agreed to redeem notes for not more than the cost of collection.

---

of the United States (Washington, D.C.: Blair and Rives, Printers, 1945), leaned heavily on Gallatin for 1811-1830 estimates and offered additional ones for the years 1830-1840. The Treasury began to collect bank data from the states in 1834 and pushed the series back into the past on the basis of the Gallatin and Blodgett estimates. Most of the Gallatin and Treasury data are reprinted in Historical Statistics of the U.S.

The Suffolk System's success meant that all New England bank notes circulated at par throughout New England, but it also meant that the New England area experienced a mild deflation that was not experienced in the other regions. Yet the other sections of the United States also desired the safety and solvency that appeared in New England. In New York the city banks chafed under the same country bank irritants that had bothered Boston, but in the city the problem was solved by the use of correspondent banks, notably the Isaac Bronson banks and the Mechanics' Bank. And later, in 1851, the Metropolitan Bank copied the Suffolk System; at the same time, Pennsylvania instituted a similar collection system, but it was not all-embracing.

New York also introduced a separate innovation in the interest of protecting the bank customer. In 1829, it created a Safety Fund, an idea patterned after an arrangement originated by the merchants of China under which the stronger merchants supported the weak. Banks had to contribute ½ of 1 percent of their capital annually for six years to a fund that was to be used to pay off the creditors of insolvent banks. The Safety Fund was, therefore, the forerunner of the present Federal Deposit Insurance Corporation (FDIC).

In time, as has been said, the banking system would have improved by itself. But the process of improvement would have been long, and the American people were impatient. With great faith in the magic power of legislation, they preferred trying to make commercial banking "sound" by passing laws.

These laws differed from state to state and ran the gamut from severe restriction to extreme leniency. Some states formed and ran their own commercial banks. Others, after an especially painful experience with bank failures, prohibited commercial banking altogether. Thus, by 1852 there were no incorporated banks in seven Southern and Western states. Usually, however, state legislation sought to make banking safe by requiring bank notes to be secured by liquid assets, by establishing reserves against deposits, by imposing penalties for failure to redeem bank notes in specie on demand, by designating a specific place for bank-note redemption, and by providing for "free banking," that is, the privilege of obtaining a bank charter without special act of legislature. Wherever the economy was underdeveloped, regulation of commercial banking was impractical, for no matter how weak the regulations, they could be enforced only if underlying economic conditions permitted. Banks could not survive in areas with little industry and commerce. Such areas had a choice between loose banking and no banking at all, because if attempts were made to regulate banking, the inevitable result would be to drive the banks out of existence.

As industry and commerce developed, effective regulation of commercial banking became possible. But here, as in so many other phases of economic history, the development proceeded zone by zone. The first effective regulation appeared in the East in the early 1800s. Then, in later years, as the economy of each frontier area became commercialized and industrialized, effective bank regulation spread westward. But, whenever a frontier area prematurely attempted the ambitious project of creating a "sound" banking system by legislation, the result was unsatisfactory. For example, Michigan passed a free banking law, the first in the United States, in 1837. This law required banks to maintain specie reserves against deposits, and to maintain reserves in the form of securities (usually Federal or state government bonds) against note issues. But in 1837 Michigan did not have the economic foundation necesary to sustain sound commercial banking. It did not have enough specie to meet the requirements of the law. Its banks could not make many self-liquidating loans. The securities that were used as backing for the note issues were very often nothing more than the I.O.U.s of borrowers with remote prospects for obtaining liquid assets. The law was openly flouted, as it had to be if banking was to exist in the state, and inevitably most of Michigan's banks failed. But similar legislation adopted where industry and commerce were highly developed—for example, in New York in 1838—worked, and worked well.

Throughout the period before the Civil War, the Federal government, pursuing an agrarian, laissez faire philosophy, was reluctant to attempt any regulation of state banking. True, the two United States Banks had had an indirect, but potent, influence on the whole banking system; but when the Second Bank's charter expired, the government made an effort to divorce itself from the banking system. In 1846, the government adopted the Independent Treasury system, under which all debts owed to the government were to be paid in specie or in United States Treasury notes, and all moneys collected were to be deposited in subtreasuries, that is, in vaults owned by the government. Until the Civil War, the system operated unchanged and, on balance, had a stabilizing effect on the economy. As the Treasury collected money in taxes or in payment for public lands and other dues, specie was drained out of private hands, thereby reducing bank reserves and contracting credit. This trend was especially marked in periods of prosperity, when the Federal government ran large surpluses and drained the economy of its hard-money reserves. All in all, the effects were salutary in preventing speculative booms, but the system also tended to impede recovery from depression.[9]

COINAGE AND CURRENCY IN THE LATE NINETEENTH CENTURY[10]

Before the Civil War, controversies over money and banking revolved around the quantity theory of money and the state banks. Most people believed that

[9]Richard H. Timberlake, Jr., "The Independent Treasury and Monetary Policy before the Civil War," *Southern Economic Journal,* Vol. XXVII (1960).

[10]Easily the best thing that has ever been done on the monetary history of the United States from an analytical, economic point of view is Milton Friedman and Anna Jacobson Schwartz, *A Monetary History of the United States, 1867-1960* (Princeton, N.J.: Princeton University Press, 1963).

capital could be created and prices could be raised by expanding the money supply. Debtors, who would benefit from the higher prices, favored loose banking practices and an expanding money supply, while creditors, who stood to lose purchasing power if prices rose, wanted to limit the amount of money in circulation by restricting the operations of state banks. The Civil War did nothing to resolve this controversy between debtors and creditors, but it did shift the center of the controversy from the state banks to the Federal government.

During the War, specie payments were abandoned, and the Federal government for the first time in its history issued paper money. Congress, unwilling to tax or to borrow at discounts to pay for the War, authorized the issue of $450 million of fiat money in the form of United States notes, sometimes called "legal tenders" but more popularly known as "greenbacks." Congress also established a National Banking system, and immediately after the War it drove state-bank notes out of existence by imposing a 10 percent tax on them. Thus, the Federal government replaced the state banks as the major regulator of the money supply.

Immediately after the War and for the remainder of the century, prices declined secularly. Debtors, who were still seeking ways and means of raising prices, began to petition the government to increase the amount of money in circulation. Creditors, on the other hand, not only opposed an increase in the money supply, but demanded that it be reduced.

The controversy centered at first on greenback currency. Hard-money adherents wanted a speedy resumption of specie payments and insisted that the only way to accomplish this would be to retire greenbacks. They hoped to return to the *status quo ante bellum,* except that they wanted no return of state-bank notes. The easy-money group, convinced that more money meant higher prices, not only resisted the retirement of greenbacks but demanded that more be circulated. The controversy was finally settled by a compromise. By the Resumption Act of 1875, specie payments were to be resumed in 1879, and greenbacks were to be retired at a rate of $80 for every $100 of national-bank notes that were issued. This action tended to reduce the money supply because while new national-bank notes were being issued, old ones were also being retired. The severe depression of the 1870s caused a reconsideration of the retirement policy, and in 1878 greenback circulation was frozen at $347 million, the amount then outstanding, where, incidentally, it still remains.

The freezing of greenbacks was hardly a signal victory for easy-money enthusiasts. Indeed, it demonstrated to them that greenbackism could never be politically popular and that, as an inflationary tactic, it was not at all practical. A new and more promising source of monetary inflation was found in silver. In order to understand how this came about, let us recall a little of the monetary history of the previous 40 years. It will be remembered that after the devaluation of the gold dollar in 1834, silver was worth $1.29 an ounce at the mint and $1.31 in the bullion market. Because it was more profitable to sell silver in the market, very little of it came to the mint, and silver dollars disappeared from circulation. The Federal government in 1873, by an act of legislation that later came to be called "the Crime of '73," officially eliminated the silver dollar from the coinage. Immediately thereafter, vast deposits of silver were discovered, increasing the supply and depressing the market price. In a short time, the market price of silver fell below $1.29 an ounce, and agitation for the restoration of bimetallism immediately began in the silver states and farm states. Miners, facing alarming declines in the price of silver, wanted to return to the system under which they were guaranteed $1.29 and ounce for their product. Farmers, the largest group of debtors in the economy, also supported silver, for they looked upon it as the magic means that would increase the money supply and thereby raise the price level.

The Bland-Allison and Sherman Acts

From 1876 to the end of the century, free silver was a torrid political issue, with the fire burning most intensely when prices declined most sharply. At the bottom of the business cycle, many who were ordinarily only lukewarm about the wisdom of using monetary measures to combat depression were desperate enough to support any cause and joined hands with those who regarded free silver as an economic cure-all. The alliance proved just strong enough to override the "sound" money forces and to succeed in having some of its cheap-money aspirations passed into law.

The first such silver law was the Bland-Allison Act of 1878, which directed the Treasury to purchase between $2 million and $4 million of silver a month at the market price and to coin the metal into silver dollars at the old ratio of 16 to 1. Under this legislation, as the price of silver declined, more dollars were coined and more money found its way into circulation. For example, if the Treasury bought $2 million of silver at $1 an ounce, it would buy two million ounces which it would coin at $1.29 an ounce, thus adding $2.6 million to the coinage. If the price fell to 50 cents an ounce, the Treasury would buy four million ounces for $2 million. At $1.29 an ounce, this would be coined into $5.2 million.

The Bland-Allison Act was a compromise that satisfied no one, and in 1890 it was replaced by the Sherman Silver Purchase Act. The Sherman Act directed the Secretary of Treasury to purchase 4.5 million ounces of silver a month, instead of a fixed amount in dollars. In payment for the silver, the Treasury issued paper money, known as "Sherman notes of 1890," but it issued no silver dollars. Unlike the Bland-Allison Act, the Sherman Act added less new money to the circulation as the price of silver declined. Nevertheless, under the combined impact of both pieces of silver legislation, about $525 million of silver was added to the money supply between 1878, when the Bland-Allison Act was passed, and 1893, when the Sherman Act was repealed.

The Bland-Allison and Sherman Acts were small victories for the silverites. The gold-standard forces controlled the administration under the Democrats as well as under the Republicans. In 1896, however, the silverites gained control of the Democratic Party and insisted upon presenting the issue of bimetallism directly to the people. McKinley, representing monetary conservatism, defeated Bryan, the spokesman for agrarianism and easy money. Taking the vote as a mandate, the United States officially adopted the gold standard in 1900, fixing the weight of the gold dollar at 25.8 grains, 9/10 fine, or 23.22 grains pure. Although much has been made of this piece of legislation, in actual fact it merely gave legal blessing to an already existing situation. By 1900, economic conditions had changed and improved enough to eliminate the basic cause of the fight over silver and cheap money. Gold discoveries in Alaska and Africa and new methods of refining the metal had raised gold production from about six million ounces in 1890 to 14 million ounces in 1898, and because the country was on a gold standard, this raised the money supply. Deflation had run its course, and the price level had begun to rise.

THE NATIONAL BANKING SYSTEM[11]

While currency issues were being bitterly debated, the expansion of industry and the constant growth of the economy brought about important, but less spectacular, changes in the structure and operation of American banking.

In commercial banking, there were three major developments. First, dual banking was reinstituted by the adoption of the National Banking system. Second, the use of checkbook money increased steadily while the use of bank notes declined. Finally, in the years immediately after the Civil War, more and more national banks were set up, while the number of state banks declined. But by the late nineteenth century this trend had been reversed. The number of state banks was increasing while national banks were barely holding their own.

During the Civil War, in order to provide a uniform currency, eliminate the overissue of bank notes, and create a market for government bonds, the Federal government passed the National Bank Act providing for free banking and a bond-secured national currency. Any group of persons with the required amount of capital could obtain a national bank charter from the United States Comptroller of the Currency by depositing with him a specific amount of United States bonds. Against these bonds banks could issue and circulate national bank notes. National banks were required to maintain reserves against their deposits, 25 percent for city banks and 15 percent for country banks. But smaller city and country banks were permitted to deposit part of their reserves in the national

[11]Phillip Cagan "The First Fifty Years of the National Banking System" in Deane Carson, ed., *Banking and Monetary Studies* (Homewood, Ill.: Richard D. Irwin, Inc., 1963).

banks of the largest cities. The power of national banks to own real estate or to make real estate or security loans was severely limited.

In order to drive state-bank notes out of existence, a 10 percent tax was levied against them. As long as bank currency remained important, the tax discouraged state banking. But, as check transactions became more important in the economy, the tax lost its meaning. And because state banking regulations were usually more lenient than national banking laws, an increasing number of state bank charters began to be issued, until by the 1890s the business of state banks exceeded that of the national banks.

From the point of view that was orthodox in the late nineteenth century, the National Banking system ushered in a golden age of money and banking, for its emphasized the "real-bills doctrine." [12] Although the assets of most pre-Civil War commercial banks could not be turned into cash quickly, because they were neither self-liquidating nor shiftable, under the National Banking system loans were made against commercial paper and were theoretically self-liquidating, although not shiftable. It was thought by those who believed in the real-bills doctrine that, if banks made only short-term loans, they would be able to weather any crisis caused by a withdrawal of deposits, for if depositors suddenly began to demand funds, the banks, by calling in loans, would be able to obtain the cash necessary to satisfy these demands.

The National Banking system was much safer for depositors and noteholders than the old state banking system. It replaced a heterogeneous mass of bank currency with a uniform bank currency. It also tended to reduce the number of bank failures, because national banks were not as likely to collapse as were the banks in the more lenient states. On the face of it, these were immense advantages.

But the system also had some major weaknesses. By allowing smaller banks to redeposit part of their reserves, it encouraged the long-standing practice of pyramiding reserves in New York City, thereby reducing the mobility of capital funds and aggravating money-market panics. As we have already seen, even before the National Banking Act, out-of-town banks always piled up deposits in New York; then, when money was needed in the outlying areas, they rapidly drew down their deposits, forcing New York banks to call loans and setting in motion a chain reaction of credit contraction.

The most publicized weakness of national banking was that its currency tended to be inelastic. Because they were secured by Federal bonds and not by long- and short-term business debt, national bank notes did not expand readily in boom periods and did not contract readily as business activity fell off. When the economy spurted ahead, banks found loans to private business more attrac-

---

[12] The doctrine that commercial banks should make only short-term, self-liquidating, commercial loans. For a vigorous criticism of the doctrine in light of the historical development of banking theory, see Lloyd W. Mints, *A History of Banking Theory in Great Britain and the United States* (Chicago: University of Chicago Press, 1945).

tive than government bonds. Logic would seem to dictate that they sell their government bonds in order to make more business loans. If they did, they also had to retire national-bank currency. On the other hand, when the economy began to lag and the demand for business loans dried up, it was assumed that bankers would buy bonds with their excess funds, thus increasing the amount of bank currency. Far from being a disadvantage, this inverse elasticity was desirable. Elasticity would feed a boom and starve a recovery, just the opposite of what is now considered recommended monetary policy.

A third weakness, and the most important, was that national banking intensified tendencies toward money-market panics. A national bank was like a horse on a tether; it rapidly expanded its loans and deposits up to the limit of its legal reserves during prosperity, stopped credit expansion abruptly when excess reserves were exhausted, and liquidated its loans with equal speed during panics. To add to this weakness, there was no central bank that could assist individual banks when they got into trouble. There were also minor weaknesses and irritations in the system. Loans against real estate were so narrowly restricted that the national banks could not help the farmer in his efforts to raise capital. There was no national clearing house, so that check payment between different regions was crude and inexcusably time-consuming. In brief, the National Banking system made banking safer and "sounder" for depositors and noteholders, but it made the currency less elastic and capital funds less mobile, and it missed an opportunity to establish a national money market.

THE SUPPLY OF MONEY IN THE LATE NINETEENTH CENTURY

Prior to the Civil War, the supply of money consisted of gold and silver coins (specie), fractional money (cents and half cents), state-bank notes, and deposits in commercial banks. The combination was hardly ideal. Gold and silver did not always circulate. During major depressions, specie was hoarded, and at all times Gresham's Law drove one or the other of the precious metals out of circulation. State-bank notes were of every variety, size, shape, and denomination, making the whole money system confused and disorderly. It could be said that money did tend to be elastic, that its supply tended to expand and contract with the rise and fall of business activity; but this was not as advantageous or beneficial as nineteenth-century orthodox economists thought. Their sympathy for elasticity rested upon the belief that money was a passive factor that reacted automatically to market forces. In fact, however, money was often active rather than passive. At times, it influenced market forces just as at other times it reacted to them.

Although most monetary theorists in the late nineteenth and early twentieth century believed that the money supply adjusted itself to "business activity," rising when needed and falling with declines in activity, they were always uneasy when the money supply expanded. Most of them were exponents of the quantity theory of money and believed that an expansion of the money supply was inflationary. Because they feared inflation, they looked upon increases in the money stock with misgiving, despite their lip service to elasticity.

Recently, a new form of the quantity theory has taken hold. Its proponents do not ignore the connection between money and prices, but they put much greater emphasis on the relationship between income and the money supply. They believed that the business cycle and economic activity vary more or less directly with changes in the money supply. According to Milton Friedman, the theory's leading spokesman, "Apparently, the forces that determine the long-run rate of growth of real incomes are largely independent of the long-run growth rate in the money stock so long as both proceed smoothly. But marked instability in money is accompanied by marked instability in economic growth."[13]

By the 1890s, state-bank notes had long since been eliminated from circulation. But some new types of currency had been introduced. The stock of coin and currency now consisted of gold coins and gold certificates, silver dollars and silver certificates, treasury notes of 1890, subsidiary silver and fractional coins, United States notes (greenbacks), and national-bank notes. None of the currency, even though it was now regulated by the Federal government, expanded and contracted in accordance with the demands and the dictates of market forces. Instead, circulation depended on the amount of gold production, the state of international balance of payments, arbitrary acts of legislation, government fiscal policy, and market interest rates. The circulation of some types of currency increased, one declined, and some stayed the same. Up to 1893, when the Sherman Act was repealed, the amount of silver currency increased steadily as more and more was injected into the economy under the terms of the Bland-Allison and Sherman Acts. Greenback circulation was frozen by law, and after 1882 national bank-note circulation fell significantly. Gold coins and certificates, which under the gold standard were the ultimate basis for the entire money supply, followed the course of gold production and since gold production did not increase very much, the amount of gold in the money system did not vary greatly. It certainly did not increase enough to sustain a satisfactory increase in the money supply, and prices declined secularly. It should be emphasized that this was not a phenomenon confined to this country. A faltering money supply and declining prices existed throughout the Western world in the last of the nineteenth century.

The silver currency and paper money provided by the Bland-Allison and Sherman Acts were introduced in the hope that they would force an increase in general prices. Actually, neither did so. The level of expenditures did not seem to be high enough to absorb all the currency that was being issued. As prices fell,

[13]National Bureau of Economic Research, *Forty-Second Annual Report,* 1962. See also Friedman and Schwartz, *op. cit.*

consumers and investors, needing less money to take care of their everyday
needs and uneasy because of uncertainty about the future monetary standard,
converted their surplus funds into what they considered the best money,
namely, gold. Thus, the new additions to the money stock did not raise prices
but instead caused a run on gold, which went into hoarding. But after changes
took place in the late century, prices soared.

The volume of bank deposits or checkbook money, in contrast to pocketbook money, was determined much more by business demands for funds. But it
too was the slave of the reserves of the National Banking system and of the
international specie standard.

Table 24

ESTIMATED MONEY SUPPLY AND PRICES, 1867-1900
(in millions of dollars)

	Currency	Commercial bank deposits	Money supply	Savings bank deposits	Per capita money supply	Wholesale prices (1884 = 100)
1867	$ 585	$ 729	$1,314	$ 337	$38	183
1873	552	1,070	1,622	802	38	146
1879	520	1,023	1,543	803	31	100
1883	856	1,955	2,811	1,025	52	107
1884	842	1,922	2,764	1,073	45	100
1892	929	3,541	4,470	1,713	68	84
1896	832	3,434	4,266	1,907	60	75
1900	1,191	5,187	6,378	2,450	84	91

SOURCE: Friedman and Schwartz, *A Monetary History of the United States.*

THE FEDERAL RESERVE SYSTEM

Loose commercial banking, chaotic currency and coinage, and infant
investment banking characterized the early-nineteenth-century American financial scene. Monetary conservatism, orthodox banking, and robust investment banking featured the latter-nineteenth-century picture. But in the twentieth century, the trend was in the direction of ever greater government control
over the money and banking system. At the opening of the century, the National
Banking system was flourishing, the real-bills doctrine was firmly entrenched,
the gold standard was in its heyday, and the investment banker reigned supreme.
By the middle of the twentieth century, however, central banking had taken
over control of commercial banking; the real-bills doctrine had given way to a
banking system based on shiftable, rather than self-liquidating, assets; managed
money had replaced the gold standard; and corporations and insurance companies were supplying vast funds for investment.

The twentieth-century trend toward increased central control over the exchange system was well illustrated by the creation and evolution of the Federal Reserve System. Starting out as a quasi-central bank, the System's powers over commercial banking were gradually strengthened, while, at the same time, the Federal government's influence over the System was gradually increased.

By 1900, the weaknesses of the National Banking system were all too evident. It pyramided and immobilized reserves, it aggravated money-market panics, and under it check clearance was costly and inefficient. The belief that these weaknesses could best be corrected by the creation of some form of central banking steadily gained new adherents, and in 1913 the Federal government passed the Federal Reserve Act.

In order to make bank reserves more mobile, the Act divided the country into 12 districts, each with a district bank. Each commercial bank belonging to the Reserve System was required to maintain a reserve against deposits, either in its own vaults or in the district bank. It was expected that this change would eliminate the pyramiding of reserves in New York and would thus make the banking system much safer and less subject to panic. The first reserve requirements were 18, 15, and 12 percent for reserve-city, city, and country banks, respectively. This was a considerable reduction from the 25, 25, and 15 percent of the National Banking system, and thus very markedly increased excess reserves and potential credit expansion.

The Act provided for a more elastic currency by permitting the district banks to issue a new type of paper money—the Federal Reserve note—secured by commercial paper and gold. Thus, in periods of prosperity, when business borrowing was on the upswing, currency would expand. Oppositely, it would contract in depressions when business debt was not so heavy. It was hoped that the severity of money-market panics would be diminished by giving the district banks the power to advance reserves to the member banks by rediscounting their commercial paper. Thus, if banks were hard pressed for reserves, they could replenish them by borrowing from the district banks. Finally, the Act established a system for clearing checks without cost to the payer or payee. Before this par collection system, check clearing had been handled through correspondent banks at considerable cost in time and money.[14]

In the early years of the Federal Reserve System, executive power was concentrated in the 12 district banks, which were in turn controlled by the member banks who elected two-thirds of the directors. The central governing body, the Federal Reserve Board, was primarily an administrative agency with little control over the System's operations. Even the power to rediscount was not centrally controlled but was dispersed throughout the 12 district banks.

---

[14]Friedman and Schwartz suggested that it would have been better if the conflict over money had been resolved immediately either in favor of gold, or in favor of silver. Instead the dispute dragged on, wallowing in uncertainty for 30 years.

What seems strange today, but was not strange in 1913, is that those who wrote the Act did not seem to have any intention of using the System to stabilize the economy; its function appeared to be to improve the commercial banking machinery, rather than to exercise a major influence over the economy. It was designed to be a help to the member banks, rather than a regulator of the economy.

In its first few years, the Federal Reserve had to play a passive role. It had hardly opened before World War I broke out in Europe, and when the United States became involved, the System had to give its full support to the Treasury's war-financing program, which meant that it instituted as far as it was able an easy-money policy. Member bank reserve requirements were lowered to 7, 10, and 13 percent, and the rediscount rate on loans secured by government securities was fixed at 1.5 percent.

Early changes in the Federal Reserve's philosophy and tactics [15]

The completion of war finance gave the Federal Reserve its first opportunity to follow a more independent and more active policy. It was a golden opportunity, for monetary policy was at a high point of prestige during the 1920s. Many experts were convinced that the new central bank, with its ability to expand and contract money and credit and with its power to protect the member banks, would bury panics and depressions among the artifacts of history.

In their operations in the 1920s, Reserve authorities followed traditional orthodox central bank policy. Relying exclusively on the rediscount rate, they lowered it when gold flowed into the United States and raised it when gold flowed out. This often meant behaving in a way that did not accord with present notions of anticyclical stabilization policy. Thus, during the burst of inflation that followed World War I, the New York rediscount rate was raised to 7 percent. It was maintained at that rate when the economy ran into the severe depression of 1920-1921. Boom conditions immediately following the war gave some excuse for a high discount rate. But it is difficult to justify its maintenance all through the severe depression. Of course, the explanation lay in the fear that a lower rate of interest might cause gold to flow out in search of more attractive returns abroad.

[15]For Federal Reserve activity, tactics, and philosophy, see Friedman and Schwartz, *op. cit.*; Charles O. Hardy, *Credit Policies of the Federal Reserve System* (Washington, D.C.: The Brookings Institution, 1932); Seymour E. Harris, *Twenty Years of Federal Reserve Policy* (Cambridge, Mass.: Harvard University Press, 1933); Lester V. Chandler, *Benjamin Strong, Central Banker* (Washington, D.C.: The Brookings Institution, 1958); same author, *American Monetary Policy, 1928-1941* (New York: Harper & Row, Publishers, 1971); Elmus R. Wicker, *Federal Reserve Monetary Policy, 1917-1933* (New York: Random House, 1966); Lawrence S. Ritter, "Official Central Banking Theory in the United States, 1939-61" (*Journal of Political Economy*, Vol. LXX, 1962).

Although monetary policy did follow traditional tactics, the 1920 depression produced an extremely important addition to the Federal Reserve tool chest in the form of open market operations. When member banks did not find it necessary to borrow because of the low level of business borrowing, the System, in order to maintain its revenue, began to buy government securities and found that this tactic had an important impact on member bank reserves. At first, each district bank carried on its own open market operations; but under the leadership of Governor Benjamin Strong of the New York bank, a committee was formed in April 1923 to coordinate the activities of all the district banks.

Governor Strong was easily the most important personality among the monetary leaders of the 1920s. It was under his influence that the System veered away from traditional central bank operations toward the objective of maintaining stability and encouraging growth in the economy. By 1923, the Federal Reserve had given enough thought to a policy of "leaning against the wind" to formulate a theory of credit control. Although its statement of that year was vague, the general aim was to provide credit freely enough to encourage business expansion, but not freely enough to encourage speculation.

The Federal Reserve in the boom of the 1920s

Although the Federal Reserve was born and nurtured under most favorable conditions, it was not long before the monetary authorities were subjected to severe and penetrating criticisms from sources that carried great weight and prestige.

Table 25
MONEY SUPPLY IN THE 1920's
(dollar figures in billions)

June 30	Currency	Demand deposits	Money supply	Change in money supply	Velocity
1920	$4.5	$19.1	$23.6	—	3.8
1921	4.0	16.9	21.0	−11.0%	3.5
1922	3.6	18.0	21.6	+ 3.2	3.4
1923	4.0	18.7	22.7	+ 4.8	3.8
1924	3.9	19.3	23.2	+ 2.5	3.8
1925	3.9	21.4	25.4	+ 9.2	3.6
1926	4.0	22.1	26.1	+ 2.9	3.7
1927	4.0	21.8	25.8	− 1.1	3.7
1928	3.9	21.8	25.8	0	3.8
1929	3.9	22.3	26.2	+ 1.7	3.9

SOURCE: Friedman and Schwartz, *A Monetary History of the United States;* Federal Reserve Board, *Banking and Monetary Statistics.*

The Fed's first critical decision came as the great bull market gained momentum in 1927. As soon as stock market activity and stock prices broke into much higher ground orthodox monetary theorists expressed their uneasiness and called on the Federal Reserve to tighten credit. They contended that unless the "speculation" associated with ballooning stock market activity was brought to a halt, it would cause the economy to become overheated leading to eventual economic collapse. Their concentration on the rapidly rising stock prices led them to believe that the entire economy was in the midst of a severe inflation. It must be pointed out that their definition of inflation was different from the one that is now generally accepted. Today, inflation means a rise in the general price level. To most monetary theorists of the 1920s, inflation was an increase in the money supply, not necessarily an increase in the price level. When it was pointed out that prices in general were not rising, orthodox monetary theorists argued that price stability, rather than disproving the existence of inflation, actually proved it. According to their reasoning, the substantial gains that were being made in production during the 1920s whould have lowered prices by increasing the supply of goods. However, prices did not fall, which meant that they were being held up by increases in the money supply.

As the stock market boom continued, criticism increased commensurately. Federal Reserve authorities found themselves in a quandary, and their dilemma was intensified by the death of the strong-minded Benjamin Strong in 1928. If the Fed tightened credit to stop speculation, it might also depress general business. If it did not tighten, because of a fear that business would become depressed, the stock market would keep climbing. As the twenties wore on, the stock market moved more and more to the center of the stage, and consequently the dilemma became more and more pressing. Unfortunately, after much pondering, the Fed resolved its dilemma by deciding to stop speculation. Once the decision was made, the Fed moved full-speed ahead. The rediscount rate was raised to 5 percent in 1928 and to 6 percent in 1929. At the same time, the System reduced its holdings of government securities from $620 million to $145 million. Money supply growth slowed down perceptibly. By mid-1929, the money supply was only a little over 1.5 percent higher than in mid-1928 and mid-1927. Interest rates went up, giving the monetary authorities some cause to believe that they were achieving their objectives.

Looking back on what happened, George Harrison, governor of the New York Bank later said:

> Beginning in 1928 we raised our discount rate three times. We sold over $400 million in government securities. We lost $500 million in gold. Had anybody said two years before that it was possible to raise the discount rate three times and sell $400 million of government securities and export $500 million of gold without checking inflation, [*sic!*] it would have been thought impossible; but that is just what happened.

Harrison's view, which was shared by many others, was a misreading of what actually occurred. The 1920s *were not an inflationary period.* Aside from stocks and real estate, prices were not inflated. Indeed, the consumer price level was just about the same in 1929 as in 1924. Wholesale prices in the 1920s ranged from 56.6 of the 1957-1959 average in 1925 to 52.1 in 1929. It was also misleading to imply that the money supply increased too sharply in the 1920s and that tight money had not worked. Aside from 1924-1925, the money supply grew at a conservative rate. Nor had tight money failed in 1928-1929. Actually, it worked too well. In retrospect, the turn to extreme tight money in 1928 and its continuation in 1929 was a mistake. To be sure, the stock market continued to give signs of robust strength until September 1929, but the economy in general reached its peak in the late spring of 1929. Tight money was designed to break the back of the stock market boom. It eventually did, but in doing so it also pushed the whole economy down.

CHANGES IN COMMERCIAL BANKING STRUCTURE

No discussion of money and banking in the twenties would be complete without some mention of the important structural changes that took place within the commercial banking industry. These changes revealed themselves in three ways: first, in the sizable reduction in the number of commercial banks, from over 30,000 in 1920 to less than 25,000 in 1929, second, in the concentration of banking resources, particularly in the urban centers, and third, in a broadening of the functions of commercial banking.

The number of banks declined primarily as a result of a high rate of bank failures and a significant increase in bank mergers. Between 1921 and 1929, bank suspensions occurred at the rate of 12 to 30 percent a year. Although fewer than 1,200 commercial banks failed between 1904 and 1920, more than 5,000 failed in the years 1921 to 1929. Most of these failures were small, country, state-chartered institutions in the South and Middle West. The overwhelming majority were capitalized at less than $100,000 and almost 40 percent at $25,000 or less.

Second to bank failures in accounting for the decline in the number of banks was a sharp increase in bank mergers. Taking place mostly in the cities, the merger movement was also an important factor explaining the increase in banking concentration in urban markets. From 150 a year between 1910 and 1920, the number of bank mergers increased to between 300 and 400 a year between 1921 and 1925, and to more than 500 a year from 1926 to 1929.

Along with the decline in the number of banks and the increase in banking concentration came an upsurge in branch banking. In 1919, 464 banks operated 1,082 branches. A decade later the number of banks having more than one banking office totaled 816, while the number of branches multiplied to 3,603. More striking than the increase in the number of branch systems was the increase in the share of banking resources controlled by multiunit banks, from 16 percent in 1919 to 46 percent in 1929. Branching, of course, did not occur everywhere; a number of states continued to prohibit any form of branching. Other states allowed branching on a limited basis (for example, within the city or county of the bank's home office), and a few states, notably California, permitted state-wide branch banking.

FEDERAL RESERVE POLICY DURING THE DEPRESSION

By any standard, monetary policy during the depression was a failure. As business moved downward, the Federal Reserve was no more successful in rescuing the economy from the abyss than it had been in preventing the original depression. Perhaps it had no intention of rescuing the economy. When the depression broke, many economists and policy makers believed that it was necessary to tolerate a severe economic decline in order to wipe out the poisons that had been injected by "speculative overheating." They warned the public at large that artificial attempts to forestall the necessary liquidation would only make the depression longer and more severe.

Until late in the depression the monetary authorities, supported by many respected outside economists, took the position that to pursue an aggressive easy-money policy by mammoth open market purchases would only rekindle inflation. Still later, the System argued that attempts to pump money into the economy would not have any significant effect. Any such attempt would merely build up excess reserves, for it was just as impossible to force borrowers to borrow as it was to force bankers to lend. Sympathizers with the Fed admonished its critics and the public at large to remember that a horse could be led to water, but it could not be made to drink. Reserve authorities insisted that they were doing as much as they were able to in pumping money into the economic streams, but they also reminded their audience that "you can't push a string."

While the Federal Reserve was striving to determine what its objectives were, the money supply sank. It dropped by 4 percent by mid-1930, 6 percent by the end of 1930, 10 percent by mid-1931, and another 7 percent by the last of 1931.

The unparalleled decline in the money stock was brought about by a massive withdrawal of currency from the banks and by a sizable drop in reserves as a result of gold outflows. As the money supply shrank, it seemed evident that the Fed should institute a lenient rediscount policy and undertake large-scale open market operations. Whether such action would have reversed the depression and set the country once again on the prosperity road is a debatable question, for velocity shrank along with the money supply, and it did not recover as the money supply rose during the late thirties. (See Table 26.)

Table 26
MONEY AND BANKING IN THE 1930s
(billions of dollars)

	Number of banks	Demand deposits (adjusted)	Currency	Money Supply	Velocity
1930	23,679	$21.7	$3.4	$25.1	3.6
1931	21,654	19.8	3.7	23.5	3.2
1932	18,734	15.6	4.6	20.2	2.9
1933	14,207	14.4	4.8	19.2	2.9
1934	15,348	16.7	4.7	21.4	3.0
1935	15,488	20.4	4.8	25.2	2.9
1936	15,329	23.8	5.2	29.0	2.9
1937	15,094	25.2	5.5	30.7	2.9
1938	14,867	24.3	5.4	29.7	2.9
1939	14,667	27.4	6.0	33.4	2.7

SOURCE: Friedman and Schwartz; Federal Reserve Board.

But whether it would have worked or not, a policy of extremely easy money should have been tried. It might have triggered recovery, and it would have provided the commercial banks with the liquidity they so badly needed. In the mad rush for liquidity, the banks were compelled to sell off securities and to call in loans—actions that, in the absence of new injections of reserves by the central bank, served only to further depress security prices and to further contract the supply of money and credit. In the words of Professor Jacob Viner, the only banks that could survive were those that turned themselves into safe deposit institutions. But despite some urging by the Federal Reserve Bank of New York that the System follow a policy of positive ease, the majority within the System, and among academic economists and bankers as well, favored a more cautious policy. Between December 1929 and December 1930, Federal Reserve holdings of government obligations increased from $446 million to $644 million. By then some commentators thought that conditions were already too "easy." In the next six months, Reserve holdings of government obligations actually declined to $604 million, but then they rose to $777 million in December 1931 and to $1.9 billion by December 1932. Thus the System purchased $1.4 billion in three years, but in the first six months of 1931, it sold on balance.

Failure to act more vigorously in the open market would not have been so disastrous had the commercial banks had freer access to the discount window. To be sure, the discount rate had been lowered, in a series of stops, from a high of 6 percent in 1929 to 1.5 percent by mid-1931. Here again, however, the figures tell only a small part of the story. The monetary authorities and the bankers found it impossible to follow a straightforward policy. They were torn by conflicting objectives. The most glaring example of this conflict occurred in fall of 1931 when the administration and the monetary authorities became concerned about hoarding and the decline of reserve holdings of gold. Fearing that the gold standard was in jeopardy, they raised the rediscount rate to 3.5 percent, an action that had less economic logic than loyalty to tradition. This adventure lasted only a few months. The New York bank lowered its rate to 3 percent in February 1932 and to 2.5 percent in June.

Although overall cuts in the rediscount rate were large on the whole, member banks were both reluctant to borrow and frequently unable to do so. Reluctance to borrow was partly a carry-over from the late '20s when borrowing was discouraged by the System as, indeed, it continued to be in succeeding years. Furthermore, commercial banks were reluctant to borrow so long as depositors, fearful over the safety of their funds, were scrutinizing every bank's balance sheet to see which would be the next to go.

Most important, however, was the general attachment to the commercial loan theory. The Federal Reserve Act stipulated that only eligible paper—that is, short-term, self-liquidating, commercial paper—was subject to rediscount. Yet, commercial loans became far less important during the twenties than they had been in earlier years as commercial banks branched out into numerous diverse activities. To make matters worse, the McFadden Act of 1927 increased this departure from tradition by liberalizing the restrictions on national bank lending in order to put the national banks on a competitive par with state banks. It was no doubt desirable that banks should have gained additional flexibility to maintain their competitive position. But, unfortunately, although legislation enabled the banking system to move further and further away from adherence to the commercial loan doctrine, Federal Reserve regulations were still bound to it. Consequently, by the early thirties many banks did not have sufficient "eligible" paper to discount. Aggravating the problem was the fact that member bank borrowings in the late twenties were substantial, with the result that much of their eligible paper was already pledged. Not until passage of the Emergency Act of 1933 were Federal Reserve Banks enabled to lend to commercial banks against United States government securities and, at a penalty rate, against other forms of security.

THE BREAKDOWN OF THE GOLD STANDARD

The prestige of monetary policy, which had attained such dizzy heights in the 1920s, fell to an equally abysmal low during the 1930s. One reason for this was the apparent ineffectiveness of the central bank policy that has just been described. Another was the breakdown of the gold standard and the failure of monetary manipulation to raise prices during the depression.

As long as the world experienced no major wars and no extreme business fluctuations, the international gold standard operated surely and smoothly. International price movements and gold shipments tended to stabilize the international trade picture. If prices in one nation rose, its imports would increase, gold would flow out to pay for them, the money supply would fall, and prices would decline. As prices declined, exports would increase, gold would flow in, the money supply would expand, and prices would go up. The system never operated as the completely automatic mechanism pictured in the above example, for it was always affected by some human decisions, such as the manipulation of the rediscount rate in the London money market. But in the rational world of the first 15 years of the twentieth century, the gold standard worked well in facilitating international and domestic exchange. When the rational world began to crack under the blows of World War I and the depression of the 1930s, the gold standard broke down.

As a result of the major role she played in financing international warfare, the United States emerged from World War I as a major creditor, and Europe came out loaded with dead-weight debt. The United States, however, refused to accept her new role as a creditor, which logically entailed a willingness to allow foreign nations to pay the interest and principal on their loans in the form of goods. Instead, up went United States' tariff barriers. To protect their diminished gold and dollar reserves, European nations modified their gold standards and resorted to higher tariffs, quotas, and exchange controls. Consequently, the importance of the old connection between international prices and gold shipments was considerably modified and the free market was replaced by a manipulated one.

The disruption that World War I had visited on the international gold standard was made complete by the depression of the 1930s. In an effort to turn the tide of deflation and to raise domestic prices, nation after nation resorted to all kinds of monetary palliatives. The quantity theory of money was revitalized, and governments returned with new vigor to the notion that increasing the amount of money would raise domestic prices. But manipulating the domestic money supply in order to raise prices was incompatible with the gold standard, because price increases would result in gold exports, and gold exports were apt to depress prices, thereby neutralizing whatever benefits had been realized by money manipulation. Therefore, the gold standard was abandoned, and the nineteenth-century conviction that money was only a convenient device to facilitate trade was replaced by a revived belief in money as a tool that could be used to regulate the economy. The free movement of gold across international borders was abandoned, and governments took over control of international capital movements. International rates of exchange were no longer governed by price changes and gold movements. Each government set the rate of exchange for its currency and maintained it through a stabilization fund.

The United States was in the forefront of this new movement. In an effort to raise domestic prices, the Roosevelt administration tried various experiments with the currency. In 1933, it abandoned the gold standard and increased the quantity of pocketbook money by reducing the weight of the gold dollar from

25.8 grains, 9/10 fine (23.22 pure), to 15 5/21 grains, 9/10 fine (13.714 pure), and by remonetizing silver. The result of these monetary manipulations was disappointing, for despite an increase of 40 percent in currency in circulation (and of more than 100 percent in the total money supply) between 1933 and 1940, the price level rose less than 20 percent.

THE FEDERAL RESERVE BECOMES A GENUINE CENTRAL BANK

Some authorities believed that the Federal Reserve System had failed to smooth out the speculative boom of the 1920s and the tragic depression of the 1930s because it did not have enough power over the money market. Determined attempts were therefore made to extend the System's powers and to centralize them in the Federal Reserve Board in Washington. At first, during the Hoover administration, these attempts failed, but during the New Deal strong central banking became a reality.

The Banking Act of 1933 and 1935 not only expanded the System's powers but also centralized these powers in the Board of Governors. These acts (1) dissolved the Federal Reserve Board and replaced it with a Board of Governors composed of seven members appointed by the President for a period of fourteen years, (2) gave the Board of Governors approval power over the appointments of heads of district banks, (3) enabled the Board to vary reserve requirements within limits set by Congress, (4) gave the Board the final say over the discount rate, and (5) created an Open Market Committee composed of the Board of Governors and five representatives of the Reserve banks.

By the outbreak of World War II, the Board of Governors had at its command all the tools required to control the money market. In prosperity, the Board could, by selling government bonds to the member banks and by raising reserve requirements, mop up excess reserves and thus limit the banking system's ability to make further loans and to increase the money supply. By raising the rediscount rate, the Board could also try to discourage banks from expanding their loans. By prohibiting or restricting security loans, it could attempt to restrain speculation. In depression years, it could try to revive the economy by reducing the rediscount rate and by increasing member bank reserves through the lowering of reserve requirements and through the purchase of government bonds.

The Banking Acts of 1933 and 1935 contained other, perhaps more important, provisions. The 1933 Act established Federal Deposit Insurance, against determined opposition from most of the nation's bankers and in spite of a lack of enthusiasm on the part of monetary authorities and President Roosevelt. Under the administration of the Federal Deposit Insurance Corporation (FDIC), the deposits of any one depositor in a participating bank (all Federal

Reserve member banks were required to join) were to be insured up to a maximum of $2,500 ($5,000 in 1934).

In an effort to lessen bank failures, the acts gave the Board of Governors authority to set limits on the interest rates that commercial banks could pay on time and saving deposits (Regulation Q), and, more importantly, member and FDIC-insured nonmember banks were prohibited from paying interest on demand deposits. It was widely believed at the time that banking standards had been badly compromised by the practice of paying interest. Those who shared this belief argued that interest-rate competition for deposits, especially for correspondent balances and other large deposits, had forced banks into overly aggressive lending and investment practices that had jeopardized their safety and solvency.

Along the same lines, the 1933 and 1935 acts took a giant step away from the real-bills doctrine that had effectively kept the discount window from meeting the banking system's liquidity needs. Specifically, the new legislation made permanent what had been done temporarily by the Glass-Stegall Act of February 1932 and the Emergency Banking Act of 1933. It authorized each District Reserve Bank to make advances, at a penalty rate, to member banks on the basis of promissory notes "secured to the satisfaction of such Federal Reserve Bank," and it permitted the use of government bonds as security against Federal Reserve notes.

The Board of Governors had one opportunity to test its powers before World War II began. This came immediately after the passage of the Banking Act of 1935. By then the Fed had been feeding reserves into the commercial banks for some time, and by 1936 excess reserves and free reserves had climbed to over $3 billion. Reserve authorities, alarmed by this mass of inflationary fuel and fearing that prices would get out of hand, moved to eliminate excess reserves by tightening money. The growth of the money supply slowed down in 1936 and in 1937 the money supply actually fell, precipitating the sharp but short-lived depression of 1937.

THE FEDERAL RESERVE IN WAR AND POST WAR

In World War II as in World War I, the Board gave all its efforts to support of the Treasury's financial policies. During the War, inflationary forces were rampant, and the Board would ordinarily have resisted them by contracting the money supply through open-market operations and hikes in the rediscount rates. The Treasury, however, opposed tight-money policies, because high interest rates would raise the interest costs on the government's rapidly mounting debt. The Treasury won its point, and during the War the Reserve System followed extreme easy-money policies. By announcing that it would buy or sell any quantity of Federal obligations at a fixed price, the System guaranteed the price of government obligations. Throughout the War, a holder of a government obligation could sell it at any time for its face value. By pegging government interest rates in this way, the monetary authorities controlled interest rates throughout the money market and largely eliminated the influence of the free market. But, at the same time, stabilizing interest rates at a low figure and keeping them there by guaranteeing the price of governments, meant that government bonds were really interest-bearing money. Consequently, the System could not exercise any of its powers to check monetary inflation.

Once the War was over, the Federal Reserve argued for an abandonment of the peg on governments bonds, on the ground that maintaining artificial interest rates also meant monetary and price inflation. The Treasury contended that higher interest rates would discourage economic growth, demoralize the government bond market, and cost the government huge sums in increased service charges on the debt. In a sense, the tug of war between the Treasury and the Federal Reserve was one more incident in the never-ending difference of opinion between the adherents of sound money and those of easy money.

The debate became increasingly fervid until it was resolved in the so-called "Accord of 1951," which set interest-rate policy in the direction of a gradual return to a free market. From the Accord on, the monetary authorities followed a policy labeled by one of its principal administrators as "leaning against the wind." It tightened money in boom years by use of the rediscount rate and open market operations, and tried to ease it during recessions by lowering the discount rate, by lowering reserve requirements, and by purchases in the open market. As in the 1920s, the System stood somewhere between the adherents of sound money and the champions of easy money, with a slight tendency toward the conservative side. The yardsticks by which its position was determined were free reserves, the price level, interest rates, and the international balance of payments. The money supply received less attention until the late 1960s when more consideration was paid to the monetary base and less to free reserves.

Federal Reserve operations in money and credit markets varied a great deal during the 1950s and 1960s, which was to be expected of a system whose objective was to lean against the wind. For purposes of simplification and generalization, the two decades can be divided into six subperiods, all of which occurred as a reaction to recession and inflation. Chart 17 pictures what happened to the money supply and prices in these six periods.

The Korean episode, of course, dominated the early 1950s. The Fed followed a policy of "credit restraint" that was characterized by rising interest rates and falling reserves. At the same time, however, the money supply expanded rapidly and began to decline only when Korea was almost over.

The second stage opened in the spring of 1953 when the Fed reacted to the mild post-Korean recession. Starting off in low key with a policy designed "to avoid deflationary tendencies without encouraging a renewal of inflationary developments," it soon moved up the scale, and by the fall when its theme was "active ease," the Board had reduced the rediscount rate slightly and reserve

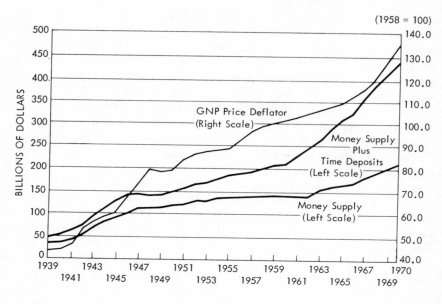

CHART 17. Money supply and prices, 1939-1970

requirements sharply while pouring some $700 million into bank reserves by open-market purchases. The money supply in these 19 months expanded by over 4 percent.

The third period of the 1950s saw the first alarm over inflation and "unsustainable growth." In the first few months of recovery in 1955, the Fed moved slowly under a policy that would "foster growth and stability" while "encouraging recovery and avoiding unsustainable expansion." But by August it had decided that "restraint was clearly appropriate," and it continued in this vein until November 1957, some three months after recovery had passed its peak. Rediscount rates were raised, open-market operations pushed free reserves into a negative position, and the money supply stood still.

The third recession of the post-World War II period occurred in the summer of 1957, and with it came another reversal in policy. In November 1957 the Fed moved "to foster sustainable growth . . . without inflation, by moderating the pressure on bank reserves." In the following seven months, it again reduced reserve requirements and the rediscount rate and bought some securities in the open market. Free reserves again ran up, long-term interest rates were down slightly, short-term rates were emphatically down, and the money supply was up sharply from its low point in January 1958.

Whether monetary policy or a large government deficit in fiscal 1958-1959 accomplished the trick or not, the economy recovered in the spring of 1958. The Fed slowly shifted into stage five. Beginning in August 1958 and continuing to May 1960, it acted to keep recovery from becoming overheated. Monetary

Table 27
MONEY SUPPLY, 1940-1969
(billions of dollars)

	Currency	Demand deposits adjusted	Money supply	Velocity
1940	$ 6.6	$ 32.2	$ 38.8	2.6
1946	26.7	80.1	106.8	2.0
1947	26.6	84.7	111.3	2.0
1949	25.6	84.8	110.4	2.3
1953	27.8	100.1	127.9	2.9
1956	28.0	107.7	135.7	3.1
1959	29.0	113.8	142.8	3.4
1960	28.9	110.5	139.4	3.6

SOURCE: Friedman and Schwartz; Federal Reserve Board.

policy was tight by any yardstick. The rediscount rate was raised from 1.75 to 4 percent. Activities in the open market and Congressional amendments to reserve requirements partially offset each other, but with the help of a steady outflow of gold, free reserves ran down to minus $550 million. Interest rates climbed to over 4 percent, and the money supply declined at an annual rate of almost 3 percent. Yet, it took almost a year to break the boom, but broken it was.

The recession of 1960 accomplished a major shift in monetary policy. Cynics insisted that the Federal Reserve Board, like the Supreme Court, followed the election returns. But whatever the reason, monetary policy in the 1960s veered away from the previous fears of inflation toward a more sympathetic attitude to easy money. Yet, the new strategy did not run any more smoothly than the old one. Monetary policy still veered from extreme to extreme.

What happened was best illustrated by the behavior of the money supply. Demand deposits adjusted and currency in the hands of the public fell by almost 3 percent between July 1959 and June 1960. Then the money supply increased at the comparatively slow rate of 2.4 percent until April 1962. In the next five months the money supply declined. Then from September 1962 to May 1965, it rose at an annual rate of 3.9 percent. In the next year, it climbed by 6.3 percent. Then rising interest rates and the beginning of galloping inflation persuaded the Fed to reverse its policy, and the money supply fell from April 1966 to January 1967. The result was a "credit crunch," which made some alarmists fear that there would not be enough money to go around. But these fears were dissipated when the money supply again began to expand. It grew at the unusually high rate of 7.6 percent for two years or until January 1969. The fast pace slowed to 3.0 percent in the next year and to 5.5 percent in 1970. But it exploded again to 13.6 percent in the first five months of 1971.

CRITICS OF THE FEDERAL RESERVE

In the half-century of its existence, monetary policy has had an excitingly rocky career. The audience has blown hot and cold, at one moment heaping extravagant praise and in the next a barrage of patronizing criticism. In the 1920s it had not been easy to steer a storm-free course through the narrow channel that separated legitimate business expansion from speculation. Yet the prestige of monetary policy reached its zenith in the 1920s. It sank to an all-time low during the depression, recovered strongly between the end of World War II and the Accord of 1951, and ran into a rising tide of skepticism as it became apparent that in navigating by leaning against the winds of inflation and deflation, it was impossible to avoid hitting numerous reefs and floundering on numerous shoals.

One of the little ironies of economics is that criticism of the makers of monetary policy—the Federal Reserve System—varies more or less in inverse porportion to the prestige of the product they are molding. In the 1920s the financial literature abounded in articles and speeches that called attention to the error of the System's ways. But there was little of this attitude in the depression, when the belief prevailed that monetary policy could accomplish very little. As the 1950s and 1960s passed into history, criticism of the Fed became steadily more devastating as the conviction grew that money and monetary policy not only mattered but mattered very much. Champions of easy money criticized the System for too much and too early. Proponents of tight money chafed under policies that they thought came too little and too late; and those in the middle criticized the Fed for both faults.

In the 1920s, many people assumed that when Senator Carter Glass et al. wrote the Federal Reserve Act, they had put an end to the business cycle. The disenchanting experience of the depression of the 1930s changed that view, but only temporarily. In the 1950s, once again, some people expressed the conviction that if only the monetary magicians would put their minds to it, they could manipulate the economy so as to produce maximum growth without inflation. Those who were responsible for monetary policy did not share this roseate view. Indeed, some of them took pleasure in downgrading the Fed's powers. At the very least, they were well aware that monetary policy could not work miracles, and they took great pains to point out the obstacles in the way. They protested that they could not do the job without the aid of fiscal policy. They also warned that monetary techniques were not overly effective in fighting inflation that was caused by pressure from the cost side. Nor could they deal satisfactorily and successfully with unemployment that was structural in nature. These caveats elicited sympathy, but they did not eliminate doubts as to the effectiveness of monetary policy or answer criticism of how it was being administered.

A more or less ubiquitous conviction that monetary policy offered little or no hope in a period of recession or depression had always existed. But the late fifties gave rise to mounting skepticism as to its effectiveness in periods of prosperity and inflation. Those who were dubious about monetary policy and those who were critical of the Federal Reserve fell into four main groups: the defeatists, the unreconstructed conservatives, those who found fault with the System's technique, and the critics of timing. First of all, there were those who believed that the institutional framework of the modern economy had reduced monetary policy to impotence. According to one line of reasoning, full employment and free collective bargaining inevitably produced rising prices, which the monetary authorities could squelch but only at the cost of recession or depression. Another group in the same school argued that the central bank's ability to neutralize inflationary pressures was fatally weakened by the existence of a large, highly liquid public debt and by the increased importance in the credit market of financial intermediaries and large corporations. When the Federal Reserve tried to tighten money, the commercial banks could increase their reserves simply by letting their short-term governments run out. But even if the banks were restrained, would-be borrowers could obtain funds from the financial intermediaries and from trade credit made available by corporations. The efforts to thwart inflation were consequently stymied before they began. What actually happened during the years after 1953 gave plausibility to this line of reasoning. For tight money or not, prices advanced throughout the period.

The skeptics just mentioned were basically sympathetic to the Federal Reserve System as well as to monetary policy. A second school of critics objected in principle to the whole concept of monetary policy. They believed that the money market should be regulated by the impersonal forces of the marketplace and not by a group which, being human, would certainly make mistakes that would have immense consequences on the whole economy. Those who argued for regulation by rule and not by men proposed that the money supply be advanced in step with the potential growth of the national product, but critical historians pointed out that something similar to this "neutral money" had been tried and found wanting in the late twenties.

The monetarists who put their faith in a marketplace philosophy were in the minority in the 1950s, when most economists were still not convinced that money and the money supply were all that important. The fifties was a period of disappointing economic growth, and most economists were still putting most of their faith in fiscal policy—that is, tax reduction, increased government spending, and budget deficits—as the best means of invigorating national income. Remembering the 1930s when an apparently easy-money policy seemed to have been ineffective, they still emphasized the axiom: "You can't push a string."

But the monetarists were not without influence, and as the 1960s raised some questions about the over-all effectiveness of fiscal policy, monetary policy naturally gained in prestige. No one any longer questioned the importance of money, but there was, of course, increased questioning about the administration of monetary policy. By the late 1960s when price inflation had replaced lagging economic growth as the paramount economic problem, the monetarists—those who believed that the money supply was immensely important—had achieved a prestige that only a foolhardy optimist would have predicted a decade before.

SUGGESTED READINGS

(On specific topics, see the readings cited in the footnotes in the chapter.)

Chandler, Lester, *American Monetary Policy, 1928-1941* (New York: Harper & Row, 1971).

Friedman, Milton, and Anna Jacobson Schwartz, *A Monetary History of the United States, 1867-1960* (Princeton, N.J.: Princeton University Press, 1963).

Hammond, Bray, *Banks and Politics in America: From the Revolution to the Civil War* (Princeton, N.J.: Princeton University Press, 1957).

Mitchell, Wesley, C., "The Role of Money in Economic History," *The Journal of Economic History,* Vol. IV (1944).

Redlich, Fritz, *The Molding of American Banking* (cited in Chapter 8).

QUESTIONS

1. Account for the enormous number of bank failures between 1920 and 1933. What was done to remedy this situation? Was it successful?
2. Describe the main trend in the relative importance of deposits and currency as means of payment. Explain by reference to such developments as those in transport, communication, and urbanization.
3. Describe the elasticity of note issue under (a) the state banking system before the Civil War; (b) the national banking system up to World War I; (c) the Federal Reserve System.
4. Describe the American coinage system before the Civil War. Why were people less interested in coinage before the Civil War than after the Civil War?
5. Compare and contrast the Bank of the United States with the Federal Reserve System.
6. It has been said that the reason why the Bank of the United States lost its charter was that President Jackson disliked President Biddle. Were there deeper and more important reasons?
7. How did the National Banking system work? What were its weaknesses? How did it affect the economy? What weaknesses of the National Banking system was the Federal Reserve designed to correct?
8. Why did the gold standard break down? What type of monetary standard succeeded the gold standard?
9. What criteria do you use to determine whether a money system is efficient or inefficient? On the basis of your criteria, how well have the American systems worked?

10. What criticisms would you make of Federal Reserve policy in its first 20 years? Is Federal Reserve policy much different today from what it was in the 1920s?
11. How did differences between sound-money and easy-money adherents influence monetary history in the period after the Civil War?
12. How was monetary policy administered in the years before the Federal Reserve System?
13. What were the weaknesses of the pre-Civil War banking system, and how did they mirror the American environment?

Chapter Ten

THE CHANGING STATUS
OF FOREIGN COMMERCE

Production and consumption are by no means the whole of economics. Commerce—distribution and transportation—also occupies a key position in economic growth and development, being both a cause and an effect of business and economic progress. In order for a nation to achieve maximum satisfaction from available resources, it must have an efficient system of marketing as well as an efficient production system.

Although one may truthfully say that man ordinarily produces in order to consume, this does not mean that individuals consume the same goods that they produce. In a young economy, producers do consume what they produce; but as economic life advances, producers and consumers take on separate identities. There begins to emerge a roundabout system of production in which producers spend less time making goods that satisfy consumer wants directly and more time in making goods that will be used to make other goods. A technological system of production emerges, and as it grows, the gap between the producer and the consumer becomes a yawning chasm. But, at the same time, the productive process becomes more specialized and, consequently, more efficient economically. Both geographical regions and individuals try to specialize in those things for which they are best fitted. Emphasizing their own comparative advantages, they exchange what they produce for the goods that other specialists produce. One region grows wheat; another manufactures iron and steel; a third plants cotton. Farmers grow crops in excess of their own consumption needs in order to exchange the surplus for goods produced by people working in industry. Workers add parts to automobiles, typewriters, and television sets in order to exchange their labor for bread, suits, and tickets to the ballgame. This process of extreme specialization would not be possible unless there were adequate means of exchange and efficient channels of distribution. Thus, the process of distribution, by enabling the economy to specialize and produce more, is as important as production and consumption; for the better the distributive process, the greater the opportunities for specialization and division of labor between different geographical areas and between different groups of men; and the greater the degree of specialization, the higher the level of living.

Early America, being a young and developing economy, did not have the prerequisites for a thriving internal commerce. Technological progress was not sufficiently advanced to permit extensive manufacturing, and transportation facilities, such as roads, could not be built until population and the demand for goods had grown enough to support them. Most of the internal commerce that did exist was conducted over natural waterways and was concerned mostly with the sale of raw materials.

But, although early America was in no position to produce its own manufactured goods, it needed them badly and wanted them badly. Fortunately, it could obtain manufactured goods fairly easily from the Old World, where they were already being produced. America had all the requisites for a thriving external trade. Her Atlantic coastline was long and dotted with many excellent harbors. In addition, this area was heavily forested and could produce the lumber, tars, and other products required by the shipping industry. The colonists thus were in an excellent position to ship the products of their farms, fisheries, and forests to Europe in exchange for manufactured goods and to other parts of the world in exchange for raw materials and semifinished products that could not be produced in America itself. Accordingly, foreign trade was of the greatest importance in the colonies and continued to be so in the United States until well after the War of 1812, when American manufacturing began to come into its own and when transportation facilities were sufficiently developed to enhance the importance of internal commerce. In his Annual Report for 1848, Secretary of the Treasury Robert Walker estimated "our" product at $3 billion, of which $150 million was exported and $500 million was traded internally.

American trade, distorted in the eighteenth and very early nineteenth century, first by its colonial status and then by the Napoleonic Wars, assumed a more normal state after 1815, permitting certain long-term trends to emerge. First, the volume of foreign trade in proportion to total trade began to decline. It never recovered the level of the late eighteenth century, but it seems to have reached its all-time low in the couple of decades just before the middle of the nineteenth century. The decline in foreign trade could be shown in many ways. One way is by the decline in tonnage. In 1790, tonnage in foreign trade was three times that of internal trade; by 1860 coastal and internal was somewhat larger than foreign. Second, over the course of time, emphasis shifted from exports of raw materials. Third, the locus of trade also shifted. Most of our early trading was carried on with Europe; but by the twentieth century, European trade, although still very important, had declined compared with the trade carried on with Canada, South America, and Japan. Fourth, our balance of trade was almost always unfavorable until 1875 and almost always favorable for the next ninety years. Fifth, the shipbuilding and shipping industries, the pride of early America, started at a point of efficiency far superior to that of the rest of the world, but declined steadily decade by decade. Sixth, our high level of productivity gave us a comparative advantage, but the gap has been closing noticeably in recent years.

THE CONTRIBUTION OF FOREIGN TRADE TO THE LEVEL OF LIVING

Historically, it would be difficult to exaggerate the importance of foreign trade in America's transition from an underdeveloped to a thriving economy. Even after it had been far superseded by domestic commerce, foreign trade remained of considerable consequence. In early America, it made a most important contribution to the national income, it was a mainstay for capital accumulation, it afforded the means by which the United States obtained badly needed manufactured goods, and it enabled the United States to exchange goods that she produced comparatively cheaply for goods that she could produce only at a high cost or could not produce at all. In later years, foreign trade represented the margin between profitability and unprofitability for many American industries. At all times, it brought into the United States a diversity of goods that added variety to the American's level of living. Then, too, the strategic materials which it provided set in motion a chain of external economies and induced investments. Silk and cloth imports, for example, brought into being domestic industries in finishing, dyeing, and the like.

When foreign trade equaled 25 percent or more of the national income, its importance in the over-all economy could not very well be denied. But even when it dropped to less than 10 percent, its marginal importance was still great, for foreign trade was not equally distributed among all goods and services. Much more than half the dollar volume of some commodities was imported or exported, and without this margin these commodities could not have been produced in such profusion and resources would not have been used as efficiently.

Having a comparative advantage in shipping, the United States made optimum use of it through foreign trade. The great American business tycoons of the eighteenth and early nineteenth century were merchants. Thomas Hancock, probably the richest man in the colonies, was a merchant. The Crowninshield family amassed about half a million in foreign trade. Derby died in 1799, leaving $1 million. William Gray was worth $3 million, and the Jacksons and the Lees, Stephen Girard, and John Jacob Astor, much, much more. Keen traders, they cast their goods on the waters and brought them back two- or threefold. Doubling or tripling their wealth, they used their profits to accumulate capital. The fortunes built up through international commerce exceeded those made in land, and eventually they became the basis for the expansion of domestic transportation facilities and industry. As foreign commerce declined, the accumulated capital of the Forbeses, Sturgises, Russells, Cabots, Lowells, and other shipping tycoons was shifted to other forms of enterprise and provided the foundation for the building of railroads and the development of manufacturing.

One further effect of international trade on the American economy needs some elaboration: the influence of the flow of gold on the domestic money supply and price level. Theoretically, under a gold standard, gold flows in or out as the domestic price level declines or increases relative to the price level prevailing in other nations. Thus, if American prices fell below those prevailing in other countries, exports would tend to increase and gold would flow into the country to balance international payments. If American prices rose above prices of other nations, imports would tend to increase and gold would tend to flow out of the country. But this movement of gold in response to changes in relative price levels would take place only if all other things were equal. Actually, all other things seldom remained equal. Wars, currency manipulation, exchange controls, restrictions on the free movement of goods, and changing international indebtedness were more common than rare and prevented the type of gold movements that would have occurred in a free market.

But whatever the reasons, this most high-powered of high-powered money had a most important effect on the money supply and thus on the whole economy. The outflow of gold tended to reduce the domestic money stock and had a deflationary influence on United States' prices. On the other hand, the inflow of gold augmented the domestic money supply and exerted an upward pressure on American prices. On the whole, the greater the quantity of gold inflow or outflow, the greater the influence on the money supply and the price level. Extraordinary gold movements were mostly associated with devaluation, war, internal political conditions, and changes in international debtor-creditor relationships. American devaluation, European wars, and European political uncertainties brought gold in; but when the United States was fighting a war, gold flowed out.

To sum up, foreign trade enabled the United States to make more effective use of specialization, division of labor, and comparative advantage. It influenced the national income, capital accumulation, the money supply, and the price level. But, most important of all, it enabled the United States to procure manufactured goods when American industry and domestic commerce were still undeveloped.

COLONIAL TRADE

The influence of British mercantilism

Colonial trade with Great Britain exceeded £700,000 in 1700, but it is estimated that this constituted only about half of total foreign trade. Some 75 years later, colonial commerce was about £2 million annually with Great Britain and about an equal amount with the rest of the world.[1] At approximately £4 million a year, this was more important than the total amount of domestic commerce; and, if allowance were made for the goods that were smuggled into the colonies, estimated by some authorities as "prodigious" and by others as "negligible," the contrast would be even greater.

Colonial foreign commerce would have been extensive in any case, but it was encouraged to greater vitality by the mercantilist policies pursued by the British government. At the middle of the seventeenth century, Great Britain had not as yet achieved her position of world economic domination. She was building an empire, but her ambitions were to some extent frustrated by the power of the Dutch and the French. In order to overcome the advantage enjoyed by the Dutch, Britain adopted a set of policies that came to be known as *mercantilism*. Designed principally to build a strong state, mercantilist policies were intended to help all parts of the Empire to compete in the world economy, but the interests of the Mother Country were favored over those of the rest of the Empire. Colonies were to be aided and assisted, but they were also regarded as producers of raw materials for Britain and as consumers of British finished products; and the British government intended to do everything in its power to keep it that way. In 1649 and 1651, Britain adopted the first navigation acts affecting the colonies, and for the next 200 years these acts were to be supplemented and modified in the interests of protecting the power of the British Empire. At first, the system of commercial regulation was meant to encourage trade. After the French and Indian War, however, the regulations began to be applied with an eye toward raising revenue. More modifications followed during the nineteenth century, until the whole system came to an end with the repeal of the Corn Laws in 1846.

In general, mercantilist legislation in commerce provided, first, that all trade to England from America, Asia, and Africa had to be carried in ships owned and manned by citizens of the British Empire; second, that all goods imported into the colonies, except wine and salt from southern Europe, had to be shipped via England; third, a long list of specific colonial goods, known as "enumerated commodities" and including such important products as tobacco, cotton, indigo,

---

[1]Trade with southern Europe equaled £629,000; West Indian trade, £1.5 million (¾ of British trade); and African trade, £172,000.

furs, rice, and shipbuilding materials, could be shipped only to England; fourth, extensive tariff regulations; and fifth, an elaborate system of rebates, drawbacks, export bounties, and export taxes.

There has been constant controversy among historians as to whether mercantilism's effects were good or bad.[2] Early American historians were sharply critical of the doctrine; those in the middle period tended to follow a middle-of-the-road position; recently, it has become more fashionable to be sympathetic toward mercantilism.

The legislation requiring that English goods be shipped in English bottoms was of little consequence, because the colonists had such a decided comparative advantage in shipbuilding that it would have been unprofitable to use any other nation's shipping facilities even if such an alternative had been permitted. The restrictions on imports and exports were economically disadvantageous to the colonists, for, if they had been allowed to buy and to sell where they pleased, they would have been able to trade more advantageously and to reap greater profits than they were able to make operating under the British restrictions. An outstanding example of a piece of legislation that frustrated American traders was the Molasses Act of 1733, which imposed prohibitive duties on imports of sugar, molasses, and rum from the non-English West Indies. Designed to protect the English sugar islands at the expense of the mainland, it was a colossal economic and political blunder.

But the system was by no means one-sided. Against the disadvantages caused by the restrictions against freedom of trade, mercantilism gave the colonists many advantages in their commercial activities. England protected colonial shipping on the high seas. She also paid generous bounties (£1.7 million by the Revolution) to the colonists on such goods as tar, pitch, hemp, silk, indigo, lumber, and high-grade cooperage materials. In some instances, this protective legislation was advantageous in that it gave the colonists an added incentive to produce some commodities, such as ships, lumber, and naval stores, in which they were most proficient. On the other hand, bounties were not altogether beneficial, for they encouraged some industries that were uneconomic and thus diverted resources into less productive channels. For example, it was not economically advantageous for the colonists to produce indigo, silk, and hemp, and when British protection was removed from these products after the Revolution, they quickly passed out of the picture and the resources that had been used in their production were diverted to more productive pursuits.

Being members of the British Empire, the colonists also had the advantage of being able to export some goods to Britain duty-free or, at least, at lower duties than were required of foreign shippers. Moreover, in some cases British

---

[2]See Oliver M. Dickerson, *The Navigation Acts and the American Revolution* (Philadelphia: University of Pennsylvania Press, 1951).

restrictions gave the colonists an almost monopolistic position. Thus, tobacco raising was prohibited in England and a prohibitive duty was imposed on non-colonial tobacco imports, giving the colonists a virtual monopoly over the British tobacco trade. Naval stores and hemp were accorded a similar monopolistic position.

Mercantilism also benefited colonial economic development in yet another way. It made it comparatively easy for the colonists to raise capital. Within the closed trade system that mercantilism fostered, the Mother Country supplied her relatively plentiful capital funds to the colonists, such as tobacco growers, who suffered from a critical scarcity of capital. In the long run, British capital suppliers extended more credit than could be repaid under normal conditions. The American debtors tried with some success to shave down their debts by inflating the currency, and eventually they repudiated some of their debts by breaking their relations with the British Empire. Thus, one of the indirect effects of mercantilism was to give the Americans a windfall profit at the expense of British creditors.

The nature of colonial trade

On the whole, the mainland colonies of America were a disappointment to British mercantilists, for, even though trade with them increased as time passed, it was relatively less important than trade with the sugar islands of the West Indies. Moreover, the colonies never seemed to understand that their function in life was to devote themselves wholeheartedly to the interests of England, the center of the Empire. They were supposed to be producers of raw materials and consumers of English manufactures, but most of the colonies fell far short of filling their theoretic roles.

New England was the worst offender, and most English mercantilists regarded her as a burden rather than a help. Natural conditions made it impossible for New England to be a great agricultural area but did enable her to develop a thriving fishing industry. The prominent display of a codfish in the Massachusetts State House is not a gesture of aesthetic idiosyncracy, but a tribute to a generous contributor to New England's scale of living.

Because of geographical disadvantages, New England was in no position to engage in overland commerce; but, because she had a large seacoast and excellent harbors and could build ships cheaply, she was well equipped for seagoing commerce. Consequently, she competed with, rather than complemented, England's trade. New England exported fish, furs, lumber, ships, rum, and the products of her household and small-scale manufacture to the West Indies, Southern Europe, and England in exchange for sugar, molasses, and finished manufacturers. But her trade with England was much smaller than with other areas. In 1700, New England's trade with Britain was officially estimated at £133,000, about 18 percent of her total. Her trade with the rest of the world must have been considerably more. By 1769, New England's trade with Great Britain had risen to £366,000, but this was a small part of her total trade of £1.1 million.

The Middle Colonies were somewhat more attuned to mercantilism than was New England, but they were still far from satisfactory from the British viewpoint. In 1700, their trade with Great Britain was smaller than that of New England, comprising only 12 percent of the total. Because their chief exports and imports were similar to those of New England, the Middle Colonies carried on a large trade with Southern Europe and the West Indies. Early in their history, the Middle Colonies—like all the other colonies—had developed a thriving fur business; but, as the frontier became populated and animals were no longer as plentiful, the fur trade declined somewhat. An active trade in lumber and ships continued while exports of flour and provisions increased by more than enough to compensate for the waning fur trade. By 1770, the Middle Colonies had greatly increased their volume of foreign trade, handling almost one-quarter of the total of America's foreign trade and about one-seventh of her trade with Great Britain. Philadelphia was the largest trader in colonial America; Charleston was second; Boston, third; and New York, fourth.

The Southern colonies fulfilled almost perfectly the mercantilist ideal. They raised raw materials and imported manufactured goods; and what made the situation even more delightful from the British point of view, the Southern colonists traded mostly with Great Britain. In 1700, Virginia and Maryland shipped enough tobacco and imported enough manufactures to account for two-thirds of all colonial trade with Britain. The Carolinas, specializing in naval stores and rice, accounted for a very small percent. By 1769, tobacco had declined somewhat in relative importance while naval stores had increased, so that the Virginia and Maryland share of British trade had fallen to less than half while the share of the rest of the South had risen to one-quarter. In the 1760s, Virginia and Maryland exported £1 million a year; Pennsylvania, £700,000; New York £525,000; and New England, £485,000.

Eighty percent of English goods were bought on credit. Goods cost three times as much in the colonies as in England.

The colonial balance of trade

Foreign trade is usually carried on by individuals, not governments, and it is ordinarily a trade; that is, when individuals buy goods, they usually pay for them by selling goods. Where this cannot be done, the buyer may pay for his purchases by performing services or by going into debt. Thus, the citizens of one nation may for long periods of time buy more goods than they sell, paying for the difference by performing shipping, insurance, or other services or going into debt.

Two terms are used to differentiate between the exchange of tangible goods and the variety of other financial transactions that take place between nations. The "balance of payments" refers to all transactions between one nation and the rest of the world, including investment as well as the purchase and sale of goods and services. The "balance of trade" is something else again: it refers to the exchange of goods and services only.

Available statistics on trade with Great Britain show that the colonies had an unfavorable balance of trade in 33 of the 49 years between 1697 and 1745. But the balance of trade with the West Indies was probably more often favorable than unfavorable, for specie shipments from the West Indies were so frequent that in a short while Spanish dollars became the most common coin in colonial America. From 1745 until the Revolutionary War, the balance of trade with Great Britain grew more unfavorable with each passing year. In 1746 the unfavorable balance was about £200,000; in 1761 it was about £800,000; and in 1774, £1.2 million. The balance with the rest of the world was still favorable enough, however, to cover most of the deficit with Great Britain. In 1769, for example, colonial commerce, on the basis of official figures, showed a favorable balance of about £300,000.

Great Britain was prospering mightily during this era, and manufacturing progress was the key. By far the world's leading manufacturing nation, she was building up an overseas financial empire by selling more than she bought and by investing the surplus at the point of sale. It was a situation that filled English mercantilists with extraordinary glee. But actually they were living under an illusion, for it was an economic impossibility for the colonists or anyone else to buy more than they sold *ad infinitum.* For a while, deficits could be covered by borrowing, but eventually the debts became so large that they could not be paid. These debts, therefore, were one of the aggravations that fanned the anti-British feeling that eventually erupted in the Revolutionary War.

Colonial shipbuilding and shipping

The colonists partly balanced their merchandise deficit with England by shipping to their creditors specie (silver and gold) obtained from their trade surplus with the rest of the world. They covered another part of the deficit by going into debt to British nationals. A third part was met by the shipping industry, which, because of its extraordinary profitability, brought into the colonies large amounts of foreign credits. There was one overwhelmingly important reason for the high profitability of colonial shipping: the American colonists could build ships far cheaper and far better than Europeans could. America had an absolute advantage over Europe because she had an abundance of the natural resources required in shipbuilding. By the Colonial Period, Europe's timber resources for shipbuilding had been seriously depleted, but vast forest preserves existed all over colonial America.

Of all the colonies, New England made the most and best use of her timber resources, for she had no strongly competing industries to attract labor. British shipbuilders had to import timber, but the New Englander was almost surrounded by trees of all varieties. A New England ship could be built 30 percent cheaper than a British ship, and the American model was far more durable than her European counterparts. Wooden ships last from 5 to 60 years, depending on the quality of the timber that goes into them. New England built ships that lasted from 30 to 60 years, because she could pick from her wealth of timber resources the best lumber to use in ship construction. On the other hand, British ships lasted only 5 to 30 years, because poor, as well as good, timber had to be used, and even the best timber deteriorated when it was shipped in the raw state.

Because they were far cheaper and far more seaworthy, colonial ships were in great demand, and the industry grew impressively. By the end of the seventeenth century, New England was constructing 3,000 tons a year, and by 1769, 13,000 tons. The colonial shipbuilding industry supplied English as well as American shippers, and it was not uncommon for an American to sell his ship along with his cargo in British ports. The practice was, in fact, so frequent that by the eighteenth century, 30 percent of the ships in the English merchant marine had been built in America. The practice, like any other good trade, was advantageous to both parties; but England, obsessed with the mercantilist illusion that it was necessary to protect all home industries, inefficient as well as efficient, tried to prevent competition from American shipbuilding and to obtain the raw materials for her own shipbuilders. However, the cost of transporting raw materials was prohibitive in comparison with the economies of building ships within sight of the materials and then sailing the finished product across the Atlantic.

England, therefore, had to accept what it considered a not-too-satisfactory arrangement and tried as best she could to protect the long-term interests of the Empire. Aware from her own experience of the rapidity with which resources could be depleted, she attempted to conserve the best stands by marking trees with an arrow, thereby reserving them for the king's navy. The colonists, of course, paid no attention to the royal edict, for where resources are plentiful, "waste" is also plentiful. The English attempt at conservation was, therefore, abortive by 250 years.

The absolute advantage enjoyed by American shipbuilders also gave American shippers economic advantages over their European rivals. True, English shippers bought American ships and thereby neutralized to some extent the advantages of American shippers, but the whole colonial merchant marine was American-built, whereas only a fraction of the British merchant fleet was made in America. Besides being cheap (£3 or £4 per ton) and durable, American-built vessels had the decided advantage of being small. Late in the eighteenth century, British East Indiamen displaced 1,200 tons, although colonial-built transatlantic ships averaged only 160 tons and ships in the coastal trade averaged 40 to 100 tons. Ships under 400 tons were easier to handle in stormy waters, and they could sail in shallow water and in uncharted areas where large ships might run aground.

FOREIGN TRADE DURING THE NAPOLEONIC WARS

American foreign trade has always been extraordinarily influenced by war. Wars in which most of Europe was engaged and in which we were precariously neutral pushed our foreign trade to record heights. Conversely, wars fought on American soil—the War of 1812 and the Civil War—substantially reduced foreign trade.

A brisk foreign trade arose immediately after the formation of the new government and continued for the next 20 years. As one contemporary described it, there had never been "a period of such length in which foreign trade so completely absorbed the attention of a large portion of the people and exercised so vital an influence on industry in general."[3]

Between 1790 and 1807, when the first great upsurge temporarily halted, foreign trade in goods and services multiplied about five times, from about $60 million to over $300 million. There were many reasons for this extraordinary movement, including the creation of a strong government with an American "common market," the recovery from the postwar depression, and the building of a navy; but the Napoleonic Wars overshadowed all the other reasons. With the whole of Europe constantly embroiled in what amounted to a world war, the United States reaped a harvest as the world's leading shipper. "Almost the whole carrying trade of Europe was in American hands. . . . The merchant flag of every belligerent, save England, disappeared from the sea. It was under our flag that the gum trade was carried on with Senegal, that the sugar trade was carried on with Cuba, that coffee was exported from Caracas, and hides and indigo from South America. From Vera Cruz, from Carthagena, from La Plata, from the French colonies in the Antilles, from Cayenne, from Dutch Guiana, from the isles of France and Réunion, from Batavia and Manila, great fleets of American merchantmen sailed from the United States, there to neutralize the voyage and then go on to Europe. They filled the warehouses at Cadiz and Antwerp to overflowing. They glutted the markets of Emden and Lisbon, Hamburg and Copenhagen, with the produce of the West Indies and the fabrics of the East."[4]

The abnormal situation reversed itself, however, as the United States endeavored unsuccessfully to remain a neutral. In 1806 and 1807, France took

---

[3]Emory R. Johnson, et al., History of Domestic and Foreign Commerce of the United States (Washington, D.C.: Carnegie Institution of Washington, 1915), Vol. 2, p. 14.

[4]John Bach McMaster, History of the People of the United States (New York: Appleton-Century-Crofts, Inc., 1885), Vol. III, p. 225.

steps through the Berlin and Milan Decrees to break up trade between the United States and England. The British through their Orders in Council tried to do the same to American trade with France. American shipping was hamstrung, for if neutral ships stopped in France, they were subject to seizure by the British, and if they stopped in England, they were vulnerable to the other belligerent. Desperately striving to remain neutral, the Jeffersonian administrations passed between 1808 and 1810 the Non-Intercourse Act, the Embargo, and the Macon Bill, all designed to restrict trade with England and France. As a result, foreign trade fell off sharply. It fell still further when the United States finally became a belligerent. By 1814, foreign trade totaled only $30 million, the lowest amount in our whole history. There was some recovery after the War, but in 1819, total exports and imports were only about $200 million, less than two-thirds as much as in 1807.

Aggregate dollar volume is hardly the best way of measuring the importance of or the siginficant changes in foreign trade. Presumably, as the economy grows, foreign trade will also grow. But, although foreign trade may grow in dollar terms, it may not grow as fast as the general economy. To put the volume of trade in its proper perspective, it is advisable to measure it in terms of the growth of population and of the national income.

Foreign trade on a per capita basis was very high in the early United States, relatively low in the middle period, but ascended to new heights in the twentieth century. And the same generalization would apply even if the statistics were corrected for changes in the purchasing power of the dollar. Benefiting from Europe's wars and from her own comparative advantages in shipbuilding and shipping, the United States' per capita trade reached almost $50 in 1807. It then sagged; but for the whole period, it averaged $20 per capita.

Perhaps the best insight into the changes in the economic importance of foreign trade can be obtained by relating the volume of foreign trade to changes in the national income as is done in Chart 18. In proportion to national income, foreign trade declined from an initial high peak, showed some signs of recovery in the last half of the nineteenth century, and then declined anew in the twentieth century. It certainly never again equaled the importance it achieved in 1807, when merchandise exports and imports climbed above 25 percent of the national income.

The balance of payments and the composition of foreign trade, 1790-1820

In a young economy, individual citizens, possessing nothing but their own resources, talents, ideas, and initiative, make their first starts toward economic progress by going into debt to the citizens of older, more developed economies. They buy more goods than they sell. The United States was no exception. Except for two extraordinary years during the Embargo and the War, we imported more goods than we sent abroad. Ordinarily, the difference between

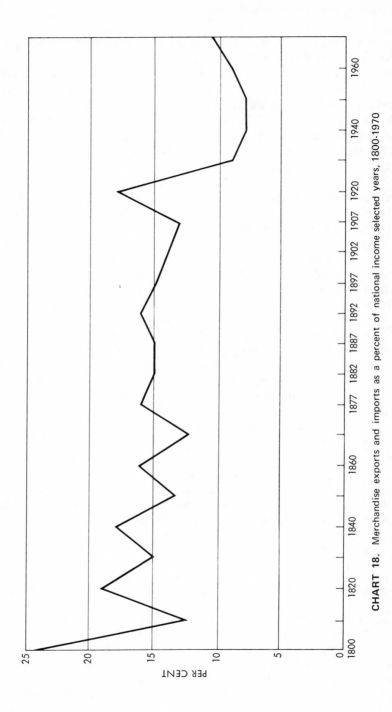

CHART 18. Merchandise exports and imports as a percent of national income selected years, 1800-1970

exports and imports was not very large; but the balance varied, and at times the gap was very large, relatively as well as absolutely. Much of the difference was made up by earnings from shipping, which loomed very large in our early commerce. A much smaller chunk was taken care of by exporting specie. The remaining deficit was covered by borrowing from abroad. In fact, the volume of such borrowing was often more than enough to equilibrate the balance of trade. Consequently, although our balance of trade was unfavorable in 28 of the 30 years between 1790 and 1820, the balance of payments was unfavorable in 19 years and favorable in 11.

In the late eighteenth century, as during the entire Colonial Period, the products of agriculture, fishing, and forestry were our chief exports. During the next century, the composition of exports changed gradually from crude materials to finished manufactures, and imports shifted from finished manufactures to crude materials.

In 1820, 6 percent of all exports and almost 60 percent of imports were finished manufactures. Not quite 65 percent of exports and a little more than 15 percent of imports were crude materials and foodstuffs.

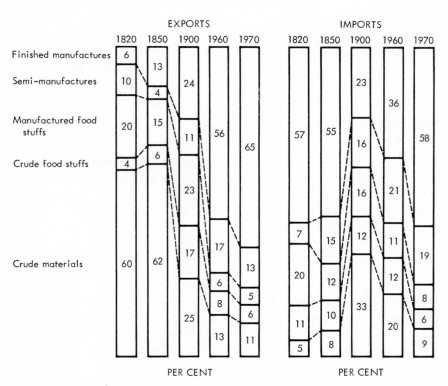

CHART 19. Composition of foreign trade, 1820, 1850, 1900, 1960, 1970

During the colonial period, tobacco, flour, fish, rice, lumber, and furs made up most of America's export trade, tobacco alone accounting for over one-third the total.

During the first half of the nineteenth century, most of the products that had monopolized the export trade in colonial times faded away and were replaced by other agricultural products, such as cotton and meat. Furs and rice became insignificant. Exports of tobacco and fish increased in dollar volume, but declined so much in proportion to total trade that they ceased to be of any relative importance. Of all leading colonial commodities, only flour and lumber continued to be of importance. This change in the composition of the export trade was the inevitable result of the rapid changes that were taking place in the nation's economic life. As the South shifted from tobacco, indigo, and rice, cotton ran far ahead of its nearest rival in the export trade. As the North shifted from the extractive industries to commercial farming and manufacturing, furs and fish became less important than wheat, corn, and meat, and the opening of the Middle West accentuated the change even more.

As early as 1790, breadstuffs represented 40 percent of total exports and exceeded tobacco as America's leading export commodity. But, although they continued to be very important, breadstuffs quickly lost their predominant position to cotton. At the beginning of the nineteenth century, the value of cotton exports was only $5 million, or less than 10 percent of all exports. By 1818, cotton exports had increased to $30 million, or sixfold. They constituted about one-third of total exports, two and one-half times as much as the exports of breadstuffs, and almost six times as great as the exports of forest products.

The direction of foreign trade in the post-colonial period

The Revolutionary War freed the United States from British mercantilist restrictions, theoretically opening all the seven seas to the American merchant marine. But the War also separated the United States from the British Empire, theoretically closing some British ports to American shipping. Anticipating a decline in their trade with Britain, which had been the backbone of colonial commerce, American merchants opened trade routes with Northern Europe and the Far East. *The Empress of China,* in which Robert Morris had an important interest, netted $37,000 from a $120,000 investment on a one-year journey in 1784-1785 to Canton, China. Elias Derby's *Grand Turk* sailed from Salem in 1785 on a long trip to Mauritius, India, and China. Voyages of two or three years were not uncommon. *The Columbia,* for example, made a three-year voyage between 1787 and 1790 that logged 50,000 miles. Profits in the trade were attractive and sometimes astounding. Boston merchants thought that trade with the East offered a moral certainty of 6 percent, a reasonable expectation of 10 percent, and a chance for 12 percent with very little hazard. Sailing from

Massachusetts with a cargo of less than $40,000, it was not impossible for a ship to return with $200,000 or more.[5]

Yet the trade with the Far East, in the early years of the Republic, was more romantic than important. In 1800, for example, trade with the Far East represented less than 10 percent of all foreign trade, and the China trade was not much greater than the trade with the British or the Dutch East Indies. Salem, the leading trader with the Far East, had 126 ships in 1812, 58 in the Far Eastern trade. Trade with Europe, especially with the United Kingdom, was by far the most important part of America's foreign commerce. Indeed, the United States was a better customer of England after the Revolution than she had been as a member of the Empire.

Economists are prone to consider economics supreme over all other considerations, especially politics. It may well be that they exaggerate. But there are a number of examples of economics triumphing over politics and one of the best is what happened in foreign trade in the early nineteenth century. At the end of the Revolution, as has been observed, trade with England dropped, and France tried to pick it up, but in a short time economic relations with England were more than restored. By 1820, trade with England was almost five times as large as trade with France, the second largest account. Although we were politically independent, we were still to all intents and purposes an economic outpost of the British Empire.

FOREIGN TRADE IN THE WOODEN SHIP ERA

The volume of trade

In the 30 years before 1850, American foreign trade was greatly influenced by the westward movement, the upsurge in domestic commerce, the varying fortunes of American shipping, the business cycle, and government tariff policy both here and abroad.

The volume of trade in the early nineteenth century was, judged by some criteria, the lowest in American history. Its magnitude ranged from about $150 million in 1821 to about $360 million in 1848. Average exports and imports were only $13 per capita, and trade in merchandise varied from 13 to 18 percent of the national income. Total trade surpassed the 1807 peak in only four of the

---

[5]See Samuel E. Morison, *The Maritime History of Massachusetts, 1783-1860* (Boston: Houghton Mifflin Company, 1921); Robert S. Albion, *The Rise of New York Port* (New York: Charles Scribner's Sons, 1939); Foster Rhea Dulles, *The Old China Trade* (Boston: Houghton Mifflin Company, 1930).

30 years, three of which, 1847-1849, surrounded the Mexican War. (See Chart 20).

Up to 1846, the factors that stimulated foreign trade were neutralized by equally powerful forces on the other side. Continuous progress in marketing facilities encouraged all trade, foreign as well as domestic. But business recessions and increases in tariff rates laid a heavy hand on international trade that was just about offset by business recovery and reductions in tariffs.

Initially, the tariff was purely a revenue-raising device. After the War of 1812, however, when war-born industries found it impossible to meet British competition, the tariff took on a protective tinge. In 1816, the first "protective" tariff was adopted. By the 1820s, sectional feeling on the issue had congealed, and tariff-making became a study in sectional politics; it was, in fact, "a local issue." The East, anxious to protect industry, favored high tariffs. The West believed that high tariffs were necessary to provide a domestic market for its raw materials and to provide the funds for internal improvement construction. Only the South, recognizing that it was destined to be an agrarian economy exporting cotton and importing manufactured goods, protested strongly against the trend toward protectionism. But the South was outnumbered in Washington, and Congress in 1824, and in the "Tariff of Abominations" of 1828, raised the tariff to new heights, twice frustrating what might possibly have been recoveries in foreign trade. From the 1830s until the Civil War, the tariff exhibited a downward trend as the West lost its enthusiasm for the "home markets" argument and the South became increasingly voluble in its demands for free trade.

Helped by tariff reductions in 1832 and 1833, foreign trade ran afoul of the 1837 panic and depression and it did not really recover until the late 1840s. Then a series of stimulative factors brought foreign trade out of its doldrums. Business prosperity was compounded by the California gold discovery in 1848 and the flood of agricultural products that began to hit the market in the late 1840s. The decline in protection that was one of the features of the mid-century international economy gave further impetus to a trend that was well under way. In 1846, Britain repealed her corn laws, and in the same year the United States reduced her tariffs. Merchandise exports jumped about 35 percent and imports about the same amount in the last years of the 1840s. This was the period when the "Atlantic Community" reached its height. In the first half of the nineteenth century, Britain sold 40 percent of what America imported and bought about the same share of American exports. The United States bought one-sixth to one-quarter of British exports and sold her about 10 to 25 percent of what she imported.[6]

Cotton was again of overwhelming importance in the export trade and, therefore, in total trade. As new lands were opened in the West, cotton culture

[6]J. Potter, "Atlantic Economy, 1815-1860: the U.S.A. and the Industrial Revolution in Britain," reprinted in A. W. Coats and Ross M. Robertson, eds., *Essays in American Economic History* (London: Edward Arnold, 1969).

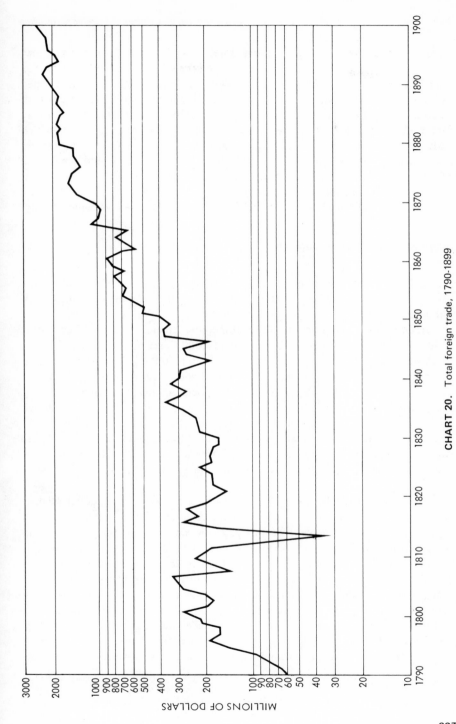

MILLIONS OF DOLLARS

CHART 20. Total foreign trade, 1790-1899

327

increased at a continuously accelerated pace. By the middle of the century, Southern patriots and political leaders had good reason to boast that cotton was king. It was the basis of the famous triangular trade in which the South shipped raw material to England in exchange for manufactured goods, and the North acted as a very prosperous middleman. So productive was this trade that it may very well be argued, as it has been, that cotton was the foundation upon which early American economic development was built. Cotton exports in 1850 were about to pass $100 million. They would, by 1860, reach the phenomenal value of almost $200 million, constituting 60 percent of all exports. Flour, wheat, corn, and meat accounted for a large part of the remainder. Finished manufactures, especially machinery, were far down the list, but were growing steadily.

Supremacy of American shipping

As has been noted, the shipping industries were a most important factor in the balance of payments. When American shipbuilding and shipping flourished, they did much to balance America's foreign trade deficit.

Relative to population and national income, American shipbuilding was at its highest point before 1807, when about 110,000 tons a year were constructed. In absolute terms, excluding war years, shipbuilding in the United States reached its peak in the late 1850s at between 500,000 and 600,000 tons a year. At the same time, the gross tonnage of the American merchant marine increased spectacularly. From less than 500,000 tons, shipping rose to more than five million tons in 1855, or more than tenfold. During this rapid climb, the American merchant marine came to almost equal that of Great Britain. In 1821, American ships carried over 90 percent of American shipping, but by 1851 this had decreased to 60 percent. Later, however, it was to fall to an all-time low of 10 percent in 1914.

There were logical reasons for the early supremacy, the gradual relative decline, and the final absolute decline of the American shipping industry. In its heyday in the early nineteenth century, American shipping enjoyed the same comparative advantages that it had possessed in the Colonial Period. American ships cost a little more than half as much to build as British ships, and were durable, small, and easily managed. They could enter and leave shallow-water ports, navigate inland rivers, and sail on uncharted waters much more efficiently than the more ponderous British ships. American ships were seldom larger than 300 tons, whereas British ships were never smaller than 350 tons. Because they cost less,[7] American merchant ships could sail more cheaply than European ships. In 1805, for example, a round trip to England cost an American ship £500

[7]For a more detailed discussion of the cost factors in international shipping, see John G. B. Hutchins, *The American Maritime Industries and Public Policy, 1789-1914* (Cambridge, Mass.: Harvard University Press, 1941), Chaps. 7-10.

and a British ship £1,000. Moreover, American labor and management on the high seas were more productive and more efficient than their European counterparts. Although a large part of this comparative advantage was offset by the higher wages paid to American labor, freight rates on American ships were always lower than in Europe and at one time were only half as much.

The decline of American shipping

America's comparative advantage in shipping fell steadily throughout the first half of the nineteenth century; and by the late 1850s, the differential between shipping costs in America and Europe had more than disappeared, for Canada and Europe were making and operating better and cheaper ships than the United States.

In brief, the reasons for this gradual shift of comparative advantage were: the rising costs of constructing wooden ships in the United States, the appearance and improvement of the iron steamship, the inertia of American shipbuilders, the elimination of the economic advantages of small ships, and the divergent policies toward shipping followed by the American and British governments.

It was inevitable that the advantage enjoyed by the United States in the construction of wooden ships would decline. The early advantage arose from the fact that European timber stands were badly depleted, whereas the United States had vast unhewed forest reserves. But in the course of time, under the pressure of population growth and large-scale building, the United States' timber reserves were also depleted, thus raising the cost of constructing wooden vessels. As early as 1800, the timber reserves of some localities had been spent, and with each passing year shipbuilders had to go farther into interior areas for timber. At the same time, the quality of the timber declined. By 1850, depletion was so widespread that the differential between America and Europe had been erased; and by 1880, the United States faced the general shortage of timber that had long plagued Europe.

While wooden ships constantly became more expensive, iron ships constantly became cheaper, and by 1850 iron was competitively as cheap as wood. Almost simultaneously, the efficiency of steamships improved, while the efficiency of sailing ships remained the same. The idea of steam as a means of propulsion was very old, but major improvements had to be made before the steam engine became a practical device for propelling a vessel. A steamship called the *Savannah* crossed the Atlantic in 1819, but its success hardly filled the operators of sailing ships with consternation. The voyage took 29 days, of which only three were navigated by steam. Aside from lack of speed, early steamships were much more dangerous than sailing ships and they could carry less cargo.

But steamships could be improved, while sailing ships had about reached the peak of their efficiency. By 1838, steamships had been improved enough to compete with sailing ships on the transatlantic voyage. In the spring of that year, the *Great Western* and the *Sirius* inaugurated regular steamship passages across the Atlantic. By 1840, when Cunard opened a regular service to Boston, a steamship could make six trips in the time it took a sailing ship to make three.

But American shipbuilders refused to accept the inevitability of steam's triumph over sail. Despite continuous improvements in steamships, which made defeat ever more certain, they built more sailing ships than steamships; and even when they built steamships, they built them grudgingly, so that construction was less efficient than in Britain. Yet even if they had built efficiently, American shippers could not have competed with Britishers once the cost curve of iron steamships passed the cost curve of wooden sailing ships. Britain could produce coal and iron more cheaply than the United States. Whereas the United States had possessed a comparative advantage in the days of wooden sailing ships, Britain now had a comparative advantage in iron steamships.

American shippers began to seek means for improving the sailing ship, and for a while they found it in the clipper ship; but even the clipper's extraordinary capabilities were quickly overcome by the progress of the steamship. The clipper ship marked the last stand of the sailing ship. First built in 1845, it was no longer being built in 1851, although a modified clipper was still being launched. Incredibly fast, aesthetically beautiful, the clipper was a thing of romance and adventure, but it was expensive and it could not in the long run compete with steam.[8]

Still another reason for the decline of American shipping was the disappearance of the economic advantages of small ships. When shipping became a large-scale industry, the advantage of large ships was enhanced; and as more waters were charted, the advantage of small ships was diminished.

Finally, government policy played a hand in the decline of American shipping. In the halcyon days of shipping and shipbuilding, the Federal government passed navigation acts and paid subsidies to encourage American shipping, but these were hardly necessary to encourage an industry that enjoyed a topheavy comparative advantage. In accordance with its position of economic supremacy, the American shipping industry was less interested in protection than in breaking down the barriers that interfered with freedom of the seas. In time, the government eased its restrictions and dropped merchant marine subsidies entirely. Meanwhile, however, cost advantages had shifted in favor of Britain, and these were further buttressed by lavish subsidies from the British government.

The organization of foreign trade

For the first two centuries of American trade, there was no such thing as a common carrier. There were half a dozen reasons for this. Industry was con-

---

[8]Clippers sometimes sailed at 21 knots and averaged 15 knots for days. *The Flying Cloud* sailed from New York to San Francisco in 89 days, a speed that compared favorably with that of the steamer.

ducted on a small scale. Trade was largely barter. Very few goods were sold in advance, sales being negotiated after the ship had docked in a foreign port. Merchants did not operate on a broad enough scale to specialize, and the early ships were general stores operating under sail. Finally, the dangers of the high seas—war, privateering, and piracy—made a regular schedule impractical.

Ships seldom represented an investment of more than $30,000, so that great merchant capitalists owned and outfitted their own ships either as a specialized business or as part of their other business ventures. Leroy, Bayard and Co., G. G. and S. Howland, N. L. and G. Griswold, A. A. Low and Brothers, and Grinnell, Minturn and Co. were exclusively in shipping in the early nineteenth century, while such merchants as Gray, Derby, Peabody, Girard, Astor, Gracie, and Ludlow carried on shipping as part of a comprehensive marketing business. Shipping ventures were sometimes an outlet for small savings. Thus, a small vessel might be divided into as many as 64 shares. Robert G. Albion cites the example of a small brig owned by four merchants, two esquires, three traders, a sail maker, a physician, a baker, a rope maker, a tailor, a cabinetmaker, a mariner, and a farmer.[9]

On the high seas, these ships were under the direction of a captain who handled the navigation and a supercargo who handled the trading.

As long as the total volume of foreign trade remained small, individual shippers could handle it in their privately owned small ships. But as the economy grew, mass-production methods became more economical than small-scale individual ventures. By the second decade of the nineteenth century, there were enough different people engaged in foreign trade to make the common carrier a feasible method for carrying on international trade. In 1817, Isaac Wright, Jeremiah Thompson, and Benjamin Marshall founded, as an adjunct to their other businesses, a packet line between Liverpool and New York. In 1818, this Black Ball Line established the first regular service to Europe, and from then on, the common carrier rapidly replaced the individually owned special carrier. Competitive lines appeared in 1821, lowering the rates and increasing service. By 1824, there were lines to London, Scotland, and France with the cost of passage running from $100 to $150. The whole organization of trade had changed. Trading houses that acted on commission had, by the second half of the nineteenth century, entirely superseded the individual merchant whose importance and methods had been steadily declining.

FOREIGN TRADE IN EMERGING INDUSTRIALISM

In the last half of the nineteenth century, America's total international trade expanded more than six times. Exports multiplied from approximately $150 million to a little less than $1.5 billion, and imports climbed less spectacularly from $200 million to a little over $1 billion. During the whole period, per

[9]Robert G. Albion, "Early Nineteenth-Century Shipowning," *Journal of Economic History*, Vol. 1 (1941).

capita foreign trade averaged about $23—about $10 more than in the previous 30 years. Merchandise imports and exports ran at a rate of 12 to 16 percent of the national income. The chief reason for this secular increase was the change from agriculture to industrialism in the domestic economy. Within the long-run movement, however, short-run ups and downs in volume were caused by war and severe downturns in the business cycle. For example, foreign trade plunged downward during the Civil War and in the great depressions of 1873 and 1893 but recovered rapidly as soon as peace and prosperity were restored.

The balance of payments, 1850-1900

The most striking feature of the era was the shift that occurred in the balance of trade. Between 1850 and 1875, there were 22 years of unfavorable balance and only three with a favorable balance. There was, by contrast, only one unfavorable balance in the years 1875 to 1900. In these years, merchandise exports greatly exceeded imports, but this was offset by shipping payments (which were now a debit rather than a credit item), insurance premiums, immigrant remittances, and tourist expenditures. The balance of payments was more often unfavorable than favorable, with the deficit being covered by an inflow of capital and an outflow of specie. In 42 of the last 50 years of the century, gold flowed out of the domestic economy, aggravating the chronic monetary problems of the era.

The composition of foreign trade

A radical change in the composition of foreign trade accompanied the radical change in the balance of payments. The whole turnabout was associated with the shift from agriculture to industrialism that proceeded rapidly after the middle of the century. Before 1900, the dollar volume of exported manufactures had come to exceed that of imported manufactures, even though total manufactured goods constituted in 1900 only 35 percent of total exports contrasted with 40 percent of total imports. Meanwhile, too, imports of raw materials had soared to almost 50 percent of all imports, whereas raw material exports, which were once the fulcrum upon which our international trade depended, had faded to a little more than 40 percent of the total. In the shift, cotton fell from its pinnacle just as tobacco had done two generations before. In 1900, cotton exports were almost $250 million; but instead of 60 percent of the total, they now constituted less than 20 percent. Breadstuffs were not far behind, with about 15 percent of all exports. Machinery occupied fifth place in the list of leading exports, accounting for about 5 percent of all merchandise shipped abroad. The days of one commodity's complete domination of the country's export market were over. True enough, some manufactured goods and some raw materials were of more than ordinary importance, but the aggregate export trade was made up of many commodities, each constituting only a small share of the whole.

Part of the decline of cotton was the result of the Civil War, but this was by no means the whole story. Even if the War had never occurred, other commodities would have rapidly overtaken cotton. The West was growing much faster than the South; and as transportation facilities were made available, the West shipped ever-increasing quantities of foodstuffs to the coast for shipment to Europe and the rest of the world. By the Civil War, the West was well on its way to becoming the bread basket of the world, but cotton had about reached the limits of its potential expansion. The Civil War did not cause the decline of King Cotton, but it accelerated it.

The decline of American shipping after the Civil War was even more precipitate than the fall of cotton. The American merchant marine declined absolutely as well as relatively, falling to almost four million tons by 1880. In the 1890s, the Federal government, in an effort to bring back the prestige of American shipping, again began to pay subsidies, but these were not large enough to close the gap between European and American ship construction and operation. To be sure, there was some recovery, and in 1900 the merchant marine, at about five million tons, was almost as large as it had been in 1860. However, it was not until World War I that American shipping showed a sizable increase.

THE UNITED STATES AS A WORLD POWER

Chart 21 gives a picture of total foreign trade in the twentieth century. The dollar volume multiplied 17 times. Goods and services moving out of and into the United States averaged $77 per capita. Total merchandise involved in American trade with the rest of the world ranged from 8 to 14 percent of the national income.[10] This was not high in comparison with the rest of the world. Foreign trade in the United Kingdom ranged from 20 to 55 percent of the gross national product. In Canada, the comparable percentage ran from 25 to 45 percent; in France, from 10 to 30 percent.

In the twentieth century, the volume of trade reflected the business cycle more than anything else. It began to move up in the 1890s despite substantial increases in the tariff in 1890 (the McKinley Act) and in 1897 (the Dingley Act). By 1913, volume was in the vicinity of $5 billion. During World War I, it more than tripled, reaching $17 billion in 1920, a record high that was not to be surpassed until World War II.

During the 1920s, foreign trade hovered around $12 billion a year, but

[10]All goods and services involved in international trade varied from 11 to 22 percent of the national income.

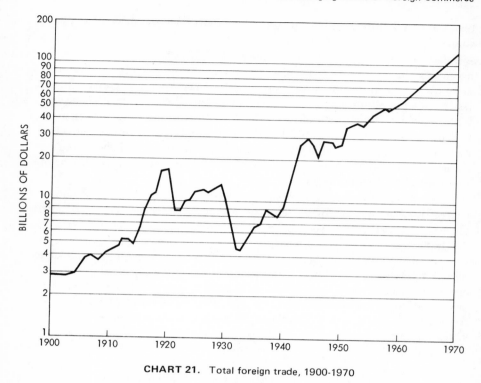

CHART 21. Total foreign trade, 1900-1970

during the depression of the 1930s it fell to the same level that had prevailed in the early twentieth century. Exports dropped to one-third and imports to one-half of what they had been. World War II brought a great resurgence and, unlike that of World War I, the rise did not stop with the end of the War. By 1950 foreign trade in goods and services alone totalled $25.8 billion, and in 1970, $122.2 billion. But in proportion to total production, it was much less important in the American economy than in other parts of the world. In 1970, imports and exports of goods and services equalled less than 10 percent of American GNP, but almost 40 percent of Canada's, 35 percent of Germany's and the United Kingdom's, and 25 percent of French product.

The balance of payments

The balance of trade was consistently favorable until the late 1960s. Exports ran far ahead of imports, and in most years the difference was not covered by services, such as shipping and insurance, or by invisible items such as tourist expenditures and immigrant remittances. During World War I, international finance became even more one-sided when the United States almost overnight changed from a debtor to a creditor nation. Under the pressure of the fight for survival, Europe imported vast quantities of food and munitions. Shipping services were not adequate to cover the deficit; immigrant remittances were of small help; and the tourist trade had stopped altogether. The balance on goods and services ran from $2 to $5 billion a year in favor of the United States. Gold flowed in at an unprecedented rate—over $500 million in 1916 and another $300 million in 1917. Because this was far from enough to balance the trade deficit, Europe borrowed heavily, and the United States emerged from the war a net creditor for about $3.7 billion. During the 1920s, the trend established by the War was accentuated. The merchandise balance ran very heavily in favor of the United States. Gold imports averaged $150 million a year, and, in addition, the United States invested about $1 billion a year abroad. By 1931, she was a net creditor for about $12 billion. The world, it was commonly agreed, was suffering from a "dollar shortage."

This dollar shortage occurred in spite of a far-reaching change in the organization of foreign trade and in international economic realtions that carried large amounts of dollars overseas. As foreign trade grew, industrial companies, especially sewing machine and farm machinery manufacturers and petroleum refiners, set up their own marketing organizations and invested in foreign-domiciled plants. By 1929, there were almost one thousand American branch houses abroad, representing an investment of something more than $350 million, and this did not include facilities for manufacturing goods or distributing petroleum.

During the depression of the 1930s, foreign trade collapsed, and America's favorable trade balance declined more than proportionately. At the same time, debtors defaulted on their debts, and widespread fear over Europe's future caused a record outflow of European gold. All these factors reduced the United States' creditor position. By 1940, we were once again in a net debtor position for about $1.3 billion.

Methods entirely different from those used in World War I were used to help the Allies in World War II. International finance had come to be more a matter of survival values than economic values. Lend-lease assistance, which was tantamount to a gift, was used instead of loans during the War; and after the War, the United States continued to provide assistance through UNRRA, the Marshall Plan, ECA, MSA, and FOA. But the favorable balance of trade climbed to cover $12 billion in 1944 and averaged about $7.5 billion for the next five years. During the war years, the United States used part of her gold to buy raw materials from neutral nations; but immediately after the War, gold imports averaged well over $1.5 billion a year. By 1949, the gold stock equaled almost $25 billion, twice what it had been in 1937 and six times that of 1929. The world, it was reiterated, was suffering from "a dollar shortage."

But then in 1950 the balance of payments turned unfavorable and, with one exception, it has continued that way. Merchandise exports continued to exceed imports, the balance ranging from a little less than $1 billion in 1959 to over $6 billion in 1957. Income from services and investment also exceeded outgo by $1.1 billion to $1.7 billion. Thus, the economy enjoyed a favorable balance of trade that ranged from $2.4 to $6.2 billion. All of this was more than consumed by government grants and loans, which gradually climbed from about $4.5 billion to $6.0 billion. In addition, American investment abroad drained the balance of payments, first by small amounts, then more substantially after 1955.

In the decade of the 1950s, the balance of payments was unfavorable by about $18 billion. We had increased our net creditor position to about $27 billion—about double what we had been owed in 1950—but we had lost $6 billion in gold. The gold stock in 1960 was only $19 billion, and its continuous decline was a source of severe aggravation to the financial community.

In the 1960s, the balance of payments continued to deteriorate. The deficit exceeded $25 billion, even though the balance of trade continued to be favorable. However, in the early 1970s, this too turned unfavorable.

BALANCE OF PAYMENTS, 1960-1970
(billions)

Trade balance	+$38.3
Income from services	+ 28.1
Transfers (private)	− 6.7
Transfers (government)	− 23.1
Investments	− 52.3
Errors and omissions	− 9.7
Balance of payments	− 25.4
Monetary movements	+ 25.4

SOURCE: International Monetary Fund, *Balance of Payments Yearbook,* 1964, 1968, 1972.

Shifts in the balance of payments were to some extent the result of government policy and activity. Traditionally, the government exerted some influence through tariffs and shipping subsidies, and in the last 20 years through a large volume of grants and loans. It is not easy to measure the effect of the Fordney-McCumber Act of 1922 and the Hawley-Smoot tariff of 1930 on the volume of foreign trade, for they both became effective at the same time that depressions were dealing a most severe blow to trade. The agreements that were instituted under the Reciprocal Trade Agreements Act of 1934 and its successive amendments reduced tariff rates over a period of time to about half of what they had been in 1930. But again, the effect of this on foreign trade is difficult to isolate.

Revitalized foreign competition was the chief cause of the shift in the balance of payments and finally in the balance of trade in the 20 years after 1950. Productivity, which had always been the secret of our advantage over other countries, ceased to increase faster than in other countries. Indeed, in some countries, notably Japan and Germany, productivity increased much faster than it did here. All of this presented the questions: were we following in England's footsteps? Would we become a service economy with our manufactures unable to compete in world markets?

The make-up and direction of foreign trade

Manufactured products continued to be of greater importance in our foreign trade in the twentieth century. Manufactures rose from 61 to 70 percent of all exports, and from 39 to 66 percent of all imports. By 1970, the seven leading exports (machinery, transportation equipment, electrical apparatus, metals, grains, chemical elements, and soy beans) made up almost 70 percent of all exports. Some of the same commodities appeared in the list of the seven leading imports (transportation equipment, machinery, metals, petroleum, clothing, coffee, and ores and scrap metals) which accounted for 55 percent of all imports.[11]

The shift from agriculture to industry also caused a shift in the direction of trade. Well over two-thirds of America's exports went to Europe in the nineteenth century; but, as the composition of exports changed, less and less went to Europe and more and more went to Canada, South America, and Asia. By the 1920s, Western Europe was buying less than 50 percent of American exports; by 1970, it was buying only 30 percent.

The trend in imports was equally striking. In the middle of the nineteenth century, about 70 percent of imports came from Europe and the remainder was scattered over three continents. By 1970, Europe was selling the United States about 30 percent of her imports; Canada provided 30 percent; South America, 12 percent; and Japan, about 15 percent. In the 1970s, trade with the United States accounted for 70 percent of Canada's total foreign trade. Canada's trade accounted for almost 50 percent of our total foreign trade.

The principal centers through which foreign trade was carried shifted with the westward movement and the transition from agriculture to industry. In 1820, New Orleans, because of the cotton trade, was first in exports, but it was a poor third in imports. New York, second in exports, was far ahead as an importer. Boston and its environs was third in exports and second in imports. By 1900, the pattern showed little change: New York, New Orleans, Galveston, and Boston were the four leaders in exports. New York, Boston, Philadelphia, and New Orleans were still the leaders in imports. In 1960, New York still led in both exports and imports, although its lead was markedly less. New Orleans, Galveston, Norfolk, and San Francisco followed New York in exports. Philadelphia, Los Angeles, New Orleans, and Baltimore followed in dollar volume of imports. Although not so spectacularly as in agriculture and manufacturing, the drive toward the West and South was also taking place in foreign commerce.

[11] Based on a three-digit breakdown.

SUGGESTED READINGS

(On specific topics, see the readings cited in the footnotes in the chapter.)

Harrington, Virginia, *The New York Merchant on the Eve of the Revolution* (New York: Columbia University Press, 1935).

Hutchins, John G. B., *The American Maritime Industries and Public Policy* (Cambridge, Mass.: Harvard University Press, 1941).

Johnson, Emory R., *History of Domestic and Foreign Commerce of the United States* (Washington, D.C.: Carnegie Institution of Washington, 1915).

Kuznets, Simon S., "Foreign Economic Relations," reprinted in Lambie and Clemence, *Economic Change in America* (Harrisburg, Pa.: The Stackpole Co., 1954).

North, Douglass, *The Economic Growth of the United States, 1790-1860* (Englewood Cliffs, N. J.: Prentice-Hall, Inc., 1961).

Taylor, Georege Rogers, ed., *The Great Tariff Debate, 1820-1830,* Amherst Readings in American Civilization (Boston: D. C. Heath & Company, 1953).

QUESTIONS

1. Was the influence of British mercantilism on the American economy completely bad?
2. What changes have occurred in the volume of American foreign trade, in the identity of the nations with which America has traded, and the composition of the trade?
3. Describe the changes that have occurred in the history of the balance of trade. Why did the changes occur? How have the deficits in the balance of trade been met? What do you consider to have been the effects of the shifting trade balance on the American level of living?
4. Was the clipper ship really important?
5. Draw a simple graph showing the trend of per capita foreign trade.
6. One of the striking features of foreign commerce has been the varying fortunes of American shipping and shipbuilding. What was the nature of this rise and fall, and what were the reasons for it?
7. How do you account for the relatively small role of international trade (as a percent of GNP) in America's economic history? Does this mean that international commodity, service, and capital flows have not had a significant impact on United States economic growth?
8. Discuss briefly the tariff history of the United States. Mention trends in rates, relation to wars, industries mainly affected, and arguments offered. How does the situation today differ from that after other wars?
9. Describe the long-term changes that occurred in the relative importance of crude materials and of manufactured goods in our imports and exports since 1830. Explain.
10. Describe the changes that occurred in the organization of foreign trade. Why did they happen?

Chapter Eleven

THE EXPANSION
OF DOMESTIC COMMERCE
BEFORE 1850

Domestic commerce or marketing, as it is now called, lagged behind foreign trade, but while foreign trade grew arithmetically, domestic trade expanded geometrically. The actual numbers describing trade are nothing more than guesses, but they do give some notion of the shift that occurred. Foreign trade in mid-eighteenth century was perhaps $10 million and domestic commerce as much as $8 million. In 1850, foreign trade was about $320 million, but internal trade on the waterways alone was estimated at $1.5 billion.

Trade loomed ever larger in every aspect of economic life. Distribution and the institutions it developed did much to determine where Americans lived, what they ate, and how they occupied their days. It so profoundly influenced the conduct of business enterprise that many authorities believe it to be the most important branch of business. All of marketing's contributions can be summed up by repeating what was said in the previous chapter on foreign commerce: an efficient system of distribution increased the scale of living by enabling people and geographical areas to benefit from the principle of comparative advantage. By specializing in those things that they could produce comparatively cheaply and by exchanging them for those things that others could produce more cheaply, individuals and groups of individuals increased their total output and thus attained a higher income. But effective specialization could exist only in a broad market area, for it would hardly pay an imaginative enterpriser to specialize in making tips for shoelaces unless there was a mass market for the product. Under specialization, moreover, producers no longer consumed what they produced. Thus, a mass market inevitably separated producers from consumers. It was the function of distribution to bridge this gap, and the crux of this problem centered around transportation.

THE MORPHOLOGY OF TRANSPORTATION

Today about 7.5 percent of the nonfarm labor force works in transportation, producing somewhat less than 5 percent of the national income. In 1870, transportation employed 5 percent of the labor force and produced something like 10 percent of the nation's income. Thus, like commerce in general, productivity in transportation has not kept pace with the fastest-growing sectors of the economy.

Yet, viewed in an absolute sense, transportation has made vast strides. As a nation moves from the primitive to the highly developed, the transportation of goods overland progresses through at least five phases. [1] First, goods are carried by human porters, then by pack animals, wagons, railways, and, finally, motor-driven vehicles. In addition, waterways, both natural and man-made, may be used. Each improvement in transportation represents a saving in time, money, and effort, and therefore contributes heavily to furthering economic progress and raising the level of living.

In the most primitive economy, efficient porters can carry 60 pounds for 15 miles a day. A line of porters at this pace can handle 1,450 ton-miles of freight a year. Such a method of transport does not lend itself to carrying bulky or perishable goods and, even at very low wages, the relative cost of transportation would be very high. Pack animals can carry two and a half times as much as humans; but, like human porters, they cannot transport bulky goods or carry perishable goods over long distances. Horse-drawn wagons offer a great improvement over pack animals, for even where roads are very poor, they can carry about ten times as much as a gang of porters. Improved roads considerably increase the speed and the load while lessening the possiblity of delay through breakdowns.

But human and animal power as means of transportation were insignificant in comparison with the railroad. Trains on a broad-gauge railway could carry 4,500 tons per hour, 22 hours a day, 365 days a year, or 3.6 million tons a year. With an annual capacity 240 times as great as a horse-drawn wagon, they vastly increased the market area that could be covered.

In their ability to carry bulky goods, waterways were equal to railways, and

[1] See the excellent analysis by J. Edwin Holmstrom, *Railways and Roads in Pioneer Development Overseas* (London: P. S. King and Son, 1934), Chap. 2.

they were originally far cheaper. Thus, where waterways existed, the potential market area was very large. Whereas a farmer could cover a market area of 40 miles by horse-drawn wagon over poor roads, he could cover 100 miles over good roads, 200 miles by railway, and 400 miles by waterway. But speed and convenience were also considerations. Traffic on natural waterways was cheaper than any other form of transportation, but railways were faster and more practical in the sense that they operated year round and could connect areas not traversed by waterways.

In early American history, when the economy was agriculturally oriented, the problem was to get farm products from the many widely scattered growers to the few marketing centers. Later, when industry replaced farming as the main economic pursuit, the problem was to get manufactured products from the few centers of production to the many scattered market areas. Intelligent observers early recognized that each improvement in transportation broadened the market area, making possible greater specialization and division of labor. They therefore urged the rapid construction of a systematic network of transport facilities to connect the major urban markets and to give the farmer an easier way of marketing his produce.

The advice of these farsighted commentators did not go completely unheeded. In the American experience, arteries of commerce were built in great haste, occasionally ahead of population and traffic and long before they could promise an adequate return on investment. Market factors—the weighing of costs against revenue—were important in determining where and when to build turnpikes, canals, and railroads. But these factors were by no means the only things considered. Indeed, they may not have been even the primary considerations. The gains from the productivity increases produced by marketing improvements were spread over the whole community. Consumers got more, producers got more, and the government got more. Consequently, an enterprising citizenry, impatient to get its goods to the market, clamored for more efficient and more dependable facilities regardless of the cost. Governments of different regions, locked with each other in an intense rivalry for the custom of different areas, sought victory by building better means of transport. Thus, as George Rogers Taylor has expressed it, there developed a sort of metropolitan mercantilism in which canals and railroads, rather than merchant fleets, were the chief weapons of warfare. However, the process, crude as it was, did much to raise the scale of living.

COLONIAL DOMESTIC COMMERCE

The colonies carried on very little domestic commerce. One of the reasons for the lack of a thriving domestic commerce was that each colony was an independent unit, priding itself on its own nationalism and erecting trade barriers to prevent competition from the other colonies, much as individual nations erected and still erect artificial barriers to prevent the free flow of goods in international trade. But the main reasons for the small volume of colonial internal trade were economic rather than political. The colonists did not have anything remotely resembling an orderly monetary system which would enable them to carry on trade in an efficient manner. Moreover, because of a sparse population and insufficient capital, they could not construct the transportation facilities that would have enabled them to exchange goods over a broad market area. Yet, in an effort to raise their level of living, colonists used, wherever possible, arteries supplied by nature—the Atlantic Ocean and the innumerable rivers and bays that ran through the Atlantic coastal plain. The large cities on the coast acted as marketing centers engaged primarily in the business of foreign trade and as a link between Europe and the interior. Outside the big cities were clusters of towns, each one serving an area limited to the distance that could be covered by horse and wagon. Although these towns were small and close together, they lived in relative isolation. The inhabitants of each area were much more concerned with getting to town than with getting from one town to another.

Where possible, goods were transported to the interior by water, for natural waterways were cheap and relatively convenient. Boats were small, which meant that almost any waterway or body of water was navigable. Boston, New York, and Philadelphia sent goods north and south along the Atlantic Coast. Baltimore had an outlet through the Chesapeake Bay. From all the big market centers, goods were transported via the Hudson, Delaware, Susquehanna, James, Savannah, and other rivers, large and small. But waterways could not carry goods to towns that were not located on navigable waters. The commerce that brought goods to these places traveled over broadened Indian trails by pack horse or shank's mare, and was so expensive that it discouraged trade and obstructed efforts to raise the level of living. It cost as much, for example, to ship goods 35 miles inland as it did to ship them across the Atlantic. To ship by pack horse from Philadelphia in eastern Pennsylvania to Erie in western Pennsylvania cost $250 a ton, compared with only $9 a ton to ship across the Atlantic. The cost of shipping a cargo from Pittsburgh to New Orleans by way of the rivers (2,000 miles) was less than the cost of sending the same cargo 60 miles by land. Even after the Colonial Period, Tench Coxe, one-time Assistant Secretary of the Treasury and prolific commentator on the passing economic scene, reported that many merchants spent one-fifth to one-half their costs for transport. During the blockade set up by England in the War of 1812, a barrel of New York flour that had cost 75 cents more in Boston when sent by water cost $5.00 more when sent by land.

THE TURNPIKE ERA

The American traveling across the country today can, with a little imagination, easily see the amazing progress that the development of transportation has contributed to the level of living. Today's modern highways offer little challenge. Driving over them is merely an incidental event in getting from place to place. But in the late eighteenth and early nineteenth century, traveling was a major adventure, featured by high cost and minimum comfort. At the time of the Revolution, it took a day and a half by fast coach to get from New York to Philadelphia. In 1825, it still took "only" two days from Boston to New York, 11 hours from New York to Philadelphia, five days from Philadelphia to Pittsburgh, and 15 hours from Philadelphia to Washington. So-called roads were streaks of dust in dry weather and a line of ruts and mudholes after a storm. Making a road in the pioneer days meant removing only large boulders and cutting down large trees, leaving stones, stumps, and the small wood. An act of the Ohio legislature in 1804, for example, provided that stumps left in the road should not be more than a foot high.

In 1800, there was only one good road in the whole United States: the 60-mile turnpike from Philadelphia to Lancaster, Pennsylvania. Completed in 1794 at a cost of about $7,000 a mile, it was much superior to the ordinary dirt road that was nothing more than a broadened Indian trail. A horse could carry 150 pounds over an ordinary trail but it could pull 1,500 pounds over a dirt road, and a ton over a turnpike. Freight costs over a dirt road were 30 to 70 cents a ton-mile and the pace was frustratingly slow. It cost, for example, $1,000 and took 115 days to ship a wagon load of goods from Augusta, Maine, to Savannah, Georgia. On the other hand, freight on turnpikes cost about 15 cents a ton-mile. The cost per 100-weight from Pittsburgh to Philadelphia was $9.50 in 1817; $6.50 in 1818. Passenger rates were 5 cents a mile in the 1820s.

Because they were quicker and cheaper and could handle more goods, turnpikes were built as fast as capital could be accumulated. In the decade after 1800, the halcyon years of Eastern turnpike construction, Pennsylvania chartered 86 companies that built over 2,000 miles of road at a cost of some $37 million; New York had 135 companies with 1,500 miles of road; and New England chartered 180 companies. By 1820, all the major cities in the United States had been connected by turnpikes, and wagon trains and stagecoach companies were feverishly active in carrying freight, passengers, and the United States mail. The first long step had been taken in making specialization effective. By 1830, when the first great era of turnpike building came to a halt, 15,000 miles of surfaced roads had been constructed in a little more than 30 years. More charters had been granted to turnpike companies than to any other form of business. Although most of them were financed privately by the sale of common stocks, governments also shared in the business, as they would in every later transportation development. Pennsylvania, for example, subscribed $1.9 million of the $6.4 million turnpike capital raised by 1822.

THE EARLY DEBATE OVER GOVERNMENT AID

Even before the Constitution, governments were contributing funds to build roads, bridges, and canals. In 1785, for example, Pennsylvania appropriated £2,000 for a road from Cumberland County to Pittsburgh. Almost from the beginning, too, governments on all levels gave philosophical encouragement to the whole internal improvement movement. Despite widely held laissez faire sentiments, there was surprisingly little debate over whether government should participate. What argument did take place centered around the question of which government—local, state, or Federal—should participate and what form the participation should take. State and city governments quickly became involved, with Pennsylvania, New Jersey, and the city of Albany being among the first to build turnpikes. But the Federal government initially acted through the states. When Ohio was admitted to the Union in 1803, Congress allocated to internal improvements 3 percent of the proceeds from the sale of public lands in the state.

The first great departure from this aloof attitude came in 1808. At that time Secretary of the Treasury Albert Gallatin, anticipating the imminent retirement of the national debt, proposed that future surpluses be used to finance a ten-year $20 million internal improvement program that would cover the country with a gridiron of turnpikes and canals. Ordinarily, Gallatin wrote, improvements might be left to "individual exertion," but in the United States there were two obstacles that only the general government could remove: "the relative scarcity of capital" and "the extent of the territory compared to the population." Although Gallatin presented his proposal in his usual painstaking and logical manner, it was too much ahead of its time. It was not adopted, but neither was it completely forgotten. It was resurrected in the years of great change that followed the War of 1812. The population explosion, the westward movement, the wave of nationalism, and the valiant efforts to found a domestic manufacturing system that distinguished the era enabled Henry Clay to formulate a comprehensive program which came to be called "The American System." One of the cornerstones of this program was the construction of internal improvements to extend the market area. Clay argued that in a new country, society might be ripe for public works long before individuals could accumulate the necessary capital. He contended that transportation facilities helped everyone, not just those who used them and those who invested in them. Society, Clay said, might reap rewards of 15 to 20 percent while investors might receive 3 percent or less.

The "American System" had some effect. The most famous turnpike of all, the Cumberland Road, was financed by the Federal government. This "National Road," now Route 40, followed the original trail from the Potomac to the Ohio that General Braddock had broadened into a so-called "road." The first strip was completed from Cumberland, Maryland, to Wheeling, West Virginia, in 1818. The cost was high—$13,000 a mile—but it cut in half both the time and the cost of shipping goods from Baltimore to Wheeling, the gateway to the West.

But the Cumberland Road was an exceptional piece of behavior by the Federal government. During most of the first half of the nineteenth century, the White House was occupied by Presidents who opposed Federal intervention because of deep-seated agrarian distrust of centralization or because of constitutional scruples. Madison and Monroe each vetoed bills for the financing of internal improvements, and Jackson's veto of a bill to construct a road from Maysville to Lexington, Kentucky is one of the most famous in constitutional history.

Yet, even though the dreams of Gallatin and Clay fell far short of realization, governments did contribute importantly to transportation construction. In the nineteenth century alone, they contributed perhaps as much as $760 million in cash and credit, not to mention substantial additional help through land grants, land surveys, and other means. But governmental aid came in an erratic fashion. It was never given where private enterprise was unquestionably adequate. It never followed a carefully formulated plan, but proceeded in a typically American pragmatic piecemeal fashion. For turnpikes, for example, government aid was much smaller than for canals. Pennsylvania's 30 percent was highest.

THE TURNPIKE'S LIMITED SUCCESS

Because turnpikes cut the cost and time of shipping goods by 50 to 75 percent, they were heavily used. A new industry of overland freighting sprang up. Hundreds of canvas-covered wagons, tugged along by double and triple teams of horses and oxen, pounded the roads from Salem and Boston to as far away as Augusta and Savannah. It was estimated that as early as 1814, 4,000 wagons and 20,000 horses and oxen were involved in domestic commerce over the turnpikes and roads of the United States. At the same time, stagecoach companies appeared in great profusion, 67 in Boston alone, to carry eager travelers in a wild ride from city to city. Thus, turnpikes encouraged specialization by making markets more accessible, mobility by making it easier for people to travel, and manufacturing by giving a great impetus to the wagon-building industry.

Good roads were much superior to the old country roads, but there were far more of the latter than of the former. Farmers were willing to accept the inconveniences of unbelievably bad roads rather than to make them fancy by an investment of scarce capital and labor, which they thought could be better used elsewhere. Moreover, the turnpikes, the best of all roads, still presented many severe problems. Costing anywhere from $1,000 to $15,000 a mile, they represented such huge sunk costs that it is questionable whether they were a good investment for a capital-sparse economy. To be sure, they increased productivity by cutting time and cost, but they were still expensive and time-consuming. At 15 cents a mile, it did not pay to ship grain or flour more than 150 miles. Some teams averaged only 20 miles a day or two miles an hour. It still took 26 days to ship goods from Boston to Baltimore, and a week from Philadelphia to Pittsburgh.

Turnpikes also fell far short of the anticipations of the entrepreneur and the capitalist. Like most means of transportation, they were not a good investment. In New England, for example, only a handful of the more than 200 turnpikes that appeared ever paid a reasonable return. The Lancaster Pike netted less than 3 percent; 5 percent was about as much as any earned. Heavy toll revenues were required just to meet the interest costs on the capital investment. But users of the toll roads were ingenious in figuring out ways and means to avoid paying tolls. When they approached a toll gate, they shifted to "shunpikes," alternate routes that charged no toll. Some shippers traveled after sundown, when toll collectors had gone home. The stagecoachaes, which were important to the turnpikes, also ran into financial difficulties. Aggravating rate wars, in which passengers were sometimes carried free, occurred frequently and always ended in the elimination of a large number of operators through consolidation or bankruptcy. Under the circumstances, toll revenues rarely met fixed costs, and even more rarely were they large enough to yield a profit. By 1825, the financial structure of the turnpikes was already very bad, and as competition from other means of transportation increased, the situation became so desperate that the states took over and the day of privately owned roads virtually came to an end.

WATERWAYS IN TRANSPORTATION

Natural waterways were the chief arteries for the commerce of the early United States just as they had been in colonial times. Producers living along navigable waters floated their goods on flatboats or keelboats downstream with the tide. Settlers in the Northwest Territory who lived near streams sent goods down the Miami, Wabash, and Ohio Rivers to the Mississippi and thence to New Orleans. Although the trip was dangerous, it was manageable and cheap, and downstream traffic was very heavy. Some keelboats were 80 or 90 feet long. Upstream traffic was something else again. Boats had to be poled or bushwhacked against the tide, a slow, tedious process that taxed the strongest backs. It took 20 to 30 days to send goods from Louisville on the Ohio to New Orleans, but it took 30 men more than three months to work a boat back from New Orleans to Louisville. Consequently, there was little upstream traffic, especially on the strongest-flowing streams. There were about 20 trips a year up the Mississippi, less than 10 percent of the downstream traffic. Shippers usually sold the boat as well as the cargo at the end of their trip and worked their way home as best they could.

Water traffic had some outstanding advantages over road travel. Waterways were a gift of nature and did not have to be constructed. Thus, they did not absorb capital and labor as road construction did. Moreover, water traffic was far cheaper than overland commerce. It was estimated, for example, that it cost seven times as much to ship flour by wagon as by water. But inland waterways also had glaring disadvantages. Traffic depended on the location of navigable streams, and waterways could be used only by those who were close to them. And, as has been already pointed out, upstream travel was virtually impossible. In addition, water was too slow for shipping perishable goods; and in most cases, rivers and streams froze in the winter, temporarily stopping traffic of any sort. Dependable navigation on the Mississippi-Missouri, for example, was limited to six months of the year. Western waterways offered an additional problem. They were too shallow, too winding, and too narrow for efficient use of sail. Canals alleviated some of the disadvantages and brought many more producers into market areas. The steamboat eliminated other disadvantages by increasing speed and at the same time enabling shippers to travel upstream as easily as downstream. But water traffic could never be flexible enough for maximum economic development.

STEAMBOATS ON THE RIVERS AND LAKES

Although steamboats had been built long before Robert Fulton ran the *Clermont* from New York to Albany in 1807, he was the first to demonstrate that they could be made a paying investment. Yet, like most innovations, it took some time for the steamboat to catch on. It was not until a decade after Fulton that steamboats became common on the Mississippi River.[2] As early as 1811, the *New Orleans* made the "voyage" from Pittsburgh to New Orleans, but the first trip by steam up the river from New Orleans to Louisville did not take place until 1815. The trip took 35 days, compared with 90 days on the old flatboat. At the same time, it took 32 hours to make the trip from New York to Albany on the Hudson.

The early steamboats were flimsily built and operated far below maximum efficiency. Constant improvement was inevitable. Once the monopoly that Ful-

[2]See Louis C. Hunter, *Steamboats on the Western Rivers* (Cambridge, Mass.: Harvard University Press, 1949), pp. 3-37 and 52-60.

ton and his associates had fashioned was broken, the efficiency of the boats improved, and transportation time fell significantly.[3] As early as 1824, one boat made the trip from New Orleans to Louisville in ten days. By 1850, it took only five days. Consequently, many goods formerly brought into the interior overland from Eastern markets were carried up the River. At the same time, the downstream traffic increased even more. Steamboating required little capital—a medium or large boat cost $20,000 to $60,000—and shortly steamers took over a larger and larger share of river and lake traffic. There were 69 steamboats with 14,000 total tonnage on the Mississippi in 1820; by 1850, there were 740, with a tonnage of 142,000. Total tonnage on the Great Lakes[4] and on the Mississippi was twice as much as all the shipping at New York, and the total tonnage on the Western waterways was almost as large as the total in the whole British Empire. Yet the older forms of water transportation not only failed to disappear, but continued to grow. In the 1820s, one could expect to see a keelboat arrive each day at Pittsburgh. By the late 1840s, three came in every two days. In 1816, almost 1,800 small boats came to New Orleans; by 1846 there were over 2,700. These small boats could serve the isolated areas better than the early steamboat, but in time small steamboats were developed, and they pushed out the flatboat and the keelboat almost completely.

In the early nineteenth century, no other single factor was more important than the steamboat in raising the level of living in the western United States. What it did to the cost of transporting goods was even more important than the time it saved. Before 1820, it cost $5 to ship 100 pounds to Louisville from New Orleans. With the steamer, the cost immediately dropped to $2, and by 1839 it was down to 62 cents. In the same year, it cost a passenger only $45 for excellent accommodations on the 2,000-mile trip from Pittsburgh to New Orleans.

Lowered transportation costs brought greater returns to the Western producer, encouraging him to increase his production. At the same time, the Westerner benefited as a consumer, for with steam, goods could be sent to him upstream much more cheaply and much more quickly. Coffee cost 16 cents more a pound in Cincinnati than in New Orleans in 1816, but only 2.6 cents more in 1830. On sugar, the difference per 100 pounds fell from $10.33 to $2.64. A barrel of Western pork that would exchange for 30 pounds of coffee in 1816 would buy about 52 pounds in 1830.

Better methods of river transportation also encouraged specialization among men and regions. The emergence of a marketing pattern that combined specialized economic activity and easily discernible streams of commerce may be dated

[3]Shreve broke the monopoly on the Mississippi before the Supreme Court (in 1824 in *Gibbons* vs. *Ogden*) held that the monopoly on the Hudson was in violation of the Federal government's control over interstate commerce.

[4]Steamboats accounted for 140,000 tons on the Great Lakes in 1860, but sailing vessels still had a tonnage of over 250,000. Steam did not surpass sail until the 1880s, and in the coastal trade not until the 1890s.

roughly with the appearance of the first steamboat on the Western rivers.[5] For the next two decades, this improved method of marketing enabled the West to ship most of its farm produce down the Mississippi to the South. The South shipped its products up the river to the West or up the Atlantic Coast to the Northeast and Europe in exchange for foreign or eastern manufactures. As the amount of traffic on the rivers increased, cities emerged as major or subordinate marketing centers. With more and more paddle wheels churning the Mississippi, New Orleans became the nation's leading export center. In 1807, the volume of goods received at New Orleans from the interior was hardly $5 million; by 1816, it was $9 million; by 1830, $26 million.

In 1810, Cincinnati, St. Louis, and Louisville were villages. In 1850, at the height of river traffic, three of the eight cities with a population of over 50,000 were on the Mississippi system. Cincinnati had a population of 115,000; St. Louis, 77,000; and Louisville, 43,000. The river ports were twice as large as the Great Lakes ports: Chicago, Buffalo, and Duluth.

The steamboat also had its unattractive side. The fastest traveled at a speed of only 15 miles an hour and, like all water traffic, it was very inflexible: it could not be readily adapted to changes in the volume of traffic. Shipping or traveling by steamboat was also dangerous. The average life of a boat on the Western rivers was five years, and 30 percent of all that were built before 1849 were lost in accidents.

For the most part, too, the business was unprofitable. To be sure, the *New Orleans* cleared $20,000 in a little over a year, but she charged $25 upriver and $18 downriver. Competition appeared very quickly, for steamboating required little capital, and when it appeared it was rough. Rate wars were a common Mississippi pastime, and attempts to maintain customers by offering more aesthetic services did not pay off. When the railroad invaded the West, the mortality caused by what Schumpeter called creative destruction became awe-inspiring.[6]

THE CANAL ERA

There were some canals in the United States in the eighteenth century, but the great era of canal building occurred in three waves between 1815 and 1840.[7]

[5]See Louis B. Schmidt, "Internal Commerce and the Development of National Economy before 1860," *Journal of Political Economy,* Vol. XLVII (1939); Douglass C. North, *The Economic Growth of the United States, 1790-1860* (Englewood Cliffs, N.J.: Prentice-Hall, Inc., 1961), Chap. 9.

[6]See Robert C. Toole, "Steamboat on the Rocks," *Business History Review,* Vol. XXXVI (1961).

[7]The relationship between canals and economic development has been best described in Carter Goodrich, *Government Promotion of Canals and Railroads, 1800-1890* (New York: Columbia University Press, 1960); and Carter Goodrich, ed., *Canals and American Economic Development* (New York: Columbia University Press, 1961).

During those years, almost $190 million was invested and over 4,000 miles were constructed, most of them in New York, Pennsylvania, and Ohio. By the decade of the 1850s, because of competition from the railroads, more miles of canals were being abandoned than constructed, and by 1880 almost 2,000 miles had been abandoned, leaving about 2,500 miles in existence.

Canals were extremely effective in reducing the costs of shipping goods. Tolls charged on canals varied from ½ to 3 cents per ton-mile, compared with 15 cents on turnpikes. In some cases, canals also reduced the time required for shipping goods; and at all times they offered a more convenient and less strenuous method of transportation. But with all their advantages, many obstacles had to be overcome before they could be constructed. Canals required a great deal of capital—much more, indeed, than was usually available from private investors. Most of them were therefore assisted in the years 1815-1860 by state, local, and Federal government grants of land and cash that amounted to almost three-quarters of canal investment. The Federal government gave four and a half million acres of land. It also subscribed, during J. Q. Adams' administration, to $2 million of stock in four companies. But state and municipal governments gave much more. They supplied almost 70 percent of the $190 million that was invested in canals in the years before 1860. In additon, they granted to canal companies tax exemptions, rights of way, and permission to conduct lotteries and to issue paper money—all this in an era usually regarded as one of the golden ages of *laissez faire*.

Besides the problem of raising capital, canal companies had to overcome some difficult construction problems. There were neither engineers nor big construction companies in the early nineteenth century. Consequently, experts in other lines of endeavor had to be enlisted to supervise canal work. The Erie Canal, for example, was built under the direction of lawyers, not engineers. Indeed, the Erie had to train its own engineers, and became known as a school for engineers. In addition to the scarcity of expert personnel, there was no excavating machinery. Canals had to be built by manual labor through forests and swamps.

Finally, canals, like all economic improvements, had to face obstacles arising from habit, tradition, sectional jealousies, and conflicting economic interests. Every economic improvement must hurt someone; and, in the last analysis, the question of whether the improvement will be accomplished or not depends on how much power the injured interests can wield. In the case of canals, the opposition was not strong enough to prevent their construction.

Canals were built in order to bring more producers into the market area served by waterways, and to bring hitherto inaccessible natural resources such as coal and iron into production. They were, therefore, constructed as feeders or links for the great rivers, bays, and lakes. At first, canals covered short distances, but "dreamers" had in mind a grand pattern: the construction of an all-water line from the Middle West to the Atlantic Ocean. The most logical method of accomplishing this was to connect the Great Lakes with the ocean in the East and with the Mississippi River system in the West. The cornerstone in this plan was, of course, the Erie Canal.

Among all the canals, the Erie was in a class by itself. Before its construction, there were about 100 miles of canals in the whole country. The longest canal was 28 miles long; the Erie would be 364 miles. More than any other canal, the Erie help to raise the level of living by reducing shipping costs, encouraging geographical specialization, acting as an incentive for other canal building, and inducing foreign investment in the United States. As Carter Goodrich has said, "The opening of the Erie Canal may be regarded as the most decisive single event in the history of American transportation."

The Erie opened an all-water line from New York to the Middle West and greatly reduced the costs of shipping. Prior to its completion in 1825, it cost $100 to ship a ton of goods from Buffalo to New York. The Canal immediately reduced this cost to $15 and eventually to $9. To put this another way, before the Canal the cost of transporting wheat from New York to Buffalo was three times the New York price; after the canal, it was one-quarter of the price. Great as this contribution was, it was almost equaled in importance by what the Erie did for geographical specialization and division of labor. It was the strategic factor in the growth of the Great Lakes cities: Buffalo, Cleveland, and Toledo. Much more important was its effect on New York. If there had been any doubt that New York would become the leading marketing center of the East, that doubt was removed by the completion of the Canal.

The Erie opened the Eastern markets to the grain belt of the Middle West, helping to accelerate the growth of commercial farming in the Middle West and of industry in the East. By thus encouraging specialization, the Erie helped to make possible a great increase in productivity and in total production.

The Erie also contributed indirectly to the nation's rising level of living. Costing $11 million, it was a tremendous financial success, paying for itself in ten years. It was so successful, in fact, that it encouraged other states to construct canals. Moreover, because British investors provided most of the capital, the financial success of the Erie encouraged further foreign investment, helping the United States to obtain capital more rapidly than would otherwise have occurred.

Once the Erie connected the Great Lakes with the Atlantic Ocean, it became feasible to build canals connecting the Great Lakes with the large Midwestern rivers. In 1832, the Ohio Canal, costing $3 million, provided a connection between Portsmouth, on the Ohio River, and Cleveland, on Lake Erie. The Illinois River was connected with Lake Michigan in 1848; in 1851 the Wabash Canal, the longest in the United States, connected Toledo and Evansville; and the Sault Ste. Marie, one of the world's busiest canals, was opened in 1855, providing a link between Lake Superior and Lake Michigan. The completion of this canal system provided a cheap waterway for shipping goods from the Mississippi Valley through the Great Lakes, along the Erie, and down the Hudson to New York. This inexpensive, all-water route from the West to the East was the opening chapter in a major transformation of the stream of commerce. Before the canals, East-West traffic was not economically feasible except for goods with very high specific value. After their completion, direct traffic offered greater advantages—advantages that the railroad was to make overwhelming. The canal system was also the initial event in the breakdown of the uneasy economic entente between the West and the South, which had depended so much on the Mississippi.

Not to be outdone by New York, Pennsylvania and Maryland engaged in feverish canal-building activity to maintain the competitive market positions of Philadelphia and Baltimore. Pennsylvania embarked on the almost unbelievable project of attempting to connect Philadelphia with the West 400 miles away through a complicated system of two canals, two portage railways, and a series of inclined planes. A horse railway carried goods from Philadelphia to Columbia on the Susquehanna (about 75 miles). A canal ran along the Susquehanna and Juniata Rivers to Hollidaysburg, from where a portage railway and inclined planes took the goods over about 35 miles of mountains. On the Western side of the Alleghenies, a second canal connected the Conemaugh River to the Allegheny and thence to Pittsburgh. Although the Pennsylvania "canal" enabled Philadelphia to hold some of its trade, it was never as successful as the Erie, and in 1857 the state sold it to the Pennsylvania Railroad at an enormous loss.

Meanwhile, other Eastern centers constructed canals to link up the many natural waterways along the Atlantic Coast. The Morris Canal connected the Hudson at Jersey City with the Delaware at Phillipsburg, and the Delaware and Chesapeake were connected by the canal of the same name.

Cheap as they were, canals were far from the most satisfactory means of shipping goods. They were subject to many natural disadvantages, such as floods and freezing weather, and travel was slow. In addition, they cost anywhere from $20,000 to $30,000 a mile to build—twice as much at it cost to construct turnpikes. Moreover, they were often poorly constructed, and maintenance costs were high. Therefore, although they greatly benefited society, they were not a good business investment and seldom provided an adequate return. The Middlesex Canal was typical. One of the first in the United States, it cost $554,000, raised by the sale of 800 shares of stock. In time, each share was assessed another $740, although the company did pay dividends of $30 a share annually in the boom years 1834-1837.

THE RAILROAD

Roads, canals, and the steamboat extended the market area and encouraged trade, specialization, division of labor, the growth of manufacturing, and a general rise in the level of living. But much could still be done, for, as important as all these improvements were, they still did not approach the ideal method of shipping goods and people. Too many producers were still outside the great market areas. Goods traveled slowly, and bulky goods could not be shipped easily. The railroad provided an answer to these problems.[8] It was fast; man, not nature, determined its location; it had a greater carrying capacity than other forms of transportation; it traveled in all sorts of weather; it could carry bulky goods; and it was immensely romantic.[9]

Yet, despite their decided advantages, it took a comparatively long time for railroads to get started. The early railroad promoters had to overcome the same obstacles faced by the canal builders. Those who had a stake in older forms of transportation opposed the new rival. Canal and turnpike owners feared that railroads would put them out of business; stagecoach operators and tavern owners thought that railroads would certainly cut their business. Eastern farmers though that the railroads would flood their markets with Western farm products. Then, too, there were the misgivings aroused by the human dislike for change. Some doctors warned of wholesale insanity and apoplexy, and a group of distinguished Boston physicians predicted that traveling by rail at 15 to 20 miles per hour would result in many cases of brain concussion. Those who followed a gloomy interpretation of God's will thought that if He had wished man to travel by railroad, He would have provided the rails. At least in one town, the city fathers accused railroad promoters of being subversive and refused them the use of town facilities for the purpose of publicizing a projected railroad on the ground that it was a satanic device. That man's essential resistance to change acted as a stumbling-block was more than clear to Oliver Evans, the multi-talented inventor. In 1809, he attempted to form a company to construct a steam railroad from New York to Philadelphia. In 1812, he wrote:

> When we reflect upon the obstinate opposition that has been made by a great majority to every step toward improvement; from bad roads to turnpikes, from turnpikes to canals, and from canals to rail-ways for horse carriages, it is too much to expect the monstrous leap from bad roads to rail-ways for steam carriages, at once. One step in a generation is all we can hope for. . . . I do verily believe that the time will come when carriages propelled by steam will be in general use. . . travelling at the rate of fifteen miles an hour.

But all these obstacles were minor matters and certainly would not have long delayed the coming of the railroad. The chief difficulty was the high cost of

---

[8]There is a voluminous literature on the railroads. Every major railroad has a history or two. There are also general histories on regional development. See, for example, Robert Riegel, *The Story of the Western Railroads* (New York: The Macmillan Company, 1926); Edward C. Kirkland, *Men, Cities and Transportation, A Study in New England History, 1820-1900* (Cambridge, Mass.: Harvard University Press, 1948).

[9]Most scholarly works do immense injustice to the rich color of the railroad. It has probably been best described by Stewart H. Holbrook, *The Story of the American Railroads* (New York: Crown Publishers, Inc., 1947).

construction—in most cases, at least $30,000 a mile—and the comparative scarcity of capital and capital funds. At the peak of extraordinary booms, it was not so difficult to find capital; but in depressions it was an almost impossible task to raise any money at all, and at such times, the phrase "indigestible railroad securities" became a cliché in financial circles. Even when funds were available, it was not easy to persuade their owners to invest enough to finance an efficient railroad. Railroads by nature were large-scale enterprises over which the individual investor had little control. Moreover, returns from some already established businesses were very high, discouraging many would-be investors from providing capital for a new and untried industry. So it was that John Stevens, in 1811 and again in 1815, applied for a charter to build a railroad in New Jersey, but he could not raise the capital. It was not until 12 years later that the Delaware and Hudson Canal Company ran the first steam railway.

Where the capital came from [10]

Despite all the obstacles, capital was raised in sufficient quantities to construct a railroad network in an amazingly short span of years. Enough money was raised to pay the $15 million cost of the Baltimore and Ohio, $30 million for the New York Central, and $25 million for the Erie. Funds were attracted in a variety of ways, depending upon the section of the country, the nature of the individual entrepreneurs, and the condition of the money market, which in turn depended on the state of the business cycle.

Private sources provided most of the capital that flowed into the early railroads, although the government contribution was by no means picayune. Most of the private funds came from domestic savings. Foreign capital was rarely important in initiating a venture, but substantial amounts poured in later. It is estimated that foreign capitalists owned about one-fifth of all railroad property in 1873 and perhaps one-third in 1890. Their holdings, it is said, amounted to about $50 million in 1850 and $250 million in 1870.

Railroad promoters depended, of course, on speculative capital. Construction ahead of population, which was the way some American railways were built, did not offer the kind of investment in which savings banks, educational institutions, and prudent trustees would entrust their funds. Promoters had to appeal to those who were willing to take substantial risks for a possible capital-gains windfall. Few early railroads sold bonds. They relied more on stock, most of which was sold on the installment plan or paid for in land, labor, and materials.

[10]See Jules I. Bogen, *The Anthracite Railroads* (New York: The Ronald Press Company, 1927); F. A. Cleveland and F. W. Powell, *Railroad Promotion and Capitalization in the U.S.* (New York: David McKay Co., Inc., 1909); Stephen Salsbury, *The State, the Investor, and the Railroad: the Boston and Albany, 1825-1867* (Cambridge, Mass.: Harvard University Press, 1967).

In seeking capital funds, no prospective investor was ignored. A part of the large fortunes accumulated by the merchant families of New England and New York was attracted by the prospect of a further increase of principal; but promoters also went after the $5 and $10 savers by peddling stock from door to door in the manner that funds are now solicited by the Community Chest or the Red Cross. Much railroad stock eventually proved worthless, but prices over the short run fluctuated widely, enabling some speculators to do quite well even while the majority lost everything they had invested. Many of the small fry subscribed to stock in exchange for a promise that a railroad would be built through their town or in close proximity. They did not really expect any direct financial return, and they were usually right.

Gradually, especially after governments took a hand, bonds became increasingly popular because of their superiority to stock in attracting distant investors. By 1850, bonds supplied most railroad capital, even in New England. The Philadelphia and Reading built in 1844 issued $6.6 million in bonds and $2.0 million in stock. Bonds were often sold at heavy discounts, or stock was thrown in as a bonus. Roads often paid enormous prices for money. Western roads, for example, sold 6 to 7 percent mortgage bonds at anywhere from 50 to 90 and sometimes included nine or ten shares of stock with every bond. At the same time, farmers in the same area were borrowing at 10 to 18 percent.

In addition to selling common stock and bonds, railroads were the first to issue preferred stock, a practice that began in the 1840s. Preferred stock was issued either to refund bonds or because it became necessary to pay a "guaranteed dividend." Rates varied from 3.5 to 30 percent, but 10 and 12 percent were not unusual. These early issues were cumulative and nonparticipating, but they had the same voting rights as common stock.

Railroad men also borrowed large amounts of short-term capital either on their own account or on the credit of the railroad. Naturally, financial intermediaries, investment bankers, and commercial bankers played a vital role in railroad financing. In the early days, the railroads were assisted by the Bank of the United States and by agents and correspondents of European houses that specialized in the export and import business and in foreign exchange. The firm of Winslow and Lanier became active somewhat later, and Morgan, Speyer, Fisk and Hatch, and Kuhn, Loeb, still later. Through their financial legerdemain, unusually able railroad entrepreneurs attracted much speculative capital from individual capitalists. Indeed, the ability to raise capital funds often distinguished able entrepreneurs from those who failed.

Other devices besides securities were used to raise capital. In the West, the construction-company strategy was very popular. Ordinarily, it worked somewhat in this way. The promoters of a railroad also formed a separate construction company, whose stock was sold to the public. The proceeds were used to buy the stocks and bonds of the "parent" railroad. The railroad bonds were sold to the public, and the stock was retained by the entrepreneurs in the hope of a capital gain. The whole maneuver seemed to be a piece of financial hocus pocus, but it did have a practical purpose. Railroad men were well aware that a construction company could attract capital from men who would not pay par for stock in a railroad where the chance for profit was low. Thus, the strategy had the advantage of enabling railroads to be built through sparcely populated areas; but it had the disadvantage of being enormously costly.

The most famous or infamous example of the use of a construction company appeared in the building of the Union Pacific Railroad. Because it was to be constructed across the Great Plains, its prospects for immediate prosperity were dim. One could not, therefore, realistically expect investors to buy Union Pacific stock at par. But Dr. Thomas Durant and his associates in the U. P. worked out a way to circumvent this difficulty. They formed a construction company, somewhat grandiosely named after the French financial institution, the *Crédit Mobilier,* to take over the building of the Union Pacific. The Union Pacific paid $90 million to the *Crédit Mobilier,* which in turn paid subcontractors $51 million. The difference of $39 million was not all profit, because some of the $90 million was in stock; but the actual profit was at least $14 million to $15 million, and this was not a mere bagatelle. As Professor Ripley put it, "$111 million of securities were issued in order to raise $74 million of cash to construct a railroad, which actually cost about $60 million."[11] Despite its cost, the road was poorly constructed. All this raises a number of questions: Should the road have been built if the market did not demand it? Were the railroads built ahead of demand? Were the profits exorbitant in the sense that they were in excess of what was necessary to call forth the efforts of the entrepreneur? To what extent was government help necessary? The answers to these questions depend on the individual's own evaluation of the circumstances. Certainly, however, the road would not have been built at the time it was built without the financial machinations of the entrepreneurs.

Government aid before 1850

When private capital did not flow freely, which was more often than not, railroad promoters were not averse to seeking financial assistance from governments. Indeed, many of them went to considerable lengths to get the government involved, using the argument that public aid to the railroads would benefit society more than it would benefit the railroad owners.

At first, governments responded with enthusiasm, but heavy financial losses and revelations of skulduggery, bribery, and graft on all levels chilled the initial ardor, and public aid stopped. Most state governments dropped out of the game in the depression of the 1850s, the Federal government quit in the 1870s, and most local governments had stopped giving aid by the 1890s.

[11]William Z. Ripley, *Railroad Finance and Organization* (New York: David McKay Co., Inc., 1923); Robert W. Fogel, *The Union Pacific Railroad* (Baltimore: Johns Hopkins Press, 1960).

It is not possible to state exactly how much governments contributed, because their assistance took many forms that could not be measured in cash. Governments made outright gifts, but they also subscribed to stock, much of which was lost. They also made loans, which were not all paid back. They guaranteed credit, an activity which was often a prerequisite for obtaining capital funds but on which no money value could be set. They remitted taxes, provided and paid for surveys, offered drawbacks (reduced rates) on tariffs, gave roads the privilege of issuing paper money, and made them gifts of land. The Federal Coordinator of Transportation in 1940 very conservatively estimated government assistance for the whole of American history, excluding the purchase of securities, at $1.4 billion, a large amount in absolute terms, but small in proportion to the total cost.

Before 1850, the Federal government provided much engineering assistance,[12] but its other aid to railroads was negligible. State and municipal governments, on the other hand, provided some $300 million, probably about one-third the cost of the pre-Civil War network. The nature and magnitude of this help varied from section to section. In New England, Massachusetts was the only state that contributed, although towns and cities were active. Government aid was much more important in the Middle Atlantic states. Most of the capital for the construction of the Erie Railroad, for example, came from government loans. The city of Troy built its own railroad. Pennsylvania, as part of its canal system, built two railroads, including the Philadelphia and Columbia, called the "first railroad undertaken in any part of the world by a government." In the Middle West, governments began with generous support, but this diminished abruptly because of heavy losses during the depressions of 1837 and 1857. Nevertheless, government aid made a substantial contribution in Ohio, Indiana, Illinois, and Michigan; and Missouri contributed almost as much to internal improvements as did New York.

Governmental assistance was far more important in the South than in any other section. Over half the cost of Southern railroads was paid by states, cities, and towns.[13] South Carolina subscribed for as much stock as did private investors. Maryland, Virginia, Georgia, and North Carolina paid for much more than half. The ways in which this aid was given varied widely. Tennessee provided funds for completing roads after the beds had been laid. Georgia and Virginia constructed roads and then turned them over to private operators. In most states, however, gifts and loans were made directly to the road. But no matter what form it took, government help was profoundly important. In 1840, the South, where government played the major role, had more railroad mileage than any other section, a phenomenon that was, to be sure, short-lived.

[12]On this little-published activity, see Forest Hill, "Government Aid to Railroads before the Civil War," *Journal of Economic History,* Vol. XI (1951).

[13]Milton Heath has estimated that governments supplied almost $150 million (56.7 percent by the states, 26.0 by municipalities, 12.6 by counties, and 4.7 by the Federal government). *Journal of Economic History,* Vol. X (1950).

Government assistance after 1850

The Jacksonian philosophy that prevailed in the early years of the railroads effectively prevented the Federal government from playing an important role in the construction of the Eastern roads. But in the 20 years after 1850, Federal aid became much more important. To be sure, the only financial help given by Washington was $65 million of loans to the Union Pacific and Central Pacific railroads, and these were first-mortgage loans which in time were paid off. They were greatly overshadowed by $95 million in state aid and $175 million in local help. However, the Federal government also made huge land grants, about 180 million acres in all. These grants, which were designed to encourage the construction of railroad lines through the vast, sparsely populated West, were for 100 feet of right of way and six square miles on alternate sides of the track before the Civil War, and for 10 miles in the states and 20 miles in the territories after the War. One road, the Northern Pacific, got a grant of 20 miles in the states and 40 miles in the territories. Seventy railroads shared in the government's largesse. Four (Northern Pacific, Santa Fe, Southern Pacific, and Union Pacific) received 73 percent of the total. Immense as the grants were, however, they contributed to less than 20,000 miles, or only 8 percent of the country's total railroad mileage.

Land grants gave an immense psychological impetus to railroad building. They nourished the promoters' usual optimistic belief that any road would pay. It came to be assumed that free land meant the difference between a tidy and a vast fortune. The success of the Illinois Central, which received the first land grant, buttressed this feeling. But in most cases the faith in land grants was a delusion, for the roads were not able to sell land quickly enough to meet construction costs. It is true that the Illinois Central sold $15 million of its land within one year of its construction, but it was fortunate because it was located where land was in great demand. The Central Pacific, on the other hand, sold only $100,000 of land, and its experience was more typical. Thus, the grants failed to fulfill the principal goal that the government had in mind. But the misinterpretation of what the land grants would do also accelerated the building of a Western railroad system. Attracted by the prospect of profits from land grants, many entrepreneurs rushed in to build railroads long before railroads would ordinarily have been constructed. Moreover, in their anxiety to turn their lands into cash, railroad companies engaged in aggressive and elaborate sales campaigns here and abroad. They publicized and advertised. They sold on credit at prices ranging from $1.25 to $20 an acre. Although the money did not roll in, settlers did, and the West was populated more quickly than it would have been without the land grants.[14]

[14]The land policies of the railroads have been painstakingly covered in a series of histories. For a general summary, see W. S. Greever "A Comparison of Railroad Landgrant Policies," *Agricultural History*, Vol. 25 (1951); on the land grants themselves, see Lloyd J. Mercer, "Land Grants to American Railroads: Social Cost or Social Benefit?" *Business History Review*, Vol. XLIII (1969).

The Eastern roads were not built ahead of population; some middle western roads and most western roads were. Since the Western railroads were built sooner than would have happened in an economy directed solely by market forces, construction was usually very sloppy and inefficient. Emphasis was on speed, not stability, and many of the Western roads had to be rebuilt shortly after their original construction. To those who believed that the market should be the sole determinant of economic development, and that economic progress should be slow, steady, and "unwasteful," the land grants were, on balance, economically harmful. Those who emphasized the short run and believed that speed was of the essence thought the land grants made a most significant contribution to economic development.[15]

The pattern of railroad development

Because of the general lack of capital, the importance of water travel, the low density of population, and the primitive state of technology, railways were at first considered to be no more than a set of improved roads that could act as feeder lines for waterways. But this idea was quickly abandoned as railroads began to cut into canal business. By the 1850s, the whole notion had been dropped. By then, railroads were recognized as the most important form of transportation. Railroad construction in the East became very active. Construction on the Baltimore and Ohio, the first common carrier in American railroading, began in 1828. When the line opened in 1830, there were only 23 miles in the whole country. By 1840, there were almost 3,000 miles; but the longest line, the Central of Georgia, extended less than 200 miles. In the 1840s, construction picked up, and railroad mileage measured 9,000 miles in 1850. At the same time, there were about 3,700 miles of canals.

In building the early railroads, the general idea was to broaden the market area by linking producers of raw materials, manufacturers of finished products, importers and exporters in the harbor cities, and consumers in the large urban centers. Thus, in the East, the main lines connected the large market cities with one another and with the transport facilities of the interior. The first railroads connected Baltimore with Washington and with the Ohio River, Charleston with the Savannah, the Chesapeake and Delaware Bays, the Delaware and Hudson Rivers, Boston with the Hudson, and so forth. In the Middle West, railroads were constructed to carry goods east and south to be exchanged for finished products. Beyond the Mississippi, the goal was to link the Pacific Coast with the Middle West by means of transcontinental lines. The railroad pattern, when it was finished, resembled an intricate latticework in the East and a series of horizontal lines beyond the Mississippi.

[15]On the question of building ahead of population, see the excellent study by Albert Fishlow, *American Railroads and the Transformation of the Ante-Bellum Economy* (Cambridge, Mass.: Harvard University Press, 1965).

The primitive nature of the early railroads

Because of the lack of capital, railroads, like agriculture and manufacturing, first developed extensively; intensive development came much later. Most early railroad promoters had two alternatives. They could concentrate what little capital they had or they could spread it thinly; they could construct short, well-built railroads, or long, poorly built railroads; they could look to the long run and use a great deal of capital per mile, thereby keeping annual maintenance costs low, or they could favor the short run by using less capital per mile at the expense of high annual costs. Most early railroad builders followed the latter strategy. They constructed a railroad network with incredible speed; efficiency and safety were left for later. Economically, this was a wise decision, for it was better to have many "poor" roads than too few good ones.

In retrospect, one may wonder why human beings entrusted their lives and their goods to the early railroads. The first railroads were often a peril to life, limb, and property, as well as being unpredictable and uncomfortable. But the railroad, unlike its only rival the horse, could be improved. Its potential was stupendous, and in time it realized its potential.

It could be suggested that most early railroads were poorly built because the builders were sloppy or because promoters were engaged in gigantic swindles, but the fundamental reasons were that capital and capital funds were scarce and that technology and engineering skills were comparatively primitive.

In New England, where capital was not so scarce and where lines were short, the first railroads were built to last forever. Some roadbeds were laid on granite and had no elasticity. On one road, the Boston to Lowell, granite crossties were used. These experiments with native granite did not work out well, for they resulted in excessive wear and tear on the equipment. In other sections of the United States, however, railroad construction ran to the other extreme. Fixed capital outlays were kept low even though this meant high operating costs. In order to save money, and because they didn't know any better, engineers followed existing trails instead of making new ones. Consequently, sharp curves, steep grades, and winding courses were characteristic. Roadbeds were defective, tracks were poorly laid, and locomotive and rolling stock were not even reasonable facsimiles of the luxurious affairs of today. For example, the first practical locomotive, which appeared in 1831, weighed only three and one-half tons.

In order to save iron, wooden rails faced with a strip of iron were sometimes used, but not with the best of success. Under the weight of cars, passengers, and freight, the iron stripping came loose, penetrated the floor, and sometimes impaled an innocent passenger to the wall. Locomotives were feeble affairs in which no one had confidence. Some road operators, resigned to the likelihood of breakdowns, kept relays of horses along the track. Sometimes passengers were even requested to get out and push to get the train started. Some railroads experimented with sails, and the mechanically minded patented many gadgets intended to give locomotives more traction.

Poor construction also posed aggravating traffic problems. Lacking capital, most railroads were single-track with sidings at convenient distances. But there were no signals, and time was in a state of chaos. Each road presumably ran by the time of its terminal city. Actually, trains started when the spirit moved the engineer. In the absence of a signal system, and because of the curves and sharp grades, it was not easy to know the whereabouts of a train at any given moment. Only the fact that speeds were slow prevented a constant stream of accidents, but even at speeds of less than 15 miles per hour, fatalities were heavy. By the 1850s, railroad accidents were so common that they became a national scandal. There is no way of telling how many accidents there were, for records were not kept until 1891. During that year, 7,000 were killed, including 300 passengers and 2,700 employees. Thereafter, the historical trend was steadily downward. There were less than 4,000 fatalities in 1950 and less than 2,500 in 1970; and of these, almost 1,500 were the result of automobile-grade crossing accidents.

Derailing, collisions, impalement, and physical exertion by no means exhausted the list of indignities suffered by railroad passengers on the first American railroads. Locomotives burned wood, and sparks flew in all directions, including on the passengers. In a superlative outburst of misguided provincialism, many states passed laws and railroads adopted policies under which gauges varied so widely that cars could not be shifted from line to line. New England and the Middle West used the English standard (4 ft. 8½ inches). Five feet prevailed in the South, although some used a six-foot gauge. Confusion reigned in the Middle Atlantic states. Consequently, passengers and freight were constantly "changing," even though traveling short distances.

THE ORGANIZATION OF DISTRIBUTION

Selling goods before 1850

Distribution requires not only transportation facilities, but also organizations of businessmen to provide the mechanisms through which goods may be exchanged. In addition to railroads, trucks, roads, and waterways, distribution requires a variety of wholesale and retail outlets and ancillary services, such as advertising, to expedite the transfer of goods from the producer to the consumer.

Trade is an immense business. Wholesale and retail selling account for over 15 percent of the national income and employ almost 20 percent of the labor force. This was not always the case. In 1870, trade employed only 6 percent of the labor force, although it accounted for about the same percent of the national income as it does today. Its importance in the economy was probably much lower during the Colonial Period and in the early decades of the nineteenth century. According to one estimate, trade originated only about 5 percent of the national income and employed perhaps 4 percent of the labor force in the early 1800s.[16]

In the late eighteenth century, the distributive organization was very amateurish as judged by today's standards. But it nevertheless fulfilled its function of serving an economy characterized by small population, primitive transportation facilities, a crude money system, and household industry. At that time it was not uncommon to find one firm occupying all the steps between production and consumption. It handled wholesaling and retailing and all the ancillary institutions connected with distributions. Thomas Hancock, for example, was an importer, wholesaler, retailer, and banker. Like all the merchants of his time, he dealt in all manner of goods and services. He had many different interests and fulfilled many different jobs.[17] But gradually, merchants began to specialize in one or a few commodities—metals, for example. There were two main reasons for this evolution: the market was continually expanding, and with its expansion, diversified trade needed more capital than was practical. Specialized houses stepped in and took over each of the subordinate steps in trade that had previously been handled by one merchant. Before the nineteenth century was very old, the organization of wholesaling had become quite complicated. Sedentary merchants in the large seaport cities continued to import goods and sell them for their own account, but they dealt in fewer lines. In domestic trade, wholesalers (commission merchants and selling agents) disposed of goods made by foreign and domestic producers. Jobbers, whose function was to handle smaller lots than the wholesaler, vended dry goods to country retailers. Factors, who were already thriving in colonial times, financed producers and acted as agents in the sale of goods, especially cotton and cotton textiles. Wholesalers of one type or other occupied the strategic link in the chain of trade; it is not too much to say that because of their position, they dominated business in the first part of the nineteenth century.

The usual trade channel for foreign goods was from the importer to the wholesaler, to the jobber, to the retailer, to the consumer. But the auction system flourished from the end of the War of 1812 to about 1830. It was most widely used in distributing imported goods, for British manufacturers resorted to it in an effort to destroy American manufacturing. As Lord Brougham said, "It is well worth while to incur a loss upon the first exportation in order, by the glut, to stifle in the cradle those rising manufacturers in the United States which had been forced into existence, contrary to the natural course of things." Auctions were, however, also used to sell domestic manufactures. Under the auction system, producers sold their goods through agents to retailers who came to the

[16]Theodore Marburg, in *Trends in the American Economy in the 19th Century,* National Bureau of Economic Research, *Studies in Income and Wealth,* Vol. 24 (Princeton, N.J.: Princeton University Press, 1960).

[17]W.T. Baxter, *The House of Hancock* (Cambridge, Mass.: Harvard University Press, 1945). See also Virginia D. Harrington, *The New York Merchants on the Eve of the Revolution* (New York: Columbia University Press, 1935), Chaps. 2 and 3.

market cities about twice a year. The system was especially economical for British producers who had a large volume of goods to sell, for eliminating the importer and the jobber could save as much as 25 percent of the costs of distribution.

So long as imported goods were so predominantly important, and so long as retailers continued to come to the Atlantic seaboard cities in large number, the auction system worked very well. But when domestic production began to catch up to foreign production, and when competition forced producers to adopt more aggressive selling methods, the auction system began to fail. Cincinnati and St. Louis developed as wholesale centers in the late 1840s, and as wholesaling became established in the West, Western retailers no longer found it necessary to take the long journey east to buy goods. Moreover, by buying at private sale rather than at auction, buyers could obtain better credit terms.

Although wholesale trade was already specialized in the early 1800s, it took longer for most retail trade to become similarly specialized. Because of poor transportation facilities, most domestic trade in the Colonial Period was conducted in limited market areas and, because of an inadequate money system, usually by barter. Ordinarily, buyers and sellers traded directly, and much business was transacted at weekly and semiweekly public markets. The smaller volume of trade that was conducted over wider distances was usually handled by peddlers who owned one or two pack horses and traded goods for goods, carrying as much as $300 worth of merchandise on one trip. It would be wrong to belittle their contribution. They played an especially important part in the brass, clock, silver-plate, and hardware industries. Traveling along remote trails, they called on the farmers in outlying regions, trading pots, pans, thimbles, needles, and other things for farm products, rags, and other articles. Occasionally, these petty capitalists were large-scale operators, employing as many as 200 horses and 100 men and supplying trading posts and country stores in the outlying areas with goods from the market centers on the Atlantic Coast. Both the peddler and the community market have survived to the present day, but by the early nineteenth century, they had already been surpsssed by the small-town general store and the city specialty shop. As early as 1840, there was one store for every 300 people, which meant a severe curtailment of the peddler's opportunities.

As its name implied, the general store sold a wide variety of goods, for the demand for any one commodity or class of commodities was not large enough to permit specialization. Except in the large cities, retail stores carried a miscellaneous stock of imported manufactures, tropical goods such as sugar and spices, and the staples of the surrounding country. Thomas Ashe's description of a Western Pennsylvania store in 1806 would apply equally well to any frontier retail store at a later date:

> These storekeepers are obliged to keep every article which it is possible that the farmer or manufacturer may want. Each of their shops exhibits a complete medley; a magazine where are to be had both a needle and

an anchor, a tin pot and a large copper boiler, a child's whistle and a pianoforte, a ring dial and a clock, a skein of thread and trimmings of lace, a check frock and a muslin gown, a frieze coat and a superfine cloth, a glass of whiskey and a barrel of brandy, a gill of vinegar and a hogshead of Madiera wine.[18]

Although the general stores carried a wide variety of articles, their total stock was quite small. Many stores occupied only a few square feet, and a box or a chest held the entire stock. The stock of luxuries or finery was especially small, because the demand for them was limited, because it was difficult and expensive to transport them, and because the store owner did not think the turnover large enough to warrant putting much money into them.

Usually, the general store proprietor went in person to the large market cities—Philadelphia, Baltimore, and New York, in the early nineteenth century, and also to Cincinnati and St. Louis around the middle of the century. He bought goods at auction or from wholesalers on very liberal credit terms, usually six months, payable in 12, with interest at 6 to 10 percent after six months. The cost in time and money for this annual or bi-annual visit was very high. It cost, for example, $300 and took anywhere from one and a half to three months for a merchant to make the trip from Cincinnati to Philadelphia around 1820. The average country store did about $15,000 to $20,000 worth of business a year, but sales ran as low as $1.25 a day and as high as $60,000 a year. Because the operation was so small, markups had to be very high—25 percent was insufficient, 50 percent was fair, but prosperity required 75 percent.[19]

Business depressions, the appearance in the 1840s of credit agencies, and the Civil War changed the terms of credit. Francis Skinner & Co., prominent selling agents, illustrated what happened. At first, they sold on eight to nine months credit. After the panic of 1857, they cut the time to four to eight months, and in the Civil War they reduced it to 30 days.

Most country stores' trade was conducted on a barter basis, but there were certain "cash articles" that could not be bought except with money. These included tea, coffee, leather, iron, powder, and lead. But linen, cloth, feathers, beeswax, deerskins, and furs were regarded as money when offered by the would-be purchaser. Because of the prevalence of barter, storekeepers had little cash, but wholesalers and manufacturers accepted as pay the goods that the storekeepers had acquired in trade, and the storekeeper disposed of any surplus by shipping it down the river to a commission merchant. In time, of course, this practice of barter between the retailer and the wholesaler became outmoded, but

[18]Quoted in Fred Mitchell Jones, *Middlemen in the Domestic Trade of the United States, 1800-1860* (Urbana, Ill.: University of Illinois, 1937), p. 44.

[19]For the Western general store, see Lewis E. Atherton, *The Pioneer Merchant in Mid-America* (Columbia: The University of Missouri, 1939). For the Southern general store, see Lewis E. Atherton, *The Southern Country Store, 1800-1860* (Baton Rouge: Louisiana State University Press, 1949), and Thomas D. Clark, *Pills, Petticoats and Plows* (Indianapolis: The Bobbs-Merrill Company, Inc., 1944).

it was still common in the late 1830s and had not completely disappeared by the 1850s.

Transactions in frontier stores were more often than not a matter of bargaining between the store owner and the shopper. In the sale of specialized products like dry goods, haggling was universal. On basic commodities, many stores followed a one-price policy; but in places where a proprietor had a monopoly position over a relatively wide area, it was customary to bargain. In such extreme cases, something as basic as coffee sold anywhere from 25 cents to $1.25 a pound, depending on the financial status of the buyer.

There was little competition among stores, chiefly because few storekeepers were interested. There was no price competition, because the general stores usually had a monopoly in the small, local market areas. To most storekeepers, nonprice competition seemed pointless because of the shortage of goods. If the supply was limited, there was no reason to make any special effort to drum up demand by the usual strategies of product differentiation, such as special packaging, service, advertising, and emphasis on brand names. But more alert, more talented, more aggressive merchants realized that imaginative merchandizing could persuade consumers to buy more or to save less, and they acted accordingly.

The general store, even though primitive, made a solid contribution to the rising level of living. In every small town, especially on the frontier, it was an economic and social institution, as important as the church and probably more important than the school. The country-store proprietor was an unusually influential citizen. No specialist himself, he enabled others to specialize. He was often banker as well as merchant. By buying goods on long-term credit and selling them to customers on open-book account, he brought capital to the outlying regions from the better-developed areas. To be sure, the system was very expensive. Prices were about twice as high as back East, but this was the price that had to be paid for small-scale operations, the large volume of credit business, and the high cost of shipping goods.

In the big cities, these disadvantages either did not exist or were much less important, thus permitting specialized retailing to develop fairly early. Certainly, by 1850, the general store had disappeared in the large cities. As early as 1650, Boston had apothecaries and tobacco shops. By 1750, there were wine, grocery, and book shops and a millinery, a seed, and a window-glass store. And by 1850, the cities had books; boots and shoes; carpetings; china and glassware; clothing; combs and fancy goods; cutlery and hardware; dry goods; feathers and mattresses; furniture; "gent's furnishings"; hats, caps, and furs; hosiery and gloves; house or kitchen furnishings; india rubber goods; laces and embroideries; saddles, trunks, and harness; silks and ribbons; tea and coffee; tobacco and snuff; upholstery; watchmaking and jewelry.

To advertise what was for sale, there were in the early 1700s at least seven newspapers, half the contents of which were advertising. In 1850, there were 200 papers.

SUGGESTED READINGS

(For suggested readings, see the next chapter.)

QUESTIONS

1. Why did domestic commerce develop so much later than foreign commerce?
2. No factor was as important in American economic development as the "Transportation Revolution." Comment.
3. How important were Federal land grants in building the Western railroads? How were these grants made? As a taxpayer in the 1860s, would you have objected to the land grants?
4. Contrast the building of the Eastern railroads with the building of Western railroads.
5. Which was more important in its influence on the American standard of living—the turnpike, the canal, or the railroad? Why?
6. Did turnpikes pay? Did canals pay? Did railroads pay?
7. A well-known economic historian has said that the opening of the Erie Canal may be regarded as the most decisive single event in the history of American transportation. Do you agree or disagree, and why?
8. Discuss the most important business problems of early railroad development.
9. Comment on the following statement: Vanderbilt made no contribution to economic development because he never built a railroad; on the other hand, the promoters of the *Crédit Mobilier* built a railroad and thus advanced economic progress.
10. From what sources did the early railroads obtain most of their capital funds? Was this typical of other businesses of the period? What were the reasons for the relatively slow growth of mileage in the early history of the railroads?

Chapter Twelve

DOMESTIC COMMERCE
SINCE 1850

THE GROWTH OF THE RAILROADS AFTER 1850

Railroad construction first emerged as a spectacular enterprise in
the 1850s. At the beginning of the decade, no Western city had
direct connections with the Atlantic Coast. The Erie, in 1851, was
the first to reach the Great Lakes. In the following year, the Pennsylvania completed its route from Philadelphia to Pittsburgh, and
in the year after that a direct connection opened between Chicago
and New York. By the end of the decade, over 20,000 miles of
road had been completed—more than twice as much as the total
in existence ten years before. From then until the end of the
century, interrupted only by the Civil War and the great depression of the 1870s, track was laid at a phenomenal rate. The
Union Pacific and the Central Pacific, forming the first so-called
"transcontinental railroad," met at Promontory Summit, Utah, in
1869. The Northern Pacific reached the Coast in 1883, and the
Atchison, Topeka, and Santa Fe in 1887. By 1890, the nation had
164,000 miles of railroad—more than five times as much as there
had been 30 years before.

After 1890, by one criterion or another, railroad expansion
slowed down. To be sure, rails continued to be laid. The Great
Northern reached Seattle in 1893, and the Chicago, Milwaukee,
and Saint Paul, the last of the transcontinentals completed its

route in 1909. But the pace of construction was more leisurely than it had been. For two generations, the railroads had put down track faster than the growth of population. But this was no longer true after 1890. The proportion of rails to population reached its peak in that year, when there were 2,600 miles of road owned (that is right of way, whether single, double, or triple track) per one million of population. The peak of building came in 1887 with 12,900 miles. The high in total miles covered came in 1916, at 254,000. Total track reached a record high in 1930, when it passed 425,000 miles. That the railroad industry was in state of decline became quite obvious during the Great Depression. Since 1930, some 40,000 miles of track have been abandoned. In proportion to population, total mileage is about the same today as it was in 1870, and in the older states there is less mileage today than there was in 1900.

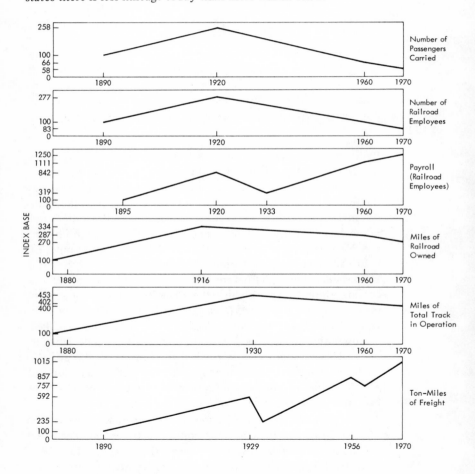

CHART 22.   The growth and maturity of railroad transportation.

Other criteria show the same picture of decline. In 1890, almost 750,000 people—1.8 percent of all the employed—were working on the railroads. This army continued to increase until 1920, when railroads employed over two million, or almost 3 percent of the working force. In recent years, total railroad employment has been cut back to the 1890 level and represents less than 1 percent of the labor force.

Despite major attrition in the number of workers, freight handling has stood up very well, for no other means of transport has been able to surpass the practicality and efficiency of rail in carrying bulky goods. Except for recession and depression, which cut business substantially, and war, which increased business abnormally, the railroads steadily increased their freight business until recently, when that, too, began to erode. In 1947, rails carried almost nine times as much freight as in 1890. In the 1950s freight traffic declined, but it more than recovered in the 1960s. Passenger traffic, as everyone knows, has had a much more woeful experience. Early railraods counted on passenger traffic for one-quarter to one-third of their revenue. But from the beginning, passenger service advanced much more slowly than freight, and from 1920, because of the automobile, it began to fall absolutely as well as relatively. Today's railroads carry fewer passengers than in 1890, but they carry them much farther, some 20 billion miles—about as much as in 1904 but less than half as much as in the peak year, 1920.

TECHNOLOGICAL ADVANCE

Some substantial improvements in railroad construction and operation had taken place by the middle of the nineteenth century. The 1830s brought the bogie truck, which helped locomotives stick to the rails, and the equalizing beam, which equalized pressure on the drive wheels and prevented uneven wear much as wheel balancing does on today's automobile. The 1842 tariff encouraged large-scale domestic iron production, and iron rails soon began to replace wooden ones. Locomotives were rapidly improved as more information about the principles of friction and traction became available. A spark arrester appeared in 1845, and signal systems, double tracking, and the first bridge over the Mississippi in the 1850s. But even greater changes came after the transition from extensive to intensive development that occurred in the late years of the nineteenth century. Then some of the capital funds that had previously been invested to extend the railroad system began to be used to improve existing systems. Greater emphasis was placed on increasing the size of cars, the pulling capacity of locomotives, and the safety of the whole system.

The extensive stage of railroad development had improved the level of living by connecting producers and consumers; the intensive stage improved the level of living by making the connecting links speedier, safer, and more efficient. To be sure, this was not entirely the work of the railroads. Occasionally, as was illustrated by the rather hesitant acceptance of the air brake and the automatic coupler, it took some serious urging by the government to overcome the railroads' reluctance to spend money on improvements that did not produce direct and immediate revenue.

The chaos of different gauges was still prevalent in 1870, the steel rail was still not common, a locomotive's traction power was about 15,000 pounds, an average coal car could carry 10 tons, freight trains traveled at a maximum speed of 15 miles an hour, and passenger trains sometimes attained 20 miles an hour. Today's locomotive has a traction power of over 66,000 pounds, the capacity of a freight car is 60 tons, and trains travel at 60 to 90 miles an hour. Much of this improvement took place gradually; but the 1870s, the first peacetime decade after the virtual completion of the Eastern system, saw many of the most important innovations in railroad history. Some of these, like the sleeping and dining cars, contributed to passenger amenities. Others, such as the coal-burning locomotive, the steel rail, the rapid spread of uniform gauges, and the flanged wheel, resulted in increased speed and efficiency. Still others, like the automatic signal system, made railroads much safer and much more productive.

Of all the innovations in the 1870s, three deserve a somewhat more detailed description. The first of these was the Westinghouse air brake, which was patented in 1869 but was not adopted on any broad scale until many years later. Before the air brake, it had taken 1,600 feet to stop a train from a speed of 30 miles an hour. Moreover, the process of bringing a train to a halt was extremely dangerous to a freight train crew and most uncomfortable to those who traveled on passenger trains. The air brake cut the stopping distance to 500 feet and incalculably reduced the danger and the strain for crew and passengers. Yet the roads did not rush to adopt Westinghouse's invention. Nor did they rush to adopt the Janney automatic coupler, which made an equally important contribution to safety and efficiency by eliminating the extraordinarily dangerous and clumsy coupling of cars by hand. Janney patented his mechanism in 1868. The Pennsylvania adopted it for its line in 1876, eight years later, and even then it was the lone pioneer. [1]

Time, too, was reorganized in the 1870s. By then, there were 54 different times in existence, and none had any real basis of logic. In 1873, it was proposed that these be consolidated, but it was not until ten years later that the present time zones were created.

Through invention and innovation, the railroads by the late nineteenth century could carry far more goods over much greater distances, more safely, more cheaply, and at a much faster rate of speed than the horse-drawn wagons and

---

[1]Fortunately, the air brake and the coupler attracted the attention and absorbed the energy of a persistent and determined individual named Lorenzo Coffin. Coffin became fascinated by the railroad business and, especially, by the need for improving safety. Largely through his dedicated efforts and continuous agitation, the Federal government in 1893 passed a law making air brakes and automatic couplers compulsory equipment.

steamboats that had preceded them. But innovation did not cease. Carrying capacity continued upward. In the 1930s, the diesel was introduced. By 1950, diesels comprised about one-third of all locomotives, and by 1960 they had almost entirely replaced steam. Better methods of laying track also cut the costs of railroading. Thus, the market was greatly broadened and the level of living immeasurably raised. Less track, better equipment, faster service, and more efficient management also produced dividends in the form of higher productivity. In 1880, railroads handled 88,000 ton-miles of freight per employee. This had doubled by 1915 and increased tenfold by the 1960s.

THE RAILROAD'S CONTRIBUTION

All transportation innovations influenced profoundly the pace and course of economic growth and development. The turnpike and the canal each broadened the market area by lowering costs and speeding distribution; but the railroad's influence dwarfed all that had gone before.[2] They completely broke down the triangular stream of commerce that had originally been created by natural waterways. They speeded the distributive process and made it possible to ship much larger quantities of goods. They lowered freight costs, accelerated manufacturing growth, provided a large investment outlet for savings, increased the mobility of the factors of production, pioneered in business administration through their innovations in accounting, management, and corporation finance, fed the ancillary institutions of business, and enhanced land values. They not only affected fundamentally the individual's income, but also, to a large extent, determined where he lived, what he ate, and how he spent his leisure time.

Nothing more succinctly expresses the railroad's great economic influence than the fact that it would take a fully employed labor force 60 years to carry the freight shipped over the railroads in one year, and the cost would be 200 times as great. But this is only a summary of a very long story.

In 1817, it required 52 days to ship goods from Cincinnati to New York by boat and wagon. Twenty years later, it took only 20 days by railroad alone. Much faster than the canal, the railroad was almost as cheap. As early as 1835, it cost $58.60 to ship a ton of goods 200 miles by team, $7.90 by canal, and $12.00 by the Baltimore and Ohio Railroad; 125 years later, it cost only $2.68 to ship a ton 200 miles by rail. It cost 83 cents per 100 pounds to ship grain from Chicago to New York in 1865; 9.6 cents in 1910. Rail freight rates fell from 2.2 cents per ton-mile in 1870 to less than one cent in 1910. A traveler spent one month in getting from New York to Chicago in 1836. Fifteen years later, he could make the same trip by rail in less than two days, and 50 years later he could travel twice as far, from Chicago to the Coast, in less than two

[2] Alfred D. Chandler, *The Railroads: The Nation's First Big Business* (New York: Harcourt, Brace & World, Inc, 1965).

days. When the Far West opened up just before the Civil War, John Butterfield's Overland Mail traveled the 2,700 miles between St. Louis and San Francisco in 24 days at a cost of $200; the Pony Express, a miracle in its time, did the trip from St. Joseph, Missouri, to Sacramento in nine days, about the same time it had taken the Persians to carry the mail in 500 B.C.

Railroads were American's first really big business in every sense of the word. As such, they introduced or gave exceptional impetus to almost every economic institution that is well recognized today. In manufacturing, the scattered shops that the railroads set up were often the medium that first brought industry to rural America. Moreover, just as the automobile was to do later, the railroad created a series of external economies. That is, it induced accelerated economic progress in a number of different industries whose products were jointly or complementarily demanded. The railroads ate immense quantities of iron, steel, coal, and lumber. They took 7 percent of pig iron in 1840-1850 and 25 percent in 1860. It was the railroad that supported Andrew Carnegie's steel mills. Rails comprised 50 percent of Bessemer steel production in 1867-1890 and at times the proportion was as high as 80 percent.

The railroads also caused a revolution in financial and business administration. They were the first to use convertible bonds and preferred stocks. They introduced the first sharp uptrend in stock market activity and, by so doing, they nourished investment banking, brokerage, and bank specialization. They also stimulated the profession of cost accounting and, by developing ratios of one sort or another, they gave the investor a tool by which to measure efficiency.

Railroads were also the initiators of many of the "firsts" in management. It was in the railroad that the professional manager first replaced the owner-manager. It was the railroad that first gave important employment to the corporation lawyer and to the office worker. And it was the railroad that first employed the holding company. None of these adventures was in any sense sterile, for each acted as a model for subsequent action by business firms in manufacturing, trade, and utilities.

Railroads also contributed to economic growth in more indirect and less measurable ways. First, by making it possible to ship perishable foods such as milk, vegetables, and meat from the farms to the city, they improved the diet and extended the span of life. Second, by broadening the market area they brought producers from different regions into competition with one another. Faced by the prospect of declining profits, businessmen made greater efforts to reduce costs and focused more attention on methods of increasing productivity, with consequent increases in real income and the level of living. Third, by being the largest industrial consumer of capital they were the most important industry in determinging the course of economic activity during most of the nineteenth century. Railroads accounted for perhaps one-eighth of total investment in the 1870s. Between 1860 and 1910 gross investment in the railroad industry ranged between $9.1 and $15.9 billion. In 1900 the $10 billion of railroad capital equalled one-sixth of the country's reproducible wealth. It was, therefore, the ups and downs of railroad building more than any other factor except housing that caused the ups and downs in nineteenth-century business. When railroad construction expanded, prosperity ruled. When railroad investment spending was in the doldrums, the nation experienced extreme depression. Last, among its indirect effects, the railroad enhanced land values, regardless of whether the owner used the rails or not.

Thus, many individuals—indeed, the majority—reaped important economic benefits over and above the direct contribution that the railroads made to the scale of living. Some of these benefits, like the increment in land values, inured only to the individual and not to society. But most of the railroads' benefits were social benefits. Society gained even though individual railroads might not make money and though individual investors might suffer losses.

The ramifications of railroad development penetrated deep into the social structure. It was the railroad that made possible the very existence of most American communities. It was the railroad that nourished the mushroom growth of some of the nation's largest cities. Chicago, for example, was nothing but a country town before the railroads reached it. In the late 1840s, hogs ran wild in the center of town and wolves were seen at Wabash and Adams Streets. Less than ten years later, the city had ten trunk railways and its population had passed 80,000.

The towns that the railroads built formed a pattern entirely different from the one created in the older pre-railroad era. In the newer areas, towns did not appear in clusters. Because the rails brought the people, rather than vice versa, towns were located relatively far apart. The whole complex developed in dumb-bell fashion. Whereas a map of the East consisted of a mass of dots, the rest of the country resembled a series of beads loosely strung on a ribbon of rail. The local isolation of the individual town broke down as its inhabitants expanded their goals beyond the primary one of getting to town and began to think in terms of going from town to town.

The developments in transportation that came after the railroad had an entirely different effect on society and the way people lived. The newer methods of transportation and communication—the automobile, the telephone, and the airplane—eliminated distance and telescoped time. By so doing, they broke down geographic specialization and set in motion a trend back toward decentralization. The decision maker in a large company no longer had to have his office in the manufacturing plant. Plants could be spread around the country far removed from each other and from the head office, for they could be instantly reached by telephone and personally visited in a few hours by plane. What specialization continued was due to the location of natural resources or to such intangible factors as the need for constant face-to-face relations such as those that helped to make New York the nation's office headquarters. The plane, auto, and telephone were the marketing tools for a new era of decentralization and diversification just as the railroad had been the mechanism for an era of centralization and specialization.

The newer means of locomotion also changed the way people lived. The horse and buggy had meant closely grouped towns. The railroads brough separated cities. The automobile took the people out to the suburbs and replaced the interspersed cities with a series of metropolitan areas, the urban sprawls of the mid-twentieth century. The whole process of evolution took place so quickly that the successive stages are lying next to each other in contemporary America. One can easily see what happened by contrasting the appearance of New York, originally a product of foreign trade in an era of human and animal locomotion; Chicago, the market center of the railway age; and Los Angeles, a metropolitan area of the automobile age.

Given the enormous contribution that the railroads made to the economy and to the way people lived, it was easy to believe that the railroad was indispensible. But this conclusion, which at one time was considered obvious, turns out to be not obvious at all. It has been impressively challenged by Professor Robert Fogel.[3] Combining linear programming and economic theory with painstaking research, Fogel concluded that the railroad produced in 1890 a social saving (the difference between actual national income and what the national income would have been in the absence of the railroad) of at most 5 percent of GNP.[4] But this is not to say that the railroads were not important. As Fogel wrote: "The discussion should not be interpreted as a statement of the unimportance of railroads." The railroads were clearly of great importance. They were not indispensible, but that is a matter for the games that economic historians play. After all, to some, even God is dispensible.

THE RAILROAD ENTREPRENEUR

Juggernauts with the awesome economic and social impact that has just been attributed to the railroads did not run themselves. They had to be planned and directed in some fashion and, in the kind of economy in which we live, this meant by businessmen.

[3] Robert W. Fogel, "A Quantitative Approach to the Study of Railroads in American Economic Growth: *Journal of Economic History,* Vol. XXII (1962); "Railroads and the Axiom of Indispensibility," Ralph Andreano, ed., *New Views on American Economic Development* (Cambridge, Mass.: Shenkman Publishing Company, 1965; *Railroads and American Economic Growth: Essays in Econometric History* (Baltimore, Inc.: Johns Hopkins University Press, 1964).

[4] Albert Fishlow says 10 percent. "Internal Transportation," Lance E. Davis, et al., *American Economic Growth* (New York: Harper & Row, 1972).

The men who built and ran the railroads came in all sizes and shapes. They fitted no stereotype. They did not conform to the prototypes of N. S. B. Gras' stages theory of business history, nor to Schumpeter's innovating entrepreneur, nor to the robber baron of Henry Demarest Lloyd and Matthew Josephson. The owner-manager (Gras' industrial capitalist) was rare in railroading, because even the smallest railroad was usually much too big for one-man ownership. The petty capitalist, of course, never appeared. On the other hand, professional management, which is usually assumed to have been a very late development in business, appeared very early in railroad history.

Railroad business men could be categorized in still other ways. There were the promoters, like Thomas Durant of the Union Pacific and Cyrus K. Holliday of the Santa Fe; the builders, including James J. Hill of the Great Northern and Collis P. Huntington of the Central and Southern Pacific; the financiers, ranging from Commodore Vanderbilt of the New York Central to John Murray Forbes of the Chicago, Burlington, and Quincy; the consolidators, such as J. Pierpont Morgan, Edward Harriman, and Jay Gould; and the managers, like Charles Francis Adams and Charles Elliott Perkins. But, like all attempts at separation, the lines of demarcation are very blurry. Huntington was promoter, builder, financier, and consolidator. Morgan financed consolidation. Forbes financed building. Most railroaders played not one, but many, roles.

How railroad entrepreneurs are labeled is not nearly so important as what they did. In economic theory, the entrepreneur is defined as the one who makes crucial business decisions. He puts the factors of production together or, in more sophisticated language, he reshuffles the production function. The railroad man certainly conformed to the economist's model. He had to raise capital, decide where and when to build, attract a labor force, cope with construction problems, forestall or meet competition, put together an administrative structure, and—need it be said?—make a profit.

These functions were not of equal importance at all times in railroad history. It always behooved the head of a railroad to make a profit, but whether he did or did not depended upon how well he performed his other functions. In the early years of any railroad, raising money and the problems of construction absorbed almost all of the railroad man's time. Indeed, at this stage the ability to raise capital meant the difference between success and failure. Huntington's extraordinary ability to dig up money when it seemed absolutely unavailable enabled him to maintain a precarious hold on his railroad empire. On the other hand, Jay Cooke and Henry Villard each lost the Northern Pacific because neither was able to keep coming up with the capital funds that were needed. But, once a network was finished, construction problems ceased to bother anyone. At the same time, financial decisions were no longer concerned with merely raising money, but with the more sophisticated area of corporation finance.

Administration by professional management[5]

As the railroads grew, problems of administering the emerging empires absorbed more and more attention. By the late 1800s, the largest railroads had become as big as businesses could become. They covered vast stretches of territory and handled a staggering volume of business. They employed huge work forces and were owned by many stockholders. As early as the 1850s, the Illinois Central, with its 700 miles, was the longest road in the world. The Delaware and Hudson employed over 4,000 people and the New York Central was owned by over 2,500 stockholders. By the 1880s, the Pennsylvania Railroad, then the largest business organization in the world, had 30,000 employees and operated 3,500 miles of main track. These long lines were responsible to so many diverse groups and their span of influence covered such a wide geographical area that their managers could not function efficiently with the kind of structure that had sufficed for the turnpike, the canal, the small factory, or the short railroad. The short line could make money under the old structure; the long line could not. This fact was clearly recognized by some railroad superintendents, such as Benjamin Latrobe of the Baltimore and Ohio and Daniel C. McCallum of the Erie, long before management emerged as an academic science. In the early 1850s, McCallum wrote:

A superintendent of a road fifty miles in length can give its business his personal attention and may be constantly on the line engaged in the direction of its details; each person is personally known to him, and all questions in relation to its business are at once presented and acted upon; and any system however imperfect may under such circumstances prove comparatively successful. In the government of a road five hundred miles in length a very different state exists. . . . I am fully convinced that. . .the disparity of cost per mile in operating long and short roads is not produced by a difference in length, but is in proportion to the perfection of the system adopted.[6]

The railways were not very old before they produced a set of full-time career men. Usually, these professional administrators were not important stockholders, but they were interested in orderly management with a minimum of interference from the board of directors. By the 1840s, according to Leland Jenks, these officials were talking among themselves about systems by which

5This was long a neglected aspect of economic history. Recently, however, a number of excellent studies have appeared. See Thomas C. Cochran, *Railroad Leaders, 1845-1890* (Cambridge, Mass.: Harvard University Press, 1953), especially Chaps. 5 and 6; Alfred D. Chandler, Jr., *Henry Varnum Poor* (Cambridge, Mass. Harvard University Press, 1956), Chaps. 6 and 7; Leland H. Jenks, "Early Railway Organization," *Business History Review,* Vol. XXXV (1961).

6Chandler, *op. cit.,* p. 146.

construction, maintenance, and accounting could be carried out. They were aware of the need for formal organization, and by the 1860s some of them had worked out much of the managerial apparatus: an organization chart, systematic record-keeping, allocation of authority and responsibility, and a system of departmental control. In the 1860s and 1870s, the Pennsylvania established departments in traffic, transport, and accounting under the direction of a central office. What was happening was well illustrated by the career of Henry Varnum Poor, the able and influential editor of the *Railroad Journal*. When Poor first started in 1849, he focused his attention on the problems of construction. By the early 1850s, he was also writing about intricate matters of corporate finance. By the late 1850s, management and administration were absorbing more and more of his attention.

This early interchange of ideas about the need for a managerial structure was a venture in pioneering and, like all pioneer efforts, it was largely unheeded by railroad men in general. It was not until after the Civil War that managerial administration really came into its own. By the 1880s, it had definitely arrived, for in 1886 Charles Francis Adams lectured at Harvard on railroad management as a profession. Four years before, Charles Perkins had threatened to write a book on the subject. As Cochran has pointed out, "Success in the railroad business came to be seen in a bureaucratic setting." Managers "followed the book" and performed their duties as part of a nine-to-five routine. Thus the so-called "Organization Man" appeared in railroading at least 50 years before the date usually given as his birthday. His appearance was an inevitable result of large-scale operations, but it presented all the many, well-publicized disadvantages that came to be associated with bureaucracy and the separation of ownership and control. Management offered an attractive area for empire building and internecine warfare. Very often, the technical manager—the man who had the responsibility for running the railroad—was opposed by the financial men, who felt themselves responsible for raising capital and making a profit. The latter often emerged as victors, usually with disastrous results, for the colorless man in the office was the only one who really could operate the road. The spectacular freebooter on the stock exchange, whose interesting exploits have so often been described as typical in the literature, was really the atypical railroad man.

The problems of competition

One of the most important functions of the railroad entrepreneur—perhaps his very reason for existence—was to price transportation services to yield a profit. But in doing this, he was hampered by the necessity of forestalling competition or of meeting it when it could not be forestalled.

Over the course of railroad history, the complexion of the competitive problem changed markedly. When railroads were growing extensively, there was little serious competition from other means of transportation. Competition came from other railroads. In later years, however, competition was more and more a struggle among different means of transportation. It was not so much railroad against railroad as railroad against truck, airline, and inland waterway.

In the early years, when the only thing the railroads had to fear were the railroads themselves, parallel lines or lines serving the same terminals often engaged in frenzied price competition. These rate wars were the most striking aspect of competition, but by no means the only one. The other, and perhaps the more important, was the need to anticipate and forestall potential or future competition. This aspect of the competitive struggle rose from the very real fear that, unless one could serve an extensive market area, a rival would usurp it and thereby gain a fatal strategic advantage. Unless a railroad ran between two important market centers, such as New York and Chicago, it could not feel safe. Another railroad might accomplish the trick first. Even if this did not happen, the road was always at the mercy of feeder lines. Feeders which touched two roads could favor one or the other by adjusting rates. The unfavored road would be in a precarious competitive position and sooner or later would feel compelled to free itself by extending its line to a logical terminal market place.

The need to forestall competition was the most important motivating force behind the rapid expansion of the railroads. Railroaders were much less concerned with short-run profits than they were with their long-run competitive position. They grossly underestimated the costs of construction—a habit that seems to have been an occupational disease. Then they rushed to build many miles of road in excess of what the existing volume of traffic could be reasonably expected to support.[7] For reasons that had little to do with the good of society, businessmen and railroad entrepreneurs piled an additional oversupply on what was already excessive. Thus, Carnegie threatened to build a road rivaling the Pennsylvania because he learned that the Pennsylvania was charging him discriminatory rates. He enlisted the aid of the Vanderbilts in the proposed construction; the Pennsylvania retaliated by building the West Shore Railroad as a rival to the Vanderbilts' New York Central. A worse example of predatory behavior was the construction of the New York, Chicago, and St. Louis, the "Nickel Plate". Its only reason for existence was to blackmail the New York Central. Such incidents as these were harmful both to society and to the railroad. For society, they represented a waste of economic resources; for the railroad, they reduced profit margins and laid the basis for financial disaster.

In "good times" the supply of transportation was not in excess of demand. This was evidenced by relative stability of rates. But equilibrium was so finely balanced that any slight recession, any slight decline in demand, threw the

---

[7]The extension of the Chicago, Milwaukee, and St. Paul was, for example, a most disastrous undertaking. See its interesting case history in N. S. B. Gras and Henrietta Larson, *Casebook in American Business History* (New York: Appleton-Century-Crofts, 1939), pp. 421-37.

market into a state of chaos. Then frantic rate cutting became an industry habit. Each road had a very large capital investment and, therefore, very heavy fixed costs. Under competitive pressures, it was willing to lower its rates to a point where they barely covered variable costs rather than lose the business altogether. Indeed, if the pressure were severe enough, it might in its anguish go even further and reduce rates far below its over-all break-even point. In the years of great expansion after the Civil War, rates fell until, in 1888, they were one-third of what they had been in 1865. To be sure, some of this reduction was the result of cost-reducing technological developments, but much of it was the effect of a greatly expanded supply. Proof of this was the fact that railroad operation on the whole was not profitable. The fortunes that the railroads produced came out of construction or security speculation, not from running a railroad. During the last century of railroading, there has hardly been a year when more than half the railroads paid dividends. To be sure, substantial fortunes were made in railroading. One need hardly be reminded of the riches of Vanderbilt, Harriman, Huntington, Gould, James and others. But the return on stated capital seldom exceeded 5 percent, though this too should be qualified. Much of the nominal capital existed only on paper. Most railroad securities were originally sold at a discount, but returns were calculated on face value. Moreover, because of the industry's cyclical nature, capital gains could be substantial. In the 1890s, for example, railroad shares were very depressed, selling mostly around two-thirds their price in 1900. Then in the early 1900s prices rose sharply, and those who had bought in the 1890s enjoyed substantial gains.

Attempts to solve the competitive problem

There were various ways out of the competition trap, but none was completely satisfactory. The least satisfactory, but the one that occurred most often, was wholesale bankruptcy. In the years before World War I, there were never less than 800 miles of road in receivership, and most of the time there were over 10,000, reaching a high of over 40,000 during the severe depression of 1893. From World War I until 1955, the number of miles of road in bankruptcy ranged from 5,250 to 77,000, but there were only nine years in the whole 40-year period when less than 10,000 miles were in receivership.

In theory, bankruptcy should have cured itself by reducing the supply of transportation facilities. But this could not work in the railroad business because it was not easy, for economic and social reasons, to pick up a few thousand miles of road and throw them away. Bankrupt railroads did not go out of business; they went through a financial reorganization. Part or all of the equity was eliminated. The debt owed to the bondholders was scaled down by replacing existing bonds with stock or bonds of lower face value. After going through the wringer of reorganization, a road re-entered the competitive arena much more vigorously because of its new, lower-cost structure.

There were other ways of avoiding the disastrous results of competition. Where a road had a territorial monopoly, it tried to charge rates high enough to offset the skimpy returns from the section where competition was intense. This resulted in a well-known anomaly of the business—the discrepancy between long- and short-haul rates. At one time it cost 30 cents to ship a tub of butter from Elgin, Illinois, to New York City, and 65 cents to ship it 165 miles from upper New York State. Pittsburgh paid 25 cents on Chicago grain, whereas New York paid 15 cents.

Whatever else one might say for it, the long- and short-haul discrepancy did irreparable damage to public relations. Most farmers and most shippers found it impossible to understand why it should cost twice as much to send goods half the distance, or why it should cost more to send goods 50 miles to Chicago than it cost to send them 900 miles from Chicago to New York.

Because railroad men as a group had little to gain from competitive rate wars, it could be expected that they would attempt to come to some form of cooperative agreement. Pools and gentlemen's agreements were commonly made. Roads agreed to split territory, to desist from rate cutting, and to give drawbacks or finders' fees on business brought by one road to another. But, as was usually the case in other industries, agreements among railroads were more easily broken than observed. Freight agents, desirous of maintaining their business volume, often broke agreements by giving rebates to shippers. Sometimes this was not known to the roads' executives, but, if it was known it was winked at. For example, John Murray Forbes, the unusually high-principled president of the C. B. and Q., remarked when he heard of an under-the-counter rebate, "We can stand a great deal of cheating better than competition."[8]

Voluntary cooperation having failed, railroaders, like businessmen in general, attempted to consolidate competing lines. As one corporation lawyer expressed the prevalent feeling, consolidation was necessary because of the inability of the roads to meet fixed charges, " an inability that was due to the ruinous reduction of rates, partly through legislation and partly through ruinous competition." The consolidation movement started in a serious way soon after railroad construction reached a peak in 1887. By the early 1900s, most of the nation's railroad network had been consolidated into some six systems. The Pennsylvania and the New York Central dominated the East. The New Haven had consolidated New England. Morgan had reorganized the South. The Great Northern, the Northern Pacific, and the Chicago, Burlington, and Quincy formed an entente in the Northwest. The Far West had been welded into the Harriman empire. Only the Southwest continued to be a set of individual baronies, although at one time Jay Gould seemed well on the way toward creating one system.

At first, consolidations seemed to offer the answer, but, like the efforts of the early medieval kings, they did not endure. The New Haven fell apart because

[8]Cochran, *Railroad Leaders,* p. 166.

it was uneconomic. The Great Northern-Northern Pacific alliance was broken up when the Supreme Court in the *Northern Securities* case of 1904 held it to be in violation of the Sherman Anti-Trust Act. The Harriman and Morgan empires gradually disintegrated, but the idea of consolidation did not die. It returned in the 1920s and again in the 1950s, when railroads faced a different type of competitive problem.

Consolidation in the 1920s for the most part followed the route of the late nineteenth century. Mergers were impossible because of legal restrictions and popular opposition, but individual empire builders, using the holding-company device, tried to weld railroads together in vast systems. The Pennsylvania Railroad formed the Pennroad Corporation to organize part of the East. The Van Sweringen Brothers created the Allegheny Corporation to hold the Chesapeake and Ohio; the Denver, Rio Grande, and Western; the Missouri Pacific; and others. But these ambitious aggregations had more to offer financially than economically, and with the depression, they collapsed as their predecessors had.

In the 1950s, when transportation again failed to participate in the general national prosperity, harassed railroad and airline managers produced plans for large-scale mergers and consolidations. The public at large was much more willing to accept the idea than it had been in previous periods of stress and strain. Some mergers were, in fact, accomplished. But the hostility of the railroad brotherhoods and of some legislators who feared the evils of monopoly was still strong enough to prevent or delay consolidation through merger.

TRUCKS AND AIRLINES; PIPELINES AND INLAND WATERWAYS

The slackened pace of railroad growth did not mean that transportation was becoming less important in the general economy. On the contrary, year by year Americans traveled more miles and shipped much more freight. Today, the volume of ton-miles of freight shipped is at least three times what it was 50 years ago, and the number of passenger-miles traveled is at least 30 times as much. The bulk of this increase has accrued to the newer means of transportation: the truck, the bus, the automobile, the pipeline, the revitalized inland waterways, and the airplane. Today there are as many miles of pipeline as of railroad, and there are twice as many miles of paved primary highways.

Transportation offers an excellent illustration of what the late Joseph Schumpeter described as progress through creative destruction. In 1916, railroads carried more than three-quarters of the country's freight. Today they carry less than half. Trucks, on the other hand, carried almost nothing in 1916 but handle almost one-quarter of today's total. Inland waterways carry somewhat less than 20 percent of what they once carried. The pipelines carry more than the waterways, and the airlines are still a negligible factor.

As a demander of capital, transportation would never again account for

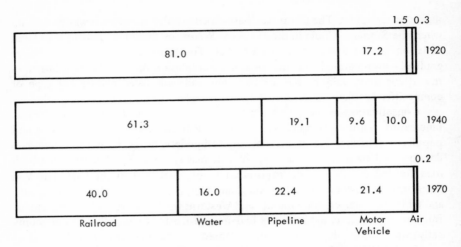

CHART 23. Interstate freight traffic by different means of transportation.

more than 15 percent of capital formation as it did in the 1870s. In 1902-1906, highway capital expenditures averaged $100 million a year and railroad capital expenditures averaged $500 million. By 1960, both were expending much more but the relative amounts were reversed, with highways accounting for $5.5 billion and railroads for $1.5 billion. Together the two amounted to less than 10 percent of gross capital formation.

In passenger traffic, buses, private automobiles, and airlines have done as much damage to the railroad as the railroad once did to the canal, the turnpike, and the steamboat. In 1922, railroads carried 40 times as many passengers as buses did. Today, buses carry three times as many as the railroads, which carry less than 1 percent. The private automobile far overshadows all other means combined, accounting for almost 90 percent of intercity passenger travel. Planes carry about 10 percent.

Starting early in the century, the influence of the automobile quickly pervaded the whole of economic life. The nation literally took to wheels. By midcentury, when production ran at the rate of 7 million to 9 million vehicles, there were almost 80 million cars, buses, and trucks registered in the United States—almost ten times as many as in 1920, and more than double the number at the end of World War II. Americans are the most automobiled people in the world. They operate two out of every three of the world's motor vehicles. They travel about 720 billion miles a year by motor vehicle, or about one and a half million round trips to the moon.

In a period of less than 50 years, the automobile has become in many respects the common denominator of marketing. Even before the end of the 1920s, more than 50,000 towns had no direct access to either railroad or waterway. By the 1950s, many sizable cities had divested themselves completely of the last vestiges of their once bustling public transportation systems.

The effect on marketing was particularly striking in agriculture. Before the truck, the middlewestern farmer lived, on the average, about eight miles from his market. With the truck, the average distance was extended to 18 miles—more than doubled. The average cost of hauling wheat by horse was 30 cents a ton-mile; by truck it was 15 cents a ton-mile. Along with this enlargement of the market area and the reduction in the cost of marketing, new possibilities of geographic division of labor appeared. Freed of some of the chores of marketing, the farmer could devote himself more efficiently to growing crops and raising animals.

The automobile also illustrated how technological change tended to transform traditional concepts and activities of government. By mid-century, Federal, state, and local governments were collecting $13 billion a year in motor vehicle taxes, and expenditures for highways were $16 billion. In addition, the automobile made possible intermunicipal authorities, breaking down the traditional separation of municipality, county, and borough.

The railroads argued that much of the shift of business was the result of unfair exploitation by government and labor. They argued that their costs were lower than those of other modes of transport. But in the labyrinths of sophisticated accounting, it was a wise man indeed who knew exactly how much it cost to ship goods and bodies. Certainly, operating costs by rail were lower, averaging one-third to one-quarter of the cost by truck. Rails carried about 200 ton-miles per employee; trucks carried less than 200,000; and airlines, less than 50,000.

To be sure, cost figures require severe qualification. Actual costs of transportation have always been disguised by government aid. Instead of falling altogether on the shipper, costs have been socialized. Land grants and financial aid helped the turnpike, the canal, and the railroad. More recently, governments have assumed the costs of much of the capital construction for the automobile, the truck, the airline, and the renovated inland waterway. The Federal government, for example, spent $11.7 million for river and harbor improvements in 1890, $33.0 million in 1916, and $545.0 million in 1960—almost 50 times as much as 70 years before. Government expenditures for highways (much of which is raised by motor vehicle and gasoline taxes) began on a small scale in New Jersey in 1891 and now amount to over $16 billion a year. Governments also expend over $1 million a year to defray the costs of airports.

If costs were the only factor that governed the travel of freight and passengers, railroads and waterways would handle almost all traffic. But costs have been only one part of the explanation of why one method of transport has superseded another. Speed, service, and convenience are equally if not more important. Motor vehicles are more expensive than rail, but they are also much more convenient; the airline is much faster; and these factors have made arguments about costs somewhat academic.

GOVERNMENT REGULATION OF TRANSPORTATION

Government regulation of transportation is not a recent invention. It goes back as far as government financial assistance, and government financial assistance began in colonial days. From the beginning, transportation was the product of a mixed economy. Governments regulated the turnpikes and the canals. Indeed, most of the latter were government-owned. But regulation first became formalized with the railroad. The first railroad commission was created in Rhode Island in 1839. The idea quickly spread to the other New England states, and by the time of the Civil War it was widely adopted. The function of the early commissions was to regulate fares, rates, and earnings, but states also interposed their authority in other ways. New York had a substantial stake in canals, and until 1851 it tried to protect that stake by limiting the amount of freight that railroads could carry. Pennsylvania, until 1861, levied a charge on railroads that it used to subsidize its canals. Massachusetts and Illinois had state representatives on the boards of the Boston and Worcester and the Illinois Central. To be sure, most of this regulation and control was not pursued aggressively. Nevertheless, it showed that laissez faire was more a matter of words than of behavior.

The rationale on which early regulation was based had a logical simplicity. Railroads were monopolies and had to be regulated or society would lose the benefits that competition produced. At least, this was the picture as portrayed in the widely accepted classical economic theory. Ideally, regulation would produce a quantity, quality, and price roughly the same as that which would have appeared under conditions of pure competition. But it soon became clear that it was impossible to simulate a condition of pure competition. States therefore veered toward the more realizable objective of protecting the weaker party in the bargaining process. In this case, the weaker party was the consumer of transportation services, the shipper or the farmer. Out of this desire to protect the weak grew the so-called "Granger Laws," which spread through the Middle West in the 1870s. The Granger movement, often pictured as a symptom of agrarian discontent, was a lot more than that.[9] It represented a collective effort on the part of farmers and shippers to secure relief from what they considered monopolistic exploitation by various businesses, especially the railroads. Typical Granger laws, such as that of Illinois in 1871, set up commissions and gave them powers to set maximum rates, to prevent discrimination, and to veto consolidations of competing lines.

The constitutionality of the Granger laws was quickly challenged on the ground that they deprived citizens of property without due process of law.

[9]Lee Benson, *Merchants, Farmers, and Railroads* (Cambridge, Mass.: Harvard University Press), 1955. For the forces responsible for the ICC, see Edward A. Purcell, Jr., "Ideas and Interests: Businessmen and the Interstate Commerce Act," *The Journal of American History,* Vol. LIII (1967).

However, the Supreme Court, in the famous case of *Munn* v. *Illinois* (1876), held that the laws were constitutional. But then, exactly ten years later, the Court reversed itself and, in the equally famous case of *Wabash, St. Louis, and Pacific Railroad* v. *Illinois,* it held that a state could not regulate the intrastate part of interstate commerce. This left a vacuum in railroad regulation that pleased very few. It not only dissatisfied farmers; it also dissatisfied the merchants and those railroad managers who thought that if regulation was an evil, it was a lesser evil than the individualistic, competitive chaos of unregulated railroading. The Federal government, which had been toying with the idea, now wasted no time in stepping into the void left by the *Wabash* case.

Congress in 1887 passed the Interstate Commerce Act, which prohibited rebates, pools, long- and short-haul differentials, and unreasonable rates. A commission was established to administer the law, but it soon became clear that the Commission had little power. The burden of proof in a controversy between the Commission and a railroad was on the former, and the judicial process was extremely slow. Furthermore, the Commission could declare a rate to be unreasonable, but it could not set a reasonable rate even if it knew what such a thing was. Then, too, it was assumed that rebating was an individual act for which the railroad was not liable.

To close the loopholes in the original act, Congress eventually extended the scope of regulation. The Elkins Act (1903), largely initiated by the railroads themselves, made railroads liable for rebates. The Hepburn Act (1906) gave the ICC power to fix maximum rates and to require annual reports. The Mann-Elkins Act (1910) completed the process by empowering the Commission to veto changes in rate. The burden of proof was thereby shifted to the railroads. The Commission was no longer required to prove that rates were unreasonable, but it was up to the railroad, which had announced a change in rates, to prove that the new ones were not unreasonable.

What was a reasonable rate, however, was a matter of considerable uncertainty. Theoretically, it was a rate that would give a fair return on a fair value. But how was fair value to be determined, and what was a fair return? In the celebrated case of *Smyth* v. *Ames* (1898), the Supreme Court tackled the problem and laid down the following edict:

> . . . in order to ascertain value, the original cost of construction, the amount expended in permanent improvements, the amount and market value of its bonds and stock, the present as compared with the original cost of construction, the probable earning capacity of the property under particular rates. . .and the sum required to meet operating expenditures, are all matters for consideration, and are to be given such weight as may be just and right in each case.

This left no one any wiser than he had been before. It was so vague and so complicated that evaluation became, in the words of one wit, "a calculated, studied uncertainty reflecting the conviction that fair value must be made to be the unpredictable product of incalculable consideration." But the ICC set itself to the problem, and under the authority of the Valuation Act of 1913, it began to calculate the value of the railroads. The whole awe-inspiring task was interrupted when the government took over the railroads in World War I. It returned them under the Transportation Act of 1920, an omnibus measure that began with a statement that railroads were entitled to a fair rate of return on fair value and continued by giving the ICC power to fix minimum as well as maximum rates. Any earnings in excess of a fair return were to be divided half and half between the railroad and the government, and the government was to use its share to make loans to the weaker roads. The Act also gave its belated blessing to consolidation by instructing the ICC to work out a plan for railroad unification. The Commission, in 1929, did emerge with a blueprint for consolidating the whole national network into 21 systems. The proposal immediately aroused the ire of the brotherhoods, the fears of the shippers, and the veto of the railroads.

But by this time the Transportation Act was rapidly becoming a dead letter. The first evaluation made by the Commission was rejected by the Supreme Court in the case of *St. Louis and O'Fallon Railroad* v. *the United States* (1929) on the ground that insufficient consideration had been given to reproduction costs. The depression of the 1930s swept away all that was left of the Act. The whole concept of fair value was abandoned in the Emergency Railroad Transportation Act of 1933. The 20 years of time and the $188 million of money that had been expended in attempts to calculate value were unceremoniously dumped in the historical graveyard.

By the time the Transportation Act was laid to rest, it was well recognized that the railroads were no longer the only means of transportation available to the public. In 1935 Congress passed the Motor Carrier Act to regulate commercial interstate motor vehicle traffic, and in 1940 it extended regulation to inland waterways.

Although the authority of the ICC now covered all forms of land and water interstate commerce, the Commission continued to follow the time-honored American tradition that the objective of regulation was to protect the weak, or at least those who appeared to be the weak, in the economic market place. Much of nonrailroad transportation remained unregulated. It has been alleged that, in the years since World War II, exempt trucks have increased their volume five times; exempt barges, four times; but regulated truckers and barges have just about tripled their volume. Under a notion that competition means complete equality, the ICC refused to allow railroads to cut rates below those of trucks. "Rates of all respondents," said the Commission, "must be on the same level if respondents are to effectively compete and fairly share in the traffic." But this peculiar view of competition was abrogated in 1958, when Congress decided that rates did not have to be held up to a particular level to protect any other mode of transportation. Today, the ideal is a rate that will give investors a return equal to what they might have received in an alternative investment. This is a far cry from the policing of monopolies that marked the beginning of transport regulation.[10]

PROGRESS IN COMMUNICATION

What the railroad and motor vehicles did for transportation, the telegraph and the telephone did for communication. And in each case, the evolution was much the same. The telegraph began in 1844 when S. F. B. Morse, with the help of a Federal subsidy of $30,000, ran a telegraph line from Baltimore to Washington. But it was not until the railroads encouraged the telegraph that it made real progress. There were only 50,000 miles of telegraph in 1860. But then the railroads gave Western Union a right of way, transported men and materials without charge, and provided housing for three-fourths of all telegraph offices. In return, Western Union gave the rails free wire service. By 1878, there were over 200,000 miles of wire. Western Union's growth was so remarkable that its president was moved to tell the stockholders: "Successful competition with your company is improbable if not actually impossible." The president had forgotton the dangers from what economists call cross-elasticity. He was thinking in terms of another telegraph company. He did not anticipate a wholly new device, the telephone, which would offer more than successful competition.

The telephone was "invented" by Bell in 1876, but it did not make any real progress until Theodore N. Vail, a brilliant entrepreneur, took over its management in 1878. At first, subscribers paid $20 a month for a personal phone or $40 for a business phone. There was no central exchange, but lines ran from one subscriber to another, with the subscribers paying the costs of construction—$100 to $150 a mile. The potentials of the phone business under such arrangements were clearly limited. When Vail took over, there were less than 50,000 phones in the whole country, and the company's assets were about $10 million. Vail reorganized the management, established an engineering and experimental department, and began to put telephone wires underground. But his most important innovation was to use copper wire, which for the first time made long-distance phoning practical and feasible.

Vail, who served the company intermittently for 34 years, laid the groundwork for the company's progress. The telephone became an indispensable part of an American's physical equipment. By 1929, there were 17 million telephones, and the Bell System's invested capital had passed $3 billion. By the 1960s, there were more than 70 million phones, and the System's capital had passed $20 billion.

[10]Albro Martin, *Enterprise Denied: Origins of the Decline of American Railroads, 1897-1917* (New York: Columbia University Press, 1971) offers a provocative account of the ICC's responsibility for railroad decline.

TOWARD MORE SOPHISTICATED MARKETING

At the middle of the nineteenth century, for reasons inherent in an undeveloped economy, trade was at a low level of sophistication. With rare exceptions, the merchant's countinghouse, the wholesaler's warehouse, and the retailer's store were emporia devoted more to taking orders than to selling goods. Advertising was not so much a business-getter as a method of conveying information. Some outdoor advertising appeared in the large cities, and newspaper advertisements were inserted in the local newspapers and in the national magazines. Newspaper ads wasted no space. In fine print, they announced the place of sale and the list of products in stock. They seldom mentioned price and hardly ever carried a description of the article. Installment selling was not very common, but it did exist. As early as 1807, a New York dealer was selling furniture at so much down and so much a month. The McCormick reaper was sold "on time" almost from its beginning, but the terms—20 percent down and four months to pay—were considerably more conservative than those now practiced. A most important innovation in consumer credit came in September 1856, when Edward Clark of the Singer Sewing Machine Company began to sell on much more liberal terms. His sewing machine sold for $125—$5 down and $3 a month.

Crude as marketing was, the seeds that produced the glamorous art of today had already been planted and were just sprouting by the time of the Civil War. A half-dozen factors were responsible for the rapid progress of trade and its auxiliary institutions. The miracles of transportation—the railroad after 1850, the streetcar somewhat later, and the auto toward the end of the century—made it easier to move people and merchandise. Continuous population growth filled up the cities and eventually spilled over into suburbia. Gradually, an impressive number of Americans came to earn more than what was needed for sheer necessities. They were bringing in what the economists call *discretionary income.* Whether to buy or not to buy became a matter of choice, that is to say, the demand for many of the goods for which consumers shopped became income-elastic. With larger discretionary income and a more pervasive demand elasticity, the business of buying and selling became less a task in economics and more a lesson in psychology. To maximize profit, it became necessary to persuade people to buy. Fortunately, the media through which people could be persuaded multiplied and replenished the earth. The cheap newspaper grew spectacularly in the 1830s, and an advertising man was quick to take advantage of it. Volney B. Palmer is credited with having formed the first advertising agency in 1841.

The mixture of transportation progress, population growth, expanding income, and widely circulating means of communication was ready to ferment. All that was needed was the yeast, and this quickly appeared in the person of the merchandising entrepreneur, who could adapt himself and his business to the rapidly evolving economic environment.

As better transportation and communication pushed wholesaling westward, as capital accumulated and population grew, and as mass consumption and mass production appeared, Eastern producers reorganized their distributive methods to meet the pressures exerted by increased competition. They developed, especially in the two decades around the middle of the century, more sophisticated and more aggressive selling methods. Organized produce exchanges, which diffused risk and relieved producers from some of the chores of marketing, replaced direct negotiations between buyers and producers of raw materials. The drummer, a traveling man whose original function was to "drum up" trade, broadened his activities and began to take orders, eventually emerging as the traveling salesman. By 1860 there were about a thousand such salesmen in the country. Most important of all, large-scale manufacturers began to market their own wares. McCormick and Singer sold directly to consumers before the Civil War. Swift, early in the 1870s, invaded eastern markets and sold directly to retailers. A few years later, W. L. Douglas, the shoe manufacturer, opened a chain of retail stores. In 1890, Dan River Mills eliminated one of the middlemen and sold directly to retailers. The wholesaler, who had dominated the business world, was now pushed aside in the move toward vertical integration. He did not disappear altogether, but much of what he had done in acting as the middleman between producer and consumer was now performed by the manufacturer himself.

The department store

The mid-nineteenth century was an opportune time for innovation in retailing as well as in wholesaling. In the big cities, retail stores had grown to substantial size and were ready to branch out. In the 1840s, Boston's Oak Hall, the largest clothing store in the country, did a half-million-dollar business. A. T. Stewart, the world's most famous dry-goods specialty shop, often took in $10,000 a day in the 1850s. These stores were already buying from the producer instead of the wholesaler. What this meant was that the tendency toward specialization, so impressive in the first half of the century, was reversing itself. Shops such as Lord and Taylor and R. H. Macy in New York, John Wanamaker in Philadelphia, and F. and R. Lazarus in Columbus, were gradually expanding into department stores. At the same time, many businesses in the rapidly growing medium-sized cities, like Gimbel Brothers in Milwaukee, were outgrowing the general-store classification and achieving department-store status.

Technically, a store in which both merchandising and management were organized along departmental lines was a department store. But according to John Wanamaker's definition, a department store was nothing more than a blown-up general store. Because of the uncertainty of definition, there has been much useless dispute over which department store was the first. To be sure, some pioneer department stores began operations in the 1830s and 1840s, but the great growth period occurred in the 1870s and 1880s. In that period the house of A. T. Stewart was by far the largest retail business, although technically it was not a department store. When Stewart died in 1876, his sales were $40 million to $50 million a year. It was said that his firm bought one-tenth of all the imports that entered the Port of New York.[11]

Credit for originating every important idea in department store merchandising has been given to Stewart, or to John Wanamaker, or to R. H. Macy, or to Marshall Field. This is a slight exaggeration. The policy of selling for cash only appeared as early as 1806. The one-price policy is at least as old as 1820. The money-back guarantee existed in the 1840s. What the innovaters did, however, was very important. They made these retailing novelties standard practice by publicizing and pressing them upon their competitors. Nor were they mere imitators. Stewart was the first to make a successful effort to attract women shoppers; and he was also the first to manufacture some of the goods he sold. Wanamaker opened a series of branches, shortened hours, and pioneered in new kinds of advertising. Macy's, under the ownership of the Strauss family, introduced a series of innovations in the management of a department store. By 1900, Macy's contained 50 different departments, plus sizable manufacturing and delivery adjuncts. The business was much too big for personal supervision, and the Strausses proceeded to reorganize it in order to achieve more efficient means of gathering information, coordinating, planning, and making decisions. In 1905, a controller's office was established to gather accounting information which would be helpful in current operations as well as in describing past performance. In 1908 and 1914, two committees were created to give advice and to supervise operations.[12]

Chains and mail order

The 1870s saw not only the department store emerge as an important institution, but also the chain store and the mail-order house. Both were in existence long before they became solidly established in the prosperity years of the erratic 1870s.

Chain stores have been traced all the way back to the ancient Romans, and they certainly existed in the early nineteenth century, though they did not become important until late in that century. But the Atlantic and Pacific Tea Company, founded by George F. Gilman, a leather dealer, is the oldest existing chain store in the United States. It goes back to 1859, but the A. and P. did not really become a chain until George H. Hartford took over operations in 1878. Hartford was a marketing genius. By door-to-door selling, the use of trading stamps, constant opening of new stores, and rigid economy, the A. and P. soon

[11]Harry E. Resseguie, "Alexander Tunney Stewart and the Development of the Department Store, 1823-1876" *Business History Review,* Vol. XXXIX (1965).
[12]See Ralph M. Hower, *R. H. Macy and Co.* (Cambridge, Mass.: Harvard University Press, 1943).

became one of the largest business firms in the world. A second highly successful chain began its career in 1879, when the F. W. Woolworth chain quickly achieved a volume of $100,000 and a profit of $10,000 a year.

Mail-order selling is as old as the post office but, like the other retail institutions, it did not attain any great stature until the 1870s when rural mail delivery gave it a forward thrust and Aaron Montgomery Ward opened his firm. The first Montgomery Ward catalog was a single 8-by-12-inch sheet, but the business was an immediate success. Catering to the discontented farmer, Ward was soon doing an annual business of over $1,000,000—enough to attract many able competitors: Spiegel, May, Stern in 1882; National Bellas Hess in 1888; and Sears, Roebuck and Company in 1893.

Sears actually started a mail-order watch business in Minneapolis in 1886, but he sold out for a temporary career in banking. In the late 1890s, Julius Rosenwald, a clothing dealer, entered the business. His talents tended to balance the colorful but erratic genius of Richard Sears, and the firm embarked on a giddy rise.[13] Its sales passed $50 million in 1907 and $100 million in 1915. After World War I, the Sears management was persuaded that the automobile and the decline of agriculture had permanently crippled the catalog mail-order business. In 1925 it began to open retail stores on the outskirts of town and, by 1929, it was operating over 300 of them. Montgomery Ward did not adapt itself to the new social and economic environment with the same enthusiasm. Viewed from the advantage of hindsight, it is quite clear that its more conservative policy was a mistake. By 1970, Sears, with $10 billion in sales, was a giant in American business, more than three times the size of Montgomery Ward, which was, of course, no pigmy. This divergent performance offered one of history's best and most publicized illustrations of the difference in the adaptability of business entrepreneurs.

Advertising and consumer credit

Modern developments in retailing would not have been possible without a gigantic expansion in advertising and consumer credit. These two institutions have fanned America's propensity to consume and kept the rate of consumption at fever pitch. It is estimated that in 1867, something like $50 million was spent for advertising of one sort of another. When George P. Rowell founded the American Newspaper Directory in 1869, advertising agencies bought and sold space. Their objective was to buy space from the publishers at the cheapest price possible and sell it to advertisers at the highest price possible. Thus, the agents

[13]For an exhaustive history of Sears, see Boris Emmet and John E. Jeucks, *Catalogues and Counters* (Chicago: University of Chicago Press, 1950). For some of the management problems, see Alfred D. Chandler, Jr., *Strategy and Structure* (Cambridge, Mass.: MIT Press, 1962).

were the leading participants in an intensely high-pressure, competitive economic game. Like many competitive games, this one pleased no one except a few spectators. In 1875, the N. W. Ayer agency instituted a radical change by inaugurating the open contract, under which the agency handled all the advertising for an account in return for a stipulated commission—in this case, 12.5 percent of the budget.

By the 1890s, merchandisers and some businessmen who realized that the utopian days of a virgin market were numbered had become fascinated by the miraculous powers of advertising. One enthusiastic adherent went so far as to say, "Advertising is the medium of communication between the world's greatest forces—demand and supply. It is a more powerful element in human progress than steam or electricity." One manufacturer spent $750,000 for one year's advertising, and Richard Sears spent more money on advertising than on wages. Innovations came rapidly. In 1899, N. W. Ayer broke new ground by organizing for the National Biscuit Company the first completely coordinated national advertising campaign, incorporating special packaging, a brand name, a slogan, and the combined resources of all known communications media. This pioneer effort was successful beyond the most optimistic expectations, for when it was finished, hardly any American was unaware of "Uneeda Biscuit." By then, total advertising expenditures had passed $500 million, ten times as much as a generation before. But even greater strides were yet to be made. National magazines, radio, television, and the challenge of sated appetites carried advertising appropriations to over $10 billion in the 1960s, 2 percent of the GNP, compared with perhaps nine-tenths of one percent in 1870. Yet advertising remained a highly cyclical industry; its expenditures varied directly with the business cycle, multiplying in boom, falling drastically in depression, and declining even in a mild recession.

The other stimulant to consumption, consumer credit, first became really important in the 1920s, when consumer durables, especially the automobile, became a significant part of consumer spending. Total consumer credit, divided about half and half between installments and charge accounts, amounted to about $6 billion in 1929, about 12 percent of retail sales and 7.5 percent of disposable income. By the 1970s, consumer credit had grown to almost $60 billion, more than one-third of retail sales and about 18 percent of disposable income.

Despite the larger scale of its organization and the constant reductions in shipping costs, distribution absorbed more and more economic resources as time passed.[14] Trade probably absorbed 6 percent of the labor force in 1870, 10 percent in 1929, and 19 percent in 1970. There were a number of reasons for this. For one thing, as discretionary income grew, more resources in the form of more attractive packaging and more sophisticated advertising were required to

[14]See Harold Barger, *Distribution's Place in the American Economy Since 1869* (New York: National Bureau of Economic Research, 1955).

attract marginal consumption expenditures. But much more important, productivity in trade did not rise as much as in other economic pursuits, and hours of work declined much more. If there are many economies of scale in retailing or, to express it differently, if large-scale operations can cut the cost of doing business, there is little chance for this to exert itself. There is little evidence to indicate any decline in the importance of the small retailer. Department stores handle about the same volume of business as in 1929, and so do the chain stores. Retail establishments that employ one hundred or more people have increased somewhat in relative number, but their share of total business is slightly less now than in 1929. Shops that employ 20 or more are, as one might expect, much more common in this much larger economy than they were in 1929 (5.2 percent, in contrast with 1.7 percent), but their share of total sales has not grown commensurately. They handled about 30 percent of the business in that other era of prosperity, compared with about 40 percent today. In any event, it is estimated that output per man-hour in distribution has risen about 1 percent a year since 1869, compared with better than 2.5 percent a year for the economy as a whole. The performance in the twentieth century has been even less satisfactory; output in manufacturing increased at an estimated rate of 3 percent a year, whereas in distribution it fell short of 1 percent. Meanwhile, hours of work in trade declined from 66 in 1869 to 54 in 1929 and to 35 in 1970, while they declined much more moderately from 56 to 44 to 40 in manufacturing.

Because productivity rose more slowly in trade, the costs of distribution had to rise. There are no reliable estimates of how much it cost to distribute goods in early America, but in 1929 it cost more to distribute goods than to make them, and there has been little change in the ratio since then. Although this is often condemned as an unconscionable situation, the high costs of distribution do not necessarily mean that middlemen are gouging the innocent consumer. High distribution costs are one of the prices paid for an advancing level of living for, as an economy progresses, the problems of primary and secondary production become less imposing. Then, in man's continuous economic struggle, attention is focused on gaining leisure and in improving service. If all the gains of economic progress that accrued after the initial conquest of the basic problems of primary and secondary production were taken in the form of increased leisure, distribution costs would not be so high, but neither would the level of living, measured in terms of material things.

SUGGESTED READINGS

(On specific topics, see the readings cited in the footnotes in the chapter.)

Callender, Guy S., "The Early Transportation and Banking Enterprises of the States in Relation to the Growth of Corporations," *Quarterly Journal of Economics,* Vol. XVII (1903). This classic essay has been reprinted in

Joseph T. Lambie and Richard V. Clemence, *Economic Change in America* (Harrisburg, Penn.: The Stackpole Company, 1954); Frederic C. Lane and Jelle C. Riemersma, *Enterprise and Secular Change* (Homewood, Ill.: Richard D. Irwin, Inc., 1953).

Cochran, Thomas C., *Railroad Leaders, 1845-1890* (Cambridge, Mass.: Harvard University Press, 1953).

Goodrich, Carter, et al., *Canals and Economic Development* (New York: Columbia University Press, 1961).

Fishlow, Albert, *American Railroads and the Transformation of the Ante-Bellum Economy* (Cambridge, Mass.: Harvard University Press, 1965).

Fogel, Robert W., *Railroads and American Economic Growth* (Baltimore, Md.: The Johns Hopkins University Press, 1964).

Jenks, Leland H., "Railroads as an Economic Force in American Development," *Journal of Economic History,* Vol IV (1944). Reprinted in Thomas C. Cochran and Thomas B. Brewer, eds., *Views of American Economic Growth,* Vol. II (New York: McGraw-Hill Book Company, 1966) and in Alfred D. Chandler, et al., *The Changing Economic Order* (New York: Harcourt, Brace and World, 1968).

Jones, Fred M., *Middlemen in the Domestic Trade of the United States* (Urbana: The University of Illinois, 1937).

Lively, Robert A., "The American System," *Business History Review,* Vol. XXIX (1955). Reprinted in Chandler, et al., *op. cit.,* and in Stanley Coben and Forest G. Hill, *American Economic History* (Philadelphia: J. Lippincott Company, 1966).

Martin, Albro, *Enterprise Denied: Origins of the Decline of American Railroads, 1897-1917* (New York: Columbia University Press, 1971).

Porter, Glenn and Harold C. Livesay, *Merchants and Manufacturers: Studies in the Changing Structure of Nineteenth Century Marketing* (Baltimore, Md.: Johns Hopkins University Press, 1971).

Shapiro, Stanley J. and Alton F. Dooley, *Readings in the History of Marketing, Settlement to Civil War* (Homewood, Ill.: Richard D. Irwin, 1968).

Taylor, George Rogers, *The Transportation Revolution* (New York: Holt, Rinehart & Winston, Inc., 1951), Chaps. 2-5 and 9.

QUESTIONS

1. In the early stages of railroad building, extensive development was emphasized. More recently, the development has been more intensive. What do these statements mean? Do you think any other type of development would have been more conducive to economic growth?

2. (a) What were the causes of the efforts on the part of the railroads to avoid competition?

   (b) What devices were used to escape or minimize competition?

3. Some people think that railroads are now a declining industry. Do you agree? Why, or why not? Are the problems of today's railroads different from those of the railroads a century ago?

4. The railroad industry's economic difficulties in this century are largely due to the way they were constructed, financed, and managed in the 1800s. Do you agree or disagree?

5. Compare and contrast the principal means of transportation around 1860 with those of today. How has the economic life of the nation been influenced by the change?
6. By reference to the history of transportation, describe:
   (a) How new industries encroach on the business done by old industries. Is the initial encroachment on all types of business done by the old industries or only on certain types? Do new industries eventually take away all the business, or do they leave something?
   (b) Why the process of encroachment is gradual rather than abrupt. Indicate the bearing of this on developments in the rest of the economy.
7. In what major ways has public policy affected the growth of American transportation in the twentieth century?
8. How has the process of distribution changed in American history?
9. Does it appear, from the historical evidence, that distribution costs too much?
10. Why is it said that modern business administration first began in the railroads?
11. How important do you think the railroads were?

Chapter Thirteen

THE INDUSTRIALIZATION
OF THE ECONOMY

Throughout most of American history, agriculture dominated the economy. In the Colonial Period, over 90 percent of the population made its living from farming. Factory production, as we know it today, did not exist, and most of the manufactured goods that were produced domestically were made by hand in the home. During the next two centuries, the economy gradually became industrialized, and today manufacturing is far more important than agriculture, the scene of production has shifted from the home to the factory, and the machine has replaced handcraft.

This chapter and the next will deal with four questions about the general development of manufacturing: How much did manufacturing grow? What were the reasons for the growth? How did industry change from a household, handcraft process to one in which the factory and the machine are typical? and What was the nature of the industrialization process? The answers to these questions should give an insight to manufacturing's vitally important impact on the level of living.

THE GROWTH OF MANUFACTURING

One way of measuring the growth of manufactures is in terms of the gross value of output. In 1810, when the largest plant in the country was worth less than $250,000, Tench Coxe estimated the gross value of manufactured product at $200 million, almost all produced at home. Admittedly, this estimate was only a guess and is hardly reliable as a measure of the extent of manufacturing. Better data did not appear until 1849, when the government took its first census of manufactures. Gross value of manufactured product was then estimated at a little over $1 billion. By 1860, it was almost $2 billion. But manufacturing was still far from what it was to become. Entrepreneurs had not transferred their allegiance to manufacturing. Caleb Cushing, for example, had only one-third of his $2.5 million estate invested in manufacturing when he died in 1862, and Cushing was a widely diversified capitalist. By 1899 manufacturing produced $11 billion. During the last half of the nineteenth century, therefore, gross value doubled every 15 years. In the first third of the twentieth century, total output rose at a slower rate, increasing slightly more than five times between 1900 and 1939. The pace accelerated in the next 20 years, total manufacturing sales reaching $650 billion in 1970.

Value added by manufacturing

Gross value of product is admittedly a very unsatisfactory method of measuring industrial growth, because it does not take into account the cost of the raw materials used in production, and thus does not represent the real value added by manufacturing. Manufacturing industry actually adds to the nation's product an amount equal to the gross value of manufactured output less the value of the goods used in the process of manufacturing. As shown in Chart 24, this net value, or "added value," as it is usually called, grew consistently decade by decade, except during the Great Depression. By 1970, value added by manufacturing, measured in terms of dollars of the same purchasing power, had climbed to over $260 billion from the 1849 figure of a little less than $2 billion.

These figures describe how much total manufacturing has increased. They measure the "extensive growth" of manufacturing. But they do not tell us very much about the "intensive growth," that is, the increase per unit of population or per unit of the labor force. Here, the rise was somewhat less spectacular. Between 1850 and 1970, population multiplied about nine times, but value added by manufacturing multiplied 130 times, or 14 times as fast as population.

Concealed within the secular growth of industrial production were precipitous increases and declines associated with the ups and downs of the business cycle. It took anywhere from 4 to 20 years for industrial production to double. It doubled in the general prosperity from 1860 to 1873. It slowed down during the depression of the 1870s and did not again double until 1888. The depression of the 1890s again dampened progress, and production did not double until 1902. After World War I, it took 20 years to double output, chiefly because manufacturing ran into the doldrums associated with the depressed 1930s. Indeed, by 1932, the depression had eradicated all the gain achieved in the previous

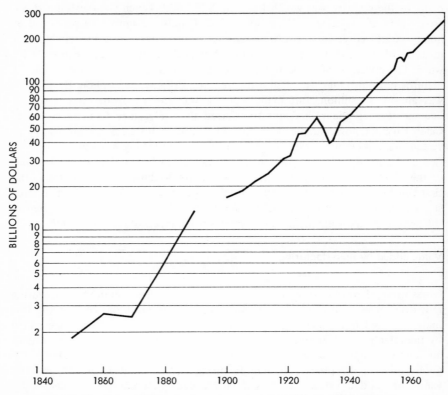

CHART 24. Value added by manufacturing, 1850-1970, in 1957-1959 prices.

20 years. The economy had sunk so far that it took only five years (1932-1937) to double the index. Thereafter, development proceeded at a much more encouraging rate. The index of industrial activity doubled between 1938 and 1942, again between 1941 and 1960, and rose another 60 percent in the 1960s.

Manufacturing's contribution to income and employment

The remarkable growth of manufacturing can be shown in still other ways, such as in its contribution to national income and to the labor force. Manufacturing accounted for perhaps 5 percent of income in 1800 and 14 percent (about two-thirds as much as agriculture) in the decade 1869-1878. Manufacturing continued to gain on farming, and by the last decade of the century, its contribution to income was about equal to that of agriculture. By the decade 1919-1928, the factory was producing about 22 percent of the national income, twice as much as agriculture. In the 1960s, manufacturing contributed about one-third of the national income, ten times as much as agriculture.

In like manner, manufacturing employed an increasing part of the nation's labor force while agricultural employment declined. In 1820, perhaps 8 percent of employed workers were involved in manufacturing. Steadily and gradually the share rose, until it reached about 25 percent in 1920. Since then, it has fallen slightly, dropping to about 23 percent in 1970.

By the end of the nineteenth century, when the net value of manufactured product exceeded the net value of the agricultural product, the United States had become not only an industrialized nation, but the largest industrial nation in the world. One of the few heartening economic trends during the otherwise gloomy "gay nineties" was the fact that in that decade America's industrial production came to exceed the combined production of Great Britain and Germany.

SOME CAUSES OF MANUFACTURING GROWTH

If we eliminate the effect of the business cycle, the growth of manufacturing did not take place in spurts and starts, but rather as a part of a steady process. This was to be expected, because most of the factors that discouraged growth were eliminated steadily rather than sporadically, while technology, the cause of most of the growth, advanced equally gradually and equally inexorably.

Every young economy must devote most of its resources to agricultural production, for food is the basic necessity of life and, until a good supply is assured, manufactured goods must remain the stuff of dreams. But the American people were determined to make the dream a reality. They were able and willing, indeed eager, to use technology. An almost limitless supply of land stocked liberally with natural resources lay before them, and in the cities and towns there were many merchants and shopkeepers who were potential business entrepreneurs. But to make the most of all these advantages, many obstacles had to be overcome.

Population in early America was too small to make the construction of good transportation facilities economically feasible. And because transportation was lacking, market areas were localized and too limited to permit specialization and division of labor. Even the most enterprising businessmen were reluctant to risk the prohibitive costs involved in shipping goods by pack animal and wagon train over roads that were no more than Indian trails. Early manufacturing was therefore limited to small-scale production.

A small population also meant a small labor force, and the lure and attractiveness of other types of work further diminished the skilled labor available for manufacturing. Some who had the skills tended to become petty capitalists rather than to work for someone else. For others, there was so much land in proportion to population that it seemed easy to become a landed proprietor—an ambition that was much more appealing than working as a skilled laborer.

The American businessman who wanted to enter manufacturing also faced a shortage of capital goods and capital funds. All in all, he had, if anything, too much enterprise and ambition. Nature had endowed the country with ample supplies of most of the essential raw materials. There was plenty of iron and timber; cotton could be cultivated on a large scale. To be sure, wool was in short supply, but in time this shortage would be easily corrected. Like the Ancient Mariner who was surrounded by water that he could not drink, the entrepreneur found himself swimming in raw materials but lacking the capital goods with which to process them, the capital funds with which to acquire tools and equipment, or the transportation with which to collect them.

The obstacles in the way of industrial growth were overcome not overnight and not even in a decade, but as part of a long, gradual, continuous process. Some of the factors involved in this process contributed more to the growth of production than to the growth of productivity, that is, they made possible extensive growth of manufacturing. Other factors gave a forward push to intensive manufacturing growth, contributing more to raising man-hour output than to raising total output.

One of the things that did the most to feed over-all manufacturing growth was the natural increase in the factors of production. Gradually, the labor force, the land area, and capital expanded to make possible a steady and gradual climb in total manufacturing output. At the same time, these factors and others were operating to give an impetus to productivity in the whole economy, especially in manufacturing, through technological development and improvement.

Technology

Technological progress made possible roundabout production, specialization, division of labor, and economies of scale. It gave the factors of production more hands than ordinarily they would have had and enabled them to use those hands with greater dexterity. In technological progress, therefore, lies an important clue to an understanding of the industrial growth and, consequently, the economic development of the United States.

Before explaining how this worked, it would be advisable to say what technology is. Technological progress is a complicated, many-sided movement that includes the substitution of natural energy for human exertion; the mechanization of industry, transportation, and agriculture; the standardization of equipment; and the development of mass production by means of specialization, division of labor, and scientific management. It incorporates the application of brains and skill to improve physical property—plant, tools, and equipment. Perhaps even more importantly, it also encompasses the multitudinous advances in managerial knowledge: the concept of interchangeable parts, assembly-line techniques, time and motion study, and design of factory buildings. In brief, technological progress means the application of analytic methods of science to the industrial arts.

Anything that speeded up the process of invention, encouraged business entrepreneurs to experiment with new devices, or improved the skills of labor accelerated technological change and industrial development. As the American economy advanced, numerous influences contributed to make this change progressively more rapid. The accumulation of capital, the creation of a workable money system, and the enlargement of the market area through more efficient transportation facilities certainly contributed. But of all the myriad influences that were at work, three were basic: the scarcity of labor, the expansion of education, and the prospect of profit. To this, the encouragement of an interested government could be added, but in a more subordinate position.

Scarcity of labor was the fundamental cause in carrying technology forward, for it was through the use of nonhuman energy, tools, machines, and capital goods in general that the small labor force could be made to produce more. The perceptive and oft-quoted de Tocqueville observed that the United States "was able to invent methods that may enable the worker not only to work better, but more quickly and more cheaply." Thus, it was technology that enabled the economy to produce and to use the capital goods needed to bridge the gap between the abundance of land and the scarcity of labor.[1]

Despite the unprecedented growth of American population, the labor supply remained scarce in proportion to the other factors. But population growth did quicken the demand for goods and did provide a versatile labor supply that could easily be adapted to new machinery, new methods of work, and new forms of division of labor. Moreover, the increased demand for goods was more than a function of the increase in numbers. This growing population had a high propensity to consume. It was a "young population," exerting greater demand than an "old population." Then too, the American culture encouraged the accumulation of material things. Because the population was not divided into social strata, there were no peculiar class tastes or needs. Anyone, regardless of his status, could buy goods, no matter how luxurious, provided he had the price. To satisfy this high propensity to consume, new capital goods in the form of tools, machines, and equipment were being demanded and added continuously, thus offering powerful incentives for constant technological progress.

The growing population also meant that a larger labor pool could be maintained from which recruits could be drawn to man the new machines. With minor exceptions, American workmen did not oppose technological innovation; the revolt against the machine that characterized the European industrial revolu-

[1]The relationship between labor scarcity and technology is exhaustively discussed in H. J. Habakkuk, *American and British Technology in the Nineteenth Century* (London: Cambridge University Press, 1962).

tion had no counterpart in American history. Of course, one of the reasons for this was that in Europe the machine was a substitute for labor, whereas in the United States, where labor was scarce, the machine was an addition to labor. Here, machinery increased production as well as productivity and added to the worker's wages rather than to his unemployment.

Tools fitted naturally into the American way of life. The American value system frowned upon leisure. It made work a fetish and production a religion. The oft-quoted European commentators, who observed so much, were quick to note this as an unusual trait. Said de Tocqueville, "The notion of labor is presented to the mind on every side as the necessary, natural, and honest condition of human existence. Not only is labor not dishonourable amongst such a people, but it is held in honour. In the United States, a wealthy man. . .would think thimself in bad repute if he employed his life solely in living." Another European, Friedrich von Raumer, remarked: "In America everyone is made to know that it is labor in some specific pursuit that alone gives life its value and importance."

Education and the change in the inventive process

The chronic scarcity of labor predetermined that technology would do well in the United States, but the rate of progress would depend on the facility with which men conceived new ideas and the rapidity with which they put those ideas into practice. This was a function of education, but the potential was slow in developing.

Although much scientific information had been accumulated even as early as the first half of the nineteenth century, it had not yet been integrated into college instruction, which still emphasized classical studies above all else. There was little organized education in mechanics or engineering. In fact, engineering education was largely confined to the Military Academy at West Point. As a result, scientific findings had not yet begun to filter down to industry. During the second half of the century, however, engineering and mechanical education progressed rapidly. In 1850, the Rensselaer Polytechnic Institute, which had been founded in 1824, became an engineering school. In 1862 the Federal government, through the Morrill Act, began to subsidize colleges for the agricultural and mechanical arts. In 1864, the National Academy of Sciences was founded; and in the following year, instruction began at the Massachusetts Institute of Technology. By the end of the century, there were 147 higher institutions offering technical education. Of this number, 66 were supported wholly or in part by the Federal or state governments.

As more and more technical schools opened, a growing stream of students began to enroll. Between 1830 and 1930, the number of engineering students increased almost 100 times as fast as the population, making the absolute increase almost a thousandfold.

Technological progress was speeded not only by the expansion of technical educational facilities, but also by changes that occurred in the inventive process. The inventive process had never been an individual one in the sense that one indicidual conceived an idea, elaborated it, and then carried it through by overcoming seemingly insurmountable obstacles. As J. F. Flexner aptly put it, "The term inventor has a meaning only if taken in the sense of a man who was slightly in advance of the procession at the crucial moment when his civilization was already on the verge of the discovery he was about to make."[2] But neither had the process ever been an organized group affair. Instead, each individual inventor built upon the work of innumerable other inventors, not in a cooperative or orderly fashion, but largely by hit-or-miss, trial-and-error methods.

As the roundabout method of production became more common, each single invention became less valuable. To meet the potentials imbedded in technology, each invention had to beget other inventions in an orderly sequence. The whole process became more conscious for, in the words of Professor Usher, "The inventor realized more or less clearly that the fulfillment of his purpose required several related inventions and discoveries, and not merely a single innovation."[3] The inventive process moved into the laboratory. It became more systematized, more disciplined, more orderly and less intuitive, more collective and less individual. It became a profession, with a good share of it organized on a group basis and financed by business enterprise and, to a lesser extent, by government. In 1925, 30,000 patents were granted to individual inventors; today, about half as many are issued to individuals. Meanwhile, the total of patents granted to corporate inventors crept up on those to individual grantees, passing them by in the early 1930s and rising in the process from less than 10,000 in the 1920s to 25,000 today. (See Chart 25.)

As it shifted more in the direction of the corporation, the inventive process became more efficient and more productive. This was so because commercial ventures had more success than individual ones. Something like 40 to 50 percent of individual inventions achieved commercial success, compared with 55 to 65 percent for corporate inventions. In addition, the time between invention and commercial success, although still very long, diminished as the corporation became more important. It has been estimated that in the England of the Industrial Revolution, it could take up to a century between the invention of a machine and its general adoption. In the late nineteenth century, it took about 33 years for the average successful patent to become fully developed. Today it takes about 17 years. What happened was that the inventors and technicians were spending less time in hunting will-o'-the-wisps and more time in finding ways to accomplish some predetermined goals. But here, again, there is a temptation to

[2]James F. Flexner, *Steamboats Come True* (New York: The Viking Press, Inc., 1944), p. 378. See also S. C. Gilfillan, *The Sociology of Invention* (Chicago: Follett Publishing Co., 1935).

[3]Abbott Payson Usher, *A History of Mechanical Inventions,* 1st ed. (New York: McGraw-Hill Book Company, 1929), p. 20.

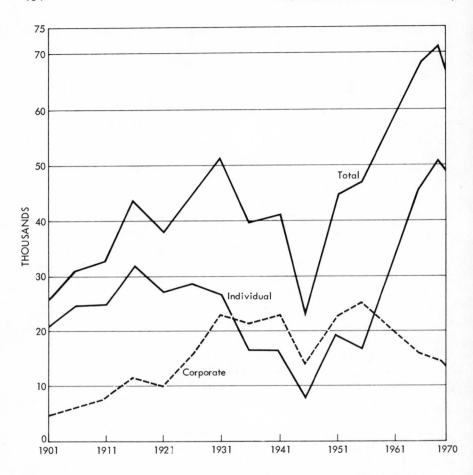

CHART 25. Patents issued to individuals and to corporations, 1901-1970, shown in thousands.

exaggerate the nature of the change in the inventive process. "The modern view about invention in the nineteenth century," writes John Jewkes, "is based on the assumption that science and the spread of formal scientific education have transformed the methods of invention, whereas they have only modified them; and that, in consequence, no previous inventors can have worked in the same manner as modern inventors, whereas they could and did."[4]

[4]John Jewkes, David Sawers, and Richard Stillerman, *The Sources of Invention* (New York: The Macmillan Company, 1958), p. 70.

The contribution of business to technological progress

Thus far we have said nothing about the fact that technological progress paid. It offered the prospect of a profit. In a sense, therefore, economic forces—the rule of the market place—brought forth invention.[5] But, what is more important, the more enterprising businessmen recognized this, found it fascinating, and took ample advantage of it. Of course, not all businessmen were equally daring. Many—probably most—hung back and resisted change. The annals of business history are thick with sentiments similar to the following: "Anything approaching an automatic machine was frowned upon. . . . Mr. Webster may be credited with forcing automatic machinery to the front as he constructed a machine to run half automatically against the positive orders of management."[6] It seems, however, that the more adaptive American businessmen were much quicker to make use of technological developments than were their European peers. Although there is no conclusive proof, it appears that Americans scrapped machinery faster than the British did. Part of the reason for the relative rapidity of scrappage was that from the beginning American machinery had more in-built obsolescence. But this really reflected a different set of values: the American was more intrigued by novelty. It was this contrast between European and American ways that probably led Friedrich List to say in the 1820s, "Everything new is quickly introduced here . . . .There is no clinging to old ways, the moment an American hears the word 'invention' he pricks up his ears."[7] Professor Nathan Rosenberg points out that mid-nineteenth-century English observers were astonished that American products were often designed to suit the machine rather than the customer. Of course, if the consumer refused to accept the product, it could not long be produced. Professor Rosenberg also points out that some firms and industries showed a greater willingness and ability to undertake technological innovations. Besides illustrating once again the differences between people, the disparate rate of adaptability goes far to explain why it is not possible to find a precise correlation between the rate of capital formation and economic growth.

Business enterprise also accelerated the adoption and development of machinery by emphasizing mass production and mass consumption. Without large-scale business, the type of technological evolution the United States experienced would not have occurred, because only large-scale business enterprises could afford to adopt the complicated and expensive machinery that technology even-

---

[5] Jacob Schmookler, "Economic Sources of Inventive Activity," *Journal of Economic History,* Vol. XXII (1962).

[6] C. W. Moore, *Timing a Century* (Cambridge, Mass.: Harvard University Press, 1945), p. 59.

[7] Quoted in Habakkuk, *op. cit.,* p. 49; Nathan Rosenberg, "Technological Change in the Machine Tool Industry 1840-1910," *Journal of Economic History,* Vol. XXIII (1963): same author, *Technology and American Economic Growth* (New York: Harper and Row, 1972).

tually produced. But large-scale business enterprise itself could not exist without mass production, which in turn was economically dependent on mass consumption. Very early in American history, the American businessman realized that his opportunities for expansion rested, in the last analysis, on the expansion of mass consumption, and he set his sights accordingly. As early as the Jacksonian period, some observers were suggesting that selling at a low price to all, rather than at a high price to a few, was a characteristic feature of American business.[8]

Thus, it was a combination of labor scarcity, education, and entrepreneurial initiative that gave an impetus to the machine and all it meant. In 1851, Sir Joseph Whitworth, the British machine builder, said, "It is this condition of the labour market, and the eager resort to machinery wherever it can be applied to which, under the guidance of superior education and intelligence, the remarkable prosperity of the United States is due." But this was not all. Over and over, the British commissioners explained the American system in terms of the American character with its restless energy, its rejection of class rigidity, its refusal to be bound by traditional ways of doing things, its goal of economic success, and its optimistic confidence in its ability to handle things mechanical. At times, the British commissioners themselves were swept along by the zestful atmosphere of the New World. In their enthusiasm, they often accepted the American dream as a reality and judged the Horatio Alger tale of rags to riches to be much more universally true than it actually was. "It may be said," the commissioners wrote, "that there is not a working boy of average ability in the New England states, at least, who has not an idea of some mechanical invention or improvement in manufactures, by which, in good time, he hopes to better his position or rise to fortune and social distinction."

Government aid to industrial growth

By subsidizing transportation facilities and fostering education, government did much for technological progress and industrial growth, but other government contributions were not particularly significant.

The Federal government early adopted a policy of encouraging industry by levying tariffs against European manufactured goods, but this trend was reversed when agrarianism became entrenched in the politics of the first half of the nineteenth century. After the Civil War, when the government's attitude toward industry had again changed, tariff rates were continuously pushed up to encourage manufacturing.

The tariff's influence on economic development was never as great as either protectionists or free-traders contended. Without tariffs, American manufacturing would still have grown to a position of world supremacy, for America's natural resources, enormous land mass, innovating entrepreneurs, efficient labor

[8]DeTocqueville, *op. cit.*, Vol. 2, p. 52.

supply, technological potential, and economic philosophy, not the tariff, made manufacturing successful in the United States. Nevertheless, certain specific tariffs did encourage economic progress by giving protection to some American industries in their infant stage, enabling them to survive the onslaughts of competition from other more industrialized areas. Tariffs helped the textile industries after the War of 1812, the iron industry in the 1840s, the steel business during the 1870s, and the tinplate business in the 1890s. Time after time, as new tariffs were imposed, commission merchants and wholesalers shifted from their foreign sources of supply and gave business to local manufacturers.[9] On the other side of the coin, tariffs also encouraged some industries that had no good economic reason for existence. They kept alive the lace business, watchmaking, and fine handicraft manufacturing that had difficulty competing with foreign products.

It has often been assumed that the patent system encouraged invention and thereby hastened technological progress, but this is a rather doubtful thesis. Actually, the government's contribution to technological progress through the patent system was less substantial than the contribution it made by encouraging education and by assisting in the building of transport facilities. The patent system is based on the heroic interpretation of history. It assumes that inventions are the work of one individual toiling away in the isolation of a garret. But each invention rests on existing knowledge, and virtually all important inventions have been made almost simultaneously by different individuals, indicating that the basic elements of each had already been discovered and that the time for synthesis had arrived. Thus, the patent system in itself did little to encourage invention. Furthermore, because nine-tenths of the patents issued not only failed to make money but did not even pay for their legal and other fees, some inventors gave up taking out patents because fighting to protect them consumed too much time and money. Cross-licensing agreements and patent pools, as used in modern industry, also represented essentially an abandonment of patenting. As a result, since the latter part of the nineteenth century, the American patent rate has not increased any faster than the population. In the late 1880s, the rate for patents issued to domestic inventors was one for each 2,760 people. The rate in the 1920s was one for each 3,930; in the 1940s, one per 3,530; and in the 1950s, one per 2,880. A similar decline in the rate in which patents have been applied for and granted has occurred in every country where industrialization has occurred. We may, therefore, conclude that the patent system has been a minor factor in technological progress. It was rather the American value system, the expansion of population, the accumulation of capital, the construction of transportation facilities, and the institutional framework of the American economy that predetermined a technological civilization and a very rapid industrial growth.

[9]Elva Tooker, *Nathan Trotter* (Cambridge, Mass.: Harvard University Press, 1955), p. 91.

A CENTURY AND A HALF OF TECHNOLOGICAL CHANGE

Early American industry was small and, compared with that of Great Britain, exceedingly primitive. To be sure, there were scattered throughout the colonies fairly sizable flour mills, breweries, distilleries, sugar refineries, and other processing industries which used some mechanical equipment and division of labor. But there was no such thing as a factory, that is, one plant that fabricated material by machinery from the raw state to the finished product. There were no complicated machines, and human energy was the chief source of power. Even the iron industry, the basic heavy industry of the day, was organized on a small-scale, rural basis.

This was the case despite the fact that a considerable portion of the American public was eager to encourage industry and manufacturing. The will to manufacture existed long before efficient methods were actually started. Quite early, strenuous efforts were made to stimulate an industrial consciousness, and in these efforts Americans fully exploited their peculiar gift for forming associations, but mostly to no avail.[10] The difficulty lay in the fact that ambitions far exceeded the means of satisfying them. Many of the things that we take for granted today were unheard of in 1776. This was especially true of machine tools, which constitute the very foundation of industrial technology. Watt's steam engine and Arkwright's water frame were already in existence in England, but the only equipment the mechanics who worked on these machines had were simple hand tools: hammers, chisels, and files. The only measuring devices were simple calipers and wooden rules. Although hand forging was fairly well advanced, metal-cutting appliances were still replicas of the tools of the Middle Ages.

Today, by contrast, the factory has become deeply entrenched. It has left the rural environs for the outskirts of the cities. Production has become thoroughly mechanized and organized, with intricate specialization and division of labor. Electricity, natural gas, oil, and the atom provide the power once supplied only by water and steam. Precision instruments measure in millionths of an inch. Machine tools work automatically, and the whole is overseen by the arts of scientific management.

These changes in technology occurred gradually and continuously rather than sporadically. Although it is impossible to measure the rate of change, it probably was relatively the same generation by generation. Almost every era in American history was rich in invention and innovation. Technological development was, therefore, evolutionary rather than revolutionary. Yet, as we shall see, each period was dominated by a particular type of technological development: the early years, by the accumulation of machines and tools; the late nineteenth

[10]See Samuel Rezneck, "The Rise and Development of Industrial Consciousness in the United States, 1760-1830," *The Journal of Economic and Business History,* Vol. IV (1932).

century, by the intensive development of bigger machines, better metals, and new sources of power; the early twentieth century, by scientific management and research and development.

PIONEERING IN AMERICAN MECHANIZATION

The first industries to introduce the factory system, large-scale machine operation, mass production, and intricate division of labor were armaments and consumer-perishable goods. Here the prospects for mass consumption were most encouraging. In the one case, it was the government that exerted a mass demand. In the case of consumer-perishables, such as textiles and food products, the demand was as large as the population, the cost of production was relatively low, the products were essentially standardized, and they absorbed only a small share of consumer income. Moreover, Europe had already performed much of the pioneer work, and on this Americans built, for it must be pointed out that, in mechanizing the economy, the American forte was not so much invention as innovation. American businessmen were always adaptive. They acquired technological processes, especially in the initial stages, from abroad and then experimented with them, often greatly improving on Old World originals. American business enterprise had well-developed talents for shaping other people's inventions to fit more closely into the practical world. Europeans themselves were the first to recognize that the American approach was different from theirs; they coined the term *American System,* by which they meant a system of mass production of standardized interchangeable parts, with heavy emphasis on utility and a general disregard for aesthetics.

The first serious moves toward standardization and interchangeable parts were made in government armories and arms factories, because government orders for muskets, arms, and ordnance offered one of the first ready-made mass markets. As early as 1717, an attempt was made in France to manufacture firearms with interchangeable parts. Nothing came of this abortive attempt, and it took almost another century before interchangeable parts manufacture became permanent. In 1798, Eli Whitney obtained a contract from the United States government to manufacture within two years ten thousand stands of arms, which in that day meant muskets and the various appurtenances thereto. Whitney understood that to fulfill his contract would require roundabout methods of production with machinery taking the place of skilled labor. As he somewhat prosaically put it, "A substitute for European skill must be sought in such an application of mechanism as to give all that regularity, accuracy, and finish which is there effected by a skill." Whitney spent two years building machinery before making a musket. In fact, it took him eight, not two,[11] years to satisfy the original contract. Yet, the experiment was a great success.

[11] Constance M. Green, *Eli Whitney and the Birth of American Technology* (Boston: Little, Brown and Co., 1956).

While Whitney was involved with muskets, Simeon North began to manufacture small arms with interchangeable parts. In 1808, he wrote the Secretary of the Navy: "I find that by confining a workman to one particular limb of the pistol until he has made two thousand, I save at least one-quarter of his labor."[12] But despite clear evidence of its feasibility, interchangeable parts manufacture was slow in being accepted. It was not until 1813 that the government signed a contract with North to make 20,000 pistols specifically with interchangeable parts. Even then, considerable skepticism remained, and it took until the late 1820s before the War Department fully accepted the idea. By then, however, the practice had spread beyond the arms industry, and Connecticut artisans were making clocks with interchangeable parts. By the middle of the century, agricultural machinery and watches had also joined in, with immense gains in productivity.

Textile machinery

The emphasis on the pragmatic and the practical was clearly outlined in the early beginnings of the armaments industry, but perhaps the best illustration of the process of building on someone else's foundation was to be found in textile machinery, for here the American entrepreneur's adaptive abilities had to overcome special obstacles. Long before the seeds of manufacturing had taken hold in America, England had performed the pioneer work in textile machinery, producing the fly shuttle, the water frame, the spinning jenny, the power loom, and the mill for roller spinning. From the beginning of the Industrial Revolution, Great Britain tried to keep secret her recipe for industrial success. She made valiant attempts to prevent the emigration of skilled artisans out of a fear that workers would carry their knowledge of English techniques to other lands where, in time, they might be utilized to Britain's disadvantage in world trade. Like all bans on people's movements, this one was not a complete success. A few English workmen did come to America and joined hands with American entrepreneurs in constructing and using textile machinery.

The very early attempts were unsuccessful, principally because of faulty memories and a lack of skilled labor. However, toward the end of the eighteenth century, Samuel Slater, an English workman, learned that prizes and bounties were being offered in the United States for information on the construction of textile machinery. He sailed secretly, and in 1791, after a disappointing venture in New York, he moved to Rhode Island where, with the help of two capitalists, Almy and Brown, he began to operate a small enterprise to spin cotton yarn by machinery. Subsequently, in 1811, a Bostonian, Francis Cabot Lowell, traveling through Great Britain made a painstaking study of English textile-manufacturing

[12] Felicia Deyrup, *Arms Makers of the Connecticut Valley* (Northampton, Mass.: Smith College Studies in History, 1948).

machinery. Upon his return to the United States, he turned his information over to Paul Moody, an able mechanic, whose job was to convert the raw data into a working machine. Moody succeeded in building a power loom, which, although admittedly imperfect, was at least equal to the looms then being used in England. Then, in 1814, Lowell and his brother-in-law, Patrick Tracy Jackson, began large-scale manufacture of cotton textiles in their famous plant at Waltham, Massachusetts.

In similar fashion, the woolen industry became mechanized and moved from the home to the factory. In 1793, John and Arthur Scholfield left Yorkshire for the United States, where they built a carding machine and began to spread information about the techniques and the machinery used by the British in spinning and weaving woolens. Building upon this base, American mechanics and businessmen, chiefly by accelerating the speed of operation, replacing wood with metal, and making processes automatic, steadily improved textile machines. By 1820, the United States had taken the lead in innovating textile machinery. A decade later, the technical equipment in textiles had achieved its modern form. In the woolen industry, according to Arthur H. Cole, "Within forty years, improvements, chiefly of American origin, had given a new significance to the power-driven carding machine borrowed from England; had made the spinning operation quasi-automatic by a development unknown abroad; had harnessed the loom to power, for the most part independently of foreign advance; and had largely removed hand processes from the cloth–finishing operations through the invention of machines so valuable that they were frequently copied by other nations in subsequent years."[13]

Meanwhile, some quite amazing behavior was taking place in food processing. Contrary to popular notion, the automobile industry was not the first to use the mechanized conveyor and the moving assembly line. The honor belongs to Oliver Evans, an extraordinarily talented inventor, perhaps the most talented in American history. Evans in 1785 put together a complicated system of flour-milling machinery. Run by water power, his plan included elevators, conveyors, hoppers, drills, and descenders. The whole process was entirely automatic, a century and a half before the word *automation* was invented. In fact, the whole idea was so revolutionary and so far ahead of its time that Evans never really succeeded in getting it adopted.

Machine tools and precision instruments

Wooden machines were made by hand and, as long as mechanized industry was relatively uncommon, machines could be custom-built rather than mass-produced. With the spread of mechanization and the expansion of the market

[13] Arthur H. Cole, *The American Wool Manufacture* (Cambridge, Mass.: Harvard University Press, 1926), Vol. I, p. 86.

area, however, mass production of machinery for the few mass-consumption industries—armaments, clocks, textiles, and agricultural implements—became a possibility. This meant that it was necessary to have machines to make the machines that made the machines. But before the full fruits of this roundabout process could be realized, standardization of products had to be worked out, machine tools and high-precision instruments had to be invented.

Machine tools are the devices that do the turning, grinding, boring, milling, and planing that is a prerequisite in building metal machinery. The industry has always been small. Even today it consists of 325 companies, employing 60,000 with sales of less than $1 billion. But, small as it is, it is infinitely important, for without it mass production would not be possible.

One of the reasons why the machine-tool industry has always been small is that it has been very closely knit, with all its parts and all its actors intricately intermeshed. Each new tool created a need and a demand for a series of other tools. The talented minds who invented and created there tools were all inter-related. They worked with each other and learned from each other. Knowledge was handed down from master to apprentice, generation after generation. The family tree began in England, where Joseph Bramah, who made an almost un-pickable lock, trained Henry Maudslay, whose slide rest made the lathe a much more accurate tool and was therefore one of the most important "inventions" in all mechanical history. The same ladder descended in the United States from Eli Whitney and Simeon North to the modern toolmakers.

Samuel Colt used the Whitney plant in making his automated revolver. Colt's superintendent, Elisha K. Root, trained Pratt of Pratt and Whitney. The firm of Robbins and Lawrence was the lineal ancestor of Jones and Lamson. William Sellers, the Philadelphia machine builder, was head of the Midvale Steel Company in which Frederick W. Taylor was trained. Henry M. Leland, who introduced interchangeable parts into the automobile business, worked in the Springfield Armory, in the Colt plant, and for Brown and Sharpe.

The evolution of the machine-tool industry took place in an incredibly short time as time is measured by the historian. In the late eighteenth century, the best-equipped machinist possessed nothing but the simplest tools. His precision instruments were incapable of producing fine tolerances. Even as late as 1813, the best tolerance that an experienced toolmaker strove for was one-thirty-second of an inch. Yet, by 1850, a little more than 50 years after the beginnings, the general principles of machine tools were well established. The evolution in form was largely complete, and since then further progress has been mostly in improvements and refinements. Up to about 1850, the progress was one of extensive development; since then, it has been one of intensive development. In more economic terms, it may be said that before 1850, machine tools was a capital-using industry. Thereafter it became a capital-saving industry; instead of new machines, existing machines were improved in size, speed, versatility, and automaticity. One machine replaced many machines.

We can only mention a few of the many contributions that were made to the industry, for they came thick and fast—so fast, in fact, that Colt in the 1850s was using 1,400 different tools to make his revolver. Among the most important contributions were the steady and spectacular improvements in lathes, the machines that controlled the operation of machine tools. Power-driven lathes were already in existence at the opening of the nineteenth century. Shortly thereafter, Maudslay's slide rest infinitely improved their accuracy. Then Christopher Soener produced the cam control, which made lathe operation automatic. The final stage came in 1854, when F. W. Howe and D. D. Stone of Robbins and Lawrence, the Windsor, Vermont, gunmakers, built a turret lathe. By then the lathe had become an early example of advanced automation.

Milling machines also evolved quickly. Both Eli Whitney and Simeon North used milling machines, but the first one made for sale was designed by the same F. W. Howe of Robbins and Lawrence. Brown and Sharpe, in 1862, are credited with being the inventors of the universal milling machine. The work of Joseph R. Browne was especially important in the improvement of precision instruments. He built a linear dividing engine in 1850. This first automatic machine for graduating rules was so practical that it is still in use. In 1851, Brown, working on principles borrowed from the French, made the first inexpensive caliper, giving the machinist a piece of everyday equipment that could measure within one-thousandth of an inch.[14]

Toward the end of the century, Frederick W. Taylor succeeded in producing high-speed steel tools that led to a general redesign of the whole industry, enormously increasing the durability, cutting power, and speed of machine tools. In the middle of the nineteenth century, steel could be cut at a rate of 50 feet a minute. With high-speed steel, this had been raised to 120 feet by 1890. Chips could be cut from metal at four ounces per minute in 1850. Today, machine tools chip away 20 pounds per minute. The modern tool is about ten times as accurate as well as 80 times as fast. In addition, it is multiple: some modern precision tools can measure at 32 different points simultaneously, and a multiple-spindle drill can bore 98 holes at the same time.

In the race toward machine-tool progress, the Americans quickly took the lead. The British readily acknowledged American superiority. In London in 1851 an exhibit of guns made with interchangeable parts by Robbins and Lawrence attracted so much attention that a visit was made to American factories in 1853 by a British Commission whose members were, as you will recall, most impressed by the "American System." They did point out that American goods often appeared crude, but this was more than balanced by their simplicity, originality, effectiveness, and, above all, their cheapness. As a result of the Commission's visit, the British government "resolved to introduce the American System." It

---

[14] See Nathan Rosenberg, "Technological Change in the Machine Tool Industry," *Journal of Economic History,* Vol. XXIII (1963).

ordered 20,000 interchangeable-parts rifles and thoroughly equipped the Royal Small Arms factory at Enfield with American machine tools. Nor was this all; other governments joined in, and the resulting orders opened up world markets to American gunmakers and tool builders. But the American superiority in machine tools should not be exaggerated. In 1850, the English were still far ahead in most manufacturing fields, but what was most impressive was that a nation that was just getting off the economic ground should excel in any field.

Why did the United States do so well in mechanized mass production? To a great extent, it was because of the usual sterotyped reasons: expanding markets, improving transportation, the attitude of a sympathetic government, and a great labor shortage. But this is not a complete explanation. As Sawyer has pointed out, "All this had emerged before the 'big' explanations became operative and at a time when principles of comparative advantage might have argued for other lines of growth—before the transcontinentals and the open hearths; before the ores of the Mesabi or the opening up of oil; before the great capital accumulations associated with later decades; and, most important, before that always-cited bigger American market had come into existence."[15] As English observers seemed to have recognized, much of the explanation for the rapid growth of the "American System" lay in the American environment and the American character.

STEEL REPLACES IRON

Each generation is tempted to think that its contribution to technological history is uniquely rich. But this is not true. Every period has produced a wealth of inventions that seemed miraculous at the time. The late nineteenth century was no exception. It saw: "mechanical reapers, mowing and seeding machines, the steamplow and most other eminently labor-saving agricultural devices; the Bessemer process and the steel rail; the submarine and transoceanic telegraph cables; photography and all its adjuncts; electroplating and the electrotype; the steamhammer; repeating and breech-loading firearms, and rifled and steel cannon; guncotton and dynamite; the industrial use of India rubber and gutta-percha; the steam-excavator and steam-drill; the sewing machine; the practical use of the electric light; the application of dynamic electricity as a motor for machinery; the steam fire-engine; the telephone, microphone spectroscope, and the process of spectral analysis; the polariscope; the compound steam engine; the centrifugal process of refining sugar; the rotary printing press; hydraulic lifts, cranes and elevators; the 'regenerative' furnace, iron and steel ships, pressed glass, wire rope, petroleum and its derivatives, and analine dyes; the industrial use of the metal nickel, cotton-seed oil, artificial butter, stearine-candles, natural

15 John E. Sawyer, "The Social Basis of the American System of Manufacturing," *Journal of Economic History,* Vol. XIV (1954).

gas, cheap postage, and the postage stamp."[16] But, of all the technological changes of the last generation of the nineteenth century, the triumph of steel was the most important.

High on the list of Little-Known Facts in American History is the surprising intelligence that there were more ironworks in the colonies than there were in England. In 1700, the colonies produced one-seventeenth of the world's total output, and in 1775, when every colony except Georgia possessed an iron mill, America's share had risen to one-sixth. With 80 blast furnaces, the colonies actually exported iron to England. Yet total production was very small, the entire output in 1775 coming to something like 30,000 tons. The average iron-works operated for no more than 20 or 30 weeks of the year and produced at most ten tons a day, about as much as can now be turned out in half a minute. Only the best-grade iron ore could be used. The ore was reduced by being smelted in a small blast furnace; charcoal provided the fuel, and bellows and blowing cylinders kept the fire roaring. When the furnace cooled, a few poinds of crude iron were found at the bottom in lumps known as "pigs." This was refined by innumerable heatings in a forge and interminable beatings under a water-driven hammer. The resultant wrought iron, known as *merchant bar,* was sold through country stores to blacksmiths and other fabricators, who converted it into finished products, such as horseshoes, nails, and tools.

Production fell off sharply following the Revolution and really did not pick up again until the 1820s. Then the spread of mechanization accelerated improvements in the metal industries. As machine production became more prevalent, experimenters began to use iron instead of wood to construct machines. Wood lasted just as long as iron, but it could not be used in larger machines. Furthermore, iron did not warp, but wood did. In the textile industry, warped machinery could not be used satisfactorily because it broke the thread and caused periodic breakdowns in production. As early as 1820, some machinery built of iron was being used in making woolens. Although it took some decades for the new idea to permeate the industry, the transition from wood to metal was entirely completed in textiles by midcentury.

As more machines were made of iron, the demand for iron naturally increased. By then, too, railroad building had begun in earnest, creating a gigantic demand for metal for rails and equipment. Consequently, improvements had to be made in both the quantity and the quality of iron and steel production. The old processes of smelting and refining iron by beating it under a triphammer gave place early in the nineteenth century to puddling and rolling. Coal replaced charcoal as fuel around 1840. This transition occurred considerably later than in England where coke was widely used as early as 1810. When the transition did take place in the United States, it involved anthracite rather than bituminous as in England. Because we were ordinarily quick to adopt British innovations, the

[16]David A. Wells, *Recent Economic Changes* (New York: Appleton-Century-Crofts, Inc., 1889), pp. 64 ff.

late shift and the use of hard rather than soft coal deserves an explanation. Coal appeared late in American iron making for three reasons: 1) iron made with charcoal was superior to that made with coke and iron made with anthracite was superior to iron made with charcoal, 2) bituminous coal was not readily accessible in the absence of good transportation facilities, and 3) it was not until the late 1830s that the problem of igniting anthracite was satisfactorily solved. When it did come into general use, coal broke the fetters that were holding back the spread of factory production.[17]

Immense strides were also made in the late nineteenth century in producing steel. In 1855 and 1856, Henry Bessemer in England and William Kelly in the United States independently hit upon the idea of blowing a blast of air through molten iron, thus removing the excess carbon that differentiates iron from steel. The first attempts to use the Bessemer process on a big scale failed because the iron ore that was used was heavy in phosphorus. This difficulty was corrected when Robert Mushet developed spiegeleisen, an alloy of iron and manganese that, when added to the recipe, regulated the amount of carbon that steel had to contain in order to be durable. With the Bessemer process, it became possible to produce a much larger volume of steel at a much lower price. The puddling process, which, it will be remembered, was an improvement over the colonial method, could produce 500 pounds of iron in three to five hours; the Bessemer converter could produce five tons of steel in half an hour.

Meanwhile, too, bigger and better blast furnaces were turning out more and more pig iron. A typical furnace could belch forth about 20 tons a week in 1800, 60 tons in 1850, 2,400 tons in 1890, and 7,000 tons in 1960. Total pig iron production increased about five times between 1810 and 1840, and about seven times between 1850 and 1880.

Improvements in steel making did not end with the Bessemer process. Even before Sir Henry read his famous paper on a new method of cooking iron, Williams Siemens, a German-born Englishman, had demonstrated the advantages of the open-hearth process. The open-hearth furnace, a rectangular furnace lined with lime and magnesium, enabled steel producers to use low-grade coal and produced a greater heat, increasing pig iron output by 20 percent. The Thomas-Gilchrist process, which came in the late 1870s, made it possible once and for all to use the highly phosphoric ores that could not be used in the Bessemer process. By the early twentieth century, the open-hearth method had quite clearly bypassed the use of the Bessemer converter. Subsequently, the modern electric furnaces produced new types of steel for special purposes. Manganese steels and other alloy steels of unusual hardness were used in railroad frogs, battleships, and scientific instruments. High-speed steels could be operated without damage at red-hot temperatures.

[17] Peter Temin, "A New Look at Hunter's Hypothesis about the Antebellum Iron Industry," *American Economic Review,* Vol. LIV (1964); Alfred D. Chandler, Jr., "Anthracite Coal and the Beginnings of the Industrial Revolution in the United States," *Business History Review,* Vol. XLVI (1972).

CHART 26. Pig iron production, five-year moving average, 1855-1956.

Table 28

STEEL PRODUCTION, 1900-1970

(millions of net tons)

	Open-hearth	Bessemer	Electric	Basic Oxygen	Total
1900	3.8	7.5	—	—	11.3
1908	8.8	6.9	—	—	15.7
1920	36.6	9.9	0.6	—	47.2
1929	54.2	8.0	1.1	—	63.2
1932	13.3	1.7	0.3	—	15.3
1944	80.4	5.0	4.2	—	89.6
1960	86.4	1.2	8.4	3.3	99.3
1970	48.0	—	20.1	63.3	131.5

SOURCE: William T. Hogan, *Economic History of the Iron and Steel Industry* (Lexington, Mass.: D. C. Heath and Company, 1971).

In other branches of metallurgy, more and more nonferrous and light metals began to be used. Aluminum, magnesium, chromium, and others became increasingly popular because of their lightness, resistance to corrosion, reflectivity, or workability.

Under the pressure of technological improvements plus an intense demand for steel for railroads, bridges, and other structures, production soared at an almost unbelievable rate. In 1870, Great Britain turned out something like 650,000 tons of steel, the United States produced about 200,000 tons, and Germany about 100,00 tons. By 1900, Great Britain was producing a little less than five million tons, but United States production was almost twelve million and Germany's was about eight million.

Once again, the United States had accomplished this more by innovation than by invention. Aside from Kelly's converter, which, justly or unjustly, was never accorded much credit, what the Americans did was well described by Captain Billy Jones, Carnegie's superintendent. In 1881, Jones told the British Iron and Steel Institute: "While your metallurgists . . . have been devoting their time and talents to the discovery of new processes, we have swallowed the information so generously tendered and have selfishly devoted ourselves to beating you in output."

In steel, the United States never did take the lead in innovation. Because of this and for other reasons, we lost our position of world superiority. In 1947, the United States produced over 56.7 percent of the world's steel. From then on its share fell rapidly until 1960 and more slowly thereafter until it had shrunk to 22.5 percent in 1969.

THE EVOLUTION OF POWER

Like the development of mechanization, the evolution of power was a long-drawn-out and continuous process. Manpower was replaced by water power, and water power by steam, electricity, oil, and natural gas. And eventually these sources may be replaced by atomic energy. This gradual improvement in power was a most potent influence in American economic development, for today it would require the labor of five billion slaves, or about twice the world's population, to accomplish the work done by the harnessed energy resources of the United States.

Although the steam engine was older than the United States, early American industry made little use of it. Even when Oliver Evans in 1801 built an inexpensive and remarkably efficient engine, American industry was not impressed. New England, the cradle of American industrialism, had a water supply more than ample for its needs. Although water power was not as expansible as steam because it was limited to those areas where streams ran and rivers flowed, it did not require the complex machinery used by steam and it was much cheaper. As late as 1840, the cost of generating one horsepower by water was $12 compared with $90 for steam. Watt's steam engine commanded 14 horsepower—not much more than other forms of power. A man turning a crank handle could generate about seven-hundredths of one horsepower; a bullock, three-tenths of a horsepower; a horse, one-half; and water wheels and windmills, with few exceptions, ten horsepower. Once a dam and wheel were built there were, aside from maintenance, no energy costs. Hence, water power was much cheaper than steam, especially if only small quantities of power were needed or if power was not needed in places removed from streams.

As industry continued to grow, available water-power sites became scarcer and scarcer. Accordingly, attempts were made to make more efficient use of water power. The pitchback wheel, with 75 percent efficiency, was developed. Then the water turbine was put into use on a larger scale. By 1840 Fall River and Lowell were using turbines that were 88 percent effective. But, as industry moved with markets away from waterways and as existing and available power sites were utilized to capacity, new sources had to be pressed into service. At the same time, technology had just about exhausted the possiblities of human energy and water power. But the vast potentials of steam had hardly been tapped. By 1850, a steam engine could be expected to turn out 50 horsepower. Steam began to overtake water as the principal agent of power, although as late as 1869, water power still accounted for 50 percent of all industrial power consumed.

The steam engine represented a vast improvement over water power, but it had some of the same basic weaknesses. It could not transmit power beyond the range of its belts and shaftings any more than streams could beyond their banks. It often led to excessive industrial centralization because it had to be used fairly near to coal deposits. It could not be used effectively to propel small vehicles, and it was not very practical on the farm. Moreover, there were limits to the efficiency of the reciprocating engine, which was the chief means for utilizing steam at the middle of the nineteenth century. The power that it could generate varied directly with the size of the engine, and in most cases it was impractical to build an engine of a size that could generate very large amounts of power. All this was changed by a series of events that occurred in the last quarter of the century. The invention of the steam turbine, the invention of the internal combustion engine, and the application of new devices to the generation of electricity created far more flexible sources of energy than before.

As with most "inventions," the utilization of electricity was a gradual process. Michael Faraday, the British scientist, had discovered the principle of induced current as early as 1831, but not much was done with it until Edison in 1876 devised a method of using electricity for illumination. Electricity was, however, very expensive and not practical for industrial use because it could not be transmitted over long distances from low-cost generating plants. George Westinghouse finally solved this problem by building a transformer that could reduce voltage at the point where current was used, thus permitting electricity to be transmitted at high voltages. As with all inventions, it took time for the transformer to be adopted, but once it came into use, electricity became feasible as a major power source. In 1900 electricity and steam each supplied about equal percentages of industrial power, but by 1960 seven-eighths of the nation's industrial power came from electric motors. Instead of being chained to water power or to their own steam-power plants, factories could now avail themselves of electric power generated by water power or steam hundreds of miles away. This meant substantial savings in capital, resources, and space and allowed greater flexibility in the use of power within a factory. It also meant a vast increase in the total amount of power available for production, because coal, water, fuel oil, and natural gas could be used to generate electricity.

But electricity was not too satisfactory for use for vehicles or mobile machines. Here, however, what electricity could not do, the internal-combustion engine could, because its unit size did not limit the total amount of energy it could create. Compact gasoline engines, in automobiles, trucks, and tractors, provided an almost incomprehensible volume of horsepower available for use on the nation's highways and farms. In 1800, a flourmill worker commanded about 1.66 horsepower. Oliver Evans raised this figure to 5; by 1910, it had reached 22 and today it is about 40.

SCIENTIFIC MANAGEMENT AND RESEARCH AND DEVELOPMENT

More and increasingly complex machines made it necessary to devise improved managerial techniques and better organization of physical facilities in order to achieve a more intensive application of mass-production methods in fabrication and assembly. Under old organizational forms, these methods had reached the point of diminishing returns. But a new race of engineers was already at work on this problem. The solution, they believed, lay in scientific management, which they confidently believed held the key to greater efficiency and productivity.

Scientific management represented the utilization of research as an approach to the solution of management problems. It was a nonmechanical aspect of technological progress. It stressed standardization of product and process; better organization; coordination and control of men, materials, and machines; rigid production planning; time and motion studies; incentive plans; and selection and training of workers.

The term *scientific management* was first used in 1910 at hearings before the Interstate Commerce Commission, but the movement itself was a gradual development, growing out of a preoccupation with management problems that first manifested itself in 1886 when Henry Towne read a paper on "The Engineer as Economist" before the American Society of Mechanical Engineers. The management movement, as this forerunner of scientific management was called, at first paid particular attention to differential wage systems; later it stressed cost finding; and about 1900, it shifted its emphasis to organization and system. Although interest in the movement spread, especially among engineers, it had relatively little influence in the practical business world.

At about the same time that the management movement was getting under way, Frederick W. Taylor, the pioneer in creating a widespread interest in scientific management, was making his initial experiments as assistant foreman in the machine shop of the Midvale Steel Company. Taylor had by the 1880s already concluded that the usual method of using force instead of knowledge to increase factory output caused antagonism and waste and defeated its essential purpose. He proposed to study each job in order to ascertain scientifically the "one best way" of doing it. The next step was to build the "one best way" into a set of rules that each worker had to follow in order to earn premium pay for outstanding productivity.[18]

Taylor's initial goal was to measure and specify a proper day's work for each operation and, in line with this, he began to experiment by controlling all the variables in the actual production process—shafting, belting, machine adjustments, tools, and disposition of materials—in order to discover the most productive working conditions for one group of workers engaged in one particular task. He immediately achieved a remarkable increase in output without any additional effort on the part of the worker. Having succeeded in increasing the productivity of a single group of workers, Taylor broadened his sights. He perceived that jobs in all work places could be standardized and that operations behind the worker could be coordinated in order to facilitate the flow of work. This not only meant that the output for each job could be measured against a standard, but it also meant that men and machines would no longer stand idle between job operations. To carry out his ideas, Taylor found it necessary to institute special training in order to secure the most effective performance and coordination of all operations at each work place. Thus, planning, preparation, training, and cooperation were added to measurement and standardization as elements of managerial technique.

In its initial stages, scientific management as promulgated by Taylor was concerned chiefly—almost exclusively—with production. But in time, this appeared inadequate. It was not working out as well as had been hoped and expected. Scientific management began to be obsessed with "the breakdown of morale in workers." As Taylor expressed it, "Few seem to want to work any more than is absolutely necessary. Many want something for nothing, do not care how they do their work and constantly seek to 'pass the buck.'" After World War I, the movement broadened and began to aim for more rational utilization of all the elements in the business process—materials, labor, and machinery. The various problems of management were approached analytically and studied in more detail than ever before. Business enterprise began paying greater attention to sales forecasting, cost accounting, statistics, quality control, budgeting, personnel administration, and industrial psychology. Just as the latter half of the nineteenth century saw the growth of formalized education for engineers, so the twentieth century witnessed a great acceleration of formalized education for businessmen. Between 1900 and 1910 alone, 240 volumes on

---

[18] Reinhard Bendix, *Work and Authority in Industry* (New York: John Wiley & Sons, Inc., 1956), pp. 274 and 282.

business management were published; and in 1908, Harvard University founded its Graduate School of Business Administration. By 1960, collegiate schools of business granted 50,000 undergraduate degrees and another 5,000 advanced degrees. In a complicated economy, it was no longer feasible for an entrepreneur to proceed along lines that were in vogue 50 years previously. It was freely recognized that leadership and success in business depended on education as well as on experience.

Science moved into business in other ways in the twentieth century, ways that were spectacular enough to lead to gross exaggeration. Typical was the movement that came to be referred to in twentieth-century shorthand as "R and D." It is reported that in the early 1900s, a DuPont executive said that his company required no basic research; it could buy all it needed in Europe. Business leaders were not really as parochial as this statement implied. Standard Oil had done much research in the use of by-products and the Carnegie Company employed a chemist to give it a better mix in producing steel. But it is true that, although there were some organized research facilities in Europe, the first American laboratory did not appear until General Electric established it in 1900. By then a great transition was taking place in the market. Years of progress in the level of living were beginning to produce significant discretionary income; years of manufacturing progress had filled a substantial part of the market. Competition put less stress on price and more on product differentiation. Management was forced to seek new products and new lines. In an atmosphere of scientific management, diversification led naturally to research and development. American business was changing slowly and more or less unconsciously from "know-how" to "know-what."

Yet the growth of research was far from sensational. There were perhaps 100 private laboratories at the outbreak of World War I. By 1920, there were perhaps 300, employing around 7,000 and spending less than $50 million. By 1970, research and development employed over half a million and expenditures amounted to a little less than 3 percent of the gross national product. But of this, the largest fraction was financed by the Federal government. In 1970, over half of all estimated research spending was paid for by the government, whereas industry paid for about 40 percent.

A negligible sum was spent for basic research, about 20 percent for applied research, and 80 percent for development. Four industries accounted for 75 percent of all spending: aircraft and missiles for 35 percent, electronics for 23 percent, and about 17 percent was divided almost equally between the chemical and machinery industries.

TECHNOLOGY'S CONTRIBUTION

Technology and industrialism radically influenced all segments of the American economy, and the rapid speed at which the growth took place intensified the influence, so that it permeated social as well as economic life.

Table 29

RESEARCH AND DEVELOPMENT EMPLOYMENT AND EXPENDITURES

	Number of employees	Expenditures (millions)	Percent of GNP
1920	7,367	$ 48	.05
1931	32,830	214	.28
1940	107,033	336	.33
1950	235,609	1,980	.70
1960	387,000	10,507	2.08
1970	555,000[1]	26,287	2.70

[1] 1969 estimated.
SOURCE: National Science Foundation, *National Development Resources,* 1953-1972.

To begin with, technology boosted man-hour output. In an exhaustive study of manufacturing made in 1832, respondents paid close attention to the question of what had happened to costs and productivity. According to a typical answer, "The various articles manufactured in the country are probably produced at something less than 50 percent of their costs in the earliest days. This saving has resulted partially in diminished expense of raw materials; something has been saved in the expense of labor; but the principal difference has resulted from the introduction of improved machinery." It is hard to say what happened in the next 20 years, but from 1850 there are various estimates of the improvement in productivity. According to one, manufacturing productivity gained 40 percent between 1850 and 1890. In other words, five men could produce in 1890 what it had taken eight men to produce in 1850 and 16 men in 1790.[19] An estimate of the gain in manufacturing productivity for the period 1899 to 1937 concluded that total output had almost quadrupled, the number of employees had barely doubled, and working hours were down one-third.[20] Consequently, man-hour output had increased two-and-a-half times, enabling two men to do what five had done. Combining these two estimates, we may conclude that one man in 1937 could do the amount of manufacturing for which five men had been needed in 1850. The 30 years after the 1930s witnessed further substantial gains. Output more than doubled, employment was up about 60 percent, and hours of work fell slightly. Productivity, therefore, was more than twice as high in 1970 as in 1937. This, in turn, meant that one man could accomplish as much in 1957 as one dozen men in 1850 and two dozen men in 1790.

Random samples of production gains in specific industries demonstrate even more vividly the progress that was made. The cotton weaver in 1800 could make

[19] United States Secretary of the Treasury, *Documents Relative to the Manufactures in the U.S.,* Executive Documents, 22nd Congress, 1st Session, No. 308, Washingtin, D.C., 1833; David A. Wells, *Recent Economic Changes, op. cit.,* p. 29.
[20] Solomon Fabricant, *Employment in Manufacturing, 1899-1939* (New York: National Bureau of Economic Research, Inc., 1942), pp. 8-19.

Table 30

**MANUFACTURING OUTPUT, PRODUCTIVITY, WAGES,
EMPLOYMENT, AND HOURS, 1909-1970**

(1947 = 100)

Year	Value added	Output per man-hour	Wage earners	Production workers	Hourly earnings (prod. wkrs.)	Real hourly earnings (prod. wrks.)	Weekly hours worked (prod. wkrs.)
1909	11	37	50	54	15	38	51.0
1919	32	42	69	74	36	49	46.3
1929	41	72	68	73	43	58	44.2
1933	19	76	47	50	33	60	38.1
1939	33	91	67	68	48	80	37.7
1947	100	100	100	100	100	100	40.0
1956	176	132	114	108	149	128	40.4
1958	127	144	114	93	160	130	39.2
1970	415[1]	191	134	114	260	157	37.1

[1] 278 based on 1947 wholesale prices.
SOURCE: Kendrick, *Productivity Trends in the United States;* Bureau of Labor Statistics.

a pick a second; his successor in 1900 could make 60. A cotton-textile worker in 1840 turned out 10,000 yards of cotton sheeting in a 13-hour day; in 1900 he produced three times as much in an 8-hour day. An average ironworker produced 5 tons of pig in 1830, 15 tons in 1850, and 130 tons in 1960. Machines made much of this possible, for, like the sewing machine which cut the time to make a man's shirt from 14 hours to one hour, they lowered production time and thus immensely raised productivity.

Technological progress influenced the population and the labor force in other ways besides contributing to higher productivity. It gave rise to a multitude of new occupations and created a need for a specialized labor force. Rural society had no need for accountants, salesmen, public relations experts, personnel consultants, advertising copywriters, and computer programmers. Workers in home and household manufacture were jacks-of-all-trades. But in mass-production manufacturing, few workers saw a product through from start to finish. The productive process was broken down into a number of intricately specialized jobs. In the business firm that appeared with technological progress and industrial growth, the entrepreneur had to focus greater attention on coordinating the enterprise, on distributing his products, and on providing services. There was not only a place, but also a crying need, for specialists outside the field of primary and secondary production. Technicians, engineers, and research men, personnel and public relations experts, salesmen and advertising men, lawyers, economists, accountants, and millions of clerks filled the ranks of modern mass-production industry. Without them, business would be chaotic; it simply could not operate without an intricate administrative organization.

Among its other benefits, technological change in the manufacture of a commodity cut costs of production drastically and resulted in a quick and substantial price reduction. But this reduction in price occurred only in the initial stage of development. As soon as early technological difficulties were ironed out, emphasis shifted toward quality improvement, not price reduction. Thus, when Connecticut manufacturers began to mass-produce clocks with machinery and interchangeable parts, the cost of a clock fell from $50 in 1820 to $6 in 1840 and to 75 cents by 1860. Cotton sheeting cost 18 cents a yard in 1815 and 2 cents in 1860, while the general price level fell by half. But when later technological changes lowered costs, the benefits tended to be distributed among the factors of production in the form of increased money income rather than lower prices.

The benefits of technology—increments in productivity, an expanded level of living, wider job horizons, lower prices, and better quality—did not come painlessly, nor were they achieved without cost. In every industry successive waves of machines and tools cost more than their predecessors, and their life span was shorter. Moreover, there is a limit to the economies of scale that can be achieved by the substitution of machines for human beings. As more and more manpower is eliminated from the manufacturing process, there will come a time when no further substitution is possible, simply because a process has become completely automated.

The costs of technological progress fell especially heavily on labor. Labor became dependent on the machine, a fickle master whose whims filled the worker's life with doubt and insecurity. As the machine replaced human energy, work became more monotonous, and even though the worker could escape in daydreaming, the machine presented a multitude of alleged problems, such as stunted personality growth, fatigue, and discontent. The machine also created more leisure and, because people found it difficult to occupy their time, increased leisure was perhaps a more important cause of neuroses than the monotony of operating a machine.

Whether the machine eliminated workers became a hotly debated economic question. Most economic theorists believed that increased use of machinery did not cause a net increase in unemployment. They argued that technological progress, either by lowering costs or by bolstering demand, added to the amount of goods and services sold. Moreover, the machines themselves had to be made, and workers were needed to make them. The most that these economic theorists would admit was that workers in a given industry might be temporarily displaced; but, they argued, the unemployed would presently be reabsorbed by the expansion of the economy. Many other writers and thinkers who believed that man's material wants were not infinite insisted that technology resulted in displacement of labor permanently, rather than temporarily. Some condemned the machine itself as the cause of technological unemployment; others held that the economic system rather than the machine was responsible. But all of history supported those who argued that the machine created rather than destroyed jobs.

Regardless of whether the machine caused technological unemployment, it did require that the worker make swift adjustments to new tasks and new methods. An especially heavy burden was placed on older workers, who were not able to make the required adjustments in speed and coordination that machine production required, and on unskilled workers, who did not have the aptitudes or the education necessary for a world wrapped in technology.

Technological change and manufacturing growth also increased the economy's vulnerability to radical swings in business activity. More than twice as many workers were employed in machine-producing industries in 1970 as in 1900. And workers so employed could easily be laid off in a business recession, for machine-making was elastic and could be stopped altogether if demand fell. On the other hand, the production of necessities could not cease altogether, no matter how far the economy dropped. This is best illustrated by a few figures. On a base of 1919 equaling 100, the production index for producers' durable goods rose to 110 in 1929 and then dropped to 29 in 1933. Perishable goods did not fluctuate nearly as much. The index rose to 102 in 1929 and dropped to 60 in 1933. Thus, labor was much more vulnerable to cyclical unemployment and to increased insecurity. It sought to regain this lost security by joining unions, by supporting paternalism in government, and by demanding pension and welfare programs from employers.

SUGGESTED READINGS

(For suggested readings and questions, see the next chapter.)

Chapter Fourteen

THE INTERNAL EVOLUTION OF MANUFACTURES

Thus far, we have been talking about some of the external influences that operated on manufacturing. As a result of these external forces, the internal structure of manufacturing underwent a series of basic changes. Its focus shifted from the home to the factory, and its habitat spread to all sections of the country, South and West as well as North and East. At around 1800, Tench Coxe described American manufacturers as farmer craftsmen; in 1830, they were village artificers; by 1850, they were fast becoming city operatives. Thus, in a period of about 50 years, industry had shifted from home to factory, from skilled hand industry to highly specialized machine production. But this change hardly disrupted the economy and created little suffering among the people. There was no industrial revolution in the true sense of the word in the United States. The American economy started to industrialize almost from its very beginnings. Production moved from the home into the factory as fast as the stern restrictions of each section's economy would permit. And the movement was repeated over and over again as each frontier area matured. There was no large labor supply to be cast into the ranks of the unemployed as manufacturing moved from home to factory; there were no large market areas to be disrupted; and there were no established industries to be cut down by the demands of economic progress.

A second very important aspect of evolutionary transition

was the constant reshuffling of the industries that constituted manufacturing's leadership. Industries, like Shakespeare's man, passed through stages. Some of them did not survive a precarious infancy. But those that did experienced a long life. They grew strong in prosperous adolescence. In middle age, they settled down to enjoy the fruits of their past accomplishments. Eventually, they became old and broken down and were gradually replaced by more robust, competing industries. Thus, the roster of the leading manufacturing industries in the middle of the twentieth century differed significantly from what it had been in the early nineteenth century. But, in the process of change, the emerging industries and the emerging plants were bigger than the industries and plants they had replaced.

IN THE COLONIAL PERIOD

In the 150 to 200 years of the Colonial Period, Americans made marked progress in manufacturing, even though at the beginning of the nineteenth century industry was, by and large, still far from an advanced state of development.

In the early Colonial Period, when even the economy of the East was still very underdeveloped, most industries were in the homespun stage of production, that is, goods were made at home for home consumption. By the close of the Colonial Period, this type of industry had given place to household manufacturing, that is, making goods in the home for sale outside.[1] Homespun industry, however, did not die completely. It was solidly entrenched in making wearing apparel and household textiles. On the other hand, it was not long before a sawmill, a gristmill, a distillery, and a brewery appeared in a frontier settlement. Handcraft-itinerant workers and specialists, like blacksmiths, carpenters, coopers and shoemakers, arrived in frontier towns very early. Pittsburgh was a frontier settlement in 1790, but of its 130 families, 37 were manufacturers. At about the same time, Lancaster, Pennsylvania, had 700 families, of which 234 were manufacturers, including 36 shoemakers, 30 smiths, 28 weavers, 25 tailors, 17 saddlers, 14 hatters, and 11 coopers.

Some historians have made much of the ways in which British mercantilism acted to impede the progress of colonial manufacturing. Viewing the colonies as a source of raw materials and as a market for British manufactures, Great Britain tried to discourage American manufacturing and to encourage America's extractive industries. The Woolen Act of 1699 prohibited the inter-colonial export of wool; the Hat Act of 1732 did the same for hats. The Molasses Act of 1733 imposed a prohibitive duty on molasses, the principal ingredient of rum, which was one of the mainstays of the New England colonial economy. The Iron Act of 1750 limited iron manufacturing in the colonies. There were other laws besides these, and the colonists chafed under the restrictions. But it is easy to exaggerate their effects. The acts were half-heartedly enforced and consequently

[1]The classic study is still R. M. Tryon, *Household Manufacture in the United States, 1640-1860* (Chicago: University of Chicago Press, 1917).

had little influence on American industrial progress. Indeed, it can be argued that merchantilism had more of an encouraging than a discouraging effect on American home manufactures. Under the Empire system, Great Britain gave direct encouragement to certain industries; trade with other manufacturing nations was forbidden; and some American manufactures were permitted to enter Empire markets under the preferential terms reserved for the in-group. Then, too, the adverse balance of trade stimulated manufacturing as a means of cutting down on the liabilities incurred by imports.

Despite English mercantilist obstructions, the colonists tried to encourage manufacturing. Colonial governments offered bounties to foster manufacturing. They also passed a long list of typically mercantilist laws, such as prohibiting the sale of ships, prohibiting the sale of sheep, and requiring each family to plant flax or hemp and to spin or provide a spinner. Late in the Colonial Period, collective efforts were made to further America's manufacturing progress. In 1764, a "Society for the Promotion of Arts, Agriculture, and Economy" was founded in New York. In the same year, Philadelphia tried to establish a linen manufactory. The United Company of Philadelphia for Promoting American Manufactures appeared in Philadelphia in 1775.

Once independence was achieved, state governments made renewed efforts to turn mercantilism to their own use. They tried to encourage large-scale manufacturing with bounties, prizes, tax exemptions, public loans, and lotteries. Most of these inducements were not particularly effective either before or after the Revolution. To be sure, small industry did very well. As has been pointed out, iron was produced in such quantities that it was exported to England, but the industry was small, both absolutely and in comparison with flour milling, brewing, distilling, sugar refining, leather tanning, and cooperage. Attempts to found large-scale industries did not do very well. Before the Revolution, Peter Hasenclever, a German manager for an English company, imported 500 workers to operate an ironworks, but his ideas were much too grandiose and he was shortly relieved of his position. After the Revolution, a number of attempts were made to found large-scale manufacture. A cotton plant was established in Beverly, Massachusetts; a woolen company at Hartford, Connecticut; and a textile business (The Society for Establishing Useful Manufactures) at Paterson, New Jersey. But none of these three was a success. The first died during the Embargo of 1807, and the other two never began production, principally because of a shortage of skilled labor and the impossibility of wide-scale marketing.

IN THE FIRST HALF OF THE NINETEENTH CENTURY

As has already been said, the first thriving manufacturing industries in the United States relied on domestic raw materials and produced consumer-perishable goods, like processed foodstuffs and textiles. These had an elastic demand because they were low-priced necessities that could be easily standard-ized. Of the ten leading industries by net value in 1860, seven were concerned with processing raw materials and two were manufacturing food and clothing. (See Table 31 page 437.)

The stalwarts of an advanced industrial society—steel, heavy equipment, machinery, and finished tools—were mere pygmies. The steel industry produced a net value of only $1 million in 1860, and American manufacturers of finished steel goods imported most of their raw steel. There were, of course, exceptions to the general absence of heavy industry. Cincinnati was exporting steam engines to South America as early as 1830, and by then machine shops had made castings of four tons and had forged five-ton anchors for the Navy. In 1860, one machine shop in Philadelphia bored castings 16 feet in diameter and 18 feet long. In the same year, the country produced 470 locomotives, three-quarters of them in Philadelphia and Paterson, New Jersey. But these phenomena were not typical. To be sure, the steam-engine industry turned out a net product of almost $30 million, but cotton textiles produced twice as much.

As in heavy machinery, the United States in 1860 was also rapidly increas-ing its production of precision tools and equipment, but it still had a long way to go before it would be the world's leading producer. Before 1830, most of the goods sold in hardware stores were imported, although the axe had always been an American specialty. By 1850, about half the hardware sold was fabricated domestically. Those special tools and implements which were in greatest demand were produced domestically, but others were still imported, and in 1860 the gross value of manufactured tools was less than $4 million, and the manufacture of textile machinery grossed approximately $5 million. On the other hand, the American system of mass production was already easily discernible in the manu-facture of agricultural equipment. Valued at $17.6 million, farm implements were among the top 20 in manufacturing, almost equal to tobacco and paper production.

Each of the nation's leading industries at the middle of the century pro-duced $20 million or more of added value, but manufacturing was still very small-scale. Cotton textiles, the pioneer in factory production, was by far the leading industry throughout the first half of the century.[2] It produced in added value almost $60 million in 1860, or more than the Federal government's entire annual revenue. Judged by the standards of the day, it was a large-scale industry, but by today's standards, it was not. There were 8,000 spindles in operation in 1807, 800,000 in 1825, and 5.2 million in 1860. Typical Massachusetts factories in 1833 employed from 12 to 100 workers, although there were a couple that had payrolls of 1,400 each. The 800 establishments in the industry in 1860 employed an average of 143 workers each and represented an average investment

[2]See Caroline Ware, *The Early New England Cotton Manufacture* (Boston: Houghton Mifflin Company, 1931).

of $116,000. Though huge in American eyes, the textile industry was very small in comparison with Britain's, which operated 6.5 million spindles in 1813 and 30 million, or almost six times as many as the United States, in 1860.

Woolen manufacture in 1860 was far smaller than cotton.[3] Raw wool was scarcer than raw cotton, and woolen manufacturing methods lent themselves more readily to home production than did cotton manufacturing methods. As early as 1816, the woolen industry's product was valued at about $20 million, and there were some large firms in operation, notably the Middlesex Company at Lowell, capitalized at $500,000. But mill manufacturing of wool did not become dominant until the 1830s, and the industry in 1860 was ninth in net value. Its net annual product was $25 million, produced by 1,200 establishments (half again as many as cotton) with an average investment of less than $25,000.

How extremely small-scale American manufacturing was at the time of the Civil War may perhaps best be gathered from some figures on the lumber and flour-milling industries. In terms of net value, lumbering was the second largest industry and flour-milling was fifth. In the lumber business, 20,000 establishments, employing four people each, turned out $54 million of added value on an average investment of $4,000. Employing two workers each and with an average investment of $6,000, 14,000 flour mills produced $40 million.

Even though manufacturing industry was still small, it was moving very rapidly out of the home and into the factory. Average per capita household manufactures dropped from $1.70 a year in 1840, to $1.18 in 1850, and to 78 cents in 1860. There were three principal reasons for the fall in home manufacturing. The supply of labor, which had always limited factory production, rose rapidly because of native population increase, immigration, and a marked spurt in agricultural productivity. Marketing continuously improved with better transportation facilities and the opening of more and more wholesale and retail outlets. Third, the more efficient factory system reduced prices so sharply that it no longer paid to manufacture in the home.

As could be expected, it was in the East that production first moved from the home to the factory. Later on, as each frontier area entered the widening marketing areas, the same process of transferring manufacturing from the household to the factory was repeated. As early as 1830, household manufacturing was on the wane in New England, and by 1850 household manufactures were estimated at less than 25 cents a year per capita in New England. But at the same time in Illinois, household manufactures were valued at $1.36 per capita. By 1860, the nation's household manufactures were only $24 million out of a total of almost $2 billion; yet in Tennessee, nine-tenths of the population still wore homespun.

In a sense, the shift away from the home was the same move from self-

[3]See Arthur H. Cole, *The American Wool Manufacture* (Cambridge, Mass.: Harvard University Press, 1926).

sufficiency to commercialization that was occurring simultaneously in agriculture. In both instances, the country store was a kind of *deus ex machina*. As soon as it appeared in any outlying community, it eliminated some of the more complicated household chores. Before the country store, the pioneer tanned his own leather and worked it up into clothing. Animal skins were thrown into a vat of lye to remove the hair. Then the hides were soaked for several months in liquid made from black-oak bark. Then they were scraped and rubbed with bear oil and tailored with thread from deer sinews. As soon as a store appeared, the pioneer could abandon tanning and instead trade his animal skins for the goods in the country store proprietor's larder.

Whole industries also moved gradually from the home to the factory. Boot and shoe manufacturing was one of the earliest and best examples of this production and marketing evolution.[4] Most of the early colonists made their own shoes, but by 1750 the handicraft stage had already appeared. Work was done under one roof without division of labor by individual cobblers, journeymen, and apprentices on a "bespoke" basis, that is, for individual order. Even before the end of the Colonial Period, handicraft production had been superseded in importance by the second phase of household manufacture, the putting-out system. Under the putting-out system, general merchants controlled the industry. They supplied their workmen with leather, binding, thread, and other materials for shoe manufacture, but seldom provided tools. The workmen were independent artisans who, with the help of their families or apprentices, fashioned the shoes at home from the raw materials furnished by the merchant capitalist. The workmen cut the leather, fitted the uppers, sewed them together, attached the soles, and delivered them to the merchant, who sold them either on special order or for general sale. There was virtually no specialization and the process was wasteful, but there was little else that could be done, because transportation facilities and distribution channels by which the market could be exploited were sorely lacking.

As markets expanded, merchants extended their operations and began to insist upon some degree of specialization in order to reduce costs. The shoe merchant set up a central shop and parceled out some instead of all the work. At first, around 1820, the leather was cut in the central shop. The uppers were put out to artisans who did the fitting and to makers who finished the shoe by applying the sole and sewing the parts together. In time, the market broadened to such an extent that the commercial product became more important than the made-to-order product. This development in turn required greater specialization to increase production and to reduce costs. Each part of the shoe became the special enterprise of a particular workman and, under the circumstances, the old business of putting-out ceased to be practical, for if one workman made the sole and another the heel and a third bound them to the shoe, too much time was

---

[4]See Blanche E. Hazard, *The Organization of the Boot and Shoe Industry in Massachusetts Before 1875* (Cambridge, Mass.: Harvard University Press, 1921).

required in transferring the shoe from place to place. Moreover, output was not uniform, and there was no method of supervising the household laborers. Consequently, the whole process was now incorporated under one roof, and workers were brought to the factory instead of doing the work at home.

Between 1840 and 1860, cutting, rolling, and sewing machines were introduced to speed the productive process. Each addition of machinery required the entrepreneur to maintain continuous production, for idle machines meant lost interest on a large capital investment. Together with the constant widening of the market area, this increased production led to more intense competition, necessitating constant improvement in the product and constant lowering of costs of production. By the 1850s, the boot and shoe industry was organized on its modern lines, for by then the productive process had become mechanized and distribution facilities—wholesaling and retailing—had become organized. Most shoes were now made for the retail trade, rather than for the custom buyer. And for the first time right and left shoes appeared. They were no longer packed willy-nilly in a barrel and bought by the buyer through a process of tedious picking and long-drawn-out trial and error, but were packed neatly in boxes and made according to sizes. Thus, the boot and shoe industry had changed from household "bespoke" work to mechanized factory production. The change, like all transitions from home to factory, significantly raised the level of living. It produced a standardized product. It enabled entrepreneurs to accomplish savings through wholesale purchase of materials and the avoidance of unnecessary transfers. It required less skilled labor and it increased labor's output.

In this era of emerging manufactures, the Eastern part of the United States had such great absolute and comparative advantages over the other sections that it automatically became overwhelmingly dominant in industry. In 1860, the Middle Atlantic states accounted for 43 percent of all added value. These states were exceedingly rich in the natural resources, like iron and coal, which were too bulky to be processed far from their source. They had an ample labor supply, some capital funds, and adequate means of transportation, and their excellent harbors made them ideally suited as market places. New England, which produced 26 percent of manufacturing net value, had a comparatively dense population, apt and eager in the use of tools, vast amounts of water power, a thriving commerce, and a large pool of capital funds. It also had the advantage of being unfit for prosperous large-scale farming, so that its industry did not have to overcome serious competition from agriculture. In addition, the East had a group of entrepreneurs with mechanical aptitude, imagination, confidence in the ultimate triumph of hard work, and a readiness to adapt themselves and their businesses to an altering pattern of life. The West's population was still too small for large-scale enterprise, but its states nevertheless produced 18 percent of all added value. The 11 Southern states were too absorbed by "King Cotton" to produce more than 8 percent of the national total. The Pacific Coast was responsible for the remaining 5 percent.

Within the sections, some states were far more important than others. Nine states produced a net value of $20 million or more a year. New York, with its thriving men's clothing, cabinet-making, flour-milling, leather-working, shipbuilding, and machine-making industries, was the leading manufacturing state in the Union, producing a net value of $164 million a year. Pennsylvania accounted for $137 million of added value, augmenting her vast iron manufacture with shipbuilding and machine-making. Massachusetts, the nation's leading cotton textile producer, added $120 million to manufacturing. Ohio, fourth among industrial states in the nation, was nevertheless far behind the three leaders. A mammoth manufacturer of farm implements and a prodigious slayer of hogs, she produced $52 million a year. The gold-mining industry made California the fifth largest industrial state with an annual net value of $41 million. Connecticut, with her clocks and armaments, was close behind. New Jersey was seventh with $35 million of annual production. Illinois was eighth with $22 million, and Virginia, a leading flour miller, was ninth with $20 million of annual production.

LARGE-SCALE MANUFACTURING IN THE SECOND HALF OF THE NINETEENTH CENTURY

Mass production was not yet a reality in manufacturing in 1850. There were 123,000 establishments, employing a little less than one million people and producing almost $500 million of net value. By 1900, mass production had arrived. By then there were 205,000 establishments, employing about five million people and turning out $5.5 billion. Including neighborhood industries, the number of plants had quadrupled and the number of workers had quintupled, but value added had risen 12 times. This meant that the average establishment was doing three times as much business in 1900 as in 1850.

Manufacturing in 1900 was no longer so closely confined to providing food and clothing but had moved into producers' goods as well. By 1900, there were 26 industries with a net product of over $50 million a year, compared to three in 1850. Of the ten leading industries, three were in the business of manufacturing food, drink, and allied products, two were in textiles and clothing, one was concerned with processing raw materials, and four were in producers' goods.

During the late nineteenth century, manufacturing joined in the westward movement that had been initiated by population 50 years before and carried on by agriculture a generation before. By 1900, as shown in Chart 27, the share of the Middle Atlantic states and New England had dropped by 20 percent, whereas that of the West had risen sharply, and the South's share to a lesser extent.

There were solid reasons for the progress of the Middle West and the South in manufacturing. Improved transportation facilities, technological innovation, and capital accumulation made it possible to develop the Middle West's vast stores of natural resources—iron, coal, and petroleum—and to give that section manufacturing supremacy. At the same time, the South was moving away from cotton culture and into industries that her natural resources made possible—

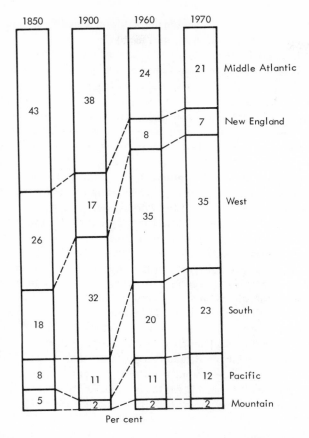

CHART 27. Comparative location of manufactures, 1850, 1900, 1960, and 1970

cotton textile manufacturing, tobacco processing, lumbering, and petroleum refining.

In addition to reshuffling the sections of the nation, the westward movement of manufacturing also resulted in a realignment of the leading manufacturing states. In 1900, the two leaders, New York and Pennsylvania, were far ahead of the next four, Illinois, Massachusetts, Ohio, and New Jersey, which were closely bunched.

IN THE TWENTIETH CENTURY

The nineteenth-century trends in manufacturing continued unabated in the first half of the twentieth century. The size of the average plant became more and more gigantic. The industrial composition of manufacturing leadership underwent a further metamorphosis, and manufacturing activity continued to flow southward and westward without interruption.

Between 1900 and 1960, productivity advanced astoundingly and the value added by manufacturing soared upward, but the number of manufacturing establishments did not grow similarly. Value added in 1970 was 60 times as much as in 1900. The number of workers was more than 13 times as large, but there were only 50 percent more plants. Clearly, manufacturing in 1960 was much more a mass-production operation than it had been in the early 1900s, for in the later period the average factory was doing 30 times as much dollar volume.

During much of the twentieth century, the largest manufacturing firms grew much faster than the average. One way of measuring this is by the number of wage earners employed. In 1914, half the workers were employed in 3.4 percent of all plants; in 1958, half were employed in 2.5 percent. Concentration could also be measured by the share of value added turned out by the largest firms. Here, there seems to have been a close correlation between concentration and the state of the business cycle. In years of high-level activity, concentration was less marked than in periods of recession or depression. In the prosperous year 1929, for example, the plants that produced $1 million or more of net value comprised a little less than 1 percent of all plants and produced 41 percent of all value added. This was about the same situation as prevailed in 1904. But it was decidedly different from what happened in the less prosperous years 1923 and 1939, when about 5 percent of all factories produced over $1 million each and accounted in the aggregate for around two-thirds of net manufactured product. Similar data are not readily available for the period after World War II. But since then, concentration apparently increased, although this is by no means certain.[5] The largest 50 firms accounted for 17 percent of all net value in 1947 and for 23 percent in 1954 and again in 1958. The 200 largest produced 30 percent of the total in 1947, 38 percent in 1958, and about the same in 1970.

By 1970, 52 different industries each produced more than $2 billion of added value a year. Of the ten largest, five made producers' goods, two were in household goods, one was a consumer-durable industry, and the others defied classification. Only one of the leading industries of 1860 and two of the leaders in 1900 were still at the top in 1960. Indeed, four of 1970's ten leaders were either totally unknown or known only to a select group at the beginning of the century.

Some industries that operated on a small scale still produced a large aggregate quantity of manufactures. There were over 13,000 establishments in the various divisions of the women's clothing industry, producing $2.0 billion of

[5]See pp. 196ff.

Table 31

THE LEADING INDUSTRIES IN MANUFACTURING, 1860-1970, BY VALUE ADDED

Rank:	1860	1900	1970
1.	Cotton textiles ($60 million)	Foundry and machine-shop products ($435 million)	Automobiles ($14.5 billion)
2.	Lumber	Lumber	Blast furnace and basic steel
3.	Boots and shoes	Printing and publishing	Aircraft
4.	Iron	Iron and steel	Basic chemicals
5.	Flour milling	Malt liquors	Communications equipment
6.	Men's clothing	Tobacco	Beverages
7.	Gold mining	Cotton goods	Structural metals
8.	Steam engines	Men's clothing	Newspapers
9.	Woolen goods	Bakery products	Drugs
10.	Leather ($20 million)	Cars and general railroad construction ($108 million)	Soaps ($5.1 billion)

SOURCE: Census of Manufactures; *Survey of Manufactures.*

added value and employing an average of 40 persons per establishment. Men's clothing produced $2.0 billion in 4,500 firms. The lumber business, with all its subdivisions, was still almost as small-scale as it had been in 1860, employing an average of 15 wage earners in 38,000 establishments and producing $3.5 billion of added value.

What had happened to the giants of 1860 and 1900? Boots and shoes, steam engines and woolen goods, were far down on the list. Carriages had, to all intents, disappeared, and linens and pianos were no longer of any importance. Shipbuilding and railroad equipment produced about $550 million each.

The location of manufacturing activity changed as leadership shifted. By 1970, as can be seen by Chart 27, the West was clearly in first place and the South was rapidly overtaking the Middle Atlantic states; whereas New England's position had declined markedly.

There was less of a transition among the leading states than among the geographic sections. New York still held first place, with $28 billion of added value. But California ($27 billion) was the closest competitor that New York had met in 150 years. Ohio, Illinois, Pennsylvania, and Michican with net product of 20.3 to 24.2 billion were closely bunched. But the last four states ran down from 14.4 billion in New Jersey to $9.6 billion in Massachusetts.

Table 32

TEN LEADING MANUFACTURING STATES,
1860, 1900, 1960

	1860	1900	1969
New York	1	1	1
Pennsylvania	2	2	5
Massachusetts	3	4	10
Ohio	4	5	3
California	5	—	2
Connecticut	6	7	—
New Jersey	7	6	7
Illinois	8	3	4
Virginia	9	—	—
Indiana	10	9	9
Michigan	—	8	6
Texas	—	—	8
Wisconsin	—	10	—

SOURCE: Census of Manufactures; *Survey of Manufactures.*

THE AUTOMOBILE BUSINESS—A CASE IN INDUSTRIALIZATION

Thus far in this chapter, the process of industrialization has been treated in its broadest aspects. Its long historical evolution has been telescoped into a few pages. But manufacturing growth is a practical rather than an abstract development; its story might better be told specifically than generally. The long histories of the iron and steel industry, cotton textiles, or boots and shoes offer specific examples of the obstacles in the way of manufacturing growth, the nature of the industrialization process, the development of technology, the transformation of business administration, and the effects of industrialization. But no case offers a better illustration of the sweep, the dynamism, and the effects of industrialization and technological development than the history of the American automobile industry.[6]

Born late in the nineteenth century, the automobile industry developed

---

[6]There is a vast literature on the automobile business. Though dated, Ralph C. Epstein, *The Automobile Industry* (Chicago: A. W. Shaw Co., 1928) is very valuable. See also Lawrence H. Seltzer, *A Financial History of the American Automobile Industry* (Boston: Houghton Mifflin Company, 1928). More recent and very helpful are: Allan Nevins, *Ford: The Times, the Man, the Company; Ford: Expansion and Challenge;* and *Ford, Decline and Rebirth* (New York: Charles Scribner's Sons, 1954, 1957, 1963); Alfred P. Sloan, Jr., *My Years with General Motors* (Garden City, N.Y.: Doubleday & Company, Inc., 1964); John B. Rae, *American Automobile Manufacturers* (Philadelphia: The Chilton Co., 1959); same autauthor, *The American Automobile* (Chicago: University of Chicago Press, 1965); Alfred D. Chandler, Jr., *Giant Enterprise: Ford, General Motors, and the Automobile Industry—Sources and Readings* (New York: Harcourt, Brace and World, 1964).

within the span of a single generation into a colossus of mass production, representing the acme of division of labor, mechanization, and scientific management. To describe how this change was accomplished is to describe the essence of industrialization; the factors that made industrialization possible, the long inventive process, the fulfillment of mass production, the appearance of scientific management, the adaptation of business enterprise, and the effects of manufacturing growth on everyday social and economic life.

The creation of the automobile gives substance to the thesis that there is no such thing as an "invention" in the true sense of the word. The idea of a self-propelled vehicle is very old. Leonardo da Vinci in the fifteenth century had the germ of the idea. Roger Bacon before him and Isaac Newton after him both considered the possibility of a steam-propelled vehicle. In 1769 Joseph Cugnot, a Frenchman, actually constructed such a vehicle. So did the American Oliver Evans in 1784, and Richard Trevithick, an Englishman, in 1801. By 1860 scientific experiment had gone far enough to allow inventors to turn from steam to gas as a propelling fuel. In that year Lenoir, another Frenchman, built an internal-combustion engine. A decade later, G. B. Brayton put together a two-cycle engine. But the basis for the gasoline-driven automobile of today really came in 1876, when Otto, a German, patented the four-cycle engine. Gottfried Daimler applied it to motorcycles in 1885 and Karl Benz built a motor car in the same year. Thus, the inventive process behind the automobile combined the contributions of amateur and professional scientists and technicians from the leading industrial countries.

The United States adopted these foreign contributions, elaborated them, and added the "American System" of mass produciton. To be sure, the French Panhard Company, in 1891, was the first organization to make automobiles commercially, but in a short while America became by far the largest producer. The reasons for American leadership were the same ones that explained this country's rapid technological development and manufacturing growth. The vast area of the United States lent itself ideally to the use of the automobile, and a road system would be quickly laid out to take advantage of this. The American middle class, far greater in number than that of any European nation, offered a potential mass market. Scattered among the population were innumerable tinkers with a facility for adapting and improving mechanical devices. The raw materials necessary for automobile manufacture were either available in the United States or could be easily imported and the facilities for mass-processing could be easily constructed. Finally, there were industries already in existence that could contribute either directly or indirectly to the growth of the automobile business. These industries had developed a number of well-established wood- and metal-working enterprises that were equipped with capital goods capable of producing parts for automobiles. They had also evolved intricately organized shop procedures to carry on the productive process. Armories had taken the pioneer steps in developing tools and methods; sewing-machine manufacturers had made further advances; and by the late nineteenth century, the bicycle business had emerged as a most important force in technological development. It was already on a mass-production basis, using heavy, complicated, and special-purpose machinery, such as the chain-shaver, the chain-riveter, and the slot-cutter. Great pains were taken to manufacture special machine tools, and tolerances were measured to 1/2,000 of an inch. The industry had made remarkable strides in the fabrication and use of such items as ball bearings and gears, parts that were to be indispensable in automobile production. The bicycle people were experimenting with the use of new metals, and the Pope Company had already established a metallurgical laboratory in 1892. In addition, the bicycle business had systematized the entire manufacturing process through the use of orderly procedures, departmentalization, and specialization. With all these developments, it was able to manufacture efficiently a variety of parts, such as spokes, wheels, tires, sprockets, and chains, that could be used in the automobile.

The bicycle industry also contributed in a more indirect fashion to the advance of automobile manufacture. The four million cyclists in the United States had already begun to lobby for roads and, in 1891, had succeeded in persuading the State of New Jersey to help finance highway construction. But more important than this, the bicycle mania broke down in the late 1890s, and many of its leaders turned to making automobiles. Of course, this was not enough to make a giant out of the automobile. Substantial obstacles still had to be overcome before the business emerged from infancy. A labor supply had to be procured, the inertia that interfered with capital mobility had to be overcome, and extensive technological innovations had to be made.

The pioneer phase

For convenience, the growth of the automobile industry can be roughly divided into four periods: the pioneer phase, from 1892 to about 1900; the beginnings of mass production, from about 1900 to about 1908; the expansion of mass production, from 1908 to around 1927; and the era of full expansion.

During the pioneer period, the automobile was largely hand-produced for a localized market. This was a stage analogous to "household industry," the putting-out system, or petty capitalism. Entrepreneurs were not determined businessmen, but mechanics like the Duryea Brothers and the Appersons, or refugees from other businesses who treated the automobile as a hobby. In the latter group were Pope, the bicycle manufacturer; Winton, an engineer; Steinway, the piano maker; Haynes, who had done well in the gas business; Packard, a success in electric cables; and Buick, who had invented a process for installing bathroom fixtures. These early makers did "bespoke" work, and in time most of them disappeared from the industry. Those who placed their faith in electric and steam-propelled vehicles failed because electricity was impractical, requiring constant battery recharging, and steam was dangerous, requiring a boiler and a fire.

But most of the early experimenters with gasoline-driven automobiles also left the industry very quickly. Some, like the Duryea Brothers, who made the first American automobile in 1893, did not have the vision or the ability to adapt themselves to the needs of a new and different industry. Others, like Winton, failed because they lost interest as soon as a project appeared to be achieving success.

Perhaps the most common reason for the lack of success of the early gasoline-driven automobile companies was the difficulty of raising capital funds; or, to state the problem more precisely, success eluded many because they could not raise capital in sufficient volume to carry on a desired rate of expansion. As was the case in other infant industries, savings did not flow readily into the automobile business, nor was capital readily withdrawn from other businesses to be invested in the pioneer automobile industry. This problem of capital raising not only characterized the early pioneer period but remained all through the stage of initial mass production. In fact, automobile securities were not distributed publicly until General Motors offered some five-year notes in 1910.

Early automobile manufacturers tried to overcome their lack of capital by entering into credit arrangements with body builders and parts manufacturers. Parts and bodies would be bought on credit and paid for when the automobile was sold. This made the pioneer automobile industry a small-scale assembly business. Manufacturing by factory methods was impossible, and every automobile was virtually a custom-built job, which goes far toward explaining why there were only about 300 cars built by 1900.

The beginnings of mass production

Ransom E. Olds was the first man to attempt to manufacture rather than build automobiles. He owned a machine shop in which he built gasoline engines, and, like most of the pioneers, he became interested in automobiles as a hobby. Being an expert workman, he built a gasoline-driven automobile, and in 1897, with the financial assistance of local bankers, he began to build automobiles in Lansing, Michigan.

Olds had visions of mass production. He believed that the principles used in manufacturing carriages could be adapted to the automobile. This meant buying the parts in quantity and assembling them. But Lansing could not supply the labor, the money, or the housing for the large-scale project that Olds had in mind, and his motor vehicle company quickly failed. Olds then contemplated opening a plant in Newark, New Jersey, but Eastern capitalists considered his ideas wildly impractical, and they rejected his request for a loan. However, he succeeded in enlisting the help of a Detroit capitalist, S. L. Smith, who wanted to set his sons up in business. In 1899, Olds opened in Detroit with $200,000, $400 of which was his own.

The first Olds factory turned out a complicated car with a pneumatic clutch, cushion tires, and an electric starter. Not only was it too far ahead of its day but, priced at $1,250, it was also too expensive. After one year, Olds moved back to Lansing, and in 1901 he began to produce a $650 Oldsmobile on a mass basis, buying the parts in quantity and assembling them on an embryonic assembly line. Olds was an immensely important pioneer, for he was the first in the industry to use division of labor, the first to use the moving assembly line, and the first to bring the materials to the worker instead of the worker to the materials. With his improved processes, Olds sold 5,000 cars in 1904 and paid 105 percent in dividends in three years.

Meanwhile, substantial headway was being made in introducing mass-production methods into the making of engines, bodies, and parts. Olds bought most of his engines from the Leland Faulconer Manufacturing Company. Its owner, Henry M. Leland, who had had long experience as a machinist in the Colt arms factory and later with Brown and Sharpe, believed that it was possible and practical to manufacture a standardized engine with interchangeable parts. Unable to persuade Olds or other automobile makers to build automobiles with interchangeable parts, Leland decided to do it himself. He took over the Henry Ford Company in 1903 and began to manufacture the Cadillac, which represented a radical change in auto building. It was not the first automobile to have a steering wheel or a gear shift (the Packard had a steering wheel in 1900 and a gear shift in 1902), but it was the first to make the double departure of breaking away from the horse and buggy and of adopting interchangeable parts successfully.

In 1908, Leland performed an amazing experiment to prove the worth of a machine-made product with interchangeable parts. He sent three Cadillacs to England, tore them down, and threw the parts in a heap. Then Cadillac mechanics, equipped only with wrenches, hammers, screwdrivers, and pliers, proceeded to assemble the parts into three complete automobiles that were then driven on a 500-mile test. The test demonstrated that, with assembly-line production and interchangeable parts, automobile production would be limited only by consumer purchasing power.

To produce interchangeable parts required precision instruments and machine tools. Leland therefore imported a set of "Jo blocks"—steel blocks that were accurate to within four-millionths of an inch—named after their producer, Carl Johansson, a Swedish technician. Meanwhile, specialized machine tools, such as multiple-drill presses for boring cylinder blocks, cylinder-grinding machines, and turret lathes to turn flywheels, had been developed. By 1903, the pioneer work in mass production had been accomplished. The assembly line, interchangeable parts, precision instruments, machine tools, material routing, and machine layout had all been conceived. The automobile industry was ready to expand mass production. But this had not been achieved without tremendous financial casualties, for three-fifths of the automobile companies that were formed between 1900 and 1908 ended up as failures.

The expansion of mass production

Olds and Leland were the pioneers in introducing mass-production methods, but Henry Ford carried mass-production much further. Ford did not originate standardization and the assembly line. His great contribution was the emphasis he placed on an expert combination of accuracy, including standardization; continuity; the moving assembly line; and speed, through careful timing of manufacture, material handling, and assembly.

Ford had already failed twice in the business (in 1899 and 1900) when, in 1903, he formed the Ford Motor Company with the help of Malcolmson, a coal dealer of some means. The enterprise was capitalized at $100,000, but only $28,000 in cash was paid in immediately and only $14,000 more (or $42,000 in all) was paid in in 1904. Ford never again raised new money, but financed all his future expansion through retained earnings.

At first the company was an assembler, not a producer. It bought chassis for $250, bodies for $52, cushions for $16, wheels for $26, and tires for $40. A dozen workers, at $1.50 a day each, put these parts together. The car sold for $850, yielding a profit of $246.

But Ford had other ambitions. By 1908, most automobile manufacturers were tending toward high-priced cars. Ford, going against prevailing opinion, determined to produce low-priced cars in immense volume. As he put it, "We were going to build one model . . . The chassis would be exactly the same for all cars, and I remarked, 'Any customer can have a car painted any color he wants so long as it is black.' I cannot say that anyone agreed with me." He bought out some of his more recalcitrant partners and began to manufacture the Model-T, a completely standardized product that retailed well within the price range of America's middle class. Ford completely dominated the industry in these early years, but there were rivals. W. C. Durant had bought the Buick company in 1904 and, in 1908, when Buick was the largest auto producer, he combined Buick, Olds, Cadillac, and a number of others in a holding company named "General Motors." Ford's stategy was to integrate vertically through internal growth. Durant chose to grow more by merger and consolidation. The rivalry between the two was very intense, but Ford prevailed. In 1915, with the help of associates who were extraordinarily able businessmen and engineers, Ford produced 35 percent of the national output of 880,000 motor vehicles. In 1923, he produced 57 percent of four million cars and trucks.

The Ford Company showed some glaring weaknesses. Ford was an empire builder who insisted upon having his finger in every pie. He had no use for records, refused to admit his own errors, and was skeptical of those who had some knowledge. Ford lavished almost all his love on the Model-T. He had little left over for the rest of the company. When the Model-A appeared at a later date, he treated it as an unwelcome stepchild. He did make some attempts to diversify both within the auto business and by entering other industries, but these attempts failed, and they always seemed halfhearted. Research was run in an eccentric fashion, and the company's financial policies often resulted in a dangerous shortage of cash. But in a virgin market in which price was important, Ford did very well, especially because his chief rival had an organization that was even more chaotic. Durant was interested in growth for growth's sake. He had no financial management, no clear lines of authority, no budgeting of appropriations, and no consistent strategy or tactics. He once said that he "believed in changing policies just as often as my office door opens and closes."

Led by Ford, the automobile business embarked upon the most spectacular mass-production operation in history. This was the heroic age, the year of the industrial capitalist and a virgin market, a period of rapid plant expansion, wholesale technological innovation, and substantial increases in productivity. In less than 20 years, the automobile business emerged from nowhere to become by far America's leading industry. Only 200,000 autos were registered in 1908; there were over 23 million in 1927.

Technological development

Even before the Model-T, Ford had begun his efforts to produce a standardized product. In 1906, he hired Walter E. Flanders, one of Frederick W. Taylor's students, to increase production to ten thousand cars a year. Flanders applied line-production theory to automobile manufacturing. Machines and tools were rearranged according to function instead of type. Waste motion in the laborer's work and movement was thereby eliminated. The job, as well as the parts, became standardized.

It was split down again and again in order to have the worker do only one simple routine task with as few motions as possible. Two technicians, C. W. Avery and William Klann, took over from the meat-packing industry the idea of a moving conveyor. In 1913, they applied the principle to the job of making a flywheel magneto. Previously, the whole job had taken one workman 20 minutes. By splitting the job into 29 different operations and putting it on a mechanical conveyor, Avery and Klann cut production time to a little over 13 minutes. Experiments with the height of the conveyor soon cut the time to five minutes. In other words, one man replaced four in assembling a magneto. Adapting the same principles to the task of assembling a motor, Ford technicians broke the process down into 84 different jobs and cut production time by two-thirds.

The production of automobile parts increased astonishingly, but the assembling process could not keep pace with the production process. Under the original system, parts were brought to a chassis and assembled there. This took 12 hours and 28 minutes and remained the bottleneck that had to be removed. In the late summer of 1913, Avery and Klann were ready to mechanize the final assembly of the car. Assemblers worked on a chassis as it was dragged across the floor by means of a windlass at a speed of 8 1/2 inches a minute. This took only 5 hours and 50 minutes. Ford technicians soon developed a mechanized overhead conveyor, an endless belt that elevated the whole final assembly line to the height of a man's waist. By constant time and motion studies, the speed and height of the conveyor were improved, and assembly time was finally cut, by April, 1914, from the original 12 hours and 28 minutes to 93 minutes.

Ford wanted to eliminate still more of the human influence in the production line. Automatic equipment had to be developed to take the place of human energy. Ford engineers lent themselves to this task with enthusiasm, and by 1922 Ford could announce that his plant in Highland Park was completely mechanized.

Standardization spread throughout the industry. "Inventions" developed by one company became freely available to other firms when, in 1915, cross-licensing of patents was instituted under the auspices of the National Automobile Chamber of Commerce. The automobile itself became a standardized product. The 800 different lock washers used in early cars were reduced to 16, the 1,600 types of steel tubing were cut to 17, and the 230 different alloy steels were standardized at 50.

Consumer credit, originally introduced in 1905 and common by 1916 when the industry first produced one million cars a year, further increased effective demand and gave greater impetus to mass production. New tools and new processes continuously simplified procedures. Before World War I, automobiles had been painted with natural enamels, and so many coats were needed that it took about two weeks for the car to be painted and then to dry. After the war, nitrocellulose lacquers were introduced, cutting the drying period and thus reducing the painting process from weeks to days. One-piece stamping processes for bodies also were introduced, thus eliminating 18 different parts in the underbody alone.

The effects of these improvements in mass production were prodigious. The number of plants in the automobile business increased from 178 in 1904 to 2,471 in 1923, when the automobile industry became the largest industry in the country. The number of man-hours required to produce a car underwent a startling reduction. Based on 1914 equalling 100, productivity increased to 270 in 1923. In 1914 it took 4,664 man-hours in one plant, 1,260 in another, to produce a car. By 1923, required man-hours had been reduced to 813 in the first plant and to 228 in the second. But the increase was obtained at some expense. Labor turnover was greater than in other industries. During the 1920s, the Ford plant had to hire 53,000 workers to maintain a constant corps of 14,000.

Compensating for this, wages increased as productivity rose. In 1903, skilled workers received $2.25 and unskilled $1.50 for a nine-hour day. In 1914 Ford adopted the famous five-dollar, eight-hour day. About 200 workers got $7 a day; 1,000 got $6; and 1,500, $5.

Prices also declined. In 1908, a Ford runabout cost $700 and a six-cylinder luxury car over $2,500. By the middle 1920s, the small Ford was down to $260 and the luxury car to $1,700. The quality of the automobile had also been greatly improved. The self-starter had replaced the crank; the sedan had replaced the touring car. The demountable rim, forced-feed lubrication, the cord tire, the four-wheel brake, and other innovations had been adopted.

It was possible for the heroic business entrepreneur to make prodigious profits in the automobile business. Consider the Maxwell, for example. The sedan was sold to an agent for $1,200 and the runabout for $500. The cost of production was $636 in one case and $225 in the other. The sale of 1,500 cars brought a gross profit of $557,000. After deducting $231,000 for fixed charges, the company had a net profit of $326,000 on a capital of $1.2 million. Yet the Maxwell eventually went out of the automobile business. On the other hand, Ford made $900 million between 1903 and 1927. What these examples and others showed was that it was the daring entrepreneur who made the spectacular profits and the spectacular failures. He who dared and won, won magnificently. He who did not dare was certain to end in failure, but his failure would come considerably later than for him who dared and lost.

The era of full expansion

By 1923, it was clear to the most farsighted that the heroic age of the automobile business was just about over. An omen of things to come occurred when Durant was forced out of General Motors as the result of the precipitous business decline of 1920-1921. After an interregnum under the DuPonts, Alfred P. Sloan, Jr., took over the direction of the company and basically revised its objectives and reorganized its structure and administration. Sloan's approach to business was altogether different from Durant's or Ford's. Durant was hypnotized by growth for growth's sake. Ford was obsessed with production to the exclusion of all other aspects of the business. Each ran his company in a state of anarchy. Under Durant, General Motors operated under a quixotic decentralization that approached chaos. At the other extreme, in the Ford organization, centralization approached chaos. Sloan followed a middle course. He instituted a managerial structure which he described as "decentralization under coordinated control."[7] He enlisted his executives in a real partnership. The entrepreneurial decision makers in General Motors were concerned with long-run objectives rather than with day-to-day activities. The whole managerial hierarchy attempted to approach problems in a systematic, orderly fashion. They were not "hunch players." They emphasized forecasting, coordination of production to demand, statistical data, accounting, and long-range planning in "a constant

[7]Alfred P. Sloan, *My Years with General Motors;* Ernest Dale, *Great Organizers* (New York: McGraw-Hill Book Company, 1960).

search for the facts . . . and their intelligent unprejudiced analysis." Ford had nothing but contempt for this new view of management. As he put it: [8]

> To my mind, there is no bend of mind that is more dangerous than that which is sometimes described as the "genius for organization." This usually results in the birth of a great big chart; showing, after the fashion of a family tree, how authority ramifies. The tree is heavy with nice round berries, each of which bears the name of a man or an office. Every man has a title and certain duties which are strictly limited by the circumference of his berry. It takes about six weeks for the message of the man living in a berry on the left-hand corner of the chart to reach the President or the Chairman of the Board, and if it ever does reach one of these august officials, it has by that time gathered to itself a pound of criticisms, suggestions, and comments . . . .The buck is passed to and fro and all responsibility is dodged by individuals—following the lazy notion that two heads are better than one.

Ford's comments were a justifiable criticism of the general evils of bureaucracy in the large organization; but as a dismissal of what was happening in the administration of his chief competitor, they were far off the mark. Times had changed, and Ford was very much behind them. Twenty years of high-volume production in the automobile industry had ravished the virgin market to which Ford was still attuned. Originally, automobiles had been price-elastic, that is, price reductions resulted in a more than proportionate increase in the number sold. But the used-car market, installment credit, and a partially saturated market made them price-inelastic and income-elastic. Replacement demand had become the strategic factor, and the purchase of an automobile could now be postponed. Competition switched to the marketing department. To maintain quantity production, it was necessary to emphasize quality and doo-dads, not price. Advertising, production differentiation, and credit became much more important in a world that inexorably shifted to what the economist called a market structure of "monopolistic competition." Sloan understood this; Ford did not. In 1926, General Motors sold more automobiles than Ford, and by 1927 it had become clear to even Ford that his idea of one model in vast volume at lower and lower prices could not continue to dominate. Reluctantly, he shifted to the Model-A, but he never surrendered his prejudices against a decentralized managerial organization, and he therefore never could regain his leadership. To be sure, there were occasional years in which the Ford Company led in sales. But these years were salutes to tradition rather than a resurgence of old managerial concepts. That they were exceptions was made clear when the Ford Company, after Henry's death, reorganized along the General Motors' lines under an executive who had been trained in the GM organization.

[8] Henry Ford, *My Life and Work* (Garden City, N.Y.: Doubleday & Company, Inc., 1922), pp. 91-92.

As the industry matured, it became in every way more concentrated. At one time or an other, there were 2,900 different makes of autos in the United States. Perhaps 181 companies produced cars between 1903 and 1926. Only 11 survived the entire period. There were, altogether, 40 different makes in 1926. Since then, 34 new ones have entered and 55 have left: of the 19 still being made, only four go back to 1904. In 1917, 10 of 76 active companies manufactured 75 percent of total output. By the 1960s, three companies produced well over 90 percent. From the 1920s on, less stress was placed on expansion and production and more thought was given to new problems, such as the great importance of the replacement, the used car, and the foreign markets.[9] As early as 1927, Sloan said, "The industry has not grown much in the past three or four years. What has taken place is a shift from one manufacturer to another." But the automobile, like many other phenomena of economic history, progressed in long swings. The industry sold 5.3 million vehicles in 1929. Then came the depression, and it was not until the years after World War II that production and sales took off in a new burst of activity. The 1929 figure was finally surpassed in 1949; and in 1955, dealers sold over 9 million cars and trucks, a record that was not again exceeded until 1963. Then in 1965, a record 11.1 million were sold.

There were other signs of maturity. Foreign competition suddenly loomed as a decided threat to American manufacturing. As late as 1960, exports of automobiles, trucks, and parts exceeded imports by $1.2 billion to $627 million; in 1970, imports exceeded imports by $5.1 billion to $2.9 billion.

If it was true that the industry had ceased to be a growth industry, prices did not evidence it. Up to the mid-1920s, automobile prices fell regardless of what was happening to the general consumer price index. After the mid-1920s, the price of a care showed a greater upward slope than the so-called "cost of living." Between 1925 and 1940, the cost of living dropped by almost one-third, whereas the price of a best-selling automobile went up 40 percent. In the postwar period, the price of this same automobile rose 50 percent while the general index climbed 25 percent. But more than a word of caution about these conclusions is necessary. Quoted prices on automobiles were not the prices that were actually paid after the higgling and haggling in the actual market. Quoted prices, furthermore, made no allowance for quality change and, as the automobile business became older, it was apparent that prices were becoming less important in motivating consumers, whereas subjective considerations, such as quality, style, and status, were becoming more important. In 1925, the age of an average motor vehicle was six and a half years and its mileage, 25,000; a generation later, the average age was about the same, but average mileage had quadrupled. At the same time, technological development had become more intensive than extensive. Innovations were more refined than fundamental. The emphasis was less

---

[9]As early as 1905, the United States exported more automobiles than she imported; but between 1922 and 1926, when the industry manufactured more cars than in its entire previous history, foreign markets really became important.

on cost reduction than on demand induction through changes in design and improvements in comfort. Faster-drying paints appeared and consumers were offered a wide choice in colors. The automobile, which once contained less than one hundred parts now contained eight thousand. For those who were interested only in driving, there was shatter-proof glass, heaters and ventilators, balloon tires, automatic transmission, power steering, and power brakes; for the aesthetes, the teardrop body had made the automobile a work of art.

As automobiles ceased to be price-elastic and became more income-elastic, automobile pricing also became much more sophisticated. Price making did not become an art until Donaldson Brown developed a complicated formula for General Motors in the mid-1920s. Subsequently, something similar was adopted by all the other companies. Unit costs were estimated on the basis of standard volume (around 55 percent of capacity), and a profit margin was added to yield a target rate of return of about 20 percent on net worth.

Some economic and social effects of the automobile

No other economic innovation, including the railroad, surpassed the automobile in its effect on economic and social life. The ways in which motor vehicles influenced the marketing of goods and the transportation of people have already been discussed.[10] But the auto permeated every aspect of life, not just marketing. It rehabilitated old industries, like the toll road and the roadside inn, and it created wholly new industries and institutions, such as billboard advertising, the gas station, the motel, and the outdoor movie. One business in every six became intimately related to the automobile industry. Motor vehicles used more than 60

Table 33

PRODUCTION FACTORS IN THE AUTOMOBILE INDUSTRY
(dollar figures in millions)

	No. of vehicles sold (thousands)	Value added	Average employment	Payroll	Weekly hours	Weekly earnings	Real weekly earnings (1947-1949 dollars)
1904	22	$ 16	12,000	$ 7	51	$ 11.43	$ 28.50
1909	127	117	75,700	48	50	12.37	30.00
1919	1,876	809	343,000	491	46	27.53	37.20
1946	3,089	3,819	544,000	1,431	38	50.61	60.70
1960	7,869	10,100	571,000	3,492	40	114.11	91.30
1970	8,239	14,524	580,000	5,146	38	177.40	131.12

SOURCE: *Census of Manufactures; Automobile Facts and Figures; Survey of Manufactures.*

[10]See pp. 382.

percent of the country's plate glass, 70 percent of its upholstery leather, 60 percent of its rubber, and 18 percent of all steel.

Ever since 1920, the automobile industry has employed approximately 3.5 percent of all manufacturing workers. Perhaps another 10 percent of all nonagricultural workers were in jobs that the automobile had created. With constant improvements in productivity, money and real wages climbed upward. By 1946, despite two wartime inflations, real wages were more than twice what they had been in 1904. By 1970, they had doubled again.

The automobile also made profound changes in where people lived and in how they spent their money. It made possible the drift toward suburbia and exurbia and the transmutatuion of the city into the metropolitan area. Before long, those who lived in the suburbs and a smaller number who lived at the core were spending 5.5 percent of their disposable income for the purchase and maintenance of automobiles.

Economists were certain about the benefits that were brought by the automobile. Some other thinkers, putting more emphasis on social factors, were not quite so sanguine. Old moral cliches lost their meaning as the automobile became the distinguishing mark of conspicuous consumption. Sociologists were also dubious about the effects of the automobile on mental life, for the auto was synonymous with the assembly-line process and epitomized the monotony of a machine society. But, in time, much of this criticism lost its bite as the automobile became older and much more ubiquitous. Even the automobile's reputation as a public enemy and a ruthless killer improved. Long the seventh most important cause of death, autos killed 25,800 in 1927 and 55,000 in 1970. But in terms of population and of miles traveled, automobile fatalities were decreasing. The fatality rate per 100 million miles dropped from 16.3 in 1927 to 0.5 in 1971. It jumped from 21.8 per 100,000 of population in 1927 to 30.8 in 1937, and then slipped back to 25.5 in 1971.

Beyond doubt, the automobile disrupted the pattern of existence by its influence on family living in the urban-suburban environment, but there was also little doubt about the upward thrust it had given to the level of living.

SUGGESTED READINGS

(On specific topics, see the readings cited in the footnotes in the chapter.)

Clark, Victor S., *History of Manufactures in the United States* (New York: McGraw-Hill Book Company, 1929).

Gilfillan, S. C., "Invention as a Factor in Economic History," *Journal of Economic History, Tasks,* Vol V (1945).

Roe, J. W., *Early British and American Tool Makers* (New Haven, Conn.: Yale University Press, 1916).

Strassmann, W. Paul, *Risk and Technological Innovation* (Ithaca, N. Y.: Cornell University Press, 1959).

Usher, Abbott Payson, "The Balance Sheet of Economic Development," *Journal of Economic History,* Vol XI (1951).

QUESTIONS

1. Describe the factors that contributed to American manufacturing growth.
2. What factors gave rise to factory industry in America? Where did the early entrepreneurs secure capital and labor?
3. What were some of the steps by which technological progress improved the level of living?
4. Why were cotton textiles the first products manufactured by factory methods?
5. What shifts have occurred in the type of manufactured goods produced in the United States?
6. What have been some of the most important effects of technological change and manufacturing growth?
7. Describe the evolution of the American automobile business, showing (a) the reasons for its rise, (b) stages in its evolution, (c) its economic problems, (d) the effect of technological change, and (e) its effects on the standard of living.
8. Discuss the reasons why Britain put obstacles in the way of manufacturing growth in the colonies. What were the effects of such British action?
9. What were the factors that retarded and the factors that accelerated American manufacturing growth?
10. Describe by illustration or by general discussion the historical progress of technology.
11. An authority described American manufacturing in 1794 as that of farmer craftsmen; in 1825, as that of village artisans; and in 1900, as that of factory operatives. Explain what he meant, using any one industry as an example.
12. Trace the long-term shifts in the structure of United States manufacturing. Why did these changes occur?
13. Describe the long-term changes that have occurred in the following aspects of manufacturing: its growth; the types of goods produced; the location of manufacturing activity.
14. Why was the Industrial Revolution in the United States more of an evolutionary development than the Industrial Revolution in Great Britain? Why did it begin in textiles rather than in other industries? What was its effect on Southern cotton cultivation and on the daily life of the American people?
15. Describe the changes that took place in the business organization of the automobile business. Why did they take place?

Chapter Fifteen

THE WORKER
AS A PRODUCER
AND AS A CONSUMER

Previous chapters have stressed the importance of the man-land ratio in the economic development of the United States. In marked contrast to most of the nations in the rest of the world, where land is limited and labor plentiful, labor in America has been scarce relative to land. In a sense, this scarcity of labor was an obstacle to economic growth. It prevented farmers from making full use of their land. It impeded the development of manufacturing. It obstructed specialization and division of labor; and, by keeping the market area from expanding, it interfered with the growth of trade.

In another and more important way, however, the low man-land ratio encouraged economic development. The gap between scarce labor and plentiful land and natural resources acted to stimulate technological innovation. In labor-scarce America, marginal productivity was high and wages were high, a fact that was clearly recognized almost as soon as settlement began. In 1633, Governor Winthrop complained in Massachusetts Bay: "The scarcity of workmen has caused them to raise their wages to an excessive rate." One hundred years later, Benjamin Franklin said the same thing in a different way: "So vast is the territory of North America that it will require many ages to settle it fully; and till it is fully settled labor will never be cheap here, where no man continues long to work for another." Gradually, each worker in agriculture, manufacturing, and the so-called service industries was given more tools, more education in how to use them, and more managerial direction. With these helps, he was able to produce more per man-hour worked; and as his productivity increased, and as the national level of living improved, his income and his level of living also improved. Although this improvement applied to all workers, whether in agriculture, manufacturing, distribution, or the office, the bounty of economic progress was not showered equally on all.

As history spun its course, the manufacturing worker's scale of living rose much more than that of the agricultural worker. Both his money and his real wages (what his money income could buy) moved continuously upward. Although the work week was at first extremely long, eventually it declined substantially. Similarly, as we shall see later in the chapter, working and living conditions were at first abominable, but ultimately great progress was achieved; housing conditions were improved; educational and medical facilities were supplied on an ever-increasing scale; and the worker as a consumer also benefited by improvements in the quality of the products he bought.

THE LABOR MARKET IN THE EARLY NINETEENTH CENTURY

The supply of labor

In the United States, as deTocqueville observed more than one hundred years ago, "The notion of labor is presented to the mind, on every side, as the necessary, natural, and honest condition of human existence. Not only is labor not dishonorable, but it is held in honor." Because work was something of a fetish, one would expect that a high percent of the population would be in the labor force.[1] This, however, was not altogether true, despite the relative scarcity that prevailed in America and despite the restless obsession with activity that characterized American life. Because of the relatively low median age of the population, and because the American economy did not make as full use of some of its potential labor supply as did some other nations, the American labor force was not unusually high at any time. Almost all males between 25 and 65 were in the labor force; but women, children, and the very old were not fully employed. Apparently, America expanded the effectiveness of the labor force more than its quantity. It did this through technological innovation, using less of its human energy and more power-driven machinery and equipment to satisfy its desire to raise the level of living. Actually, the proportion of the population in the labor

---

[1] "Labor force" includes all those who are working or looking for work—the manager, the teacher, the doctor as well as the bricklayer, the typist, and the truck driver. The concept of "gainfully occupied" that was used in census data before 1940 included all those who had an occupation regardless of whether they were working or looking for work.

force has remained about the same. In the early nineteenth century, it was about 35 percent of the population; today it is about 40 percent. The difference is largely a function of the increasing age of the population, for the ratio of the labor force to the population of 14 years old and over has been consistently stable.

Industrial and commercial workers, or labor as it is usually thought of, hardly existed in colonial America or in the early nineteenth century. Even in 1800, it is hardly likely that independent wage earners, other than farmers, exceeded 10 percent of the labor force; and as late as 1850, they still constituted only 12 percent. The working class consisted mostly of slaves and, in the colonial period, bonded servants. It is estimated that more than 60 percent of the people who came to the colonies were bonded,[2] and in the early nineteenth century, or as long as slavery existed, slaves made up about 35 percent of the labor force.

As on every frontier, many of the gainfully employed were independent farmers—perhaps one-third in 1800 and one-fifth in 1850. Manufacturing was, for the most part, carried on in the home, and handicraft artisans supplied village and urban consumers with the manufactured goods that were not made at home or imported from abroad. Usually, these artisans employed one or two journeymen and an equal number of apprentices in their workshops. Here and there were some large concentrations of employees, especially in such trades as carpentering, cabinet making, and, at a later date, clothing. One house carpenter in New York City just before the Revolution employed as many as 20 journeymen and three apprentices. The largest clothing manufacturer in the country at about 1850 employed 200. These instances were, however, exceptional.

In the early factory, the typical worker was a child. Children in 1820 made up 43 percent of Massachusetts and 55 percent of Rhode Island workers. It was said that 15 percent of the children under 16 in Paterson, New Jersey, in 1835 worked in manufacturing. As a result of the prevalence of child labor throughout the country, many "men" reached positions of responsibility at an unusually young age. Many, and sometimes all, of the officers of the New England ships that circled the globe in the early nineteenth century were 17 to 21 years old. In manufacturing, 13- and 15-year-olds often held positions of great responsibility. One 15-year-old boy set up and superintended a mill in Rhode Island. The superintendent of the Pawtucket Thread Company in 1826 was 19 years old and had already had 11 years' experience.

The employment of women was high in manufacturing, domestic service, and teaching. Most office workers, of which there were, in any case, very, very few, were men. As industry moved from the home to the factory, farmers' daughters, who had played a prominent part in household manufacture, moved

2 Richard B. Morris, *Government and Labor in Early America* (New York: Columbia University Press, 1946), p. 315.

to the city. In the Massachusetts cotton mills in 1832, there were three women for every two men. In the woolen mills, a little less than half were women, but in the carpet factories only one out of five was a female. For manufacturing as a whole, it was estimated that one of every three workers was a woman. Yet only about 5 to 10 percent of American women worked for an income before 1850, which attests to the overwhelming importance of farming and self-employment in the economy of that day.

Money and real wages

Generalizations are always difficult, but it is especially difficult to generalize about the worker's life in the early 1800s. We do not know enough about wages, the occupational mix of the labor force, employment and unemployment, and the cost of living. Instead of a set of statistics, we have a series of examples gathered from a variety of sources. The views of these sources conflict sharply on wages, hours, working conditions, and anything else that pertains to life

Table 34

WAGES AND SALARIES, 1800-1850

	About 1790	About 1800	About 1820	About 1850
Farm labor (monthly with board)	$10.00	$ 10.00	$ 10.00	$ 12.00
Nonfarm labor (daily)	.50	.75 - $1.00	.75 - $1.00	.87
Carpenter (daily)	1.07	1.50	1.50	1.50 - 2.50
Able seaman (montly)	28.00	20.00	11.00	15.00
Sailor (monthly)	—	11.70	9.00	10.00
Clerk (annually)	—	300-500	300-500	500-600
Business executive (annually)	—	1,500	2,000	3,000-5,000

among the working classes. According to some, wages were so high that some mill women saved thousands of dollars; according to others, wages were so low that hundreds of mill women were forced into prostitution. Some mill women could not escape from the factories; but, on the other hand, there was no permanent factory population.[3]

[3]Ray Ginger, "Labor in a Massachusetts Cotton Mill, 1853-1860," *Business History Review,* Vol. XXVIII (1954).

As best we are able, we gather that wages were 30 to 100 percent higher than in England in colonial days, 25 to 50 percent higher around 1830, and 50 percent higher in 1850. Most labor made 75 cents to $1.25 a day. The skilled commanded twice as much as the unskilled. New York tailors, for example, were getting $8 to $10 a week in 1840, and carpenters in the McCormick plant in 1849 were being paid $2.50 a day. Women were paid one-half to one-third as much as men. Children were paid one-half to three-quarters as much as women. To state this a little differently, nonfarm male labor earned about $1 a day, women made 50 cents, and children, 25 cents.

On the whole, the price of labor did not vary much, except on the higher paying jobs. As one manufacturer reported to the Treasury in 1832: "On the introduction of manufactures in this country, mercantile information and mechanical skill could not be conveniently obtained. Hence, the compensation to clerks, agents, and superintendents was extravagant. The information at that time possessed by few has now become the common property of many; and agents who could have obtained an annual compensation of $1,000 can now be obtained for less than half while the compensation to common laborers remains nearly the same."

Departures from the mode, because of geographical location, occupational differences, and the bargaining position of the employer, were much wider then than they are now. The labor market was not as competitive on either the demand or the supply side—if for no other reason, because of the limited distance one could walk and the inadequacy of communications. Wage rates varied from 37 1/2 cents to 63 cents within a few miles. Sectional differences were especially large. The lowest rates were paid in the South; and, as a general rule, the further West a person went, the more money he could expect to make. Ohio in 1850 paid farm hands $8 a month with board, Illinois paid $12, and California paid $60—a rate that reflected a Gold Rush bias.

Factory workers' wages were two or three times as high as those of domestics. Indeed, factory workers did as well as or better than some professionals. The average wage for a mill girl in Lowell was $3 a week; the first school mistress at Lowell got $2 plus board, which was valued at $1.25. The school year, however, was much shorter than it is now, and the school mistress was employed for only 18 weeks.

Many industries were still in the domestic or handicraft stage of production. Workers in these industries earned much less than factory workers. Shoe workers earned 75 cents to $2 a week. Seamstresses in the big cities earned as little as 14 cents for a 15-hour day. Yet there was an ample supply of them, as is evidenced by an advertisement in the Philadelphia *Public Ledger* in 1848: "Wanted by a young girl . . . the loan of $100 for which she will give one year and a half of her time as a dressmaker and seamstress."[4]

---

[4]Norman Ware, *The Industrial Worker, 1840-1860* (Boston: Houghton Mifflin Company, 1924), p. 52.

Large-scale enterprise often found it necessary to offer higher rates than normal to attract a sizable pool of labor. Lowell mills paid 50 percent more than smaller mills in the immediate environs. McCormick also paid wages considerably above the mode. Here again, however, it would be dangerous to carry the generalization too far. Not all "big businesses" paid well. A Paterson manufacturer of sail duck, for example, employed 265 workers and paid $3.90 a week to men, $2.38 to women, and $1.38 to children, about two-thirds the rate in Lowell.

What did all this mean as far as the worker's real wages were concerned? The course of real wages in the first half of the nineteenth century appears to have been somewhat as follows: Prior to 1820, there is little evidence of any apparent increase. Money wages did not improve; if anything, they fell, whereas prices were much the same in 1819 as in 1802. From about 1820 to 1850, the gain in real wages was impressive. Prices fell to about 60 percent of their 1820 level, and money wages, especially for those with high skills, increased markedly. The real wages of some skilled workers, for example, armory workers, quadrupled over the first 50 years of the century. It was said that a skilled worker at the beginning of the period could buy a 15-pound turkey with his daily pay; in 1850, he could buy five turkeys with what he made. A contemporary observer, commenting on the changing way of life under conditons of thriving industrialism, wrote in 1850: "Wages have raised about 100 percent (since 1829) while articles of furniture are very much lower and $100 will go much farther. . . . This change is owing largely to labor-saving machinery. . . . The rise in wages creates new wants and former luxuries have become necessities." Life was very kind to the skilled mechanic, but for workers in general, the unskilled as well as the skilled, the exploited and those who were more fortunate, the rise in real wages was less dramatic—probably between 50 and 60 percent.[5]

The whole concept of real wages and what they meant to the worker was clearly quite different in the early 1800s from what it is today. A 50 percent increase in a wage of $1 a week would hardly make a needle worker into a Cinderella. Yet there were some mitigating circumstances. The number of commodities and services the worker could buy was limited, and the demand on the

[5] Wage data are scattered in a great many business histories and in social and economic histories. There is a mine of information in Report of the Secretary of the Treasury, *Documents Relative to the Manufactures in the United States* (House Executive Documents, 22nd Congress, 1st Session, 1833). See also Walter B. Smith, "Wage Rates on the Erie Canal, 1828-1881," *Journal of Economic History,* Vol. XXIII (1963); Roland Gibson, *Cotton Textile Wages in the United States and Great Britain* (New York: Columbia University Press, 1949); Robert G. Layer, *Earnings of Cotton Mill Operatives, 1825-1914* (Cambridge, Mass.: Harvard University Press, 1955); Donald R. Adams, Jr., "Wage Rates in the Early National Period, Philadelphia, 1785-1830," *Journal of Economic History,* Vol. XXVIII, Sept. 1968. Some attempts have been made to estimate real wages in the period. See Harold Moulton, *Controlling Factors in Economic Development* (Washington, D.C.: The Brookings Institution, 1949); Jurgen Kuczynski, *A Short History of Labor Conditions Under Industrial Capitalism,* Vol. II (London: Frederick Muller, Ltd., 1943); Stanley Lebergott, *Manpower in Economic Growth* (New York: McGraw-Hill Book Company, 1964).

worker's income was much smaller than it would be at a later period. It was estimated that about 55 percent of his income went for food and another 30 percent for rent and clothing. Prices for these necessities were low. In 1818, bread was about 3 cents a pound; beef, 7 cents; milk, 8 cents a quart; and coffee, 18 cents a pound. Horace Greeley's *Tribune* printed, in 1851, a budget of $10.37 a week for a family of five; and the *Times,* not to be outdone, estimated that a family of four could live, though moderately, on $600 a year.

Most workers received their board along with the job, and many of the others lived in boardinghouses, where lodging was cheap. A French traveler, in 1802, reported that he was "profusely served" at the best boardinghouse in Lexington, Kentucky, for $2 a week. In Philadelphia, about 1820, workers averaged about $1 a day and it cost $4 a week to live. Female workers in the Chicopee mills in 1825 averaged about $2.50 a week, of which $1.25 went for board. These figures were, of course, deceiving. "Steady work" was the exception rather than the rule, for the methods of distributing goods were so poor that gluts very often developed in marketing commodities, resulting in wholesale layoffs of workers. Workers were not paid regularly. Sometimes as many as three to six months intervened between paydays. Then, too, employers took advantage of the shortage of coin and currency that characterized the early American economy. Usually, they paid wages in store orders or in depreciated paper money. In either case, the worker was the loser, for both methods deprived him of a sizable fraction of his nominal wage. The store-order system encouraged unscrupulous employers to charge workers higher prices than they normally would have paid for products and to falsify accounts by charging the worker for goods he had never purchased.

To augment income, workers often hired out their whole families. Slater's mill in 1816 employed 68 people, consisting of 13 families of three to eight members each, eight single men, and four single women. One Denis Rice made a contract in 1815 with a cotton mill for himself, three sons, one daughter, a sister, and a niece at rates of pay ranging from 75 cents to $5 a week. The whole family's income was about $13.66 a week. Under such an arrangement, a family could eke out a precarious existence. If no one fell ill or lost his job, the family might even be able to save a little money.

There is no way of telling how much workers saved. Of 1,976 depositors in the Lowell Savings Institution, 978 were factory girls. Their deposits totaled about $100,000, and it was not uncommon for an individual worker to have $500 in the bank. Patrick Tracy Jackson, the prominent Boston entrepreneur, stated that in one of his mills with a payroll of $60,000, workers' savings amounted to 11 percent of wages. Account books, however, show a different story. In the Slater Company, of a dozen families with from three to seven children each, only two managed to keep out of debt. The only people who continually came out ahead were the skilled workmen with no families, the single women with high relative earnings, and the small families with grown children.[6]

Hours and working conditions

The improvement in hours and working and living conditions in the early nine-teenth century was less encouraging than the improvement in wages. Because of the scarcity of labor, the generally accepted belief that idleness was immoral, the employee's desire to make as much money as possible, and the employer's desire to get maximum work out of his hired help, hours of work were very long, usually 12 to 14 hours a day, or from sunup to sundown. Vacations were unknown, and there were few holidays aside from Sundays, Fourth of July, Christmas in the South, Fast Day and Thanksgiving in New England. However, by modern standards, employees worked comparatively slowly, and both the employer and the employee gave relatively little thought to productivity.

By 1850, hours had hardly been reduced at all. Textile workers still worked 75 hours a week, compared with 69 in Great Britain. The working pace was much faster than in the previous generation, for entrepreneurs were forced, because of increased competition and lack of reserves, to try to cut costs. Con-sequently, factory workers operated three or four looms, compared with two in the 1820s and two in contemporary Great Britain. But some few skilled trades had achieved the 10-hour day, and in government service the 10-hour day was theoretically the rule after 1840. Although relatively long hours were the rule, the average worker still lost about one-quarter of his potential working time because of layoffs caused by inadequate methods of distribution.

Many employers were completely indifferent to the working and living con-ditions of their labor force, for the spread of the factory system had weakened the paternalistic attitude that had characterized the early American entre-preneur. The average employer regarded labor as no more than a commodity. He believed that the longer a laborer worked, the more he produced. The factory owner apparently was unaware of the fact that reductions in hours might in some cases result in greater production.[7] Most businessmen believed that wages

[6]For additional reading on the industrial worker in this period, see Caroline F. Ware, *The Early New England Cotton Manufacture* (Boston: Houghton Mifflin Company, 1931); Vera Shlakman, *Economic History of a Factory Town* (Northampton, Mass.: Smith College, 1935); Hannah Josephson, *The Golden Threads* (New York: Duell, Sloan, and Pearce, 1949); U.S. Department of Labor, Bureau of Labor Statistics, *History of Wages in the United States from Colonial Times to 1928,* Bulletin 604 (Washington, D.C., 1934).

[7]Although other experiments were probably made earlier, the first known attempt to measure scientifically the relation between hours of work and productivity was made by the English industrialist, Sir William Mather, in 1893.

were determined by supply and demand, and that the freedom of the market should determine what workers should earn. They paid little attention to the relationship between hours of work, working conditions, and production. Nor did it commonly occur to them that labor represented the hard core of consumer demand. One Fall River factory owner came as close to this automatic economic-man view as anyone could:[8]

> I regard my work-people just as I regard my machinery. So long as they can do my work for what I choose to pay them, I keep them, getting out of them all I can. What they do or how they fare outside my walls, I don't know nor do I consider it my business to know.

It was, however, difficult for either man or government to adhere completely to this Social Darwinism. In 1842, Massachusetts passed a law establishing a maximum 10-hour day for children under 12. Five years later, New Hampshire established a 10-hour day for women. At the time, the committee that recommended the law said that shortening the work week would be advantageous to employers, who "would realize a greater profit, even in less time, from laborers more vigorous and better able to work, from having had suitable time to rest." Like all pioneer attempts, however, these laws were mostly ineffective. The Massachusetts law was not enforced, and there was a clause in the New Hampshire law that, by permitting workers to contract for longer working days, made the legislation of only academic importance.

Working conditions under the circumstances were abysmal, although here again, the views of contemporaries contradict each other. A careful analysis by a medical man revealed that even the model factories at Lowell were poorly ventilated and unhealthy. Indeed, the Lowell mill workers petitioned the Massachusetts Legislature as follows in 1845:[9]

> We the undersigned peaceable, industrious, hardworking men and women of Lowell, in view of our condition—the evils already come upon us, by toiling from thirteen to fourteen hours per day, confined in unhealthy apartments, exposed to the poisonous contagion of air, vegetable, animal and mineral properties, debarred from proper *Physical* exercise, time for *Mental* discipline and *Mastication* cruelly limited; and thereby hastening us on through pain, disease and privation, down to a premature grave.

Living conditions were just as bad if not worse. The flood of immigrants

---

[8] Ware, *The Industrial Worker,* p. 77.

[9] Ware, *The Early New England Cotton Manufacture,* p. 251. See also Constance McLaughlin Green, *Holyoke, Massachusetts: A Case History of the Industrial Revolution in America* (New Haven, Conn.: Yale University Press, 1939).

during the late 1840s and the even greater migration from the farm packed the cities and intensified urban problems. In seven wards of downtown New York, the density of population per block climbed from 158 in 1820 to 273 in 1850. Urban American slums were as foul as those of Europe; housing was hopelessly inadequate; and medical care was almost unknown. There are many extreme examples that illustrate just how gruesome life could be in mid-nineteenth-century industrial America. In Lowell, two families occupied one room, with one of the families consisting of a man, his wife, eight children, and four boarders. Thirty-nine persons slept in a cellar in Half-Moon Place in Boston. Among the poor in New York, the average number of people living in one room was six and the maximum 20. One cellar, ten feet square and seven feet high, was home for two families of ten people. Though these conditions were not typical, neither was the following homey picture drawn by an English observer of American industrial life. "On entering the house of a respectable mechanic," he wrote, "one cannot but be astonished at the apparent neatness and comfort of the apartments, the large airy parlors, the nice carpets and mahogany furniture, and the tolerably good library." Much more realistic were the grim figures of the 1850 census that showed 18,500 families living in 8,141 cellars in New York City, and the even grimmer medical estimate that the average length of life of the Boston Irish was 14 years.[10]

Traditionally, it has been assumed that formal education's contribution to economic growth was as important or even more important than any other factor but, as the Scotch might say, this is not proved. It is probable that education's contribution has been grossly exaggerated. But whatever its contribution, educational facilities steadily improved. Some strides were made during the first half of the nineteenth century, but much still remained to be done. By 1850, labor's demand for tax-supported school systems had been pretty fully granted on the primary level, except in the South. Government-supported secondary schools, however, were still rare, and free colleges were unknown. But the mere fact that free primary schools existed did not mean that they were being attended. In 1860, the average American had less than three years of schooling. Nevertheless, this was about five times as much as in 1800 and exceeded the figures for all European countries except Germany.

Many reformers urged the urban worker to flee from his miserable housing and working conditions and to move westward where land was cheap and opportunity unlimited. But in the 1850s, even the skilled worker did not have enough money to go west and establish a farm. Moreover, as miserable as his life was, the average city worker was compelled by habit, custom, and general inertia to continue his mean existence. As one worker expressed it:[11]

10Ware, *The Industrial Worker, 1840-1860*, pp. 13-16.
11*Ibid*, p. 37.

We have always been used to live in a town where we could get what
little things we want if we have money and it is only those who have
lived in the wilderness who know what the horrors of wilderness life
are.

THE WORKER'S PROGRESS IN THE LAST HALF
OF THE NINETEENTH CENTURY

The 25 years between the end of the Civil War and 1890 were years of great
technological innovation and extraordinary economic progress. This phenomenal
growth had a mixed effect on the American worker. His hours of work and his
living and working conditions remained substantially the same, but the composition of the labor force and money and real earnings changed significantly.

Industrial labor commonly worked a 10-hour day in 1890, as compared
with 11 hours in 1860. There was, however, a much more determined movement
toward shorter hours, a movement which employers strenuously resisted. The
comment of a cotton-mill manager was certainly shared by many. He thought
that a reduction in working time would "increase crime, suffering, wickedness,
and pauperism. . . . Yes, I verily believe, there are a large number of operatives in
our cotton mills who have too much spare time now."[12]

Living conditions were, if anything, worse than in 1860, for urban manufacturing areas became steadily more congested, and labor was no more mobile at
the end of the century than it had been at mid-century. It still took a lot of
money to go west, and the frontier was fast losing its appeal. A Fall River
worker, when asked in the 1880s why he did not go west, gave a typical answer:
"Well, I never saw over a $20 bill. . . . If someone would give me $1,500, I would
go."

The composition of the labor force

One of the more substantial changes that occurred during the last of the 1800s
was a decline in the number of self-employed. In 1850, almost half of all the
nonslave labor force was self-employed. In the succeeding decades, the decline in
farming and the appearance and growth of large-scale business cut sharply into
the ranks of the self-employed. By 1900, only 34 percent of the entire labor
force and by 1970, less than 10 percent of the labor force was self-employed.

Other changes in the composition of the labor force that we have come to
regard as spectacular still lay in the future. The white-collar occupations were
more unusual than common, including not many more than one out of every ten

[12]Shlakman, *Economic History of a Factory Town*, p. 185.

workers. The growing urban labor force was fed during these years, as it had been fed for two generations, by immigrants, departing farmers, and a continual influx of children. Those between 10 and 15 made up 13 percent of the gainfully occupied in 1870 and 18 percent in 1890.

The great female invasion of the labor force had not yet begun. In 1880, only one out of every six workers was a woman. Less than 20 percent of all females and less than 5 percent of married females were in the labor force. Spinsters, widows, and the daughters of the very poor were almost the only ones who worked for an income. Almost half of working women were in domestic service. Another 40 percent were divided about equally between the farm and the factory, leaving 10 percent for the professions, the government, and the clerical occupations. In the latter, which we have come to regard as the peculiar province of the female, men outnumbered women three to one at the close of the last century.

Money and real wages

Money wages were considerably higher in 1890 than in 1860, but not as high as in 1865. Money earnings followed the business cycle. They multiplied during the Civil War, fell abruptly in the first postwar recession, gained some lost ground in the early 1870s, sank rapidly in the depression, and regained in the 1880s part of what had been lost.[13]

There continued to be wide differences in pay among the different industries, among the different occupations, and between the sexes. Women were paid about half as much as men. Workers in the highest-paying industries earned two

Table 35

MONEY WAGES IN SELECTED OCCUPATIONS, 1860-1890

	1860	*1870*	*1890*	*Change, 1860-1890* *1860 = 100*
Farm (per month with board)	$13.70	$20.00	$13.90	101
Skilled	1.67	3.00	2.92	175
Steel	3.20	4.50	3.96	124
Carpenter	1.70	2.97	2.37	139
Unskilled	1.00	1.50	1.45	145
Steel	1.37	2.25	1.67	122
Women	.50	1.19	.92	184
Executive (annual)	5,000	10,000	15,000	300
Clerical	500	600	850	170

[13]In addition to the references in footnote 5, see David E. Novack and Richard Perlman, "The Structure of Wages in the American Iron and Steel Industry, 1860-1890," *Journal of Economic History,* Vol. XXII (1962).

to three times as much as in the lowest-paying. The differences among occupations were even greater. Salaries in clerical occupations ranged from $600 to $1,500 a year. An unskilled worker made two-thirds as much as a skilled worker in 1860, but only half as much in 1890.

Although money wages declined somewhat between 1865 and 1890, prices went down sharply. Depending on whose estimate is used, the cost of living fell as much as 60 percent. Real wages were, therefore, higher in 1890 than in 1860 and much higher than in 1865.[14] According to Clarence Long, whose estimate is the one most widely accepted, real annual earnings in manufacturing increased about 50 percent between 1860 and 1890. Long estimated that, in 1860 dollars, average earnings in manufacturing were $297 in 1860 and $434 in 1890. The Civil War did nothing to improve the lot of the urban worker, but his monetary circumstances improved splendidly in the 30 years after the War. Perhaps the best evidence of this can be found in how the worker spent his income. In 1860, he spent 80 percent of his income on food, rent, and clothing. In 1890, these took only 75 percent. In 1870, when Reed and Barton, the silversmiths, paid unskilled workers $1.25 a day, skilled workers, $3 to $5, and foremen, $6, room and board cost $4.50 a week for men and $3.00 for women. In 1890, carpet workers made only $400 a year, but one could rent six rooms for $4 to $9 a month.

THE WORKER IN THE TWENTIETH CENTURY

By the end of the first quarter of the twentieth century, the United States had become an urban, industrial economy. Mass production had become "the American system"; the great factory had long since emerged as the focal point of production; bigness had come to characterize the whole of American economic society. In this new era of mass production and colossal economic units, a change occurred in the composition of the labor force, as well as in the benefits that labor gained from economic growth. Labor placed greater emphasis on the less measurable rewards than it had ever done before. Wages rose, but all income, tangible and intangible, multiplied.

The composition of the labor force

The proportion of the population age 14 and over in the labor force continued to remain remarkably steady. Since 1890, it has varied only 2.2 percentage points, from 52.2 to 54.4 percent, but during the same period the percent of the total population in the labor force has ranged between 30 and 40 percent. The

---

[14]The lowest estimate of the increase in real wages between 1860 and 1890 is 12 percent, and the highest is 80 percent.

An example of labor conditions around 1870[15]

difference in the trends was the result of a gradual increase in the median age of the population.[16]

The internal composition of this relatively stable labor force has undergone

[15]This set of admonitions was apparently widely used; it has been credited to at least a dozen companies.

[16]Gertrude Bancroft, *The American Labor Force: Its Growth and Changing Composition* (New York: John Wiley & Sons, Inc., 1958); John Durand, *The Labor Force in the United States, 1890-1960* (New York: The Social Science Research Council, 1948); Clarence Long, *The Labor Force Under Changing Income and Employment* (Princeton, N.J.: Princeton University Press, 1958).

a radical transformation. The number of self-employed has dwindled to less than 10 percent of all those who earn an income. The primary and secondary occupations that were most prevalent in 1890 have faded, whereas the tertiary occupations have multiplied. Those who grow and process goods are now fewer than those who distribute goods and offer services.

Urbanization, the extension of education, higher wage rates, pensions, and a general upgrading of skills removed many of the very young and the old from the labor force. In 1890, when most Americans still lived "in the country," when unskilled labor was in much greater demand, and when pensions were a rarity, almost 70 percent of the males over 65 were in the labor force. In the urbanized, industrial, highly educated, and well-pensioned environment of the mid-twentieth century, only one out of three of Social Security age was working or looking for a job. Voluntary retirement had become much more common. Then too, the speed-up of production and the increasingly technological nature of the economy put a premium on mental and physical agility and adaptability and threw many of the older workers into the industrial scrapheap of involuntary retirement.

The family system of hiring that characterized early American industrial history was abandoned long ago, but the earning of income continued to be a cooperative rather than an individual enterprise. Among working-class families during the early part of the century, the father's income was augmented by the earnings of his children and often by income obtained from boarders. A survey in 1909 of some 300 New York City working-class families showed that less than half were supported entirely by the father's income. In time, child labor diminished, but as it did, it was replaced by increased employment of women. Married women stopped working "unproductively," that is, for nothing, around the house. They entered the labor force in an effort to supply the additional family income needed to meet the ever-rising standard of living. By the 1930s, husbands were the sole earners in only three-fifths of American families and in a far smaller percentage of working-class families.

The proportion of children between 10 and 15 among the gainfully employed began to drop in 1900. It was then about 20 percent. After 1930, when it had dropped to less than 5 percent, the census discontinued collecting the data. Here again, urbanization and industrialization had much to do with the exodus, but the most important catalyst was the continued spread of education. A change was taking place in the American philosophy and the "American Way of Life." The thesis that man was born only to work and then to die no longer seemed so clear. The Horatio Alger, Jr., script telling that success could be expected only through hard work and diligence began to be subtly modified. Success, hard work, and thrift were still important, but many people began to see that with a good education, success would come much more quickly. The average American youth began to give more of his time to education, and to postpone the day when he would "go out into the world and seek his fortune."

The change from an agrarian to an industrial society intensified the trend. On the farm, only a rudimentary education was essential, but in the new professions and in the careers that were rapidly opening up, further education was a prerequisite. Consequently, most of the young attended school, and full-time child labor virtually disappeared.

As the working child became increasingly rare, the working woman became increasingly typical. Urbanization, the multiplication of so-called "nonproduction" jobs in the clerical, sales, and professional occupations, and, above all else, technological progress broadened the economic opportunities for women. As early as the 1830s, the impact of technology could readily be seen. In carpet manufacturing, for example, 80 percent of the operatives in 1832 were men but in 1850, after the machine, 47 percent were women. The influence of the machine was even more striking in the late nineteenth century when the typewriter and the telephone swelled the importance of the office and changed its composition from male to female. More and more women began to take jobs despite a solidly entrenched middle-class prejudice against it. It is generally assumed that a great revolution took place in the status of women in the 1920s with the suffrage movement or in the 1960s with the outburst of "women's lib." But this is a caricature of the truth; "the emancipation of women" began in the early 1900s.

In October 1910, a well-known feminist wrote:

> The four great curses of working women have been insufficient wages, intense and unfair competition, long hours, and the lack of any incentive to acquire and display ability. There is good reason to believe that the turning point has been reached.

In the intervening 63 years, two of the disabilities have been removed. There is no doubt, of course, that women have entered the labor force and the fact is well accepted. In 1870, 15 percent of women were employed; in 1973, 45 percent were employed. In 1870, women made up 13 percent of the labor force; today, they account for 40 percent. But the influx into the labor force was not a steady progression. After a substantial gain, up to and including the 1920s, the surge was rudely interrupted by the depression of the 1930s only to burst forth in a more accelerated movement from World War II on. Thus, from 15 percent in 1870, female employment jumped to 21 percent of all women in 1900. Then it slowed to 29 percent in 1940 and soared to 45 percent in 1973. And the employment of married women increased about twice as fast as the employment of women in general. In 1900, one out of every eight working women was also a wife; in 1973, five out of every eight were married. To some extent, the multiplication of the number of working females was more a matter of semantics than of reality. Much of the increase represented a shift of housewives, who by definition are not included in the labor force, to income-earning jobs. Some of it could also be considered a form of "moonlighting," that is, holding more than one job—being a housewife in addition to working for an income.

The whole mix of what females do in the labor force has changed impressively. In 1870, 60 percent of working females were domestics; in 1970, it was less than 10 percent. In 1900, less than 20 percent of working females wore white collars; 100 years later, 60 percent were in so-called white collar occupations. To be sure, most of the jobs are still of the clerical and kindred variety. Less than 2 percent are professional, a little more than 5 percent are in the managerial class, 7 percent of working females are in sales, but almost 80 percent are in clerical and kindred occupations.

The length of the work week

Along with the shifting composition of the labor force, the twentieth century witnessed a drastic reduction in the hours of work. It was hardly likely that the work week dropped as much as 15 percent in the last 30 years of the nineteenth century, but the trend toward leisure picked up speed in the 1900s. From the end of the Civil War to the end of World War I, the work week shortened about 3/10 of one percent a year; from 1919 on, it fell about 6/10 of one percent annually. The drop was especially noticeable in trade and manufacturing; and less so in clerical occupations and in agriculture, although farm laborers did cut their hours. In 1890, the average work week for the whole economy was about 53 1/2 hours. In farming, it was 45 1/2 hours; in manufacturing, 53 1/2 hours; clerical help worked about 50 hours; and those in trade, at least 60 hours. By 1970, the work week was not so variant. It averaged 34 to 42 hours across the board.[17] Farmers gained four hours; clerical workers, ten; manufacturing workers, 14; and those in trade, 20 hours.

At first blush, it would seem that any reduction in hours could be achieved only by a reduction in earnings or an increase in prices, for less hours worked could only mean less production. But this was not always true. Some reductions in working time were accompanied by such sharp increases in man-hour output that total production went up even with less hours worked. It is obvious, however, that at some point this fortunate result could no longer occur. It is also clear that in certain sectors of the economy, such as trade, the possibilities for increased productivity were not very bright. Drastic reductions in hours in these areas had to increase costs and, because wages did not fall, prices had to rise.

THE TWENTIETH-CENTURY SPURT IN WAGES

In the three generations after 1890, money wages multiplied more than ten times. Price inflation, however, took some of this gain away. Consequently, real hourly earnings in manufacturing rose about five times. And, because workers

[17]Farm owners, it was said, worked 52 hours and managers, 50 hours.

spent fewer hours on the job, real weekly earnings multiplied about four times.[18] This progress in wages did not proceed steadily and smoothly from 1890 to 1970. On the contrary, it was interrupted by war and jolted by severe depression.

Table 36

MONEY WAGES IN SELECTED OCCUPATIONS, 1900-1970

	1900	1930	1950	1970	1900-1970 (1900=100) increase
Farm (annually with board)	$ 178	$ 369	$ 1,200	$ 3,600	202
Skilled (weekly)	18	39	75	157	870
Unskilled (weekly)	9	22	50	110	1222
Clerical (weekly)	12	35	52	109	900
Male	—	—	58	132	—
Female	—	—	46	86	—
Retail clerks (weekly)	10	23	48	82	820
Male	—	—	—	93	—
Female	—	—	—	25[2]	—
Teacher (weekly)	6	27	58	160	2666
Male	—	—	—	176	—
Female	—	—	—	117	—
Executive (annually)[1]	25,000		209,000	317,500	1530

[1] President of Standard Oil of New Jersey.
[2] Includes part-time employees.

From 1890 to 1929

Although the economic status of the average worker had improved vastly by the beginning of the twentieth century, his life was far from utopian. Judged by any standard, his wages were not sufficient to permit him to live in comfort. Few workers were paid as much as $18 a week in 1900, and at least two-thirds of the adult male workers made less than $600 a year. To be sure, prices were low. Beef could be bought for 18 cents a pound, and housing could be had in New York City for $14 a month. Nevertheless, it was estimated that $825 a year was the minimum necessary for a family of five to maintain a reasonably adequate living standard in New York City. If the main breadwinner's earnings were not enough to achieve this standard, family income was increased by additional income from other members of the family and from lodgers. So well did this arrangement work that among 318 families surveyed in New York City in 1909, only 86

[18] Albert Rees, *Real Wages in Manufacturing, 1890-1914* (Princeton, N.J.: Princeton University Press, 1961). See also Lebergott, *Manpower in Economic Growth.*

found it impossible to "make both ends meet" and 116 were actually able to save a little money.

Wages improved slowly in the 25 years after 1890. By 1913, average non-farm wages were $675 a year. A skilled worker earned $750, clerks and stenographers $15 a week, accountants, $30, a banker, $7,700 a year, a lawyer, $4,200, physicians, $3,900, and college professors, $2,900. But one could go around the world for $639 or rent a five-room apartment in New York City for $50 a month, which was considered high.

When Henry Ford announced his $5 day in 1914, the announcement literally shocked the world. The *Times* estimated that the move meant doubling the rate of pay and called it "distinctly Utopian," while the *Wall Street Journal* labeled it "unscientific." Wages spurted upward sharply when war began in Europe; they stabilized when the United States became involved, and then spurted again in the 1920s. By 1929, real wages were about 40 percent higher than in 1890. The average annual earnings of the American manufacturing worker were $1,300. Prices were about twice as high as in 1900, and it took about $1,700 to take care of a family. Yet, some workers still found it possible to save money. In one survey of almost 4,000 families averaging $1,344 annually, average savings were $83 a year, or more than 6 percent.

From the depressed 1930s to 1970

The four decades after 1930 were years of extreme ups and downs for wage earners as well as for most of the rest of society. The greatest gains during this period came in the form of increased real wages. Real weekly wages more than doubled between 1929 and 1960—from almost $40 to over $90—and then increased another 13 percent in the 1960s to over $100. But neither money nor real wages went up continually. During the gloomy years of the Great Depression, hourly money wages fell almost 20 percent, but the cost of living fell more than 30 percent, so that the real wages of those who had full-time jobs actually increased. Few, however, were in such a fortunate position. Allowing for time lost because of unemployment, average real wages fell more than 30 percent. Thus, during the depression, industrial workers lost all the gain in real wages that they had achieved in the previous 25 years.

After the depression, progress in money wages was the most spectacular in history. At the same time, another windfall came as pension and welfare benefits became part of the usual order of things. These fringe benefits averaged only $18 a year in 1929 and $20 in 1933, but they had passed $900 before the 1970s were far along. Under this double impact, the average annual earnings of a full-time employee rose from a little over $1,000 in 1933 to $8,200 in 1970, and in manufacturing, from $1,100 to $8,600. Meanwhile, however, prices had more than tripled, and, as usual, the standard of living had expanded much faster than the level of living. It was estimated, for example, that it required $3,200 to

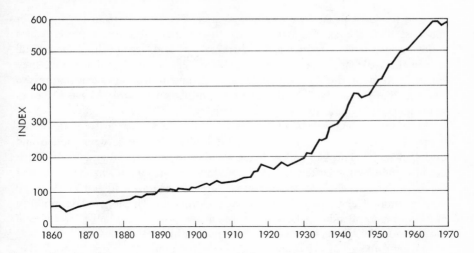

CHART 28. Index of real hourly wages in manufacturing, 1860-1970 (1890=100)

keep a family of four in "modest but adequate" bed and board in 1947, but $11,000 in 1972, even though the price level had not quite doubled in the 25 years. Despite the higher prices and the greater ambitions, money wages had increased so magnificently that real wages were up very impressively. In the generation after 1929, real wages more than doubled, and after 1933, after allowing for unemployment, they quadrupled.

Disparities in wages and salaries among different groups and among different occupations still existed, but they were not quite so marked as in the past. This could be expected, for continuous improvements in transportation and communication meant more mobility. Immigration was much less important after 1929 than it had been before. The demand for labor was much more intense in the period after World War II. And, finally, some old social shibboleths had been replaced with some new clichés.

For the last reason, women found it easier to join the labor force, but the pay differential between men and women did not narrow except among the self-employed and in the managerial occupations. Women still earned half or less than half as much as men, and in the 1960s, despite all the talk about "women's lib," the disparity in pay between the sexes actually widened. On the other hand, new concepts of education, the prestige of a white collar, and the general low repute of the blue collar had rather remarkable effects on the spread between clerical salaries and manufacturing wages for both men and women. Clerical salaries were substantially higher than wages in 1900, and perhaps twice as high in 1915. During World War I, wages rose much more rapidly; but in the 1920s, salaries regained some of the lost ground. By 1939, they were probably 30 percent higher than wages. World War II changed all this; the extraordinary demand for labor pushed wages above salaries. But from 1948 to 1970, as after the first War, salaries again rose faster than wages. Other wage patterns also followed long-wave movements. Teachers' salaries had lagged behind the general movement for many years. Then because of sharply increased demand, they spurted ahead in the 1960s. Similarly, government workers made impressive gains so that for similar jobs the average monthly salary in 1973 was higher in municipal employment than in private industry.

The extraordinary demand for labor and the increasing rarity of the immigrant also did something to the long-established spread between skilled and unskilled wages. This gap had widened steadily between 1850 and 1929, but it began to narrow thereafter. In 1907, the skilled in manufacturing made twice as much as the unskilled; in 1930, almost three times as much; and in 1960, 50 percent more. Geographic differences also narrowed with the increase mobility and the spread of industrialization. Wages in the South were half as much as in the North in the 1920s, but two-thirds as much in the 1950s.

Among the groups that are usually collected under the word "labor," that is, industrial workers, farmers, and occasional white-collar workers, the disparity between wages in the same occupation became increasingly small. Among executives, however, the difference remained surprisingly substantial. In 1900, a typical salary for a businessman who had an ownership stake in the business he was running was $25,000 to $30,000 a year. Hired top executives in the large insurance companies earned $100,000. Salaries jumped in the twentieth century as the professional manager became more common. By 1950, the average salary of the head of a large company was about $165,000, but the disparity was immense, ranging from $50,000 to over $500,000. In the executive positions next to the top, the range was equally great, from $33,000 to well over $300,000. By 1970, the salary of a chief executive of one of the country's largest companies, together with bonuses but not including stock options, averaged $400,000. Again the range was immense, from $120,000 to $767,000.[19]

WAGES AND SALARIES IN THE NATIONAL INCOME

Changes in real wages offer the best criterion for measuring what labor received for its production, but labor's rewards can also be measured in terms of its share of the national income. Since 1929, this has ranged from 58 to 74 percent. Going back even further and using annual averages by decades, labor's share has ranged from 53 to 67 percent.[20] Concealed within this range, however,

[19]Based on data collected by *Business Week,* May, 1955; May, 1961; June, 1971. See also Leonard R. Burgess, *Top Executive Pay Package* (New York: The Macmillan Company, 1963); Wilbur G. Lewellen, "Executives Lose Out, Even with Options," *Harvard Business Review,* January-February 1968.

[20]D. Gale Johnson, "The Functional Distribution of Income in the United States, 1850-1952," *Review of Economics and Statistics,* Vol. XXXVI (1954). Using a different

is a secular rising trend. Thus, in 1900-1909, labor's share averaged about 55 percent of the national income, whereas in the 1950s and 1960s it averaged 65 percent.

Prior to World War II, the share of the national income that went to wages and salaries varied inversely with the rise and fall of business activity. In periods of prosperity, when aggregate income was high, labor's share was low; in periods of recession, when aggregate income was low, labor's share was high. Labor received only slightly more than 50 percent of the even higher national income of 1929. On the other hand, its share was over 70 percent in 1921 and 1933, years of deep depression. In short, labor shared relatively less in prosperity, but suffered relatively less in depression. This dismal set of rewards offered labor dubious prospects for economic advancement; but in the period after World War II, there was some evidence of a change. Labor's share in the national income showed no signs of declining despite the existence of unprecedented prosperity. From a wartime peak of slightly more than 65 percent in 1945, labor's share of the national income dropped to slightly less than 65 percent in 1946 and was back to over 70 percent in 1973. It no longer seemed so certain that labor had to accept either a smaller share of the large national income associated with prosperity and full employment or a larger share of the low national income associated with recession and unemployment.

Because of fundamental changes in the economy, labor's share in the national income was bound to go up even though the individual worker might be no better off relative to other members of society. First of all, the number of self-employed has been declining drastically. This has transferred income out of unincorporated enterprise into the wage and salary category. Consequently, part of the rise in wages and salaries, a far from insignificant part, has resulted from an increase in the proportion of wage and salary recipients. A second reason has been the increased participation of government in the economy. Under the peculiarities of national income accounting, only that part of government expenditures that is paid out in salaries and wages is included in national income. It is assumed that government contributes nothing to saving and capital formation, and certainly it does not make a profit. Therefore, as government spending increases, it tends to bloat the wage and salary items in the accounts. Taking these things into consideration, most authorities think that the wage and salary share of national income has been remarkably stable. And from this they further deduce that neither government nor labor unions can much affect what labor receives.

---

definition of labor's share, Dennison concluded that it ranged from 67 to 75 percent. Edward Dennison, *The Sources of Economic Growth in the United States* (New York: Committee for Economic Development, 1962).

LIVING AND WORKING CONDITIONS IN THE 1900s

The rise in real wages enabled the worker to enjoy a way of living he would not have believed possible a few decades before. In the early years of the century, housing conditions were still wretched. Only 18 percent of the families surveyed in a 1909 investigation had inside bathrooms, and more than half lived in homes that averaged one and a half persons to a room. A settlement-house worker described a typical working-class apartment as one which housed eight people in a tiny kitchen, a combination living and bedroom, one bedroom (6'×7'), and one closet. Four water closets in the yard each served three families. The father in this case was a derrick lifter, usually unemployed in the winter, but earning up to $3 a day when working.

Working conditions were just as bad. In one large corporation, which even its "severest critics praised for its labor policy," sanitary facilities were very primitive. The company allowed each worker one bar of soap a week. Toilets were improvised sheds covering a scantling with holes. Although the basic hours of employment were supposed to be nine, the working day lasted as long as the foreman decided. Employees had to eat when they could. It was a system that has been described as "patriarchal, although benevolent."

By the middle of the century, wretched housing conditions had not been completely eliminated, but the average worker lived in far better state. Over half of the nation's labor force owned their own homes, compared with less than 20 percent at the beginning of the century. Working conditions had, if anything, improved more than living conditions. But granted that life was better, it was still not without adversities. The chief of these was the specter of unemployment, apparently a product of advancing urban industrialism. Educated guesses estimate that in the worst depressions of the early nineteenth century, the unemployment rate varied between 3 and 8 percent. In the severe contraction of 1876, unemployment exceeded 10 percent and in the last depression of the century, it passed 15 percent. Between 1890 and 1929, unemployment exceeded 6 percent of the labor force in 13 of the 40 years, although during the prosperous 1920s, it averaged much below 6 percent. During the depression, unemployment rose to over 25 percent. Thereafter, it exceeded 6 percent in every year between 1929 and 1941. The picture was assuredly much better after World War II, for unemployment exceeded 6 percent in only two of the years between 1942 and 1974. A mythical worker who had worked the first 60 years of the twentieth century spent 16 of them under conditions of severe unemployment, 21 in moderate unemployment and 23 in minimum unemployment. The 1960s were quite different. Average annual unemployment was below 6 percent except in 1961, and in one year (1969) the rate fell as low as 3.5 percent. But the performance satisfied neither the most militant critics of the system nor the most idealistic. Even though there had never been a peace-time year between

1929 and 1964 when unemployment did not at some time *during the year* pass 6 percent, the definition of full employment was reduced to 4 percent with the understanding that it would be further reduced to 3 percent as soon as feasible.

UNEMPLOYED AS A PER CENT OF THE LABOR FORCE, 1900-1970

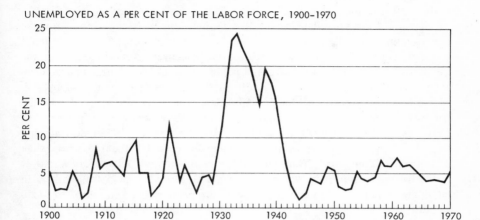

CHART 29. Unemployment as a percent of the labor force, 1900-1970

GOVERNMENT REGULATION OF HOURS AND WAGES

Labor—its working conditons, wages, and hours—has been one of the most important areas of government regulation and illustrates how governments tried to help the relatively weak members of the economy. From the ineffectual pioneer beginnings in New England in the 1840s, government regulation of hours expanded rapidly. By the 1870s, many states had passed laws regulating the hours of labor, and by 1939 there were 44 such statutes. Minimum-wage legislation in the states started much later, for it took a long time to convince the Supreme Court that such regulation was constitutional. Massachusetts first regulated wages in 1912, but as late as 1938, only half the states had minimum-wage laws. Unemployment insurance legislation was adopted still more slowly, Wisconsin passing the first such law in 1932, shortly before the Federal government took over the initiative.

Although it adopted a ten-hour day for its employees in 1840 and an eight-hour day in 1869, the Federal government did not enter generally into labor regulation until the twentieth century. Once having entered the field, however, it broadened its activities rapidly. In general, the objective was the same as that of the states: to protect the weaker party in industrial bargaining. In 1916, Congress, under the urging of President Wilson and in order to prevent a nation-wide railroad strike, established an eight-hour day for trainmen. During the 1920s, Federal attempts to regulate labor conditions centered on child labor, and two child labor laws were passed. One prohibited the use of child labor in interstate commerce; the other imposed a tax on goods produced by child labor and shipped in interstate commerce. However, the Supreme Court struck down both statutes as unconstitutional.

Not until the early days of the New Deal did the Federal government make any attempt to regulate hours and wages on a broad national front, and then it was a gradual process. The National Industrial Recovery Act of 1933 began the trend by setting minimum wages and maximum hours for workers covered by codes, but these regulations, along with the other provisions of the NIRA, collapsed when the Act was held unconstitutional. The NIRA was succeeded by the Walsh-Healy Act, which set minimum standards for workers on government contracts. It was, however, the Fair Labor Standards Act of 1938 (the Wage and Hour Law) that set the first permanent and wide coverage. Including more than 25 percent of employees, its initial terms set a maximum work week of 40 hours by 1940 and a minimum wage of 40 cents an hour by 1945 for workers in interstate commerce. Subsequently, the minimum was raised in jumps to $1.60 an hour.

PRODUCTIVITY—THE KEY TO THE WORKER'S PROGRESS

Government intervention and trade unionism may have contributed to the worker's rising level of living. Certainly, they had an effect on relative rates of pay. But for labor in general, most of the progress resulted from increased productivity, that is, from more output per man-hour. Over the long run, as labor's contribution to production increased, labor's share in the total product increased commensurately. Not every increase in productivity, it is true, was immediately followed by an equal increase in labor's tangible or intangible income. At times, productivity increased faster than labor's economic share; at other times, labor's benefits were greater than the increase in man-hour output. In general, however, labor reaped larger benefits as the nation's productivity increased.

Available data on output per man-hour in the early nineteenth century are too fragmentary to be of any value. Estimates based upon better data begin with the last decade of the 1800s. They show that, over the 70 years between 1889 and 1957, output per man-hour in the private economy increased about 2.4 percent a year, or 1.5 percent a year if government is included. Contrary to what many people believe, the performance was better in the later than the earlier years. Up to 1919, the rise was about 2.0 percent a year; after that it was 2.6 percent a year, a rate that would double output in something like 25 years.[21] In

[21] Using weighted averages per unit of labor input and disregarding the contribution of capital, Kendrick concluded that the annual increase in man-hour output was 2 percent from 1889 to 1957, and 2.3 percent from 1919 to 1957. John W. Kendrick, *Productivity*

the late 1960s, however, the rate of productivity increase fell sharply. For the whole decade, output per man hour rose by 33.3 percent, but 60 percent of the increase occurred in the first five years. Moreover, the performance of agriculture was far more impressive than that of the nonfarm economy. And finally, the gains for the whole decade were far less than those achieved by some of our international competitors.

What caused the rise in productivity, and why did the increase accelerate in the 1920s and fall off in the 1960s? A quick answer is increased capital goods, but this is not adequate, for the productivity increase far surpassed the input of new capital. What must have taken place was a better use of existing and new capital as well as manpower—in short, better techniques of management and more research and development. We also know that productivity goes up faster in expansion than in contraction and much faster in the earlier years of expansion than in the later years. Finally, we also know that the possibilities of productivity gains are much greater in agriculture and manufacturing than in the so-called service industries. All of which goes far to explain the poor performance of the 1960s.

LONG-RUN TRENDS IN THE WORKER'S ECONOMIC STATUS

The data in this chapter have been so scattered that they may have blurred what really happened to the worker over the 150 years of American history. It seems advisable, therefore, to sum up the long-run trends in the worker's level of living.

In the last 150 years, real wages have increased almost eight times, but this is not to be interpreted to mean that the worker is in a state of giddy affluence. Like most Americans, his scale of living has been chasing a standard of living, and the gap, although narrower than a generation ago, is by no means closed.

Real wages increased at a rather steady rate. Our best guess is about 20 times. But hours of work followed a more erratic course. Ignoring the paid vacations, disability time, and holidays, which are in themselves a great boon, the average working week has been cut in half since the early 1800s.

A third feature of the worker's changing life that requires emphasis is the change in occupation. It is an error to think of the labor force under the same heading as it was thought of 30 or 50 years ago. Agriculture employs far less than a generation ago. There are many more white-collar workers, a somewhat larger number of blue-collar wearers, and far fewer self-employed. The enormous increase in the non-self-employed formed an army out of which came battalions

---

Trends in the United States (Princeton, N.J.: Princeton University Press, 1961). See also Solomon Fabricant, "Basic Factors on Productivity Change," NBER *Occasional Paper,* No. 63, 1959.

of trade-union members. The twentieth century was not long in being before the term "big labor" became as common as "big business," and to that aspect of labor history we now turn our attention.

THE EVOLUTION OF TRADE UNIONISM

Labor's gains—increased wages, shorter hours, and improved working and living conditions—were not achieved without a struggle, and this struggle was expressed most noticeably in the varying fortunes of labor unionism.

Like all economic institutions, American labor unions reflected the constantly changing American cultural and economic environment. More specifically, the union movement reflected such social and political factors as the American's affinity for organization, the difference in interests between the skilled and the unskilled, the changing attitudes toward property rights, and the government's more active role in economic matters. Unionism was also deeply influenced by such fundamental economic phenomena as the business cycle, the widening of the market area, the disappearance of free land, the decline of agriculture, and the change from small- to large-scale business organization.

THE AMERICAN ATTITUDE TOWARD LABOR UNIONS

During their early history, American labor unions found it difficult to gain a firm foothold; but in time the attitude of society changed, and if unions were not welcomed as honored guests at the economic table, they were at least accepted.

At first, the majority of society was either violently opposed to or apathetic toward labor unions. Trade unionism in essence represents an attempt to reduce the absolute rights of private property. But the sanctity of property rights was deeply ingrained in American culture, and early trade unionism, therefore, aroused considerable opposition from the community at large.[22]

Farmers, who formed the bulk of society, were strongly opposed to labor unions, for their objectives were far different from those that the unions were seeking. Farmers favored inflation, whereas labor tended to oppose inflation; farmers wanted low-priced manufactured goods, while labor unions wanted high wages that would tend to raise the price of manufactured goods.

But agrarian opposition was as nothing compared to the hostility the unions met from employers. The mid-nineteenth-century American businessman was

[22]The most exhaustive history of labor unions is John R. Commons, et al., *History of Labor* (New York: The Macmillan Company, 1918-1935). The most recent is Philip Taft, *Organized Labor in American History* (New York: Harper & Row, Publishers, 1964).

paternalistic and disregarded the relationship between wages and the demand for goods—if he was aware that any such relationship existed. As he viewed matters, labor organizations were ethically and economically unjustifiable. They not only violated the rights of private property, but they were without point. According to business opinion, "going wages" were determined by market forces and could not be influenced by labor unions without creating economic chaos that would hurt the laborer as well as the rest of society. Businessmen insisted that, if unions were successful in raising wages, they would increase costs, reduce business activity, and create unemployment, thus injuring the laborer rather than helping him. They followed the nineteenth-century "wages-fund" theory, which taught that wages were determined by the ratio between the labor force and available capital funds. Because the imagined wages fund was a fixed amount, it followed that if wages were raised for some employees, the wages of the others would have to go down, or some unemployment would have to result. Strangely enough, labor unions to some extent accepted the arguments underlying the wages-fund doctrine. Time and again, labor leaders argued that an increase in the labor supply would reduce the individual's share of total wage payments. This was the same as saying that there was only so much work to go around, only so much money in the wages fund, and that this fixed amount divided by the total number of workers determined the average wage.

Because of the influence of farmers and businessmen, unionism throughout most of its early history had to face persistent political opposition, for the state and national governments often were quite sensitive to business and farm opinion expressed through farmers' organizations, political parties, and various businessmen's trade associations. But even labor itself was apathetic toward the early unions. Land was plentiful, labor was scarce, economic opportunity seemed almost unlimited, and there were no sharply defined class lines that acted to prevent a worker from moving up the economic ladder. The laborer, especially the skilled laborer, shared the American dream of economic advancement. He did not consider himself destined to drag out his years as a permanent member of the laboring class, but looked forward with confident optimism to the day when he would be a landowner, a small businessman, or a substantial entrepreneur. Because he expected some day to be a member of the employer class, he could not develop a feeling of hostility toward employers, nor could he generate a devotion to the employee class. His attitude was middle-class not proletarian, and consequently differed from the attitude, beliefs, and outlook of the continental European worker.

Because of the vast economic opportunities that existed in America, and considering the worker's middle-class attitude, the early American labor movement could scarcely pretend to represent a struggle by a downtrodden and economically exploited group to achieve economic progress or status. Labor's tactics, therefore, were quite different from those developed by the continental European labor movement. In order to placate social opposition, American unionism was conservative rather than radical, and whatever success it achieved came, not because it tried to maintain the worker's status as a worker, but because it acted as his champion whenever his status as a property owner or would-be property owner was threatened.

As the economy developed and became more complicated in the nineteenth and twentieth centuries, unionism gradually gained strength. The rise of industrialism meant an increase in the number of manufacturing workers and provided more potential members for labor unions. As the productive process became increasingly complex and roundabout, the worker had less contact with his employer and with the ultimate consumer of the goods he was making. Thus, his job became less real and less meaningful to him. At the same time, the spread of mass production, division of labor, and large-scale enterprise associated with the roundabout process convinced the worker that it was increasingly difficult for him to become an important entrepreneur. More and more workers lost their faith in the American dream of economic advancement, resigned themselves to a working-class status, became less indifferent to labor unions, and accepted them as spokesman for labor not as defenders of middle-class aspirations.

Unionism itself took advantage of changing economic conditions. Eminently realistic and practical, it gradually placed more stress on "business unionism," a system of tactics that placed more emphasis on short-run objectives—higher wages and shorter hours—than on long-range welfare or political objectives. To keep the opposition of the other elements in the community at a minimum, unionism began to concentrate on stable organizations with conservative rather than radical principles. At the same time, the process of organization itself became easier. Organizers became more expert, and better means of transportation and communication made it easier for officers to keep their fingers on every union pulse.

The economic factors that made the worker more amenable to the idea of unionism also diminished the public's prejudices and changed the government's attitude. The real or fancied abuses of corporate enterprise, the growing power of "big business," antagonized public opinion and led many people to regard the threat from this quarter as much more serious than any danger the unions ever posed. People were becoming more tolerant of unions, more sympathetic to union efforts on behalf of the underdog worker. The businessman continued to oppose labor unions, but his attitude also showed signs of changing. He had long since discarded the wages-fund theory, which was really a sham, and for the most part he had also long since abandoned paternalism, which was ill-suited to a mass-production economy. His antagonism toward labor unions now rested chiefly on a belief that such union tactics as the closed shop, the sympathy strike, the boycott, and opposition to the adoption of new machinery interfered with the rights of management.

Employers insisted that labor had no natural "rights in the job," and that wage decisions were a prerogative of management with which labor had no right to interfere. They objected to action on the part of the laborer to raise or maintain wages, on the ground that it was dangerous aggression, but they defended their own attempts to reduce wages as defensive actions necessary to safeguard the investment that their businesses represented. To the individualistic businessman, wages were simply one of the costs of production, and he was inclined to pay little attention to the influence of wages on consumer demand. Accordingly, with few exceptions, he regarded wage increases as dangerous because they increased his costs of production. What he overlooked was the fact that wage increases also increased the money income of a large group of consumers and thus increased the demand for products.[23] On the other hand, labor spokesmen tended to overemphasize the importance of wage increases in raising purchasing power and to underemphasize wages as a factor in the cost of production. Each side tended to take an extreme position, and although the extremes often lent themselves to a workable compromise, such settlements rarely satisfied either party.

LABOR UNIONISM IN THE EARLY NINETEENTH CENTURY

Although they were better off than the average European worker, American laborers in the early nineteenth century were far from satisfied with their lot, and they occasionally resorted to organizations to improve their status. But because manufacturing was still in its infancy, there were few workers to join unions. Most laborers were more like independent artisans and, because there was little labor mobility, early labor unions were local, opportunistic organizations devoting their main efforts to maintaining the worker's opportunity to achieve a propertied status. Politics and welfare unionism, which emphasized long- rather than short-term goals, were most popular.

During these years, labor as a group had no rationale—no economic theory it could emphasize in presenting its case. As was to prove the case so often in the future, progress in unionization depended almost completely on the vagaries of the business cycle. Prosperity meant expansion; depression meant disaster.

The first labor oganizations in American appeared in the late eighteenth century among the highly skilled workers—among the carpenters and shoe-makers in Philadelphia, printers in New York, and tailors in Baltimore. These early labor organizations were contemporaneous with the rise of the wholesaler who was a bargaining specialist acting as an intermediary between producers and consumers and widening the market area. Being in a strategic position, he played producers off against one another, forcing them into competition. The producers, in turn, were forced to cut prices and, consequently, tried to reduce their

---

23In the 1920s a change in viewpoint among businessmen seemed to place more emphasis on demand. Many businessmen preached the doctrine of higher production, higher wages, and lower prices, but the doctrine may have been expressed more in words than in action.

costs by beating down wages. To meet this threat, workers began to organize. But these early organizations were not trade unions in the true sense of the term. Skilled workers merely banded together to meet specific grievances. Once a problem had been solved, the organization disintegrated.

Yet the goals and tactics that characterized this era of "dormant unionism," as John R. Commons called it, were similar to those of all the subsequent job-conscious unions that sought short-run gains. Workers bargained over wages and hours; demanded the closed shop; tried to restrict the use of apprentices; engaged in strikes, boycotts, and picketing; and set up benefit funds. They fought an uphill battle against public opinion, meeting resistance chiefly in the shape of adverse court decisions. Using as a precedent the English common law interdiction against conspiracy, the courts held that most labor unions were illegal. This doctrine had its most extreme expression in the famous conspiracy case against the Philadelphia shoe-makers in 1806. The court held that "a combination of workmen to raise their wages may be considered from a twofold point of view; one is to benefit themselves, the other to injure those who do not join their society. The rule of law condemns both." The court fined the defendants $8 each, but the decision never became accepted law. There were only 12 conspiracy cases brought against unions between 1821 and 1842, and only five resulted in convictions. A milder form of disapprobation prevailed. It was aptly expressed in 1821 by a Pennsylvania court, which held that an act that was legal for an individual became illegal when committed by a group if there was a direct intent of inflicting injury or if the act benefited the group to the "prejudice of the public or the oppression of individuals." The case of *Commonwealth v. Hunt*, in 1842, clarified this doctrine by holding that unions in themselves were not illegal and that union tactics were not illegal if their purposes were not illegal. This still remains the generally accepted viewpoint.

As time passed and the labor market expanded, job-conscious trade unionism or unionism "of the pure and simple type" gained ground. But its progress was gradual, and throughout the 1820s and early 1830s the most prominent workers' organizations put their faith in long-range goals and in political tactics.

Local crafts began to coalesce into city trade unions. In 1827, the trades in Philadelphia organized the Mechanics' Union of Trade Associations, and presently similar organizations were formed in other urban areas. At first, these federations of trade unions turned to politics because the nature of many of their demands was socioeconomic, not purely economic. They were opposed to monopolies. They were hard-money enthusiasts, disliking paper money and banks in general. They demanded that compulsory service in state militia and imprisonment for debt be abandoned. They urged governments to institute free public education and mechanics' lien laws. They tended, in short, to support middleclass interests that the farmer and small businessmen could also support.

To drive home their demands, members of the federations began forming workingmen's parties in the principal cities. The first labor party in the world was organized in Philadelphia in 1828. Although these early parties enjoyed some success, all had disintegrated by 1831 and 1832. They failed, as all American labor parties have failed, primarily because the major American political parties, always opportunistic and flexible, quickly adopted the main planks of the labor platform as their own. And, in addition, the average American worker was not interested in political objectives, but in short-run gains. Moreover, political activities created internal dissension and weakened the workers' organizations.

Unionism, however, was kept alive by the various local organizations that survived the breakup of the early labor parties and, in the speculative boom of the early 1830s, these locals made great progress. By 1836 there were 58 in Philadelphia, 52 in New York, and lesser numbers in other cities. These organizations forsook politics and emphasized business unionism, setting their sights on achieving higher wages and the ten-hour day. Making excellent progress, they formed, in 1834, a National Trades' Union, which at the height of its career claimed a membership of 300,000. But in forming this national organization, the trade-union movement temporarily lost sight of its concrete and practical goals and became engrossed in more grandiose aims. The declared purposes of the National Trades' Union, set forth in somewhat glowing terms, were "to advance the moral and intellectual condition and pecuniary interests of the laboring classes, promote the establishment of trades unions . . . ; and . . . publish and disseminate such information as may be useful to mechanics and working men generally."

Employers were disturbed by the success of the trade-union movement, and they in turn organized to frustrate it. They were particularly bothered by the demand for the ten-hour day, which they opposed on the ground that it would "lead to debauchery" and would curtail production. By circulating the names of workers who were associated with unions, they instituted a black-list in an attempt to strangle the embryonic labor unions, but they might just as well have saved their ammunition, for the whole labor movement collapsed in the depression that began in 1837.

UNIONISM IN DEPRESSION AND RECOVERY

Unions could not resist employers' wage cuts in the face of heavy unemployment, nor could they offer the worker any other concrete advantages, such as shorter hours or better working conditions. Unions therefore declined, but highly mystical and radical movements dominated by intellectuals sprang up. The years of the depression became, in the phrase of Van Wyck Brooks, "the God-Intoxicated Forties," or, in less sophisticated terms, the "hot air" period of American labor history. Idealistic reform philosophies, such as the socialistic Fourierism, and communistic experiments, such as Brook Farm, achieved a varied following. In 1844 George Henry Evans began the Land Reform Movement, which attracted many urban workers with its promise of a free homestead to every would-be settler. Cooperatives also enjoyed a wide following; producers' cooperatives were organized in almost every skilled trade, and consumers' or distributive cooperatives sprang up in various parts of the country. In the political field, workers who were becoming apprehensive at the prospect of having to compete with ever-growing numbers of immigrant laborers flocked to the standard of the Native American Party, the "Know-Nothing Party," whose platform was chiefly distinguished by extreme anti-foreignism.

Although they represented another phase of the continued attempt by labor to preserve its opportunities to achieve propertied, middle-class status, the reform, cooperative, and political movements of the depression years had little lasting effect on the economy. The land-reform movement did accelerate the trend toward a more liberal land policy, which the Federal government had been following since 1820. Cooperatives were in most cases economic failures, and the reform movement, given concrete expression in the socialistic phalanxes and "farms," soon disappeared from the scene.

Economic recovery in the 1850s not only raised the worker's economic position, but also brought business unionism permanently into the labor movement. Instead of confining itself almost exclusively to cooperatives, reform, and the "one big union," the labor movement began to concentrate more on collective bargaining, shorter hours, higher wages, and other short-run objectives. Under these circumstances, trade unions—organizations of skilled workers who had come to accept their status as laborers—were formed and gained a foothold they never lost. The first national union, the National Typographical, was formed in 1852, but there was no marked evidence of growth until late in the Civil War.[24]

By the 1850s, unions were no longer looked upon merely as organizations that sprang up sporadically whenever workers' grievances needed airing; they were now regarded as permanent spokesmen for the skilled worker. But anything resembling a united labor front was still far from being realized. Labor was split into two camps, with one part expressing the working-class ideas of the skilled worker and the other part speaking for the ambitions of labor in general. Trade unions were emphasizing short-run goals, but other labor organizations were still attempting to bolster middle-class aspirations by supporting homestead legislation and by opposing monopoly.

On the whole, the welfare unions were more successful than the trade unions in the years before the Civil War. They played an important role in accelerating public education, homestead legislation, and antibank legislation; it is questionable whether the trade unions were as successful with their purely economic aims, such as raising wages, reducing hours, and improving working conditions.

[24]Lloyd Ulman, *The Rise of the National Trade Union* (Cambridge, Mass.: Harvard University Press, 1955).

THE ECLECTIC UNIONISM OF THE POST-CIVIL WAR ERA

Labor's position improved greatly in the quarter-century of rapid economic development that followed the Civil War. But the very conditions that created economic progress also created a sense of uneasiness among workers and made this era one of great ferment in labor-union history.

These were years of phenomenal growth in manufacturing, in mass production, and in machine techniques; and, although productivity and real wages were rising, more intersectional competition, greater division of labor, closer-knit employer organizations, and a constant influx of immigrant workers were clouding the rosy picture. As the economic process became more intricate, the gulf between production and consumption yawned wider and wider. The worker, performing an increasingly specialized task, found it more difficult to associate what he was doing with the final product turned out by the factory. This difficulty contributed to the worker's insecurity and prompted him to place greater emphasis on trade unionism and to try to maintain closer control over the job. Workers joined unions not only in the hope of raising their wages and shortening their hours, but also to satisfy their need for status and recognition.

Unionism, therefore, continued to be eclectic. It sprang from widely diverse aspirations and expressed itself in broad aims and goals of a social as well as an economic nature. Unions agitated for the eight-hour day but also for the prohibition of Oriental immigration. They succeeded in achieving the first collective bargaining agreement—the Iron Puddlers' Agreement—in 1866, but they also founded the first permanent political labor lobby around the same time.

The trend toward national unions of skilled workers continued, the most important new union being the Knights of St. Crispin, which eventually was able to boast a membership of 50,000. To obtain greater bargaining power on a national basis, the various local and national trade unions formed, in 1866, a weak federation, the National Labor Union, under the leadership of William H. Sylvis of the Iron Moulders.[25] Sylvis was an intellectually curious and restless person, and the union's aims were, therefore, always in at state of confusion. At first, it sought to promote cooperatives, abolish convict labor, restrict immigration, establish progressive taxation, create a Federal department of labor, and bar everyone except actual settlers from the public domain. But its chief aim was the eight-hour day, which for the first time was given an economic rationale. Ira Steward, a Boston machinist, was the economic theorist of the movement, which he popularized with the famous couplet: 'Whether you work by the piece or work by the day, decreasing the hours increases the pay." But Steward also had a more scholarly set of arguments at hand. He denounced the wages-fund theory

[25]Gerald N. Grob, "Reform Unionism: The National Labor Union," *Journal of Economic History,* Vol. XIV (1954).

as altogether fallacious and held that wages depended on the habits, customs, and standard of living of the worker. He believed that laborers would not work for less than enough to maintain their standard of living. Shortening the hours of work, Steward believed, would increase the wage earner's leisure, his wants, and, consequently, his standard of living, and this would automatically raise wages. Actually, this was the purchasing-power theory turned on its head.

Steward believed that the eight-hour day could be achieved more quickly and more easily by political means than through usual trade-union activities. The National Labor Union was therefore diverted into the political arena. Although the Union enrolled many members, estimated at 600,000 to 800,000, but more probably 200,000 to 400,000, or less than 5 percent of the nonfarm gainfully occupied in the 1870s, it had little success in achieving its aims. It did succeed in obtaining Federal legislation establishing the eight-hour day for government employees, but, Steward's theory notwithstanding, the reduction in hours was also accompanied by a reduction in wages.

The National Labor Union also became embroiled in the post-Civil War controversy over inflation. Union officials lent their voices to the greenback crusade for more paper money. This weakened the organization, for the rank and file of the workers were not in favor of inflated money. The union was further weakened when employers, their fears aroused by labor strikes, joined hands across the nation in a concerted antiunion effort. Michigan employers started the movement in the early 1870s with a widely publicized statement charging that the continuation of unionism and the use of the strike would result in "widespread beggary." Employer organizations sprang up to reinforce the movement, using the lockout and the black-list to implement the drive. The National Labor Union was, therefore, already defunct when the depression of 1873 delivered the *coup de grace*.

THE TWILIGHT OF WELFARE UNIONISM

With the depression, labor turned again to a type of welfare unionism, although the national unions of skilled workers continued to exist. In 1869, some Philadelphia garment workers formed a secret society, known as the Noble Order of the Knights of Labor.[26] During the succeeding nine years, the organization grew slowly, but in 1878 it was reorganized as a permanent, open labor organization under the leadership of Terence V. Powderly, Grand Master Work-

---

[26]One of the best studies of the Knights of Labor within the context of the working and living conditions of the period is Norman J. Ware, *The Labor Movement in the United States, 1860-1895* (New York: Appleton-Century-Crofts, 1929). See also Gerald N. Grob, "The Knights of Labor and the Trade Unions, 1878-1886," *Journal of Economic History*, Vol. XVIII (1958). Reprinted in Alfred D. Chandler, Jr., et al. *The Changing Economic Order* (New York: Harcourt, Brace & World, Inc., 1968, and in Thomas C. Cochran and Thomas B. Brewer, *Views of American Economic Growth*, Vol. II (New York: McGraw-Hill Book Company, 1966).

man. The Knights was to become the most spectacular labor movement of the period, but its growth was sporadic and fortuitous and it left little imprint on the economy.

The Knights emphasized education, legislation, and mutual benefits through cooperation. The Order was extremely idealistic, for its long-range goal was the abolition of the wage system. For the short run, it sought "to secure to the workers the full enjoyment of the wealth they create, sufficient leisure in which to develop intellectual, moral, and social faculties." More specifically, it sought to establish a bureau of labor statistics, a weekly pay day, and the eight-hour day, and to abolish contract labor and child labor below the age of 14. The new organization planned to devote most of its energies to producers' cooperatives and to arbitration, and it looked with disfavor on the strike and direct political action.

The Knights was a "one big union" type of organization, membership being open to everyone except doctors, lawyers, bankers, and saloonkeepers. The chief authority rested ostensibly at the top in an executive body composed of five members, but this body did not exert strong leadership, and the rank and file often took over control. Paradoxically, the great successes and the great failures of the Order stemmed from the rebellion of the rank and file.

In 1884, 15 years after it had been founded, the Knights had only 60,000 on its membership rolls. Two years later, this number had soared to 700,000, mainly, but not solely, as a result of the prestige the Order had gained by conducting a successful strike against Jay Gould's Western railroad system. But the subsequent decline of the Knights was, if anything, more spectacular than its rise.

Many causes contributed to the organization's breakdown. The heterogeneous membership, all with mixed interests, disrupted its *esprit de corps*. A second strike by the rank and file against Jay Gould's Southwestern railroad system failed completely. The producers' cooperatives organized by the Knights were financial failures, because most of them were in mining, cooperage, and shoemaking, industries that required heavy capital investment and managerial talent beyond the Knights' abilities.

Compounding the Order's difficulties were the sanguinary controversies between capital and labor in the years after the Civil War. Differences of opinion were rarely settled around the conference table in the give-and-take of bargaining. More frequently they resulted in strikes that were much more violent than those that took place in Europe at the same time. Especially violent were the long coal strike of 1874, the railroad strikes of 1877, and the Haymarket Affair of 1886. Public opinion was horrified by these events, and although employers were far from blameless, there was little sympathy for the worker. It was still quite commonly believed that, if a man were poor, it was his fault or his destiny, and that the best he could do was exert his ambition, live frugally, and not complain. The Reverend Henry Ward Beecher spoke for the respectable when from the eminence of his $20,000-a-year income, he pronounced, "I do not say that a dollar a day is enough to support a working man. But it is enough to support a man! Not enough to support a man and five children if a man insists on smoking and drinking beer. . . . But the man who cannot live on bread and water is not fit to live."[27]

Whether justified or not, public opinion held the Knights responsible for the labor-capital violence. The conservative press fanned the popular prejudice. The New York *Sun,* exaggerating the power of the Knights' Executive Board, wrote: "Five men . . . control the chief interests of five hundred thousand workingmen, and can at any moment take the means of livelihood from two and a half million souls." Finally, and most important, the Knights of Labor did not adapt itself to the American wage earner's desires and interests, which emphasized short- rather than long-term objectives. When the Knights attempted to absorb the independent trade unions, the trade unions, in turn, took the offensive and pushed the Knights out of the skilled trades. By 1900, the Knights' membership had dwindled to 100,000, consisting mainly of farmers, independent mechanics, and small merchants.

THE AMERICAN FEDERATION OF LABOR—THE VICTORY OF BUSINESS UNIONISM

By 1890, the conflict between welfare unionism, as represented by the Knights of Labor, and business unionism, as represented by the national trade unions, had been resolved in favor of the business unions: the iron and steel workers, the cigar makers, typographers, and other organizations of skilled workers. The victory of trade unionism of the pure and simple type was most clearly demonstrated in the progress of the American Federation of Labor.[28] The A. F. of L. was founded in 1886 by Samuel Gompers, Adolph Strasser, and P. J. McGuire, but it grew directly out of the Federation of Organized Trades and Labor Unions formed in 1881.

From the beginning, the AFL represented the aspirations of the skilled laborer, who by this time had accepted his working-class status and had pretty much resigned himself to the fact that the economy had grown so large that his own opportunities to climb by his own efforts were distinctly limited. The Federation devoted itself completely to a policy of business unionism. It was job- and wage-conscious. Concluding that the American worker was interested in immediate gains in hours, wages, and working conditions and not in the creation

[27] Foster Rhea Dulles, *Labor in America* (New York: Thomas Y. Crowell Company, 1949), pp. 114-25.

[28] See Lewis L. Lorwin, *The American Federation of Labor* (Washington, D.C.: The Brookings Institution, 1933); Philip Taft, *The A. F. of L. in the Time of Gompers* (New York: Harper & Row, Publishers, 1957); same author, *The A. F. of L. from the Death of Gompers to the Merger* (New York: Harper & Row, Publishers, 1959).

of a new society, its leaders emphasized short-run objectives. Their philosophy was pragmatic, not idealistic. As early as 1883 Adolph Strasser said, "We have no ultimate ends. We are going on from day to day. We are fighting only for immediate objects—objects that can be realized in a few years." Similarly, the leaders of the AFL were disinterested in theory. "We are opposed to theories," said Strasser. "We are all practical men." And Gompers wrote, "At no time in my life have I worked out definitely articulated economic theory. [29]

In fighting to win immediate improvements in the status of the skilled laborer, the AFL paid no attention to the plight of the unskilled. It emphasized "control of the job" through control of the supply of skilled labor. Formed in an era when industrial consolidation was becoming a prominent feature of economic life, the leaders of the AFL early asserted that trusts in industry were inevitable and could not be controlled by government but only by strong labor unions. Thus, they very early adopted and made their own a theory similar to what John Kenneth Galbraith called the doctrine of countervailing power.

Although the Federation's chief leaders had been trained in the school of socialism, they quickly abandoned any radical ideas and followed a conservative approach. They also avoided direct political action for attaining their goals. "Foremost in my mind," said Gompers, " is to tell the politicians to keep their hands off and thus to preserve voluntary institutions and opportunity for individual and group initiative." Even as late as the great depression of the 1930s, the AFL continued to be suspicious of politics and opposed the whole concept of legislated social welfare, including Social Security and minimum-wage and maximum-hour legislation. But this did not mean that the AFL supported *laissez faire,* for the Federation's platform demanded liberal doses of government intervention. The right to organize and the shorter work week were always the chief planks in the platform. But at times the Federation also stumped for government ownership of public utilities, limitation of child labor, regulation of corporations, Federal housing, and drastic restrictions on immigration.

Nor did opposition to political methods mean that the Federation was free from political battles. For 50 years, with the exception of the years of World War I, unionism encountered government opposition. The Sherman Antitrust Law hit labor unions especially hard. The Supreme Court in case after case held that certain forms of picketing, boycotts, and even the organization of labor unions violated the Sherman Act; these were accordingly prohibited by injunction and punished by heavy fines. Altogether, between 1880 and 1931, almost two thousand injunctions were issued against labor unions. The United States used the Sherman Act to break the railroad strike of 1894, and in the *Danbury Hatters* case (1908), the *Buck Stove and Range* case (1911), and the *Hitchman Coal* case (1917), unions were effectively stopped from engaging in secondary boycotts or from organizing workers employed under nonunion contracts.

[29] Samuel Gompers, *Seventy Years of Life and Labor* (New York: E. P. Dutton & Co., Inc., 1925), Vol. II, pp. 17-18.

The AFL tried to combat this hostility as discreetly as possible. It seldom took a definite stand on political issues, but through its lobbies and its occasional support or denunciation of political candidates, it fought the use of the injunction, the application of the Sherman Antitrust Act in labor disputes, and legislation that seemed detrimental to its interests. On the whole, however, the struggle accomplished little; the injunction and the antitrust acts continued to be used in labor disputes until the Norris-LaGuardia Act was passed in the Hoover administration.

THE AFL'S ADVANCE AND RETREAT, 1890-1930

The Federation's techniques included initiation fees, high membership dues, and financial help to members during strikes. Insofar as its internal structure was concerned, the federation allowed the individual unions a substantial degree of autonomy, at the same time stressing the need for strong discipline within the unions. But loose control at the top was hardly conducive to good discipline at the bottom. Soon the individual unions began to jockey for position, and then contests for power began to appear within the unions themselves. Internal politics became as important as economic considerations. As unions gained in strength, they very often pursued policies designed to build prestige and maintain organizational stability, even though the economic benefits that their members might reap from such policies were obscure. The strongest emphasis was always placed on union recognition, collective bargaining, and the written trade agreement. Strikes and boycotts were used cautiously, both because they alienated public opinion and because they disrupted the union.[30] The AFL tended to resort to the strike only to achieve its principal aim—the control of the job through union recognition and the trade agreement. Available data on the strikes at the turn of the century show that labor succeeded in winning all its demands in almost half the strikes called and some of its demands in an additional 15 percent of the strikes it engaged in. As a result of aggressive action, organized labor succeeded in achieving written agreements for many of its skilled workers. By 1900, typographers, machinists, iron molders, granite workers, and the building trades were operating under restrictive trade agreements.

Confining itself almost exclusively to skilled laborers, organized labor, as represented by the AFL and by the more specialized railroad brotherhoods, enlisted only a small fraction of the total labor force. In 1900, only 4.5 percent of the workers were organized; and in 1920, the peak year in union membership for the period 1890 to 1929, less than 20 percent.

---

[30]Although in theory the strike was a last resort, there were bitter and bloody strikes at the end of the nineteenth century. The history of the most sensational ones is covered in Samuel Yellen, *American Labor Struggles.* (New York: Harcourt, Brace & World, Inc., 1936).

The Federation, representing the majority of the organized workers, enjoyed two great periods of growth in the years before 1929. But, unlike previous periods of labor history, the rise and fall of union membership did not follow the movement of the business cycle so closely, seeming rather to be more closely correlated with the peculiar conditions of a wartime economy. Federation membership mushroomed during both the Spanish-American War and World War I. From 275,000 members in 1898, the AFL grew to 1.7 million in 1904. True, the growth was confined to a comparatively small number of occupations, but the increase was not confined solely to urban areas. Indeed, union membership increased at a faster rate in many small towns than it did in many of the large cities. After 1904, membership remained rather static; but during World War I, the number of names carried on the Federation's rolls leaped to 4.1 million.

Just before the war, most trade-union members were in the building trades, railroads, and printing. There was a somewhat lesser representation in the coal, glass, and stone industries, but manufacturing workers were largely unorganized. World War I created an extraordinary demand for labor, thus creating a labor scarcity that was made more acute by the virtual halt in immigration. As part of its wartime activities, the government encouraged collective bargaining to promote smooth industrial relations. Under the powerful impetus of the great demand for labor and because of government encouragement, unionism began to spread extensively in manufacturing industries, especially among textile, meat-packing, metal, and water-transport workers.

With the end of World War I, the decline in the demand for labor and the widespread public spirit of antiradicalism, which at times verged on hysteria, posed great difficulties for the trade unions. It may be that union leaders did not read the public pulse correctly, for in the first years of peace, as employers resisted attempts to renew collective-bargaining agreements and as money wages failed to keep step with the cost of living, more and more strikes were called. Public opinion grew hostile; membership began to tail off. Nor could the unions recoup their losses during the remainder of the decade—in some respects the most prosperous in the history of American manufacturing. Between 1920 and 1930, total trade-union membership declined from 5 million to 3.4 million; the Federation did somewhat better, but its membership still fell from 4.1 to 3 million.

Paradoxically, the prosperity of the 1920s was one of the most important reasons for the trade-union decline. With prosperity came higher wages for all workers, nonunionized as well as unionized. Prosperity also resulted in increased mechanization, which displaced many manufacturing workers but increased the demand for white-collar, semiskilled, and unskilled workers. The trade unions, as they existed in the 1920s, were totally unable to cope with the problem of organizing white-collar workers, and they showed little enthusiasm for organizing the less skilled. Finally, and by no means of least importance, the trade unions declined during the 1920s because of a strong and effective attack from the right and a strong but less effective attack from the left.

LEFT-WING UNIONISM

Attacks on labor from left-wing and dissident groups had little influence on conservative unionism. If the program of the AFL occasionally lost its appeal for the American laborer, Marxist doctrines were never able to leap in and fill the vacuum.

Representing a minority of employees, radicals at times attempted to found competing unions. But these were universally unsuccessful, and radicals always reverted to the tactic of "boring from within"; that is, they joined conservative unions and attempted to convert them to their own radical principles. In general, radical labor movements, like welfare unionism, achieved some small successes in periods of business depression. But during prosperity, radicalism had little appeal and little success.

Radicalism had its greatest vogue among the unskilled, for whom there was no place in the more conservative unions. It also wielded great influence among the immigrants. Although the great majority of immigrants were more conservative than native-born laborers, there was a minority among the newcomers that was extremely radical. German radicals undertook to form the Social Party in 1867, and immigrants in Chicago organized the Metal Workers' Federation Union of American in 1885. Neither was successful, and the radical group attempted to infiltrate the Knights of Labor. Terence V. Powderly, the leader of the Knights, had been a socialist; but as the Knights grew, his enthusiasm for socialism waned, and he led a successful movement to stamp out radicalism in the Order. Later attempts to bore into the AFL were likewise frustrated, even though Gompers and others also had been at one time sympathetic to socialism.

Excluded from the Federation, the radicals, led by Daniel DeLeon, organized the Socialist Trade and Labor Alliance in 1895 to compete with the AFL. But many of the radicals, convinced that boring from within offered a better possiblity of success, abandoned DeLeon's group, joined the older unions, and formed the Social Democratic Party (later the Socialist Party) in 1898. Other attempts by radicals to create competing unions, such as the Western Federation of Miners (1893) and the Western Labor Union (1898), had only indifferent success.

The radical unions, organized to compete with the AFL, combined in 1905 to form the Industrial Workers of the World. The IWW was America's most militant attempt at dual or competing unionism. Its career was short but unusually violent. From the beginning, the IWW was split among three factions: those who wanted to turn it into an active labor organization, those who were devoted to syndicalism and revolution and wished to use the IWW for direct action, and those who wished to pursue political ends. By 1908 the conflict had been resolved in favor of the direct actionists, and the IWW became an almost completely opportunistic group. It led, often brilliantly, many of the most spectacular strikes of the period, strikes that expressed the aspirations of the unskilled for whom there was no place in the conservative trade unions. But it never became an organizer as much as a supplier of strike leaders. Its membership was never large. Altogether, in 11 years of existence, it issued 200,000 membership cards, but its membership probably never exceeded 70,000 at any one time; and many of its members among the unskilled turned to it in desperation simply because they had no other place to go.

Meanwhile, the socialists, boring from within, gained control of many individual unions in the Federation. During World War I, however, socialism split into factions and disintegrated. It lost its capacity for aggression; and its position as a proponent of revolutionary action, as a radical borer-from-within, was taken over by the communists. William Z. Foster had initiated the communist movement in the United States in 1911 with the formation of the International Educational League of North America. It did not take the communists long to take an aggressive part in union activities. By 1919, Foster was leading the strike against the United States Steel Corporation. In 1922, he affiliated his organizations with international communism. But shortly thereafter, communist infiltration was brought to a sharp halt when the trade unions expelled the communists and forced them to go underground.

Labor radicalism left no lasting imprint on the American economic scene. It accomplished little, if anything, insofar as the individual worker's level of living and conditions of work were concerned. The American laborer has never shown himself to be particularly captivated with theories—social, economic, or political. Marxist and socialist economics found very few converts in the New World, among skilled or unskilled workers. Even when radical groups gained control of individual unions, union policy showed no significant change. Union recognition, higher wages, and shorter hours—the goals of conservative unionism—remained dominant. Radicalism seems to have left no imprint whatsoever on the status, condition, or consciousness of the skilled. But it possibly contributed toward improving the lot of the semiskilled and unskilled by focusing public attention on the plight of these groups in a succession of dramatic strikes.

COUNTERATTACK BY EMPLOYERS

Attacks by organized employers always had a more devastating effect on conservative trade unions than attacks launched by radical or competing unions. In fact, the greater the intensity of employer campaigns against unions, the greater the decline in the rate of growth of union membership.

There was little in the early history of the AFL to arouse employer opposition. To be sure, in the same year that the Federation was formed, businessmen organized the first employers' organization on a national scale, The Stove Founders National Defense Association. Its purpose was the "unification of its members for protection and defense against unjust, unlawful, and unwarranted demands of labor." Then, too, there had been violent strikes at Homestead, Pennsylvania in 1892, and against the Pullman Company in 1894; but the Federation managed to remain pretty much aloof from these, even though the Homestead strike involved one of its affiliates. Indeed, relations between the Federation and management were so amicable that the period up to 1900 came to be called the "honeymoon period between capital and labor." in 1900, affable relations were formalized when representatives of management and labor cooperated in forming the National Civic Federation, an organization devoted to encouraging collective bargaining, mediation, and arbitration in industrial disputes.

Public opinion seemed to grow more tolerant of trade unions after the National Civic Federation was set up. But the honeymoon ended, especially insofar as small businessmen were concerned, when union membership began to grow and then multiply at the turn of the century. The precipitating event seems to have been the anthracite coal strike of 1902. Businessmen feared that, as organizations like the AFL grew, they would insist upon participating in making business decisions, a function that management considered its exclusive preserve. Under the direction of men with a flair for public relations, such as John Kirby, Jr., and J. West Goodwin, small businessmen in the Middle West formed organizations that were frankly and openly designed to combat unionism. From local Citizens' Alliances, the movement quickly became more formalized. In 1902, the American Antiboycott Association was organized, and, in 1903, D. M. Parry succeeded in converting the National Association of Manufacturers from a protective-tariff association to a militant anti-union organization.

Under Parry's leadership and the NAM's aegis, antiunion businessmen organized the Citizens' Industrial Association in 1903. By 1904, the nation was studded with antiunion business organization, including the National Founders' Association, the National Metal Trades Association, the Structural Erectors' Association, the League for Industrial Rights, and many others. These organizations were determined, serious, efficient, and effective. They fought militantly against union efforts to obtain contract agreements, and when unions resorted to strikes and boycotts, they resisted with money, strikebreakers, and lawsuits. More than anyone else, they fought the Federation in the courts. Their attitude toward unions was, in short, unmistakably antagonistic, although at times they tried to smoke-screen their aims. In 1903, D. M. Parry gave their philosophy its most typical expression when he said, "We are not opposed to good unionism. The American brand is un-American, illegal, and indecent."

The most successful tactics used by employers' associations included the black-list, pledges by members not to enter into closed-shop agreements, financial assistance to employers during strikes, opposition to legislation supported by unions, and campaigns to arouse public opinion in favor of the open shop. In addition, employers were helped in their campaign by the anti-union attitude of government.

But once their drive achieved top momentum and began to show results, employers relaxed their efforts. Then, during World War I, the scarcity of labor and government encouragement of collective bargaining made anti-unionism inexpedient. But as soon as the War was over, employers once again took up the cudgels. Using both positive and negative tactics, management tried throughout the 1920s to prevent the spread of trade-union membership.

Shortly after World War I, a national industrial conference was called to formulate a set of principles to be used as a basis for amicable industrial relations. Labor representatives insisted as a *sine qua non* that labor be guaranteed the right to bargain collectively through representatives of its own choosing. The employer representatives refused to agree to this demand, and the conference broke up, having accomplished nothing. All through the early postwar period, antiunion employers resisted, successfully in most cases, recognizing unions as accredited collective-bargaining agents. Up and down the nation, an enthusiastic and eminently successful crusade to sell the open shop to the American people was carried on. Gradually, as union membership contined to fall off, the antiunion forces shifted to more positive techniques. The tools of the "tough policy"—the labor spy, the injunction, the black-list, and the *agent provocateur*—were still retained, but major emphasis now was placed on welfare plans and "industrial democracy." Many employers began to publicize the purchasing-power theory, insisting that it was necessary to pay high wages in order to maintain a high level of demand. Welfare plans, embracing improvements in working conditions, insurance, pensions, and recreational activities, were extended. High hopes were held for profit-sharing and employee-stock ownership plans, but in most cases the results were disappointing. In 1929, some 364 firms had pension plans covering 3.75 million employees, most of whom were managers.

Scientific personnel programs and company unions, on the other hand, proved most effective in the new antiunion offensive. Personnel programs were built around scientific management and introduced centralized hiring and promotion systems as well as wage-incentive plans. About 600 company unions were established in the 1920s. By 1929, there were about 400 in operation, covering one and one-half million employees. The majority of them were under management control and offered little opportunity for labor to bargain collectively. They were also useless as instruments for solving industry-wide or area-wide economic problems. But they did offer an opportunity for group relations to the unskilled, the semiskilled, and other groups whom the conservative unions regarded as untouchable. In addition, some company unions were really sincere about giving the worker an opportunity to practice industrial democracy.

Although trade-union leaders scoffed at welfare capitalism and industrial democracy, their criticisms fell largely on deaf ears. They were unable to offer any convincing reasons why the worker should scorn welfare capitalism and join a trade union. On the other hand, the employers' counteroffensive impressed the worker and convinced him, rightly or wrongly, that he was receiving more from management than he could receive from the union. The policy of United States Steel set a good example. Steel introduced a series of welfare projects that eventually included a pension plan, some company housing projects, and a variety of devices for improved safety and convenience. The benefits covered those employees who had been with the company for a period of years and had shown an interest in the company's welfare and progress. Judge Gary explained the rationale of the company's policy to some of the junior executives. Labor organizations exist, he said, either because an employer foolishly recognizes them or because the workers feel abused. He therefore admonished his audience to "make it certain all the time that the men in your employ are treated as well, if not a little better, than other men who are working for people who deal and contract with unions. . . . So far as you can, cultivate a feeling of friendship, and influence your men to the conclusion that it is for their interests in every respect to be in your employ."

LABOR UNIONS AND THE DEPRESSION OF THE 1930s

The depression years following 1929 accelerated the decline that trade unions had been suffering during the boom years. Having little to offer to the laborer during prosperity, trade unions had even less to offer him during depression. Membership in the AFL declined to around two million and total trade-union membership to less than three million.

In an effort to protect their members, unions resorted to a share-the-work movement and endeavored to establish the 30-hour week. The AFL supported efforts to break down the antitrust laws and to establish a "planned society," but it gave little enthusiastic support to a program of government-sponsored public works. On the whole, trade unions followed a floundering policy during the depression and became vulnerable to boring from within by radical groups, who gained control of some individual unions. Yet, considering the malaise of the period, radicalism made astonishingly little progress among labor groups.

The depression was not, however, without its beneficial effects. A gradual change took place in the public's attitude toward unions. Organized labor was viewed more sympathetically, and the government tended to do the same. In 1932, under the Hoover administration, the Norris-LaGuardia Act prohibited the use of the injunction in labor disputes except under limited circumstances. It was not until the New Deal, however, that sympathy was translated into outright friendliness. Under the National Industrial Recovery Act of 1933, labor was guaranteed the right to bargain collectively through representatives of its own choosing. The AFL regarded the legislation as an official government blessing and encouragement to organize, but employers, always sensitive to the union problem, hastily organized company unions to meet the challenge.

The company union seemed to be having the best of it in the struggle with the AFL when the NIRA was declared unconstitutional in 1935 and its Section 7a was replaced by the National Labor Relations Act (the Wagner Act). The new legislation virtually outlawed the company union. Much broader in scope than the NIRA, it forbade employers to refuse to bargain collectively, to interfere with labor's right to organize, to discriminate against union members, or to dominate a union. It also set up machinery to supervise elections of bargaining representatives and to enforce the provisions of the Act. As soon as the Act was put into operation, it was attacked ineffectively by spokesmen for employers on the ground that its administration and enforcement not only equalized labor's bargaining power, but actually increased it above that of the employers.

Meanwhile, unskilled workers, cognizant of the AFL's traditional attitude of coolness, wondered who was going to act as their bargaining agent. Their answer came in 1935, when a group of Federationists, opposed to the AFL's craft-union orientation, split from the parent organization to form the Committee for Industrial Organization. Under the leadership of Lewis of the Mine Workers, Hillman and Dubinsky in the garment trades, and Murray in steel, the CIO immediately launched an aggressive organizational campaign that had the incidental effect of opening the AFL to the unskilled. Membership in both organizations swelled, and by 1940 total trade-union membership was over 8.7 million.

UNIONISM SINCE WORLD WAR II

With World War II, union expansion continued on an even more pronounced scale, and at the war's end, 35 percent of the nonfarm labor force was unionized. Thereafter, however, unions failed to hold their position. Their share of the labor force began to slip in the early 1950s, and by 1970, it was down to 27.9 percent. The main reason for this decline was the swelling of the ranks of the white-collar groups, traditionally outside the reach of the unions' persuasive powers. If most of these were not counted, organized labor still had within its folds more than half the nation's workers. What was more important, more than 80 percent of the wage earners in a score and more of the nation's most important industries (building, automobiles, steel, and clothing) were members of a labor union. Area-wide and nation-wide bargaining between collective labor and collective management had replaced the old system of bargaining between individual employees and individual employers. Business unionism had become universal, and in the process philosophical differences had been obliterated—a fact that was well illustrated by the merger of the AFL and CIO in 1955. Even radical unionism had become enamored of business unionism. Paradoxically, those labor unions that succeeded best in invading what had always been considered management's exclusive area were the very ones with the strongest sympathy for capitalist institutions.

In the first few post-depression years, public opinion was not adverse to the growth of unionism. It was commonly thought at the time that labor had a right to organize and to bargain collectively. But the friendliness toward unions began to cool with the sit-down strikes of 1937. Then, during the War and immediately thereafter, because of the so-called wage-price spiral and many strikes, popular opinion turned against labor. The belief spread that unions were achieving too much power. This belief was expressed legislatively in the Taft-Hartley Act of 1947, which sought, as one of its authors said, to make labor as responsible in labor-management relations as the Wagner Act had made management.

The Taft-Hartley Act not only retained the unfair labor practices of the Wagner Act but in addition designated certain union policies as unfair. It prohibited labor unions from coercing employees to join them. It also prohibited unions from engaging in secondary boycotts, sympathy or jurisdictional strikes, and "featherbedding." The Act outlawed the closed shop but permitted the union shop. Employers were guaranteed the right of free speech. The Act also restored the use of the injunction in labor disputes by giving the Attorney General the power to issue an injunction postponing for 80 days a strike or lockout in those labor disputes that the President certified as threatening the national health and safety. Finally, the Act created a new Federal Mediation and Conciliation Service to act as mediator and arbitrator. With the Wagner and Taft-Hartley laws, Federal regulation of labor-management relations had become specific rather than general. It spelled out the rules, whereas previously the area of regulation had been nebulous.

Labor denounced the Act as "slave legislation." Whether it was or not, union membership continued to grow, but not at the same pace as in previous years. Union leaders themselves had much to do with union growth. They were essentially pragmatic in their tactics, and were no more given to defending any particular ideology than the labor leaders of the past had been. Yet they still did not represent labor as a whole; they represented groups of workers—steel workers, miners, teamsters, garment workers, and so forth. The leaders were still highly opportunistic, and all unions, conservative and radical, continued to emphasize the goals of business unionism and the tactics that had always been used by that type of unionism: the collective bargaining agreement and control over the labor supply

But the post-1935 labor leaders also departed from the policies of the past. They presented labor's case more effectively, and they missed no opportunity to employ experts to support their arguments. Recognizing that far fewer workers now believed that they would some day leave the ranks of labor, the unions, especially the CIO, entered politics and openly supported candidates of their choice for the Presidency, the Congress, and occasionally for local office. They also broadened labor's goals to include pension arrangements, disability benefits, supplementary unemployment benefits, the guaranteed annual wage, and paid vacations. In short, these leaders looked at labor as a way of life, and were therefore philosophically closer to William Sylvis than to Samuel Gompers.

A change in the attitude of businessmen also contributed to union growth, although naturally in a more passive way. Employers were not so militantly antiunion as they had been in the 1920s, nor did they make such valiant attempts as they had in the "welfare capitalism" of the 1920s to outbid the unions for the favor of the workers. Partly because of a change of heart and partly because of government legislation, most businessmen had come to recognize that unions were here to stay. There were, of course, many spectacular exceptions, such as Ernest Weir and many of the mill owners of the South; but even before the end of the 1930s, such rugged individualists as Henry Ford and Tom Girdler had accepted the inevitability of unionization. And, no matter how reluctantly they did so, these die-hard businessmen conceded that a great change had occurred in American's beliefs and attitudes toward unionism. After a century of struggle, and after many ups and downs, trade unionism had become an integral part of American life.

THE UNIONS' INFLUENCE OVER WAGES AND HOURS

How much unions can influence labor's income has been the subject of much deabate. Most economists believe that unions have not *materially* affected labor's share in the national income, for that share has remained relatively constant over the years. Whether labor or any other factor of production can increase its income depends on what happens to the size of total income and that depends in turn on increases in productivity.

What then can unions do? They certainly have influenced the wages of specific segments of the labor force. In two painstaking, thoroughly researched studies of labor-management relations at McCormick Reaper-International Harvester,[31] Robert Ozanne concluded that unions "were the chief force behind the reduction in the work day and week" and that "in the long history of the company the strike and the threat of strike have been the primary forces raising wages." Ozanne did not discount the important role played by productivity. But "productivity was a relatively constant factor that did not explain the widely varying wage movements. . . . These short-run movements varied in close relation to union activity."

Labor union leaders were limited in what they could deliver to their members. They could offer more job security and higher wages than were paid in nonunion jobs, but it did not seem that they could raise all wages or labor's share in the national income. Where there was a conflict between job security and high wages, some unions deliberately chose the latter. In the mines, for example, the unions deliberately set their demands so high that operators were

[31] Robert Ozanne, *Wages in Practice and Theory: McCormick and International Harvester, 1860-1960* (Madison, Wisc.: University of Wisconsin Press, 1968); *A Century of Labor-Management Relations at McCormick and International Harvester,* 1967, especially pp. 139-51.

forced to substitute capital for labor. Productivity was maintained at a high level by constantly putting pressure on management. In choosing between relatively low wages for all, or relatively high wages for some, union leaders decided, as one would expect them to decide, in favor of more for some rather than less for all.

SUGGESTED READINGS

(On specific topics, see the suggested readings cited in the chapter footnotes.)

Allen, H. C., and C. P. Hill, *British Essays in American History* (New York: St. Martin's Press, 1957), essay by Henry Pelling.

Bernstein, Irving, *The Lean Years, a History of the American Worker, 1920-1933* (Boston: Houghton Mifflin Company, 1960).

Lebergott, Stanley, *Manpower in Economic Growth* (New York: McGraw-Hill Book Company, 1964).

Ozanne, Robert, *A Century of Labor-Management Relations at McCormick and International Harvester* (Madison, Wisc.: Univ. of Wisconsin Press, 1967).

——, *Wages in Practice and Theory* (same publisher, 1968).

Perlman, Selig, *A History of Trade Unionism in the United States* (New York: The Macmillan Company, 1922).

——, *A Theory of the Labor Movement* (New York: the Macmillan Company, 1928).

QUESTIONS

1. What basic changes, if any, took place from 1800 to 1860 in (a) the supply of labor, (b) labor organization, (c) hours, wages, and working conditions? What economic conditions caused these changes?

2. Who, in your opinion, fared better in American history: the farmer, or the laborer?

3. The American worker's real wages have been consistently higher than those of the worker of other nations. How high have they been? Was it because of a "safety valve," unionism, or something else? Explain.

4. "The present status of the American worker is immeasurably better than it was in the early 19th century." Do you agree? Why? What factors tended to raise the worker's status? In what periods were these factors most influential?

5. Why do economic historians call labor the "scarce factor"? How can you tell when a factor is scarce? Has or has not labor always been short in this country? Explain.

6. Describe the trends, over the past 60 years, in the proportion of gainful workers among persons: (a) under 15, (b) over 65, (c) females 16 to 65. Explain the preceding trends.

7. Describe the main trends since 1870 in the relative importance of the following occupational groups: proprietors other than farmers, professionals, clerks and kindred workers. Explain by reference to changes in industry.

8. Would you say that the risk of unemployment has probably increased since 1820? Discuss the relation between this trend and the rise in the relative importance of nonagricultural industry.

9. Rank the following in order of their percentage rise since 1800: (a) average hourly money wages, (b) average hourly real wages, (c) average weekly real wages, (d) average annual real wages. Explain your ranking.

10. Describe changes in the conditions of industrial work since 1820; in the conditions of agricultural work. Would you say that they have worsened or improved? Explain.

11. How have wages and salaries compared since 1900? Can you cite any change in the circumstances of the worker in trade that may throw light on the statement, "Distribution costs too much"?

12. During American history, marked changes have occurred in the attitude of the public, the worker, the government, and the businessman toward labor unions. What were these changes?

13. What were the essential differences between the Knights of Labor and the American Federation of Labor? Which had more success? Why?

14. Under what conditions did the first unions appear? How did the "unions" of the first half of the nineteenth century differ from those that appeared after the middle of the century?

15. Selig Perlman pointed out that American labor organization differed sharply from that of Europe. What was the difference, if any?

16. Explain the influence of (a) marketing developments and (b) the activity of businessmen on trade-union development.

17. Describe the problems of labor organizations in the 1880s. What factors were responsible for the erratic growth in trade unions?

18. Describe the main lines of labor legislation between 1860 and 1914. Why have many economists described the New Deal legislation relating to labor as involving a "social revolution"?

19. Describe the changing nature of trade unionism since the Civil War. What were the periods of unusually rapid growth in trade unionism? Why did they occur? What brought them to a halt?

20. Discuss the early trade-union movement, 1800-1850, in regard to (a) reasons for its appearance, (b) aims, (c) success, and (d) reasons for its decline.

Chapter Sixteen

GOVERNMENT'S ROLE
IN THE ECONOMY:
THE ECONOMICS OF WAR

Economic historians have never been as fascinated by war as political and social historians have been. Yet, war is such a disrupting force that it can hardly be ignored.

During World War II, it became fashionable to use the phrase "the economics of war." If we consider economics as dealing with the satisfaction of material wants, there is no economics in war. War, of course, demands a high degree of resource allocation, but economic values must be ignored in the interests of survival. As few resources as possible go into the satisfaction of material wants and as many as possible are devoted to the necessities of survival.

Because war uses up economic goods without satisfying material wants, it is difficult to understand the widely held belief that war creates economic prosperity. One school among those who hold this view rests its argument on a fear that overproduction is an ever-present menace and that economic activity is always in danger of bogging down under the pressure of an abundance of goods that cannot otherwise be sold in the market place. They hold that war, by eliminating these excess goods, makes it possible for an economy to maintain full employment. Very few argue that wars actually increase the level of living, but there is a belief, best articulated by the German economist, Werner Sombart, that war causes economic progress by creating a great demand for capital and large-scale enterprise. There is still a third school who, although sympathetic to the arguments about overproduction and the mobilization of resources, place great stress on the changes in the economic, social, and political environment that war may bring. Wars, they point out, create a huge backlog of demand which enables the economy to roar forward as soon as the war is over. They also insist that wars, notably the Civil War, enabled those who believed in rapid economic growth to throw off the restraining influence of those who placed less value on economic goals. Those who do not think that war creates prosperity regard the menace of overproduction in a world where the average level of living is pitifully low as a naïve illusion. To them war is economic waste and must result in a lowering of the general level of living; and it is impossible for them to understand how economic progress can be achieved by destroying the goods and services that mean economic progress.[1]

But whether they accelerate economic progress or retard it, wars "break the cake of custom" and thereby disrupt the economy; and the greater the degree of economic development, the greater the disruptions caused by war. Total war was impossible in an underdeveloped economy. Subsistence took such a large part of income that little was left over for fighting wars. As incomes grew, subsistence took a smaller fraction of income and a greater share was available for luxuries, including the luxury of war. The Napoleonic Wars, world-wide as they were, probably siphoned off an insignificant amount of the national income of the nations involved. The American Revolution, fought by only a fraction of the population, probably absorbed not even 5 percent of the national income of the colonies. In like manner, the War of 1812, fought when the American economy was relatively underdeveloped, did not involve a large part of the population and certainly only a small part of the national income.

As the American economy grew, however, wars became greater in scope, involving more people, a greater volume of resources, and a larger percentage of the national income. Each of America's major wars progressively required a more extensive conversion of industrial facilities from the production of peacetime goods to the production of goods needed in war. Agricultural production, excessive in peacetime, became inadequate for war needs and had to be expanded. The labor force, reduced by enlistments and the draft, had to be greatly augmented in order to meet the goals of increased production. To cover the stupendous costs of a war program, government fiscal affairs were reorganized, greatly affecting the cost of living and the distribution of income. To offset the essentially inflationary influences of war finance, government resorted to direct controls over prices, wages, and production, thereby vastly increasing its area of activities.

[1]For a discussion of the pros and cons of the above, see John U. Nef, *War and Human Progress* (Cambridge, Mass: Harvard University Press, 1950); Stephen Salsbury, "The Effect of the Civil War on American Industrial Development," in Ralph Andreano, ed., *The Economic Impact of the American Civil War* (Cambridge, Mass.: Schenkman Publishing Company, Inc., 1962).

Nor did war's effects end with an armistice or peace treaty. Wars continued to affect the economy long after hostilities had ceased. Indeed, some of their influences became permanently embedded in the pattern of economic life, and, although the public wistfully longed to return to the "good old days" of normalcy, it was impossible to do so.

MONEY EXPANSION AND PRICE INFLATION IN THREE WARS

As the next chapter will show, highly inflationary methods were used to finance our major wars. Consequently, the amount of currency and coin (pocketbook money) in circulation and the amount of bank deposits (checkbook money) increased radically. Money in circulation more than doubled from $14 per capita in 1860 to $30.35 per capita in 1865. Only scattered data on bank operations are available for the Civil War period, but from what we have, we can assume that per capita commercial bank deposits also increased by at least 100 percent. Fed by this larger money supply, increased government spending pushed wholesale prices up to more than twice the prewar level, while the cost of living increased by some 70 percent.

During World War I, money in circulation rose from $22.25 per capita in 1917 to $35 per capita in 1919. Commercial bank demand deposits, not including interbank deposits, went from $141 to $178. While the money supply was expanding by about 25 percent per capita, the output of goods and services declined somewhat. The old story of more money chasing less goods pushed wholesale prices up about 20 percent and the consumer index up about 35 percent.

World War II saw a repetition of the wartime pattern of higher spending, money expansion, and price inflation. The per capita money supply more than doubled, from $560 to $1,200. Thus, at the end of the War, there was twice as much money for each man, woman, and child as there had been at the beginning of the War. But production was relatively high. Consequently, wholesale prices increased by only 38 percent and the cost of living by only 33 percent between 1941 and 1946. But in both world wars, monetary and price inflation started long before the nation entered the war. Wholesale prices doubled between 1914 and 1919 and increased by 60 percent between 1939 and 1946. The cost of living increased about 70 percent between 1914 and 1919 and almost 40 percent between 1940 and 1946.

In only one case did war's end bring a simultaneous decline in prices. Following the Civil War, the rapid rise in the money supply slowed down perceptibly. Federal revenues substantially exceeded expenditures, and the surplus was used to reduce the number of greenbacks in circulation. At the same time, the creation of the national banking system and the levying of a prohibitive tax on state-bank notes also had a deterrent effect on the supply of money. Accompanied as it was by a decline in total spending, the reduction in the money supply tended to push prices down.

Following both world wars, the peacetime developments that were expected to reverse wartime monetary and price inflation did not occur, and the price level continued upward. Prices reached their high points in May 1920 and in February and September 1948. It was expected that the Treasury would have a substantial surplus that it would use for debt repayment with deflationary results. Although the Treasury did accumulate surpluses after both wars and used this surplus to repay debt, the deflationary influences were not forthcoming, for the Treasury surplus was more than offset by increases in private, state, and local debt. At the same time, gold, which flowed out of the country during the war years, began to flow back in, increasing bank reserves and making possible a further expansion in the stock of money. Combined with increased spending by businesses and consumers and the abandonment of price controls and rationing, this monetary expansion pushed prices even higher than they had been during the actual war years.

HOW WAR AFFECTED INCOME

The methods used in financing the Civil War tended to make the rich richer and the poor poorer, but the financing of the two world wars had the opposite effect.

Production during the Civil War did not increase sufficiently to offset the amount of goods used in fighting the War. Consequently, after deducting from total production the amounts used for war, there were less goods and services available for the civilian economy than there had been in the previous peacetime period. In other words, part of the real costs of the War were paid for by a decline in the level of living. Because of the prevailing method of taxation, almost all this burden was borne by the lower-income groups. Excise taxes and customs duties, which provided the bulk of Civil War revenue, were passed on to the consumer in the form of higher prices and fell most heavily on those at the bottom of the income scale. But lower-income groups received a relatively smaller share of government expenditures. Thus, the burden of Civil War financing was regressive in that it shifted income from the poor to the wealthy.

World War I also resulted in a reduction in the amount of goods available for the civilian population. Total production of goods and services increased from $60.5 billion in 1917 to $75.2 billion in 1919, but 25 percent of the new total represented materials of war. Moreover, a large part of the increased production was unreal, because it represented only increased prices. After subtracting war costs and correcting for changes in the price level, there were less goods and services available for consumers than before the War.[2]

[2]John M. Clark, *The Costs of the War to the American People* (New Haven, Conn.: Yale University Press, 1931).

If this was so, which groups in the economy suffered most and which groups least? Because of the extraordinary increase in income taxes, the burden fell most heavily on those in the upper-income brackets. In addition, individuals in the lower-income groups were much heavier buyers of bonds in World War I than in the Civil War. Indeed, it was estimated that 30 percent of the Liberty Bonds were bought by people with incomes of $2,000 or less. The entirely different war-finance policy of World War I, therefore, had an entirely different effect on income distribution. Instead of incomes being shifted from the bottom to the top, with the lower-income groups bearing the brunt of war costs, the lower-income groups improved their relative position during World War I, and the major burden of war costs fell on the wealthy. Wages and salaries received the same percentage of national income in 1918 as they had received in 1914, and real wages remained approximately the same throughout the war period. Business profits were abnormally high in 1916 but, under the impact of wartime taxation, they declined by the end of the War. Nonfarm entrepreneurial net income declined from about 17 percent of the national income in 1916 to 13 percent in 1918. On the other hand, farm income increased sharply. From 10 percent of the national income in 1914, it jumped to 11 percent in 1916 and to 15 percent in 1918. In short, industrialists and capitalists were no better off at the end of the war, wage earners maintained their position, and farmers improved their lot substantially.

During World War II, gross national product more than doubled. From a little over $100 billion in 1940, it rose to $213.7 billion in 1944. Government purchases in 1944 amounted to $96.5 billion, leaving $117.2 billion for the civilian economy. Even after allowing for changes in prices, the civilian economy had at its command approximately the same amount of goods and services as it had before the War. However, because of government spending and heavier employment, World War II shifted income downward. In 1941, the lowest 40 percent of the population received 13.2 percent of the total income after taxes. In 1947, after taxes, they received 14.7 percent of a much larger total income. The upper 40 percent obtained 70.9 percent of the income after taxes in 1941 and 69.1 percent after taxes in 1947.

THE EFFECT OF WAR ON INDUSTRIAL PROGRESS

In prehistoric times men fought one another in wars in which a club was the only weapon. Manpower at the front was the important thing, and not technology or production. But economic progress, by enabling people to devote more resources to war, enhanced the importance of weapons and armor, while the importance of manpower as a fighting instrument remained approximately the same. War, therefore, became a mechanized business, and victory came to depend more on the mobilization and utilization of economic resources than on the amount of manpower in the armed forces. Yet, with the possible exception of World War II, the wars in which the United States has been engaged seem to have discouraged, not encouraged, technological progress. Whatever wartime increases in production did occur resulted not from increases in man-hour output but from the employment of previously unemployed resources, for each defense effort began in a period of depressed business when unemployment prevailed.

If American wars have had relatively little effect on technology, the same cannot be said of their influence on industry. Before the era of mechanized warfare, it is true, war mobilization had little direct effect on industry. The plan of war was to throw as much manpower at the enemy as possible and most of the little manufacturing that existed continued to function on a "business as usual" basis. Modern mechanized war, however, has had profound effects on industry, and each increase in mechanization has affected industry more sharply, for the goal in modern war is to throw as much armor at the enemy as possible. Thus, mechanized war fundamentally influenced the short- and long-run development of manufacturing industry and, therefore, of the economy as a whole.

To meet the demands of modern war, it is necessary to gear most of the economy to the needs of war production. Decisions about what and how much to produce are not determined by ordinary economic criteria, but by the necessities of survival. Production must be expanded, not in order to provide a higher level of living for civilians, but to provide the military sinews for war. Existing industrial facilities are converted from producing civilian goods to producing war materials. New industries, many of which are economically inefficient, have to be created to provide goods that were formerly imported or were unnecessary. It's not the cost, but the goods, that count.

The War of 1812 or, more accurately, the neutrality legislation that immediately preceded the war, encouraged the growth of American manufacturing more than anything else that the Federal government did in early American history. The embargo acts, which the Jeffersonians passed in the hope of keeping the United States out of European wars, restricted American trade and reduced the importation of manufactured goods and therefore encouraged the growth of American industry, especially in textiles and iron. But this was more the result of an attempt to preserve peace than a result of war itself.

Industry in the Civil War

It has become commonplace to refer to the Civil War as the first total war in history, but it was a total war only in the sense that it subjected the Southern civilian population to the sufferings of war and in the sense that it was fought by large masses of ordinary citizens and not by professional soldiers. It was not a "total war" as the term is understood today, for it did not require a wholesale shift to war production, and it emphasized manpower more than mechanization.

When the War started, those who were considered experts about such things prophesied a quick victory for the North because of her vast economic superiority. But the North never made maximum use of these advantages, and she won the War primarily because she had more manpower, rather than because of her economic superiority.

In fact, although the Civil War stimulated certain industries, it seems to have retarded rather than to have accelerated over-all manufacturing progress. Available data show that, by comparison with the immediate prewar years, the War did very little to raise production. This is especially significant because deep depression characterized the pre-Civil War era. Entering the war with unemployed economic resources, the economy should have been able merely by the use of available resources to produce a much greater quantity of goods. Actually, the rise in value added by manufacturing was lower during the ten years from 1859 to 1869 than for the previous two decades. In addition, total production, as measured by the only available index, rose only 13.3 percent from 1863 to 1865, but 34 percent in the first year after the war.

Production of certain war commodities increased, but this was almost entirely offset by declines in civilian goods production. The annual consumption of wool rose from 85 million pounds in 1860 to 213 million pounds at the height of the War. The number of sets of machinery in use in wool manufacturing rose 50 percent between 1860 and 1865. Wool, as well as munitions, was a staple of the war economy, for the Union's armed forces used 75 million pounds in 1865 and production was on a 24-hour seven-day-a-week basis. Profits were, of course, enormous, and dividends of 10, 25, and even 40 percent were frequent. Meat packing also showed great progress, the number of hogs packed increasing from 270,000 to 900,000 during the war. The production of iron rails increased from 205,000 tons to 335,000 tons, but in the five years of the War, railroad construction was considerably less than half of what had been built in the prior five years. There was some progress in pig iron production—from 800,000 tons in 1860 to one million tons in 1864—but hardly any increase in coal production: nine and one-half million tons were mined in Pennsylvania in 1860 and only ten million tons in 1864. The cotton industry, cut off from its raw material, suffered heavily in the first two years of the War, when mills operated at 25 to 50 percent of capacity. Thereafter, however, production increased as the North's occupation of the South once again allowed raw cotton to flow north to the mills.

The country's failure to make a better production showing stemmed from the decline in technological progress. It is true that because of government demand and the shortage of manpower, great progress was made in standardizing clothing, tents, tools, and munitions. On the other hand, the number of patents increased at a much slower rate than before the War. Between 1855 and 1860, the number of patents granted more than doubled. But, during the War itself, the increase was less than 50 percent. Even in armaments, where technological progress should have been most pronounced, the results were meager. Throughout the War, both sides continued to use the muzzle-loading rifle, although the newly developed breech loader was demonstrably faster and more effective. The Gatling gun, predecessor of the modern machine gun, was patented as early as 1862, but was never widely used during the Civil War.

There was some extension of the factory system and mass production, but only in the essentials of war—in the munitions, clothing, meat-packing, and food-processing industries. Here the long-run effects were quite significant, for mass production became a permanent characteristic of these industries and provided models on which the system was later extended. On the other hand, very few industries converted from peacetime to wartime production, and what conversion did take place had little effect on the economy. Cotton and carpet factories were converted to wool production. Saw factories turned to the manufacture of sabers, and jewelry manufacturers began to turn out uniform buttons.

Although reconversion to peacetime production did not present a critical problem and was quickly accomplished, the Civil War continued to influence industry long after peace had been restored. The tariff, which had been raised from an average rate of 20 percent to 45 percent during the War, continued at approximately the same rate throughout the postwar period. Even though its effect on industry as a whole was probably not very great, it had important repercussions on specific industries, such as steel. The War also increased the amount of saving available for investment, first of all because of the high profits earned by business, and second because of the methods used in financing the War. Relying mostly on loans, the Federal government had incurred an enormous amount of debt, most of which was owned by upper-income groups who could save a large part of their incomes. In the postwar years, the interest and principal on the debt were paid by levying regressive taxes. Thus, Federal fiscal policy transferred money from consumers to savers, augumenting the amount available for investment and encouraging the expansion of industry. For an economy that was still in the early stages of development, this policy encouraged economic growth and a rising level of living.

Industry in World War I

Much more armaments, munitions, and war machines were used in World War I than in the Civil War. The weight of metal fired in just one offensive in 1918 equaled the entire amount fired by the North during the whole Civil War. Being far more mechanized than the Civil War, World War I required a greater industrial effort and much more planning. New industries had to be created, old industries converted, and new facilities built to provide the necessary tools of war. The Federal government for the first time engaged in economic planning and set up elaborate controls to regulate the economy. The whole civilian population was affected to a far greater extent than in any previous war in American history.

The great expansion in production that marked the World War I era in the United States had already been accomplished by the time this country actually entered the War. When Franz Ferdinand was assassinated at Sarajevo, the United States was entering a period of business depression, and the outbreak of hostilities at first intensified the economic decline. However, European orders for armaments and war goods soon began to revitalize the American economy, and by 1916 much of the nation's unemployed resources had already been put to work to manufacture war supplies for Europe. In 1916 alone the United States exported over $1 billion worth of munitions. Industrial production increased by almost 20 percent between 1915 and 1916. Steel production jumped from 32 million to 43 million tons, and copper production from 694,000 to 964,000 tons during the same year. Capital expenditures for manufacturing plant and equipment increased from $616 million in 1915 to $1.1 billion in 1916, and industrial profits were the highest in history.

When the United States entered the War in April 1917, the demand for war supplies became appreciably greater and new problems in economic planning presented themselves. Mechanized warfare required different types of goods from those that had been used in previous wars. There was a far greater demand for coal and petroleum and for new types of strategic materials, such as diamond dies and abrasives, alloy steels, and aluminum sheet and castings. New industries had to be created to build the newly invented airplane and to manufacture chemicals that formerly had been imported. Shipbuilding, long an inefficient American industry, had to be expanded to provide transportation to carry men and materials to a war being fought three thousand miles away. In 1916, aircraft production was $1.5 million and ship production was at the rate of $104 million. By 1918, $175 million worth of aircraft was being produced, and in 1919 shipbuilding reached almost $1.4 billion.

Although the production of war goods increased remarkably, there was no similar increase in total production, largely because of declining productivity and material and manpower bottlenecks. Indeed, industrial production increased less than 1 percent between 1916 and 1917, and in 1918 and 1919 it was actually lower than it had been in 1916. Value added by manufacturing, when corrected for changes in the price level, was not much greater in 1919 than in 1914, and probably not as high as in 1916. Steel production did not increase substantially. In 1917 steel produciton stood at 45 million tons, compared with 43 million tons in 1916. Copper production declined from the peak reached in 1916. But the production of manganese ore, chromite, and aluminum substantially increased.

For the whole economy, technological progress once again failed to maintain a fast enough pace to enable the nation to take war production in its stride. Capital expenditures for new manufacturing plant and equipment were $2.5 billion in 1918 and $1.1 billion in 1916; but because the wholesale price level had increased by over 50 percent, capital equipment was not growing much faster at the end of the War than it had been at the beginning. The number of patents granted declined during World War I, just as was the case during the Civil War. In 1911, 34,000 patents were granted; in 1916, 46,000; but in 1919, only 39,000.

The failure of production to expand sufficiently to take care of the increased demand for war supplies necessitated extensive conversion of industrial facilities from civilian to war production. Carpet factories began to turn out uniforms; horseshoe plants made trench picks; stove businesses manufactured grenades and bombs. Standardization was greatly accelerated, and the variety of goods available for civilians was cut drastically. Attempts were made to institute economies and to eliminate waste in industrial processes. The yardage used in the manufacture of clothing was reduced 15 percent in men's and 25 percent in women's. Shoe styles were cut about two-thirds. The number of planters and drills fell from 784 to 29, and the variety of buggy wheels from 232 to 46. Economies in packing goods were supposed to save 17,000 carloads of freight space, 141 million cartons, and 500,000 packing cases a year. The paper used by daily and weekly newspapers was reduced 15 percent, and the amount used by Sunday newspapers was cut by 20 percent.

Because World War I was more a mechanized struggle than the Civil War, industry faced a greater reconversion problem than it had in 1865. The transition, however, was accomplished quickly. Industry entered the postwar years with greatly improved plants and equipment and with a backlog of saving that could be used to finance further capital expenditures. Industrial productivity increased rapidly. By 1923, and in some cases as early as 1921, industry had far surpassed its wartime performance, as evidenced by the fact that the index of manufacturing production was 30 percent higher in 1923 than in 1919.

The War had created or reinvigorated some manufacturing industries, and these continued to flourish after the return of peace. The chemical industry, unknown domestically in 1914, prospered more than most others during the War and received protection from foreign competition after the War under the aegis of the Fordney-McCumber Tariff. Although the chemical industry proved in time to be of benefit to the country's economic development, the same could not be said of the merchant marine, which was kept alive by government subsidies.

Industrial progress in World War II

In every respect, World War II was a more total war than either the Civil War or World War I, and it therefore affected the economy and the process of economic development more fundamentally. Whereas the Civil War had little effect on civilian life in the North, and World War I had a limited effect on the pattern of consumption, World War II had extensive repercussions on everyday life. Moreover, World War II was a much more mechanized war than any other conflict the nation had fought. In World War I about 3,500 mechanical horsepower was required to keep an infantry division moving. In World War II, 400,000 mechanical horsepower, or more than a hundred times as much, was required to keep an armored division going.

As a result of increased mechanization, war required a greater quantity as well as a greater variety of minerals. During the Civil War, war goods requiring minerals were responsible for perhaps 25 percent of industrial production, but in World War II such war goods required 75 percent of the total industrial effort. During World War II, new materials formerly unknown to the layman were introduced in the economy with far-reaching implications for the future. The required amounts of strategic and critical materials used in World War II, including such esoteric items as quartz crystals, loofa sponges, synthetic resins, and uranium-235, were approximately two and one-half times the 1935–1939 requirements. Yet, the resources of the United States and the world in general were so great that these increased requirements did not result in a critical depletion of total resources.

In contrast to World War I and the Civil War, the American economy made great progress during World War II, as well as during the prewar defense period. Gross national product in constant prices increased 70 percent between 1939 and 1944. Industrial activity expanded beyond the dreams of the most optimistic, increasing 48 percent between 1939 and 1941 and rising another 45 percent by the end of the War. Steel production jumped from 47 million tons in 1939 to 80 million in 1944; copper, from 713,000 tons to over 1 million; and aluminum, from 327,000 to 1,840,000 tons. American factories produced fantastic amounts of war materials: 300,000 planes, 124,000 ships, 41 billion rounds of ammunition, 100,000 tanks and armored vehicles, and much else.

The war economy at its peak took roughly half of total production and 80 percent of durable goods production. Yet the increase in total production was so great that there was enough left over to furnish the civilian economy with approximately the same income as it had received in the year before the War. But this increase was not achieved without considerable cost; the American people worked far harder during the War but received the same amount of income.

The amazing World War II production record could not have been achieved without an extensive mobilization of the entire economy. For industry, mobilization meant the maximum utilization of existing resources, the creation of new facilities, the conversion of industrial plants from peace to war production, multishift operation, and heavier reliance on technology.

As in previous defense periods, most of the increase in production came from the use of resources previously unemployed. The United States in 1939 had a large number of unemployed workers and extensive unused plant and capital equipment. Before the end of the defense period, most of these resources had been put to work, and by the end of the War existing resources were operating at capacity. Further expansion of production occurred as a result of the expansion of industrial plants, that is, the construction of new facilities and the addition of large amounts of equipment. Expenditures for construction and new equipment between 1940 and 1945 exceeded $60 billion, and included $10 billion for direct military construction, $13 billion for expansion of nonmanufacturing facilities, and $25.5 billion for manufacturing facilities. Of the total war-material expansion, 75 percent was publicly financed. Thus, the government[3] for the first time became the chief financier of expansion for war production.

Although the expansion of production took place at a remarkably rapid rate, it still took almost three and a half years for the economy to reach maximum production. In the interim, the needs of total war could be satisfied only by converting most of the nation's industrial facilities from civilian production to war production. Many of the gadgets to which civilians had long been accustomed suddenly became scarce or disappeared altogether. Bobby pins and white shirts, nylon stockings and rubber bands became collector's items. Radios and electric devices for civilians were not produced at all, the plants being diverted to the production of military electronics equipment. But the most remarkable example of conversion from peace to war production occurred in the automobile industry, which became the center of war production. Production of automobiles for civilian use ceased in February 1942, and one thousand plants engaged in the industry began to make war goods. Existing automobile plant facilities were expanded by more than $1 billion, 80 percent government-financed. The automobile industry, by itself or through subcontracting with small businesses previously producing cash registers, steam shovels, outboard motors, and so forth, turned out more than 10 percent of all war production, producing all the tanks and combat vehicles and a large part of the aircraft engines and machine guns.

World War II was the first war in which science was mobilized for warfare. It was also the first war to contribute to technological progress and "the first war in history to be affected decisively by weapons unknown at the outbreak of hostilities."[4] Although the number of patents granted declined greatly, just as it had in- the Civil War and in World War I, the number of new devices and processes developed during the War was most impressive. Great strides were made in producing synthetic rubber and synthetic gasoline. Antibiotic drugs fundamentally changed the whole process of medical care. Radar and other electronic devices appeared. Above all, scientists during the War opened up the field of atomic energy, the full effects of which would not be fathomed for generations to come.

Industry as a whole emerged from World War II with much more efficient plants and equipment than it had possessed in 1940. Manufacturing production

---

[3]Of all the money spent by the government for war purposes, more than 10 percent was used for new construction; more than 30 percent for pay, subsistence, and so forth; and over 50 percent for munitions.

[4]Irwin Stewart, *Organizing Scientific Research for War* (Boston: Little, Brown & Co., 1948), p. ix.

was inconceivably higher. Indeed, by 1947 the United States produced half the world's manufactured output. But, obviously, World War II influenced the peacetime development of certain strategic industries much more than it influenced industry in general. The demands of national defense that followed World War II caused a massive expansion in the capacity of the critical industries, especially steel and petroleum. Steel capacity, for example, was raised to 120 million tons, half again as much as at the peak of World War II production. $\times$

GOVERNMENT PLANNING FOR WAR

Modern warfare, involving as it does vast outlays of men and materials, must be intricately planned by a central agency. Only the government can provide this necessary central agency. In war, therefore, the government becomes the regulator of the economy, and war creates the atmosphere for a wide extension of government power.

Ordinarily, in a free-enterprise economy, goods are allocated through the mechanism of market prices. But total war creates problems in the allocation and pricing of goods that cannot be solved satisfactorily in the market place. The need for specific goods for war and the curtailment of civilian production create extreme scarcities. The expansion of the money supply and the great increase in government spending result in inflationary pressures. With less goods and more money, prices would skyrocket, causing social injustice and a loss of morale. The government would be forced to bid against civilians for commodities necessary to the war effort. This cannot be permitted, and, in a war economy, the market mechanism must be abandoned temporarily in the best interests of defense and survival. Government directives replace free choices by sellers and buyers in determining the allocation and pricing of goods. Economic values are subordinated to the needs of defense, and the more total the war, the more complete the abrogation of ordinarily accepted principles and the more pervasive the rule of government decree.

Although the power and importance of the Federal government increased as a result of the Civil War, the government's influence over the economy was exerted indirectly rather than directly. Scarcities were not a major problem, and there was relatively little need for government planning for war. The Union government did not impose any direct controls and relied almost exclusively on private enterprise to provide the essentials of war. The government did not help to finance any private manufacturing enterprises, but it did conduct a few establishments under its own auspices: a clothing factory, three laboratories to produce drugs and medicines, and a few meat-packing plants.

The direct controls exerted by the Federal government over the economy in World War I were probably less important for their influence during the War itself than for their long-run effects. A good part of the War was spent in developing administrative machinery, and controls were never imposed widely enough to have a great effect on the War itself. But the controls that were fastened on the economy acted as precedents and models for later attempts at peacetime planning, such as the NRA, and for the much more ambitious planning program of World War II.

When World War II began, there was no existing master plan of mobilization. At first, the organization of agencies to direct and control the nation's economy followed the model set by World War I, but it was quickly learned that World War II, being a more total war than World War I, required more extensive planning and far wider government controls. For a time, however, planning evolved on a piecemeal and opportunistic basis, resulting in a complicated succession of agencies and programs.

In May 1940, the President created the Office for Emergency Management and resurrected the Council of National Defense originally established in World War I. Neither of these two agencies could plan effectively for war mobilization, however, because their powers were too nebulous. The first important unit set up in the OEM for active planning was the Office of Production Management, created in January 1941. OPM was responsible for advising, planning, coordinating, and stimulating production of materials necessary for defense. Because it could not change the stated requirements of the War and Navy Departments, and because it had no authority over the civilian economy, its power rested entirely on its authority to control priorities. This left a gap in the planning machinery, for the issuance of priorities in the interests of defense provided the military with basic commodities but diminished the supply of goods available for the civilian economy, created extreme scarcities, and caused sharp price increases. In order to alleviate this critical difficulty, the administration, in April 1941, created the Office of Price Administration and Civilian Supply to stabilize prices and to maintain a flow of essential goods for the civilian economy. Like all new government agencies, however, it lacked the power to enforce its decisions. The agency was forced to rely on persuasion and cooperation to keep prices down, and "jawbone" price control, as it was called, was ineffective.

The administrative machinery created during 1940 and early 1941 was so awkward that it was questionable whether it helped or hindered the defense effort. The OPM could not formulate an over-all plan for directing the entire economy, and the OPACS lacked enforcement powers. Moreover, the OPM was headed by a partnership, not by a single individual, and there was no clear-cut differentiation of powers between it and the OPACS. The rivalries that existed all along the line interfered with efficient administration. In order to eliminate some of the difficulties, the Supply Priorities and Allocations Board was superimposed on the OPM in August 1941. However, this attempted solution only made a bad situation worse, because there were now three organizations (OPM, OPACS, and SPAB) vying with one another for top position.

Once the nation became an actual belligerent, the awkward and clumsy administrative machinery proved intolerable. In January 1942, therefore, President Roosevelt abolished OPM and SPAB and created the War Production Board under a single administrative head. At the same time, the Office of Price Administration, a subdivision of OPACS, was placed on a statutory basis.

The WPB was given very wide powers over production, including the general direction of procurement and production, the administration of priorities, and the allocation of materials and production facilities. The OPA's powers were also extremely broad: it could fix prices for all nonfarm commodities and ration civilian goods. And although price controls had many disadvantages and spawned black markets, the OPA had considerable success in restraining price inflation. It resorted to general rather than specific controls and rationed the civilian supply of meats, fats, gasoline, fuel oil, shoes, sugar, and other commodities.

The administrative machinery set up under the WPB and OPA, although far superior to its predecessors, was still not satisfactory, for, in the course of time, other agencies, such as the War Manpower Commission and the Office of Defense Transportation, became important, and no single agency existed to coordinate all the different plans and activities of the war effort. For example, there was no single head who could determine the allocation of manpower among the military services, industry, and agriculture. Nor was there any over-all agency to supervise the vast problem of economic stabilization. In order to unify the direction of the entire war economy, the President, in May 1943, created the Office of War Mobilization, setting up the war administrative machinery in its final form. By the end of the War, government activity had been enormously intensified and covered the whole economy. Basic commodities and manpower were subject to priorities and were allocated among the different sections of the economy according to the needs of war. Civilian goods were price-fixed and rationed. The government had complete control of new construction, prohibiting it except where essential and financing a large portion of it.

POPULATION AND WAGES IN WAR

Major wars affected labor just as fundamentally as they influenced government and industry. Whether mechanized or not, they created an extraordinary demand for manpower. By influencing the death rate, the birth rate, and immigration, wars changed the rate of population growth and, thereby, the supply of labor for many years thereafter. Wars also transformed the composition and function of the labor force, altered the trend in wages and hours, accelerated unionization, encouraged mobility, and reduced productivity. Some of these effects had enduring reactions on economic development, even though their full impact did not appear until after peace had been restored. Other effects were ephemeral, disappearing with the completion of the war and only temporarily interrupting or accelerating economic development.

As in every war, manpower was the essential element in the Civil War. But the demand for men came largely from the armed forces. The demand for workers to produce war goods was relatively low, because technological warfare was still in the infant stage. Probably four million men or 10 percent of the population served in the armed forces at one time or other during the Civil War; but, at its peak, the Union Army consisted of about one million men, and the Confederate Army numbered perhaps 666,000. The number of workers needed to supply the troops with war goods was probably less than the number serving in the armed forces, but it must have totaled at least one million. Consequently, the Civil War increased the demand for labor by at least two and one-half million. Much of this increased demand was met by immigrant labor. The remainder was covered by the reemployment of previously unemployed workers, the natural growth of population, and the shifting of workers from peace to war production.

Although the demand for labor rose substantially during the Civil War, population growth was not maintained at its previous rate. Total war casualties from battle and disease were about 635,000. Immigration was much lower than it had been and the birth rate declined, so that population increase during the decade 1860-1870 was about 1.3 million less than might have been normally expected. This decline in the rate of population growth had long-run repercussions on the economy, for it reduced the nation's productive capacity by cutting the scarcest factor—labor.   Although the demand for labor was much higher during the Civil War than it had been previously, the worker, peculiarly enough, did not benefit. Money wages did increase, but because of the expansion in the money supply, the vast increase in spending, a decline in labor productivity, the smaller amount of goods available for civilians, and the type of taxes levied by the Federal government, wages did not rise as rapidly as prices. The cost of living went up 68 percent whereas money wages increased only 50 percent. The decline in real wages in the midst of full employment did not go unresisted by the worker. There were numerous strikes, most of them successful, throughout the War, and membership in labor unions increased at a much faster rate than in the prewar years.

Labor in World War I

The increase in the mechanization of war between 1865 and 1917 did not reduce the demand for manpower, but it did change the nature of the demand. Mechanized war required a smaller number of men in uniform and a far greater number in overalls. By the end of World War I, 4.8 million men had served in the armed forces. This was roughly 5 percent of the population, compared with the 10 percent that served in the Civil War. At the peak of the War, there were about one million men in the armed forces, but it was estimated that three to five men were required in industry and transport to produce and ship the equipment and supplies needed by one man at the front. On the basis of this estimate, at least three million workers were needed for war production, making the total demand for manpower four million.

At the outbreak of the War, the nation was in a recession, and the initial demand for war workers was satisfied by reemploying the unemployed. Thereafter, the government, through the United States Employment Service and state and local agencies, actively took a hand in mobilizing labor for war production. From Puerto Rico and the Virgin Islands, 100,000 laborers were imported; 300,000 boys were enlisted for farm work; and almost one million women were added to the gainfully occupied working force.

Yet there were offsetting factors in this expansion of the labor force, for immigration virtually ceased during the War, and the average work week in manufacturing declined from 55 hours to 53.6 hours. Because the supply of labor, even with full employment, was not increased sufficiently to take care of the war demand, a reallocation of the existing labor force became necessary. Workers were shifted from peace to war production chiefly by the inducement of higher pay, and the composition and function of the labor force were fundamentally affected. The number of farm workers decreased by more than 10 percent, the small number of workers in forestry and fishing was further reduced, the number of manufacturing workers increased by more than 10 percent, and the number of workers in the service industries expanded by 33.3 percent. These changes in the occupational make-up of the labor force did not disappear with the return of peace, but were one of the long-run repercussions of war. In addition, World War I again changed the rate of population growth. The increase in population between 1910 and 1920 was 3.3 million less than expected, chiefly because of the halt in immigration, and, to a lesser degree, because of war mortality.

Because the demand for labor was so great, there was active competition for workers, and a spectacular increase in turnover rates and labor mobility occurred. Prior to the War, labor turnover in typical industries averaged 300 percent annually, but during the War, 10 percent a week was common. Laborers flocked to the centers of war production from all over the country, and the government encouraged the movement by setting up an agency to construct housing and to provide transportation for them.

Major wars have always reduced productivity, that is, the output per man-hour, and World War I was no exception. The change from peace to war shifted workers from familiar to unfamiliar production processes. Marginal workers—the old, the very young, and the partially disabled—entered the labor force and tended to reduce man-hour output. Marginal equipment was also brought back into use. Because speed and total production were more important than costs, businessmen had little incentive to spend time in developing more efficient methods of production to increase productivity.

Productivity declined so much during World War I that the total amount of goods also declined. Meanwhile, spending, fed constantly by money expansion, increased sharply, with resultant jumps in the price level. Money wages also shot upward because of the great demand for labor, but they chased rather than led the rise in prices, so that annual real wages in manufacturing remained approximately the same during the War.

The failure of wages to rise as rapidly as prices once again gave impetus to industrial unrest, and the number of strikes was more than twice as high as it had been in the previous peacetime period. Trade-union membership also expanded. Workers flocked into the unions in an effort to raise their economic status, and the government, in order to mitigate industrial unrest, recognized unions as the logical representative of labor in collective bargaining. Union membership jumped from 2.6 million in 1915 to four million in 1919.

Total war's impact on American labor

In World War II, the armed forces, fighting on two fronts, required more than three times the manpower needed in World War I. Approximately 14 million individuals served in the armed forces at one time or other. This figure represented more than 10 percent of the population and was, therefore, a relatively greater mobilization than had occurred even during the Civil War. In addition, approximately two million civilians worked for the government in war-connected jobs. Moreover, the demand for manpower to supply the technological equipment necessary for mechanized war was much greater than in World War I. For each man at the front, approximately 12 men in industry and transportation were required, for an armored division used 400,000 mechanical horsepower to keep it going, and eight tons of shipping were needed to send one man to the fighting front and an additional one ton a month was required to keep him supplied. Even in the combat zones, one and one-half to three men were required behind the lines for each man at the front.

Normally, the American labor force constitutes 40 percent of the population, but this amount was far from sufficient to meet the extraordinary demands of war, and strict economizing and broad allocation of labor were necessary. Unemployed manpower, eight million in 1940, was rapidly put back to work. The labor force grew rapidly, and, at the peak of the war economy in 1944, it held 66 million or about 47 percent of the population. Roughly seven million of these workers were persons who ordinarily would not have been gainfully employed but were in the labor force because of patriotic motives or because they could not resist the high wartime wage rates. About 2.8 million of the seven million were from 14 to 19 years old and had interrupted their schooling or had taken part-time jobs. Another one and one-half million were recruited housewives, 800,000 were persons who had delayed retirement, and the remainder were marginal workers. The manpower pool for war production was further increased by shifting workers from peace to war production and by increasing the length of the average work week. By 1942, eight million workers had shifted to war production, and hours of work had increased from 38 per week in 1940 to 45 per week in 1944.

The addition of new workers and the shift from peace to war production again wrought vast changes, seemingly permanent, in the composition and function of the labor force. In 1940, only 14.2 million females were in the labor force, constituting 25 percent of the total. By 1945, there were 19.3 million female workers, 30 percent of the total labor force. "Rosie the Riveter" was as famous a personage in World War II as the "Shipyard Worker" had been in World War I.

As in World War I, farm workers were especially eager to move into war plants, and farm employment declined by almost one million, or approximately 10 percent, between 1940 and 1945. The number of workers in mining, contract construction, and finance also fell, but only slightly. On the other hand, the number of workers in manufacturing increased by almost 50 percent, and the number of government workers increased similarly.

Unlike the Civil War and World War I, World War II accelerated rather than retarded the rate of population growth. Our casualties were small compared with those of other nations, (201,000 killed)[5] Nonbattle deaths were lower for the armed forces than for similar age groups among civilians. Moreover, the birth rate during World War II was higher than it had been at any time since the middle 1920s. Because the civilian death rate remained about the same as it was in 1940, a much larger increase in population resulted.

Labor mobility was more evident during World War II than at any other time. Because of competitive bidding by war plants, difficulties in getting to work, inadequate housing, and dissatisfaction with working conditions, labor turnover, which had been extremely high in all previous wars, reached an annual rate of 87.2 percent in 1943. The experience of the Boeing plant was not unusual; in three years it hired 250,000 workers, but it never employed more than 39,000 at any one time. The War also increased the geographic mobility of labor by accelerating the movement of industry toward the South and West.

Because of the great demand for labor, wages spiraled upward from a little more than $25 a week in 1940 to $46 in 1944. After allowing for the concomitant rise in the cost of living, real weekly wages were almost 50 percent higher at the end of the War than they had been at the beginning. Much of this remarkable increase was caused by higher rates of pay for overtime, for real hourly earnings did not rise as sharply as weekly earnings, increasing less than 25 percent between 1940 and 1944.

Although the American manufacturing worker enjoyed a remarkable rise in real wages, his good fortune did not stem from an increase in productivity. If anything, manufacturing productivity declined during World War II. The more likely causes of the improvement in real wages were the increase in total

[5] Britain lost 306,000; France, 200,000; Germany, 2.9 million; and Russia, 7 million.

production that raised the supply of goods, the relatively high rate of saving that held down the demand for goods, the government's success in controlling the cost of living, and the expansion in the power of labor unions, resulting from a great increase in their membership and their control over strategic industries. Labor union membership rose from 8.9 million in 1940 to 14.8 million in 1945, and in the heavy industries 90 percent or more were unionized.

Throughout the War, the most insistent demands by unions were for wage increases and the union shop. Both of these objectives were accomplished to a large extent through strikes and because the government, fearing interruptions in production, encouraged recognition of union demands. Work stoppages during the War involved an annual average of 7.5 percent of employed wage earners. This percentage had been exceeded only three times in the previous 20 years and was far higher than the rate in World War I. Recognizing that industrial disputes could seriously damage war production, the administration, soon after the United States entered the War, created the National War Labor Board and instituted what amounted to compulsory arbitration. To protect the unions as collective-bargaining agents, the Board established the "maintenance of membership clause" which required union members to maintain their membership for the duration of a union contract. To protect the economy from running amuck in a spiral of inflation, the administration froze wages by the "Little Steel Formula," under which any group of workers whose straight-time hourly earnings had increased by less than 15 percent since January 1, 1941 became entitled to wage increases bringing them up to that level but no further. Exceptions, however, occurred frequently.

The two pseudo-wars of the 1950s and 1960s—the Korean police action and the Vietnam involvement, expensive and unpopular as they were, were far from being total wars. At the height of Vietnam, 7.8 million were involved in the military or in military production. This amounted to 10.2 percent of total employment and 5.5 percent of private employment.

THE INFLUENCE OF WAR ON AGRICULTURE

Wartime changes in the demand for and supply of foodstuffs, the number of agricultural workers, the quantity of land under cultivation, the amount of capital utilized on the farm, and the farmers' debt position left a permanent impact on the long-term development of agriculture. Each war multiplied the demand for foodstuffs. Higher money income increased the civilian demand. Then too, the armed forces used a far greater amount of food than an equivalent number of civilians. In World War II, for example, the members of the armed forces used 50 percent more food than they had as civilians. Finally, in global war, food was needed in greater quantities to supply our allies and to feed liberated areas where military campaigns had made food production impossible.

In each major war the inflated demand for food was met partly by increasing aggregate agricultural production. During the Civil War, farm production expanded relatively little; in World War I, it increased about 11 percent; and in World War II, about 23 percent. Each wartime increase in agricultural production was accomplished despite a decline in the number of agricultural workers.

With less labor, farmers increased production to some extent by bringing new lands under cultivation, especially during the Civil War and World War I. Cropland probably increased by 10 percent during the Civil War, and the number of acres harvested increased by an equal percentage during World War I. During World War II, however, the number of acres harvested increased by only 6 percent, and farmers were actually cultivating less acres than were under the plow in 1932. It was not, therefore, more acres, but wider use of machinery and more intensive cultivation of the soil that raised agricultural output in World War II. The amount of agricultural equipment, measured in constant prices, increased by about 50 percent, and the use of fertilizer increased even more. Consequently, output per farm worker, which had not improved markedly during either the Civil War or World War I, rose by a third between 1939 and 1944.

The methods by which the farmer increased agricultural production in each of the three wars had a major disruptive effect on the nation's economy. The expansion of land under cultivation in the Civil War and World War I added to the farmer's mortgage debt, and he emerged from these wars in a precarious economic state. But in World War II he used his increased income to pay off debt rather than to buy new land. Of even greater importance, the war economy forced the farmer to use better methods of cultivation, so that soil was conserved, not wasted. The farmer's economic position, was, therefore, extremely good after World War II, and the level of living of the average American in the short and long run gained from agriculture's experience in the War.

PROFITS IN WARTIME

In general, war had a salutary effect on commerce and trade. Profits were high and business failures, low.

Data for the Civil War period are sparse, but contemporary commentators cited high profits in textiles, iron, and other manufactured articles. It was estimated in early 1864 that the value of regularly listed stocks on the New York Stock Exchange had risen $200 million in two years, and that the price of railroad stocks had doubled during the War. There were very few business failures: 6,000 in 1861, but only 500 in 1864. Liabilities of failed firms were estimated at $180 million in 1861, but at less than $10 million in 1864. Despite the small number of failures, however, there were fewer firms at the end of the War than at the beginning, for the War encouraged business consolidation.

Profits during World War I were high, but not so high as in the preceding neutrality and preparedness periods, and in addition, actual involvement in the war had a depressing effect on stock prices. Reflecting the rise and fall of profits, stock prices increased about 20 percent between 1914 and 1916, but they dropped sharply thereafter, so that *they were lower in 1918 than at any time since 1904.* Business failures, on the other hand, declined steadily. Total liabilities of business failures were at a rate of $20 million per month in 1914, but only $8 million in August 1918.

In World War II, corporate profits after taxes rose from $6.4 billion to $10.8 billion. Stock prices climbed almost 60 percent between 1940 and 1946. Standard and Poor's industrial average (1941-1943=100) rose from 87.80 in 1942 to 170.8 in 1946. Liabilities resulting from business failures were less than $1 million in April 1945, contrasted with $14 million in May 1940.

As the Federal government increased its debt, other debt declined relative to the high rate of business activity. In one year of the Civil War, three times as much debt was paid off as in any single previous year. In World War I, nonfederal debt increased from $86 billion to $101.1 billion; but in World War II, nonfederal debt declined absolutely as well as relatively. In 1941, the net debt outside the Federal government was $156.3 billion; in 1945, it was $154.6 billion, The Federal government was replacing other debtors and sometimes turning them into creditors.

SUMMARY

America's major wars, with the possible exception of World War II, appear to have retarded rather than accelerated the rise in the average level of living. To some extent, wars caused a better postwar allocation of resources; but on balance, they interrupted technological innovation, deterred population growth, reduced output per man-hour, diminished the quantity of goods and services available for consumption, and threw the economy off balance by introducing price inflation and by encouraging high-cost industry and expanded agricultural output. Together with the wastes of natural resources that total war inevitably brings, wars slowed down economic progress. Superficially, it might appear that wars made the economy run faster, but whatever imporvements appeared were the result of employing previously unemployed factors of production. Peace and periods of preparedness played a much greater role than war in the remarkable economic development experienced by the United States.

SUGGESTED READINGS

(On specific topics, see the readings cited in the footnotes in the chapter.)

Cochran, Thomas C., "Did the Civil War Retard Industrialization?" *Mississippi Valley Historical Review,* Vol. XLIX (1961).

Fabricant, Solomon, *The Trend of Government Activity in the United States Since 1900* (New York: National Bureau of Economic Research, 1952).

Fine, Sydney, *Laissez-Faire and the General Welfare State* (Ann Arbor: University of Michigan Press, 1956).

Gilchrist, David T. and W. David Lewis, eds., *Economic Change in the Civil War* (Wilmington, Del.: Eleutherian Mills-Hagley Foundation, 1965).

Kimmel, Lewis, *Federal Budget and Fiscal Policy* (Washington, D. C.: The Brookings Institution, 1959).

Lively, Robert A., "The American System, A Review Article," *The Business History Review*, Vol. XXIX (1955).

Murphy, Henry C., *The National Debt in War and Transition* (New York: McGraw-Hill Book Company, 1950).

Rozwenc, E. C., ed., *The New Deal: Revolution or Evolution*, Amherst Readings in American History (Boston: D. C. Heath & Company, 1959).

Stein, Herbert, *The Fiscal Revolution in America* (Chicago: The University of Chicago Press, 1969).

Studenski, Paul and Herman E. Krooss, *Financial History of the United States*, 2nd ed. (New York: McGraw-Hill Book Company, 1963).

Vartanian, Pershing, "The Cochran Thesis: A Critique in Statistical Analysis," *Journal of American History*, Vol. LII (1964).

Wright, Chester W., "The More Enduring Economic Consequences of America's Wars," *Journal of Economic History*, Vol. III, Supplement (1943).

QUESTIONS

1. It has been argued that war retarded economic development. The opposite has also been argued. Which side do you take? What are your reasons?
2. How did the worker fare in the three major wars?
3. What influence did the major wars have on the farmer?
4. Discuss the influence of the Civil War on industrial progress.
5. How did wars affect profits and security prices?

Chapter Seventeen

GOVERNMENT'S ROLE IN THE ECONOMY: FISCAL AFFAIRS

One of the most persistent maxims in the series of abstractions known as "the American Way" is that government should refrain from interfering with the economy. Accompanying this is a persistent legend that in the United States of yesterday the government did refrain from interfering with the economy. In reality, however, American governments of one kind or another—Federal, state, and local—have always played a role in the economy, from the building of the $5 million Cumberland Road to the $100 million Glen Canyon Dam, from the Lewis and Clark expedition to sending a man to the moon, from $20,000 for education in one state in 1790 to $3.25 billion in another state in 1970. *Laissez faire* of the extreme type envisioned by some classical economists never characterized the American scene. Nor, indeed, did the less extreme form that Adam Smith had in mind in his *Wealth of Nations*. The United States has always had a mixed economy, that is to say, one in which private enterprise and government have each played a role, often a cooperative one, in fostering economic development.

To be sure, the government's role has grown appreciably. Its place in the economic process has expanded with the growth of the American economy, and it has no doubt expanded more rapidly than the general economy. Governments first exerted their economic influence in the role of policemen and, to a lesser extent, as redistributors of economic resources. They afforded protection to life and property, encouraged colonization, and contributed to the advancement of business, agriculture, and social welfare. In time, they took on new and more complicated functions, finally becoming conservators of resources, business entrepreneurs, and economic stabilizers, as well as policemen and income redistributors. In the process, the Federal government, which once played a minor role, expanded its old functions and took on new ones in a continuous acceleration of influence. At the same time, the state governments, which had always pioneered in opening up new areas for government activity, continued to grow, but not as fast as the Federal government. They therefore ceded their position as innovators and came to play a much smaller part in shaping the economic milieu.

This expansion of government influence was not the result of the scheming of a group of Machiavellian politicians or of the conniving of a clique of power-hungry insiders. As with all aspects of economic history, the expansion of government influence was intimately connected with the other factors in the economic process, especially technological progress, population growth, urbanization, and the business cycle. In general, the increasing complexity of the economy was responsible for the great expansion of government, but more specifically its causes were wars and their aftermath, including the demands of national security; the evolution of transportation and communication, which shortened distances and nationalized economic problems; the emergence of the United States as a world power and the acquisition of overseas territory; and the public and group pressures exerted on the government to contribute capital, to coordinate economic resources, to resolve group conflicts, and to spread the costs of economic risk among the various members of society. If government has grown in the United States, it is because the people have wanted it to grow.

The spread of government influence did not follow any preconceived plan. Instead, it proceeded in the American traditon of pragmatic muddling through. With few exceptions, the purposes, goals, and objectives of political parties and of statemen were very hazy, but if any one theme dominated, it was the idea of protecting the weaker members of economic society. At times this meant shoring up the competitive structure; but at other times it meant ripping it down.

In previous chapters there was much evidence of how government participated in the economy through land policy, transportation subsidies, business regulation, tariff policy, and legislation on labor and for the farmer. This chapter will concentrate on government fiscal operations.

GOVERNMENT IN THE ECONOMY BEFORE 1800

Governments were thoroughly immersed in economic activity during the Colonial Period and the first few years of the new Republic. This was readily understandable, for mercantilism was the dominant economic philosophy in these early years, and mercantilism was primarily concerned with increasing the power of the state.

The colonies closely regulated the lives of their citizens, their health, their status, and their clothing, as well as their business lives. Before the Colonial Period was over, governments were using a mass of laws and administrative regulations designed to achieve economic growth without the costs and the pains that usually accompany such growth. The activities that are ordinarily associated with "government in business" had become stereotyped even before the end of the eighteenth century. Bounties and tariffs, land grants, and the right to a legal monopoly were used to encourage entrepreneurs to get on with the business of advancing economic development. But there were also inspection laws and laws regulating banks, transportation, and industry in general to see that entrepreneurs did not get out of hand. Legislators fixed prices and wages. Thinking that they could augment the supply of capital and the quantity of wealth, they formed banks and issued paper money to increase the quantity of money in circulation. Then they passed laws to force the people to take paper money when it was offered.

Protecting the weaker members of society against economic difficulties became one of the permanent functions of American government. The colonies, like medieval governments, passed laws prohibiting "regrating" (buying goods for speculation); "forestalling" (obtaining a corner on commodities); and "engrossing" (obtaining a monopoly). Cities, towns, and counties provided some form of relief for the poor, the aged, and the infirm. As early as 1789, some states established charitable institutions, contributed to the support of private welfare institutions, adopted public health measures, and made land grants to veterans.

On the whole, these experiments did not turn out as ideally as was hoped. Inflation did take place in many colonies, and the laws against so-called "speculative" abuses were not enforceable. But the colonies did build a thriving commerce, and the bustling activity in the towns soon brought some of the more annoying problems of boom prosperity. It is ironically amusing that in this bucolic life there were complaints about traffic, its accidents, noise, and the difficulty of finding a place to park.

Whatever its weaknesses, mercantilism continued to dominate economic and political philosophy in America's first decade. Federalism, the political creed for which Alexander Hamilton was the leading economic spokesman, regarded economic growth and development as society's primary goal. Federalists believed that this could best be attained by a workable alliance between government and business, represented in this era mostly by the merchants. They therefore supported a strong central government and substantial government intervention. Hamilton, as Secretary of the Treasury, persuaded Congress to charter a national bank and to encourage industry deliberately and positively through tariffs, bounties, commercial treaties, and navigation laws, rather than to allow it to follow the natural course of development.

The Federalist administration was not particularly opposed to government spending. On the contrary, Federal expenditures tripled, reaching $10 million in 1800, 45 percent of which went for interest on the debt and 40 percent for the army and the navy. To meet these expenditures, Congress set up a tax system that was essentially regressive (that is, its burden fell more heavily on the low-income than on the high income groups) in that it emphasized tariffs and excise taxes. However, revenues, despite extensive taxes, did not quite match expenditures, so that the debt, which was already considered huge at the end of the Revolutionary War, rose to about $83 million in 1800. Yet, the government's credit apparently did not suffer for Federal bonds sold at close to par in the late 1790s contrasted with a 90 percent discount at the end of the Revolution.

Clearly, the Federalists were more concerned with the nonfiscal than the fiscal objectives of fiscal policy. Hamilton made no particular effort to pay off the debt. In fact, unlike his successors, he regarded it with equanimity and used it as a tool to influence the economy. When money was tight, he accelerated payments on the debt; and when opposite conditions prevailed, he postponed debt payments. Similarly, taxes were esteemed more for their broad economic and social impact than for their efficiency as money raisers. The whiskey tax, for example, was favored because it would make people work harder, and the rationale for tariffs was the protection of infant industries.

State and local governments played a poor second fiddle to the Federal government during the Federalist era. The Federal government spent about $2 per capita in 1800, when spending in New York State was 65 cents and in New York City, $1.80. Local governments offered very few of the services that are now commonly expected. Even in the largest cities, only the main streets were paved and had drains or sewers. There were no day police, and fire protection was supplied by volunteers. No city or town had an organized water supply, but pumps and wells were generally erected in the city square. Public-health control was almost nonexistent and few localities maintained schools. State governments did contribute to social welfare, but not on an immense scale. They initiated public health measures, operated the prisons, and contributed to educational institutions. Around 1800, New York spent about 7 percent of its budget for charity, 7 percent for prisons, and 5 percent for public health. At the same time, about 3 percent went toward internal improvements.

GOVERNMENT IN THE AGRARIAN ERA

In retrospect, it is hard to understand how Federalism and its mercantilist doctrines achieved political success. They appealed to the merchants, but certainly not to the feelings of most Americans. The small farmers and the small businessmen and artisans who constituted the majority of the population in the early nineteenth century had little to gain from Federal intervention. Like their colonial ancestors, they believed in home rule, limited government spending, low taxes, balanced budgets, and rapid debt repayment.

Hamilton envisioned a wealthy and powerful nation. The opposite political creed, led by Thomas Jefferson, preached the good life. It looked forward to the *status quo:* a nation of small farmers, "a happy rather than a wealthy nation." Part of the Hamiltonian vision had a broader appeal than the ideology of the Jeffersonians; but, on balance, Jeffersonianism and later Jacksonianism had a much greater appeal, and from 1800 to the middle of the century they clearly dominated the political scene. Indeed, some contemporary Americans still pledge their faith to many Jeffersonian tenets—the belief in limited government, low taxes, overbalanced budgets, and rapid debt retirement.

In the age of agrarianism that Jefferson ushered in, the power of the Federal government diminished. This was especially true of its direct influence through spending, tax collection, and debt management. Per capita expenditures were only $2.00 in 1860, the same as in 1800. This, however, did not mean that the agrarian age was one of complete *laissez faire,* for although the power of the Federal government did not increase, state and local governments constantly broadened their activities. In addition to exerting their police powers and extending their welfare services, the latter governments advanced credit to private business and sometimes formed and operated their own business enterprises.

Federal spending gradually inched up from about $8 million in 1802 to almost $75 million in 1858; but, in proportion to population, there was, as has just been said, no increase at all. Defense took anywhere from 35 to 60 percent of all spending; but for the whole 60 years, its share was a little over 50 percent. Interest payments were very high at the beginning of the period but disappeared temporarily in the 1830s and did not again become significant until after the Civil War. As interest payments fell, pension payments climbed almost equally. At the same time, spending for public works showed a secular rise, increasing from an insignificant amount to about $3 million a year in the Jackson days and to $6 million a year in the 1850s.

In line with the political philosophy of interfering as little as possible with the ordinary workings of the economy, each administration tried to hold down expenditures and at all times to balance the budget. If it were forced to borrow by unavoidable circumstances, such as war or depression, the accepted idea was to pay off the debt as fast as possible. Thus, the debt arising from the Revolution, the Louisiana Purchase, and the War of 1812 was all repaid by 1835.

Although the goal was to have income exceed outgo, in practice government expenditures and tax revenue were playthings of the business cycle. During business booms, customs brought in much more revenue than in less prosperous times, even though tariff rates were reduced rather regularly. At the same time, the sale of public lands soared. Thus, in 1835 and 1836, the sale of public lands brought in $40 million, almost half of all Federal income, and in 1855, it brought $12 million, or about one-fifth of all revenue. Under the combined impact of bloated customs and booming land sales, revenue spurted upward, but expenditures were held down until the very height of the boom, when spending for internal improvements and pensions became much more liberal and expenditures skyrocketed. A somewhat opposite course of events was spun out during the depression phase of the cycle. Revenues sank very rapidly as public land sales ground to a halt and as the decline in foreign trade cut customs income. Then, despite the fact that all administrations were strongly opposed to deficits and took great pains to try to cut expenses, the Federal government could not make ends meet and ran into debt.

The 1830s and the 1850s offer two very good examples of the pattern of fiscal policy in the nineteenth century. As the economy roared upward in the heady exuberance of the early 1830s, Federal revenue also roared upward from $25 million to $50 million. Expenditures, however, were kept under tight rein at around $17 million to $18 million until they broke out of their bonds in 1836, when over $30 million was spent. The Treasury used the annual surpluses to pay off the entire national debt, and when revenues continued to exceed expenditures, provision was made to distribute the cash surplus to the states. But then came the depression of 1837, which immediately cut revenues in half and eventually to less than $20 million. Expenditures could not be cut with equal rapidity and did not show any decided reduction until 1839 and 1840. Debt, which had been obliterated in 1835, gradually mounted to about $30 million by the end of the depression.

In the 1850s, the economy again took off, and as it did, the Federal government's income mounted from around $50 million to $75 million. Expenditures showed a gradual increase throughout the early 1850s, not because the administration wanted it so, but because it was not strong enough to withstand Congressional pressure. Nevertheless, receipts were substantially in excess of spending, and the debt which had been built up by the depression of the 1830s and the Mexican War was sharply reduced. Then in 1857, panic and depression hit the economy. Income fell sharply from around $70 million to less than $50 million, but expenditures continued upward and reached a peak in 1858. It was not until 1860 that significant cuts finally emerged.

It must again be stressed that what happened in the 1830–1844 and 1852–1860 cycles was not at all in accord with the intentions or desires of the administrations that were then in office. During the first recognized depression, that of 1819, the executive branch thought that depressions were none of the government's business. President Monroe ignored the panic and took little notice of the subsequent depression, except to call for economy and simplicity. During the panic of 1837, Martin Van Buren told Congress: "Those who look to the action of this government for specific aid to the citizen . . . lose sight of the end for which it was created and the power with which it is clothed . . . . The less government interferes with private pursuits, the better for the general prosperity." In the 1850s, the administration tried to hold the fort in the interests of

"fiscal conservatism" against the onslaughts of those who were tempted by
rapidly rising revenues to demand expenditures for social welfare. To be sure,
the Federal government had upon rare occasions appropriated money for those
who had suffered from natural disaster: $50,000 was contributed to the victims
of a Venezuelan earthquake in 1812 and $20,000 was given to the victims of a
fire in Alexandria, Virginia, in 1827. But these were to be taken as exceptions,
not as precedents. In 1854, Congress made a land grant to the states for the care
of the indigent insane; President Pierce vetoed it. A few years later, Buchanan
vetoed a bill giving Federal land to the states to support education. Said he:
"When the state governments look to the Federal Treasury for the means of
supporting themselves and maintaining their systems of education . . . the character of both governments will be greatly deteriorated." During the depression
of 1857, Buchanan dismissed those who argued for freer spending. "No statesman," he said, "would advise that we should go on increasing the national
debt."

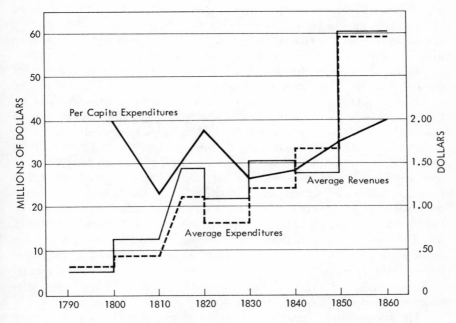

CHART 30. Federal expenditures and revenues, averages for selected periods, and per
capita expenditures, 1789-1860

It could be said that the administrations of this period tried to follow a
noncompensatory fiscal policy, that is, they increased spending in prosperity and
tried to reduce it in recession. To the extent that they succeeded, they intensi-

fied both the boom and the bust phases of the cycle. They added marginal expenditures to an already swollen income stream at the height of prosperity and thus accentuated booms. They tried to reduce spending and balance the budget during depressions and thus added weight to the economic downturn. Fortunately, however, economic forces prevented them from achieving their objectives. They were not able to balance the budget in the depressions of 1819, or 1837, or 1857. Despite their intentions, government fiscal policy turned out to be compensatory, but not nearly as compensatory as most modern theory would recommend.

State and local activity

State and local governments were much more eager to broaden their activities. Their increased expenditures, especially in the 1840s and the 1850s, more than made up for Federal passivity. Whereas the Federal government was spending about $2 per capita in 1860, state governments probably spent 50 cents and local governments over $5. The latter figures, of course, varied widely, depending upon the section of the country, the population, and the degree of development. A city like Providence, Rhode Island, spent over $7 per capita; but on the frontier, conditions were most primitive, even though activity hummed and the streets were dense with pedestrians. As late as 1834, in the thriving city of St. Louis, there were no sidewalks, and dead horses, hogs, and cows lay on the streets for days. It was reported that in 1843 an ox team drowned in one of the holes on the streets of Montgomery, Alabama. A typical frontier town at the middle of the century supported itself by a poll tax of $1, a property tax of 25 cents per $100 of real estate, a tavern and store license of $5, and a few excise taxes on admissions, carriages, drugs, groceries, and liquor.[1] On the other hand, the larger cities and the states relied heavily on property taxes and on borrowing. Debt piled up, especially during prosperity. By 1860, state debt amounted to over $250 million and local debt added another $200 million, more than three times as much as the national debt. Each major crisis—1837 and 1857—was accompanied by wholesale state and local defaults. Yet in the subsequent recoveries, foreign and domestic lenders rushed back into the capital markets in which local and state governments were borrowing.

The most popular expenditures on the state level were for internal improvements and education. Investments by states in transportation facilities and other public improvements were as old as the Colonial Period, but they became really important when New York financed the $11 million construction of the Erie Canal in 1817–1825. The success of the Erie fired popular imagination in the other states, and later this eagerness spilled over into railroads. But enough of

[1]Everett Dick, *Life on the Dixie Frontier* (New York: Alfred A. Knopf, Inc., 1948, pp. 152 ff.

this story has been told in another context, so that a further account of it here would be repetitious.

State educational support began on a broad scale when Massachusetts began to support schools with taxes in 1800. Two years later, when Ohio entered the Union, the Federal government agreed to set aside out of its public lands one section of each new township to be used for education. In 1805, New York set up a common school fund. Free education for everyone, however, first appeared in 1834 in Pennsylvania. Thereafter, it spread fairly rapidly, and by 1850 free schools were common, except in the South. Of course, the demand for this type of government service was immense, but here and there, public schools were regarded as an unwarranted invasion of private life and a dangerous breech of self-reliance. Perhaps by coincidence, this feeling seemed most prevalent in those areas which appeared to lag in economic growth.

City governments went in heavily for services. Among operating expenses, those for police protection, streets, and education grew most rapidly. Boston established the first round-the-clock police department in 1854. Boston and Cincinnati had the first paid fire departments in 1860. New York did not have one until 1865 and Philadelphia, not until 1870. Among the most spectacular projects were the construction of waterworks. New York spent $9 million on the Croton Reservoir system in the late 1830s and early 1840s. Boston spent $5 million on a water system in 1846. By 1860, there were 68 public waterworks, but all of them charged a fee or a rate. To some extent, the construction of these works was part of a policy of using public works to alleviate suffering during business depressions, a practice which is traceable at least as far back as the Romans. In the United States, cities used it as far back as anyone can remember, and it became increasingly popular with each successive business depression. In the relatively minor crisis of 1807, New York City extended its streets and drained some of its ponds, primarily to give work to the unemployed. Again in 1857, the city graded Central Park and tore down a number of obsolete buildings in the lower section of town. But these programs were unsystematized and were, of course, far less ambitious than what has since become customary.

FISCAL AFFAIRS IN A PERIOD OF NASCENT INDUSTRIALISM

The long-lived agrarian, small-business dominance over Federal politics came to an end with the rise of industrialism around the middle of the nineteenth century. All political parties were regarded with suspicious disdain by industrialists and bankers, but the Republican Party, which controlled the Federal government almost without interruption in the late nineteenth century, succeeded about as well as any party could in overcoming this hostility. Although it insisted that it was the champion of *laissez faire,* it defined the term peculiarly, interpreting it not literally, but broadly to mean refraining from any action which blatantly interfered with the progress of industrialism. The Republican Party believed that what was good for business was good for America. Under its leadership, the Federal government established the National Banking System, pushed the tariff to new heights, supported regressive taxes, subsidized several Western railroad systems, and subsidized the merchant marine. The only fissures in this solid entrenchment of the business ethos were the government's obsession with sound money and a volume of spending for veterans' pensions which many thought overgenerous. In the days of Queeen Victoria and William McKinley, government policy was still being steered according to a set of aphorisms based on *Poor Richard's Almanac,* but without the emphasis on "the good life" that had been so essential a part of the *Almanac* in Jefferson and Gallatin's day. In the late nineteenth century, there was an implicit conviction that economic riches, economic success, and economic progress were the desiderata of all existence. So persuasive was this belief, and so well did the policy work, that most of the doctrines of Republicanism were taken over by the Democratic Party, so that changes in political administrations during the late nineteenth century had little effect on the Federal government's activities.

Meanwhile, state and local governments, largely because of the extraordinary urbanization that so spectacularly characterized the late nineteenth century, embarked on a very active program of expenditures. Here there was no illusion of *laissez faire,* but instead a frank acceptance of the idea that government should play an important role. The colonial emphasis on home rule was still embedded in American thought, and the citzenry did not allow their distrust of central government to impinge upon their faith in state and local government.

One way of demonstrating the trend in government activity is to trace what happened to government employment. Federal employment, not including the military, multiplied a little over five times between 1821 and 1861, compared with almost seven times in the next 40 years. Total government civilian employment (Federal, state, and local) rose from 2 to 3 percent of the labor force between 1870 and 1900. Government employed one out of every 50 workers in 1870, and one out of every 30 in 1900. Public activities and services were continuously expanding, and government influence over the economy was constantly increasing. But this, of course, hardly meant that government was as yet a very important force in the total economy. Its total employment was still very low. Government expenditures, except in time of war, at most, amounted to 8 percent of GNP. Federal expenditures were about $5 per capita in 1889, the states spent about $1, and local governments added another $8, making a total of about $14 per capita, an amount much too small to make much of a difference in the total economy, even if that had been the general intent.

Federal fiscal affairs in the late 1800s fluctuated narrowly, except for the business cycle. Expenditures ranged from somewhat less than $250 million in 1878 to a little over $380 million in 1893. Revenues were at their lowest in 1878 at a little over $250 million, and at their highest in 1882 at a trifle more than $400 million. Revenues fluctuated under the pressure of two forces: first, a continuous series of tax reductions between the end of the Civil War and the early 1880s; and second, the effect of the severe cycles of the period. In prosperity, revenues climbed somewhat faster than the general business index, whereas the opposite was true in recession and depression. As in the early part of the century, expenditures tended to rise in booms, and some attempt was made to cut them when depression succeeded prosperity. The one sharp divergence from the early period was that the time lag was considerably shorter, that is, expenditures rose much more quickly in booms and were cut much faster in recession.

In the rational world of the late nineteenth century, military expenditures as a percent of the total were the lowest in our history, taking only 20 cents out of every dollar spent. Interest charges and pension payments each consumed a half-dollar. Public works took a little less than a dime, while the other 20 cents went for general operation, foreign service, and so forth. As before, interest payments traveled downward all through the period, whereas pensions proceeded upward, so that in the 1890s veterans were receiving more money than any other function of government. Customs continued to supply most of the revenue—about 55 percent—but this was much less than in the early period, for excise taxes of one sort or another provided another 35 percent, with sales of public lands, bank taxes, and miscellaneous sources making up the remainder.

Because revenues ran consistently ahead of expenditures up to the 1890s, the government acquired a massive surplus that was, to whatever extent possible, applied to the retirement of the debt. The interest-bearing debt fell from $2.3 billion to $610 million. By the 1890s, the surplus had become a source of annoyance rather than comfort. For by then, all the outstanding debt was in noncallable bonds, which could be retired only by purchase in the open market at high premiums. There was an additional complicating factor: the national bank currency rested on government bonds, and continued debt retirement might further reduce the amount of currency, which was already embarrassingly low. Steps were therefore taken to eliminate the surplus. The McKinley tariff reduced receipts and raised expenditures, dissipating most of the surplus. The remainder was taken care of by increased payments to veterans and the depressing influence of the depression of 1893. By 1897, the interest-bearing debt was again in the vicinity of $850 million.

In the aggregate, expenditures on the state level were not very high, but, as had always been the case, they varied widely in different sections of the country. By the end of the century, states were putting about 25 percent of their expenditures into health services. Another 15 percent, approximately, went for education as states established free secondary schools (especially after 1880), placed more emphasis on vocational schools, and established colleges and universities. Public welfare accounted for almost 10 percent; 20 percent went to general operation; and the rest was expended on highways, natural resources, interest, correction, and miscellaneous accounts. The larger states in the industrial, urbanized areas were, however, much more concerned with regulation and welfare than were the rural states.

In 1860 New York State spent only $50,000 for regulative services other than public health; by 1880 it spent $300,000 and by 1900, $900,000. It established a railroad commission for the regulation of rates in 1882, a Bureau of Labor Statistics in the same year, and a Board of Mediation and Arbitration and a Board of Factory Inspection four years later. Mine inspection was instituted in 1890; and sweatshop and bakery inspection in 1892–1895. A state Board of Health was established in 1880, with powers to collect vital statistics, enforce pure-food laws, and investigate disease. State expenditures for the mentally ill and for social welfare increased from $263,000 in 1860 to $1,230,000 in 1880 and to $6,500,000 in 1900. A state Agricultural Experiment Station was established in 1880 and a Department of Agriculture, inaugurating cattle inspection and eradication of bovine tuberculosis and plant and nursery diseases, in 1893. Conservation of state resources started in 1868 with the creation of Commissioners of Fisheries, and a Forest Reserve Commission was established in 1885.

Local governments, which were the heaviest spenders of all, spent much of their money (almost 30 percent) on education. General operation and utilities took 25 percent; streets, 20 percent; police, fire, and sanitation, 15 percent; and health and welfare, 10 percent.

Cities everywhere opened and paved miles of new streets; enlarged their water works and sewer systems; built scores of new police and fire stations; reequipped their police and fire forces; constructed new public schools; added high schools (and in New York City, free municipal colleges); erected giant bridges, imposing city halls, and courthouses; and founded or laid out municipal museums, zoological and botanical gardens, and public parks. The larger cities annexed tremendous suburban areas and, having become super-cities, proceeded, at large additional capital investment and operating costs, to unify and enlarge the municipal facilities throughout the entire area on a metropolital basis.

Government tax systems around 1900 were the end result of a long period of improvisation, but they were still extremely regressive; that is, they took a much larger percentage of the incomes of those in the lower brackets than of those in the upper brackets. The property tax provided three-quarters of local revenue and almost half of state revenue. On all levels of government, excises were important, and fees and licenses produced at least something.

On the Federal level, the tax system was regressive, and expenditures for the lower-income groups were not relatively large. These groups, therefore, paid a larger share of their incomes than they got back in benefits. Federal fiscal policy during the nineteenth century thus tended to shift income from those in the lower-income groups, who had a high propensity to consume, to those in the upper-income brackets, who had a high propensity to save. State and local fiscal activities probably benefited middle-income groups the most, for, although state and local tax systems were also regressive, expenditures benefited upper-income groups less than the middle class or the poor. For the over-all economy, and from the point of view of long-run economic progress, the effects of over-all government fiscal operations in the nineteenth century were probably more advantageous than disadvantageous; consumption expenditures were probably lower than they would otherwise have been, but saving was higher, and in a period of capital scarcity there was a greater need for saving and investment than for consumption spending. But it is also important to point out that the impact of government fiscal affairs on the distribution of income and on the saving-consumption mix should not be exaggerated. Government spending amounted to only 10 percent of total production, and not all of the 10 percent represented a transfer of income from low-income groups to high-income groups, or from consumers to savers. How much the actual shift amounted to is impossible to tell, but it hardly could have exceeded 3 percent of the national income.

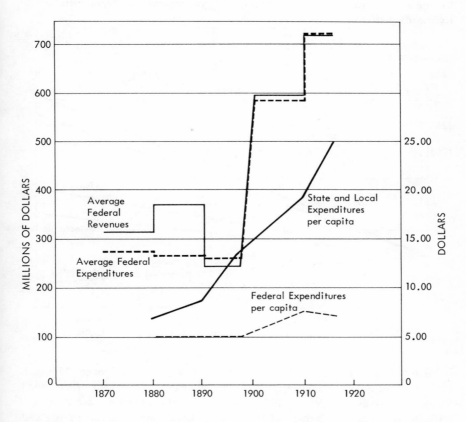

CHART 31. Federal expenditures and revenues, and per capita expenditures by Federal, state, and local governments, 1871-1920

GOVERNMENT FISCAL POLICY IN THE TWENTIETH CENTURY

The enhanced importance of government

As is common knowledge, the economic influence of government, especially the Federal government, has increased immensely in the twentieth century. Around 1900, governments spent about $20 per capita, or 8 percent of the GNP. In 1927, they spent 12 percent of GNP. In 1960, per capita spending was over $700 and in 1970, over $1,350 for a total of $333 billion or more than 35 percent of total output. In 1900, governments employed one out of every 30 workers; in 1970, one out of every six. Of every 100 civilians employed by government, 57 worked for local government, 21 worked for the state, and 22 for the Federal government. State and local government had become the country's leading growth industry.

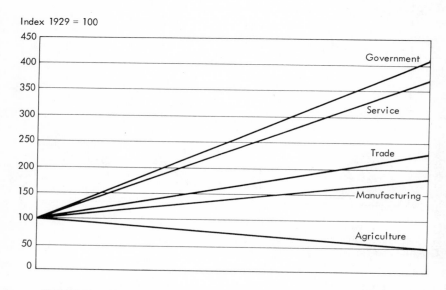

CHART 32. Changes in employment by selected industry groups, 1929-1970

There were logical reasons for this rise in government influence. Although the policies of the Federal government in the late nineteenth century encouraged business and industrialization, and were thought to contribute more than normally to the economic growth of the nation, public opinion became more and more uneasy about the course of events. Bigness was becoming a prominent feature of economic life, and the weaker members in the economy desired some control over its growth in order to protect their real or fancied self-interest.

Farmers, small businessmen, and many big businessmen wanted protection against the rigors of the competitive system; workers wanted government to provide greater security; and consumers desired the government to act as a buffer against the real or imagined evils of monopoly. A second reason for the new importance of government was that the United States was becoming a world power, extending its territories to the far points of the globe, and its new responsibilities dictated that the Federal government take a more active role in economic matters. As the country grew politically in the international scene, it also grew economically, and businessmen and bankers with world-wide interests looked to the Federal government for services and protection.

Not only was the world getting smaller, but the nation itself was contracting as improved methods of transportation and communication shortened distances. There was an ever-growing trend toward interstate industry, and in time it came to be realized that state boundaries were more geographic than economic. Railroads and automobiles brought East and West, North and South, closer. The telegraph, telephone, and other public utilities transcended state lines. As interstate commerce grew, so did the Federal government, for it alone had the power to regulate interstate commerce.

Regardless of whether public opinion was in or out of tune with reality, it exerted very real pressures around the turn of the century for greater Federal participation in economic activity. These pressures quickly affected American political developments, and the Progressive Era of the early 1900s ushered in an era of neomercantilism. During the Roosevelt, Taft, and Wilson administrations, the government broadened its regulation of business, increased its contributions to agriculture, built a strong navy, entered business enterprise, adopted a deliberate policy of conserving natural resources, and raised its expenditures. At first, however, what was happening was not clearly recognized, but then two world wars and a catastrophic business depression made the existing trend toward greater Federal intervention clear to almost everyone.

Gradual change in economic and political philosophy

Admittedly, the government had taken a somewhat more active role in controlling the economy in the last third of the nineteenth century than it had taken in the middle third. The Grant administration, for example, took action to increase the supply of money during the panic of 1873. But this action was taken as an emergency measure, and there was no intention of really controlling the economy either in the short run or the long run. True, many people on the farms and in the offices that supervised the factories believed that the government should use its powers over money and banking to raise prices. However, the notion that government not only could but should shape its monetary and fiscal policies so as to influence the national income and the distribution of wealth, to eliminate unemployment, and create a balance between inflationary and deflationary forces, was in the nineteenth century too fantastic for any reasonable person to give it credence.

Of course, government controls over money and banking and over its own revenue, expenditure, and debt policies always affected the economy, whether it was so intended or not. But before 1900, two factors tended to obscure this fact. Government expenditures and revenues constituted a small part of the national income, and their economic impact was, therefore, not very great. Second, governments either tried to divorce themselves from influencing the economy or they followed rather than led changes in business activity.

Around 1900, some government officials began to express skepticism concerning the traditional theory of government fiscal operations. They were not sure that the rules that applied to an individual's financial operations should apply to the government's. Some went so far as to question whether the government should live within its income, that is, balance its budget. But in 1900 these ideas were still rare indeed. Much more common was the belief that, if the government was to interfere at all, it should do so by creating a central bank to control the banking system.

Gradually, more people of influence became converted to the belief that government could conduct its fiscal affairs in ways that would soften the impact of business recessions. In the early 1900s, Secretary of the Treasury Shaw asserted that it was just as much the government's duty to protect the people from financial panics as to protect them from yellow fever. A little later, Secretary Cortelyou questioned whether a balanced budget was always advantageous. In 1915, when it seemed that a full-scale depression was about to descend on the economy, the Federal government began to make plans to meet the problem of unemployment. In 1923, Secretary of Commerce Hoover urged Congress to correlate its appropriations for public workers with the business cycle, and in 1928 a bill to that effect was introduced but was defeated in the House.

It was the depression of the 1930s that gave reality to the events foreshadowed at the beginning of the century. Then the Hoover administration broke with the past and somewhat reluctantly accepted the view that the government should take an important, positive, and active part in trying to lead the country out of the depression. It used monetary techniques; it adopted legislation such as that embodied in the Reconstrucion Finance Corporation and the Home Owners' Loan Corporation to assist banks, insurance companies, and businesses; it proposed a moratorium on international debts; it increased the government's public works expenditures; and it gave state governments financial assistance in taking care of the unemployed.

The Roosevelt administration went further. Some of its tactics were extensions of what the Hoover administration had already started. Thus, it used monetary techniques and expanded Federal expenditures, especially in providing relief. But it also attempted to "plan" the economy by passing such legislation as the NIRA and the AAA. At first, the Roosevelt administration, like the Hoover administration before it, pledged its faith to the orthodox balanced-budget philosophy, but then in the recession of 1937, after much soul searching, it reluctantly turned its back on the balanced budget and switched its allegiance to the idea of using fiscal policy as a means of controlling and stabilizing the economy. By World War II, the role of government as an economic stabilizer was generally, if not unanimously, accepted.

Fiscal activities in the Progressive Era

Compared with some of the more important general indexes of economic activity, not much change occurred in government affairs in the years before World War I. Only a little over 3 percent of the labor force worked for the government in 1900 and in 1910. In 1900, all governments spent about $18 per capita ($5 by the Federal government, $3 by the states, and $10 locally). By 1913, the total had risen to $26 per capita ($7, $4, and $15, respectively). Although this was certainly a substantial increase, the total still remained below 10 percent of the gross national product.

The dollar volume of Federal expenditures and revenues showed a steady rise during the years immediately before World War I. Expenditures rose from a low of a little less than $500 million in 1902 to over $750 million in 1915. Revenues rose at about the same rate from $540 million in 1904 to $780 million in 1916. Over the whole period, 1901–1916, total spending and total income were almost equal, so that almost no change took place in the interest-bearing debt.

Viewed in an approximate way, the sources of revenue and the things on which money was expended were about the same at the outbreak of World War I as they had been in 1901. In both years, customs produced about 40 percent of income, defense took about 35 percent, and veterans' pensions between 25 and 30 percent. But looking below the surface, it was apparent that some fundamental changes were occurring. Excise taxes provided over 50 percent of income in 1901 but only 40 percent in 1913. The difference was offset to some extent by the appearance of a corporation income tax in 1909 which produced about 5 percent of all income in 1913.

On the spending side, public works expenditures, which had for years run at a rate of about 8 percent of all spending, shot up to almost 15 percent just before the War. Then too, the government added many functions which were small as a percent of total spending but large in dollar amounts. During the Progressive Era, the government established a Department of Commerce and a Department of Labor. It entered the business of conservation and reclamation. Relief payments to victims of cyclones, floods, earthquakes, and fires became much more common. The Public Health Service enhanced its prestige. Spending for agriculture was greatly stepped up by the addition of experiment stations, meat and food inspection, and attacks against disease and insects. These new functions, each for a small amount, added up to enough to account for a large share of the $275 million increase in Federal spending in the early years of the century.

Federal policy in the prosperous 1920s

The 1920s are usually regarded as a period of fiscal conservatism. On the Federal level, this was substantially—but not entirely—true. The effects of World War I were too great to be sloughed off even in a generation, and the more impatient among those who wanted to turn back the clock were forced to chafe under what they considered the very slow pace of the return to normalcy.

The features of Federal fiscal affairs in the 1920s that deserve emphasis are: (1) the stability of expenditures and revenues, (2) the numerous reductions in tax rates, (3) the amount of debt repayment despite the sizable tax reductions, and (4) the contrast between the 1920s and previous periods in respect to the nature of expenditures and revenues.

Federal expenditures ranged from $2.5 billion to $5 billion and revenues from $3.5 billion to $4 billion. Because income continuously exceeded outgo from 1921 on, substantial headway was made in retiring the debt, the interest-bearing debt dropping some $8 billion to approximately $16 billion in 1930. The surplus that enabled the Treasury to retire about one-third of the debt in ten years was entirely the result of economic expansion, for there were six substantial tax reductions during the decade. Yet there was no return to the indirect and regressive tax system that had existed since the nation's beginnings. In the last years of the 1920s, income taxes produced almost two-thirds of all tax revenue. Customs, which just ten years before had brought in half of all revenue, now produced only 15 percent, and excises were responsible for 20 percent.

The changes in the kinds of expenditure were not nearly so spectacular as the changes in taxes. The old standbys continued to absorb most government funds. Interest on the debt remained a very heavy charge, as did military spending and veterans' pensions. The first took almost 30 percent of the budget and the other two split about 40 percent. Highways accounted for 15 percent, and social welfare, 5 percent.

Federal fiscal policy since the depression

The 1920s did not succeed in returning to the good old days of small government and home rule, but they did succeed in holding the line. That line collapsed totally during the depression of the 1930s. Thereafter, government employment and spending became more important in the economy, and the Federal government became far more important than it had ever been before.

By 1932, governments were spending an amount equal to about 20 percent of the gross national product. Between 1930 and 1940, government employment rose from 3.2 million to 4.5 million and to 8.8 million in 1960. In these years, too, Federal expenditures, which had been traditionally far lower than local spending, came to equal half again as much as the combined total of state and local outlays.

Federal fiscal activity became so intricate and so influential that new and more sophisticated methods of accounting were devised to better describe their impact. By 1960, the Budget Bureau was operating with three different sets of accounts: the administrative budget, which covered the expenditures for which the government was liable; the cash budget, which included only those expenditures and those revenues that had been paid and collected in cash; and the national-accounts budget, which included only those transactions that entered the national income and which was therefore largely dominated by outlays for goods and services. The following table gives some idea of the wide disparity between the various types of government accounts.

Table 37

GOVERNMENT EXPENDITURES, SELECTED YEARS, 1930-1967
(in billions)

	Administrative budget	*Cash payments*	*National income account*	*Spending for goods and services*	*Direct state and local expenditures*
1930	$ 3.3	$ 2.9	—	$ 1.4	$ 8.4[1]
1940	9.1	9.6	—	6.2	11.2
1948	33.1	36.5	—	19.3	21.3
1950	39.6	43.1	$ 42.4	19.3	27.9
1960	76.5	94.3	91.3	52.7	61.0
1970	—	—	197.2	99.2	148.1

[1] 1932.

During the depressed 1930s, budget expenditures jumped from about $4 billion to almost $9 billion. Revenues, which fell to less than $2 billion at the bottom of the depression, were running at a rate in excess of $5 billion in 1940, primarily because of continuous and drastic increases in tax rates. But despite the rise in income, every year featured an unbalanced budget. The continuous deficits in these years, equal to three-quarters of total revenue, pushed the interest-bearing debt to beyond $40 billion.

The composition of expenditures and revenues also underwent a radical change. In 1940, relief and welfare took the largest share (25 percent) of the $9 billion of expenditures. Defense and agriculture each took about 20 percent, and public works and interest on the debt, about 10 percent each. One of the strange things that occurred during the New Deal was that the tax system became somewhat more regressive. In 1940, less than 40 percent of tax revenue was paid in income taxes. The remainder came from customs, excises, and employment taxes.

For a while after World War II, it appeared that what had taken place in fiscal affairs following every previous major war would be repeated after this one. Traditionally, one could expect drastic cuts in spending, continuous tax reductions, large surpluses, and steady debt retirement. But Korea ended all these illusions, chiefly because of the so-called "cold war" that kept defense spending high. Federal expenditures, which had dropped to below $35 billion in 1948, climbed to $75 billion in the last year of the Korean action. They fell back to $65 billion in 1955, but climbed steadily thereafter, reaching $80 billion in 1959, approximately 17 percent of the GNP. Meanwhile, there were few tax reductions, and most of these had been cancelled by increases during the Korean years. In the first few years after the War, revenues were stabilized at around $40 billion to $45 billion. After the Korean conflict, revenue was much more influenced by the business cycle and fluctuated between $60 billion and $80 billion. In most years, receipts were short of expenditures, so that the debt came to exceed $300 billion.

The nature of Federal tax collections and expenditures was quite different from what it had been in the New Deal days. In the 1950s, income taxes brought in three-quarters of all revenue. In absolute dollar amounts, the Federal government spent a sizable amount on social welfare—at least $8 billion in 1960. As a percent of total spending, however, social welfare was small. As had always been the case, defense expenditures swallowed by far the largest share of Federal outlays, accounting for more than 60 percent of government spending, or over $250 a year for each man, woman, and child. Indeed, when total Federal spending fell, as in the years immediately after World War II, it was because of cuts in military spending.

By the 1970s, the mix of Federal spending had again changed. Defense was taking 30 percent of the budget, and human resources consumed 45 percent of approximately $270 billion of total outlays.

Further changes in fiscal philosophy

From the depression on, fiscal philosophy had been undergoing a significant transformation. Once government expenditures and receipts had grown to the point where they equalled a high proportion of total output, government influence over the economy assumed new significance. It became clear that variations in government spending or shifts in government taxation would profoundly affect the whole economy. The vague concepts of "fiscal policy," if one may use that term, that had been adequate when public finance was a passive economic factor had to be changed when public finance became an active force in determining the course of the economy.

New philosophies do not develop over night, but by 1938 a theory of fiscal policy had been fairly well formulated. In brief, the new goals were: to use fiscal and monetary techniques to stabilize the economy, to vary government spending in order to maintain full employment, to use the government's tax policy to achieve a more equal distribution of the national income, and to use monetary techniques to assure an even flow of purchasing power throughout the economy.

The new goals of public finance were based upon the theory that total spending determined the level of employment, and that government expenditures could be used as a balance wheel to stabilize the economy at the full employment level. The Employment Act of 1946, often misnamed the Full Employment Act, expressed the new trend in theory and policy:

> It is the continuing policy and responsibility of the Federal Government to use all practicable means consistent with its needs and obligations . . . to utilize all its . . . resources for the purpose of creating and maintaining, in a manner calculated to foster and promote free competitive enterprise. . . .conditions under which there will be afforded useful employment. . . .and to promote maximum employment, production, and purchasing power.

In periods of declining business activity, the policy, often described as "compensatory fiscal policy," called for increased government spending, reduced taxes, and a rising public debt to assure the aggregate expenditures necessary to create full employment. On the other hand, when inflationary pressures were rampant, the theory demanded reductions in government spending, increased taxes, and repayment of public debt in order to reduce total expenditures and resist inflation.

Although the theory provided for a countercyclical policy, it was difficult to put the theory into practice, because the world was not conducted on economic values alone. Political and survival values were just as important—indeed, sometimes more important. Principally for reasons of national defense and, to a lesser extent, because of political considerations, it was often impossible to reduce government spending when countercyclical theory called for a reduction. On the other hand, total government expenditures were not raised to sufficient heights in periods of deflation. Changes in taxes were often also cyclical rather than countercyclical. Existing rates were raised and new taxes added in the midst of deflation, and taxes were reduced in inflationary periods when the theory called for an opposite policy.

In the 1950s, disillusion with compensatory fiscal policy led to some flirting with what was labeled the automatic budget stabilization policy, according to which tax rates should be set high enough to balance the budget at a 6 percent unemployment level. Once set, tax rates were to be left alone unless there was a major change in national policy. The concept was not officially adopted, but it kept cropping up in the next couple of decades.

In the late 1950s, dissatisfaction with the rate of economic growth and recurring unemployment led to a new attack on existing fiscal policy. Liberal economists indicted national fiscal policy as "a fiscal drag." They argued that as full employment (now defined as 4 percent unemployment or less) came into view, government surpluses appeared depressing the economy and preventing it from achieving its potential growth.

The fiscal-drag concept quickly took over center stage in the early 1960s, but toward the end of the decade, the "full employment budget," reminiscent of the automatic budget stabilization policy, was adopted by the Nixon administration. Under this concept, the budget was supposed to be balanced at full employment, that is, expenditures would be held to a level equal to what revenues would be *if the economy were fully employed.* [2]

New concepts of fiscal policy offered an excellent rationale for much higher levels of government spending. Federal expenditures in the late 1960s and early 1970s hovered between 20 and 22 percent of the gross national product. But the dollar volume exceeded $150 billion by 1967, $200 billion by 1971, $250 billion in 1973, with prospects of $275 billion by 1975. Since revenue trailed expenditures in six years of the 1950s and in eight years of the 1960s, Federal debt held by the public climbed to almost $300 billion.[3] There is another way of looking at the 1950-1970 deficits in perspective. In the eight years of the Truman administration, the total deficit was $500 million; in the Eisenhower years, it climbed to almost $20 billion; and in the Kennedy-Johnson years, to almost $30 billion. It was estimated that the deficit would be $25 billion in 1973. Yet total spending as a percentage of GNP remained about the same.

State and local finance

Federal spending multiplied 400 times in the twentieth century, whereas state and local expenditures increased 150 times. In the early part of the century, state and local governments spent $2.50 for every $1.00 out of Washington. By the middle of the century, the Federal government was spending $1.30 for every $1.00 expended by all the states, counties, cities, towns, and villages.

Aside from the impressive increase in total spending, the most striking developments in twentieth-century state and local finance were: (1) the relative

[2] See Herbert Stein, *The Fiscal Revolution in America* (Chicago: The University of Chicago Press, 1969).

[3] Gross debt in 1970 was $389.2 billion and in December 1972, $450 billion.

decline of the property tax as a source of income, (2) the drop in the cost of ordinary government operation, (3) the rise of the sales tax, and (4) the increase of spending for social welfare and for education. At the beginning of the century, state and local spending was divided somewhat as follows: 25 percent for education, 15 percent for streets and highways, 15 percent for general operation, and 10 percent for health and welfare. By 1970, the distribution gave 40 percent to education, 12.5 percent for streets and highways, but 20 percent for health and welfare (including urban renewal), and only 3 percent for general operation. In 1900, the property tax raised about 75 percent of state and local income. By 1970, the property tax brought in 40 percent of ordinary income;[4] sales taxes, another 35 percent; and income taxes, 15 percent. Although the dollar volume of revenue was much higher than at the beginning of the century, state and local governments had to resort to ingenious borrowing operations to meet their burgeoning expenses. By 1970, state and local debt was over $143 billion, almost ten times as much as in 1946.

A DIGRESSION ON WAR FINANCE

Of all the activities in which governments have engaged, wars have had the most influence on the government's position in the economy. The major wars fought by the United States did more than anything else to add to government power, for in each major war, government clearly became the preeminent player on the economic stage; and when the war was over, the government never completely reverted to the status of a bit player.

The rising costs of war

Even in peace time, defense expenditures represented a substantial percentage of Federal spending—35 to 40 percent in the first half of the nineteenth century and 20 percent in the second half. However, the costs of actual wars multiplied these percentages.

There seems to be a destiny that plays with the costs of war, for each of America's three major wars cost ten and one-half times the cost of the previous one. Four and one-quarter years of Civil War cost the Union $3.2 billion,[5] two and one-quarter years of World War I cost $33.4 billion, and six years of World War II cost $360 billion. Whereas it required $3,200 to outfit and maintain a

[4]In 1970, state and city governments collected $150 billion; of this, $22 billion came from grants-in-aid, $31 billion represented charges for services, and $10 billion was trust fund income. It is the remaining $87 billion that is here considered ordinary income.

[5]Senator Sumner in 1870 quoted estimates that the total destruction of wealth as a result of the Civil War amounted to $9 billion. *Congressional Globe,* January 12, 1870, p. 378.

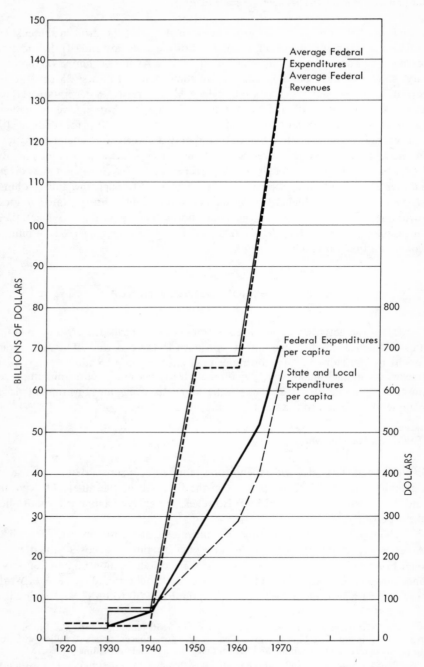

CHART 33. Federal expenditures and revenues, and per capita expenditures by Federal, state, and local governments, 1921-1970

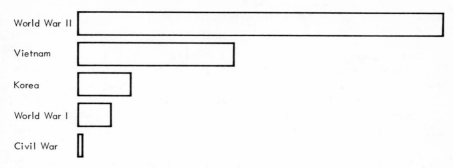

CHART 34. The cost of war

member of the armed forces in the Civil War, it took $33,000 in World War II. Even the minor wars and police actions involved huge sums. It is estimated that Vietnam cost $150 billion and Korea, $50 billion, but of course no one really knows. Then too, in terms of GNP, both actions were much cheaper than the major wars. At the peak of war spending, World War II took 50 percent of total output; World War I and the Civil War, 25 percent; Korea 6 percent; and Vietnam, 4 percent.

But the costs of war did not stop when fighting ceased Each war also entailed very large indirect costs that continued long after the fighting was over and that multiplied government money expenditures. Even if government activities had not expanded at all and had merely returned to the *status quo antebellum,* the costs of government would have gone up because of the price inflation that resulted from the methods used in financing wars.

Wars also entailed mammoth transfer payments that raised money expenditures without a commensurate increase in total social costs. Borrowing increased the public debt, so that interest payments were much higher after each war than they had been before. Even though interest payments were a transfer from taxpayers to interest recipients, and therefore left the whole of society in the same position it had been in before, they increased the money costs of government. Similarly, pension payments were transfer payments but required ever-greater money outlays. The last pension from the War of 1812 was paid in 1945. Civil War pensions did not reach their peak until 1921, and payments to Spanish-American War veterans reached their highest point in 1940.

With new unavoidable obligations, total Federal expenditures after each war were between four and four and one-half times as high as in prewar years. Before the Civil War, Federal expenditures were approximately $65 million annually; by the 1870s, they were approximately $260 million. World War I raised Federal spending from $700 million to $3 billion. As a result of World War II, annual Federal expenditures rose from $9 billion to $40 billion. No similar increase in government expenditures ever occurred in peacetime. It was, therefore, war more than anything else that raised the level of government expenditures.

HOW THE COSTS WERE MET

Governments can cover the costs of war (1) by taxing; (2) by borrowing from noncommercial-bank investors, that is, individuals, corporations, savings banks, and insurance companies; (3) by borrowing from commercial banks; (4) by borrowing from the central bank; (5) by printing paper money; or (6) by using any combination of the above. Each of the six methods has a different effect on the national income, the distribution of income, the price level, the amount of spending, and the amount of saving.

Taxes transfer money from individuals to the government. Because they do not increase the amount of money or the aggregate purchasing power of the economy, they are usually noninflationary. [6] But although they do not affect the price level significantly, they still have great economic effects, because they may change the distribution of income by transferring purchasing power from savers to consumers or from consumers to savers. If the government levies most of its taxes on those with high incomes, and if its expenditures benefit the lower-income groups more than the upper-income groups, there will be a transfer of money from persons in the upper-income brackets, who would ordinarily save substantially, to persons in the lower-income brackets, who spend most of their incomes and save little. The net effect will be to increase consumption and reduce saving. Conversely, regressive taxes, that is, those that take a larger percentage of low incomes will siphon off purchasing power from consumers and tranfer it to savers.

In general, borrowing from individuals has the same economic effect on society as taxation, for it neither increases nor decreases total purchasing power. When individuals buy bonds, they surrender purchasing power in exchange for noncash assets. At the same time, the government gains purchasing power but also increases its liabilities. Because individuals and the government are the same, the net effect is a permanent reduction in civilian purchasing power, for the bonds that represent an asset to the individual citizen also represent a liability to him in his role as part owner of the government. This point can best be illustrated by an oversimplified example. Suppose there are only two persons in a society. Assume that the cost of their government is $100 a year. If, instead of taxing themselves $50 each, they should decide to cover the costs of government by each buying a $50 bond, the effect on both of them would be the same as if they had resorted to taxes in the first place, for, if both bought bonds, they would surrender purchasing power that they could regain only by levying taxes on themselves. From a social point of view, borrowing is, therefore, disguised taxation; but it is voluntary rather than involuntary and is much cruder than genuine taxation, for it affects income distribution in a different way from taxes.

[6] In some cases, taxes transfer money from savers to spenders and thus increase total spending. Moreover, it may be argued that taxes are inflationary in themselves, because in many cases, they are passed on by sellers in the form of higher prices for goods and services.

Obviously, when a government issues paper money, it increases the money supply and adds to the total amount of purchasing power, thus inviting price inflation. The same thing will result, but in a more complicated fashion, if the government borrows by selling its securities to commercial banks or to the central bank. When an individual buys securities, he pays for them in cash, and the transaction represents nothing but a transfer of cash from the buyer to the seller. Consequently, there is no net increase in the money supply. However, when a commercial bank or the central bank buys securities or makes a loan, it does *not* transfer cash. Instead, it creates a deposit for the security-selling borrower, enabling him to write checks. This results in a net increase in the money supply and in purchasing power. Thus, when the Treasury sells bonds to the commercial banks or to the central bank, it obtains bank deposits or, in other words, a supply of checkbook money that represents a net addition to the total purchasing power of the economy. Because all this new money will be spent, the net effect will be to increase the demand for goods, to raise prices, and to increase the cost of the war. Borrowing from commercial banks is, therefore, inflationary, and in this respect it is the same as issuing paper money.

Fortunately, inflationary methods of war finance create offsetting deflationary pressures. Inflation raises the national income in money terms, and most tax revenues rise without any increase in rates. Moreover, as the national income rises, personal saving increases and it becomes easier to sell bonds to individuals.

In covering the costs of its major wars, the United States has resorted to all methods of financing. In every major war and a few minor ones as well, taxes were greatly increased and the government borrowed large sums from individuals. But, in each war, the government also borrowed from commercial banks. In one case, the Civil War, it also issued paper money. In both world wars, it borrowed from the central bank, that is, the Federal Reserve banks. Thus, each war was paid for to a greater or lesser extent by inflationary methods. Of the total costs of war, the government raised by taxes 22 percent in the Civil War, 30 percent in World War I, and 46 percent in World War II. Although a larger percentage of each war's costs was raised by taxation, this did not necessarily mean that each war was financed by less inflationary means. In fact, more inflationary methods were used to finance the Civil War than World War II, whereas the least inflationary methods were used in World War I.

In the Civil War, 13 percent of the total cost was covered by issuing paper money. There are no adequate estimates of just how much the government borrowed from the commercial banks, but it must have been at least another 40 percent. No paper money was issued during World War I, but approximately 14 percent of the War's total costs was financed by borrowing from the commercial banks and the Federal Reserve System. In World War II, loans from commercial banks covered approximately 15 percent of the total war costs and another 5 percent was raised by borrowing from the Federal Reserve System. To summarize, at least 50 percent of the Civil War's costs was raised through inflationary methods, compared with 20 percent in World War II and only 14 percent in World War I.

HOW WARS INCREASED TAXATION

Although loans provided most of the money used in financing the major wars, each war revolutionized the American tax system. When the Civil War began, the Federal government had no internal tax system of any kind. Tariffs produced 95 percent of nonborrowed receipts, with the remainder divided about equally between the proceeds from the sale of public lands and various minor miscellaneous sources. The War not only increased total revenue from $56 million to $334 million, but also produced a full-fledged internal revenue system. By 1865, customs duties were providing only 25 percent of total Federal revenue. Excises, including taxes on alcoholic beverages, tobacco, and manufacturers' sales, contributed approximately 45 percent of the total. Income taxes were adopted for the first time in 1863 and were not completely repealed until 1872. By the end of the War, they were producing almost 20 percent of all Federal revenue.

World War I not only increased Federal revenue from less than $750 million to $4.7 billion but, in addition, sharply accelerated an incipient trend toward direct and progressive taxes. Just before the War, 40 percent of all Federal revenue came from customs duties. Excises produced slightly more, and the newly introduced peacetime income tax provided less than 10 percent. By the end of World War I, income taxes were producing 56 percent of the greatly expanded Federal revenue.

The trend toward progressive taxation inaugurated by World War I was further accelerated during World War II, for by its end Federal tax revenues had jumped to $44 billion, of which direct taxes contributed 75 percent.

THE EFFECTS OF GOVERNMENT FISCAL POLICY

Despite forty years of more-or-less deliberately planned fiscal policy, it is still not clear whether government spending, taxation, and debt management influence the economy to any significant extent. The vast majority of economists readily agree that government policy, whether determined by sound economic theory or necessitated by considerations of military survival or sheer expediency, fundamentally affected the course of the economy and the business cycle. But an articulate minority disagree, and even among the majority, the question of precisely how and to what precise extent the government influences economic conditions remains murky. In theory, as every beginning economics student knows, tax reductions are supposed to reduce government revenue; government deficits are supposed to be inflationary; and government surpluses are said to be deflationary. Yet, history offers many examples that contradict these logical conclusions. Substantial, across-the-board tax reductions after the Civil War, World War I, and, to a lesser extent, World War II, were not followed by a decline in Federal revenue. Tax increases passed in the 1960s in order to combat inflation were not followed by price declines; indeed, prices rose at a faster rate than before the tax increases.

But looking at government policy in a different way leads to the conclusion that it unquestionably affected the general level of living by its encouragement to education, by its contribution to transportation, by its land policy, and by the services it provided. But it is difficult to place a money value on these contributions because government producion consisted mostly of intangible services rather than tangible goods. Moreover, most of the services, although necessary in an urban economy, would have been unnecessary in an agricultural society. Thus, instead of representing a net addition to the level of living, many of the services were part of the price paid for the industrialization of the economy. As far back as the early part of the century, this was clearly seen by students of government affairs. At that time, the evolution from do-it-yourself to outside performance was taking place in urban living just as it had taken place in home manufacture before and as it would take place on a Federal level later. In 1915, Carl Plehn wrote:[7]

> Much of the work done by cities is . . . cooperative or semi-socialistic. That is to say, the cities provide for the individual citizens things which they might—and for a long time did—provide for themselves, or which might be provided by private enterprise. The big motor-driven street sweeper has taken the place of the primitive rule "let every man sweep in front of his own door."

Then, too, the benefits from government service did not accrue equally to all groups. During the nineteenth century, government finance effected a small shift in income from those in the lower-income groups to those in the upper-income groups. In the twentieth century, the combination of a relatively progressive tax structure and the enormously increased scale of government activity resulted in a considerable shift of income from upper- to lower-income groups.[8] The United States had become to a great extent "the welfare state." Paradoxically, it was capitalistic society that was giving practical application to the Marxist dictum, "from each according to his ability, to each according to his need," proving once more that social welfare succeeds best in societies that emphasize production and business vitality, for welfare is a function of an expanding economy, not of a social, economic, or political ideology.

[7] Carl C. Plehn, *Government Finance in the United States* (Chicago: A. C. McLurg & Co., 1915), p. 85.

[8] To attempt to measure the shift quantitatively requires great courage, but attempts have been made. See Kenyon Poole, *Fiscal Policies and the American Economy* (Englewood Cliffs, N. J.: Prentice-Hall, Inc., 1951), p. 396. For a comparison with Great Britain, see the much more extensive study by Tibor Barna, *Redistribution of Incomes Through Public Finance in 1937* (London: Oxford University Press, 1945).

SUGGESTED READINGS

(For suggested readings, see the previous chapter.)

QUESTIONS

1. Comment on the statement: There has never been such a thing as *laissez faire* in the American economy.
2. Why did the Federal government's economic role increase? Would you say that this increase has advanced or retarded the level of living?
3. Describe the nature of government expenditures and revenues (Federal, state, and local) around 1900. Did the ways in which government raised money and spent it have any effect on income, prices, and output? Explain.
4. Why do some people consider Hamilton the ancestor of the New Deal?
5. How do you explain why the government viewed the balanced budget so differently in 1900 and in 1960?
6. During the depression of the 1930s, President Hoover was accused of "doing nothing." Was this justified?
7. Contrast the revenue system of the Federal government in 1850-1900, and 1960. How did the differences affect the economy?
8. In the last few years, state and local governments have been expanding faster than the Federal government. Is this something new? Explain.
9. It has been argued that government fiscal activities have no effect on the economy. On the basis of history, do you agree?
10. The financing of major wars—the Civil War, World War I, and World War II—demonstrated steady improvement. To what extent do you agree or disagree? For what reasons?

INDEX

Avery, C. W., 444
Ayer, N. W., 392, 393

B

Bacon, Roger, 439
Baker, George F., 193, 261
Balance of payments, 278, 317, 322-23
   (*chart*), 330-31, 333-35 (*table*)
Balance of trade, 224-25 (*chart*), 333-34
Bank notes, 245, 255
Bank of the United States, 245-48, 252, 275,
   277-79
Banking:
   commercial, 244-45, 269-71 (*chart*), 273
   investment, 252-53, 254, 261, 271-73
   regulation of, 249-51, 300-2
   savings banks, 253-54, 261
   structure of, 18
   trust companies, 253, 254
Bankruptcies, 225
Baring Brothers, 252-53, 277, 279
Barksdale, H. M., 189, 190, 202
Bayard, Col., 176
Beecher, Henry Ward, 487
Belmont, August, 193
Benson, Ezra Taft, 163
Benton, Thomas, 91, 93, 278
Benz, Karl, 439
Bessemer, Henry, 416
Bicycle industry, 439-40
Biddle, Nicholas, 248
Big business, 193-94, 196-98, 203, 219-21,
   228-29
Bimetallism, 271
Bingham, William, 27
Birth rates, 74-78 (*chart*), 147
Black Ball Line, 331
Bland-Allison Act, 160, 285-87, 290
Blodgett, Samuel, 235
Bookkeeping, 175
Boston Associates, 176
Boston Manufacturing Co., 225
Boycotts, 488, 489, 494, 497
Bradstreet's Commercial Agency, 252
Bramah, Joseph, 412
Brayton, G. B., 439
Brennan, William J., Jr., 217
Bristed, John, 67
Brown Brothers, 176
Brown, Donaldson, 448
Browne, Joseph R., 413
Bryan, William Jennings, 168
Burchard, Horatio, 235
Bureaucracy, 221-22, 259, 447
Business cycle:
   historical pattern in, 14-17 (*table*)
   and volume of trade, 332, 373
Business enterprise:
   ancillary institutions, 190-91
   bibliographies on, 173
   big business, 193-94, 195-97, 203, 222-
   24, 229-30
change and, 168, 178, 199, 223

Business enterprise (cont.)
   competition, 65, 181-82, 203, 213, 377-
   80
   concentration and control, 202-4
   consolidation in early 1900's, 492-99
   diversification and decentralization, 201-2,
   373
   failures, 224, 257
   investment banker, 191-92
   in late 1800's, 177-85
   and mergers, 193-94, 203-4
   mortality rate, 224-25
   organization in late 1800's, 184-90
   philosophy, 169, 209
   separation of ownership and control, 184-
   90
   since 1920, 199-207
   size of, 169, 195, 204
   and technological progress, 415-16
Businessmen:
   antecedents of, 180
   education of, 180
Business unionism, 479, 487-89, 497

C

Cairncross, A. K., 25
Call Loans, 253
Callendar, Guy S., 4
Canal era, 44, 346, 345-48
Canby, Henry Seidel, 167
Capital:
   and economic progress, 4, 70, 232
   definition of, 232-33
   money value of, 233
Capital accumulation:
   capital imports as source, 243-44
   financial institutions and, 248-50
   volume of, and saving, 234-37 (*table*)
Capital/output ratio, 234
Capitalism, finance, 192, 196
Career executives, 220-21
Carnegie, Andrew, 85, 177, 178, 179, 180,
   185, 187, 189, 191, 192, 194, 197, 220,
   223, 372
Cartel agreements, 181-82
Chain stores, 390
Chandler, Alfred, 171, 177, 201
Chapman, William S., 98
Child labor, 454, 460, 462, 466, 475
Cities (*see Urban areas*)
Claims to wealth, 11
Clark, Edward, 183, 192
Clay, Henry, 90, 344
Clayton Act, 212, 216
Clerical occupations, 38-40, 221, 259, 468
Cleveland, Grover, 95
Cleveland Trust Company, 14
Clews, Henry, 262, 263
Closed-shop, 494-97
Cochran, Thomas C., 169, 221, 377
Coffin, Lorenzo, 370
Coinage:
   colonial, 239-40